Environmental Economics

KARPAGAM M.

STERLING PUBLISHERS (P) LTD.
Regd. Office: A1/256 Safdarjung Enclave,
New Delhi-110029. CIN: U22110DL1964PTC211907
Tel: 26387070, 26386209
E-mail: mail@sterlingpublishers.in
www.sterlingpublishers.in

Environmental Economics

© 2019, Karpagam M.

ISBN 978 93 86245 42 7
First Edition 1991
Second Revised Edition 1999
Third Revised Edition 2019
Reprint 2022, 2023

All rights are reserved. No part of this publication may be reproduced, stored in a retrieval system or transmitted, in any form or by any means, mechanical, photocopying, recording or otherwise, without prior written permission of the original publisher.

Printed and Published in India by

Sterling Publishers Pvt. Ltd.,
Plot No. 13, Ecotech-III, Greater Noida - 201306, U. P. India

Preface

When the first edition was published in 1992, there was a paucity of introductory text books on environmental economics by Indian authors. Over the past two decades there has been a boom in research on environment related themes in social sciences in general and economics in particular and this necessitated frequent revision of introductory text books on environmental economics. Further environmental studies has gained the status as one of the core papers in undergraduate programmes in social sciences, particularly in economics. Updation of content and change in narration are two essential criteria for this third revised edition, of course, thanks to the continuous support of students and teachers to this book.

I am happy that this revision has been achieved due to the sustained interest of the publisher Sterling Publishers (P) Ltd in this project. The objective of the third edition is to update the second edition and make the book more informative, besides encouraging the students to take up short projects or to write articles on environment related issues.

This third edition is an enlarged version of the earlier editions and changes have been made in almost all chapters besides the newly added chapters. To inform students about the development of ideas in this subject, I have rewritten almost all the chapters of the earlier editions incorporating latest ideas and information from academic and policy documents in appropriate contexts. Environmental Ethics, Energy and Environment, Environmental Kuznets Curve, Welfare Criteria for Evaluations of Policies and Projects, Theories of Corporate Environmental Management and Principles of Environmental Policy Making are the new additional chapters. Extensive enlargement of existing chapters complement the new chapters, particularly those on policy instruments, and practice of environmental policy at national and international level and sustainable development. The concept and theories in the various chapters are supported with suitable case studies.

Students are encouraged to explore new ideas through solving exercises given at the closure of the chapters. The reference list is exhaustive on every aspect of this subject. Exclusives lists of websites accessed, books, reports and articles referred to are given at the end. A comprehensive glossary is also provided.

This revised edition has relied a lot on articles by eminent scholars in reputed journals and websites, on reports by the United Nations and FAO , working papers and reports by World Bank and information from many text books on environmental economics and environmental management. There are numerous quoted remarks, figures, tables and case studies to elucidate concepts and theories. I am grateful to all those whose work I have quoted and summarized. The book "Green Management –Theory and Applications" which I co-authored with my colleague Dr.Geetha Jaikumar in 2010, was very useful in bringing out this revised edition.

This third edition of the book provides a clear easy-to-understand overview of the subject that is gaining importance among present day teachers, students and researchers in economics. Awaiting your feedback.

20th October, 2018 **Karpagam M.**

Contents

SECTION 1
ECONOMICS, ECOLOGY AND ETHICS

1. BASIC ECOLOGY 2
1.1 What is an Ecosystem 2
1.2 Components of Ecosystem 3
1.3 Functioning of an Ecosystem 5
1.4 Classification of Ecosystem 7
1.5 Forest Ecosystem—Mangrove forests 7
1.6 Wetland Ecosystem– An example of an Aquatic Ecosystem 9
Conclusion 13
Questions 14
Exercise 14

2. ECONOMICS–ENVIRONMENT INTER-LINKAGES 15
2.1 Economics - Environment Trade Off 15
2.2 Economics, Environment and Ecology—Interlinkages 16
2.3 Economic Functions of the Environment 17
2.4 The Economy and the Environment – The Circular Flow 18
2.5 The Material Balance Approach - Law of Thermodynamics and Environment –Economics Inter Linkages 20
2.6 Boulding's Spaceship Economy 21
Conclusion 22
Questions 22
Exercise 22

3. ENVIRONMENTAL ETHICS 23
3.1 Intrinsic Value and Instrumental Value 24
3.2 Theoretical Foundations of Environmental Ethics 25
3.3 Evolution of Environmental Thinking 26
3.4 Approaches to Environmental Ethics 27
Conclusion 31
Questions 31
Exercise 32

4. ENVIRONMENTAL MOVEMENTS 33
4.1 Evolution of the Environmental movement before 1962 – before the publication of Silent Spring: 34
4.2 Environmental movement from 1962 to 1992: 37
4.3 Environmental Movement since 1990 to the present day 49
Conclusion 52
Questions 52
Exercise 52

SECTION 2
ENVIRONMENTAL DEGRADATION

5. AIR POLLUTION 54
5.1 Structure of the Atmosphere 54
5.2 Gas Composition in the Atmosphere 55
5.3 Definition and Classification of Air Pollution 56
5.4 Specific Air Pollutants 58
5.5 Effects of Air Pollutants 61
5.6 Air Pollution Case Study 67
5.7 Control of Air Pollution 69
Conclusion 70
Questions 70
Exercise 70

6. WATER POLLUTION 71
6.1 Global Distribution of Water Resources 71
6.2 Definition of Water Pollution 72
6.3 Classification of Water Pollution 72
6.4 Sources of Water Pollution 74
6.5 Measures of Water Pollution 78
6.6 Effects of Water Pollution 78
6.7 Control of Water Pollution 82
Conclusion 84
Questions 84
Exercise 84

7. POLLUTION BY SOLID WASTES 85
7.1 Pollution by Solid Wastes 85
7.2 Thermal Pollution 94
7.3 Pesticidal Pollution 96
Questions 97
Exercise 97

8. POPULATION AND ENVIRONMENT 98
8.1 The Population Data 98
8.2 Impact of growing Population on Global Environment 101
8.3 Environmental Limits and Population Growth 103
Conclusion 107
Questions 107
Exercise 107

9. URBANISATION AND ITS IMPACT ON ENVIRONMENT 108
9.1 Trends in Urbanisation 109
9.2 Urbanisation by Regions 110
9.3 Urbanisation by Development Group 111
9.4 Pace of Urbanisation 111
9.5 Impact of Urbanisation 112
9.6 Specific Pollution Problem in Some of the World's Large Cities. 114
9.7 Proliferation of Slums 115
9.8 Quality of Urban Environment in India 116
Conclusion 119
Questions 120
Exercise 120

10. ENERGY AND ENVIRONMENT 121
10.1 Forms of Energy 121
10.2 Energy Data 123
10.3 Environmental Impact of Various Sources of Energy 125
Conclusion 130
Questions 131
Exercise 131

11. FORESTS AND ENVIRONMENTAL QUALITY 132
11.1 Forest Cover Data 132
11.2 Role of Forests 133
11.3 Effects of Deforestation 134
11.4 Climate and Deforestation 135
11.5 Situation in India 136
Questions 139
Exercise 139

SECTION 3
ECONOMIC DEVELOPMENT AND ENVIRONMENTAL QUALITY

12. ECONOMIC GROWTH AND ENVIRONMENTAL QUALITY 142
12.1 Environmental Impact 143
12.2 Accounting for Environmental Degradation 143
12.3 Boulding's Spaceship Economy 144
12.4 Limits to Growth 144
12.5 Trade-off between Environment and Economic Growth 145
12.6 Environmental Kuznet's Curve 146
12.7 Ecological Foot print 147
Conclusion 148
Questions 148
Exercise 148

13. LIMITS TO GROWTH 149
13.1 Club of Rome 149
13.2 Basic Thesis of the Model 150
13.3 Factors Affecting Growth in the Model 151
13.4 Predictions of the Model 152
13.5 Criticisms 152
13.6 Policy Implications 154
13.7 Update on the Limits to Growth Model 154
Conclusion 155
Questions 155
Exercise 155

14. ENVIRONMENTAL KUZNET'S CURVE 156
14.1 Growth Vs Environment 156
14.2 The EKC Concept 157
14.3 EKC and the I = PAT Equation 157
14.4 Shape of the EKC 158
14.5 The Three Effects 158
14.6 Existence and Turning Point of the EKC 159

14.7 Policy Relevance of EKC 161
Conclusion 162
Question 162
Exercise 162

15. ECONOMICS OF SUSTAINABLE DEVELOPMENT 163
15.1 Definitions of Sustainable Development 163
15.2 Components of Sustainability 166
15.3 Models of Sustainable Development 168
15.4 Strong Vs Weak Sustainability 174
15.5 Theoretical Approaches to Sustainable Development 177
15.6 Realising Sustainable Development 185
Conclusion 186
Questions 187
Exercise 187

SECTION 4
WELFARE ECONOMICS AND ENVIRONMENTAL ECONOMICS

16. PARETIAN WELFARE ECONOMICS 190
16.1 Welfare Economics – Pareto Optimum and Pareto Efficiency Conditions 190
16.2 Efficiency in Consumption 191
16.3 Efficiency in Production 193
16.4 Efficiency in Product Mix 193
Questions 195
Exercise 195

17. MARKET FAILURE 196
17.1 Causes of Market Failure 196
17.2 Missing or Incomplete Markets 198
17.3 Correction of Market Failure 199
Questions 200
Exercise 200

18. CONSUMER'S SURPLUS AND PRODUCER'S SURPLUS 201
18.1 Marshall's Concept of Consumer's Surplus 201
18.2 Marshall's Concept of Consumer's Surplus Using Indifference Curves 201
18.3 Hicksian Four Measures of Consumer's Surplus 202
18.4 Compensation Variation Measure of Consumer's Surplus 202
18.5 Equivalent Variation Measure of Consumer's Surplus 203
18.6 The Concept of Producer's Surplus 204
18.7 Application of Consumer's Surplus and Producer's Surplus 204
Questions 205
Exercise 205

19. WELFARE CRITERIA 206
19.1 Pareto Improvement Criterion 206
19.2 The Compensation Criterion or the Kaldor – Hicks Criterion 207
19.3 Scitovsky Criterion 208
19.4 Bergson Samuelson Criterion 209
Conclusion 210
Question 210
Exercise 210

SECTION 5
ENVIRONMENTAL ECONOMICS

20. ECONOMICS OF POLLUTION 212
20.1 Economics of Pollution 212
20.2 Problem of Second Best 215
20.3 Solutions to Externality 217
20.4 Environmental Quality as a Public Good 218
20.5 Optimal Provision of Public Good 220
Question 222
Exercise 222

21. NATURAL RESOURCE ECONOMICS 223
21.1 Classification of Natural Resources 223
21.2 Evolution of Resource Economics – A Brief Summary 224
21.3 Theories of Natural Resource Use 226
21.4 Discounting 227
21.5 Renewable Resources 227
21.6 Non-Renewable Resources 232

21.7 Conservation of Resources 235
Conclusion 239
Questions 239
Exercise 239

22. ACCOUNTING FOR ENVIRONMENT 240
22.1 Shortcoming of Traditional National Income Accounting with Reference to Environmental Issues 241
22.2 Adjustments to National Income to Incorporate Environmental Degradation 243
22.3 Greening India's National Income 245
Conclusion 247
Questions 247
Exercise 247

23. THE ENVIRONMENT AND INTERNATIONAL TRADE 248
23.1 Trade – Environment linkages 248
23.2 Economic Theory of Trade and Environment 250
23.3 Role of Unilateral Measures 253
23.4 Trade, Environmental Policy and Economic Relationships 254
23.5 Multi-lateral Agreements 255
23.6 GATT and Environment 259
23.7 WTO and Environment 260
Conclusion 262
Questions 262
Exercise 262

SECTION 6
ENVIRONMENTAL POLICY

24. ENVIRONMENTAL POLICY – AN INTRODUCTION 264
24.1 Economic Foundations of Environmental Policy 265
24.2 Optimum Pollution or Zero Pollution 266
Conclusion 269
Questions 269
Exercise 269

25. PRINCIPLES OF POLLUTION CONTROL 270
25.1 Polluter Pays Principle 270
25.2 The Precautionary Principle 272
Conclusion 276
Questions 277
Exercise 277

26. ENVIRONMENTAL POLICY TOOLS –COMMAND AND CONTROL 278
26.1 Environmental Policy Instruments 278
26.2. Direct Regulation or Command and Control 279
Conclusion 283
Questions 283
Exercise 283

27. POLLUTION CONTROL: MARKET USING INSTRUMENTS 284
27.1 Meaning and significance of Market Based Instruments (MBIs) 284
27.2 Evolution and Components of MBIs 285
27.3.Market Using Instruments: Charges286
27.4 Market Using Instruments - Subsidies 293
27.5 Refundable Deposits and Environmental Performance Bonds 297
Conclusion 299
Questions 299
Exercise 299

28. POLLUTION CONTROL - MARKET CREATING INSTRUMENTS 300
28.1 Definition of Property Rights 300
28.2 Coase Theorem 301
28.3 Market Creating Instruments – Pollution Permits 302
28.4 International Offset System 308
Conclusion 310
Questions 310
Exercise 310

29. COMPARISON OF POLLUTION CONTROL POLICY INSTRUMENTS 311
29.1 Dependability 312

29.2 Permanence and Adaptability to Growth 312
29.3 Equity 312
29.4 Economy 313
29.5 Inducement to Maximum Effort 313
29.6 Minimal Interference with Private Decision 314
29.7 Incentive to Innovate 314
29.8 Political Acceptability 315
29.9 Uncertainty 315
Conclusion 316
Question 316
Exercise 316

30. ENVIRONMENTAL PROTECTION – VOLUNTARY PARTICIPATION 317
30.1 Moral Suasion 317
30.2 Voluntary Agreements 318
30.3 Information Disclosure 320
30.4 Product Labelling /Ecolabelling 321
30.5 Certification 321
Conclusion 322
Questions 322
Exercise 322

SECTION 7
COST - BENEFIT ANALISIS

31. COST BENEFIT ANALYSIS –AN INTRODUCTION 324
31.1 Steps in Cost Benefit Analysis 324
31.2 Theoretical foundation of Cost Benefit Analysis 326
31.3 Rules of CBA 327
31.4 A Simple Cost Benefit Analysis 327
31.5 Limitations of Cost Benefit Analysis 329
Conclusion 330
Questions 330
Exercise 330

32. ECONOMIC EVALUATION OF ENVIRONMENTAL BENEFITS 331
32.1 Components of Total Economic Value 331
32.2 Techniques for Valuation of Environmental Benefits 332
32.3 Direct Methods 334
32.4 Revealed Preference Methods 343
32.5 Household Production Function Approach 345
32.6 Cost Based Methods 348
32.7 Conventional Market Approach 349
32.8 Benefit Transfer Method 350
Conclusion 350
Questions 351
Exercise 351

33. ENVIRONMENTAL IMPACT ASSESSMENT 352
33.1 Evolution of EIA 352
33.2 Definition of EIA 353
33.3 Objectives of EIA 354
33.4 Principles of EIA 354
33.5 EIA Process 355
33.6 Methodology of EIA for Identification and Prediction of Impacts 359
33.7 Benefits of EIA 362
33.8 Limitations of EIA 363
33.9 EIA in India 364
Conclusion 365
Questions 365
Exercise 365

SECTION 8
CORPORATE ENVIRONMENTAL MANAGEMENT

34. SUSTAINABLE INDUSTRIALISATION 368
34.1 Production Paradigms 368
34.2 Sustainable Industrialisation 370
34.3 Challenges to Companies 373
34.4 Business Charter for Sustainable Development 374
Conclusion 374
Question 374
Exercise 374

35. CORPORATE STRATEGIES FOR ENVIRONMENTAL MANAGEMENT 375
35.1 Theories of Corporate Environmental Response 375

35.2 Tools of Corporate Environmental Management 378
Conclusion 391
Questions 392
Exercise 392

SECTION 9
ENVIRONMENTAL POLICY IN PRACTICE

36. ENVIRONMENTAL CHALLENGES AND POLICY IN INDIA 394
36.1 A Profile of India's Major Environmental Issues 394
36.2 India's Environmental Policy 398
36.3 Environmental Legislation in India 403
36.4 Environmental Protection under Twelfth Five Year Plan – a brief note 409
36.5 Fiscal Incentives for Environmental Protection in India 411
Conclusion 411
Questions 411
Exercise 411

37. GLOBAL ENVIRONMENT: PROBLEMS AND POLICIES 412
37.1 Global Warming 413
37.2 Ozone Depletion 421
37.3 Biodiversity Loss 424
37.4 Hazardous Wastes 435
37.5 Major International Conferences on Environmental Protection 438
Conclusion 440
Questions 440
Exercise 440

Glossary 441
References – Websites 448
Articles, Books and Reports 459

SECTION 1

ECONOMICS, ECOLOGY AND ETHICS

1

BASIC ECOLOGY

To halt the decline of an ecosystem, it is necessary to think like an ecosystem.

—*Douglas P. Wheeler*

Ecology is the study of how organisms interact with the other living organisms and the non-living components (e.g., sunlight, soil, water, air) in their surrounding environment. The word 'ecology' was first used by German biologist "Ernst Haeckel" in 1869 in the following statement:

"By ecology we mean the body of knowledge concerning the economy of nature—the investigation of the total relations of the animal both to its inorganic and organic environment."

Websters dictionary defines ecology as "the totality or patterns of relations between organism and their environment". The shortest and least technical definition is to consider ecology as "environmental biology".

The word "ecology" is derived from two Greek words, oikos ("house"), and logos ("study of", or "governing rules"), literally, meaning "the rules of the house." The "rules" refer to the relationships and interconnections between organisms and their environment. The term environment refers to all the external conditions and factors, both living and non-living, that affect an organism. Ecology is the study of ecosystems.

1.1 What is an Ecosystem

The term "ecosystem" was first coined by Roy Clapham in 1930. In 1935, the British ecologist Arthur Tansley defined the term ecosystem to denote the physical and biological components of an environment considered in relation to each other. The word ecosystem is an abbreviation of the term, "ecological system." Odum has defined ecosystem as the basic fundamental unit of ecology which includes both the organisms and the non living environment, each influencing the properties of the other and each is necessary for the maintenance of life. S. Mathavan (1974) defined ecosystem as the sum total of living organisms, the environment and the process of interaction between various components of the system.

An ecosystem is a dynamic complex of plant, animal and micro organism communities and the non-living environment, interacting as a functional unit. Ecosystems include the biotic organisms (that is, the living organisms) the abiotic environment (non-living) within which the living organisms live and exchange elements (such as soil, water and the atmosphere) and the interactions among the components. Ecosystem provides a variety of services such as supply of food, fresh water, fuel wood, and fiber, the control of frequency and magnitude of floods and droughts, and maintenance of local as well as global climate.

Ecosystems embody the concept that living organisms continually interact with each other and with the environment to produce complex systems with emergent properties, such that "everything is connected". Interactions between the living organism with the non-living components are crucial for sustaining the system and for allowing it to respond. Each ecosystem has a definite structure and components and each component part of the system has a definite role to play in the functioning of the ecosystem. There are many examples of ecosystems -- a pond, a forest, an estuary, a grassland. Ecosystems exist on a variety of scales. An example of a small scale ecosystem (micro) is a pond. A medium scale ecosystem (messo) could be a forest. The tropical rainforest is an example of a very large ecosystem (biome).

1.2 Components of Ecosystem

The ecosystems mainly consists of the living, or biotic components and the non-living, or abiotic, components.

Biotic Components of the Ecosystem: The biotic elements of an ecosystem are its organisms like plants, animals microbes which together form the communities of the ecosystem. The biotic living components of the ecosystem can be categorised into *producer, consumer* and *reducer* components.

1.2.1 Living Components of an Ecosystem

a. **Producers or Autotrophs** (i.e., self - feeders) are those that produce carbo hydrates from CO_2 through photosynthesis. Typically they are the chlorophyll bearing plants, algae of a pond, grass of a field, trees of a forest etc. Producers produce carbo hydrates and not energy. They convert radiant energy into a chemical form. Hence they are also called as *converters* or *transformers.* The producer organisms are *autotrophic,* i.e., self feeding. In terrestrial ecosystems, mainly the rooted plants are the autotrophs. In aquatic ecosystems, floating plants called phytoplankton and shallow water rooted plants called macrophytes are the dominant producers.

b. Consumer organism on the other hand, are heterotrophic, i.e., organisms whose nutritional requirements are met by feeding on other organism. Consumers, depending on their food habits, can be further classified into three types. Consumer organisms could be either primary consumer, or secondary consumer.

- **A Primary Consumer** more commonly referred to as **herbivore or a heterotroph** derives its nutrition directly from plants. Examples include deer, rabbits, cattle, etc., They are plant eaters and they feed directly on producers.
- **A Secondary Consumer or Carnivores** are meat eaters and they feed on herbivores (primary consumers). They are animal eaters, e.g. lions, tigers.
- **Tertiary Consumers or Omnivores** eat both plants and animals, e.g. pigs, rats, and humans.

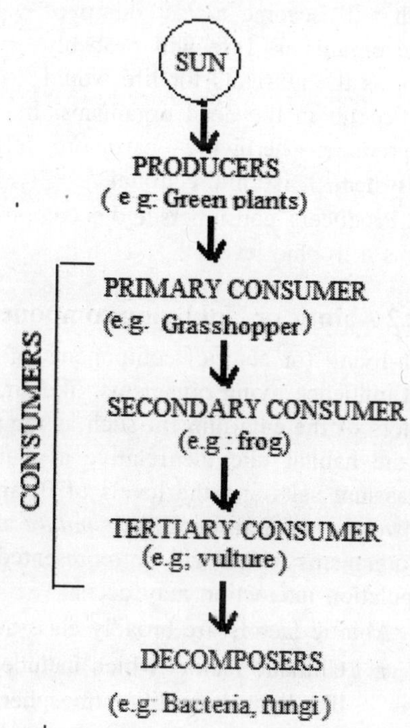

Fig. 1.1 Biotic Components of an Ecosystem

c. **Decomposers** (primarily bacteria, fungi; nematodes like tapeworms; mites and certain insects) are organisms that feed by degrading organic matter. They are essential components of all nutrient cycles and food chains.

Decomposers or reducers consists chiefly of bacteria and fungi. Generally in the territorial ecosystems bacteria act on animal tissue and fungi on plant tissue. These decomposers consume food by absorption. The enzymes produced within their bodies are released into dead plant and animal material. Enzymes act upon the organic compounds of the dead matter. Decomposers absorb a part of the decomposition products for their own nourishment and the remaining substances are mineralized. Released minerals are reused (utilised) as nutrients by the plants (producers). The decomposers perform an invaluable service to the ecosystem by mineralising the organic matter. If decomposers are removed from the biosphere, the earth will become a vast dump of dead organisms. Life will probably stop, as the nutrients for life would be tied up in the dead organisms. Implicit in this autotroph—heterotroph or producer—consumer or producer—herbivore—carnivore, relationship is the direction of energy movement through the ecosystem. It is unidirectional.

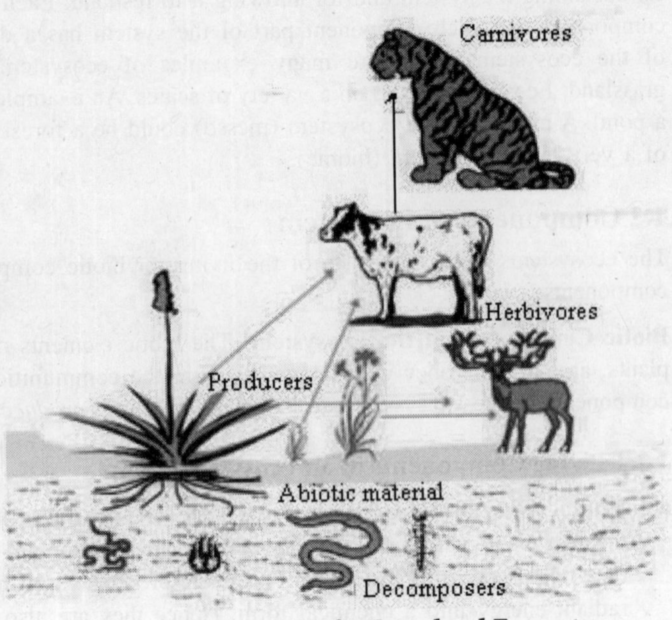

Fig. 1.2 Components of a Grassland Ecosystem

Source: http://www.tutorvista.com/content/biology/biology-iv/ecosystem/ecosystem-components.php

Producers, consumers and decomposers are linked together by the food chain where each category forms a trophic level.

1.2.2 Abiotic or Nonliving components

Non-living (or abiotic) components of an ecosystem include all the physical and chemical factors that influence living organisms, like air, water, soil, rocks etc. The abiotic element includes physical factors of the environment such as temperature, moisture, light etc., together with chemical features of the habitat like the relative availability of essential nutrients, especially nitrates, phosphates, potassium salts and the levels of 0_2 and $C0_2$. These various abiotic elements affect the ecosystem in two ways determining their *nature* and their *function.* Nature of an ecosystem refers to the range of organisms which will be represented in its population, while function refers to the rate at which population interaction may occur.

Abiotic factors are broadly classified under three categories.

a. Climatic factors which include the climatic regime and physical factors of the environment like light, humidity, atmospheric temperature, wind, etc.

b. Edaphic factors which are related to the structure and composition of soil including its physical and chemical properties, like soil and its types, soil profile, minerals, organic matter, soil water, soil organisms.

c. Inorganic and organic substances: Inorganic substances include water, carbon, sulphur, nitrogen, phosphorus and so on. Organic substances include proteins, lipids, carbohydrates etc.

Each of the abiotic factors listed in table 1.1 act as a limiting factor, determining the types of organisms that exist in the environment. Example:

- a low annual temperature determines the species of plants that can exist in that area
- the amount of dissolved oxygen in a body of water determines the specie of fish that can live in it.
- the dry environment of desert regions limits the organisms that can live there.

Table 1.1 Biotic and Abiotic Components of an Ecosystem

Abiotic Components	Biotic Components
Sunlight	Primary producers
Temperature	Herbivores
Precipitation	Carnivores
Water or moisture	Omnivores
Various types substratum (soil or rock type)	Detritivores
Inorganic substances such as minerals	
Gases such as oxygen, carbon di oxide and nitrogen	
pH	

The carrying capacity of the environment is limited by the available abiotic and biotic resources, as well as the ability of ecosystems to recycle the residue of dead organisms through the activities of bacteria and fungi. An ecosystem involves interactions between abiotic (physical) and biotic (living) factors to maintain a balance. An ecosystem is self-sustaining if the following requirements are met:

- A constant source of energy and a living system capable of incorporating this energy into organic molecules.
- Cycling of materials between organisms and their environment.

1.3 Functioning of an Ecosystem

The two major functions within an ecosystem are:

- the transfer of energy *through the ecosystem*
- the cycling of nutrients *within* the ecosystem.

The energy flow and the nutrient cycle within an ecosystem are explained using the food chains. A food chain is a simple pathway of the flow of nutrients in an ecosystem. It is called a 'chain' because each living organism provides a link in the chain and each organism depends on the organism that comes before it. One organism will feed upon another in a sequence of food transfers. Food chains links or **trophic levels** usually start with a primary producer and end with a predator. An example of a very simple food chain is:

grass → grasshopper → frog → snake → Vulture

In this food chain, grass is the primary producer. It uses energy from the sun to grow and reproduce. The grasshopper is the primary consumer, or herbivore, because it eats different kinds of weeds. The frog is the primary carnivore because it eats the grasshopper. The snake is the secondary consumer because it eats the frog and the vulture which feeds on the snake is the tertiary consumer. When the vulture dies, its remains are consumed by the decay-causing bacteria and fungi.

Organisms of an ecosystem are linked together in food chain. As stated in the example given in the last paragraph, the grasshopper eats grass and in turn it is eaten by the frog. A mouse may eat some grain and in turn may be eaten by an owl or hawk or cat. Autotrophs form the only link between biotic and abiotic components of an ecosystem. They draw water and mineral from the soil and combine them with sunlight and CO_2 from air to produce carbohydrates, fats and proteins. Small herbivores such as caterpillars and field mice consume the nutrient rich vegetable matter and convert it to animal matter. They then become food to meat eating (carnivore) animals which in turn are eaten by large carnivores. This sequence of 'eating and being eaten' with the resultant transfer of energy is known as food chain. A food chain describes the transfer of matter and energy from one organism to another organism as one individual eats another or dies and decomposes. Food chains are normally arranged according to trophic levels.

An autotrophic organisms (producers/ plants), convert light energy and inorganic substances (carbon dioxide, water and various mineral nutrients) into organic (carbon based) molecules, (carbohydrates) by photosynthesis. Photosynthesis is the process by which energy from the sun is absorbed by plants, blue-green algae and certain bacteria to produce new plant cell material, which forms the food source for plant eating animals (herbivores). The carbohydrates produced by photosynthesis are:

- Combined with elements such as nitrogen, phosphorous and sulphur to produce proteins and nucleic acids.
- Converted into starch and stored in the plant.
- Converted into cellulose (the main plant structural material).
- Used by the plant for respiration i.e. biochemical processes, cell maintenance and growth.

In the energy cycle, when herbivores such as caterpillars and field mice consume the plant, carbohydrates and the chemical energy from autotrophs is transferred to them. When carnivores consume the herbivores, energy is transferred to the next trophic level, where the chemical energy is transformed mostly in to mechanical energy and heat.

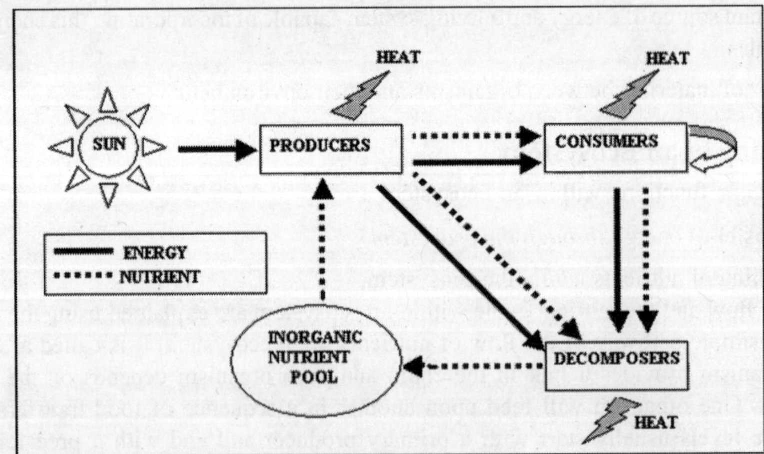

Source: http://web.ead.anl.gov/ecorisk/fundamentals/pdf/ecofund.pdf

Fig. 1.3 Energy and Nutrient Movement in an Ecosystem

It is estimated that 90 percent of the energy is used up at each trophic level and only 10 percent of it is transferred to the next trophic level. Finally at the last trophic level there is no more energy available for recycling. Thus all energy available to organisms originates in plants; ***Herbivores*** obtain their energy by consuming plants or plant products, ***carnivores*** eat herbivores, and ***detritivores*** consume the droppings and carcasses of all. The energy flow from the sun through producers to consumers is unidirectional and is non-cyclic. A second major process linking the biotic and abiotic constituents of an ecosystem is the flow of nutrients. Unlike energy, which is not cycled, inorganic nutrients are cycled in ecosystems. Producers obtain inorganic nutrients from the inorganic nutrient pool, which is usually the soil or water surrounding the plants or algae. Inorganic nutrients are passed from organism to organism as one organism is consumed by another. Ultimately, all organisms die and become detritus, which serves as the food source for decomposers. At this stage, the inorganic nutrients are returned to the soil or water to be taken up again.

Figure 1.3 shows how energy flows through an ecosystem. The solid arrows in Figure 1.3 represent the movement of this energy between trophic levels. All the energy is initially derived from the sun, and the ultimate fate of all the energy in ecosystems is to be lost as heat. Energy does not recycle. The movement of inorganic nutrients is represented by the dashed arrows in Figure 1.3. While the inorganic nutrients are recycled, the energy is not recycled.

1.4 Classification of Ecosystem

Ecosystems may be classified as terrestrial ecosystem and aquatic ecosystem. Terrestrial ecosystems include that of forests, grassland, semi arid areas, deserts , mountains and islands. Aquatic ecosystems include pond ecosystem, lake ecosystem, Wetland ecosystem, River ecosystem, Delta ecosystem, and Marine ecosystem. Table 1.2 gives list of the terrestrial and aquatic ecosystems. Section 1.5 and 1.6 explains mangrove (forest) ecosystem and an aquatic ecosystem respectively.

Table 1.2 Types of ecosystems

Terrestrial Ecosystem	Aquatic ecosystem
Forest Ecosystem	Pond Ecosystem
Ecosystem of the semiarid areas	Wetland ecosystem
Desert ecosystem	River ecosystem
Mountains ecosystem	Delta Ecosystem
Island ecosystem	Marine ecosystem

1.5 Forest Ecosystem—Mangrove Forests

A forest is a large area of land covered by a thick growth of trees and other plants. It is the home of many different birds, insects and other animals. The forest ecosystem is a terrestrial unit of living organisms (plants, animals and microorganisms), all interacting among themselves and with the environment (soil, climate, water and light) in which they live.

The term mangrove refers to a diverse group of salt-tolerant trees and other plant species that are found along sheltered tropical and subtropical shores and estuaries. Mangrove wetlands are home to many rare animals and plants, and have wider ecological and economic importance, and provide numerous services to humans. A large proportion of coastal populations in tropical regions depend on mangroves for their subsistence, either directly through the extraction of wood and non-wood forest products, such as fuel wood, charcoal, timber, food and medicines, or indirectly through the many aquatic and terrestrial species for which these ecosystems provide nutrients and a habitat. Mangroves serve as spawning grounds and nurseries for a variety of fish and shellfish, playing a significant role in the marine food system. Destruction of mangrove forests results in decline in local fish catches. Mangrove forests store and process huge amounts of organic matter, dissolved nutrients, pesticides and other pollutants that are dumped into them by human activities, and by absorbing excess nitrates and phosphates prevent the contamination of coastal waters. In so doing, they play a vital role in protecting coral reefs and sea grasses from siltation and eutrophication. Although they are not particularly species rich, mangrove ecosystems are important nursery areas and habitats for commercially valuable shrimp, shellfish, and fish species.

Mangrove forests have been rapidly disappearing from Southeast Asian coastlines in recent decades to make way for vast shrimp farms and tourist resorts. About 15.2 million hectares of mangroves currently exist worldwide, down from 18.8 million hectares in 1980, with the largest extent found in Asia, followed by Africa and South America. Half the global area of Mangrove forests are found in just five countries: Indonesia, Australia, Brazil, Nigeria and Mexico. Over the last 25 years, 3.6 million hectares of mangroves (or about 20 percent of the total extent found in 1980) have disappeared worldwide. The mangrove ecosystems also play an important role in preventing and reducing coastal erosion, providing nearby communities with protection against the effects of wind, waves and water current.

Mangrove forests reduce the impact of tsunamis by reducing both the height and the velocity of the incoming waves, and by distributing water among the canals and creeks of the mangroves, thus decreasing the level of inundation, and acting as a bio shield. The development of shrimp aquaculture poses the gravest threat to the world's mangroves forests. Thailand, Indonesia and India are among the world's top producers and exporters of farmed shrimp, but the substantial wealth generated by the industry has been offset by numerous and significant negative environmental impacts.

In the post 2004 Tsunami period many research studies were undertaken to study the impact of Tsunami in the affected countries. It was observed that the conversion of mangrove habitat into shrimp farms, tourist resorts, agricultural and urban land over the past decades contributed significantly to the catastrophic loss of human lives and settlements during the 2004 tsunami. In several affected countries, the mangrove forests played a crucial role in saving human lives and property when the Tsunami hit them in 2004. Where mangroves and other coastal habitats had been destroyed the waves were able to penetrate far inland, destroying homes, inundating farmland and washing away people and livelihoods. The four countries that were worst affected by the tsunami – Indonesia, Sri Lanka, India and Thailand – have experienced recent net losses of mangrove cover. Between 1980 and 2000, the total area of mangroves in these four countries was reduced by 28%, from over 5million to 3.6 million hectares.

It is estimated by a study that in India mangrove cover has been reduced from 600,000 ha in 1953 to 200,000 - 300,000 ha in 1989. In the southern Indian states of Kerala, Tamil Nadu and Andhra Pradesh, and the Union Territories of Pondicherry and the Andaman and Nicobar Islands, hundreds of coastal communities were devastated by the tsunami, which claimed over 10,000 lives.

In Tamil Nadu, mangrove forests are relatively sparse and patchily distributed, and are in various stages of degradation with only about 1000ha considered to be 'dense. An international team of researchers coordinated by the Nordic Agency for Development and Ecology (NORDECO), have found that in the Cuddalore District of Tamil Nadu, mangroves and other types of coastal vegetation significantly minimised tsunami waves and protected the shoreline against damage. The study revealed that villages located behind dense mangrove stands suffered no destruction, whereas in areas located an equivalent distance from the shore but unshielded by dense vegetation were seriously inundated.*It was reported that* the tsunami did less damage to lives and property in Tamil Nadu in the regions of Pichavaram and Muthupet, which are both shielded with dense mangroves, than in areas where mangroves had been cleared or were absent. Mangroves not only broke the impact of the waves, but also trapped debris and prevented people from being washed out to sea, which was a major cause of death.

Source: Mangroves – Nature's Defense Against Tsunamis – A Report by the Environental Justice Foundation (2004) Avaiable at *http://ejfoundation.org/sites/default/files/public/tsunami_report.pdf.PdfCompressor-1022348.pdf*

Box: 1.1 Mangroves and the Impact of Tsunami in Tamilnadu, India

The tsunami that hit Asia in December 2004 revealed the devastating consequences of this loss. It was demonstrated during the 2004 tsunami in Asia, that, in locations in which extensive areas of mangroves existed, coastal villages suffered less damage. All of the countries that were hit by the tsunami – Indonesia, Sri Lanka, India and Thailand – had experienced net losses of mangrove cover. This underlines the protective role of coastal forests in reducing damage, including from regular storms, such as the typhoons that batter the Philippines every year.

1.6 Wetland Ecosystem – An example of an Aquatic Ecosystem

A wetland is an area of land that is either covered by water or saturated with water. Wetlands are areas of marsh, fen, peat land or water (permanent or temporary), with water that is static or flowing. According to the Ramsar Convention that defines international standards on wetland,

"Wetlands are areas of marsh, fen, peatland or water, whether natural or artificial, permanent or temporary, with water, that is static or flowing, fresh, brackish or salt, including areas of marine water the depth of which at low tide does not exceed six meters."

Wetlands ecosystem as defined by the Ramsar Convention on Wetlands, include:

- inland wetlands such as swamps, marshes, lakes, rivers, peat lands, and underground water habitats;
- coastal and near-shore marine wetlands such as coral reefs, mangroves, sea grass beds, and estuaries;
- human-made wetlands such as rice fields (paddies), dams, reservoirs, and fish ponds.

The soil must remain water logged or submerged for whole or part of the year. They can be natural or manmade. The classification of wetlands is given in Table 1.3.

Table 1.3 Classification of Wetland

Inland Wetlands	
Natural	Lakes/Ponds Ox-bow lakes/ Cut-off meanders Waterlogged (Seasonal), Playas Swamp/marsh
Man - made	Reservoirs, Tanks, Abandoned quarries Ash pond/cooling pond
Coastal Wetlands	
Natural	Estuary, Lagoon, Creek Backwater (Kayal), Bay Tidal flat/Split/Bar, Coral reef Rocky coast, Mangroove forest Salt marsh/marsh vegetation Other vegetation
Man made	Salt pans, Aquaculture

Source: http://www.indiaonline.in/About/Profile/Geography/Wet-Lands/index.html

1.6.1 Functions of Wetland Ecosystems

Wetland ecosystems perform several vital functions that enhance human welfare. These functions include:

- Supply of fresh water
- Water purification and detoxification of water
- Supply of fish which is a primary source of animal protein for rural communities in any economy.
- Regulation and mitigation of climate
- Cultural services

Inland wetlands such as lakes, rivers, swamps, and shallow groundwater aquifers are major **suppliers of renewable fresh water** for human use. Supply of groundwater is recharged through wetland. It is estimated that nearly 1.5–3 billion people depend on ground water for drinking water. Wetlands **treat and detoxify** waste products. They remove excess nutrients and other pollutants.

Wetlands control climate change by sequestering and releasing a major proportion of fixed carbon in the biosphere. For example peatlands are estimated to hold 540 gigatons of carbon, which is nearly 1.5% of the total estimated global carbon storage. Wetlands, such as mangroves can play a critical role in the physical buffering of climate change impacts such as rise in sea level and increase in flooding. The loss of wetlands increases the risks of floods occurring. It is reported that nearly 2 billion people live in areas of high flood risk. This risk will be increased if wetlands are lost or degraded. Coastal wetlands play an important role in reducing the impacts of floods due to coastal storms.

Cultural services: Wetlands provide significant aesthetic, educational, cultural, and spiritual benefits. They provide opportunities for recreation and tourism. Recreational fishing and nature-based tourism, like scuba diving and snorkeling are significant sources of revenue to the countries.

Table 1. 4 Ecosystem Services Provided by Wetlands

Provisioning Services	
Food	production of fish, fruits, and grains.
Fresh water	storage and retention of water for domestic, industrial, and agricultural use
Fiber and fuel	production of logs, fuelwood, peat, fodder.
Biochemical	extraction of medicines and other materials from biota
Genetic materials	genes for resistance to plant pathogens, ornamental species, and so on.
Regulating Services	
Climate regulation	source of and sink for greenhouse gases; influence local and regional temperature, precipitation, and other climatic processes.
Water regulation	hydrological flows, groundwater recharge/discharge.
Water purification and waste treatment	retention, recovery, and removal of excess nutrients and other pollutants.
Erosion regulation	retention of soils and sediments
Natural hazard regulation	flood control, storm protection
Pollination	habitat for pollinators.

Cultural Services	
Spiritual and inspirational	source of inspiration; many religions attach spiritual and religious values to aspects of wetland ecosystems.
Recreational	opportunities for recreational activities
Aesthetic	beauty or aesthetic value of wetland ecosystems
Educational	opportunities for formal and informal education and training
Supporting Services	
Soil formation	sediment retention and accumulation of organic matter
Nutrient cycling	storage, recycling, processing, and acquisition of nutrients

Source : Millennium Ecosystem Assessment Report on Ecosystem and Human Well-Being: Wetlands and Water, World Resource Institute, 2005

The global extent of wetlands is estimated to be in excess of 1,280 million hectares. Wetlands provide many non-marketed and marketed benefits to people; marketed benefits include supply of fish; non-marketed services include protection from storm damage and carbon sequestration. The total economic value of unaltered wetlands is reported to be greater than altered wetlands. The Millennium Ecosystem Assessment Report on Ecosystem and Human Well-Being: Wetlands and Water (2005) reports that in Thailand, intact (that is unaltered) mangroves have a total net present economic value ranging between $1,000 per hectare to $36,000 per hectare, compared with about $200 per hectare when converted to shrimp farms.

1.6.2 Threats to Wetland Ecosystems

Primary factors responsible for loss of wetlands are rising population and economic development. The specific factors causing significant loss of wetlands are infrastructure development, land conversion, water withdrawal, pollution, overharvesting and overexploitation, and the introduction of invasive alien species. Half of world's wetlands have disappeared since 1900. The loss of wetlands over years is significant and causing concern. For example, the area of the Mesopotamian marshes located between the Tigris and Euphrates Rivers in southern Iraq is reported to have decreased from an area of 15,000–20,000 square kilometers in the 1950s to less than 400 square kilometers today due to excessive water withdrawals and industrial development.

Coastal ecosystems, highly threatened systems in the world, are experiencing some of the most rapid degradation and loss. About 35% of mangroves have been lost over the last two decades, mainly due to aquaculture development, deforestation, and freshwater diversion. The volume of water in the Aral Sea basin has been reduced by 75% since 1960 mainly due to large-scale upstream diversions of the Amu Darya and Syr Darya river flow for irrigation. Loss of wetland ecosystem increases the threat to wetland dependent species which in turn affects the stability and resilience of the ecosystem.

A major threat to wetlands comes from the draining of wetlands for infrastructure and commercial development and for tourism development. The water drained form these wetlands, which are nature's underground aquifer, outpaces its ability to replenish itself. Due loss of flora and fauna which depend on these, wetlands are threatened. Vast areas of wetlands are drained for the sake of agriculture too.

Introduction of alien invasive species affect the species dependent on wetland ecosystems leading to their extinction. Discharge of effluents from industries and fertilizer run off and pesticides from agriculture makes the water toxic and unfit for the regular uses. They affect the ecosystem's efficiency and balance. Global climate change strengthen the adverse impact of other factors that cause destruction of wetlands.

To focus attention on the importance of wetlands for the environment and the people, since 1997, every year, **February 2**, is observed as the World Wetlands Day. On February 2nd 1971, the Ramsar Convention on Wetlands was signed in Ramsar, Iran, by 18 countries. Today the convention has 135 members. It is the only global environment treaty dealing with a particular ecosystem. The countries that signed the contract are committed to include internationally important wetlands in the Ramsar list and ensure the maintenance of the ecological character of each site.

1.6.3 Wetland Ecosystems in India

India has a varied terrain and climate that supports a rich diversity of inland and coastal wetland habitats which are unique ecosystems. Table 1.5 is a list of wetlands that have been declared as internationally important and hence are known as "Ramsar Sites."

Table 1.5 Wetlands in India

S No	Wetland Site	Area (KM^2)
1	Ashtamudi Wetland, Kerala	614
2	Bhitarkanika Mangroves, Orissa	650
3	Bhoj Wetland, Madhya Pradesh	32
4	Chandertal Wetland, Himachal Pradesh	0.49
5	Chilika Lake, Orissa	1165
6	Deepor Beel, Assam	40
7	East Calcutta Wetlands, West Bengal	125
8	Harike Lake, Punjab	41
9	Hokera Wetland, Jammu and Kashmir	13.75
10	Kanjli, Punjab	1.83
11	Keoladeo National Park, Rajasthan	28.73
12	Kolleru Lake, Andhra Pradesh	901
13	Loktak Lake, Manipur	266
14	Point Calimere Wildlife and Bird Sanctuary, Tamil Nadu	385
15	Pong Dam Lake, Himachal Pradesh	156.62
16	Renuka Wetland, Himachal Pradesh	0.2
17	Ropar, Punjab	13.65
18	Rudrasagar Lake, Tripura	2.4
19	Sambhar Lake, Rajasthan	240
20	Sasthamkotta Lake, Kerala	3.73
21	Surinsar-Mansar Lakes, Jammu and Kashmir	3.5
22	Tsomoriri, Jammu and Kashmir	120
23	Upper Ganga River (Brijghat to Narora Stretch), Uttar Pradesh	265.9
24	Vembanad-Kol Wetland, Kerala	1512.5
25	Wular Lake, Jammu and Kashmir	189

Source: http://www.indiaonline.in/About/Profile/Geography/Wet-Lands/index.html

Development needs of a rising population have caused degradation of most of the wetlands in India. Table 1.6 gives details on some of the degraded wetlands in India.

Table 1.6 Degraded Wetlands in India

Wetland	Degradation cause
Ladakh	These wetlands face dangers from the nomadic tribes, growing demand for Pashmina wool, over-grazing in the pasturelands, non-biodegradable garbage thrown into the lakes, pollution, cars washed in water bodies, off track driving by tourists, all is harmful for the balance of the eco-system.
Wular Lake, Jammu and Kashmir	This lake in is grossly encroached by farmers who convert vast catchment area into agricultural land. Besides, pollution from fertilisers and animal waste, hunting pressure on waterfowl and migratory birds and weed infestation has led to problems.
Ropar Lake, Punjab	Siltation from the adjoining barren and soft hills cause threat to the lake. Water quality degradation is caused by fertilizer and thermal power plants in the vicinity.
Point Calimere, Tamilnadu	Illegal extraction of timber and non-timber produce has led to an ecological imbalance in this wildlife and bird sanctuary which already faces danger from industrial pollution and poaching.
Sambar Lake, Rajastan	Grazing pressure from the 20-odd villages around the lake causes desertification.
East Calcutta Wetlands, West Bengal	Waste water effluents of the industries are emptied into the city outfall channels, illegally, resulting in metal deposition in the canal sludge. This waste water is incapable of ensuring the edible quality of fish and vegetables grown in the wetland.

Source: http://www.wwfenvis.nic.in/pdf/land.pdf

Government initiatives through various conservation programmes have been adopted to save the wetland ecosystems. The forest Ministry is working with the state governments to protect the wetland ecosystems. Twenty four wetland sites have been identified by the forest ministry as those requiring urgent conservation and management.

Conclusion

Human demands for ecosystem services are growing rapidly. The capability of ecosystems to provide many of these services is being restricted due to human intervention in ecosystem functioning. The impacts of human activities on ecosystems has resulted in adverse changes in the functioning of ecosystems which are becoming more and more apparent – air and water quality are increasingly compromised, oceans are being over-fished, pests and diseases are extending beyond their historical boundaries, deforestation is eliminating flood control around human settlements. It is reported that approximately 40-50 percent of Earth's ice-free land surface has been heavily transformed or degraded by anthropogenic activities, 66 percent of marine fisheries are either overexploited or at their limit, atmospheric CO_2 has increased more than 30 percent since the advent of industrialisation and nearly 25 percent of Earth's bird species have gone extinct in the last two thousand years. Unless and until we take steps to protect our ecosystems we will not be able prevent the environmental crisis that looms large on our planet earth and on our own survival.

Questions

1. Define an ecosystem and enumerate its components
2. What are the functions of an ecosystem.
3. Account for the threat to major ecosystems.

Exercise

1. Download the MEA report Millennium Ecosystem Assessment, 2005 on " Ecosystems and Human Well-being: Synthesis" and highlight the trend in the state of global wetland ecosystems.
2. From the Millennium Ecosystem Assessment Report 2005 and FAO's Forest Resources Assessment Report (2015) prepare an write up on state of global forests and the role of forest ecosystem.
3. Make a descriptive note on the profile and status of any ecosystem in India.

2

ECONOMICS–ENVIRONMENT INTER-LINKAGES

"No longer is economics merely a science of production and distribution, it has to take into account the ecological repercussions of economic activities that could affect both production and distribution".

- *Arun Balabubramaniam*

Environmental economics analyses the inter relationship between economic agents and environment. The economic activities of humanity have a profound impact on the natural environment in the form of a rapid depletion of natural resource stock as well as through pollution. Such use and abuse of resources have raised many moral as well as practical questions concerning the present and future generations. Environmental economics analyses the allocation problem posed by the use of environmental resources.

2.1 Economics - Environment Trade Off

Economic theory studies aspects of economic life that answer questions like: what to produce, how to produce and for whom to produce, so that the scarce resources may be efficiently allocated to maximise human happiness. So long as natural resources were available in unlimited quantities, environmental issues were simple social issues. It is only with the transformation of environmental goods into economic goods that economists started applying economic principles and theories to environmental issues. The abuse of environmental resources has transformed environmental resources into economic goods, through a reversal in the supply demand relationship of environmental quality, i.e., the demand for environmental quality has registered a sharp increase while the supply of clean air, water and other resources have declined.

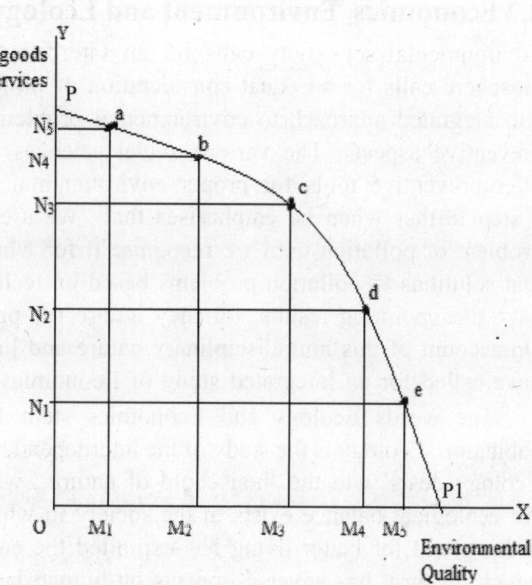

Figure 2.1 Production Possibility Frontier

The increase in demand for environmental resources is attributed to the affluence that accompanies economic growth and development. At the verge of subsistence, people seldom worry about the quality of the environment in which they live. Only when man is assured of his basic needs—food, clothing and shelter—does he turn his attention to other less immediate wants like enjoyment of environmental quality and the expectation of a healthier and longer life. Thus the demand for environmental quality is highly income'-elastic and environmental quality is a luxury item. This means that households with higher income are willing to pay more for a better environment. On the supply side, economic growth and development, accompanied by population growth have reduced the available supply of environmental resources, transforming it into an economic commodity. As a result society can have more of them only by giving up significant amounts of other desirable consumption goods and services. Hence there is a trade-off between environmental quality and other goods and services, i.e., the provision of environmental quality involves opportunity cost. The opportunity cost of obtaining more environmental quality for any society is the sacrifice of doing without certain other valuable commodities. This is illustrated in Figure 2.1

In the figure, PP^1 is the production possibility frontier. The different combinations of environmental quality and other goods and services that can be produced with the given technology are depicted in Figure 2.1, along the production possibility frontier by points such as a, b, c, d and e. Point 'a' shows that when OM_1 units of environmental quality are provided, quantity of goods and services is ON_5. Providing an additional unit of environmental quality, say, M_1M2 requires that the society gives up N_4N_5units of other goods and services. Thus N_4N_5 units of other goods and services given up is the opportunity cost of providing an additional unit of environmental quality. Similarly the opportunity cost of providing M_2M_3 units of environmental quality is N_3N_4; opportunity cost of providing M_3M_4 units of environmental quality is N_2N_3; of providing M_4M_5 units of environmental quality is N_1N_2.The presence of opportunity cost in the provision of environmental quality makes environmental problem an economic problem and calls for the integration of economic mechanisms and environmental issues, for the efficient management of environmental resources. This has also made economic problems a constrained one on the basis of ecological grounds. No longer is economics merely an analysis of production and distribution. It has to take into account ecological repercussions of the various economic activities.

2.2 Economics, Environment and Ecology—Interlinkages

Environmental sensitivity calls for an interdisciplinary approach. An efficient management of the biosphere calls for an equal consideration of biology, economics, physics, geology and engineering. An integrated approach to environmental problems alone will help us to identify both curative and preventive aspects. The various social sciences such as Economics, Sociology and Anthropology offer preventive tools for proper environmental planning and management. Prof Larry Ruff goes a step further when he emphasises that "We are going to make little real progress in solving the problem of pollution until we recognise it for what primarily it is—an economic problem". He adds that solutions to pollution problems based on technological, political, legal and ethical approach will have disappointing results, for they ignore the primary fact that pollution is an economic problem. On account of this multidisciplinary nature and linkages of environmental issues, several economists have called for an integrated study of Economics and Ecology.

The words Ecology and Economics stem from the same Greek root 'Oikos' which means habitation. Ecology is the study of the interdependence between living organisms and their environment. Ecology deals with the 'household of nature', while Economics deal with the 'household of man'. An ecological balance exists in the society in which man is in harmony with environment. But man in his greed for better living has exploited the environment which has upset the ecological balance, which, in turn, has adverse impacts on human beings.

Production activities by firms such as extraction, processing, manufacture, transport, and consumption and disposal activities by firms and households introduce wastes to environmental media and add stress to the environmental systems. Moreover, economic activities today affect the stock of natural resources available for the future and have inter-temporal welfare effects. The consumption and production activities of households and firms respectively, affect and are affected by the economic functions of the environment. Economic growth result in degradation and overexploitation of resources, which are evident in the decline of some fisheries, the growing number of threatened and endangered species, loss of natural habitats and inadvertent introduction of exotics. Thus economics is not only about using scarce resources to satisfy consumers' needs; it is also about how materials and energy drawn from the environment and used by production and consumption activities are returned back to the environment as wastes. The climate change and its adverse impacts that we are facing today highlights the economics- environment interdependence.

Ecology studies harmony between nature and man. Economy, in general means disharmony with nature. Use is made of nature both directly and indirectly to transform raw-materials into final goods. During this production-process nature is polluted by emission and wastes. Thus there is a conflict due to the incompatibility of the basic ecological principle of stability and the economic principles of business profitability. To restore harmony, to reconcile the interests of human beings and nature—an ecological reorientation of the economic policy is required. Unless we derive unifying principles from these disciplines— ecology and economics— any of our social and economic policies are doomed to failure.

2.3 Economic Functions of the Environment

The environment performs three vital functions that have economic implications:

- The environment is a supplier of resources – both renewable and non-renewable resources for meeting the consumption and production requirements of the economy. The natural and environmental resource input function is central to understanding the relationship between economic growth and environment. Renewable resources like water, air, biological, forest and fisheries and non-renewable resources like deposits of minerals and metals, are vital resources, whose quantity and quality helps to determine the productivity of the economy.
- the environment assimilates or absorbs wastes.
- The environment sustains life forms -maintaining biological diversity and genetic diversity;
- The environment supplies aesthetic and recreational amenities.

The first function that refers to environment as a supplier of resources is often referred to as the "source function"; the second function that refers to the waste assimilation by the environment is known as the sink function. Protecting sink functions is essential for human health. Protecting the productive or source functions is critical to mankind since livelihood depends on these resources. (Karpagam M and GeethaJaikumar, 2010).

The three functions of the environment are clearly linked. The transformation of resources to wastes caused by the economic activities of production and consumption, not only prevents environment from performing the first two functions of the environment but also hampers the third function of the environment— that of providing life support services and aesthetic services. In the absence of the first function of the environment there could be no economic activity. Absence of the second function, namely failure to assimilate wastes will affect the third function. In fact there could be no economic activity in the absence of these functions and these functions are rightly referred to as the 'economic functions' of the environment. All these functions have positive economic value. When the environment fails to perform these functions, the inevitable consequence is "environmental crisis". Reckless use of the environmental services will irreversibly reduce the carrying capacity of the planet. The ultimate inevitable result is environmental crisis. The case of the Aral Sea given in Box 2.1 proves this point. Failure to recognise these positive prices of the economic functions of the environment on account of the absence of market for environmental goods and services have resulted in misallocation and mismanagement of resources.

The destruction of the Aral sea and its ecosystems constitutes one of the greatest man-made environmental disasters in history. It was the main fresh water source for the populations of five countries: Kazakhstan, the Kyrgyz Republic, Tajikistan, Turkmenistan and Uzbekistan. Today, the lake has become a totally saline pond. The Aral Sea was once the fourth largest inland body of water on earth with a surface area of 66,000 km2. In 1960, the mean water level was 53.4 m and it contained 1090 km3 of water (Glantz 1999). The Aral Sea is sandwiched between two deserts, the Karakum and the Kyzylkum. The two main rivers, the Amu Darya and Syr Darya, enter the sea from the north and south respectively. The Amu Darya supplied about 70% of the Aral Sea's water. Nearly half of the flow of the two major rivers reached the Aral Sea.

Since 1960, the Aral Sea has lost 75 per cent of its water volume. The shoreline has receded up to 120 km from its former shore. Sea level has fallen by more than 16 meters in this already shallow sea. It is predicted that the Aral sea will disappear within 15 years. The reason for this ecological disaster is the intensive cotton and rice production introduced during the Soviet era in the delta of the two main rivers – Amu Darya and Syr Darya. Instead of feeding the Aral Sea, the fresh water brought by these rivers was diverted during four decades starting from 1950s, to irrigate and wash the fields of these water intensive crops. This caused salinisation, the disappearance of native fish species, the loss of a major fishery.

By 1990, as a result of the continuing water diversion and evaporation, the shrinking Aral divided into two and its salinity increased from 10 grams per litre to 45. In some parts of the south Aral, salinity tops out at 98 grams per litre. Average sea water salinity is 33 grams per litre. The once thriving fishing industry has been destroyed along with the fish and most of the flora and fauna. Salt pans and contaminated runoff lakes have appeared and winters have become harsher and longer and summers hotter and shorter. Of the regions 73 species of birds, 70 of mammals and 24 of fish, most have either perished or moved on. The area is now constantly subject to toxic dust storms, and desertification. The people of the Aral Sea region have 9 times the world average rate for throat cancer and infant/ maternity mortality is very high. Respiratory complications, tuberculosis and eye diseases are also rising alarmingly.

The experts agree that there is no way of rehabilitating the Aral Sea and its wetlands. However, certain parts could be saved and further damage limited if a sustainable water management system were put into place, together with more efficient irrigation systems.

Source: http://earthobservatory.nasa.gov/Features/WorldOfChange/aral_sea.php
http://visearth.ucsd.edu/VisE_Int/aralsea/index.html
http://unimaps.com/aral-sea/index.html
http://www.columbia.edu/~tmt2120/introduction.htm
http://www.dailymail.co.uk/news/article-1263516/How-Aral-Sea--half-size-England--dried-up.html
http://www.nato.int/science/publication/pdf/water-e.pdf
http://www.jcu.edu.au/jrtph/vol/v01whish.pdf

Box 2.1 The Case of the Aral Sea: Environment – Economy Interlinkage

2.4 The Economy and the Environment – The Circular Flow

Economy - environment inter-linkages is explained in this section using a simple economy consisting of only the production sector and the consumption sector. The economy is part of the environment and operates from within the environment. The environment supports the economy by supplying resources and accepting wastes, two functions which themselves are interrelated. The economy consists of firms and households (consumption and production sectors). Households supply inputs (labour) to firms while firms supply output (products) to households. The environment is involved in these production and consumption processes through its source function and sink function. It supplies raw materials to the production sector comprising of firms and products to the consumption sector comprising of households (source function). The environment also assimilates the wastes generated during the process of production and consumption (sink function). Such a *materials/energy balance* perspective of the economy differs markedly from the conventional view of the economy which focuses on the circular flow of income and the exchange of commodities in markets, and ignores linkages to the environment. The environment and the natural resources which make economic production possible do not appear in the conventional circular flow model.

When a good or service is purchased, two kinds of flow occur: the good moves from the firm to the household and a corresponding payment moves from the household to the firm. Similarly, when firms purchase factors of production, a payment of money for the use of these factors accompanies the flow of factor services from households to firms. This real and money flow between firms and households is shown in Figure 2.2.

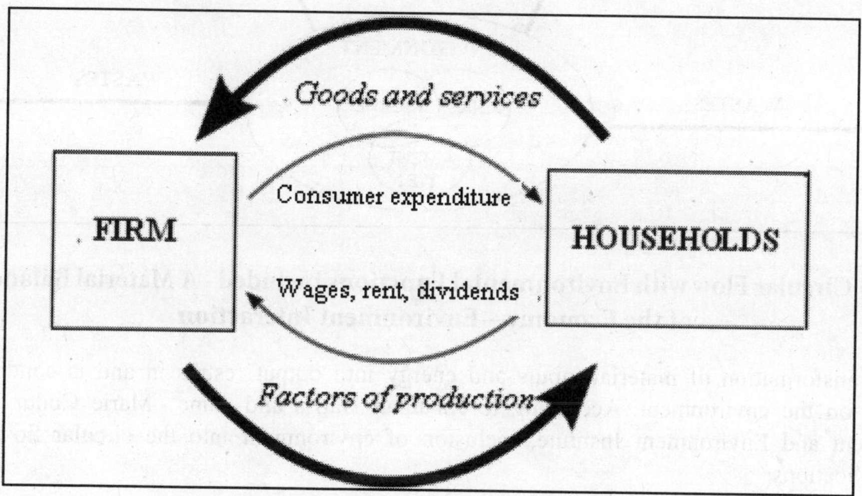

Figure 2.2 Conventional Circular Flow of Income

The transactions are shown in Figure 2.2 by the arrows going in both directions – from firms to households and vice versa. There are two kinds of flows: real economic flows and the money flows. The real flows correspond to transfers of tangible things: goods and services flowing from firms to households and factors of production flowing from households to firms. Environment which is the promoter of the whole economic "show" is ignored in the conventional model shown in Figure 2.2. We need to show the complete picture including environment and its relationship with economic activity: as a supplier of natural resources and also as the receiver of various undesirable wastes from production/consumption processes. Figure 2.3 represents the diverse flows of inputs and outputs between the environment and the economic sphere as well as within the economic sphere.

It was pointed out in section 2.3 that the environment performs three vital functions. Households and firms are linked to the environment as users of the 'source' function and 'sink' function of the environment. Households receive manufactured products from firms and firms inturn receive labour inputs from households. As mentioned earlier the waste assimilating function of the environment is limited by the volume of wastes thrown. As long as the wastes are within the assimilating capacity of the environment it does not create any adverse environmental problem. Once the wastes exceed the assimilating capacity of the environment environmental issues are felt. Hence bearing in mind the constraint of the environment to assimilate wastes, we should adopt recycling and reuse of wastes.

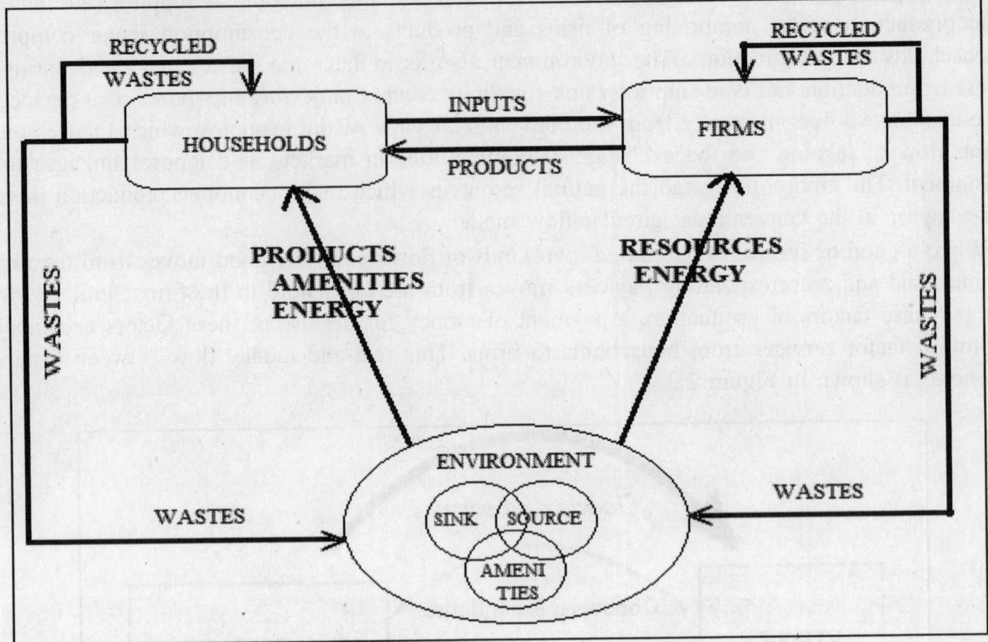

Figure 2.3 Circular Flow with Environmental Functions Included - A Material Balance Model of the Economy—Environment Interaction

The transformation of material inputs and energy into output results in and is conditioned by its impact on the environment. According to Jonathan Harris and Anne –Marie Codur of Global Development and Environment Institute, inclusion of environment into the circular flow has two major implications:

- The essential support given by the environment to human well-being that needs to be adequately taken into account in all attempts at measuring well-being.
- The capacity of the environment to perform its source function and sink function are limited and will lead to environmental crisis if over exploited.

2.5 The Material Balance Approach - Law of Thermodynamics and Environment – Economics Inter Linkages

The economic environment inter-linkage is well brought out by using the Laws of Thermodynamics by Allen Kneese and R.V. Ayres, using the Material Balance Approach. Ayres and Kneese argued that the problem of environmental degradation cannot be adequately assessed unless the complete economic materials flow is envisioned with due regard of the material balance principle. According to the materials balance approach, material cannot be created from nothing and cannot disappear into the void. The material balance approach illustrated in Figure 2.3, depicts production of output from organic and inorganic inputs, through various energy conversion and production process resulting in the discharge of solid, liquid and gaseous wastes. Similar wastes result from consumption activities too. Thus material and energy are drawn from the environment, used for production and consumption activities and returned back to environment as wastes.

Applying the first law of thermodynamic, namely, the "Law of Conservation of Matter and Energy" which states that Matter can neither be created nor be destroyed. Ayres and Kneese explained that all material resources extracted from the environment - the 'source'- eventually end up as residuals in the environment which function now as a 'sink'. Most importantly, the total weight of material is unchanged on its route from source to sink. Thus the weight of wastes entering the environment (the sink) can be inferred from the weight of materials taken from the environment (the source). In the words of Ayres and Kneese "The amount of residuals inserted into the natural environment must be approximately equal to the weight of basic fuels, food, and raw material entering the processing and production system, plus oxygen taken from the atmosphere". Thus matter only gets transformed from one form to another as it moves from source to sink.

When discharged as residuals, although their mass remains unchanged, their forms are altered and their altered forms cause significant amount of environmental damage. The law further implies that economic growth in terms of increased production and consumption levels cannot occur without the additional extraction of resources from the environment and increase in the quantity of wastes. This transformation is explained further using the Law of Entropy, the second Law of Thermodynamics.

The second law of thermodynamics known as the entropy law explains that the transformation of material and energy is an irreversible transformation of useful material into wastes. **Entropy** is a measure of unavailability or disorderliness. It describes the extent to which material or energy is organised or structured. The less structured it is, higher is the entropy of that system. Conversely, entropy is low when material and energy are highly organised and structured. A lump of coal, for example, has a low entropy before it is burnt, since the energy in it is available for use. But once the coal is burnt, it has high entropy, since energy in it has been dissipated as heat and carbon dioxide, neither of which is available for use. The second law implies that as long as there is production and consumption, i.e., as long as there is economic activity, entropy will always increase. **Entropy** is hence used as a measure of defining resources and wastes. The former have low entropy while the latter have high entropy. Economic activity converts low entropy materials into high entropy ones—resources into wastes: The importance of the second law resides in the fact that it tells us that the overall entropy of the system must increase over time; Recycling and waste management can reconvert high entropy (non-useful) matter into low entropy (useful) forms.

The second law of thermodynamics implies that the total amount of usefully concentrated energy and matter in an isolated system must decline over time. It is held by many that the entropy law implies ultimate limits to sustainability of an ecological system over time.

The second law is important because it tells us that the overall entropy of the system increases over time; Recycling and waste management can reconvert high entropy (non-useful) matter into low entropy (useful) forms.

The Laws of Thermodynamics are relevant to the economy because economic activity increases entropy. The laws together imply that the quantity of resources and wastes are ultimately the same. But they differ in entropic value.

2.6 Boulding's Spaceship Economy

In 1966, Kenneth Boulding, in his classic paper, "The economics of the Spaceship Earth" argued for a change in our perception of the nature of 'economy—environment' interactions and of measuring the economic success. In this paper he discusses a change in orientation that is required if mankind is to achieve a perpetually stable economy. He urgently recommends that the time has come to move from a throughput economy to the notion of spaceship earth. Conventional economists believe that the economy is an open system, a virtually limitless plane, where there is always some new space to move to. Boulding refers to this economy as the "cowboy economy". In a cowboy economy, no limit exists on the capacity of the outside to supply resources or receive wastes. Boulding points out that GNP or GDP that reflect the magnitudes of the material flows are the measures of economic success in a cowboy economy, and hence an increase in GNP/GDP is most desirable. Boulding has underlined the necessity for a revision in this perception of a cowboy economy to a spaceman economy. In a spaceman economy, the earth is viewed as a single spaceship, without unlimited reserves of any resource and without unlimited capacity to assimilate wastes. Within this spaceship, if civilisations should survive, every effort has to be made to recycle wastes, reduce wastes,. conserve exhaustible energy and resource sources, and tap new sources of renewable resources and energy. In such a spaceman economy, GNP or GDP is not the measure of economic performance. Boulding argues that, quality and quantity of capital stock will be the appropriate measure of economic growth.

Boulding's spaceship earth analysis was formalised in the material balance models of Ayres and Kneese (1969) and (1970). The material balance approach of Ayres and Kneese visualises the total economic process as a physically balanced flow between inputs and outputs. The materials balance approach and the Laws of Thermodynamics together warn us that continued economic activity that increases entropy and decreases the availability of useful matter and energy will result in the decline of civilisations. Halting this calls for **sustainable** development - a development path that meets the needs of the present generation without compromising the needs of the future generation. To pursue such a development path, every human being should first of all realise that there is no blue print for the planet earth, which we have borrowed from our future generation..

Conclusion

This chapter clearly explains that the economy is very clearly a part of the environment as much as the environment could be seen as part of the economy. Hence a meaningful solution of environmental problems calls for an interdisciplinary integrated approach.

Questions

1. Bring out the environment – Economics interlinkages using the Material Balance Approach and Laws of Thermodynamics.
2. Give an example of the environmental crisis due to over exploitation of the functions of the environment.

Exercise

1. Read Boulding's *"The Economics of the Coming Spaceship Earth,* in the *Environmental Quality in a Growing Economy" from the following sites prepare a comment on the same.*
   http://www.eoearth.org/article/The_Economics_of_the_Coming_Spaceship_Earth_(historical)
   http://www.panarchy.org/boulding/spaceship.1966.html
2. Read the case studies explaining Tragedy of Commons from the following site and prepare a case study from your state.
   http://welkerswikinomics.com/blog/2012/01/11/the-tragedy-of-the-commons-as-a-market-failure/

3

ENVIRONMENTAL ETHICS

"That land is a community is the basic concept of ecology, but that land is to be loved respected is an extension of ethics"

—Aldo Leopold in the foreword to Sand County Almanac (1948)

Economic growth achieved by nations have been achieved at a high cost - at the cost of the health of our Planet Earth. The pollution of the air we breathe, of the lakes, rivers and oceans, the build-up of greenhouse gases, depletion of the ozone layer and deforestation pose a serious threat not only to our own existence but also to the existence of other life forms such as the animal and plant species and ecosystems. Instead of preserving and conserving the planet earth, human beings are constantly abusing it. This is considered morally wrong not only because environmental functions are critical for both present and future generation's well-being but also because the natural environment and its various components have their own right to exist.

Environmental ethics is a new sub-discipline of philosophy that deals with the ethical problems surrounding environmental protection. It is a field of study that considers philosophical arguments for extending our ethical duties to the environment. Environmental ethics is theory and practice about appropriate concern for our duties regarding the natural world. According to Jill Oliphant (2014) environmental ethics considers the ethical relationship between people and the natural world - how humans should relate to their environment, how we should use the Earth's resources and how we should treat other species, both plant and animal. For example the following are some questions, we confront in environmental ethics:

- Should we continue to clear forests for the sake of human consumption?
- Should we knowingly cause the extinction of other species?
- What are our environmental obligations to future generations?

Humanity will not be able to save the world from environmental catastrophe unless and until the ethical reasons to protect the environment is recognised. "The goal of environmental ethics is not to convince us that we should be concerned about the environment, instead it focuses on the moral foundations of environmental responsibility (Ohara.M, 1998)." Environmental ethics examines the question: If abuse of environment by human beings is wrong, is it wrong simply because the various functions of the environment is essential for human life? Or is such behaviour wrong because the environment and its various components have their own right to exist?

Humans share this Earth with five to ten million species. Environmental ethics considers the ethical relationship between people and the natural world - how humans should relate to their environment, how we should use the Earth's resources and how we should treat other species, both plant and animal. Environmental ethics raises important questions such as:

- Does the Earth exist for the benefit of humanity?

- Do humans have the right to take all the Earth's resources for their own use?
- Do other species have a right to exist?
- If only human beings matter why should we take care of environment?
- Is it not the responsibility of human beings to take care of the environment?
- Will future generations miss what we have 'taken from them'?
- When species or landscapes or wilderness areas are destroyed, what is the loss to mankind?

According to Tongjin Yang (2006), there are atleast five distinctive features of environmental ethics. These are:

First, **environmental ethics is extended**. Environmental ethics extends the scope of ethical concerns beyond one's community and nation to include not only all people everywhere, but also animals and the whole of nature, both with respect to current as well as future generations.

Second, **environmental ethics is interdisciplinary** - the concerns addressed by environmental ethics are also addressed by environmental politics, environmental economics, environmental sciences and environmental literature. They reinforce, influence and support each other.

Third, **environmental ethics is plural.** Environmental ethics includes different ideas and perspectives explaining ethical justifications for environmental protection. Some of the various perspectives included in environmental ethics are: anthropocentrism, animal rights theory, biocentrism and eco-centrism; the approaches of these perspectives may be different but they have the same goal: it is everyone's duty to protect the environment.

Fourth, **environmental ethics is global** since environmental pollution does not respect national boundaries and solution to these global issues depends on global governance.

Fifth, **environmental ethics is revolutionary** both at a theoretical level and in practice. The theory of environmental ethics challenges the dominant and deep-rooted anthropocentrism and underlines our duty to non-human beings. At the practical level environmental ethics questions the materialistic and consumerist life style of the people and instead calls for a 'green lifestyle' that is harmonious with nature. It calls for an economic arrangement that is sensitive to Earth's limits and to concerns for quality of life'.

3.1 Intrinsic Value and Instrumental Value

The subject matter of environmental ethics distinguishes between *instrumental value* and *intrinsic value*. Intrinsic value is the value of things as *ends in themselves* while instrumental value is the value of things as *means* to further some other ends.

Ecosystems and species have instrumental value because of their source function and sink function and natural resource value, ecosystem services value, medicinal value, cultural value and spiritual value. A thing has instrumental value only if it can be used for something else. For example, a certain herb or plant is valued because it gives a life-saving drug. This is instrumental value.

Instrumental value is conditional because it changes depending on :

- the changes in the desirability of the end to which it is a means
- whether more efficient alternative means are available.

Intrinsic value on the other hand reflects the value of something for its own sake. It is the value that exists independently of any contribution; For example a tree may have instrumental value because it provides shade, fruits etc. but beyond these, even if the tree ceases to provide these, if it is considered useful, it is its intrinsic value. Since intrinsic value is unrelated to the instrumental value of a resource or ecosystem, it is also referred to as non-instrumental value. Intrinsic value depends on nothing else. To sum up, it can be said that intrinsic value is non – instrumental and non-relational;

the latter implies that it does not depend on the existence of anything else. Further the intrinsic value of a thing has a moral standing., i.e., to have intrinsic value, a thing must be morally considerable. A thing's intrinsic value generates a direct moral duty on the part of individuals to protect it or at least refrain from damaging it.

Does nature have intrinsic value or instrumental value? From the critical functions performed by nature/environment, it is doubtless that nature has instrumental value. However nature has intrinsic value too. For several centuries people recognized only the instrumental value of nature. Only human beings were considered to have intrinsic value. This view is essentially **anthropocentric or human centred.** It was much later, around 1920s, that a gradual change in thinking began which tried to establish the superiority of nature and the intrinsic value of nature.

3.2 Theoretical Foundations of Environmental Ethics

Ethics as a subject of study is a branch of Philosophy. Ethics is about giving a logical set of "rules" or principles for people to follow. Major ethical theories applied in environmental ethics are: **Teleological theories, deontological theories and virtue ethics.**

Teleological theories are characterized primarily by a focus on the consequences which any action might have. Teleological ethics focuses on the intention behind human actions. - on what the goal of a given decision is.

Consequentialism, a form of teleological ethics bases moral judgments on the outcomes of a decision or an action. If the outcomes of an action are beneficial, then that action is held to be morally right. Conversely if the outcome is likely to be harmful, then the action is held to be morally wrong. The judgement of right or wrong depends on the consequences of the decision or action.

Utilitarianism was explained by Jeremy Bentham and John Stuart Mill. It is a form of consequentialism. Utilitarianism prescribes that the morally right action is that which maximizes utility. Utilitarianism focuses on collective welfare and it identifies goodness with the greatest amount of good for the greatest number of people and is referred to as"the greatest happiness principle".

Deontological ethics is concerned with **right** action, with doing the right thing simply because it is the right thing to do. By definition, deontological theories are duty based. It holds that morality is fulfillment of moral obligations or duties. Deontological ethics holds that an action is right if it is executed according to some principle or norm.

Kanthian ethics is part of the **deontological ethics** and holds that *the rightness or wrongness of actions does not depend on their consequences* but on whether they fulfill our duty. For Kant neither environment nor non-human animals possess intrinsic or inherent value. Kant's ethics prescribes doing good for its own sake and holds that the only intrinsically good thing is a goodwill.

Virtue ethics is based on the ethics of individuals and the ethics of human character. It emphasizes the role of character and virtue rather than focusing on one's duty or acting in order to bring about good consequences. **Virtue ethics** is person based rather than action based.

Relevance of the ethical theories to environmental ethics

To see how the different ethical approaches any environmental issue let us consider the example of habitat loss resulting from some economic activity such as construction of highways. Utilitarian approaches are found to be more useful and applicable to environmental issues. Utilitarianism is commonly associated with anthropocentrism yet if habitat loss brings long-term harm to both non-human and human beings, utilitarianism would oppose any such action. Kantian ethics does not see habitat destruction as a matter of concern as long as human beings are not affected. Deontological and Virtue ethics will not be in favour of habitat loss due to their faith in ecocentric approach which recognizes the intrinsic worth of nature. Virtue ethics will hold that destroying ecosystems or habitats runs against the virtue of respect for nature and should hence be avoided.

3.3 Evolution of Environmental Thinking

One of the earliest thinking on environmental ethics is seen in the writings of the Greek philosopher Aristotle. Aristotle held that "nature has made all things specifically for the sake of man" and held that the value of non-human things in nature is merely instrumental. The early philosophers believed in the superiority of human beings and supported anthropocentric or human-centered ethical theories by assigning intrinsic value to human beings alone

Thomas Aquinas was influenced by the teachings of Aristotle and supported the view that only humans possessed intrinsic value. The early extreme supporters of anthropocentric views held that the natural world has value only as long as it useful for human beings, and when it ceases to have any value for human beings there is nothing wrong in destroying it.

During 1900s anthropocentric basis of environmental ethics was challenged, thanks to the writings of Albert Schweitzer, a theologian and a medical missionary to West Africa, Scottish emigrant John Muir and Aldo Leopold. Schweitzer published his book "Civilization and Rights" in 1923 in which he argued that every living thing in nature is endowed with something sacred or intrinsically valuable and should be respected as such. Schweitzer argued that all living things have a "will to live", and that human beings should not interfere with this will. This is his Philosophy of "Reverence for Life". This raises the question, if all living things have moral standing, or intrinsic value then what justifies destruction of non-human living things by human beings in order to live. To this Schweitzer responded that we can only harm or end the life of a living thing when absolutely necessary.

John Muir, the founder of the Sierra Club was known as the "father of American conservation" and the forester Aldo Leopold were motivated by ethical and aesthetic appeal towards nature and hence rejected the anthropocentric approaches to environment. Aldo Leopold's "Land Ethic," is the earliest expression of environmental ethics. "Land ethic" states that land is not a mere object or resource, but is a fountain of energy connecting soils, plants and animals. Hence Leopold advocates a move towards "land ethics". Land ethics granted the moral standing to land community itself. . Leopold wrote in his "A Sand County Almanac (1949) as follows:

"That land is a community is the basic concept of ecology, but that land is to be loved and respected is an extension of ethics." Leopold further adds, "A thing is right when it tends to preserve the integrity, stability, and beauty of the biotic community. It is wrong when it tends otherwise"

Leopold's Land Ethic inspired several writers who highlighted certain moral obligations towards nature. The Australian Philosopher Richard Routley, referred to anthropocentrism as "human chauvinism" and the U.S.-based environmental philosopher Holmes Rolston III, argued that species protection was a moral duty. Rolston (1989) held that "species are intrinsically valuable and are usually more valuable than individual specimens, since the loss of a species is a loss of genetic possibilities and the deliberate destruction of a species would show disrespect for the very biological processes which make possible the emergence of individual living things".

Rachel Carson's book Silent Spring exposed the impact of pesticides on the food chain. The book highlights the interconnectedness between living things and their surroundings- how the fate of one species is linked with that of all other species, including humans. It warned the public of the dangers associated with the use of pesticides like DDT, aldrin and dieldrin and emphasized the basic irresponsibility of an industrialized, technological society towards the natural world. In the first chapter of the book: "A Fable for Tomorrow," Carson described through an example, how all life - from fish to birds to apple blossoms to human beings — would be "silenced" by the insidious effects of DDT (Natural Resource Defense Council (NRDC), 2015). Silent Spring pointed out that the human beings' tendency to exploit and dominate nature will prove counter- productive and advocated an ethic that emphasized "sharing our earth with other creatures."

Several attempts have been made by philosophers over the past two decades to extend moral standing to nature. Many environmental philosophers were not for extending moral standing to animals. However since animals are part of the natural environment, extending moral standing to them is only appropriate.

Peter Singer (1974) and Tom Regan (1983) are two philosophers who support extending moral standing to animals. While Singer, advocated moral standing on the basis of sentience: the capacity to feel pleasure and pain, Regan, held that moral standing should be acknowledged in all "subjects-of-a-life".

Paul W. Taylor (1986) stated that all living organisms have intrinsic value, that is, value for their own sake, irrespective of their value to other beings. By virtue of this, all individual living things also have moral status. Taylor laid down a series of principles in the event of clashes of interest between human beings and other living things in nature. Taylor's principles include:

1. Humans are allowed to act in self-defense to prevent harm being imposed on them by other living organisms.
2. the basic interests of non-human living entities should take priority over the non-basic or trivial interests of humans.
3. when basic interests clash, humans are not required to sacrifice themselves for the sake of others.

According to Taylor, if the interests of all living things are equal, conflict in the interests of living things can be resolved with these principles.

Some of the environmental philosophers who attributed moral standing to all living organisms, proposed hierarchical moral standing differentiated on the basis of moral significance. Moral significance is different from moral standing. All living things have moral standing but moral significance varied among them. Thus some living organisms had a lower moral significance than human beings (like birds, plants for example). This hierarchical approach based on moral significance justified use and destruction of those with lower moral significance to be exploited by living things with higher moral significance. However assigning a high or low moral significance is questionable.

Thus it is clear that there were two streams of ethical thought –the earlier thought assigned superior moral standing to human beings. This anthropocentric view held that only human beings had intrinsic value and environment had only instrumental value, derived from its usefulness of human beings. The later thought beginning from 1900s, attributed intrinsic value to environment also. A biocentric and ecocentric approach in environmental ethics started slowly replacing the anthropocentric approach.

3.4 Approaches to Environmental Ethics

Literature highlights three approaches in environmental ethics, namely:

- J E Lovelock's ecological extension approach - The Gaia Hypothesis
- Preservationist's Deep Ecology Approach
- Conservationist's Shallow Ecology Approach

3.4.1 J. E. Lovelock's Gaia hypothesis

J. E. Lovelock's Gaia hypothesis (1979) questioned the claims on the uniqueness and superiority of human beings. The Gaia Hypothesis stresses the importance of viewing the earth as a living, breathing, single organism, working through a vast network of relationships to maintain a balance in which all life forms can exist and flourish. The word 'Gaia' refers to the name of the Greek goddess of the Earth. The Gaia hypothesis questioned notion of superiority of human beings and says that humans are part of a living whole – Gaia. Gaia Hypothesis holds that human life may be wiped out, but Gaia (Planet Earth) herself would survive without our presence. By abusing Gaia we are risking our own survival. Gaia owes us nothing but we owe our very existence to her.

The ***Gaia Hypothesis*** proposes that our planet functions as a single organism that maintains conditions necessary for its survival. The **Gaia hypothesis**, also known as **Gaia theory** holds that Earth's physical and biological processes are inextricably bound to form a single self- regulated complex system that maintains the conditions for life on planet Earth. According to the theory, the organic and inorganic components of Planet Earth have evolved together as a single living, self-regulating system.

James Lovelock explained the *Gaia hypothesis* as:

> "Life, or the biosphere, regulates or maintains the climate and the atmospheric composition at an optimum for itself."

Inherent in this explanation is the idea that biosphere, the atmosphere, the lithosphere and the hydrosphere are in some kind of balance. The inner workings of *Gaia*, is viewed as a study of the physiology of the Earth, where the oceans and rivers are the Earth's blood, the atmosphere is the Earth's lungs, the land is the Earth's bones, and the living organisms are the Earth's senses. Lovelock calls this the science of *geophysiology* - the physiology of the Earth

The Gaia hypothesis is being increasingly applied to studies of climate change today.

In the past 15-20 years, many of the mechanisms by which Earth self-regulates have been identified. As one example, it has been shown that cloud formation over the open ocean is almost entirely a function of the metabolism of oceanic algae that emit a large sulfur molecule (as a waste gas) that becomes the condensation nuclei for raindrops. The cloud formation not only helps regulate Earth's temperature, it is an important mechanism by which sulfur is returned to terrestrial ecosystems.

Source: http://www.gaiatheory.org/synopsis.htm
http://www.gaiatheory.org/overview/
http://www.bibliotecapleyades.net/gaia/esp_gaia01.htm

Box 3.1 Gaia Hypothesis

3.4.2 Deep Ecology or Ecocentrism

In 1970, the Norwegian philosopher Arne Næss distinguished between two ecological movements – the shallow ecology movement and the deep ecology movement in his short paper called "The Shallow and the Deep, Long-Range Ecology Movement". According to Naess shallow ecology is concerned with the "fight against pollution and resource depletion". Its central objective is the health and affluence of people – which is why it is termed as **anthropocentrism**. Deep ecology, on the other hand, is concerned with the richness, diversity and intrinsic value of the natural world - **ecocentrism**.

Deep ecology considers human beings as an integral part of its environment. The Philosophy emphasizes the interdependent value of human beings with non-human living things. The basic premise of deep ecology is that, like humanity, the living environment as a whole has the same right to live and flourish. Naess rejected the idea that humans were superior to nature and said that nature does not exist to serve humans and that all species have a right to exist for their own sake, regardless of their usefulness to humans. Naess said that from an ecological point of view " the right of all forms (of life) to live is a universal right which cannot be quantified. No single species of living has more of this particular right to live and unfold than any other species." He called this **ecosophy** – "a philosophy of ecological harmony or equilibrium".

There are three interpretations of the term deep ecology. Firstly it refers to a deep questioning about environmental issues probing the fundamental causes of environmental problems. The 'Deep' in deep ecology refers attitudes to nature. Deep ecology questions the root causes of the degeneration of the variety and richness of the world.

Second, deep ecology refers to a platform of eight principles compiled by Arne Naess and George Sessions which is referred to as the "heart of deep ecology" by supporters of deep ecology. This platform is an educational tool to assist people understanding and adding their views to ecosophy. The eight principles are:

1. All human and non-human life on Earth have intrinsic or inherent value. These values are independent of the usefulness of the non-human world for human purposes.
2. Richness and diversity of life forms contribute to the realization of these values and are also values in themselves.
3. Humans have no right to reduce this richness and diversity except to satisfy vital needs.
4. The flourishing of non-human life *requires* a smaller human population.
5. Present human interference with the non-human world is excessive, and the situation is rapidly worsening.
6. Policies must therefore be changed. These policies affect basic economic, technological, and ideological structures. The resulting state of affairs will be deeply different from the present.
7. The ideological change will be mainly that of appreciating life quality rather than adhering to an increasingly higher standard of living. There will be a profound awareness of the difference between bigness and greatness.
8. Those who subscribe to the foregoing points have an obligation directly or indirectly to try to implement the necessary changes.

Thirdly, deep ecology is characterized by the following principles:

1. **Holism.** Nature is to be seen holistically, as an integrated system, rather than as a collection of individual things.
2. **No ontological divide.** Humans are fully a part of Nature, and there is no separation between our species and other ones.
3. **Biocentric egalitarianism.** Nature has unqualified intrinsic value, with humans having no privileged place in nature's web. Emphasis is placed on value at holistic levels, such as populations, ecosystems, and the Earth as a whole, rather than individual entities.
4. **Intuition.** A sensuous, intuitive communion with the Earth is possible, and it gives us needed insight into Nature and our relationship to it.
5. **Environmental devastation.** Nature is undergoing a devastating degradation, an ecological holocaust, at the hands of human societies.
6. **Anti-anthropocentrism.** This destructiveness is rooted in anthropocentrism, a view that we are separate from and superior to Nature, which exists to serve our needs.
7. **An ecocentric society.** The goal at a social level is a society that is based on an ecocentric view of nature and that lives in harmony with the natural tendencies and the limits of natural world.
8. **Self-realization.** The goal at an individual level is to fully realize one's identification with Nature.
9. **Intuitive morality.** The moral ideal, then, is a realization of our identification with nature which yields a spontaneous, intuitive tendency to avoid harm and to flourish.

For ecological harmony or equilibrium, Naessis prescribed five points that human beings should follow. Human beings should:

- radically reduce the Earth's population
- abandon all goals of economic growth
- conserve diversity of species
- live in small, self-reliant communities
- 'touch the Earth lightly'

3.4.3 Conservation ethics – Shallow Ecology

Shallow ecology is anthropocentric. According to the shallow ecology approach the only value in animals and plants is their instrumental value for humans. The central objective of the shallow ecology movement is "the health and affluence of people in the developed countries." Shallow ecology accepts that nature may be harnessed to meet human needs and ends. Shallow ecology assumes that human beings are the central species in the Earth's ecosystem, and that other beings and parts of systems are resources for human use, and of less importance or value. Shallow ecology failed to see that non-human entities too had intrinsic value. Therefore shallow ecology does not object any environmental damaging activity if it would increase the welfare of human being. The clearing of a forest as well as the preservation of a forest were not wrong if it will benefit human beings. Ben Isacat (2015) mentions three salient features of shallow ecology:

1. The nature of shallow ecology has a utilitarian and anthropocentric attitude, based on materialism and consumerism.
2. Shallow ecology focuses on using the world's natural resources for unlimited human growth and comes up with technological solutions to offset environmental problems thus made. For example, shallow ecology promotes recycling of commercial and industrial waste instead of emphasising the prevention of the generation of waste in the first place.
3. Shallow ecology supports placing ever increasing demands on the land to produce more food instead of stressing the improvement of human birth control to reduce human numbers.

Anthropocentric approach of the Shallow ecology is the underlying principle of conservation ethics advocated by Gifford Pinchot, father of Conservation Movement who saw the Earth as a set of natural resources that need to be managed for present and future generations of humans. Conservation ethics holds that environment is useful because of its utility or usefulness to human beings. Conservation ethics chooses to conserve resource and indulge in environmentally friendly production and consumption activities only because they are beneficial to human beings. Conservation is important for our welfare and that of future generations. Pinchot sought to protect natural resources from short-sighted exploitation arising from irresponsible production method and advocated rational, long-term management of natural resources.

3.4.4.Antropocentrism (Shallow Ecology) Vs Ecocentrism (Deep Ecology)

Ecocentrism is based on the intrinsic value of a thing or being. Anthropocentrism on the other hand is based on instrumental value of a thing or being. Anthropocentrism holds that human beings are the central or most significant entities in the world. It regards human beings are superior to nature and hence the exploitation of other entities such as animals, plants mineral resources etc are justified. Ecocentrism and anthropocentrism are the guiding philosophies of deep ecology and shallow ecology. As pointed out already shallow ecology accepts that nature may be exploited to meet human needs and ends while deep ecology completely rejects any belief that the human beings are in some way superior to any other species or nature itself. According to the deep ecologist Arne Naess, anthropocentrism is the root cause of the ecological crisis, human over population and the extinction of many non-human species. Ecocentrism focuses on the biotic community as a whole and strives to maintain ecosystem composition and ecological processes. Anthropocentrism held that nature was designed exclusively, to serve the needs of humanity.

Ben Isacat (2015) in his online book "How to do Animal Rights" gives eight tenets for shallow ecology contrasting with the eight tenets of deep ecology given above. Table 3.1 gives Isacat's eight tenets of shallow ecology in contrast to the eight tenets of deep ecology.

Table 3.1 Deep Ecology Versus Shallow Ecology – the Eight Tenets

No	Deep Ecology*	Shallow Ecology
1	All creatures on Earth have intrinsic value	All creatures on Earth have value only for their usefulness to humans.
2	The whole diversity of living beings, human and non-human - contributes to life's richness.	Human beings are more important than other living beings.
3	Humans should use other beings only to satisfy their basic needs.	Humans should always use all resources for their material and economic advantage.
4	The health of non-humans depends on decreasing the number of humans.	The human population can increase without restraint.
5	Human interference with the world is excessive and worsening.	Technological progress will solve all problems
6	Human policy (economics, technology and ideology) must change radically.	Materialism and consumerism should govern human society.
7	Quality of life is more important than standard of living.	The standard of living should keep rising.
8	Every human who believes in these points must work for change.	Leave environmental problems for the experts to solve.

* summarized and interpreted version

Source: reproduced from online version of the book "How to do Animal Rights" by Ben Isacat (2015)

Conclusion

Environmental ethics is concerned with the issue of protecting our environment and treating nature cautiously. Untill the beginning of 1900, the negative impact of human actions on the environment were not felt, probably because they were too small compared to the powers of the environment for self-cleansing or because we were not aware of the damages we are inflicting on the environment and we could not foresee the long-run implications of such continued impacts. At present the negative consequences of our actions are obvious and the awareness of such consequences are also high. We know that only we are to be held responsible for the mess we have created. Therefore we have a moral obligation to "to act with care, foresight and at times, with forbearance and constraint". Nobel Laureate Wangari Maathai, the environmentalist form Kenya, said "... the environment is very important in the aspects of peace because when we destroy our resources, they become scarce and we fight over that...". It is time realized our environmental responsibility and we signed a peace treaty with environment.

Questions

1. Distinguish between intrinsic value and instrumental value.
2. Summarise the salient features of environmental ethics.

3. Give a brief note on Gaia hypothesis
4. Briefly state the main theoretical approaches to ethics and explain their applicability to environmental issues through an appropriate example.
5. Environmental ethicists have taken either an anthropocentric approach or an ecocentric approach to Nature. How do these approaches differ? Which one do you support? Why?
6. The concept of Sustainable development 'seeks to create a balance between the best naturalistic values, as well as good humanistic ones for respecting ecosystems'. Discuss

Exercise

1. What are the feelings that come to your mind first when you think of the environment? What are the factors that shape these? Why?
2. Examine the ethics of any development activity - local, national or global in terms of its environmental consequences.
3. Go to the website that gives an account on pollution of River Ganges and also visit other similar sites on Ganges and make a case study of environmental ethics.
4. http://www.all-about-india.com/Ganges-River-Pollution.html
5. What should corporations do to prevent another Bhopal? Relate your answer to environmental ethics.
6. From the website down load information on the issue of mining using cyanide based technologies by Roşia Montana Gold Corporation at Apuseni Mountains in Romania. Discuss the ethical implications of the issue.
7. *"The greatest threat to people is ignorance; the greatest threat to animals is ignorant people"- Discuss.*
8. Download the online book "How to Do Animal Rights" from the site http://www.animalethics.org.uk/How-to-Do-Animal-Rights-2015.pdf

Read the book and prepare a write up on the Ethics of Animal Rights quoting examples of flora and fauna which have extinct or which are endangered.

4

ENVIRONMENTAL MOVEMENTS

"The rise of global environmental movement has made sure that the relationship between humans and their environment will never be quite the same again."

—*John McCormick*

Environmentalism is defined as the promotion of values, attitudes and policies aimed at reaching an accommodation between human needs and the limits of natural environment. In simple terms, environmentalism aims at popularising the basic truth about the inter-relatedness of the biosphere and at alerting the homosapiens that the mismanagement of the finite resources of the planet earth will ultimately threaten our own existence. Today, environmentalism has spawned into a mass movement, with millions of followers and has provoked a rethinking of our economic and social priorities. Environmentalism has brought a fundamental change in human values and human behaviour— a change that is environmentally friendly.

Environmental movements are people's response to the threat to their survival and to the demand for the conservation of the vital life supporting system. The environmental movement is a diverse scientific social and political movement for addressing environmental issues born out of the conviction that environment can be protected from man when and only when man realises his responsibility towards nature. Environmental and ecological movements are "expressions of the universal socio – ecological impacts of a narrowly conceived development based on short term commercial criteria" (Vandana Shiva, 1991). Gadgil and Guha define environmental movement as an "organized social activity consciously directed towards promoting sustainable use of natural resources, halting environmental degradation or bringing about environmental restoration" (Gadgil and Guha, 1995). Environmental movements reveal how the resource intensive demands of current development have ecological devastation built into them. They also stress that the issue is not merely one of a matter of money but it is a matter of life itself. The three important objectives of Environmental movements are:

- Creating awareness about the need to preserve/conserve natural resources
- Prevent environmentally destructive activities.
- Promote environmental rehabilitation and restoration through sound natural resource management, (eg: afforestation and soil conservation initiatives)

The environmental movement addresses a variety of issues from the protection of forests to the protection of penguins—from the disposal of toxic wastes to the dangers of global warning and ozone hole; from the effects of affluence to the effects of poverty. The environmental groups are also different in character. On the one hand we have non-governmental organisations (NGOs) like Green Peace, World Wide Fund for Nature, having an office in London, a multi-million budget, over 100 paid employees and so on. On the other hand there are environmental groups that have no full time or part time paid employees and occupy a very borderline position in terms of their organisational characteristics. The approach adopted by the groups are also different; ranging from creating awareness through public education to a careful and sustained lobbying in national and local legislatures. The philosophy of the different groups, though aiming towards conservation of nature, differs in application; while some groups develop an attitude of an uncompromising anti-growthism, others work towards sustainable growth. The former are called as preservationists and the latter as conservationists.

The global environmental movement grew out of a series of independent responses to local issues, in different places at different times. In the mid to late 19th century individuals formed local groups which subsequently became national movements. These national movements have shaped into global movements today, thanks to the improved scientific understanding, increased personal mobility and spread of human settlement.

The causes for the rise of environmental movement of the developed nations differ from that of the developing and underdeveloped nations. Environmental movement of the advanced industrialized nations, referred to as "full stomach" environmentalism, is the "direct consequence of affluence" with the focus on preserving the wilderness and flora and fauna and maintaining the quality of the environment. The objective of the environmental movements in developing countries are not necessarily for greening the earth or for saving the endangered species, as in the west, but for the very survival of the local poor. Hence environmentalism of the south is called as "empty – belly" environmentalism (Sharma, 2007). In the underdeveloped nations environmental movement arise out of scarcity of resources, the movement initiated by the marginal population – hill peasants, tribal communities, fishermen and other underprivileged people who fight for their right to manage these resources on which their livelihood is dependent. The Chipko movement in India (Box 4.2) and the movement to save the Brazilian rain forests (Box 4.5) are examples of conflicts initiated by local people dependent on, and in, control of the resources.

The earliest expressions of environmental movement mostly seen in the 18th century, in the advanced countries, particularly in Europe and the United States arose primarily out of concern for protection of countryside and wilderness; Modern environmental movement in most countries is said to be a consumer movement that demand a clean, safe, and beautiful environment as part of a higher standard of living. The evolution of the environmental movement to its various manifestations today clearly reveals three distinct phases categorized as follows:

- the period before 1962
- the period from 1962 to 1990
- the period from 1990s to the present day

4.1 Evolution of the Environmental movement before 1962 – before the publication of Silent Spring:

Concern about the impact of environmental problems on human life is not new. There are many historical evidences of misuse of environment. Nearly 3700 years ago, the Sumerian cities were abandoned on account of the increased salinity and water logging of irrigated lands. Plato's writings mention of the effects of deforestation and soil erosion in the hills of Attica, caused by over grazing and felling of trees. The decline and fall of many civilizations can be traced to environmental deterioration. Many commentators of Roman history have attributed the decline of Roman empire to over exploitation of land and soil deterioration. The fall of the 400 year old Mesopotamian civilisation in the 7th century and the Mayan civilisation in the 10th century are similarly attributed to mismanagement of natural environment. However, such concerns did not give rise to public activism. The industrial revolution that made England the foremost economic power in the world brought with it chaos to the natural environment. William Wordsworth, the English poet, described the darker side of industrial revolution as the "outrage done to nature". John Evelyn, a naturalist, complains of London as "the suburb of Hell". Sewage and chemical effluent poured into the Thames from the rivers along its banks during 1950s. In 1858 Queen ElizabethI had to live out of London on account of the stink in the River Thames which had become a vast sewer, and the stink was referred to as the 'great stink of Thames'. In the early 19th century the Rhine River, one of Europe's great river systems, was a byword for pollution. As industrialization developed, the Rhine became a vast sink for pollution. In 1828, after a visit to the city of Cologne Samuel Coleridge wrote:

The river Rhine, it is well known
Doth wash your city of Cologne
But tell me, Nymphs, what power divine
Shall henceforth wash the river Rhine?

Prior to the 19th century, for several hundred years, the dominant world view regarded humans as superior to other creations and hence advocated the use and exploitation of all aspects of nature to meet the growing needs of the population. This view was, however, criticised by many philosophers, poets and religious leaders. Philosophers Henry David Thoreau, John Muir, Ralph Waldo Emerson and Aldo Leopold developed an ethical view of nature and environmental protection to them is a "right" of the planet. From the 19th century onwards, the environmental movement is referred to as the "cult of wilderness". This period highlighted the need to preserve nature based on the deeply held values on nature. The main policy proposal emerging from the first current of environmentalism is the preservation of nature through the creation of nature reserves or natural parks.

Henry David Thoreau (1817 -1862), wrote extensively on the beauty of nature. Thoreau called for the preservation of wilderness and believed that in wildness is the preservation of the world. He wrote "the earth I tread on is not a dead inert mass. It is a body, has a spirit , is organic and fluid to the influence of its spirit". In his book "Walden" he provides an inspiring environmental virtue ethics, which links environmental protection to human happiness. Thoreau advocated restraint in our dealings with nature and said that such restricted use of nature will help us to lead better lives. Thoreau is a leading critic of anthropocentrism: the view that "only human beings have rights or intrinsic value"

John Muir, (1838-1914), an ecological patriot, and the founder of the Sierra Club, in 1882, was of the view that wilderness is a necessity and that mountains, peaks and forests are fountains of life. John Muir believed that "nature's object in making animals and plants might possibly be, first of all, the happiness of each one of them not the creation of all for the happiness of one .." and added that "the universe would be incomplete without man; but it would also be incomplete without the smallest trans microscopic creatures …" Muir stated that "everybody needs beauty as well as bread, places to play in and pray in, where nature may heal and cheer and give strength to body and soul alike". He added that these places needed to be protected for their own sake and as sacred places. His writings and philosophy strongly influenced the formation of the modern environmental movement. Muir believed in the equality of all entities in nature's dominion.

Gifford Pinchot, (1865–1946) called as the "apostle of conservation," helped to cast conservation as a moral crusade for environmental management. The aim of conservation, according to Pinchot was the greatest good for the greatest number for the longest time. Pinchot was a proponent of a practical environmentalism. He advocated that natural resources may be used for the good of the society provided the resources are used on a sustainable basis. Conservationists advocated wise use of natural resources since not using the natural resources was a waste. Pinchot advocated application of scientific principles for the maintenance and use of forests and rivers, which would enhance human welfare.

Aldo Leopold (1887-1948) a conservationist and wildlife ecologist was deeply concerned about the speed and impact of industrialization on the natural world and human-nature relationships. He advocated the preservation of wildlife and wilderness areas. In 1939 he wrote an essay titled "A Biotic View of Land." In this essay he conceptualized land in a holistic way and stated that "land was not a mere economic resource, but a living community". He described land as a "biotic pyramid," with "soil at the base, plants and herbivores in the middle, and carnivores at the top. Energy from the sun is channeled from the base to the apex. At the end of an organism's life, the nutrients in its body are returned to the soil through decomposition" (Leopold quoted by Lin Qi Feng, 2013).

Figure 4.1 Eminent Early Environmental Thinkers

The concept of land ethic was coined by Aldo Leopold in his book *"A Sand Country Almanac" published in 1949*. Leopold's Land Ethic, considers humans as a part of nature and not separate from it. Therefore Leopold suggested that human beings should consider ourselves as a part of the natural community and not as rulers of the natural world. Land Ethics suggests that the natural world has a right to exist in its natural state as an end in itself. In "The Land Ethic", Leopold wrote: "Conservation is a state of harmony between men and land." One of the well-known quotes from the book is: A thing is right when it tends to preserve the integrity, stability, and beauty of the biotic community. It is wrong when it tends otherwise.

Ralph Waldo Emerson (1803-1882), through his essay entitled "Nature" set out his belief that all elements in nature and man are interrelated and interdependent. He said: *"In the presence of nature, a wild delight runs through the man, in spite of real sorrows.*"

The dominant world view was questioned by the 'preservationists' and the conservationists. The preservationists advocated a life style in line with natural rhythm. They favoured ecocentrism. The conservationists like Gifford Pinchot, Garret Hardin and John Passmore, advocated anthropocentrism. They viewed nature as basically a resource for human use and development and called for a wise use of nature. Their approach to resource management was scientific and professional and at the same time activist. The conservationists held the view that the goal of conservation was preventing waste and saving resources for prudent, constructive and efficient human use. Their motto was "for the greatest good, for the greatest number, for the longest time".

The early conservationist and preservationist movements focused on the protection of wild life and preservation of flora and fauna. Thus began the animal rights movement that discussed the need to prevent the increasing pressure on wild life resulting from the spread of human settlement. The world's first national environmental group known as the "Commons, Footpaths and Open Spaces Preservation Society" was founded in Britain in 1865. This and the "East Riding Association for the Protection of Sea Birds", formed in Britain in 1867, focused on the protection of animals and birds. In 1892 the *Sierra Club* was founded in the United States which today is leading a very active environmental movement with more than 70,000 members. The Scottish born naturalist John Muir's campaign in 1890 led to the creation of the Yosemite National Park, the first park specifically designed to protect wilderness.

In mid 1930's, an international *nature protection body* was formed with the joint effort of 17 European countries to collect and publish information on international protection of nature. During the years of First World War, many agreements were signed for the protection of birds and wildlife, through the efforts of the movements that warned about the extinction of species, threats faced by the migratory birds and the dangers of international trade in bird feathers and animal skin. The Second World War period strengthened the spirit of the environmental movement through the specialised agencies of the United Nations like FAO, ECOSOC, duly assisted by UNESCO. In 1948, the International Union for the Protection of Nature was formed. The IUPN, later came to be known as International Union for Conservation of Nature and Natural Resources, emphasised on conservation of resources. This period also witnessed the establishment of World Wide Life Fund, in 1961, which later came to be known as World Wide Fund for Nature (WWF); the objectives of WWF were to (a) conserve nature and ecological processes by preserving genetic species and eco-system diversity (b) to ensure sustainable use of renewable resources (c) to promote action to reduce pollution and wasteful exploitation and consumption of resources (d) to create awareness of threats to the natural environment. Thus in 1960s environmentalism entered a new phase that was more active.

4.2 Environmental movement from 1962 to 1992:

The environmental movement from 1962 to 1992, known as the period of environmental revolution, was a reaction to a series of environmental disasters and is marked by publications of environmental writing and development of new concepts. The period also saw the active involvement of the environmental NGOs, and witnessed the organization of many national and international conferences on environmental issues and policies. This period could be described as the period of 'environmental revolution'. Environmental revolution or new environmentalism, began with the publication of Rachel Carson's "Silent Spring" and culminated in Earth Day in 1970. The eight years between 1962 and 1970 saw environmentalism transformed. New environmentalism was more dynamic, more broad based and won greater public support. New environmentalism was not an organised and homogeneous phenomenon, but an accumulation of organisations and individuals with varied motives and ideas but similar goal.

The period 1966-72, witnessed a series of environmental disasters like the "Torry Canyon" oil spill and Minamata episode in Japan. These environmental disasters made people sensitive to the environmental and health costs of economic development.

Rachel Carson's Silent Spring marked the beginning of the revolution. The book detailed the effects of misuse of synthetic chemical pesticides and insecticides. The book educated the public of the implications of human activity on the environment and of the cost in turn to human society. Silent Spring exposed the dangers of widespread use of pesticide on both wildlife and humans. *Silent Spring* described how DDT entered the food chain and accumulated in the fatty tissues of animals, including human beings, and caused cancer and genetic damage. Carson concluded that DDT and other pesticides had irrevocably harmed animals and had contaminated the world›s food supply. In the chapter, "A Fable for Tomorrow" she depicted a nameless American town where all life—from fish to birds to apple blossoms to human children—had been "silenced" by the devastating effects of DDT. The public debate on use of pesticides initiated by Silent Spring continued throughout 1960s and eventually all 12 of the most toxic substances listed in Silent Spring were either banned or restricted.

A book that was equally effective as Silent Spring, was ***Stewart Udall's The Quiet Crisis*** published in 1963. The two books triggered modern environmental movement and underlined 'both the unintended and negative impact that certain human behaviors have on ecological relationships and the philosophy that humans are part of, not apart from, the rest of nature'.

New environmentalism was marked by the publication of many leading works by environmental theorists and philosophers. Some of the books and articles that created a wave of environmental awareness and environmental consciousness among the people in the 60s and 70s are:

- Kenneth Boulding's "The Economics of Coming Spaceship Earth" 1966.
- Paul Ehrlich's, 'Population Explosion'(1968)
- Hardin's "Tragedy of Commons" (1968)
- Commoner's "The Closing Circle" (1971)
- The Club of Rome's "Limits to Growth" (1972)
- Edward Goldsmith's article, "Blue Print for Survival" (1972)
- EF Schumacher's "Small is Beautiful" (1973)

All these works shared the common philosophy and faith that the present increases in production and consumption activities of human beings are threatening the very foundations of human survival by disrupting ecosystems and depleting resources.

Figure 4.2 Select Environmental Thinkers during 1962- 1990s

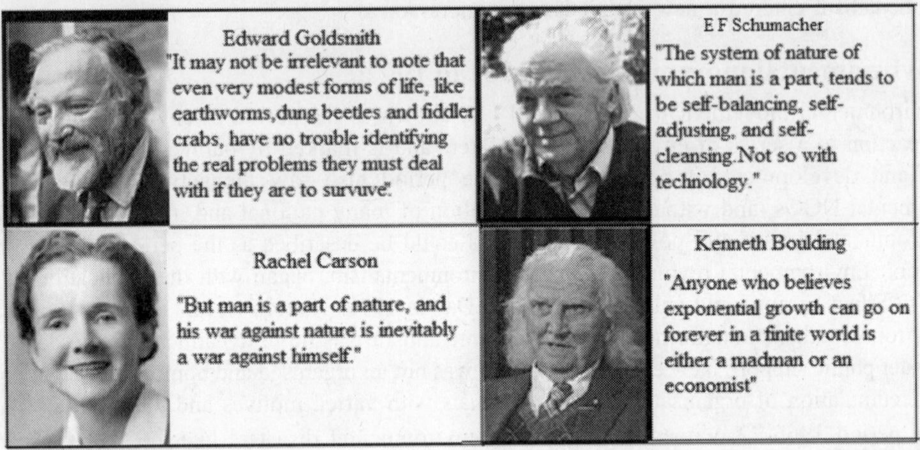

Source : A to Z quotes

Kenneth Boulding, in his classic essay, ***The Economics of the Coming Spaceship Earth***, published in 1966, described the planet earth as a spaceship. The spaceship economy is characterized by limited material and food supplies and limited capacity to assimilate wastes. The survival strategy in this case is economic use of materials, energy and the environment, and maximization of the recycling of substances, materials and products.

Boulding questioned the roles of growth and consumption as means of creating human well-being. As early as 1965 Boulding felt that the basic problem of humanity is the increased scale of its activities to a level where pollution and resource extraction can no longer be regarded as unimportant. Boulding warned that the spaceship economy had arrived already. The world economy had already run out of clean air in many cities, "many lakes have become cesspools, forests have disappeared from some regions, and the once highly productive mines have been exhausted." Boulding recommended the transformation of our increasingly (open) globalised cowboy economy into a (closed) spaceman economy.

Paul Ehrlich considered population size and growth as the most dominant reason for environmental degradation. According to him, "no changes in behaviour or technology can save us unless we can achieve control over the size of human population". Ehrlich expressed the factors responsible for environmental impact in the form an equation which is referred to as the **IPAT equation**. IPAT is an accounting identity stating that environmental impact (I) is the product of three terms: 1) population (P); 2) affluence (A); and 3) technology (T). It is stated as:

$$I = P \times A \times T$$

The Tragedy of the Commons an influential article written by Garret Hardin was published in 1968 in the journal *Science*. The essence of Hardin's story of tragedy is that herdsmen, sharing a common pasture, led by the optimizing personal gain, will ultimately overstock their herds and destroy their shared resource. The policy implication of this is that free access and unrestricted demand for a finite resource ultimately dooms the resource through over-exploitation. The solution is ensuring collective responsibility.

The Tragedy of Commons, an influential article written by Garret Hardin was published in the year 1968 in the journal "Science"

According to Hardin the unrestricted advance of private interests leads to collective ruin. The situation in which the self interest dominated rational acts of individuals destroy a common resource is referred to as the Tragedy of Commons.

Tragedy of Commons refers to the case of a pasture which is open to all herdsmen; all herdsmen would graze their cattle freely without any charge and any restriction. Any rational herdsman will want to maximize his gain. Since the personal gain from adding one more cattle on the pasture is greater than the social cost of overgrazing, each herdsman will keep on adding cattle to graze on the pasture land. Each herdsman is driven by self-interest to increase his number of herds grazing without limit. This leads to the tragedy. "Ruin is the destination toward which all men rush" remarks Hardin.

Examples of tragedy of Commons

Example 1: The Grand Banks fisheries off the coast of Newfoundland: For hundreds of years, the grand Banks was abound with cod fish. Hence cod fishing was allowed without any restriction. During the 1960s the advancement in fishing technology enabled fishermen to catch massive amounts of cod fish. There was competition among fishermen to catch increasingly larger amounts of cod. As a result the fish catch was greater than the rate of biological growth of the cod. This eventually led to the collapse of the entire cod fishing industry by 1990.

Example 2 River Ganga in India: Ganga river basin is the largest among river basins in India and the fourth largest in the world, and has a total length of 2,525 km. Around half a billion people live within the river basin, at an average density of over 500 per sq km, and this population is projected to increase to over one billion people by the year 2030. Inspite of taking a huge load of wastes Ganga remained unpolluted because the River decomposes organic waste 15 to 25 times faster than other rivers. Today however the tons of organic compounds discharged into the Ganges is far above its natural assimilating capacity. Nearly all the sewage, industrial effluent runoff from chemical fertilizers and pesticides used in agriculture within the basin, and large quantities of solid waste, including thousands of animals' carcasses and hundreds of human corpses are dumped in the river everyday. The inevitable result of this assault on the river's assimilating capacity has been an erosion of river's water quality. Large stretches (over 600 km) of the river are virtually dead from an ecological point of view. The state of the river today is a clear case of tragedy of commons.

Reference:

http://www.garretthardinsociety.org/articles/art_tragedy_of_the_commons.html
http://www.investopedia.com/terms/t/tragedy-of-the-commons.asp
http://www.ecofriends.org/main/eganga/images/Critical%20analysis%20of%20GAP.pdf
http://reli350.vassar.edu/gosselin/gangatoday.html

Box 4. 1 Hardin's Tragedy of Commons

According to Hardin the unrestricted advance of private interest leads to collective ruin. The situation in which the self-interest dominated rational acts of individuals destroy a common resource is referred to as tragedy of commons by Hardin.

Barry Commoner, a biologist and research scientist, viewed the environmental crisis as a symptom of a fundamentally flawed economic and social system. He argued that corporate greed, misguided government priorities and the misuse of technology accounted for the undermining of "the finely sculptured fit between life and its surroundings. In his book **"The Closing Circle", (1971)** Commoner blamed capitalist technologies as chiefly responsible for environmental degradation. Commoner argued that our economy—including corporations, government, and consumers—needs to be in sync with what he called the "four laws of ecology":

1. **Everything is Connected to Everything Else** which implies that there is only one ecosphere for all living organisms and what affects one, affects all.
2. **Everything Must Go Somewhere, no matter what you do and no matter what you use.** This implies the same as the first law of thermodynamics which states that matter and energy can neither be created nor be destroyed.
3. **Nature Knows Best.** The technology innovated, designed and used by human beings to improve upon nature, will be detrimental to the natural system.
4. **There Is No Such Thing as a Free Lunch**. Everything comes from something. There's no such thing as spontaneous existence. Anything extracted from the ecosystem by human effort must be replaced.

According to Commoner "The environmental crisis arises from a fundamental fault: our systems of production—in industry, agriculture, energy and transportation—essential as they are, make people sick and die." His suggestions for restoring environmental quality are:

- substituting solar sources of energy for fossil and nuclear fuels;
- substituting electric motors for the internal-combustion engine;
- substituting organic farming for chemical agriculture;
- expanding the use of durable, renewable and recyclable materials—metals, glass, wood, paper—in place of the petrochemical products that have massively displaced them.

Commoner pointed out that there is only one ecosphere for all living things. What affects one, affects all. He also noted that in nature there is no waste. We can't throw things away. Therefore, we need to design and manufacture products that do not upset the delicate balance between humans and nature. (Peter Dreier, 2017, Blog)

In 1972, members of **Club of Rome,** led by Donella and Dennis Meadows presented a world model known as the **limits to the growth model**. The model identified five factors as determining and ultimately limiting growth: population, agricultural production, natural resources depletion, industrial production and pollution. The model observed that "If the present growth trends in world population, industrialization, pollution, food production, and resource depletion continue unchanged, the limits to growth on this planet will be reached sometime within the next one hundred years... It is possible to alter these growth trends and to establish a condition of ecological and economic stability that is sustainable far into the future." The LTG model suggested that the collapse of the economic system can be avoided only by an immediate limit on population and pollution, as well as a cessation of economic growth.

Edward Goldsmith's "A blueprint for survival" (1972) was published in January 1972, in *The Ecologist* Vol. 2 No.1, and was subsequently republished in paperback by Penguin books on popular demand; The principal authors were Edward Goldsmith and Robert Allen. The article emphasised the need to conserve and preserve our environmental resources. The Blue Print observed that the world cannot accommodate this continued increase in ecological demand. The Blueprint recommended the creation of a society which is sustainable – a society that would depend not on expansion but on stability. According to Goldsmith, the principal conditions of a stable society are:

1. minimum disruption of ecological processes
2. maximum conservation of materials and energy – or an economy of stock rather than flow
3. a population in which recruitment equals loss; and
4. a social system in which the individual can enjoy, rather than feel restricted by, the first three conditions

The Blue Print recommended that invention, promotion and application of alternative technologies – intermediate technologies - which are energy and materials conservative, will have only minimum negative impact on ecological processes.

The theme of 'no growth' was taken further in 1973 by the British economist **EF Schumacher**. In his book **"Small is Beautiful",** Schumacher suggested that many of the environmental and social problems facing the world were the result of unlimited economic growth on a gigantic scale which according to him is neither desirable nor practicable for the rest of the world. Schumacher appeals to people to transform their life styles—to make transition from the belief that "more is beautiful" to "small is beautiful". Schumacher advocated the concept of "intermediate technology" known popularly as "appropriate technology" on grounds that it is "environment-friendly, non-polluting and non-exploitative of people or nature. His concept of appropriate technology is today upheld as a technology for sustainable future, as the basis for technologies of renewable energy, of recycling and of ecological restoration. Schumacher's book today is one of the bibles of the green movement.

The various books and articles mentioned above focused on the fact that, continued economic growth on a planet with finite resource was not only impossible but was also capable of destroying the vary basis of growth. The solution advocated is sustainable growth and sustainable development. It was during this period that the much discussed and debated theory – The Gaia Theory - was explained by the British Scientist and inventor, James Lovelock, in the late 1960's. The **Gaia hypothesis**, also known as **Gaia theory** holds that Earth's physical and biological processes are inextricably bound to form a single self- regulated complex system that maintains the conditions for life on planet Earth. According to the theory, the organic and inorganic components of Planet Earth have evolved together as a single living, self-regulating system (Refer Box 3,1 in Chapter 3).

During this period the Norwegian philosopher Arne Naess coined the phrase "deep ecology" in his paper 'The Shallow and the Deep, Long-Range Ecology Movement,' published in 1973, to express the idea that the human beings have no right to exploit the resources of the earth and held that a whole system is superior to any of its parts. This view is also called 'ecocentric', because it sees human beings as an integral part of planet Earth rather than at the center or on top. In contrast, shallow ecology favoured a anthropocentric approach and held that nature may be harnessed to meet human needs and ends (for a detailed discussion on shallow ecology refer to chapter 3).

The period 1966-72, witnessed a series of environmental disasters like the "Torry Canyon" oil spill and Minamata episode in Japan. These environmental disasters made people more sensitive to the environmental and health costs of economic development.

New environmentalism peaked on April 22,1970, when 'Earth day', the largest environmental demonstration in history was held in the United States, in which more than 300,000 Americans took part. The Earth Day signalled "an awakening to the dangers in a dictatorship of technology". Earth day proved that the environmental crisis was no longer a quiet crisis, but an outburst of thousands of activists who felt that the human race was rapidly using up the stock of natural resources and causing irrepairable damages to the planet earth.

Since 1972, the environmental movement worldwide has gained strength, both qualitatively and quantitatively. The momentum gained by the movement between 1960 and 1972 culminated in two international conferences; the Biosphere Conference in Paris in 1968 and the United Nations Conference on Human Environment, held in Stockholm in June 1972. The Biosphere Conference recommended the need for more and better research on eco-systems, human ecology, pollution and genetic and natural resources and on the need for an inventory and monitoring of resources, besides stressing the need for new approaches to environmental education.The theme of the Conference - "Only One Earth" - was chosen to emphasize that all living and inanimate things were part of a single interdependent system, and that man would have no other place to live if he abused the environment.

The Stockholm conference (1972) looked at wider political, social and economic questions related to environment. The Stockholm Conference was a landmark in the history of environmental movement. The Stockholm Conference was attended by not less than 113 countries and atleast 19 intergovernmental agencies and 400 non-governmental organisations. The presence of the NGOs at the conference and the role they played, marked the beginning of a more dynamic role for environmental groups.

The agreed documents of the Stockholm Conference were: the Stockholm Declaration on Human Environment and the Action Plan for the Human Environment. The Stockholm Declaration consisting of a preamble and 26 principles, addressed the major areas related to environmental issues, ranging from education and science to social and economic development and from resources to pollution. The Action Plan was a functional framework of 109 recommendations and consisted of three parts; (i) a global assessment programme (ii) environmental management activities and (iii) supporting measures, such as education and training. The 26 principles relate to:

- safeguarding and conserving the natural resource,
- international co-operation for improving the environment,
- recognizing environment – development interaction and interdependence,
- maintain pollution within the assimilating capacity of the environment,
- use of science , technology and research to promote environmental protection.

The Stockholm Conference had several important outcomes. It promoted the development of national environment policies, notably the creation in many countries of environment agencies and ministries. Several initiatives on the international environment and development issues followed in the 1970s and 1980s.

The conference led to the global participation and co-operation on solutions to environmental issues. The post Stockholm era saw renewed growth in the formation of new NGOs. Their number had grown to 2230 by 1982 in LDCs alone of which 60% were formed after the Stockholm conference. In developed countries the number of NGO's increased to 13,000 of which 30 per cent were formed after Stockholm conference. In 1972 UNEP (United Nation Environmental Programme) was set up in Nairobi, Kenya with liaison offices in New York, Geneva and regional offices in Banghkok, Beirut and Mexico. UNEP helped the NGO's and other environmental movements to carry out their mission.

In the years that followed the Stockholm conference, environmental activism strengthened, particularly in developing nations. The developing nations aspiring to achieve higher growth rate stood evidence to many environment - development conflicts most of which were seen as conflicts between the rich and poor. Examples include logging companies against hill villagers, dam builders against tribal communities and the like (Sharma, Aviram 2007). One cannot ignore the role of women in some these environment – development conflicts. The Chipko movement (Box 4.2) and the Green Belt movement in Kenya (Box 4.3) explain this point.

One woman whom future generations in Uttarkhand region are not likely to forget is Gauradevi who mobilsed women of this region to protect the trees from loggers. Women of the Uttarkhand region referred to forests as Gods.

The Chipko movement a non-violent movement based on the Gandhian philosophy of peaceful resistance to achieve goals, aimed at the protection and conservation of trees. The first Chipko action took place spontaneously in April 1973 when the villagers of the Chamoli District in Uttarkhand ,India, hugged the trees, and prevented the contractors' from felling them. In Hindi the word Chipko means "to embrace" or "to hug" and that is what the women of Uttarkhanad did to save the trees. It was sparked off by the government's decision to allot a plot of forest area in the Alaknanda valley to a sports goods company. This angered the villagers who with the support of the local non-governmental organization (NGO) by name Dasoli Gram Swarajya Sangh), under the leadership of an activist, Chandi Prasad Bhatt, went into the forest and formed a circle around the trees preventing the men from cutting them down. The success of the Chipko movement in the hills saved thousands of trees from being felled.

The Chipko protests in Uttar Pradesh achieved a major victory in 1980 with a 15-year ban on tree felling in the Himalayan forests of that state by the order of Mrs Indira Gandhi, the then Prime Minister of India. Since then, the movement has spread to many states in the country-to Himachal Pradesh in the North, Karnataka in the South, Rajastan in the West, Bihar in the East and to the Vindhyas in Central India. In addition to the 15-year ban in Uttar Pradesh, the movement has generated pressure for a natural resource policy that is more sensitive to people's needs and ecological requirements.

Several individuals have been involved in this movement and have given it proper direction. Mr Sunderlal Bahuguna, a Gandhian activist and philosopher; coined the slogan : "ecology is our permanent economy"; Mr Chandi Prasad Bhatt, is another leader of the Chipko movement. He encouraged the development of local industries based on the conservation and sustainable use of forest wealth for local benefit. Mr Ghanasyam Raturi, the Chipko poet, whose songs echo throughout the Himalayas of Uttar Pradesh. One such song says: "Soil ours, Water ours, Ours are these forests too; Our fore fathers raised these, it is we who must protect these too."

Source: http://www.apnauttarakhand.com/chipko-movement/
http://edugreen.teri.res.in/explore/forestry/chipko.htm
http://www.iisd.org/50comm/commdb/desc/d07.htm
http://www.ecoindia.com/education/chipko-movement.html

BOX 4.2 Chipko Movement

The Chipko movement, India's first Green Movement, was "direct inspiration for a series of popular movements in defense of community rights to natural resources. The Chipko movement followed the practice of the Gandhian method of satyagraha or non-violence resistance. The name of the movement comes from a word meaning "embrace": The villagers hugged the trees, saving them from the contractors' axes. The movement first sparked of in April 1973 in the village of Garhwal Himalayas of Uttarakhand valley and over the next five years spread to many districts of the Himalayas in Uttar Pradesh.

The Green Belt Movement is an indigenous grassroot non-governmental organization based in Nairobi, Kenya, that organizes women in rural Kenya to stop deforestation, to plant trees and restore to them their main source of fuel for cooking besides helping them to earn substantial income to run their family. The movement was established by Prof Wangari Maathai in 1977.

The Green Belt Movement (GBM) was founded by Professor WangariMaathai in 1977 under the auspices of the National Council of Women of Kenya (NCWK) to respond to the needs of rural Kenyan women. GBM is a non-governmental organisation based in Nairobi Kenya; it works for environmental conservation, community development and capacity building. GBM has planted over 51 million trees in Kenya. It has a network of over 4,000 community groups in Kenya that plant trees and protect the environment. GBM works at the grassroots, national and international levels to promote environmental conservation; to build climate resilience, and empower communities, especially women and girls; to foster democratic space and sustainable livelihoods. Over 30,000 women were trained in forestry, food processing and bee-keeping and other trades that help them to earn income while preserving their lands and resources. Maathai called for a new relationship with the Earth, "to heal her wounds and in the process heal our own." She called on people to "embrace the whole creation in all its diversity, beauty and wonder…."

Professor Maathai realized that behind the everyday hardships of the poor—environmental degradation, deforestation, and food insecurity—were deeper issues of disempowerment, and a loss of the traditional values that had previously enabled communities to protect their environment. In addition to helping local women to generate their own incomes through such ventures as seed sales, the Movement has succeeded in educating thousands of poor women about forestry and has created about 3,000 part-time jobs. The Green Belt Movement fought to save Nairobi's Uhuru Park from an enormous high-rise tower block to be built by the ruling party for which Maathai was imprisoned and subject to harassments in the prison. Yet Maathai was not put off. She was convinced that the environment cannot be protected in the "absence of democratic governance [or] democratic space".

Today GBM has extended to reach internationally and works for action on climate change, campaigns on the importance of Africa's rainforests in the Congo and is advocating the importance of "reduce, reuse, recycle" in Kenya and around the world. It has partnered with the United Nations Environment Programme (UNEP) in its Billion Tree Campaign.

In 2002 Maathai was elected as a Member of Parliament also served as Assistant Minister in the Ministry for Environmental and Natural Resources. In 2004, WangariMathai was awarded the Nobel Peace Prize for her work with the Green Belt Movement. She is the first African woman and the first environmentalist to ever win the Nobel Peace Prize. Greenbelt movement continues to grow as a growing tribute to ProfesssorMathai who died in Sep 2011.

Source:
http://www.greenbeltmovement.org/who-we-are/our-history
http://en.wikipedia.org/wiki/Green_Belt_Movement
http://www.care2.com/causes/how-the-green-belt-movement-in-kenya-fights-climate-change.html#ixzz22IvsbQ6J
http://www.womenaid.org/press/info/development/greenbeltproject.html
http://www.greenbeltmovement.org/who-we-are/our-history
http://www.yesmagazine.org/issues/media-that-set-us-free/the-green-belt-movement-the-story-of-wangari-maathai
http://unesdoc.unesco.org/images/0023/002301/230122e.pdf

Box 4.3 The Green Belt Movement

Narmada Bachao Andolan is a peoples movement formed from local peoples movements in Madhya Pradesh, Maharashtra, and Gujarat protesting against the building of a World Bank-funded dam project along the Narmada River. The project - which has displaced hundreds of thousands and has imposed stunning environmental costs without reaping the promised benefits of modernization - has been the source of constant controversy.

The Narmada River traverses three of India's northwestern states: Gujarat, Madhya Pradesh, and Maharashtra. In 1978, the Indian government sought the World Bank's assistance to build a complex of dams along the river as part of the Narmada Valley Development Project ("Narmada Project"). The government claimed that the Sardar Sarovar dam alone would irrigate almost 1.8 million hectares of land in Gujarat and an additional 73,000 hectares in the dry neighboring state of Rajasthan, in addition to providing potable water to over 8,000 Gujarati villages and 135 urban centers. It was also claimed that the project will generate an installed power capacity of the 3,830 MW. In 1985 the World Bank agreed to finance the Sardar Sarovar dam to the tune of $450 million, approximately 10% of the total cost of the project. However the claimed benefits excluded the social costs: the displacement of tens of thousands of individuals and considerable environmental damage. The Sardar Sarovar dam's impounding of water in a 455–foot–high reservoir would ultimately submerge 37,000 hectares of land in Gujarat, Maharashtra, and Madhya Pradesh, and divert 9.5 million acre feet of water into a canal and irrigation system. According to unofficial estimates, the Sardar Sarovar dam alone has displaced 320,000 people. Added to these human costs is the considerable environmental damage to a valley packed with plant and animal life.

The NBA employed "Gandhian methods" such as peaceful marches and protests. In 1991 the NBA announced a "non-cooperation movement" in the Narmada valley. Social activist Baba Amte provided moral leadership to the cause to preserve the Narmada River. The NBA has continually sought to encourage people-centered and environmentally sound alternatives to mega dams. The NBA has identified decentralized methods of water harvesting as a viable alternative in Gujarat that could be achieved for a fraction of the over $4 billion price tag attached to the Sardar Sarovar dam alone.

The efforts of the NBA compelled the government not only to do a Cost Benefit analysis of the Dams project but also compelled the government to admit that the Sardar Sarovar Project would displace over 100,000 people and affect over 900,000 more, contrary to its initial estimate that only 7,000 families would be affected..

The World Bank pulled out from the project in 1993. With the withdrawal of international funding it was decided to pursue the implementation of the project with domestic resources.

In 2000 Supreme Court gave approval for the completion of Sardar Sarovar Dam.

The Narmada Bachao Andolan has rendered a yeoman's service to the country by creating a high-level of awareness about the environmental and rehabilitation and relief aspects of projects to construct large dams across rivers in general and about the Sardar Sarovar dam on the Narmada in particular. But after the verdict of the Supreme court in favour of the Dam, instead of 'damning the dam' any longer, it could assume the role of vigilant observer to see that the resettlement work is as humane and painless as possible and that the environmental aspects are taken due care of." The SSP saga has forced activists to rethink the development contribution that can be expected from dams.

Source:

http://chingaree.blogspot.in/2011/10/narmada-bachao-andolan-analysis.html

http://chingaree.blogspot.in/2011/10/narmada-bachao-aandolan-case-study.html

http://www.geocities.com/CapitolHill/6027/Narmada.html

http://www.ecoindia.com/education/narmada-bachao-andolan.htmlwww.egyankosh.ac.in/bitstream/123456789/33151/1/Unit16.pdf

Box 4.4 The Movement to Save Narmada – The Narmada Bachao Andolan

The character of the environmental movement changed in the 1980s making it more policy oriented with thrust on global environmental governance. During this period the role of ENGOs like Green peace, Friends of the Earth, and the World Wildlife Fund was greatly enhanced. The growing strength of the environmental non-governmental organisations (ENGOs) increased environmental awareness of the people. This helped the ENGOs to influence policy makers to consider environmental implications of their policy decisions on development projects that had negative environmental consequences. The case of the Dam across River Kunthipuzha in the Silent Valley in Kerala proves this point. In 1970 the Kerala State Electricity Board (KSEB) proposed a hydroelectric dam across the Kunthipuzha River that runs through Silent Valley; the proposed dam would submerge 8.3 sq km of four-million-year-old untouched moist evergreen forest. It was reported that, besides providing electricity the dam would increase irrigation prospects and would provide employment to several thousand people during the construction phase and boost the economy of the state. Obviously the social costs of the dam were ignored. Several NGOs strongly opposed the project and urged the government to abandon it arguing that the entire lower valley will be submerged by the dam, destroying its biodiversity. But the Government was keen on going ahead with the project. This resulted in the outcry against the Silent Valley Hydroelectric Project – what started as a localized movement through individual and small group protests became national and international. The General Assembly of the IUCN urged the Government to conserve the undisturbed forest area. Many eminent people, wrote to the Central Government requesting that the project should not be given sanction. In **November 1983,** the Silent Valley Hydroelectric Project was called off following the strong willed determined representation from ENGOs, people near and far off, eminent and ordinary. The movement to save Silent Valley proved that people's movement successfully influenced governments to consider environmental consequences of development initiatives and that the concern for preserving and conserving the environment is beyond borders.

The 1980s is an important decade in the environmental history for yet another reason too. This period witnessed major environmental catastrophes - the Chernobyl Disaster in Russia, the Sandoz Fire in Basel, (1986) and the Bhopal Tragedy in India (1984), the Exxon Valdez oil spill(1989) and the assassination of Chico Mendes who fought to save the Brazilian rainforests (Box 4.5).

Rainforest are the most biologically diverse places of this planet: they house one half of the plant and animal life on earth. It is estimated that rainforests are being destroyed at the rate of 50 million acres per year. Amazon rainforest is the richest forest on Earth in terms of bio diversity. It is the the world's largest rainforest – over six million square kilometres and is the home to almost a million indigenous Indians and thousands of animal and plant species. Hence saving these precious areas has become an urgent environmental cause. Chico Mendes is one person who scarificed his life for the cause of preserving the Amazonian rainforests, thus becoming an ecomartyr.

Rubber tapping has been the means of livelihood for families in the Amazon for generations. It is a process whereby one harmlessly extracts sap from rubber trees, which is then used in such products as car tires, pencil erasers, and even Tupperware. It is a sustainable agricultural system. Chico Mendes was a rubber tapper who lived and worked in the Brazilian Amazon rain forest region. He worked for sustainable harvests that would protect these forests and the environment as a whole. To save the rainforest, Chico Mendes asked the government to set up reserves as they wanted people to use the forest without damaging it. The 1980s saw many Brazilians chopping down trees and converting the forest lands to cattle pastures. For the cattle ranchers in Brazil, "sustainable agriculture" impedes profit-making. In 1988 alone 30 million acres of forest were destroyed for such purposes. The Brazilian government encouraged this through tax benefits and direct subsidies for cattle ranchers, as well as by building cattle roads through forests.

Mendes opposed the destructive practices of such large companies and individuals and advocated a return to sustainable agricultural systems. He urged his fellow Brazilians to non-violent protest against corporations that would rob them of their livelihoods. In 1988, Mendes launched a campaign to stop rancher Darly Alves da Silva from logging an area that was planned as a reserve. Mendes managed to stop the planned deforestation and create the reserve. This automatically made him an enemy of cattle ranchers, especially Darli Alves da Silva. The simplest solution to them was to murder Chico Mendez. On December 22nd, 1988, Mendes was assassinated, the 19th activist to be murdered in Brazil that year and thus Mendez became an "eco martyr". The murder of Chico Mendez, illustrate the relationship between economic activity and environmental degradation. Mendes' murder made international headlines and led to massive protests in Brazil that gained an outpouring of support, eventually resulting in the arrest and conviction of Darly Alves da Silva, his son Darly Alves da Silva Jr., and a ranch hand, Jerdeir Pereia.

In April of 1989, the Brazilian government announced the suspension of all subsidies, tax-reliefs, and incentives for cattle ranching. It established many rubber preserves and nature reserves, including one named after the activist, Chico Mendes.

Mendes won several awards for his work, including the United Nations Environment Programme Global 500 Roll of Honour Award in 1987 and the National Wildlife Federation's National Conservation Achievement Award in 1988.

Reference:

http://www.myhero.com/go/hero.asp?hero=c_mendes
http://www.chicomendes.com/
http://library.thinkquest.org/26026/People/chico_mendes.html
http://greenliving.about.com/od/greenprograms/a/Rainforest-Activist-Chico-Mendes.htm

Box 4.5 The Movement to Save Brazilian Rainforests

On December 2-3, 1984, the city of **Bhopal**, in the state of Madhya Pradesh, witnessed an unprecedented tragedy caused by massive leakage of methyl-iso-cyanate (MIC) from the union carbide pesticide plant. The accident occurred because of a runaway chemical reaction in one of the tanks in which forty-two tonnes of methyl-iso-cyanate were stored (for more details see chapter 5, Box 5.2)

Explosion in the nuclear power plant at **Chernobyl** nuclear power station, eighty miles north of Keiv in USSR, has its origin in the test conducted in April 25th 1986 to check the safety systems.

The plants at Chernobyl are built with emergency diesel generators that are activated in the event of a power failure. But these generators take forty seconds to come on line. On the 25th of April, 1986, a test was conducted to determine whether the residual kinetic energy generated by the plant's turbine generators could provide electricity for vital systems during the forty seconds period for activation of the backup diesel generators. But the test ended as an explosion and fire at the nuclear power plant, leading to the evacuation of 135,000 people, hospitalisation of over 200, death of more than 30. Nearly millions of Soviet citizens and those of neighbouring European countries were exposed to significant dose of radiation from which deaths in the range of twenty thousands to forty thousands have been predicted in future. Governments in the region estimated that up to seven million people were affected by the accident. The number of individuals likely to be affected by the Chernobyl disaster was estimated as high as eleven times that of the cancer deaths expected from the combined 1945 bombings of Hiroshima and Nagasaki.

In 1986, a fire at chemical company **Sandoz** caused dangerous toxins to seep into the air and the nearby river Rhine. On November 1st 1986, fire in a building in Schweizerhalle, near Basel in Switzerland , shrouded the entire region in poisonous smoke that arose from 1,351 tonnes of pesticides and agrochemicals. It remains one of the worst environmental disasters ever to have occurred within Europe's borders. An estimated 30 tonnes of chemical products leaked into the Rhine, which turned red. The pollutants destroyed the river's flora and fauna and hundreds of tonnes of dead fish and other dead animals were found in the river in the following days. The surrounding soil and groundwater were contaminated. The Basel accident is one of the worst environmental disasters till date to have occurred within Europe's border.

During 1980s nations discussed national and international forums about protecting the ozone layer, and arresting global warming and management of hazardous wastes. The decade of 1980s was a pivotal period for advocates of global governance, particularly, environmental governance. The World Conference on Environment and Development created a World Charter for Nature. The Vienna Convention in Vienna in Austria in 1985, on Ozone Depleting Substances established the supremacy of UNEP in global environmental affairs. In 1987, the Montreal Protocol – a protocol to the Vienna Convention - banned the use of ozone depleting substances.

During the 1980s, many multi-lateral agreements were signed covering a variety of environmental issues such as trade in endangered species, management of hazardous wastes, climate change etc. Some of these are:

- United Nations Convention on the Law of Sea. 1982 (UNCLOS) – ratified on 19 July 1996
- Vienna Convention for the Protection of the Ozone Layer, 1985.
- The Montreal Protocol on Substances that Deplete the Ozone Layer, 1989 – ratified on 21 July 1988
- The Convention on International Trade in Endangered Species of Wild Flora and Fauna, 1973 (CITES) – acceded to on 10 May 1989

The World Commission on Environment and Development was created in 1987 under the Chairmanship of the Prime Minister of Norway, Gro Harlem Brundtland to focus on environmental and development problems and search for solutions. The Commission, also known as the Brundtland Commission, published the first volume of *Our Common Future*. The report of the Commission "Our Common Future" gave a complete definition for the concept of "sustainable development". Defining sustainable development as the development that meets the needs of the present generation without compromising the ability of the future generations to meet their needs, the Commission highlighted basic needs, particularly the needs of the world's poorest people and inter-generational equity as the two key concepts of sustainable development.

Table 4.1 gives time line of the environmental movement from 1962 to 1990.

Table 4.1 Time Line of Environmental Movement from 1962 -1990

YEAR	EVENT
1962	***Silent Spring*** by Rachel Carson
1963	**The Quiet Crisis** by *Stewart Udall*
1966	**The Economics of Coming Spaceship Earth** by *Kenneth Boulding*
1968	Population Bomb by *Paul Ehrlich and* Tragedy of Commons by *Hardin.*
1969	Inter National NGO **Friends of the Earth** founded.

1971	Publication of *Commoner*'s **The Closing Circle** International NGO **Green Peace** founded
1972	**Limits to Growth** by *Club of Rome* **Blue Print for Survival** by *Edward GoldSmith*
1972	United Nations Conference on the Human Environment held in Stockholm
1973	*Naess, Arne's* The Shallow and the Deep, Long-Range Ecology Movement *EF Schumacher's* **Small is Beautiful**
1973	Chipko Movement
1977	Green Belt Movement organized by Wangari Maathai in Nairobi, Kenya.
1984	Bhopal Tragedy in India (1984)
1985	Narmada Bachao Andolan
1986	Chernobyl Disaster , Russia and Sandoz Fire in Basel
1988	Chico Mendes who fought to save the Brazilian rain forests was murdered.
1989	The Montreal Protocol on Substances that Deplete the Ozone layer

(Source: Karpagam M and GeethaJaikumar, 2010 Green Management)

4.3 Environmental Movement since 1990s to the present day

The environmental movement during the 1990s mostly reflected the commitments of the Rio Summit, taking forward the road to sustainable development. The U N Conference of Environment and Development (UNCED), popularly known as the Rio Summit or the Earth Summit was held in Brazil's Rio de Janeirio in 1992 . The two major outcomes of the Earth Summit were: the Rio Declaration and the Agenda 21. The Rio declaration on Environment and Development presented 27 principles of "Environment and Development" intended to build upon the Stockholm Declaration of 1972. The Rio declaration recognised *the* sovereign rights of the countries to exploit their resources, provided such exploitation does not cause damage to the environment of other states. It recognized eradicating poverty as an indispensable requirement for sustainable development, in order to decrease the disparities in standards of living and better meet the needs of the majority of the people of the world. The Rio declaration called for global partnership to conserve, protect and restore the health and integrity of the Earth's ecosystem. It recommended that nations should develop a strong national environmental policy that included the "Polluter Pays Principle" and "Precautionary Principle." The Rio declaration directed the nations to develop national law regarding liability and compensation for the victims of pollution and other environmental damage.

The Agenda 21 is an action plan to achieve sustainable development. Agenda 21 emphasised on:

- A 'bottom-up' approach of putting emphasis upon people, communities and NGOs;
- The need for 'open governance';
- The importance of adequate information;
- The need for adequate cross-cutting institutions; and
- The complementarity between regulatory approaches and market mechanisms for addressing development and environmental needs.

The flames of Shell are flames of Hell
We bask below their blight
Nought for us to serve the blight
Of cursedd neglect and cursed Shell
- Ogoni Song

"We either win this war to save our land or we will be exterminated because we have no where to go"
- Ken Saro -Wiwa, MOSOP

The Ogoni is small region of 650 square kilometers in Rivers State Nigeria with a high population density due to more than five lakh people occupying the small area. Despite this high population density, the extraordinary fertility of the Niger delta enabled the Ogonis to make a good living as subsistence farmers and fishing people. The threat to region and its people started when Shell oil company discovered oil in the area in 1958. In 1958 Nigeria was a British colony and hence the Ogonis could not prevent the oil exploitation but the situation did not improve even after Nigeria got independence in 1960. Post independence Nigeria witnessed several coups and political instability due to conflicts between three dominant ethnic groups. The Ogoni being a minority group was systematically excluded from power and hence could not do anything to prevent resource exploitation by Shell oil company.

Shell operations in Nigeria are operated by the Shell Petroleum Development Company (SPDC) jointly with the Nigerian National Petroleum Corporation (NNPC). Almost 14% of Shell's production comes from Nigeria. For Nigeria oil accounts for nearly 80 % of the government revenue. There are more than 100 oil wells, mostly owned by Shell. The environmental impacts of these oil wells include oil spills and its impact on water bodies and land, air pollution and the consequent acid rain from gas flares and noise pollution from oil flares. Between 1976 and 1991 there were nearly 3000 oil spill incidents averaging 700 barrels each in the Niger delta.

The Ogoni people's livelihood was threatened due to the production by the multi-national oil companies.To protest against Shell's actions the, Ogoni people formed the Movement for the Survival of Ogoni people (MOSOP) in 1992 under the leadership of Ken Saro –Wiwa who was a well-known Nigerian author. The struggle was described by Saro-Wiwa as: "The Ogoni people have now decided to make a last ditch stand against the government and against the Shell that have ripped them off for the last 35 years" On the 4th of January 1993, the World Year of Indigenous People, the Ogoni people staged a mass protest against Shell oil and the environmental destruction of Ogoni land. Soon Saro Wiwa and the people fighting for the cause were subject to military prosecution and military force was frequently used against Ogoni protestors. It was reported that Shell colluded with the Nigerian government and attacked the Ogoni people.

Ken Saro Wiwa was arrested on 22nd May 1993, and was held without any charge for several months. He was finally charged with murder of Ogoni leaders and was denied legal representations or medical attention even though he is reported to have suffered four heart attacks during the detention period. On October 31st, 1995, Ken Saro Wiwa was sentenced to death along with eight co-trialists. Saro-Wiwa's last words were: ***"Lord, take my soul, but the struggle continues."*** Shock and outrage reverberated around the world, and everyone from Bill Clinton and Nelson Mandela condemned the executions. The execution of Ken Saro Wiwa and his eight co-trialists on 10th November, led to the suspension of Nigeria from the Common Wealth.

An assessment by the UNEP on the environmental and public health impacts of oil contamination in Ogoni land and Niger delata, revealed that restoring the Ogoniland will take 25 to 30 years. Researchers reported that the surface water in the Ogoni area contained 900 times the acceptable levels of cancer causing benzene. UNEP strongly recommended the establishment of a community cancer registry in Nigeria.

Source: https://ratical.org/corporations/OgoniFactS.html

https://www.theguardian.com/commentisfree/2015/nov/10/ken-saro-wiwa-father-nigeria-ogoniland-oil-pollution

http://stream.aljazeera.com/story/ogoni-vs-oil-giant-shell-0022089

Box 4.6 Shell oil Vs Nigeria's Ogoni Tribe

The Rio Summit and the International agreements that followed it gave a new direction and colour to the environmental movement and made it distinct over the earlier period movement. The most important feature that made the movement more distinct is its emphasis on inter temporal justice - the use of resources to promote development today 'without compromising the requirements and needs of future generations'. Until then the focus was on intra temporal justice – for efficient and equitable use of the resources among the rich and the poor. After 1990 the environmental movement addressed global environmental issues such as preservation of biodiversity, ozone layer and climate change besides addressing local issues. The slogan from 1990s became: Think and act locally; think and act globally. The fight by the Ogonis tribe in Nigeria against the environmental degradation inflicted by the MNC, Shell Oil Company proves this point (See Box :4.6).

From the end of 1980s, the movement became increasingly concerned about climate change. It became well known that climate change poses one of the greatest challenges facing the world in the 21st century. Many of the peoples movements and organisations, working to save the planet started educating people about the adverse consequences of climate change – its negative impact on global water supply, agricultural yields, marine ecosystems and the spread of vector-borne diseases. On the positive side these movements also educated communities about their role in averting climate change. Thus the environmental movement from the 1990s is significant for its activism related to climate change. It is in 1990s that major environmental organizations became involved in the discussions about climate. From the year 2000 several climate-specific organizations were functioning, such as Energy Action Coalition and the Global Call for Climate Action.

The presence of climate activism and the increasing awareness about climate change prompted nations across, to take necessary action. This is partly responsible for the exclusive convention on climate change at the Earth Summit in Rio in 1992.The Kyoto Protocol is one of the three conventions adopted at the Rio Earth Summit in 1992. The United Nations Framework Convention on Climate Change (UNFCCC), an international environmental treaty negotiated at the Earth Summit in Rio de Janerio from 3rd to 14th June 1992 entered into force on 21 March 1994. The framework pledges to stabilize greenhouse-gas concentrations "at a level that would prevent dangerous anthropogenic interference with the climate system".

The movement from the 90s successfully transformed public attitude in favour of environment due to which the movement came to be recognised by the decision making bodies and policymakers. Hence the environmental groups were able to exert pressure on decision makers to approve environmentally friendly projects and turndown environmentally damaging projects. Some examples in this regard are the successful attempts to close or relocate environmentally damaging industrial plants and action towards preservation of nature reserves.

After 1990, there has been a remarkable increase in the number of local / national environmental non-governmental organisations (ENGOs) and the establishment of many national ENGOS and regional ENGOs. For example 21 African ENGOs together formed the African NGOs Environmental Network (ANEN). Today more than 500 ENGOs are members in this regional network, ANEN.

Environmental movement is now oriented towards achieving sustainable economic development through efficient use of resources. Sustainable business practices – that is, eco efficiency in production and consumption is stressed by advocates of environmental thinkers and philosophers. Several concepts based on sustainable development, such as ecological modernization and industrial ecology which emerged during the 1990s, are being increasingly considered for application. Nations are taking efforts to account for environmental degradation in their national income.

In the 21st century the environmental movement has combined the traditional concerns of conservation, preservation, and pollution with more contemporary concerns like the environmental consequences of economic practices such as tourism, trade and war. There are number of environmental groups at local, national and international level working towards preservation of vital ecosystems and conservation of limited environmental resources. There is a major shift in the approach of the environmental movements – promotion of an ecocentric conservationist approach that will enable nations to grow while protecting the environment. The environmental groups are seen working with the government and corporates , convincing them of the environmental impacts of their decisions and actions and bringing about changes in their decisions.

Conclusion

Environmental problems are really social problems. They begin with people as the cause and end with people as the victims. Environmental movements work to bring about this realization in people. The environmental movements are highlighting the fact that the destruction of the environment is a matter of life sustenance. The success of the environmental movements is attributed to several factors.

- Environmental degradation is a highly visible problem today that millions can see, smell, taste and hear.
- The inherent diversity of the movement gives ample scope for expansion.
- Faith in the movement has a common objective today, that of bringing about a fundamental shift in values and in attitudes towards nature.

It has developed an 'environmental concern and consciousness' among people. The realization that environmental problems are due to the greed of the human beings has strengthened the movement. It has brought about a marked trend away from the notion of environment as divorced from humanity, towards a new focus on the costs of environmental deterioration and mismanagement—from piecemeal approach to a holistic approach—to environmental management. These movements have educated people that the environment cannot be taken for granted.

Questions

1. The nature of the environmental movement in after 1960s differed from that before 1960s. How and Why?
2. Explain the major achievements of the environmental movement after 1980s.
3. Have environmental movements improved environmental consciousness among people in the third world countries. How are the environmental movements of the rich advanced countries different from that in the poor countries .

Exercise

1. Prepare a case study of a successful effort by an ENGO.
2. List the names of atleast ten international and national ENGOS and give vital information about them. Give one case study for a national ENGO and one for an international ENGO.

SECTION 2

ENVIRONMENTAL DEGRADATION

5

AIR POLLUTION

Civilization... wrecks the planet from sea floor to stratosphere.

~Richard Bach

Environmental pollution is the introduction of contaminants into an environment resulting in instability, disorder, harm or discomfort to the ecosystems. Pollution is the undesirable change in the physical, chemical and biological characteristics of air, water and soil which may directly and indirectly affect human health, property and flora and fauna. The contamination of physical and biological components of the planet earth adversely affects normal environmental processes. Environmental pollution results when the environment is not able to perform the sink function, that is, when environment is not able to assimilate wastes.

On the basis of the component of environment that is polluted, pollution is classified as air pollution, water pollution and soil pollution.

Air constitutes about eighty percent of the man's daily intake by weight. We breath about 2200 times a day, inhaling around 16 kgs of air. It is therefore essential to know more about the air in the atmosphere and its quality.

5.1 Structure of the atmosphere

Atmosphere is the life blanket of earth, the essential ingredient for all living creatures. Air covers every part of the two hundred million square miles of the earth's surface. The atmosphere is just not the air breathed by people, animals and plants. It is also a gaseous substance enveloping the earth, protecting it from abrupt changes in temperature and protecting all living beings from harmful solar and cosmic radiation. The atmosphere of the Earth may be divided into several distinct layers.

The Troposphere

The troposphere contains eighty percent of the atmospheric mass and water vapour. The troposphere **is** where all weather related activities take place; it is the region of rising and falling packets of air.

The Stratosphere and Ozone Layer

Above the troposphere is the stratosphere where the greatest concentration of ozone is observed. This layer is primarily responsible for absorbing the ultraviolet radiation from the Sun.

The Mesosphere and Ionosphere

Above the stratosphere is the mesosphere and above that is the ionosphere (or thermosphere), where many atoms are ionized. The ionosphere is very thin and is responsible for absorbing the most energetic photons from the Sun, and for reflecting radio waves, thereby making long-distance radio communication possible. The ionosphere protects the biosphere from the harmful effects of cosmic radiation and influences the reflection and absorption of radio waves.

The **exosphere** is located above the ionosphere. The exosphere is the highest layer of the atmosphere. Together with the ionosphere, it makes up the thermosphere. The exosphere extends to 10,000 km above the Earth's surface. This is the upper limit of our atmosphere. The atmosphere here merges into space in the extremely thin air. Figure 5.1 shows the various layers of the atmosphere.

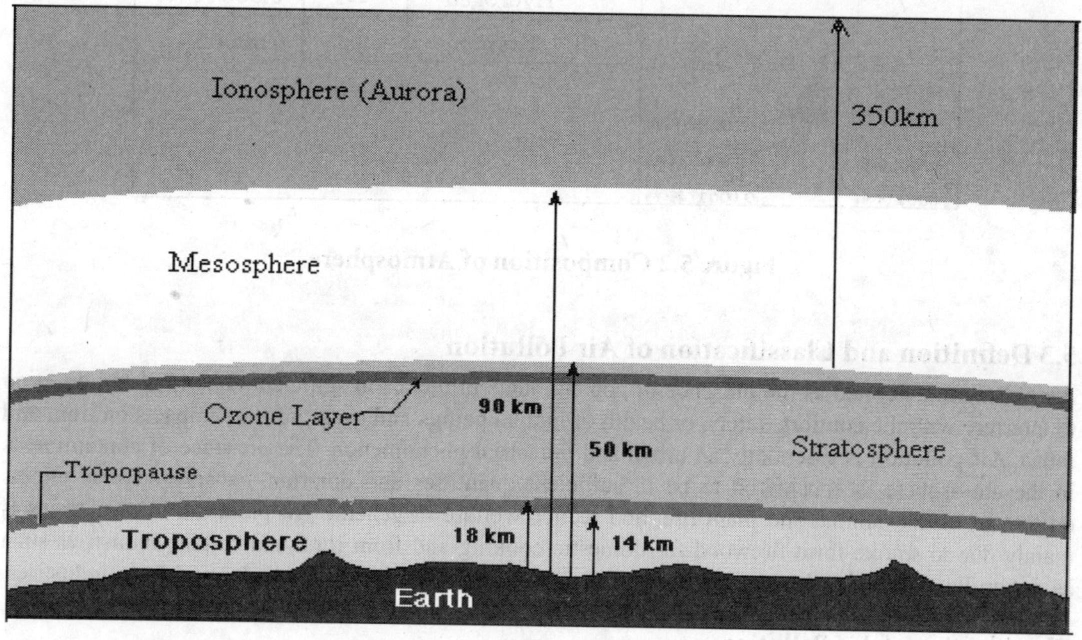

Source: http://csep10.phys.utk.edu/astr161/lect/earth/atmosphere.html

Figure 5.1 Layers of the Atmosphere

5.2 Gas Composition in the atmosphere

Air is mainly composed of nitrogen, oxygen, and argon, which together constitute the major gases of the atmosphere. The remaining gases, often referred to as trace gases, consists of the greenhouse gases such as water vapor, carbon dioxide, methane, nitrous oxide, and ozone. Figure 5.2 gives the current composition of the atmosphere.

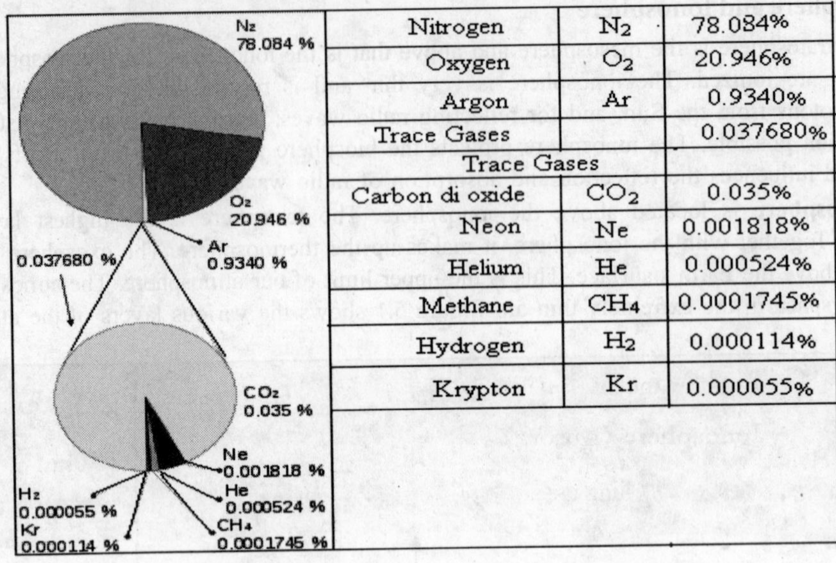

Nitrogen	N_2	78.084%
Oxygen	O_2	20.946%
Argon	Ar	0.9340%
Trace Gases		0.037680%
Trace Gases		
Carbon di oxide	CO_2	0.035%
Neon	Ne	0.001818%
Helium	He	0.000524%
Methane	CH_4	0.0001745%
Hydrogen	H_2	0.000114%
Krypton	Kr	0.000055%

Figure 5.2 Composition of Atmosphere

5.3 Definition and Classification of Air Pollution

Air pollution is defined as the presence of contaminants in the air in sufficient quantities and duration to interfere with the comfort, safety, or health of human beings and cause adverse impacts on flora and fauna. Air pollution is essentially an urban and industrial phenomenon. The presence of contaminants in the atmosphere is considered to be in sufficient quantities and duration, causing adverse effects on human health, animal and plant life, and reduce welfare in general. Air pollution in rural areas is mainly due to smoke form firewood for domestic cooking and from rural and cottage industries such as rice mills and brick kilns. In urban areas air pollution is mainly from vehicles and from industries.

Classification of Air Pollution

For a long time the problem of air pollution in cities was chiefly connected with coal burning in heating systems which emitted smoke, ashes and sulphurous gas. Today industrial enterprises and automobiles are the primary sources of atmospheric pollution. Increasing industrialisation and urbanisation have created growing demands to use the atmosphere, as a waste disposal medium. Thus the accumulation of waste gases and particles from combustion, production and other economic activities exceeds the natural dispersion capacity of the atmosphere. When air movements are unable to disperse wastes emitted in to the atmosphere, air quality deteriorates and the seemingly infinite supply of clean air diminishes. Thus air is polluted.

Air pollution may be distinguished as natural pollution and artificial or manmade pollution, on the basis of sources of pollution. Natural pollution is from sources such as volcano eruption, dust storms, forest fires etc; artificial pollution caused by anthropogenic activities include pollution from industries, burning from agricultural activities, and from automobiles.

Anthropogenic sources (human activity) include:

- Stationary sources such as smoke from stacks of power plants, factories and waste incinerators, as well as furnaces and other types of fuel-burning heating devices. In developing and poor countries, burning of traditional biomass such as crop waste, dung and wood is the major source of air pollutants.

- Mobile sources which include emissions from motor vehicles, marine vessels, aircraft and the effect of sound etc.
- Chemicals, dust and controlled burn practices in agriculture and forestry management.
- Fumes from paint, hair spray, varnish, aerosol sprays and other solvents.
- Waste deposition in landfills, which generate methane, a green house gas.

Natural sources

- Dust from natural sources, usually large areas of land with little or no vegetation.
- Methane emitted by the digestion of food by cattles.
- Radon gas from radioactive decay within the Earth's crust. Radon gas from natural sources can accumulate in buildings, especially in confined areas such as the basement and it is the second most frequent cause of lung cancer, after cigarette smoking
- Smoke and carbon monoxide from wild fires.
- Vegetation, in some regions, emits environmentally significant amounts of VOCs (Volatile Organic Compounds) on warmer days. These VOCs react with primary anthropogenic pollutants—specifically, NO_x, SO_2 and anthropogenic organic carbon compounds—and release secondary pollutants.
- Volcanic activity, which produce sulphur, chlorine, and ash particulates

Air pollutants can also be of *primary* or *secondary* nature.

Primary air pollutants are emitted directly into the atmosphere by the emitting sources, such as power-generating plants.

Secondary air pollutants are formed as a result of reactions between primary pollutants and other elements in the atmosphere, such as ozone.

Some of the main air pollutants are:

- gaseous pollutants such as oxides of sulphur and nitrogen, hydro carbons, carbon monoxide and ozone.
- aerosols such as smoke, fumes, dust and particulates.

Table 5.1 gives the sources of major air pollutants.

Table 5.1 Sources of Major Air Pollutants

Pollutant	Source
Particulates	Internal combustion engines (e g, cars and trucks), Industry (e g, factories), Burning wood.
Nitrogen Oxide (NO_2)	Motor Vehicles and other combustion processes
Sulphur di Oxide (SO_2)	Power plants, petroleum refining,
Ozone	Formed by various complex chemical reactions involving the exposure of the oxides of nitrogen and some hydro-carbons.
Carbon Monoxide	Motor vehicle exhaust and burning of materials such as coal, oil and wood. It is also released from industrial processes and waste incineration

Lead	Largely derived from the combustion of lead additives in motor fuels as well as lead smelting.
Hydro Carbons	Most fuel combustion processes result in the release of hydro carbons to the environment. The largest fuel sources are natural gas and petrol. They are also a component of the smoke from wood fires.
Ammonia	Agriculture, livestock
Air borne particles / particulates	Transport, power plants, production processes

Source: Modified from Karpagam and Geetha Jai Kumar, Green Management – Theory and Applications, 2010

5.4 Specific Air Pollutants

There are three main types of gaseous pollutants:

- Sulphur di oxide – SO_2
- Oxides of nitrogen – NO and NO_2
- Ozone

Sulfur dioxide and nitric oxide (NO) are the *primary* air pollutants, and ozone is a *secondary* pollutant. Nitrogen dioxide (NO_2) is both a primary and secondary air pollutant.

Other important gaseous pollutants are: ammonia, carbon monoxide, volatile organic compounds (VOCs) and persistent organic pollutants (POPs).

Sulphur dioxide

Sulfur dioxide is a colorless gas with a pungent, suffocating odour produced by the burning of coal, gas or fuel oil both for the domestic and industrial purposes. It is a dangerous air pollutant because it is corrosive to organic materials and it irritates the eyes, nose and lungs. The main source of this pollutant is fossil fuels which accounts for almost all anthropogenic (human-caused) sulfur emissions. Besides petroleum industry, oil refining and sulphuric acid, it is produced mostly by power plants which burn coal to generate electricity. A large power plant may burn 10,000 tonnes of coal a day. If this coal is contaminated with three per cent sulphur, some nine hundred tons of sulphur dioxide per day will be discharged. Currently, the most important sources of sulfur dioxide emissions (as a result of fossil fuel combustion) are **electric power generating plants**. The biggest sulfur dioxide emitters are US, China and Russia.

Effects: Airborne for long periods, sulphur di oxide reacts with oxygen and water vapour in the air to form sulphuric acid (H_2SO_4).The sulphuric acid is diluted by rainfall but even the rain water is said to be 10 to 100 times more acidic than normal. Rain water containing such acid is called as acid rain. Acid rain increases the corrosion rate of all metal structures such as bridges and dissolves limestone and marble. Besides causing acid rain, sulphur dioxide causes irritation of eyes and throat, suffocation and respiratory diseases.

Oxides of Nitrogen

Oxides of nitrogen are produced by combustion of all fossil fuels including coal- and gas-fired power stations and motor vehicles. The two main nitrogen oxides are nitrogen monoxide (NO), and nitrogen dioxide (NO_2) which together are expressed as NOx. Nitrogen monoxide (NO) is a colorless gas. Nitrogen dioxide (NO_2) is a reddish-brown color gas with a distinct sharp, biting odor. Combustion of fuels always produces both NO_2 and NO. But almost 90% of the NO_X combustion product is in the form of NO which is then oxidized to nitrogen dioxide (NO_2) in the air. Nitrogen oxides are mainly emitted by acid manufacturers, automobile exhaust and explosive industry. Road transport (motor vehicles) is by far the largest contributor of nitrogen emissions.

Like sulphur dioxide, Nitrogen oxides also result in acid rain and produce the associated damages. Inhalation of nitrogen oxides result in bronchitis and oedema of lungs. Nitrogen oxides damages crops.

Ozone (O_3)

Ozone (O_3) is a colorless, poisonous gas with a sharp, cold, irritating odor. In the stratosphere, Ozone occurs *naturally*, and it keeps harmful excessive ultraviolet sunlight from reaching the surface of the Earth. In the troposphere ozone occurs both naturally and as a result of human-generated emissions. In the troposphere ozone is a pollutant since it causes negative effects on humans and the natural environment. The tropospheric ozone emitted by human actions is a *secondary* pollutant because it is produced by the reaction of primary pollutants, nitrogen oxides and hydrocarbons [including VOCs], in the presence of **sunlight**. The tropospheric ozone is the main component of *the photochemical smog* which is a product of the chemical reaction between sunlight, nitrogen oxides and VOCs.

Ozone causes inflammation and damage to the lining of the lungs and aggravates asthma. It results in reduction in agricultural yields and interferes with photosynthesis and suppression of growth of some plant species. Ozone disclours leaves trees and shrubs. It damages and fades textiles and hastens cracking of rubber. Ozone irritates eyes, nose, throat and induces coughing.

Ammonia

Ammonia is a colorless, pungent, hazardous caustic gas composed of nitrogen and hydrogen. Ammonia emissions are also grouped as NHx which is a sum of NH_3 and NH_4. **Agriculture** is by far the biggest source of ammonia emissions. Livestock farming and animal waste account for the biggest percentage of total ammonia emissions which are due to the decomposition of urea from large animal wastes and uric acid from poultry wastes. The other sources are fertilizer application, vegetation and biomass burning. Exposure to very high concentrations of gaseous ammonia in the air may result in lung damage and even death.

Carbon Monoxide

Carbon monoxide is a colorless, odorless gas which is highly toxic to humans. The incomplete combustion of carbon-based fuels produces carbon monoxide. Motor vehicles and industry are among the largest anthropogenic sources of carbon monoxide emissions. Carbon monoxide is highly toxic at significant level of concentration and can cause decreased human efficiency in low but chronic doses. Exposures to carbon monoxide may lead to:

- Affect central nervous system and heart
- Carbon monoxide interferes with transfer of oxygen in the body which may be life-threatening

Volatile Organic Compounds (VOCs)

Volatile organic compounds (VOCs) are defined as organic compounds which easily evaporate and enter the atmosphere. VOCs may include a wide range of organic air pollutants, from pure hydrocarbons to partially oxidized hydrocarbons to organic compounds containing chlorine, sulfur, or nitrogen. The major anthropogenic sources of VOCs are solvent use (including paints, adhesives, aerosols, metal cleaning and printing), road transport (emissions from fuel / petroleum use), production processes and extraction and distribution of fossil fuels. Forests are the primary natural sources of VOC emissions. Some forms of VOCs are potential carcinogens and may cause leukemia.

Persistent Organic Pollutants (POPs)

Persistent organic pollutants are compounds which are resistant to degradation and are persistent in the environment. Such compounds may include dioxins, furans, polychlorinated biphenyls (PCBs) and pesticides such as DDT. POPs are used as pesticides, in industrial processes and in the production of goods such as solvents, and medicines.

Airborne Particulates

Airborne particulates are tiny fragments of solid or liquid, suspended in the air (aerosols). Particles may be *primary* – when emitted directly into the atmosphere, or *secondary* – when particles are formed in the atmosphere through the interaction of primary emissions. Solid particles between 1 and 100 μm (micrometres) in diameter are called ***dust*** particles, while solid particles less than 1 μm in diameter are called ***fumes***, or ***smoke***. The major anthropogenic sources of airborne particles are road transport, power generating plants, and production processes. Fossil fuel combustion is one of the main processes which causes vast amounts of particles to be emitted into the atmosphere. Volcano eruption, and forest fires are some of the natural sources of particulates. Particulates are dispersed and diffused by natural air movements but their structure or composition remains the same. The tiny particles reduce visibility, damage property and carry poisonous materials into the lungs.

Table 5.2 gives classification of air pollutants by source and emissions.

Table 5.2 Classification of Air Pollutants by Source and Emissions

Type	Category	Examples	Important Pollutants
Combustion	Fuel burning	Domestic burning, thermal power plant	Sulphur and nitrogen oxides
	Transportation	Car, trucks, aeroplanes, and railways	Carbon monoxide, nitrogen oxide, lead, smoke
	Refuse burning	Open burning dumps	Fly ash and particulates
Manufacturing Business	Chemical plants	Petroleum, refineries, fertilizers, cement, paper mills, ceramics	Hydrogen sulphide, sulphur oxide, fluorides and dusts
	Metallurgical plants	Aluminium refineries and steel plants	Metal fumes, (lead and zinc) fluorides, and particulates.
	Waste recovery	Scrap and metal yards	Smoke, soot, metal fumes.
Agricultural activities	Crop spraying	Pest and weed control	Organic phosphates, chlorinated hydro carbons, lead
	Field burning	Burning of refuse, fire wood, and dry cattle dung	Smoke, fly ash, soot, sulphur oxides, particulates, and organic vapours
Solvent Usage	Spray painting, solvent extractions, inks, solvent cleaning	Furniture and appliance finishing, printing and chemical separations, dry cleaning, degreasing.	Hydro carbons and other organic vapours.
Nuclear Energy Programmes	Fuel fabrication Ore preparation	Gaseous diffusion, crushing, grinding and screening	Fluorides, Uranium and Beryllium dust and other particulates. Argon and Iodine 131
	Nuclear device testing	Bomb explosions	Radio active fall out, Sr 90, CS 137 , Radio carbon C-14

Source: Zutshi, P.K, 1970

5.5 Effects of Air Pollutants

Deteriorating air quality has important consequences on human beings, animals, flora and fauna, properties and climate.

5.5.1 Effects of Air Pollutants on Human Health

Determining effects of air pollution on human health is the chief concern of this section. In the recent past there has been a dramatic rise in the respiratory disease. This is because, air pollutants attack human health primarily through the respiratory system.

Air pollutants enter the body through respiratory system. In general three factors influence the effect of a toxicant on an individual toxicity—concentration, duration of exposure, and individual susceptibility. The level where physiological reaction of humans or test animals begin to be observed is called the threshold level. In the case of some toxicants there may not be any threshold level i.e., any exposure— no matter how small—causes some reaction. Such pollutants without any threshold level are the most hazardous because even the mildest exposure to these could cause trouble. Asbestos and those that emit ionizing radiation are examples of pollutants without threshold level.

Pollutants entering the body may even affect specific organs. The ability of air pollutants to penetrate the body's natural defenses differs from one pollutant to another. Carbon monoxide and hydrogen sulphide are asphyxiating pollutants, that is, they displace the oxygen being transferred to haemoglobin molecules. Hence as increasing concentrations of carbon monoxide or hydrogen sulphide are inhaled, the quantity of life-sustaining oxygen that the blood stream transports from the lungs decrease. Several hours of exposure to carbon monoxide, 100 ppm (parts per million) results in dizziness, headache and impaired perception. With concentrations of 300-400 ppm vision problems, nausea and abdominal pain may develop and 750 ppm can be fatal. Heart patients appear to be particularly susceptible to the adverse effect of carbon monoxide and hydrogen sulphide. In very high concentrations, hydrogen sulphide impairs that part of the brain which controls chest movements essential for normal breathing and causes almost instantaneous death.

Gases that act mainly as irritants of the respiratory tract, include ozone, sulphur dioxide and nitrogen dioxide. The table 5.3 identifies the principally affected organs and the specific air pollutant.

Table 5.3 Specific Health Effect of Air Pollutants

Air Pollutant	Principally affected organs
Sulphur oxides	Eye irritation, wheezing, chest tightness, lung damage.
Nitrogen oxides	Respiratory infections, irritation of the lung and respiratory symptoms (e.g., cough, chest pain, difficulty breathing)
Quarts, silica, carbon, asbestos, cobalt, iron oxides	Pulmanory tissue - scarring of lungs, black lungs
Beryllium, hair sprays, talcum powder	Lungs
Carbon monoxide	Headaches, reduced mental alertness, heart attack, cardiovascular diseases, impaired fetal development, death.
Mercury, Fluoride, Cadmium, Chlorinated hydrocarbons, organophosphates	Nerve tissue, Brain, bowels, bones, teeth, Blood vessels, kidney, liver, fat tissue.

Formal dehyde pollen, fungi, house dust, thiocyanate, epoxy resins	Skin, respiratory tract, lungs
Strontium-90, Iodine-121, Chromium, Asbestos, Arsenic, Polyvinyl	Bones, thyroid, lungs, sinuses, nose, pleura, skin
Poly chlorinated biphenyl	Fat tissue liver
Hydrogen Sulphide	Respiratory Centre in brain, Paralysis of respiration, consequent edema, haemorrhage, death
Lead	Anemia, high blood pressure, brain and kidney damage, neurological disorders, cancer, lowered IQ.
Ozone	Eye and throat irritation, coughing, respiratory tract problems, asthma, lung damage.

Source: Adapted from Pordom and Andesron(1983) and http://www.epa.gov/apti/course422/ap7a.html

Particles or aerosols, also penetrate the body's natural defenses and pose a serious threat to health particularly if exposed to relatively high concentration levels for many years. Silica and asbestos cause fibrosis in the lungs. Silicosis caused from quartz dust generated during mining, asbestosis from asbestos fibres and byssinosis from cotton dust are serious lung diseases. Depending on the particulate type and the concentrations inhaled, impact on lungs may consist of irritation, allergic reactions or scarring of tissue. Typically, victims experience coughing and shortness of breath and in the long-run may develop pneumonia, chronic bronchitis, and lung cancer.

Certain particles are harmful when inhaled due to their interactions with other air pollutants. Some particles interfere with the functioning of cilica, thereby slowing the flow of mucus, and increasing the retention of toxic pollutants in lungs. It is in this way that carcinogenic agents are retained in the lungs increasing the likelihood of tumour formation. In addition particulates may act as carriers of other pollutants. For example, soot and fly ash and products of coal burning can transport sulphur dioxide into lungs.

Some toxic pollutants are so widely distributed in the general environment that to some extent they pose a potential health hazard to all human beings. Lead is the most notable of these pollutants. The danger of lead lies in the fact that it accumulates in the body more rapidly than it is excreted. Lead poisoning attacks the blood forming mechanism, the gastro intestinal tract and in several cases affect the central nervous system. Lead may also impair the functioning of heart and kidneys.

5.5.2 Effect on Other Species

The two air pollutants most hazardous to other species are fluoride and lead. The processing of ceramics and phosphate rock releases fluorides into the atmosphere. Some plant species are damaged by hydrogen fluoride at a concentration of only 0.1 parts per billion. When livestocks consume these plants, the organic compounds containing fluorides break down, and the fluorides released can be lethal. Dairy cattle are most sensitive to fluoride poisoning called fluorosis. Fluorides reduce milk production and attack teeth and bones producing lameness. Chronic fluorosis eventually leads to death. In Florida, substantial losses of cattle have been caused by fluoride emissions from factories processing phosphate deposits for fertilizers. Animals are also victims of lead poisoning. When contaminated by airborne lead, animals lose their appetite, develop dry coats and muscle spasms and frequently suffer paralysis.

5.5.3 Effect on Plants

Effect of air pollution on plants can be best seen near the source of pollution. For example, tree foliage along turnpikes is damaged in a band, when fumes from diesel truck exhaust, touch the leaves.

Table 5.4 Effect of select Air Pollutants on Plants

Pollutant	Indicated by	Sensitive Plants
Sulphur dioxide	Turn white to brown, bleaching, blotching between veins	Pumpkins, barley, cotton, wheat, apples
Fluoride	Necrosis on tips and edges of leaves	Tulips, Apricots, pine, cut roses
Ozone	Red brown flecks	Tobacco, tomatoes, bean, potatoes
Oxidant Smog	Silver or bronze like on underside of leave	Lettuce, oats, pinto bean
Chlorine	Bleaching, necrosis on margins and between veins, scattered spotting	Radish, cucumber, peaches, maple
Ethylene	Withering and drying of flowers, growth retardation, loss of lower buds	Tomatoes, cotton, orchids

Source: P W Purdom and Stanley H Anderson, Environmental Science, 1983

Cement dust deposited on leaves, when moistered, will form incrustations, while other dusts plug the leaf openings. When ozone concentration increases, pine needles turn brown and die. Some of the most dramatic instances of air pollution damage to vegetation have been caused by sulphur dioxide fumes from iron and copper smelters. Lettuce, barley and white-pine are particularly sensitive to sulphur dioxide. Air pollution most commonly damages the leaves of plants. Air pollution damage to plant is indicated by the yellowing of the leaves due to chlorophyll loss. This is called chlorosis which occurs when gaseous pollutants such as sulphur dioxide and ozone enter leaves and dissolve in the water that adheres to surfaces of cell walls. The pollutant can be identified by the pattern of damage to leaves. For example, fluorides accumulate at leaf tips and edges and in these areas the leaves initially turn yellow. When pollution damage is extreme, plant tissues die and leaves turn brown; this condition is called necrosis. The table 5.4 shows significant pollutants toxic to plants.

5.5.4 Effects on Material Goods

Building, fabrics and cars are also affected by particulate matter. Acids absorbed on the particles on buildings accelerate corrosion in humid areas. Sulphur oxides speed the deterioration of building materials especially marble and limestone. Fabrics, leather and steel are damaged when exposed to sulphur oxides. Ozone cracks rubber in auto tyres and reduces life of fibres. Nitrogen oxides can fade sensitive dyes. Chemically destructive gases and aerosols destroy invaluable works and monuments of culture and art. Statues and other art objects that withstood centuries of exposure in the relatively dry pollution free atmosphere of Egypt have deteriorated rapidly when exposed to acid rain.

Acid Rain

Acid rain refers to the decrease in the pH value of rain water, caused by the presence of sulphur and nitrogen emissions in the atmosphere from the burning of fossil fuels like coal, oil in power plants, industrial boilers and car engines.

The pH scale

Rainfall is acidic by nature with a pH scale of 5.6. The pH scale measures acidity and alkalinity of any liquid. A pH scale ranges from 0 to 14 and it is a logarithmic scale. A solution with a pH of 7 is neutral and anything above this is alkaline, while anything below is acidic. Since it is a logarithmic scale, every full point is equivalent to a factor of 10. Thus a pH of 6 is 10 times more acidic than neutral and a pH of 5 is 100 times more acidic than neutral (see figure 5.3).

The issue of acid rain is 'trans-frontier' because the effects of acid rain causing pollutants in one region is felt in another region. For example, acid rain in Scandinavia originates from the sulphur dioxide emissions in Central Europe or United Kingdom. Similarly about 50 per cent of acid rain in Eastern Canada is caused by emissions from the United States.

Effects of Acid Rain

Environmental effects of acid rain can be categorised as effects on aquatic, terrestrial, materials and human health. Aquatic ecosystems are seriously affected by acid rains through its impact on reproductive cycles. When exposed to acidic water, female fish, frog, salamanders and few other specie fail to produce eggs or produce eggs that do not develop normally. Besides this, acid rain alters the metabolism of fish and amphibian reptiles and kills them. Nearly a quarter of Sweden's 90000 lakes are acidified of which 4000 of them are acidified so severely that fish life is impossible in them. Nearly 80 per cent of the lakes in Norway are dead. Thousands of lakes in the US and more than 300 lakes in Canada's Ontario region are dead, thus making trout and salmon 'endangered' specie. Researches in West Germany believe that acid rain afflicts more than 50 per cent of Germany's forests. Nearly 43 per cent of conifers in the central alpine region in Switzerland are dead or dying due to the effect of acid rain. Acid rain affects forests by leaching nutrients from soil and foliage, thus inhibiting photosynthesis.

Acid rain is also the cause of material damage in many countries. The magnificent historic buildings of Krakow in Poland, the Acropolis and other marble monuments of Athens, the Jefferson Memorial in Washington DC, USA, the Cologne Cathedral in West Germany and Taj Mahal in India stand evidence to the deteriorating effect of acid rain on materials. The mobilisation of toxic metals like aluminium, mercury and lead by acid rains affect human health indirectly, when they are ingested by fish and animals, that form part of the human food chain.

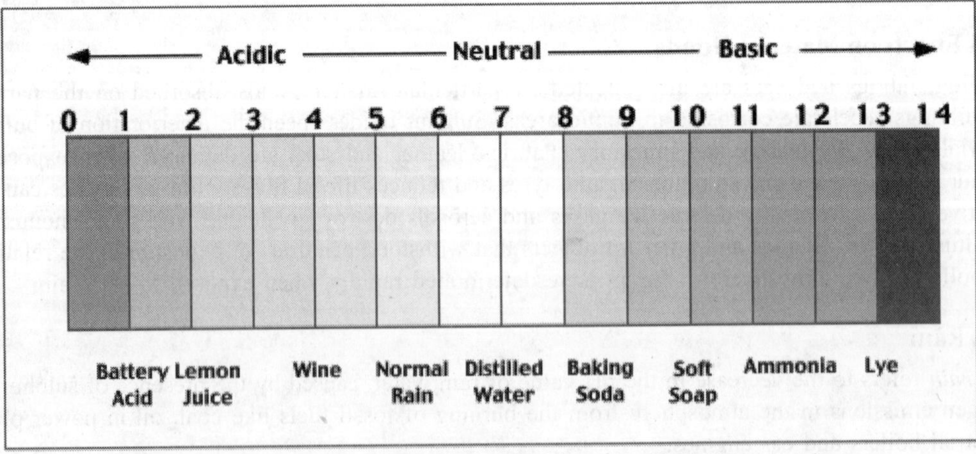

Source: http://www.edu.pe.ca/gulfshore/Archives/ACIDSBAS/scipage.htm

Figure 5.3 The pH scale

Acid rain dissolves stone and can create cracks in buildings. Statues of Greek warriors and maidens carved from marble in Athens are losing their faces, and their bodies are marred by black splotches. Some gravestones at the Gettysburg battlefield in Pennsylvania are so fragile that they bend under pressure. St Stephens Cathedral in Vienna, and Notre Dame de Paris in France are reported to be affected by air pollution. The case of Taj Mahal in Agra in India is a monument facing damages due to SO_2 emissions from the refineries and other industries located near Agra (Box 5.1).

5.5.5 Effect on Climate

There are strong indications that pollution changes the climate. The global climate has changed and is changing due to the emissions of greenhouse gases in large quantities. Increasing concentrations of carbon dioxide result in an increase in the absorption and radiation of infrared rays which warms the lower atmosphere. The atmosphere absorbs a large percentage of the infrared radiation that is emitted by the earth's surface. A portion of the infrared radiation absorbed by the atmosphere is then re-radiated back towards the earth's surface. Re-radiation by the atmosphere makes it difficult for heat to escape into space, so the temperature of the lower atmosphere is no more hospitable for living beings. The atmospheric gases that absorb infrared radiation are carbon dioxide, water vapour and to a much lesser extent ozone. Therefore an increase in the carbon dioxide content of the atmosphere (by air pollution activities) may result in more of the outgoing earth radiation being absorbed in the air and a warming of the earth's atmosphere. This warming effect is known as "greenhouse effect", even though a greenhouse behaves quite differently.

Mark Twain remarked that "the world is divided between two types of people: those who have seen the Taj Mahal and those who have not." Taj Mahal' the 'Crown of all Monuments' one of the wonders of the world and the mother of all monuments, was built by Shah Jahan in memory of his beloved wife Mumtaz Mahal and till today stands as a monument of love. It is the most beautiful creation that the Mughals gave to India. The Taj Mahal is renowned for its symmetry of proportions, its intricate details and most of all its white shining marble which changes its shades as the day approaches from dawn till midnight. While it shines pristine white at noon time, it appears whitish silver on a full moon night. Nearly two million tourists visit the Taj every year, making it a major source of revenue and foreign exchange for the region.

Unfortunately, today Taj Mahal suffers from what is termed as 'Marble Cancer' and has lost its sheen due to the air borne particles that are being deposited on it giving a yellow tinge to its pure white marble. The pollutants emitted by the industries such as the refineries, iron foundries, glass factories & brick kilns situated in and around Agra react with marble forming of a fine layer of dust over it. There is fungus in its interiors and exteriors. The sulphur dioxide emitted by the Mathura Refinery and the industries located in Agra and Ferozabad when combined with moisture in the atmosphere forms sulphuric acid and causes "acid rain" which has a corroding effect on the marble.

The Taj Trapezium (TTZ) referring to an area of 10,400 sq km around the Taj Mahal was established in 1982 to restrict pollution generating activities within an area of approximately 50 km radius around Agra. Some of the important urban centers, which are covered by the Taj Trapezium Zone are Agra, Firozabad, Mathura, Bharatpur, Jalesar and Hathras. These primary growth centers of the region influence not only the regional economy but also the environment. Besides the Taj Mahal, the TTZ includes two other world heritage monuments the "Agra Fort" and "Fatehpur Sikri".TTZ is so named since it is located around the Taj Mahal and is shaped like a trapezoid.

The industrial and refinery emissions from brick kilns, vehicular traffic and generator sets were identified by Central Pollution Control Board as primarily responsible for polluting the ambient air in and around TTZ. In response to a PIL seeking to protect the Taj Mahal from environmental pollution and after reviewing several reports by NEERI (National Environmental Engineering Research Institute) and the Varadarajan Committee, Hon'ble Supreme Court, directed, in 1996, that all the 292 industries in the TTZ must change over within time schedule to natural gas as industrial fuel or stop functioning with coal/ coke or get relocated. The court ordered 292 coal-based industries to switch to natural gas or else to relocate outside the protected zone by April 30, 1997. Gas Authority of India (GAIL) was asked to supply natural gas to the industries in Mathura. The Gas Authority of India Ltd. (GAIL) has already completed gas pipeline work for all the industries falling in priority zone. Continuous monitoring of sulphur dioxide at Taj Mahal had been initiated since 1981 and a complete ban was imposed on the establishment and expansion of air polluting activities within the trapezium area. Frequent power cuts and black outs in the area complicated the problem. In April 2002, the Supreme Court ordered the Agra Heritage Fund to set up a solar power plant to meet the energy needs of the Taj Mahal and the surrounding area. Additionally, conventional cars and automobiles are banned within a 500-meter radius of the monument.

While experts agree that some of these measures have helped to improve air around the Taj, pollution levels have not dropped to safer limits as none of the factories have actually been closed down. To date, The Tal trapezium issue is still a battle between politicians who have tended to side with industry and the judiciary which has supported the cause of the Taj.

Forest department has come up with a quick- fix project -- plant a Tulsi drive in Agra. Since Tulsi is reported to be the panacea for all problems from cosmic to cosmetic. The department is all set to launch the Tulsi plantation drive from January 2009 due to its anti- pollutant anti-oxidation and air-purifying properties. The public-private joint venture is expected to provide an eco- protection cover to the Taj trapezium zone surrounding the 17th century monument.

Reference:

Karpagam.M and Geetha (2010) Green Management, Theory and Applications
http://coe.mse.ac.in/taj.htm
http://www1.american.edu/TED/taj.htm
http://www.4to40.com/Qa/index.asp?id=3002
http://cpcbenvis.nic.in/ar2000/annual_report1999-2000-try2.htm
http://en.citizendium.org/wiki/Taj_Mahal#The_Taj_today_and_its_future
www.unesco.org/courier/2000_07/uk/signe.htm
http://www.nlsenlaw.org/air-noise/case-laws/supreme-court/m-c-mehta-v-union-of-india-air-1997-sc-734/
http://www.rrcap.unep.org/male/baseline/Baseline/India/INCH4.htm

Box 5.1 The Taj Trapezium Case

A greenhouse lets in sunlight through the glass roof to warm the surfaces and air inside and physically confines the warmed air in the glass enclosure. Thus the plants are kept warm inside a "greenhouse". The warming effect of the atmosphere by carbon dioxide is referred to as greenhouse effect. In addition, growing atmospheric concentrations of halocarbons and nitrous oxides also intensify the "greenhouse effect". The major natural greenhouse gases are water vapor, carbon dioxide CO_2, methane, and ozone, Other greenhouse gases include hydro fluorocarbons, per fluorocarbons, chloroflurocarbons, nitrogen oxides and ozone.

Different GHGs can have different effects on the Earth's warming. These gases differ from each other in terms of their ability to absorb heat and how long they stay in the atmosphere. The

Global warming potential of a gas (GWP) refers to how much energy (or heat) the emissions of 1 ton of a gas will absorb over a given period of time, relative to the emissions of 1 ton of carbon dioxide (CO_2). Since CO_2 is the reference gas, CO_2, has a GWP of 1. Methane (CH_4) has a GWP of 28 -36 times that of CO_2 for a 100-year timescale while Nitrous Oxide (N_2O) has a GWP of around 260 times that of CO_2 for a 100-year timescale. CFCs are most effective in terms of heat trapping potential. Chlorofluorocarbons (CFCs), hydrofluorocarbons (HFCs), hydrochlorofluorocarbons (HCFCs), perfluorocarbons (PFCs), and sulfur hexafluoride (SF_6) are high-GWP gases because they trap substantially more heat than CO_2. Studies report that the GWPs for these gases can be in the thousands or tens of thousands. In order to understand the effects of all the gases together, scientists consider all greenhouse gases in terms of the equivalent amount of CO_2. Since 1990, yearly emissions have gone up by about 6 billion metric tons of "carbon dioxide equivalent" worldwide, more than a 20% increase.

The two major effects of global warming are:

- **Increase in temperature:** According to the Fifth Assessment Report of the Inter-governmental Panel on Climate Change (IPCC), during the 21st century the global surface temperature is likely to rise by further 0.3 to 1.7 °C (0.5 to 3.1 °F) for their lowest emissions scenario and 2.6 to 4.8°C (4.7 to 8.6 °F) for their highest emissions scenario.
- **Rise in sea level:** Global warming is expected to bring about a rise in the sea level because of the expansion of sea water, caused by the melting of glaciers and the melting of polar ice, with a rise in temperature. According to a recent estimate sea level will rise by one foot by 2050.

The first effect of a rise in sea level would be increased flooding of many of the coastal wetlands. Shoreline losses will aggravate storm damages. Low lying island nations like Maldives and Bahamas may disappear. Studies suggest that up to 18 per cent of Bangladesh could be under water by 2050. The worst impact is on agriculture, horticulture and ecosystem. Global warming is predicted to cause a substantial decline in soil moisture due to higher temperature and reduced rainfall; besides it will also cause increased pest and weed growth due to higher CO_2 concentration in areas that are world's bread baskets. The rainfall pattern will be disrupted, varying widely among regions and between times. There will be water scarcity in some areas and increased precipitation in others. As a result in some areas severe drought and famines are bound to happen. Due to these climatic changes, areas that are already arid like Tunisia, Algeria, Ethiopia and Somalia will dry out further. Assault on ecosystem will be very severe with many speicies being driven to extinction. According to research published in *Nature*, by 2050 rising temperatures could result in the extinction of at least a million species (for a detailed discussion see chapter 37).

IPCC (2007) observed that "the peer reviewed estimates of the social cost of carbon in 2005 average US $12 per tonne of CO_2 but the range from 100 estimates is larger (-$3 to $95/t$CO_2$)". Sir Nicholas Stern, in his report on potential economic impacts suggests that extreme weather might reduce global gross domestic product by up to one per cent and that in a worst-case scenario, global per capita consumption could fall by the equivalent of 20 per cent.

Kyoto Protocol is the world's primary international agreement on reducing greenhouse gas emissions. Kyoto Protocol is an amendment to the United Nations Framework Convention on Climate Change (UNFCCC) negotiated in 1997. The Protocol now covers more than 160 countries and over 55 percent of global greenhouse gas emissions. (See Chapter 37)

5.6 Air Pollution case Study:

There are critical air pollution episodes from industrial accidents such as the leak of methyl isocyanide from Union carbide factory at Bhopal in India, (Box 5.2) and nuclear radiation caused by the nuclear power plant at Chernobyl in Russia. In addition to damaging the environment and human health, air pollution can harm buildings, monuments, outdoor statues, and other such structures. The chemicals in air pollution eat away materials such as sandstone, limestone, mortar, and different metals.

The **Bhopal disaster** or **Bhopal gas tragedy** is one of the world's worst catastrophes that took place in the Indian city of Bhopal, Madhya Pradesh. At midnight on 3rd December 1984, Union Carbide Plant at Bhopal, India, accidentally released methyl Isocyanate (MIC) gas, exposing more than 500,000 people to MIC and other chemicals. In 1969, Union Carbide (UCC-the parent company) set up a small plant (Union Carbide India Ltd.- UCIL) in Bhopal, the capital city of Madhya Pradesh, to manufacture pesticides. In the late 1960's and early 1970's, pesticide use increased dramatically in an effort to achieve self-sufficiency in agricultural production and to increase productivity of crops, in line with the objectives of India's Green Revolution programme.

Until 1979, the Indian subsidiary of Carbide used to import MIC or methyl isocyanate from the parent company. After 1979, it started to manufacture its own MIC. MIC is a dangerous chemical used in pesticide production It is a little lighter than water but twice as heavy as air, and hence it remains close to the ground when it escapes into the atmosphere .

On the night of December 23, 1984, a dangerous chemical reaction occurred in the Union Carbide factory when a large amount of water got into the MIC storage tank. The leak was first detected by workers about 11:30 p.m. when their eyes began to tear and burn. By the time any action was taken, a large amount, about 40 tons of Methyl Isocyanate (MIC), poured out of the tank for nearly two hours and escaped into the air, spreading within eight kilometers downwind, over the city of nearly 900,000 people. Thousands of people were killed (estimates ranging as high as 4,000) in their sleep or as they fled in terror, and hundreds of thousands remain injured or affected (estimates range as high as 400,000) to this day. The most seriously affected areas were the densely populated shanty towns immediately surrounding the plant and the victims were almost entirely the poorest members of the population. This poisonous gas, caused death and left the survivors with lingering disability and diseases.

The immediate cause of the chemical reaction was the seepage of water (500 liters)into the MIC storage tank. The results of this reaction were exacerbated by the failure of containment and safety measures and by a complete absence of community information and emergency procedures.

A listing of the defects of the MIC unit runs as follows:

1. MIC storage tank number 610 was filled beyond recommended capacity; a storage tank which was supposed to be held in reserve for excess MIC already contained the MIC.
2. Gauges measuring temperature and pressure in the various parts of the unit, including the crucial MIC storage tanks, were so notoriously unreliable that workers ignored early signs of trouble.
3. Failure of safety systems: The refrigeration unit for keeping MIC at low temperatures had been shut off for some time. The gas scrubber, designed to neutralize any escaping MIC, had been shut off for maintenance. The flare tower, designed to burn off MIC escaping from the scrubber, was also turned off, waiting for replacement of a corroded piece of pipe.
4. The lack of effective warning systems; the alarm on the storage tank failed to signal the increase in temperature on the night of the disaster.

Safety standards at the Bhopal plant were well below those it maintained at a nearly identical facility in West Virginia. Further, Carbide was able to operate its deteriorating plant due to lax in industrial safety and environmental laws and regulations in the state (Madhya Pradesh) and the country (India). This disaster gave rise to the world's largest lawsuit, one that spanned half-way around the world and dragged on for more than seven years. Although the final settlement of $470 million satisfied the imperatives of the company and the Government of India, it was condemned by the victims.

Source: Karpagam.M and Geetha(2010) Green Management, Theory and Applications
Cassels, Jamie. The Uncertain Promise of Law: Lessons From Bhopal. University Of Toronto Press Incorporated. 1993.
Weir, David. The Bhopal Syndrome: Pesticides, Environment, And Health. Sierra Club Books, San Francisco. 1987.
Website: http://www1.american.edu/ted/bhopal.htm

Box 5.2 Bhopal Gas Tragedy

5.7 Control of Air Pollution

Though air and water quality control programmes are analogous in effect, efforts to clean air pollution pose more of a challenge than water quality programmes, since air is more mobile than water. There are many sources of air pollution that are hazardous.

(a) point sources such as from that of a smelter

(b) mobile sources like autos, trucks etc.

(c) line sources such as a congested highways

(d) area sources, such as shopping centres.

Hence the success of air pollution abatement programme depends on the identification of the source of pollution. An understanding of the meteorological condition and topography in order to determine *the* pattern of dispersion of the emitted pollutant is also necessary. Apart from the legal measures which prescribe minimum threshold levels of pollutants and minimum standards of the quality of environment, the following general measures should be taken to control air pollution.

(1) The allowable emission rate should not be exceeded by individual plant.

(2) A continuous air pollution survey should be conducted in the concerned area and its neighbouring region.

(3) Air pollution control technology should be incorporated through legal requirement into design of the individual plant.

(4) Meteorological conditions should be considered while deciding on the location of the industry.

The above points particularly apply to air pollution in an industrial area.

Four procedures have been outlined by the World Health Organisation in its publication (Vol 12)—*Research into Environmental Pollution.* They are:

(1) *Containment:* This refers to the prevention of escape of toxic substances into the ambient air. Containment can be achieved by a variety of engineering methods like the use of pollution control equipments such as cyclones, electrostatic precipitators, scrubbers etc.

(2) *Replacement* is substitution of a technological process causing air pollution by a new process that does not pollute at least as much as the previous one. Substitution of natural gas for coal and oil would eliminate particulate emission problems from combustion, but scarcity of natural gas does render such substitution impossible.

(3) *Dilution:* Dilution is promoted by the self-cleansing capacity of the environment. The establishment of green belts in industrial areas is an attempt at diluting the concentration and effects of air pollutants.

(4) *Legislation* is the provision of legal policies and acts by the Government through its constitution to reduce pollution.

Essentially there are three approaches to air pollution-control, most of which are used simultaneously.

(1) The best solution is to ensure that there is good combustion. The combustion chamber must be well-supplied with oxygen and a good draft so that the temperature of the fire is as hot as possible. This will eliminate much of the dark smoke containing incompletely burnt dust and ashes.

(2) The second technique is to use mechanical device. Particles from combustion and dusts from manufacturing and processing can be captured by simple air cleaning equipment. Among the most used are cyclones, scrubbers, bag houses and electro-static precipitators.

(3) Chemical treatment.

One of the earliest important mechanical solution to reduce air pollution is to build the chimney stacks higher so that the fumes will be diffused at a higher level. This, however, can cause acid-rain pollution at far away distance.

Finally, some factory fumes must be subjected to chemical treatment. Only by neutralising them or forming some harmless by-product can the smoke be rendered unobjectionable. It is also possible to extract undesirable elements before combustion.

Some polluting emission can be controlled only through the modification of industrial process. Industries can lower carbon monoxide concentration by supplying more air during combustion. Levels of nitrogen oxides can be reduced by decreasing combustion temperatures.

An effective air quality control programme must not only require adequate control strategies, but also provide for proper disposal or refuse of collected air pollutants.

There are various technological devices available which can be used successfully to combat air pollution. But what is needed in addition is the presence of strict legal measures to prevent air pollution. With the problem of pollution increasing in dimensions, almost every country has its own legal measures to reduce/ prevent pollution. In the US, the Environmental Protection Agency has the primary responsibility for promoting a clean environment. The clean Air Act of 1970 and its Amendments authorised EPA to establish national ambient air quality standards for pollutants. In UK, the Modern Air Pollution Legislation dates from the Alkaline and Works Regulation Act of 1863. In Japan, the Basic Law for Environmental Pollution Control gives the national Government the responsibility to establish and implement fundamental and comprehensive policies. India is no exception to such legal measures. In India, the 42nd amendment of the Constitution has provided under articles 48A and 51A the legal foundation of environmental protection. Further the Air (Prevention and Control of Pollution) Act, 1981, prescribes emission standards for air polluting industries. We will see more of legal issues in chapter 36.

Through these legal and technical measures and adequate fiscal incentives to industries reducing its emissions, air quality can be improved.

Conclusion

Air pollution is one of the very complex problems that has come to stay with us. A point has been reached that calls for urgent action to prevent further deterioration in air quality. We need better and newer techniques of production that would pollute less; we need to update our pollution control technology. Laws and regulations should be strictly enforced. But more important, we should tackle the basic reasons of pollution: population, increasing needs and changing consumption patterns. All these need time. Do we have it? If not, as John K. Galbraith pointed out: "The penultimate western man, stalled in the ultimate traffic jam and slowly succumbing to carbon monoxide will not be cheered to hear from the last survivor that the GNP went up by a record amount".

Questions

1. What are the major air pollutants. Explain their sources effects.
2. Give a case study of air pollution and its impact.
3. What are the various measures to control air pollution

Exercise

Do micro sample survey to assess awareness, impact and health cost of air pollution in your city.

6

WATER POLLUTION

Everything originated in the water Everything is stained by water."

—Goethe

Water covers more than two-thirds of the Earth's surface. But fresh water represents less than 0.5% of the total water on Earth. The rest is either in the form of seawater or locked up in icecaps or the soil . About 97 percent of all water is in the oceans. Of the 3% which is fresh water, the majority, about 69 percent, is locked up in glaciers and icecaps, mainly in Greenland and Antarctica. Another 30% of this tiny 3 percent is held up as soil moisture and in very deep aquifers, deep below the earth. Of all the freshwater on earth, only about 0.3 percent is contained in rivers and lakes. Thus only a miniscule, less than 1 percent, of total available water is potable water. Studies have estimated that the value of services of freshwater ecosystem in purifying water and assimilating wastes is more than $US400 billion. Yet water is being misused posing challenges to future availability in both qualitative and quantitative sense.

6.1 Global Distribution of Water Resources

Table 6.1 and Figure 6.1 gives details on Global water distribution from one of the many estimates.

Water quality has become a global issue. Every day, 2 million tons of sewage and industrial and agricultural waste are discharged into the world's water - the equivalent of the weight of the entire human population of 6.8 billion people. The UN estimates that the amount of wastewater produced annually is six times more than the water that exists in all the rivers of the world. (UN WWAP 2003). It is reported that every year, more people die from the consequences of unsafe water than from all forms of violence, including war– –and the greatest impacts are on children under the age of five. Studies observe that water pollution is the leading worldwide cause of deaths and diseases and that it accounts for the deaths of more than 14,000 people daily.

Unsafe or inadequate water, sanitation, and hygiene cause approximately 3.1 percent of all deaths worldwide. According to WHO and UNICEF (2000) unsafe water causes 4 billion cases of diarrhea each year, and results in 2.2 million deaths, mostly of children under five. This means that 15% of child deaths each year are attributable to diarrhea – a child dying every 15 seconds. In India alone, the single largest cause of ill health and death among children is diarrhea, which kills nearly half a million children each year. Pollution of water is therefore a very important environmental issue that calls for very serious attention of the governments all over the world.

6.2 Definition of Water Pollution

Table 6.1 Global Water Distribution

Water source	Percent of fresh water	Percent of total water
Oceans, Seas, & Bays	--	96.5
Ice caps, Glaciers, & Snow	68.7	1.74
Groundwater	--	1.7
Fresh	30.1	0.76
Saline	--	0.94
Soil Moisture	0.05	0.001
Ground Ice & Permafrost	0.86	0.022
Lakes	--	0.013
Fresh	0.26	0.007
Saline	--	0.006
Atmosphere	0.04	0.001
Swamp Water	0.03	0.0008
Rivers	0.006	0.0002
Biological Water	0.003	0.0001
Total	-	100

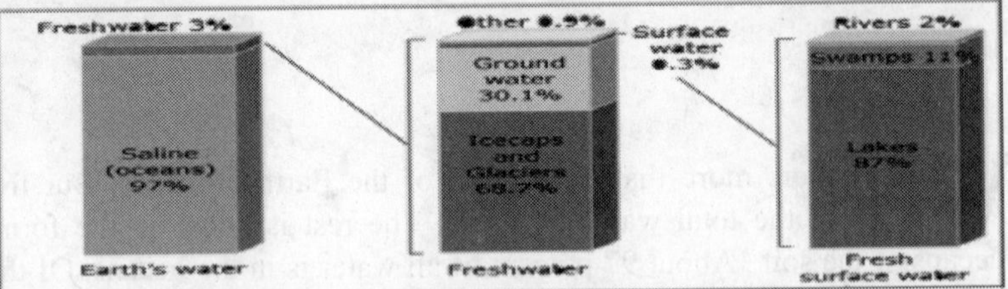

Figure 6.1 Global Water Distribution

Source: Gleick, P. H., 1996 "Water Resources" in Encyclopedia of Climate and Weather, ed. by S. H. Schneider, Oxford University Press, New York, vol. 2, pp.817-823.

Water pollution is the process of altering the properties of any water which renders it unfit or less fit for the purpose its unaltered form was used—the use being natural or artificial. It is the change in the physical, chemical and biological quality of water, caused by anthropogenic activities that are detrimental to the existing, intended and potential uses of water. Dr. Key, a British expert says: "A river may be considered to be polluted when the water in it is altered in composition or condition, directly or indirectly as a result of the activities of man, so that it is less suitable for all or any of the purposes for which it would be suitable in its natural state". Water pollution may also be defined as a natural or induced change in the quality of water which renders it unusable or dangerous as regards food, human and animal health, industry, agriculture, fishing or leisure pursuits.

Water pollution reduces the amount of pure fresh water that is available for such necessities as drinking and cleaning and for recreation activities. Water being a universal solvent readily gets contaminated by the material with which it comes into physical contact. The factors responsible for water pollution may be artificial or natural. Several natural phenomena are found to be having propensity towards polluting water. For example, drought causes water level go down in aquifers and salt water intrusion takes place. During rain, running water gathers silt and other material. Thus natural contamination occurs in the water courses. However, more than natural factors, it is the unprecedented industrial production rate that is responsible for the scarcity of pure drinking water.

Water has become a scarce commodity today on account of the innumerable ways in which human beings pollute water. As years go by human beings are making increasing demands on the world's water. Industry, agriculture, irrigation, mining, power generation and the concentration of millions of people in cities watered by one or at most two rivers, all contribute to a level of pollution that threatens to outstrip human ability to clean up afterwards.

6.3 Classification of Water Pollution

Pollutants may be classified as organic and inorganic pollutants. Organic pollutants are easily decomposable pollutants.

Organic water pollutants include:

- Detergents and disinfectants
- Bacteria from livestock operations

- Food processing wastes
- Tree debris from logging operations

Inorganic water pollutants are:

- Ammonia from food processing wastes
- Heavy metals
- Industrial discharges such as sulfur dioxide by power plants, that make water acidic.
- Chemical waste
- Fertilizers and pesticides from agricultural use
- Silt from construction sites, logging, slash and burn operation
- Volatile Organic Compounds such as solvents and hydrocarbons
- Chlorinated solvents
- Chemical compounds found in cosmetics products

Marshall I Goldman and Robert Shoop have classified water pollution on basis of nature of the pollutant as follows:

- Pollution by Putrescible (foul smelling, rotting of organic materials by bacteria) materials
- Pollution by heated effluents
- Pollution by toxic materials
- Pollution by inert materials and
- Pollution by radio-active elements and compounds.

6.3.1Pollution by Putrescible Materials

Putrescible wastes refer to foul smelling and rotting organic materials—materials like waste from humans, paper pulp plants, and canneries. Organic pollution is controlled by accelerating the process of decomposition of these organic wastes. When discharged into a stream or river or lake, the organic materials decompose by using large quantities of oxygen from water. If too much oxygen is removed and it takes too long for it to be restored, there may be serious pollution.

The amount of dissolved oxygen needed by decomposers to decompose organic materials in a given volume of water is called the biochemical oxygen demand (BOD). Thus BOD is a measure of contamination of the waste water. Human wastes are a major source of BOD. Sewage-laden waste water entering a sanitary sewer has an average BOD level of 250 ppm. This sewage-laden waste water contains only 8 ppm (parts per million) of oxygen. Hence its oxygen is quickly depleted through microbial decomposition of sewage. In fact the decomposition of the daily wastes of a single person requires all the dissolved oxygen (DO) in 9000 litres (2200 gallons) of water. Some concentrated industrial wastes have BOD levels greater than 30,000 ppm. Other sources of high level BOD wastes include run off from livestock feed lots and spoils dredged from harbours and canals.

Even in mild cases of oxygen depletion, fish such as *trout* will not have adequate oxygen for their needs. Consequently they may die or be forced to move elsewhere. Scavenger fish like carp, which require less oxygen will only survive in such waters. Wastes from paper pulp mills discharge unusually large quantities of effluent, depleting all available dissolved oxygen.

The organically polluted area of the stream may be classified into three zones. The first zone is called the Zone of Immediate Pollution. Here the dissolved oxygen content is the lowest and the odour and colour of water is affected. The second zone is Septic Zone where content of dissolved oxygen is greater than in the zone of immediate pollution. Special aquatic organisms with low oxygen requirements like snails, sewage worms, and rat tail maggots may live in this zone. Because of the odour of decomposition, the area is usually easy to find. Finally there is Zone of Recovery, where the odour begins to disappear and fish like minnows and suckers begin to appear. There is usually a large bloom of plant life or algae on the borders of Zone II and Zone III. The increased quantity of oxygen combines with decomposed organisms to break down the last traces of the organic material and create highly fertile condition.

6.3.2 Pollution by Heated Effluents

Oxygen is readily restored when the water is cool. The hotter it is, lower the oxygen holding capacity of the water. The bubbles that arise from heated water demonstrate what happens to the gases in hot water.

The discharge of clean hot water into an unpolluted stream is hence as harmful as the discharge of organic wastes. In both cases, oxygen content of **water** is reduced. It is because of this that water pollution is a serious matter in tropical countries. The temperature is always so warm that it is difficult for the streams to absorb the necessary quantities of oxygen. Hot water is discharged into water courses by industries that use water for cooling. Such heated water is extremely harmful to the fish population and many other organisms which survive only in a restricted temperature range.

6.3.3 Pollution by Toxic Wastes

Toxic wastes are those which are not easily broken down by biological means. Toxic wastes like DDT and mercury are poisonous when consumed or contacted by plants and animals. Pesticides and herbicides which wash off the land into the sewers are other examples. The mercury poisoning of hundreds of people in Minamata, Japan, is another example.

6.3.4 Pollution by Inert Wastes

Inert wastes are those which enter water as solids but are not involved in chemical reactions. Such wastes include dust, metal filings, oil films, dust and silt from soil erosion. They are removed by mechanical means such as filtering or allowing for sedimentation; these materials if not removed settle to the bottom of water course and block sunlight. As a result plant life is affected which, in turn, cutsoff the food supply for the fish and other animal populations. For example, the oyster beds off the coast of Connecticut, Rhode Island and Massachusetts have been buried with inert wastes. Pollution from inert wastes is also a serious problem in areas located near mines.

6.3.5 Pollution by Radio-Active Wastes

Radio-active wastes are produced in the processing of uranium and other radio-active substances or in testing of the nuclear devices that produce nuclides in blast devices and fall out. It may take years for the level of radio-activity in the water to fall. Practically the only way known to dispose of such materials is to dump them into ocean beyond the continental shelf or pump them into abandoned mines and deep wells. Even this may cause pollution of oceans and underground water supplies.

6.4 Sources of Water Pollution

Sources of surface water pollution are generally grouped into two categories based on their origin.

Point source pollution refers to contaminants that enter a waterway from a single, identifiable source, such as a pipe or ditch. Examples of sources in this category include discharges from a sewage treatment plant or from a factory

Non–point sources

Non-point source pollution refers to dispersed contamination that does not originate from a single discrete source. A common example is the leaching out of nitrogen compounds from fertilized agricultural lands. Non-point source of water pollution, have no obvious point of entry into receiving watercourses. In contrast, **point source** pollution represents those activities where wastewater is routed directly into receiving water bodies by discharge pipes, where they can be easily measured and controlled. Obviously, non-point source pollution is much more difficult to identify, measure and control than point sources.

All types of agricultural practices and land use, including animal feeding operations (feed lots), are treated as a non-point sources. The main characteristics of non-point sources are that they:

- respond to hydrological conditions,
- are not easily measured or controlled directly (and therefore are difficult to regulate),
- focus on land and related management practices.

Control of point sources in those countries having effective control programmes is carried out by effluent treatment according to regulations and through the use of effluent charges and discharge permits. In comparison, control of non-point sources, especially in agriculture, has been by education and promotion of more ecofriendly agricultural practices and land use management.

Table 6.2 Non Point Sources of Pollution

Activity	Pollutant	Specific Pollutant
Agriculture and allied activities, Forestry	Runoff from all categories of agriculture, leading to surface and groundwater pollution. Vegetable handling, growth of aquaculture, irrigation return flows that carry salts, nutrients and pesticides and tile drainage carrying leachates surface waters.	Phosphorus, nitrogen, metals, pathogens, sediment, pesticides, salt, BOD, trace elements.
Liquid waste disposal	Disposal of liquid wastes from municipal wastewater effluents, sewage sludge, industrial effluents and wastewater from home septic systems.	Pathogens, metals, organic compounds.
Residential, Commercial, Industrial	Urban runoff from roofs, streets, parking lots, etc. leading to overloading of sewage plants from combined sewers, or polluted runoff routed directly to receiving waters; wastes from local industries into street gutters and storm drains; street cleaning; road salting contributes to surface and groundwater pollution.	Sediments, fertilizers, greases and oils, faecal matter and pathogens, organic contaminants (e.g. PCBs), heavy metals, pesticides, nutrients, sediment, salts, BOD, COD, etc.
Sewage systems	Overloading and malfunction of septic systems leading to surface runoff and/or direct infiltration to groundwater.	Phosphorus, nitrogen, pathogens (faecal matter).
Transportation	Roads, railways, pipelines, hydro-electric corridors, etc.	Nutrients, sediment, metals, organic contaminants, pesticides and herbicides.
Mineral extraction	Runoff from mines and mine wastes, quarries, well sites.	Sediment, acids, metals, oils, organic contaminants, salts

Recreational land use	Large variety of recreational land uses, including ski resorts, boating and marinas, campgrounds, parks; waste and "grey" water from recreational boats is a major pollutant, especially in small lakes and rivers.	Nutrients, pesticides, sediment, pathogens, heavy metals.
Solid waste disposal	Contamination of surface and groundwater by leachates and gases. Hazardous wastes may be disposed of through underground disposal.	Nutrients, metals, pathogens, organic contaminants.
Dredging	Dispersion of contaminated sediments, leakage from containment areas.	Metals, organic contaminants.
Deep well disposal	Contamination of groundwater by deep well injection of liquid wastes, especially oilfield brines and liquid industrial wastes.	Salts, heavy metals, organic contaminants.

Modified from: http://fao.org/docrep/W2598E/w2598e04.htm

On the basis of sources of pollution, water pollution may also be classified as:

- Pollution by sewage
- Pollution by agricultural practices
- Pollution by Industries
- Pollution by Oil

6.4.1 Water Pollution by Sewage

One of the major pollutants of water in the urban and rural areas is the sewage that includes organic matter, animal and human excreta. The sewage most often contains organic matter that encourages the growth of microorganisms which consume the oxygen present in water. This is called oxygen depletion. The aquatic organisms like the fish cannot then survive in such waters. This increases Bio Chemical Oxygen Demand (BOD) of the water body and decreases the Dissolved Oxygen (DO) content of water.

6.4.2 Water Pollution by Industries

The industries are mostly situated along the riverbanks for easy availability of water and also for easy disposal of wastes. The wastes from industries include various acids, alkalis, dyes and other chemicals. They change the pH value of water. Industrial wastes include toxic metals like lead, mercury, cadmium, etc, and other chemicals like the fluorides, ammonia, etc. Certain industries such as power plants, refineries, nuclear reactors release a lot of hot water from their cooling plants into the water bodies without reducing the temperature. This increases the temperature in the water bodies thereby killing the aquatic life. The oxygen content of water is reduced due to increase in the temperature. This is called thermal pollution.

6.4.3 Agriculture and Water Pollution

Agriculture is the single largest user of freshwater resources, using a global average of 70% of all surface water supplies. Agricultural activities pollute water through discharge of pollutants and sediment to surface and/or groundwater, through net loss of soil by poor agricultural practices, and through salinization and water logging of irrigated land.

Table 6.3 Water Pollution from Agriculture

Activity		Pollutant
Animal feedlots Irrigation Cultivation Pastures Dairy farming Orchards Aquaculture and forestry.	Runoff from all categories of agriculture leading to surface and groundwater pollution. In northern climates, runoff from frozen ground is a major problem, especially where manure is spread during the winter. Vegetable handling, especially washing in polluted surface waters in many developing countries, leads to contamination of food supplies. Growth of aquaculture is becoming a major polluting activity in many countries. Irrigation return flows carry salts, nutrients and pesticides. Tile drainage rapidly carries leachates such as nitrogen to surface waters.	Phosphorus, nitrogen, metals, pathogens, sediment, pesticides, salt, BOD[1], trace elements (e.g. selenium). Pesticides.

Source : http://www.fao.org/docrep/W2598E/w2598e04.htm

Most of the synthetic and chemicals-based and fertilizers used in agriculture enter into the water bodies with the rain water flow and the ground water by seepage and pollute water in the lakes and rivers. Agricultural pesticides have been implicated in a variety of human health issues and as causing significant and widespread ecosystem dysfunction through their toxic effects on organisms. Table 6.3 gives information on pollution from agricultural activities.

6.4.4 Pollution by Oil Spills and Oil Leaks

Oil spill is a major problem in the oceans and seas. The oil tankers and offshore petroleum refineries cause oil leakage into the waters and causes water pollution in the oceans and seas. Oil floats on the water surface and prevents the atmospheric oxygen from mixing in the water. The United States National Research Council (NRC) published a report in 2002 that said that, globally, approximately 1.3 million tonnes of oil are released into the sea each year. The exact amount of oil pollution varies each year, generally between 470,000 and 8.4 million tonnes, depending on the frequency and severity of oil spills. Oil discharged into the seas from various sources: 363 millon gallons of used engine oil ends up in waterways while bilge cleaning and other ship operations release 137 million gallons of oil into navigable waters. Natural seeps and offshore drilling account for nearly 62 million and 15 million gallons of oil discharge into oceans every year.

Oil pollution can damage ecosystems, including plants and animals, and contaminate water for drinking and other purposes. The feathers and fur of birds and marine animals can become coated in oil; Most birds that are coated in oil would not survive. Fish can be suffocated by the thick sludge of oil on the water surface, and bottom-dwelling fish can develop liver disease, as well as reproductive and growth problems. Plants that grow in or near the water can be harmed by oil pollution. An oil spill can block the sunlight that plants need for photosynthesis, which kills plants growing in the water. Coral reefs, mangroves and marshes are highly sensitive to oil pollution. The grounding and breaking up of the Amaco Cadiz on March 17th 1978 on the French coast line and that of Torry Canyon in 1967 along English shore are examples of marine pollution by oil spills.

6.5 Measures of water Pollution

The extent of pollution in a water body is measured commonly in terms of:

Disolved Oxygen (DO), Bio Chemical Oxygen Demand (BOD), Chemical Oxygen Demand (COD), and Total Suspended Solids (TSS)

6.5.1Dissolved oxygen (DO) is measured in milligrams per liter (mg/l) or parts per million (ppm). The amount of dissolved oxygen in streams is dependent on the water temperature, the quantity of sediment in the stream, the amount of oxygen taken out of the system by respiring and decaying organisms, and the amount of oxygen put back into the system by photosynthesizing plants, stream flow, and aeration. Fish and other aquatic animals depend on dissolved oxygen (the oxygen present in water) to live. Trout need DO levels in excess of 8 mg/liter, striped bass prefer DO levels above 5 mg/l, and most warm water fish need DO in excess of 2 mg/l.

6.5.2 Bio chemical Oxygen Demand (BOD) Biological oxygen demand or BOD stands for the amount of oxygen required by the microorganisms in polluted water to complete the decomposition of organic matter present in the water. The term is usually used to know the amount of oxygen consumed. BOD is expressed in milligrams of O_2 per litre of water. A weak organic waste has a BOD less than 1500 mg/ litre, a strong one has higher than this.

6.5.3 Chemical oxygen demand (COD) is a measure of the total quantity of oxygen required to oxidize all organic material into carbon dioxide and water. COD values are always greater than BOD values; COD measurements can be made in a few hours while BOD measurements take five days.

6.5.4 Total Suspended Solids (TSS) gives a measure of turbidity of water. TSS are solid materials, including organic and inorganic, that are suspended in the water. These would include silt, plankton and industrial wastes. Suspended solids can result from erosion from urban runoff and agricultural land, industrial wastes, river bank erosion, and wastewater discharges. High concentrations of suspended solids can lower water quality by absorbing light. Water then becomes warmer and lessen the ability of the water to hold oxygen necessary for aquatic life. Because aquatic plants also receive less light, photosynthesis decreases and less oxygen is produced. The combination of warmer water, less light and less oxygen makes it impossible for some forms of life to exist.

6.6 Effects of Water Pollution

Water pollution has serious consequences not only on human health but also on flora and fauna.

Notable effects of water pollution include the effects on human health. Nitrates in drinking water affects the red blood cells of infants that sometimes results in death. Cadmium in sludge-derived fertilizer absorbed by crops and ingested in sufficient amounts causes an acute diarrhea and liver and kidney damage.

6.6.1 Effects on Ecosystem

Decomposition of organic wastes promotes the growth of oxygen consuming algae (algal bloom), especially the blue-green algae. The growth of algae, brings down the DO of water killing fish and other animals. The enrichment of water with inorganic nutrients like nitrates and phosphates is called **eutrophication.** When organic matter exceeds the capacity of the micro-organisms to break down and recycle the organic matter, it encourages rapid growth of algae. When the algae die the remains of the algae add to the already present organic wastes and eventually water becomes deficient in oxygen. Anaerobic organisms (those that do not require oxygen for their existence) attack the organic wastes releasing gases such as methane and hydrogen sulphide which pose threat to the existence of aerobic (oxygen requiring) forms of life. The result is a foul – smelling waste filled water body- death of the aquatic ecosystem. There are many water bodies which are examples of Eutrophication. One is that of River Coovum in Chennai, India.

Pollution by oil in water destroys life by obstructing sunlight which prevents photosynthesis by plants in water, thus reducing oxygen content of water.

6.6.2 Effects on Animal Health

The impact of water pollution on animal and bird life is

- Large scale death of aquatic and terrestrial animals
- Reduced reproduction rate
- Increased incidence of diseases
- Imbalances created in secondary food chains
- Accumulation of bio accumulative and non-biodegradable pollutants in animal bodies. Some organo chlorine pesticides (like DDT, BHC, Endrin) are known for bio accumulative and bio magnifiable characters.

Water pollutants pass through the food chain and food web. While passing through the organisms, the concentration of pollutants gets increased. This is called bio magnifications. For e.g., 0.5 ppm DDT in grasses gets magnified to 2 ppm in sheep. It may be magnified to 10 ppm in human beings who eat such polluted mutton.

Pollution by non-degradable broad-spectrum pesticides, cause mass destruction of aquatic life. The most famous case of pesticide poisoning through food chain is that of the bald Eagle that ate the pesticide contaminated fish which ultimately made it an endangered species. Residues of DDT built up in the fatty tissues of female eagles and affected the calcium metabolism in the eagles. As a result the shells of the egg became very thin and would break even before it was hatched. DDT affected many other species of birds most of which became extinct or endangered. The case against DDT and other pesticides was highlighted in the book Silent Spring by Rachel Carson. Figure 6.2 shows bio magnification effect of pesticides in food chain. Such organo chlorine pesticides cause health hazards like impotence, cancerous tumors beyond a threshold limit of accumulation.

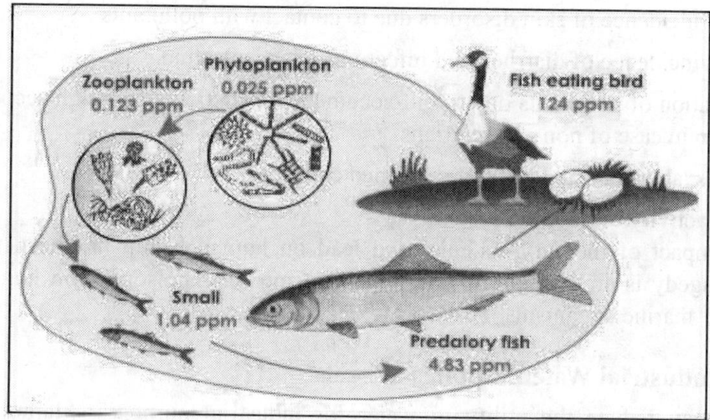

Figure 6.2 Process of Biological Magnification: DDT concentrations increase in organisms along the food chain.

Source: http://www.tutorvista.com/content/biology/biology-iv/environmental-pollution/water-pollution-effects.php

6.6.3 Effects on Human Health

Water is a significant vehicle in the transmission of disease when it contains water borne pathogens or disease producing organisms. These pathogens, which can be viruses, bacterial, protozoa (single celled animals), and parasitic worms cause such diseases as dysentery, typhoid fever, cholera, and infections hepatitis. Some of the more common water borne diseases is given in Table 6.4.

Table 6.4 Water Borne Diseases Transmitted through Drinking Water and Food

Disease	Type of Organism	Symptoms and Comments
Cholera	Bacteria	severe vomiting, diarrhoea and dehydration; often fatal if untreated
Typhoid	Bacteria	severe vomiting, diarrhoea, inflamed intestine, enlarged spleen—often fatal if untreated
Bacterial dysentery	Several species of bacteria	Diarrhoea
Para-typhoid fever	Several species of bacteria	severe vomiting, diarrhoea
Infectious hepatitis	Virus	Yellow jaundiced skin, enlarged liver, vomiting and abdominal pain—often permanent liver damage
Amoebic dysentery	Protozoa	Diarrhoea, possibly prolonged

Besides these there are other diseases which are transmitted through polluted water; urban filariasis for example, is transmitted through mosquitos breeding in polluted water.

In general, water pollution causes following health effects on human beings:

- Water borne diseases like Cholera, jaundice, hepatitis, gastroenteritis will be more prevalent due to water pollution.
- Increased incidence of tumours, ulcers due to nitrate pollution.
- Increased incidence of skin disorders due to contact with pollutants.
- Increased incidence of diarrhea and infections of the intestine.
- Concentration of pollutants due to bio-accumulative pesticides through secondary and tertiary food chain in case of non - vegetarians.
- Still births, abortions and birth of deformed children.
- Reduced activity of immune system.

The health impact of mercury, arsenic, and lead on human health has been well documented. The Minamata tragedy is an example of the impact of mercuric poisoning on human health and on other animals and marine organisms. (Box 6.1)

6.6.4 Effect on Industrial Water Supplies

Water pollution may reduce the utility of water for industrial purposes. Manufacure of a ton of sugar and steel need 4000 and 240,000 litre of water respectively. The range of quality required or desirable in industrial application is very wide. Some processes require unusually soft water; others can tolerate hard water. So polluted water can involve substantially high costs for industries—the costs of purifying the water, of repairing damaged equipment or of making extensive adjustments to industrial process themselves.

6.6.5 Aesthetic and Recreational Considerations also should be considered in an analysis of effect of water pollution. Polluted water with low DO (or high BOD) make water unfit for swimming and many water sports popular in most of the developed countries. Aesthetically it is not only the odour that is offensive but also the floating materials. Floating sewage solids especially, suspended sediments and industrial wastes reduce visual appeal of water. Dense algae growth make water both unattractive and stinking.

Table 6.5 Effects of Industrial/ Chemical Water Pollution on Human Health

Mercury	Industrial wastes	Nervous system, numbness of limbs, lips and tongue, blurred vision, deafness and mental derangement.
Lead	Industrial wastes	Absorbed into blood and affects PBCs, liver, kidney, bone, brain and the peripheral nervous system. Lead poisoning can even lead to coma.
Cadmium	Cadmium industries, fertiliser	Deposited in organs like the kidney, pancreas, liver, intestinal mucosa, etc. Cadmium poisoning causes headache, vomiting, bronchial pneumonia, kidney necrosis, etc.
Arsenic	Fertiliser	Arsenic poisoning causes renal failure and death, It can cause nerve disorder, kidney and liver disorders, muscular atrophy, etc.
Agrochemicals like DDT	Pesticides	Accumulates in the tissues of body. Adversely affects the nervous system and fertility. Carcinogenic.

*Source:*http://www.tutorvista.com/content/biology/biology-ii/environment-and-environmental-problems/water-pollution.php

Minamata, city located in Kumamoto Prefecture, Japan, on the west coast of Kyushu, witnessed the adverse impact of water pollutants due to the discharge of untreated methyl mercury into the Minamata Bay until 1966. In the mid 1950s the people of Minamata, Japan, on the coast of the Shiranui Sea, noticed that the cats in their area appeared to be going insane, and were falling into the sea. Soon the people in the town were also contracting a strange illness. Individuals began to have numbness in their limbs and lips. Some had difficulty hearing or seeing. Others developed shaking (tremors) in their arms and legs, difficulty in walking and brain damage. The disease, a disorder of the central nervous system, was termed "the Minamata Disease".

In July 1959 researchers from Kumamoto University found that organic mercury was the cause of Minamata disease. It was later discovered that Chisso Corporation, a chemical fertilizer company was responsible for the mercury poisoning. Chisso Corporation is one of the companies that made Japan's rapid postwar economic growth possible. The main products of the Chisso Minamata factory include liquid crystals, preservatives, desiccants, chemical fertilizers, and synthetic resins. It employed about 660 people as of September 2000, and is still an important company in Minamata. From 1932 to 1968 the company continued to use inorganic mercury as a catalyst in producing acetaldehyde, which was used to produce acetic acid and vinyl chloride. Methyl mercury, a by-product of the production process, was discharged virtually untreated into the sea until 1966. Several hundred tons of methyl mercury were continually discharged by Chisso's facility in Minamata between 1932 and 1966, contaminating the entire food chain and bringing about all sorts of symptoms that had never been seen in humans: trouble seeing and speaking, loss of balance and increasingly violent trembling beginning with the hands and legs then moving to the entire body. As the mercury dumping continued, babies were born with severe deformities, including gnarled limbs, mental retardation, deafness, and blindness.

According to Japanese government figures, 2,955 people contracted Minamata disease, and 1,784 people have since died.

On March 20, 1973, after a four-year trial, the court of Kumamoto condemned Chisso for its blatant neglect to set forth preventative measures. In October 1982, 40 plaintiffs filed suit against the Japanese government, saying it had failed to stop Chisso from polluting the environment, and had actually looked the other way while Chisso violated pollution laws. On October 16, 2004, the Supreme Court of Japan ordered the government to pay 71.5 million yen ($703,000) in damages to the Minamata disease victims. The Environment Minister bowed in apology to the plaintiffs. After 22 years, the plaintiffs achieved their goal of making those responsible for Japan's worst case of industrial pollution pay for their negligence. No amount of money, though, can ever make up for the lives needlessly lost to Minamata disease.

Source: http://cbcs.km.nccu.edu.tw/xms/read_attach.php?id=232 http://www.env.go.jp/en/chemi/hs/minamata2002/

http://rarediseases.about.com/od/rarediseases1/a/102304.htm

http://www.soshisha.org/english/10tishiki_e/10chisiki_3_e.pdf

Box 6.1 Minamata Tragedy

6.7 Control of Water Pollution

Policy for controlling water pollution makes a distinction is made between point sources of pollution and non-point sources of pollution. In the case of point sources of water pollution such as an effluent from a factory, either end of the pipe controls or process controls are adopted. In the case of non-point source of pollution, such as those from agriculture, the principle of "best environmental practice" may be applied to minimise non-point source pollution. Good agricultural practice is recognised by the United Nations Economic Commission for Europe (UNECE) as a means of minimising the risk of water pollution.

6.7.1 Effluent Treatment

The industrial wastes should be treated before being let into the water bodies. The toxic materials should be removed, the metallic compounds should be precipitated, the acids and alkalis should be neutralized and the temperature of the hot waters should be reduced. This includes as, said earlier, end of the pipe control and process control. **End - of - pipe** method controls only what is released from a discharge point, with little or no control of the processes which produce the effluents. **Process control** on the other hand starts at the beginning of the process and accomplishes minimisation of the effluent by promoting the use of Best Available Technology (BAT) in order to minimize the impact on the environment from the process as a whole.

6.7.2 Sewage Treatment

The sewage before being let into the water bodies must be purified.This is done in three steps as follows:

- Primary treatment
- Secondary treatment
- Tertiary treatment

Primary Treatment

During primary treatment the heavy suspended matter are made to settle down by passing through coarse sieves into the sediment tanks, after which it is passed through a bed of rocks.

Secondary Treatment

In this step, the biodegradable organic material are treated with the help of decomposers and oxygen after which the water is also chlorinated to remove the germs. In this stage 85% of Biological Oxygen Demand [BOD] and suspended solids are removed.

Tertiary Treatment

Inorganic pollutants like the nitrates, phosphates, detergents, metal ions, etc. are removed in this step by passing the water through activated charcoal that acts as a filter. It may include processes such as coagulation, flocculation and filtration

6.7.3 Methods of Treating Waste Water

Efficient effluent treatment plant for industries and sewage treatment plants is based on one of the following suitable methods:

- Reverse osmosis
- Ion exchange
- Electro dialysis
- Coagulation and Flocculation

6.7.4 Recycling of waste water for reuse

Reusing and recycling water and other alternative water supplies is a key part of reducing the pressure on our scarce water resources. **Waste Water Recycling** means recovering more wastewater for beneficial purposes such as agricultural and landscape irrigation, industrial processes, toilet flushing, and replenishing a ground water basin. **Waste Water Recovery** is the process preceding waste water recycling or reuse, recovering the waste water before you re-input the water into your system.

Water and wastewater reuse has various benefits. First, recycled wastewater can serve as a more dependable water source, containing useful substances for some applications. With adequate treatment, wastewater can meet specific needs and purposes, such as toilet flushing, cooling water, and other applications. The reuse of treated wastewater is particularly attractive in arid climates, areas facing demand growth and those under water stress conditions. The second benefit of wastewater reuse is that it leads to reduced water consumption and treatment needs, with associated cost savings. Water recycling offers resource and financial savings.

Finally, the **reuse of wastewater** can go a long way toward reducing the freshwater demand. By reusing treated wastewater for these applications, more freshwater can be allocated for uses that require higher quality, such as for drinking, thereby contributing to more sustainable resource utilization. Wastewater reuse can thus be considered as an appropriate application of Environmentally Sound Technologies (ESTs).

In addition to potential and substantial cost savings and efficiency improvements, there are the additional benefits of improving industry's image and complying with environmental regulations. With the increase in cost of water for industrial uses and with the tightening of discharge requirements, **recovery, recycling and reuse of wastewater** has become even more critical and desirable.

6.7.5 Public Awareness and legal measures

Public awareness is one of the most essential and cost effective components of water conservation. It demands the participation and cooperation of all stakeholders like consumers, suppliers and policy makers. It is also essential that the public should be made aware of the importance of water in their lives, cost of producing and delivering of water, the status of water resources availability, and its role in water resources conservation for future generations.

Besides creating awareness, sound legal measures with strict enforcement is also a must for controlling water pollution.

Conclusion

Water pollution is a very serious issue which must be controlled for the health of the nation and the economy.

With increased demand for water due to population pressure, protecting the existing sources of water is a vital step towards water security.

Questions

1. What are the sources of water pollution
2. How is water pollution measured? Examine the effects of water pollution.
3. How is water pollution controlled?

Exercise

Search internet for case studies on water pollution of a river or lake. Do a detailed study of ay one case study.

7

POLLUTION BY SOLID WASTES

"Environmental Problems are really social problems . . . They begin with people as the cause, and end with people as victims."

—*Sir Edmund Hillary*

7.1 Pollution by Solid Wastes

Solid wastes are non-liquid material that no longer has any value to the person who is responsible for it. Solid wastes are the most visible form of pollution. Most of the methods of disposing them pose serious damage to environment and hence solid waste management should be effectively handled. It is a global problem like air pollution and water pollution. Solid wastes are defined as those organic and inorganic waste materials produced by various activities of the society, from human or animal activities, discarded as useless or unwanted. It is the unwanted or useless solid materials generated from combined residential, industrial and commercial activities in a given area. It may be categorized according to its origin (domestic, industrial, commercial, construction or institutional); according to its contents (organic material, glass, metal, plastic paper etc); or according to hazard potential (toxic, non-toxin, flammable, radioactive, infectious etc). When the wastes are generated, collected, transported, and ultimately disposed off within the administrative boundary of a municipal authority, they are also known as municipal wastes.

7.1.1 Classification of Solid Wastes

A typical classification of solid waste include:

1. Garbage: Putrescible (decomposable) wastes from food slaughter houses, canning freezing industries and market refuse.
2. Rubbish: Non-putrescible wastes like paper, wood, cloth, rubber, leather etc. which, are all combustible. It also includes non-combustible items like metals, glass, ceramics, stone etc.
3. Ashes: Like fly ash from thermal plants, residues of combustion of soil fuels or residues of incineration of solid wastes by municipal bodies or industries.
4. Hospital refuse: Cotton, plaster, ampules, needles and operation theatre wastes.
5. Large wastes: Debris from construction site, old furniture, automobiles.
6. Dead animals from: Households, veterinary hospitals and zoo.
7. Sewage treatment process solids or sludge.
8. Industrial solid wastes: Chemicals, paints, sand etc.
9. Mining wastes: Tailings, slag heaps.
10. Agricultural wastes: Farm animal manure, crop residue etc.

The sources of such wastes are:

- municipal—street sweepings, sewage plant wastes
- domestic
- commercial (offices)
- industries
- mining, and
- agriculture.

Wastes are also classified as compostable wastes and recyclable wastes and residual wastes.

Compostable wastes are biodegradable wastes such as food waste, garden waste, animal waste and human waste. They undergo biological degradation under controlled conditions and can be turned into compost (soil conditioner or organic fertilizer) by mixing them with soil, water, air and biological additives/activators (optional). Examples are fruit and vegetable peelings, leftover foods, vegetable trims, rotten fish and other animal matter, leaves, flowers, twigs, etc

Table 7.1 Classification of Solid Wastes

Type	Typical waste generators	Types of solid wastes
Residential	Single and multifamily dwellings	Food wastes, paper, cardboard, plastics, textiles, leather, yard wastes, wood, glass, metals, ashes, special wastes (e.g., bulky items, consumer electronics, white goods, batteries, oil, tires), and household hazardous wastes.).
Industrial	Light and heavy manufacturing, fabrication, construction sites, power and chemical plants.	Housekeeping wastes, packaging, food wastes, construction and demolition materials, hazardous wastes, ashes, special wastes.
Commercial	Stores, hotels, restaurants, markets, office buildings, etc.	Paper, cardboard, plastics, wood, food wastes, glass, metals, special wastes, hazardous wastes.
Institutional	Schools, hospitals, prisons, government centers.	Paper, cardboard, plastics, wood, food wastes, glass, metals, special wastes, hazardous wastes.
Construction and demolition	New construction sites, road repair, renovation sites, demolition of buildings	Wood, steel, concrete, dirt, etc.
Municipal services	Street cleaning, landscaping, parks, beaches, other recreational areas, water and wastewater treatment plants.	Street sweepings; landscape and tree trimmings; general wastes from parks, beaches, and other recreational areas; sludge.
Process (manufacturing, etc.)	Heavy and light manufacturing, refineries, chemical plants, power plants, mineral extraction and processing.	Industrial process wastes, scrap materials, off-specification products, slay, tailings.
Agriculture	Crops, orchards, vineyards, dairies, feedlots, farms.	Spoiled food wastes, agricultural wastes, hazardous wastes (e.g., pesticides).

Source: World Bank, Urban Development Sector Unit, East Asia and Pacific Region, 1999

Recyclable materials refer to any waste material retrieved from the waste stream and free from contamination that can still be converted into suitable beneficial use. These may be transformed into new products in such a manner that the original products may lose their identity. Examples include newspaper metal scrap, cardboard, aluminum, glass, tin cans, office paper etc.

Residual wastes are solid waste materials that are non-compostable and non-recyclable. It should be disposed ecologically through a long-term disposal facility or sanitary landfill. Examples are: Sanitary napkins, disposable diapers, ceramics etc. Besides these there are other **special wastes** that include household hazardous wastes such as paints, thinners, batteries, bulk wastes such as large worn-out or broken furniture, lamps, book cases, filing cabinets, consumer electronics which refer to worn-out, broken and other discarded items such as radios, transistors, stereos, and white goods such as stoves, tyres etc.

A special category of wastes today is **electronic wastes** referring computer related wastes. The different categories of waste generated, their own time to degenerate as illustrated in the table 7.2.

Table 7.2 The Approximate Time Taken by Litter of Various Types to Degenerate

Type of waste	Approximate time taken for degeneration
Organic wastes such as vegetable and fruit peels, left over food stuff etc	A week or two
Paper	10 -30 days
Cotton cloth	2 – 5 months
Wood	10 – 15 years
Tin, Aluminium and other metal items such as cans	100 – 500 years
Disposable diaper	10 -20 years
Cigarette butt	2 – 5 years
Hard plastic container	20 -30 years
Rubber sole	50 – 80 years
Leather belt	40 – 50 years
Nylon fabric	30 – 40 years

Source: M K Hill, 2004 and http://edugreen.teri.res.in/explore/solwaste/types.htm

7.1.2 Generation of solid wastes –Data profile: World and India

It is reported the volume of wastes increase with the income of the nation and that there is a strong correlation between volume of solid waste generated and GNP of the nation. Two factors responsible for the dramatic increase in waste volume are - economic growth (which translates into higher income and consumption levels) and high migration from villages to cities.

Table 7.3 gives municipal solid waste generation (kg/capita/yr) grouping countries according to their gross national income (GNI). It is clear from the table that industrialized high income nations generate more wastes. The US with its affluence and high tech industrialisation is the most profligate offender. For instance, each year Americans throw away 16 billion disposable diapers, 1.6 billion pens, 2 billion razors and blades and 220 million tyres. The discarded aluminium from US can rebuild the US Commercial airline fleet every three months. It is reported that collectively, Americans throw out 160 million tons of garbage each year which could cover 1000 football fields to a depth of a 30 story building or form a convoy of 10 ton garbage trucks more than 145,000 miles long.

Table 7.3 Municipal Solid Waste-Generation Rates and Relative Income Levels

Country	Low Income	Middle Income	High Income
Annual Income (per capita/yr/ US $)	825- 3255	3256 -10065	>10066
Municipal Solid waste generation rate (tones/ per capita/ year)	0.1- 0.6	0.2 - 0.5	0.3 to > 0.8

Source: http://www.ipcc.ch/pdf/assessment-report/ar4/wg3/ar4-wg3-chapter10.pdf

Data on urban solid wastes shows that per capita wastes per day is the highest for developed nations (1.4 kg) followed by middle income developing nations (0.8 kg) , and per capita wastes per day is the least for low income developing nations (0.6 kg) . However in terms of total waste per day developed high income nations and developing low income nations generate the same amount of urban solid wastes (1.4 MM tones per day). Table 7.4 gives details on urban solid wastes for developed and developing nations.

Table 7.4 Urban Solid Wastes in Developed and Developing Countries

Country group	Total wastes per generated day	Per capita waste per day
Developed countries	1.4 mm tonnes per day	1.4 kg/per capita/ per day
Developing countries (middle income)	2.4 mm tonnes per day	0.8 kg/per capita/ per day
Developing countries (low income)	1.4 mm tonnes per day	0.6 kg/per capita/ per day

Source: World Bank, 2007 www.sandracointreau.com/CointreauComplexitiesandChallenges.ppt

The wastes generated in developing countries have a greater organic content than the wastes generated in developed industrialized nations. In high income countries the paper and plastic content is much higher than in low income countries since in higher income countries disposable material, magazines and packaged food are used in higher quantities. Table 7.5 gives relative composition of household waste in low, medium and high-income countries and Table 7.6 gives the same details for select cities in various countries.

Table 7.5 Relative Composition of Household Waste in Low, Medium and High-Income Countries

Parameter (%)	Low Income Countries	Middle income Countries	High Income Countries
Organic (Putrecible)	40 -85	20-65	20-30
Paper	1-10	15 -30	15-40
Plastic	1-5	2-6	2-10
Metal	1-5	1-5	2-13
Glass	1-10	1-10	4-10
Rubber, leather etc	1-5	1-5	2-10
Others	15-60	15-50	2-10

Source: Adapted from INTOSAI working group on environmental auditing (2002)
http://www.wgea.org/media/2905/eng04pu_guidewaste.pdf

It can be noted from table 7.6 that in Bangalore (India) and Manilla (Philippines) putrecible wastes account for more than 45 % of total wastes. The share of paper, metal, glass, plastic, rubber and, leather wastes are minimum for India while that of textiles is the least for Mexico City, Mexico and that of ceramics, dust and stone are the least for Sunnyvale, California, USA,

Table 7.6 Relative Composition of Solid Wastes in Select Cities (% wet wt)

City & Country	Putrecible	Paper	Metal	Glass	Plastic, Rubber, Leather	Textiles	Ceramics, Dust and Stones
Sunnyvale, California, USA	39.4	40.8	3.5	4.4	9.6	1.0	1.3
Paris, France	16.3	40.9	3.2	9.4	8.4	4.4	17.4
Vienna, Austria	23.3	33.6	3.7	10.4	7.0	3.1	18.9
Mexico City, Mexico	59.8	11.9	1.1	3.3	3.5	0.4	20.0
Seoul, Korea	22.3	16.2	4.1	10.6	9.6	3.8	33.4
Manila, Philippines	45.5	14.5	4.9	2.7	8.6	1.3	27.5
Bangalore, India	75.2	1.5	0.1	0.2	0.9	3.1	19.0

Source: Modified from http://www.unep.or.jp/ietc/publications/spc/solid_waste_management/Vol_I/5_6-Part1_Section-chapter1.pdf

The physical and chemical properties of wastes also differ depending on whether a country is in the low income or middle income or high income group. In the case of lower income countries waste is characterized by high moisture content, high specific weight and low calorific value since the usage of fresh vegetables and cooked food is much higher and reusable materials are largely used. Table 7.7 gives information on the relative physical and chemical properties of wastes in countries in the low income or middle income and high income group countries.

Table 7.7 Relative Physical and Chemical Properties of Wastes in Low, Medium and High-Income Countries

Physical and chemical Properties	Low Income Countries	Middle income Countries	High Income Countries
Moisture content %	40 -80	40 -60	20 -30
Specific weight kg/m3	250 -500	170-330	100-170
Calorific Value kcal/kg	800-1100	1000-1300	1500-2700

Source : Adapted from INTOSAI working group on environmental auditing (2002)
http://www.wgea.org/media/2905/eng04pu_guidewaste.pdf

Among the cities included in Table 7.6, per capita wastes per day is the highest for Sunnyvale, in California, USA, and Korea followed by Australia and France. Data on per capita wastes is given in Table 7.8

Table 7.8 Per capita Wastes in Select Cities / Country

City & Country	Per capita Wastes per day Wt (gms)
Sunnyvale, California, USA	2000
Australia	1870
Paris, France	1430
Vienna, Austria	1180
Mexico City, Mexico	680
Seoule, Korea	2000
Manila, Philippines	400
Bangalore, India	400

Source : Modified from: http://www.unep.or.jp/ietc/publications/spc/solid_waste_management/Vol_I/5_6-Part1_Section-chapter1.pdf

It should be noted that the low figure in some countries in the table does not mean that the problem of solid waste disposal is managed efficiently. It may be due to high population level as in the case of Bangalore, India.

The estimated quantity of Municipal Solid Waste (MSW) generated worldwide is 1.7 – 1.9 billion metric tons. It is estimated that the world's waste production would reach up to 27 billion tons by 2050, a third of which may be generated in Asia, with a significant percentage of that being produced in large economies such as China and India. No country on the earth is spared of this problem of garbage. HongKong with 5.7 million people and 49,000 factories within its 400 sq miles dumps 1000 tonnes of plastic a day—triple the amount thrown away in Europe. The average per capita waste generation in India is 370 grams/day as compared to 2,200 grams in Denmark, 2,000 grams in US and 700 grams in China. India's urban population grew at a rate of 31.8% during the last decade to 377 million. The per capita waste generation is increasing by about 1.3% per year in India.

A research study by R K Annepu (2012), provides the following information about waste generation in India:

- There are 53 cities in India with a million plus population, which together generate 86,000 TPD (31.5 million tons per year) of MSW at a per capita waste generation rate of 500 grams/day. The total MSW generated in urban India is estimated to be 68.8 million tons per year (TPY) or 188,500 tons per day (TPD) of MSW.
- States with minimum and maximum per capita waste generation rates are Manipur (220 grams/day) and Goa (620 grams/day). Both are comparatively small states.
- Tamil Nadu (630 g/day), Jammu & Kashmir (600 g/day) and Andhra Pradesh (570 g/day) generate large amounts of wastes per person.
- In terms of total wastes generated, Maharashtra (22,200 TPD), West Bengal (15,500 TPD), Uttar Pradesh (13,000 TPD), Tamil Nadu (12,000 TPD) and Andhra Pradesh (11,500 TPD) generate the highest amount of MSW.
- The composition of urban MSW in India is 51% organics, 17.5% recyclables (paper, plastic, metal, and glass) and 31 % of inerts. The moisture content of urban MSW is 47% and the average calorific value is 7.3 MJ/kg (1745 kcal/kg).
- Assuming a business as usual scenario (BAU), by the end of the next decade, India will generate a total of 920 million tons of MSW, landfill or openly dump 840 million tons of it and produce 3.6 million tons of mixed waste compost.

- In 2011 India will landfill:
  (1) 6.7 million tonnes per year of recyclable material which could have been used as secondary raw materials in manufacturing industries, due to the absence of source separation;
  (2) 9.6 million tons of compost which could have been used as a fertilizer supplement, due to the absence of source separation and enough composting facilities;
  (3) 58 million barrels of oil energy equivalent in residues of composting operations that could have been used to generate electricity.

Table 7.9 gives data on per capita waste generation rates and wastes generated in select Indian cities.

Table 7.9 Per Capita Waste Generation Rates and Wastes Generated in Select Indian Cities.

City	2001		2011	
	MSW generated TPD*	Per capita waste generation kg/day	MSW generated TPD*	Per capita waste generation kg/day
Greater Mumbai	7395	0.450	11,124	0.514
Kolkata	7659	0.580	11,520	0.662
Delhi	7340	0.570	11,040	0.650
Chennai	4067	0.620	6118	0.708
Hyderabad	3273	0.570	4923	0.650
Bangalore	2224	0.390	3344	0.445
Ahemadbad	1674	0.370	2518	0.422
Pune	1730	0.460	2602	0.525
Jaipur	906	0.390	1362	0.445
Lucknow	494	0.220	743	0.251
Kochi	909	0.670	1366	0.765
Patna	628	0.370	945	0.422
Amritsar	452	0.450	679	0.514
Srinagar	474	0.480	713	0.548

* Tonnes per day.

Source: R K Annepu, 2012

7.1.3 Impact of Solid Wastes: Improper solid waste management pollutes local air, water and land resources and deteriorates public health and deteriorates quality of life. It adds to global warming and climate change. Indiscriminate dumping of wastes and leachate from landfills contaminates surface and groundwater supplies and the surrounding land resources. It also clogs sewers and drains and leads to floods. Clogged sewers cause floods following a rain. Insect and rodents, attracted to MSW, spread diseases such as cholera, dengue fever and plague. Using water polluted by solid waste for bathing and food and as drinking water exposes individuals to health risks which in turn affects productivity. Improper waste management is identified as a cause of 22 human diseases and results in numerous premature deaths every year. The city Surat has suffered plague epidemic in 1994 due to improper SWM.

Open burning of MSW on streets and at landfills generates green house gases like methane, which has 24 times more global warming potential than carbon dioxide. When solid waste is disposed off on land in open dumps or in improperly designed landfills (e.g. in low lying areas), it causes the following impact on the environment.

(a) ground water contamination by the leachate generated by the waste dump
(b) surface water contamination by the run-off from the waste dump
(c) bad odour, pests, rodents and wind-blown litter in and around the waste dump
(d) generation of inflammable gas (e.g. methane) within the waste dump
(e) bird menace above the waste dump which affects flight of aircraft
(f) fires within the waste dump
(g) erosion and stability problems relating to slopes of the waste dump
(h) epidemics through stray animals
(i) acidity to surrounding soil and
(j) release of green house gas

7.1.4 Management of Solid Wastes:

Disposal of such solid wastes pose a major threat. The problem of solid wastes arises at three stages: 1. collection, 2. transport, and 3. disposal. Collection problem and transportation problem are closely linked. The type of containers in which the wastes may be stored before they are transported, and the loading/unloading provisions of the vehicle and the speed of the vehicle etc. are crucial. Disposal is even graver a problem because it leads to either land pollution if dumped in landfills, water pollution if dumped in oceans and air pollution if burnt. The endless voyage of the notorious *Pelicano* that sailed around the world for seeking a port that would accept its cargo is worth mentioning here. The ship was denied permission by all ports because its cargo was 14,000 tonnes of toxic incinerator ash that had been loaded into the ship in Philadelphia in 1986. However in October, 1988, 4000 pounds of the cargo was simply dumped off the coast of Haiti. One month later, when the *Pelicano* docked in Singapore, none of the ash was on board.

Methods of Disposal of Solid Wastes

Chief methods of disposal of solid wastes are 1. dumping in landfills, 2. dumping in ocean, 3. incineration, 4. using as cattle and hog feed 5. pyrolysis, 6. controlled tipping and sanitary landfills.

Land Filling: Many countries have made a start by locating landfills to dump solid wastes. In the US eighty per cent of solid waste are dumped into 6000 landfills. But land fill sites pose potential threat of pollution to ground water resources. Hence as landfills reach capacity, new sites have to be located which have become scarcer. In US, nearly three thousand land fill-sites were closed by 1988 and by 1993, some two thousand more is estimated to be closed. In West Germany, thirty-five thousand to fifty thousand land fill-sites have been declared as potentially dangerous.

Incineration is a very hygienic way of disposal of rubbish. It requires a well-designed incinerator that would ensure complete combustion. In incineration combustible waste is burned at very high temperature (900-1000^{0}C) to convert all combustible material to ash which along with the noncombustible wastes is disposed off in a landfill. Efficient incineration may reduce the volume of waste by 75% to 95%. In many cities incineration is generally limited to hospital and other biological wastes. Incineration however creates the problem of air pollution.

Dumping in seas is not upheld today because of the threat it poses to aquatic life and their regenerative capacity. New York still dumps its wastes in Atlantic Ocean. Nearly three million tonnes of hazardous wastes have been transported from the US and Western Europe on ships like the Pelicano to countries in Africa and Eastern Europe. Saad M. Baba, Third Secretary in the Nigerian Mission to UN observed: "International dumping is the equivalent of declaring war on the people of a country".

Hog Feeding was in practice until mid 1950s when the spread of a virus disease of hogs led many countries to regulate disposal of solid waste through this means.

Pyrolysis means an operation using intense heat to cause chemical changes but not combustion. It is a form of incineration that chemically decomposes organic materials at high temperature in the absence of oxygen. Pyrolysis typically occurs under pressure and at operating temperatures above 430 °C. Pyrolysis may yield marketable products. For example, pyrolysis of discarded rubber tyres yield two petroleum products.

Controlled tipping and sanitary land fills is the most satisfactory method of disposal of solid wastes. In this method garbage is levelled in layers, compacted and covered with earth. Where the ground is levelled trench method is followed and if there is slope, ramp method is followed. Bacteriological chemical and physical changes occur in buried refuse, and the temperature rises over 60°C in seven days, kills all pathogens and hastens the decomposition process. Today mechanical aeration method is used.

Other methods of disposal, include composting, which means degradation of putrescible material in a refuse by micro-organism. Composting is a biological process of decomposition carried out under controlled conditions of ventilation, temperature, moisture. The organisms in the waste convert waste into humus-like material by acting on the organic portion of the solid waste. This natural process of decomposition of organic waste yields manure or compost, which is very rich in nutrients. Composting is a biological process in which micro-organisms, mainly fungi and bacteria, convert degradable organic waste into humus like substance. This resulting product, is high in carbon and nitrogen and is an excellent medium for growing plants.

There are two methods of composting – aerobic composting and anaerobic composting.

In aerobic composting, the organic matter is piled with temperatures left to rise rapidly to about 70 to 80 degrees. Anaerobic composting is a process where microorganisms break down source separated organic wastes such as food scraps, manure and sewage sludge, in the absence of oxygen and recovers energy in the form of biogas, and compost in the form of a liquid residual. The ability to recover energy and compost from organics makes anaerobic composting superior to aerobic composting. Aerobic respiration, typical of composting, results in the formation of Carbon dioxide and water: anaerobic respiration results in the formation of Carbon Dioxide and methane.

Vermi-composting is one method of composting popularly practiced by house holds to convert kitchen and garden waste into manure. In this method, worms are added to the compost. These help to break the waste and the added excreta of the worms makes the compost very rich in nutrients.

Sustainable management of solid wastes prescribe adherence to the four 'R's, namely:

Refuse, Reuse, Recycle , Reduce

Refuse: Refusing to buy unwanted items – refusing to entertain buying spree.

Reuse: Opting for reusable containers, bags. Use cloth or jute bag. Using rechargeable batteries.

Recycle: Segregating wastes so that non-perishable wastes are easily collected and taken for recycling. Attempting composting of kitchen wastes.

Reduce: Reduce wastes. Carry your own shopping bag. Use refillable ball pens and not throw away pens.

Efficient management of solid wastes however means exploring the possibilities for utilisation, recovery of usable materials from them and recycling. For example, fly ash from thermal power stations is now used to make bricks. Sometimes, valuable materials can be recovered from solid wastes. Hence re-use and recovery are useful methods of disposing solid wastes.

Recycling is the most common method. It is the reprocessing of discarded materials into new useful product. Today's garbage may become tomorrow's raw material, through recycling. That is why it is said that "trash is cash". Recycling therefore is the best known way to reduce waste. Recycling refers to the removal of items from the waste stream to be used as raw materials in the manufacture of new products. Thus recycling comprises of three phases: first the waste is sorted and recyclables collected, after which the recyclables are used to create raw materials. These raw materials are then used in the production of new products.

OECD defines recycling as: *"Using waste materials in manufacturing other products of an identical or similar nature"*. Examples of recycling include industrial melting of one-way glass bottles for use in new bottles; Recycling of paper which saves tress and recycling of collected newspapers for production of sanitary paper products; aerobic or anaerobic treatment of separately collected organic household waste to produce agricultural soil. Reuse of metals will reduce the mining activities.

Japan recycles more than fifty per cent of its wastes. Western Europe and USA recycle thirty per cent and sixteen per cent of wastes generated annually. In 1988 fifty per cent of Japan's waste paper, fifty-five per cent of its glass bottles and sixty-six per cent of its beverage and food cans were recycled. Many countries have realised the potentials for energy recovery, from wastes and act according to the dictum "Rubbish is fuel for future".

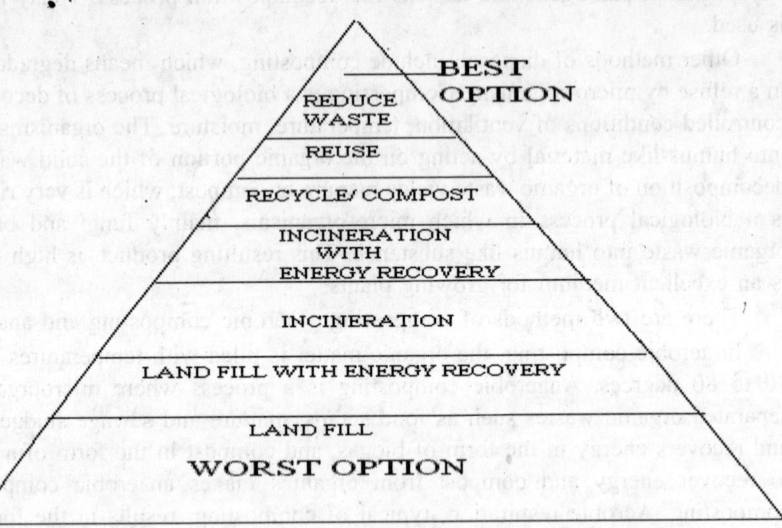

Figure 7.1 Solid Waste Management Hierarchy

Source: http://www.sustainabilityed.org/pages/example2-2.htm)

The various methods of solid waste management explained above have their own specific merits and limits. The best option it is said is waste reduction and the worst option is disposal to land fills. Figure 7.1 gives hierarchy of solid waste management.

What is needed is an integrated solid waste management. No one method can manage all the waste materials in an environmentally effective way. Hence the various options must be evaluated well and the most suitable and the best mix of the available options must be adopted. Such an integrated solid waste management method should take into consideration the social, economic, environmental and ecological impact of the mix of methods chosen. Efficient management of solid wastes is crucial. "If such wastes continue to proliferate, man will have declared war on the earth's environment— and thus in the end, on his own richest heritage." (John Langone).

7.2 Thermal Pollution

Thermal pollution is basically a form of water pollution that refers to degradation of water quality by any process that changes ambient water temperature. It is the discharge of unwanted heat energy into rivers and lakes by various industrial processes. The various industrial processes utilise water for cooling and discharge the resultant warm water into rivers and lakes. Among the industries that use large quantities of water for cooling purposes and therefore contribute towards thermal pollution of water courses are:

- Electric power generating plants
- Metal plants
- Chemical and allied industries
- Petroleum and coal products industries
- Paper plants
- Rubber and plastic plants

Electric utilities constitute the major source of the thermal pollution and lakes. The water needed for cooling purposes differs according to the local regulations and on the heat rate of the power plant. It is said that a typical power plant requires 1.5 cubic feet of water for each mega watt of installed capacity, if temperature rise is limited to 15°F. A power plant operating at full capacity requires forty gallons of water per kilo watt per hour. A nuclear power plant generating more waste heat may require 55 gallons per kilo watt per hour.

Effects: The major adverse effect of thermal pollution is on water quality and aquatic life. The temperature that a fish can withstand varies among the different types. Rapid and sudden temperature change may cause "thermal shock" and have fatal effect on the aquatic life. In a water body already containing chemical pollutants the extra warmth generated by thermal pollution will enhance the toxicity.

Thermal pollution is said to be conducive to the growth of blue-green algae, and increases bacterial multiplication rate which affects fish life. The heat discharged by thermal plants decreases dissolved oxygen (DO) content of water. If as a result of thermal pollution, the warmth of the water is limited to 4°C, then a dissolved oxygen content (DO) of 1 to 2 mg per litre of water is sufficient for most of the fresh water fish species. If however, the temperature rises to more than 15°C, then it is necessary in the interests of the aquatic life that the DO content does not fall below 3mg per litre. At these high temperatures, a DO concentration larger than 5 mg is required.

Less oxygen in the water can increase the metabolic rate of fish and other aquatic animals so they eat lot more food in a shorter time which in turn leads to imbalance in food chain resulting in significant damage to many aquatic ecosystems. Warmer water temperatures can also lead to reproduction problems for many aquatic animals, and can cause huge bacteria and plant growth. It can even lead to algae bloom resulting in even less oxygen in the water.

Control: In the past, the modifications introduced in the operation of fossil fuelled,- steam-electric stations have reduced their waste heat discharges by approximately fifty per cent by increasing steam pressure, super heating or reheating steam and by reducing exhaust pressure. One way to reduce thermal pollution is to create artificial lakes or cooling ponds. Cooling towers are also used to prevent thermal pollution. They transfer heat from cooling water to the atmosphere, generally through evaporation of water. Thermal pollution could be drastically reduced by direct conversion of heat into energy. Another method to reduce thermal pollution would be to find alternative uses for the waste heat. Aqua culture can be developed using heated water. There are certain commercially valuable species such as Pompana, Cat fish, Shrimp, Oysters and Scallops which can be produced in warm water. Warm water irrigation is also being attempted in some countries. De-salination of sea water has been accomplished in some areas with the help of the heat available from thermal discharge.

In short, the problem of thermal pollution is bound to grow in dimensions with the increased demand for power from the increasing population. This calls for efficient management of waste heat that will not alter the biological, chemical and physical quality of the water.

7.3 Pesticidal Pollution

The use of pesticides to prevent the damage caused by insects is not new. That certain chemicals would kill pests was recognised at least one thousand years before the time of Christ. The Greek epic poet, Homer, wrote of 'pest averting sulphur with its properties of divine and purifying fumigation'. We may distinguish between first generation and second generation pesticides. Many of the first generation pesticides like lead, arsenic and mercury are all inorganic chemicals and are extremely toxic. They tend to accumulate in soils to the point of inhibiting plant growth. New pesticides or second generation pesticides are found in synthetic organic chemicals. They are man-made chemicals with carbon as a principal component. The first and most famous second generation pesticide is DDT, dichloro di-phenyl trichloro ethane.

Every year pests damage crops worth billions of dollars in different parts of the globe. To prevent the damages caused by pests extensive use is made of pesticides. These pesticides may be insecticides (used to control insect pests) Nematicides (used to control round worm or thread worm) Acaricides (used to control mites) Rodenticides (used to control rodents like bandicoots, rats and mice) Herbicides (used to control weeds) Fungicides, algicides and bactericides (used to control plant diseases caused by fungi, algae and bacteria). The use of pesticides in agriculture tripled in US, between 1965 and 1985. In India, pesticide use has increased markedly from about 2000 tonnes annually in 1950 to over eighty thousand tonnes annually in the mid 1980. Some eighty million hectares of India's crop land is presently estimated to be under pesticide use as compared to a mere six million hectares in 1960. Between 1972 and 1984, there has been a threefold increase in world-wide pesticide imports.

The use of pesticides started posing problems only because they were used only with the short term benefits in mind. The harmful effects in the long run were not considered. Today people all over the world are facing the health hazards caused by extensive and persistent use of pesticides. Besides widespread poisoning of wild life and livestock, pesticides take a heavy toll on human lives—both accidental and intentional. It is estimated that at least 2.9 million people are poisoned worldwide annually at a level requiring hospitalisation and at least 220,000 of these cases are fatal. Third world countries, ironically account for only twenty per cent of global pesticide consumption but account for over fifty per cent of the pesticide poisoning and over ninety per cent of the resulting deaths. Sri Lanka provides the most stunning statistics which says that the number of deaths from pesticides poisonings in a year was twice the annual death-rate from infectious diseases like polio, diptheria, tetanus and whooping cough.

The indiscriminate use of pesticides extensively and intensively had led to widespread contamination of man and environment with pesticide residues. Contamination of ground water, food and food products are today global problem. There is new problem created by the prolonged and widespread use of these pesticides. Many pests have become resistant to these pesticides. In 1938 only seven species of insects and mites were resistant But by 1984, the number has increased to 477 species of insects and mites. Similarly, at least forty-eight species of weeds have become resistant to herbicides. Recent studies indicate that although we now use more than one pound of pesticide per person per year, only one per cent or less of the pesticides reach the targeted pests. The balance ninety-nine per cent of the pesticide only add to the poisoning and pollution of land and water.

The chief known hazard of residues of chlorinated hydro carbon from pesticide is due to their concentration in food chain. Several studies reveal that the percentage of residues in foodstuffs was well above tolerance level. Pesticides with greater persistence leave more toxic residues on treated crops and become a source of series health hazard for both human beings and domestic cattle. One pesticide which accumulates in tissue heavily is DDT.

Problems of DDT: The problems of DDT were related to its Wide spectrum effectiveness, its chemical stability, its solubility—all features which were considered virtues to start with. Pest population became resistant to DDT. Spraying of DDT on elm lices to kill the bark bettles resulted in high lethal levels of DDT in birds like Robin, Bald eagles, Ospreys, and other fish-eating birds receiving DDT from agricultural areas that leached in to water ways and thus entered aquatic food chains. At high levels, DDT impaired the reproductive function in birds. Their eggs were breaking in the nest before incubation. This was because the calcium metabolism in birds were affected by DDT which made the egg shells thin and fragile. Traces of DDT were seen in places far away from areas where it was used. Traces of DDT were detected in Arctic seals and Antarctic Penguins. Milk of nursing mothers and human fatty tissue revealed significant levels of DDT. Resurgence and upsets of pest population whereby the pest bounced back in greater numbers posing more serious problem than before the application of DDT were also reported. All these were due to the 'broad spectrum' and persistence' qualities of DDT which were once considered as virtues.

In 1962 Rachel Carson brought the hazards of DDT and other similar pesticides to widespread public attention through her classic book *Silent Spring.* Use of DDT was brought to court trial and ultimately banned in 1972.After the banning of DDT, several substitutes—synthetic organic chemical pesticides—were tried continuously—one replacing the other but not with much success. A 'natural control' method keeping in mind the eco-system balance is also suggested. In this natural control method, pests are considered as organisms within the eco-system and hence the damage by them to crops is controlled through eco-system management without completely eradicating or exterminating them. Natural control may be through any of the following three methods.

- biological control where pest control is achieved through a viral or bacterial disease;
- genetic control, which implies introduction of lethal genes into pest population;
- cultural control creates an environment unfavourable to the pest.

Besides these specific insect harmones or pheromones (chemicals working externally, affecting individuals of the same species) are also used for pest-control through their effect on reproduction of pest. Environmentalists, consider use of pheromones as the ideal method.

UN bodies like UNEP, FAO bilateral aid agencies, non-governmental organisations and also governments are today recommending Integrated Pest Management (IPM). This includes four methods.

- cultivation practices like rotation of crops and early planting that would deter multiplication of pests.
- growing insect resistant varieties of crops
- nurture of the natural enemies of the pest
- keeping the pest population below economically harmful levels through the use of chemicals but not eradicating them.

IPM approach has reduced the use of pesticides by eighty-five per cent for cotton in Brazil, by forty per cent for rice in India and by ninety per cent for cotton in China. A number of natural pesticides like extracts of neam leaves and trees, pyrethrum from chrysanthemum are also proving to be of great utility in preventing the damages by pests without the harmful effects of synthetic pesticides.

Questions

1. Classify solid wastes and highlight the problems of solid waste management.
2. Discuss the practical solutions to solid waste management
3. What are the impacts of chemical fertilisers. Suggest solutions.
4. Examine the impact of thermal pollution. Give solutions.
5. Give reasons for adopting Integrated Pest Management.

Exercise

1. Do an awareness survey on solid waste management in your neighbourhood.
2. Read Silent Spring and make a review of the book.

8
POPULATION AND ENVIRONMENT

"The explosive growth of the human population is the most significant terrestrial event of the past million millennia. No geological event in a billion years—not the emergence of mighty mountain ranges nor the submergence of entire subcontinents nor the occurrence of periodical glacial ages—has posed a threat to terrestrial life comparable to that of human over-population."

—*Paul Ehrlich*

Most of the writers on environmental crisis consider population as the prime cause of environmental problems. Lamont Cole, for example, said: "Many of the most important problems currently facing man are ecological problems arising from the unrestrained growth of the human population and the resultant increasing strains being placed on the earth's life support system". That adverse impact of growing human populations on environment is well established. Early civilizations—Mesopotamia in the Near East, Mohenjo Daro in Southwest Asia, and the Mayans of Central America are reported to have collapsed due to overpopulation and scarcity which caused depletion of arable land and water supply.

8.1 The Population Data

An examination of the population data is essential before we attempt to relate it to environmental quality. Experts believe that it took some one thousand and seven hundred years for earth's population to double from the time of Christ. Since then, the population has doubled three times in successively shorter plans. Population is projected to reach ten billion by 2070. It is said that the world must accommodate a new population roughly equivalent to that of United States and Canada every three years.

The population explosion that is witnessed today is nothing but a reminder to what Malthus said in 1878: "population, when unchecked increases in a geometrical ratio". In 1950, the world had 2.5 billion people; and in 2005, the world had 6.5 billion people. As of July 2015, global population was estimated at 7.3 billion. According to the United Nations, "World Population Prospcts" The 2015 revision, "Sixty per cent of the global population lives in Asia (4.4 billion), 16 per cent in Africa (1.2 billion), 10 per cent in Europe (738 million), 9 per cent in Latin America and the Caribbean (634 million), and the remaining 5 per cent in Northern America (358 million) and Oceania (39 million). China (1.4 billion) and India (1.3 billion) remain the two largest countries of the world, both with more than 1 billion people, representing 19 and 18 per cent of the world's population, respectively".

The total number of living humans on Earth is now greater than 7 billion. Just around 200 years ago the world population was less than 1 billion. According to M Roser and E O Ospina (2017), "for thousands of years, population grew only slowly, but in recent centuries it has jumped dramatically. Between 1900 and 2000 the increase in world population was three times greater than the entire previous history of humanity– an increase from 1.5 to 6.1 billion in just 100 years". The world population is projected to increase by more than one billion people within the next 15 years, reaching 8.5 billion in 2030, and to increase further to 9.7 billion in 2050 and 11.2 billion by 2100. The population data in Table 8.1 clearly gives a picture of the increase in global population from 1950 to 2015. (UNDBSA, 2015)

Table 8.1 World Population in Thousands

Year	De facto Population (thousands) As of 1st July of the year indicated.)
1950	2525149
1960	3018344
1970	3382488
1980	4439632
1990	5309668
2000	6126622
2005	6519636
2010	6629725
2015	7349472

Source: United Nations, Department of Economic and Social Affairs, Population Division (2015) World Population Prospects: The 2015 Revision, DVD Edition

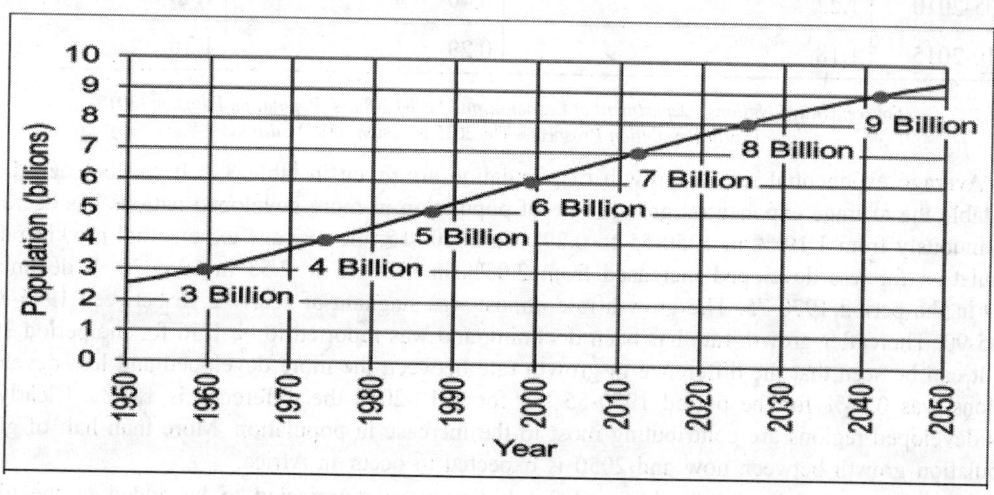

Figure 8.1 World Population 1950 -2050

Source: U.S. Census Bureau. International Data Base, July 2015.

According to recent United Nations estimates, global population is increasing by approximately 80 million — the size of Germany — each year. All of the projected growth is expected to occur in the developing world (increasing from 5.4 to 7.9 billion), whereas the developed world is expected to remain unchanged at 1.2 billion.

Table 8.2 Average Exponential Rate of Growth of the Population

Year	Average annual rate of population change (percentage)		
	World	More developed regions	Less developed regions
1950 -1955	1.77	1.19	2.03
1955-1960	1.80	1.17	2.08
1960 -1965	1.92	1.08	2.28
1965-1970	2.06	0.85	2.53
1970 -1975	1.96	0.77	2.39
1975-1980	1.78	0.65	2.16
1980 -1985	1.78	0.58	2.15
1985-1990	1.80	0.55	2.16
1990 -1995	1.54	0.44	1.84
1995-2000	1.32	0.32	1.57
2000 -2005	1.24	0.34	1.46
2005-2010	1.22	0.40	1.40
2010-2015	1.18	0.29	1.36

Source: United Nations, Department of Economic and Social Affairs, Population Division (2015). World Population Prospects: The 2015 Revision, DVD Edition

Average exponential rate of growth of population are given in table 8.2. It can be seen that in the table the average exponential growth rate of population in more developed nations has decreased continuously from 1.19 % in 1950-55 to 0.29% in 2010 -15; the average exponential growth rate of population for less developed increased from 2.03% in 1950-55 to 2.53 in 1965-70. It declined to 2.39 in the period 1970-75. The growth rate almost was stagnant at nearly 2.16 between 1975-80 to 1985-90. Thereafter growth rate has been declining and was reported to be 1.36 for the period 2010-15. It can be seen that the difference in growth rate between the more developed and less developed regions was 0.84% for the period 1950-55 but for 2010-2015 the difference is 1.07%. Clearly the less developed regions are contributing most to the increase in population. More than half of global population growth between now and 2050 is expected to occur in Africa.

It is estimated that of the additional 2.4 billion people projected to be added to the global population between 2015 and 2050, 1.3 billion will be added in Africa. Asia is projected to be the second largest contributor to future global population growth, adding 0.9 billion people between 2015 and 2050. Africa's share of global population is projected to grow to 25 per cent in 2050 and 39 per cent by 2100, while the share of Asia will fall to 54 per cent in 2050 and 44 per cent in 2100.

During 2015-2050, half of the world's population growth is expected to be concentrated in nine countries. Arranged according to the size of their contribution to the total growth of population the nine countries are: India, Nigeria, Pakistan, Democratic Republic of the Congo, Ethiopia, United Republic of Tanzania, United States of America, Indonesia and Uganda.

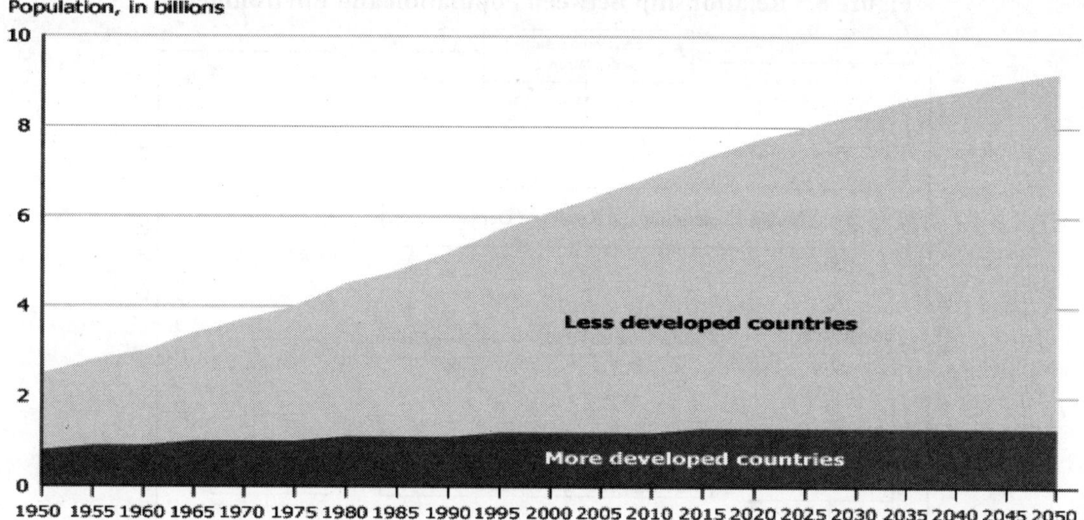

Figure 8.2 World Population Growth in More and Less Developed Nations 1950–2050

Source: *United Nations Population Division, World Population Prospects, The 2008 Revision.*

Currently, the world population continues to grow, but slowly than in the recent past. Around ten years ago, world population was growing by 1.24 per cent per year. Today, it is growing by 1.18 per cent per year, or approximately an additional 83 million people annually. The major reason for this is the decline in global fertility rates more rapidly than expected, as health care, including reproductive health, has improved faster than anticipated. Globally, fertility is assumed to decline to 2.02 births per woman (below replacement) by 2050; In recent years, fertility has declined in virtually all major areas of the world. However it is reported that about one-third of the reduction in long-range population projections, is due to increasing mortality rates in sub-Saharan Africa and parts of the Indian subcontinent.

8.2 Impact of growing Population on Global Environment

Population gained acceptance as an environmental issue, following the publication of Paul Ehrlich's book *The Population Bomb in 1968.* Between 1950 and 2000, while the world's population more than doubled, the gross world product expanded nearly sevenfold. It is observed that per capita consumption would increase four times by 2075, if percapita consumption is assumed to grow at 2% rate per annum along with an increasing population. To meet this consumption growth, economic production will have to increase six times (J J Speidel et al, 2017). Ultimately the impact is on the environment. According to the Millennium Ecosystem Assessment 60 per cent of ecosystem services are being used unsustainably. The impact of people on the eco-system is alarming. The impact of so many humans on the environment takes two major forms:

- Resource exploitation – related to the first function of the environment
- Generation of wastes. – related to the second function of the environment

The relationship of increasing population and the environmental deterioration is illustrated in figure 8.3.

Figure 8.3 Relationship Between Population and Environment

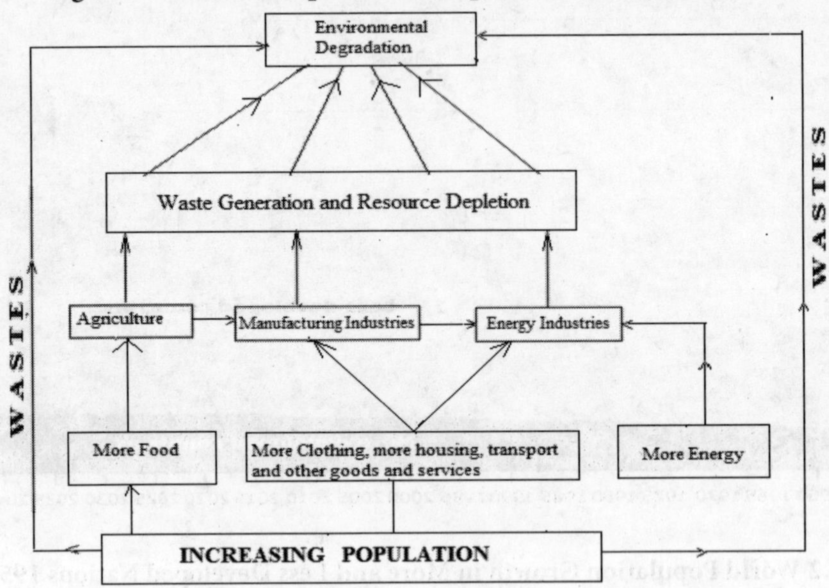

Source: Adapted from RC Sharma, 1975, Population, Resources and Environment

Ehrlich wrote that "while over population in poor nations tend to keep them poverty stricken, over population in rich nations tends to undermine the life-support capacity of the entire planet". More people need more food, more energy, housing, clothing and transport etc., all of which contribute to environmental degradation. As global population continues to grow, availability of global resources such as arable land, potable water, forests, and fisheries are fast dwindling. Few such challenges are:

- In the second half of the twentieth century, food production and hence food security has become a matter of serious concern due to decreasing farmland. Per capita requirement of land for food production has almost reached a limit. Population pressures have degraded some 2 billion hectares of arable land — an area the size of Canada and the U.S. In 64 of 105 developing countries studied by the UN Food and Agriculture Organization, the population has been growing faster than food supplies.
- Population growth reduces per capita availability of water. It is in this light that the Global International Waters Assessment listed population growth as the most important cause of the global water crisis. Global water consumption rose six fold between 1900 and 1995, more than double the rate of population growth. The supply of freshwater is finite, but demand and per capita use is increasing as population grows. The world's increase in demand for fresh water is about 64 billion cubic meters a year. According to Population Action International (PAI) by 2025, world population will reach 8 billion, and as a result 48 countries containing 3 billion people will face water shortages. By 2050, 54 countries containing 4 billion people will face water shortage.
- United Nations Estimates observe that over 1 billion people lack access to safe drinking water and two and a half billion lack adequate sanitation. Lack of safe drinking water and adequate sanitation is responsible for the deaths of more than 5 million people, more than 50% of whom are children..

- Population growth is often named as the driver of coastal and marine environmental problems. Coastal zones have higher population densities than any other ecologically defined zone in the world. Half of all coastal ecosystems are pressured by high population densities and urban development. As a result pollution is rising in the world's seas. The conversion of tropical mangroves into fish and shrimp aquaculture farms are a challenge to coastal protection and decreases the natural habitat that many fish species use for reproduction. Expanding coastal cities affects natural protection from storms and hurricanes.
- **Forests and Biodiversity**: Due to population pressure, nearly half of the world's original forest cover has been lost, and each year another 16 million hectares are cut, bulldozed, or burned. Ecosystems of all kinds are under pressure worldwide. Coastal and lowland areas, wetlands, native grasslands, and many types of forests and woodland shave been particularly affected or destroyed. The earth's biological diversity is crucial to the continued vitality of agriculture and medicine — and perhaps even to life on earth itself. Yet human activities are pushing many thousands of plant and animal species into extinction. Two of every three species is estimated to be in decline. Freshwater supply is needed to sustain marshes, rivers, coastal wetlands, and the millions of species they shelter. As more and more of fresh water is diverted to meet the needs of a growing population less is available to maintain vital wetland ecosystems. It is reported that over 20 per cent of the approximately 10,000 freshwater fish species in the world are either endangered, threatened or going extinct.
- **Energy:** More than two billion poor people in the developing world still largely rely on biomass to meet their energy needs. Developed market economies, constituting one fifth of the world's population, consume almost 60 per cent of the world's primary energy. Fossil energy is responsible for the release of the greenhouse gases which in turn is responsible for global change climate. Due to climate change growing enough food for our expanding population has become "the greatest challenge in human history."
- **Rural – Urban migration and urbanization**: Increasing population has made the world more urbanized with higher rates of migration form rural areas to urban centres. Migration takes place due to failure of agriculture and due to search for opportunities for a better standard of living. The world has become more urbanized - in 1960 less than one third of the world's population lived in cities. By 2014, that figure was 54 per cent, with a projected rise to 66 per cent by 2050. Urban centres promotes a materialistic life style that is more resource consuming. This causes environmental deterioration.

8.3 Environmental Limits and Population Growth

It cannot be denied that we are living beyond our means. There are several approaches that identify human impact on environment. In all these population size and growth is an important cause of environmental degradation or crisis. Some of these are:

- Limits to Growth Model
- I =PAT equation by Ehrlich and John Holdren
- Stockholm Resilience Centre's Planetary Boundaries Model
- Ecological Footprints
- Carrying Capacity

The I=PAT equation

The equation was developed in the 1970s by Ehrlich who argued three factors – Population, Affluence and Technology -- were important determinants of environmental impact and emphasized in particular, the role of human population growth.

The IPAT equation is a formula to measure the rising impact of population on environment in which Impact (I) equals Population (P) multiplied by Affluence (A) multiplied by Technology (T).The IPAT formula can help us realize that our cumulative impact on the planet is not just in population numbers, but also in the increasing amount of natural resources each person uses. IPAT is a useful reminder that population, consumption, and technology all impact our environmental.

$$I = PAT$$

Although the IPAT model assumed independence of each of the PAT elements, it recognizes that in the real world, these are not independent, rather they interact with each other. In underdeveloped countries population and poverty cause large scale environmental damages while in the advanced industrialised nations, high per capita rates of consumption and the large-scale use of environmentally damaging technologies greatly magnify the environmental impact.

The Limits to Growth Model in the 1970s (see Chapter 13) postulated that exponential growth in *population, industrial output, agricultural and natural resource consumption, and the pollution from all these activities* would result in severe constraints on all known global resources by 2050 – 2070. Technological innovation, population control and availability of newer alternative resources could delay the collapse. However the collapse can be avoided only by designing suitable world policies to stop population growth and stabilize material consumption.

In 2009, a group of internationally renowned scientists of the **Stockholm Resilience Centre** identified and quantified a set of **nine planetary boundaries** within which humanity can continue to develop and thrive for generations to come. The nine boundaries identified were:

- Climate change
- stratospheric ozone depletion
- land use change
- Global freshwater use
- Biodiversity loss
- ocean acidification
- nitrogen and phosphorus inputs to the biosphere and oceans
- Atmosphere aerosol loading
- chemical pollution

The Stockholm centre reported that the nine key processes are being altered by human activity which is likely to cause imbalance of the Earth system. According to the study the boundaries are strongly connected — crossing one boundary may seriously threaten the ability to stay within safe levels of the others. Respecting the boundaries reduces the risks to human beings of crossing these thresholds. The study suggested that three of these boundaries (climate change, biological diversity and nitrogen input to the biosphere) have already been exceeded. An exponentially growing population is reported to have a direct impact on the nine boundries.

Table 8.3 Ecological Footprint for Select Regions and Select Countries in Each Region

Country/Region	Population	Ecological Footprint 2008 (Global Hectares/person)
	(millions)	
High-Income Countries	1,037.00	5.6
Middle-Income Countries	4,394.10	1.9
Low-Income Countries	1,297.50	1.1
Africa	938.4	1.4
Republic of South Africa	49.3	2.6
Middle East/Central Asia	382.6	2.5
Afghanistan	29.8	0.5
Israel	7.1	4
Asia-Pacific	3,725.20	1.6
Australia	21.5	6.7
Bangladesh	145.5	0.7
China	1,358.80	2.1
India	1,190.90	0.9
North America	448.9	6.2
Canada	33.3	6.4
Mexico	110.6	3.3
United States	305	7.2
Europe	733.2	4.4
Germany	82.5	4.6
Netherlands	16.5	6.3
Russia	143.2	4.4

Source: http://www.21stcentech.com/human-population-update-carrying-capacity-planet-earth/

Ecological foot print is a concept conceived in 1990 by Mathis Wackernagel and William Rees of the University of British Columbia. The Ecological Footprint is the amount of resources needed by a single individual to survive. It is measured in hectares of biologically productive land and hence is expressed in hectares. A hectare takes into consideration cropland, grazing area, forest lands, fish habitat, carbon output and urban space requirements to sustain a human being. A key concept of footprint science is ecological overshoot. This occurs when humanity turns resources into waste faster than waste can be turned back into resources. For example, fossil fuels which took hundreds of millions of years to form are being utilized at rates far beyond the Earth System's capacity to replace them. According to Wackernagel and colleagues, it now takes the Earth one year and six months to regenerate what we use in a year. This rate of overshoot is an average for the whole globe and hides the fact that some countries are in serious overshoot while some others still have surplus biocapacity. The ecological footprint , grew from 4.5 to 14.1 billion hectares between 1961 and 2003, and it is now 25% more than Earth's "biocapacity". Moderate UN scenarios suggest that if current population and consumption trends continue, by the 2030s, we will need the equivalent of two Earths to support us.

The ecological foot print data in the last column in table 8.3 shows surprising and interesting values for some countries. For example comparing Germany with the United States, we know that both countries enjoy very high living standards but Germans consume far fewer resources to sustain their lifestyle than Americans. In Africa, South Africans use almost twice the resources of Nigerians and in Asia-Pacific Australians use more than seven times the resources of people in India and nine times of those living in Bangladesh.

Population and Carrying Capacity

Carrying capacity is the maximum population that the planet can sustain taking into consideration availability of food sources, water, and all the other necessities to sustain life. The growth of population is related to the carrying capacity of the environment. There are models that describe the population growth curve for the various species. Three shapes of the population growth curve for the various species are described by these models. 'S' shape, "J' shape and the crashing curve. The 'S" shaped curve explains that the rate of growth of population decreases even before the limits are reached. The J shaped curve implies that population overshoots the limits of the carrying capacity of the environment and then dies back in either a smooth or oscillatory way. In the case of the crashing curve the population overshoots the carrying capacity of the environment and then falls sharply. In this type of growth of population, species become extinct. Applying this to the growth of human population raises the question : whether the growth of human population will be 's' shaped or 'J' shaped or a "crash" curve; will the population growth curve for humans reach a stable level that can be sustained for an indefinite period or will it grow to a peak and collapse. Figure 8.4 illustrates the three curves.

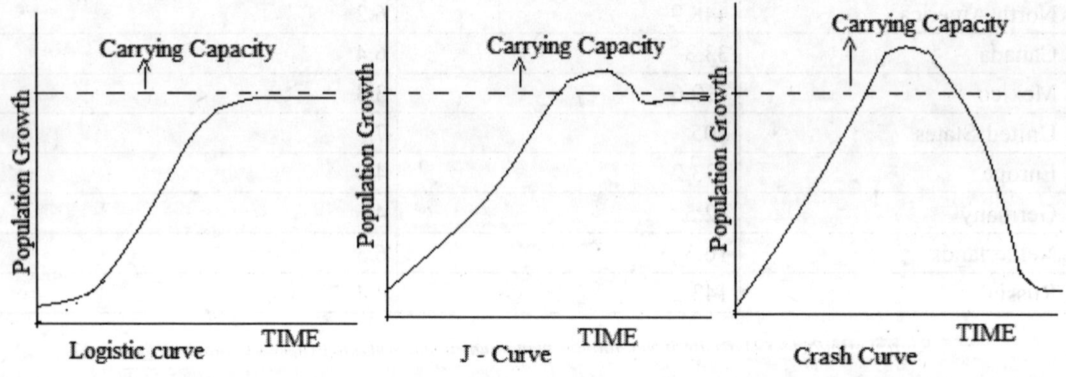

Figure 8.4 Population Growth and Limits to Carrying Capacity

Source: RC Sharma, 1975, Population, Resources and Environment

Majority of the studies that calculated estimates of Earth's carrying capacity, observe that the earth's carrying capacity is equal to or below 8 billion. Global population is fast approaching this level and is expected to get well into it at around 10 billion by the end of the century. Carrying capacity estimates are speculative estimates about a potential state and asks how many people could be supported on the planet. Carrying capacity makes assumptions about future per-person resource consumption, standards of living and "wants", productivity of the biosphere, and advances in technology.

Conclusion

The 20th witnessed an unprecedented world population growth accompanied by unprecedented change in the earth's physical environment. Increase in population growth will only increase diseases, economic inequity and environmental abuse. Hence there is no doubt that the explosion must end. Population control must be moved to the top of the policy agenda if posterity should enjoy the fruits of development.

With the threat of the population level reaching the level of carrying capacity sooner, governments are serious about stabilizing population and protecting the environment from the adverse consequences of rising population. Two lines of action are requires.

1. Policy to stabilize population level below the carrying capacity.
2. Strict environmental regulations that would promote resource and energy efficiency in consumption and production and put the economies on the path of sustainable development.

The advanced industrialised nations will have to take measures to change the resource inefficient and waste intensive materialistic life style of the people. Developing economies will have to take measures to reduce poverty so that people will include environmental conservation in their priority list.

Questions

1. Examine the trend in global population and its impact on environment.
2. "The relationship between population change and the environment vary by region"? Explain
3. Discuss the various approaches that have examined the adverse impact of population on environment.
4. Suggest measure to curb the environmental impact of a rising population.

Exercise

1. Search the website and note the ecological foot print of various nations and relate it to their population growth.
2. Prepare a write up on India's population growth and its impact on India's environment.

9

URBANISATION AND ITS IMPACT ON ENVIRONMENT

"Urbanisation now has far greater influence than ever before. A world-wide process, its impact may be found almost everywhere."

—Robert Arvill

Urbanisation means the demographic balance between rural and urban areas. In the words of Kingley Davies, urbanization is "a cycle through which nations pass as they evolve from agrarian to industrial society". Urbanisation is sometimes referred to as "location revolution" because it shifts people from smaller communities to larger communities. It is the movement of people from communities concerned chiefly or solely with agriculture to other communities generally larger whose activities are primarily centered in government, trade, manufacture or allied interest (Warren, 2005) . According to the UN Report "*World Urbanization Prospects: The 2014 Revision*" urbanization may be expressed as a condition at a point of time as well as a process occurring over time. When it is expressed as a condition prevailing at a point of time, then it refers to level of urbanization while process is the increase in levels of urbanization that is increase in percentage urban. Growth rate in the level of urbanisation is rate of urbanization.

The phenomenal increase in urbanization is attributed to:

- natural increase in population - the predominance of births over deaths among urban populations.
- migration from rural areas to urban areas
- the reclassification of previously rural areas as urban.

Three studies by the United Nations Population Division on two major components of urban growth, namely natural increase and net migration, point to natural increase as the driving force behind urban growth in developing countries. According to these studies, about 60 per cent of the growth of cities in developing countries was due to natural increase, while the remainder was due to net migration and reclassification. Natural increase was the major factor driving city growth in Africa, Asia and Latin America and the Caribbean. In essence the process of urbanization is due to:

- migration of people from rural to urban areas
- absolute growth in urban population.
- reclassification of towns by which some large village, as they grow, come under the classification of urban town.

- there are sporadic factors like wars, partitions, famines and floods which result in massive migration. For example during drought periods, rural people migrate to towns in search of better job opportunities. By and large people move to urban areas for higher income, better job opportunities and better standard of living.

9.1 Trends in Urbanisation

Urbanisation is growing at a tremendous pace, leading to a world of agglomerations; megapolis piled on megapolis'. Globally, more people live in urban areas than in rural areas. The information on urbanisation presented in this section is from the United Nations, World Urbanisation Prospects—the 2014 Revision. According to this report nearly 54 percent of the world's population lived in urban areas in 2014. In 1950, 30 per cent of the world's population was urban, and by 2050, 66 per cent of the world's population is projected to be urban. Between 1950 and 2014 world population urbanized rapidly - the proportion of population that is urban increased from 30 percent in 1950 to 54 percent in 2014. Urban and rural populations of the world are shown in table 9.1.

Table 9.1 Total and Urban Populations by Development Group Select periods (1950-2000)

Development Group	Population (billions)					
	1950	1970	1990	2014	2030	2050
Total Population	2.53	3.69	5.32	7.24	8.42	9.55
More developed Regions	0.81	1.01	1.15	1.26	1.29	1.30
Less Developed Regions	1.71	2.68	4.17	5.99	7.13	8.25
Urban Population						
World	0.75	1.35	2.29	3.88	5.05	6.34
More developed Regions	0.44	0.67	0.83	0.98	1.05	1.11
Less Developed Regions	0.30	0.68	1.45	2.90	4.00	5.23
Rural Population						
World	1.78	2.34	3.04	3.36	3.37	3.21
More developed Regions	0.37	0.34	0.32	0.28	0.24	0.19
Less Developed Regions	1.41	2.00	2.72	3.09	3.13	3.02

Source: United Nations Department of Economic and Social Affairs /Population Division, (2015) World Urbanisation Prospects: The 2014Revision, (ST/ESA/SER.A/366).

In terms of numbers the urban population of the world grew from an estimated 0.75 billion in 1950 to an estimated 3.88 billion in 2014 which implies that the world urban population in 2014 was more than five times as large as it was in 1950. In 2014 the urban population in less developed regions was 2.90 billion which is nearly 75% of the world urban population. It is reported that by 2050, 82% of the world's urban population will be in less developed areas.

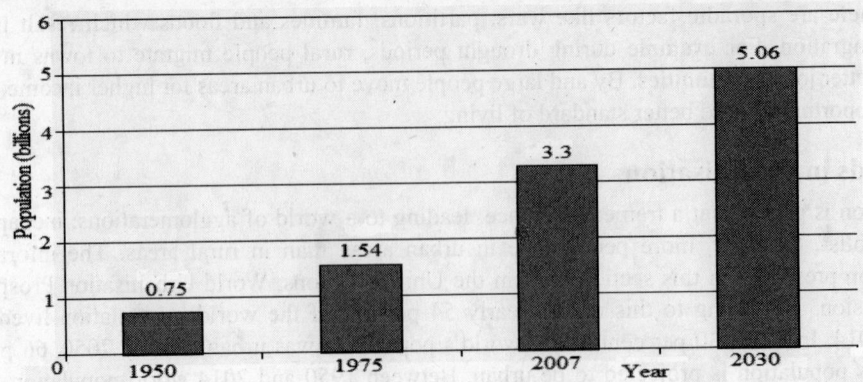

Figure 9.1 World Urban Population 1950 -2014

Source: The Johns Hopkins University and Abdullah Baqui, 2009

However the pace of urbanization is expected to slow down in the future. The increase in the annual urban growth rate (1.7 percent) is much lower than the annual urban growth during 1950-970 (3.0 percent), 1970-1990 (2.6 per cent) 1990 -2014 (2.2 percent). For the period 2030-50, the annual urban growth rate is projected to be much lower at 1.1 per cent. By 2050 nearly 66 percent of the world population is expected to be urban with urban dwellers numbering 6.3 billions. Figure 9.1 shows increase in world urban population from 1950 to 2014.

9.2 Urbanisation by Regions

Table 9.2 gives details on urbanization trends for different regions of the world. Among all the major areas of the world Africa was the least urbanized followed by Asia in 1950. In 1950, nearly 18 per cent of Asia's population lived in urban areas. Urbanisation in Asia continued to increase over time and by 2014 the level of urbanization had more than doubled to nearly 48 percent in 2014. Nearly 64 per cent of Asia's population is projected to be urban in 2050.

Africa's urbanization path is similar to Asia. In 1950, Africa was the least urbanized with 14 percent of its population living in urban areas but it experienced the fastest rate of urbanization by far during 1950-1970 and the second fastest after Asia during 1990-2014. By 2014 Africa's urban population increased to 40 per cent. It is predicted that Africa will face a level of urbanization of 56 per cent by 2050. It is estimated that by 2050 urban population in both Africa and Asia would have crossed the 50 per cent (Asia in 2018 and Africa in 2038).

Table 9.2 Percentage Urban by Major Area, (Select Periods)1950-2050

	Percentage Urban					
Major Areas	**1950**	**1970**	**1990**	**2014**	**2030**	**2050**
World	29.6	36.6	42.9	53.6	60	66.4
Africa	14	22.6	31.3	40	47.1	55.9
Asia	17.5	23.7	32.3	47.5	56.3	64.2
Europe	51.5	63	70	73.4	77	82
Latin America and the Caribbean	41.3	57.1	70.5	79.5	83	86.2
North America	63.9	73.8	75.4	81.5	84.2	87.4
Oceana	62.4	71.3	70.7	70.8	71.3	73.5

Source: United Nations Department of Economic and Social Affairs /Population Division, (2015) World Urbanisation Prospects: The 2014Revision, (ST/ESA/SER.A/366).

9.3 Urbanisation by Development Group

It is reported that the great majority in the more developed regions live in urban areas. However, the urban population of the less developed regions has been growing considerably faster than that of the more developed regions. Table 9.3 gives data on Percentage of urban population in developed and developing regions.

Table 9.3 Percentage Urban by Development Group, 1950-2050

	Percentage Urban					
Development group	1950	1970	1990	2015	2030	2050
World	29.6	36.6	42.9	54.0	60.0	66.4
More developed countries	54.6	66.7	72.4	78.3	81.5	85.4
Less developed countries	17.6	25.3	34.8	49.0	56.2	63.4

Source: United Nations Department of Economic and Social Affairs /Population Division, (2015) World Urbanisation Prospects: The 2014Revision, (ST/ESA/SER.A/366).

9.4 Pace of Urbanisation

Table 9.4 shows the time taken to add each billion to the urban population. The world urban population reached one billion in 1959 only. It took 26 years to reach the figure of 2 billion. The world population level crossed 3 billion level in 2002 and is projected to become 4 billion in 2016, 5 billion in 2029 and 6 billion in 2045. If the projections made by the United Nations are accurate then, all the expected world population growth during 2014-50 will be in urban areas. That is during this period (2014- 2050) the urban population is expected to rise by 2.5 billion while the total world population is expected to increase by 2.3 billion.

Table 9.4 Pace of Urbanisation

Urban Population	Year	Time taken (years)
1 billion	1959	-
2 billion	1985	26
3 billion	2002	17
4 billion	2016	14
5 billion	2029	13
6 billion	2045	16

Source: Based on data from United Nations Department of Economic and Social Affairs /Population Division, (2015); World Urbanisation Prospects: The 2014Revision, (ST/ESA/SER.A/366).

The discussion on trends in global urbanisation process may be summed up with the following highlights from the United Nations Report on World Urbanisation Prospects (2015):

- In 1950 about 2/3 of the world population lived in rural settlements and less than 1/3 in urban settlements. **By 2050, we will observe roughly the reverse distribution** - the world will be one-third rural (34 per cent) and two-thirds urban (66 per cent).
- World's urban population is projected to grow by **2.5 billion between 2014 and 2050**, with nearly **90% of the increase concentrated in Asia and Africa.**
- The fastest growing urban agglomerations are **medium-sized cities or cities with less than one million inhabitants located in Asia and Africa**.

- Most megacities and large cities with population between 5 and 10 million, are located in the **global South.**
- Just three countries — **India, China** and **Nigeria** – together are expected to account for 37 per cent of the projected growth of the world's urban population between 2014 and 2050. India is projected to add 404 million urban dwellers, China 292 million and Nigeria 212 millions.
- **By 2014, the number of mega-cities had nearly tripled to 28** and by 2030, 41 urban agglomerations are projected to house at least 10 million inhabitants each.
- **Tokyo** will be the world's largest city in 2030 with 38 million inhabitants, followed closely by **Delhi** with 25 million which is projected to reach the same population as Tokyo by 2030.

9.5 Impact of Urbanisation

Urban populations interact with their environment. The consumption styles and production technologies of the urban people are resource and energy intensive. While in 2014, seventeen countries with at least 90,000 inhabitants that had more than 90 percent of their populations living in urban areas it is predicted that by 2050, 32 countries with at least 90,000 inhabitants in 2014 will have more than 90 percent of their populations living in urban areas. The unprecedented growth in world population, accompanied by technological and economic growth has enhanced urbanisation.

Table 9.5 World's Top Ten Cities with Population More than 500,000

Rank - 2016	City	Country
1	Tokyo	Japan
2	Jakarta	Indonesia
3	Delhi	India
4	Manila	Philippines
5	Seoul	South Korea
6	Karachi	Pakistan
7	Shanghai	China
8	Mumbai	India
9	NewYork	United States
10	Sao Paulo	Brazil

Source: Demographia, Demographia World Urban Areas *(13th ed.).*

Arthur Lewis (1977) viewed urbanization as unavoidable but was concerned about the costs of urbanization and wrote: "Urbanization would not be inevitable if we could spread industry around the countryside instead of concentrating it in towns, but this is easier said than done. . . . One can work hard at establishing rural industries, but except in police states, this is bound to be limited."

Urban areas are engines of economic success. The world's leading cities are polluters par excellence. The 750 biggest cities on the planet account for nearly 57 percent of today's GDP, and this share is projected to rise further. It is hence not surprising that rapid urban growth has been dubbed as one of the biggest challenges by many. Table 9.5 gives details on world's top ten urban cities. The growing concern is that as cities grow larger, environmental stress multiplies. This is because cities are where action is. Cities are the focal points of opportunities. Hence there is always a movement of population to cities. This increases the pressure on existing facilities of housing and infrastructural facilities besides leading to congestion. The following quote expresses the state of cities today:

"Cities have become centers where vast numbers of people compete for the most basic elements of life: for a room within reach of employment with an affordable rent, or vacant land on which a shelter can be erected without fear of eviction; for places in schools; for medical treatment for health problems or injuries, or a bed in a hospital; for access to clean drinking water; for a place on a bus or train; and for a corner on a pavement or square to sell some goods—quite apart from the enormous competition for jobs. In the majority of cases, governments have the power and resources to increase the supply and reduce the cost of many of these". Hardoy J, Satterthwaite Hardoy J, et al (1995) .

The adverse impact of urbanisation on ecological balance is mainly reflected through deforestation. An increase in urban population increases the demand for firewood partly because of the rise in price of 'oil-based' fuels like kerosene and poor distribution system. In the tropics eighty per cent of all wood harvested—825 million cubic metres a year—is simply burned as fuel. The consumption of firewood in many cities are high because of poverty and proliferation of slums resulting from urbanisation. Besides, this increased demand for firewood, makes it commercially attractive. All these leads to deforestation.

Urbanisation depletes both renewable and non-renewable resources faster because of the excess energy requirements of urbanites. The increased substitution of machines for labour in urban cities, and the processing and transporting of additional food requirements to urban cities, creates excess demand for energy. According to an estimate the world energy use may be increased five times that of present use by 2025.

Urban Heat Island

One of the best-known impact of urbanization is the **urban heat island (UHI)** effect. Urban heat island (UHI) refers to relative warmness of the urban areas compared to nearby rural areas. It is an 'inadvertent' modification of the climate, caused by changes to the form and composition of the land surface and atmosphere. Due to urbanization, there are changes in landscapes, in the form replacement of open land and vegetation by buildings, roads, and other infrastructure. As a result land surfaces become dry and urban regions become warmer than the rural surroundings. This results in the formation of an "island" of higher temperatures in the landscape. Heat islands occur specially during clear and calm evenings and nights.

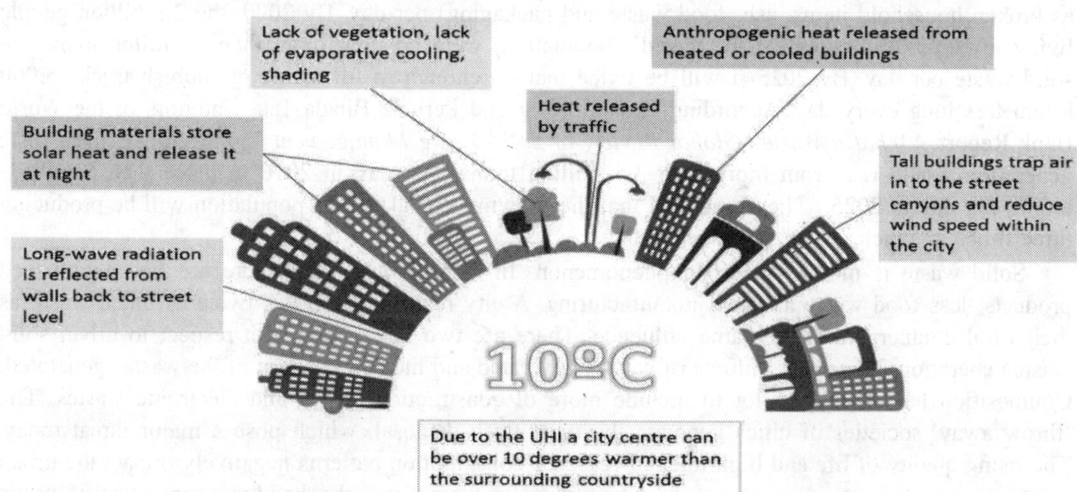

Figure 9.2 The Main Factors Contributing to the Formation of Urban Heat Island

Source: http://ilmastotyokalut.fi/kaupungin-lampotilaerot/mika-on-lamposaareke/urban-climate-research-in-the-city-of-turku/

Some of the main factors that may bring about the difference in temperatures between urban and rural areas include :

- the high heat capacity of the buildings in the urban areas compared to surrounding rural areas, resulting in more of the sun's energy being absorbed and stored in the urban areas;

- the high-density buildings in urban areas block the view of the sky and reduce the heat release back to space;
- Man-made heat emissions by buildings, air conditioning, transportation and industries in urban areas; and
- dense development in urban areas, which reduces wind speeds and inhibits cooling by convection.

Urbanization converts natural surfaces to built surfaces such as buildings and roads. As a result the thermal, radioactive, moisture and aerodynamic properties of the natural surface and the atmosphere are altered. This results in more of the sun's energy being absorbed and stored in urban compared to rural surfaces.

Urbanization impacts adversely the biodiversity across the world. The change in urban land cover results in loss of habitat, biomass, and carbon storage. By 2030, urban land cover is predicted increase by 1.2 million km^2, nearly tripling the global urban land area. This increase would result in considerable loss of habitats in key biodiversity hotspots. It has been forecast that the largest urban expansion in biodiversity hotspots is likely to be in South America, while considerable bio diversity loss is likely to occur in the Guinean Forests of West Africa, and the Western Ghats.

Urban **pollution** is the by-product of the city. Pollution in the modern cities are caused by the release of noxious substances from consumption and production activities; they are referred to as the effluents of affluence. The atmosphere in cities are filled with smoke, streets littered with wastes and water polluted with effluents in the absence of effective environmental policy and regulation.

Urbanisation and Waste Generation

Urbanization increases global solid-waste generation. In 1900, the world had 220 million urban residents (13 percent of the population). They produced fewer than 300,000 tonnes of rubbish (such as broken household items, ash, food waste and packaging) per day. By 2000, the 2.9 billion people living in cities (49 percent of the world's population) were creating more than 3 million tonnes of solid waste per day. By 2025 it will be twice that — enough to fill a line of rubbish trucks 5,000 kilometres long every day. According to Hoornweg and Perinaz Bhada-Tata , authors of the World Bank Report "*What a Waste- Global Review of Solid Waste Management* ", the global solid-waste generation would rise from more than 3.5 million tonnes per day in 2010 to more than 6 million tonnes per day in 2025. They predicted that the growing global urban population will be producing three times as much waste as it does today.

Solid waste is mostly an urban phenomenon. In rural communities there are fewer packaged products, less food waste and less manufacturing. A city resident generates twice as much waste as their rural counterpart of the same affluence. There are two key issues with respect to urban solid waste generation – the sheer volume of wastes generated and the composition of the wastes generated. Composition has changed a lot to include more of construction debris and electronic wastes. The 'throw away' societies of cities generate the most trash disposal, which pose a major threat today. The rising quality of life and high rates of resource consumption patterns negatively impact the urban environment. Generation of wastes in urban areas is far beyond the handling capacities of urban governments. As the standard of living of city dwellers increases, the amount of waste they produce goes beyond the assimilating capacity of the environment.

9.6 Specific Pollution Problem in Some of the World's Large Cities:

During the winter of 1952 London was blanketed by smog that persisted for four days. This event came to be known as the "Great Smog", and is estimated to have caused 4000 premature deaths. Los Angeles is also reported to have suffered severe smog in the 1940s. Due to these events the US and UK governments enacted stringent air quality standards as early as 1950s. Despite the advances made by London and Los Angeles, the concentration of particulate matter in these cities remain higher than the limits set by the World Health Organisation.

In Los Angeles (USA), smog fills the atmosphere very frequently that doctors have urged residents to move out of the area because smog cripples and kills. The Appollo 10 crew members made an interesting observation on their historic round trip mission to moon in December 1968. They reported that they were able to spot Los Angeles from hundreds of miles out in space by observing the large blanket of smog hovering over the Southern California metropolis.

In Beijing, pollution has soared to hazardous levels around 20 times the limit recommended by the World Health Organization. India, Pakistan and Iran are also in the list of the world's most polluted cities in terms of particulate matter, according to the most recent statistics from the WHO, compiled from more than 1,600 cities for the years 2008 to 2013.

Air pollution in Delhi is caused mainly by industry and vehicular traffic, which has released high levels of particulate matter made up of various substances—including carbon, nitrogen, sulphur and metal compounds. According to CNN, there are roughly 8.5 million registered vehicles in the city.

Air pollution, lack of proper waste management infrastructure and degradation of water bodies are the major environmental issues in Karachi. The air in the city is highly polluted by vehicle emissions from auto rickshaws and buses, industrial emissions, open burning of garbage and house fires.

Rome's River Tiber is Italy's third longest river and runs 400 kilometres (250 miles) from the hills of Tuscany to the port of Ostia on the Mediterranean. The river provided an efficient way to move goods to the city from around the Mediterranean. Rome grew to become the most important city in the world because of and in spite of the Tiber. In 2013 tourist cruises along River Tiber River was suspended indefinitely because the waterway has been judged too dirty.

Tokyo has a massive air pollution problem more pronounced than in London and Los Angeles. It is reported that school children in Tokyo have to wear masks on heavily smoggy days. Traffic police in certain parts of Tokyo must take periodic intake of oxygen breaks to keep themselves from being overwhelmed by noxious exhaust fumes.

The industrial city of Nizhni Tagil in USSR is wrapped in clouds of gaseous wastes so thick and toxic that drivers must turn on their head lights at noon. Due to such toxic gaseous emissions children are prone to skin rashes. It is said that 700,000 tons of toxic substances are spewed into the city's air.

This is the state of some of the cities in the world, witnessing urbanisation today. Shelly said, 'Hell is a city much like London'. He would perhaps have added Calcutta, Bombay, Lagos, New York or Mexico, if he was to visit them today.

9.7 Proliferation of Slums

According to UN Habitat, a slum household suffers from one or more of the following features: dwellings made of non-durable material; overcrowding; lack of access to improved water; lack of access to improved sanitation (ie, a toilet); or insecure land tenure. When urbanisation comes with lack of infrastructure, slums expand and the urban divide widens. The proliferation of slums is chiefly a problem of the Third World countries. The environment in the cities of the Third World countries are affected more by poverty and the inability of the concerned Governments to tackle its underlying and not so much by industrial or automobile exhausts. According to Jorge E. Hardy and David Satterthwaite, "most major Third World Cities are two cities: the city of the elite where Western standards are evident, and the largely self-built city of the poor". Nearly one third of the world's population is estimated to be living in either slum or squatter settlements. The largest proportion of population living in slums in the world is in the Asian region, which is also urbanizing at the fastest rate. In 2001, 60 percent of the world's total slum dwellers were in Asia.

The past few decades have seen a progressive urbanization in Asia. As urbanization continues in Asia, the region's poverty will increasingly be urban in nature. Urban poverty has similar features to rural poverty. Asia's slum population has declined significantly as a proportion of total urban population over the past decades. But about one-third of Asia's urban population still lives in slums, and the actual number of the slum population is still growing as urban populations grow. East Asia is a little better off than the regional average, with 28 percent of its urban population living in slums in 2010, down from 44 percent in 1990. China's slum population is 31percent of its total. In South-East Asia, 31percent of its urban population lived in slums in 2010, a substantial decline from 50 percent in 1990. Slum populations in poor countries like Laos and Cambodia are close to 80 percent of total urban population, while in the Philippines and Vietnam they are over 40 percent. The slum situation in South Asia is the worst in the region, with some 35 percent living in slums in 2010, well down from 57 percent in 1990.

Rapid urban population growth has outpaced the ability of city authorities to provide for housing, environmental and health infrastructure. More than a third of the Third World population lives in world's most degraded environment, without proper drinking water, sewage connection and health services. Housing is a prominent problem in all the Third World Countries leading to extension of slums. Squatter and slum settlements arise due to the inability of city governments to plan and provide affordable housing for the low-income segments of the urban population. Hence, squatter and slum housing is the housing solution for this low-income urban population. As a result communicable diseases like tuberculosis flourish, lowering resistance among inhabitants due to mal-nutrition. In most Third World slums, one child out of three dies before the age of FIVE. The proliferation of slum and squatter settlements shows that planned economic growth has to be aligned with the planned development of health services, environmental infrastructure, and housing. Yeung Y-M observes that:

"For the scale and speed of urbanization that has been taking place in developing countries of Asia, most municipal governments are unequipped physically, fiscally, politically, and administratively to tackle the problems of providing the basic infrastructure services to their people. In a situation of scarce resource allocation, the urban poor are frequently badly placed to compete for essential services. Biases in investment , standards, pricing policy, and administrative procedures, more often than not, skew services in favor of the rich, denying the poor shelter, safe water, acceptable sanitation, minimal nutrition, and basic education".

Effective action by governments, especially at the local level, is necessary to implement the necessary urban planning, and to provide infrastructure and services. A national programme that supports the efforts of the poor to rebuild and improve their habitat, at the same time providing a stable economic base to the poor alone can solve the state of environment in cities.

9.8 Quality of Urban Environment in India

In most of the developing countries of the world, urbanisation gained momentum only after the Second World War. India, accounting for more than fifteen per cent of the world population accommodated in just 2.4 per cent of the world land area, has nearly 32 per cent of its population in urban areas. Pakistan and China are said to be more urbanised than India with 38 and 54 percent of population living in urban areas. Euromonitor research observed that India had the second highest urban population in the world in 2012 and will be amongst the fastest growing urban populations globally between 2013 and 2020 in absolute terms. It took nearly 40 years for India's urban population to rise by nearly 230 million; it will take only half that time to add the next 250 million.

Urbanisation in India is due to population growth, migration of people from rural to urban areas and . reclassification of villages/towns over period. Around sixty per cent of rise in urban population is due to natural increase in population.

According to census and United Nations data, India's share of urban population in 2011 was 31 per cent, compared to around 50 per cent in China, Indonesia and Nigeria, 61 per cent in South Africa, 78 per cent in Mexico, and 87 per cent in Brazil. In the 60 years from 1950 to 2011, India's urban population share increased from 17 per cent to 31 per cent, while China's increased four times from 12 per cent to 49 per cent

India's urban population grew by 2.8% annually between 2000 and 2012, compared to the 1.6% per year rise in the total population, mainly due to high levels of rural-urban migration for better job opportunities and better lifestyles. According to the United Nations' 'State of the World Population 2007' report, by 2030, 40.76 per cent of India's population will be living in urban areas compared to about 32 per cent now.

In the 20 years from 1991 to 2011, India's urban population rose to 377 million - 160 million more than in 1991 and 91 million more than in 2001. According to the 2011 Census, the urban population registered a growth rate of 2.76 percent per annum during 2001-2011. The level of urbanisation in India increased by 3.3 percentage points from 27.7 percent in 2001 to 31.1 percent in 2011 –compared to an increase of 2.1 percentage points during 1991-2001.

In 2012, India's urban population stood at 388 million – the second highest urban population in the world. However, the country's urban population accounted for only 31.6% of the total population in the same year compared to the global average of over 50.0% of the total population; Two of India's metropolitan cities feature in the world's largest urban population by city. Mumbai is the most populated city in India and was the fourth largest urban population by city in 2012 at 12.5 million people, while Delhi – the country's capital city –was the eighth largest urban population city at 11.1 million people.

Table 9.6 Growth of Urban Population as Percentage of Total Population

Census Years	Urban population (in Million)	Urban population as percentage of total population	Number of Urban Agglomerations/ towns
1901	25.85	10.85	1827
1911	25.94	10.29	1825
1921	28.09	11.18	1949
1931	33.46	11.99	2072
1941	44.15	13.86	2250
1951	62.44	17.29	2843
1961	78.93	17.97	2363
1971	109.11	19.91	2590
1981	159.46	23.34	3378
1991	217.72	25.71	3768
2001	285.35	27.78	5161
2011	377.11	31.16	7935

Source: Census of India Report, Govt. of India 1901-2001

Shankar Acharya (2014) observes that the condition of urban India is far from being adequate and satisfactory. He substantiates his observation with the following facts of urban India :

- Twenty-five per cent of urban India dwells in slums; in Greater Mumbai the ratio is over50 per cent.
- Except few small towns in Maharashtra, continuous piped water is lacking in almost all cities. The water quality is abysmally poor. In contrast, cities in China and Brazil get much better water 24x7.

- Very few Indian towns (such as Chandigarh, Navi Mumbai and Surat) treat over 90 per cent of their sewage before discharging them into rivers, sea and lakes. In the vast majority of urban communities, the treatment rate is far lower, well below 50 per cent.
- Urban India is estimated to produce 180,000 tonnes of garbage every day, most of which ends up in huge rubbish heaps or «land hills». Overflowing garbage bins and rubbish heaps are common sights in many cities.
- Diseases like dengue, malaria, typhoid, swine flu, diarrhoea and respiratory ailments are on the rise in most towns in India.
- Urban road systems are grossly inadequate and poorly maintained. Public transport service is highly limited: only about 500 out of 8,000 cities and towns have a public bus system.

Urbanisation in India has given rise to acute shortage of housing facilities that ends up in proliferation of slums. Substantial housing shortage looms in Urban India and a wide gap exists between the demand and supply of housing, both in terms of quantity and quality. According to the Report on Urban Housing Shortage 2012-17 by the Technical Urban Group, Ministry of Housing and Urban Poverty Alleviation, India's urban housing shortage is estimated at nearly 18.78 million households in 2012. Because of this acute housing shortage, majority of urbanites live in slums. The National Sample Survey Organisation (NSSO), India, defines a slum as a "compact settlement with a collection of poorly built tenements, mostly of temporary nature, crowded together usually with inadequate sanitary and drinking water facilities in unhygienic conditions" (NSSO, 2003). Within urban India, between 1981-2001, there was a 45 percent increases in the number of people living in the urban slums. In 1981, nearly 28 million persons lived in the slums, in 1991 there were 45.7 million slum dwellers and in 2001, there were 40.6 million persons living in slums. According to the NSSO (2003), every seventh person living in the urban areas is a slum dweller. The bulk of the urban poor are concentrated in the urban slums or are squatters.

A break up of urban population reveals that slum dwellers account for nearly fifteen per cent of the urban population. In cities like Bombay and Calcutta, slum population accounts for forty per cent and in Madras about thirty per cent. One-third of the urban population in India lives in squatter settlements. Due to migration of people from rural to urban areas housing space is reduced as a result of which there is an increase in the number of families living on footpaths. The inevitable result of these is insanitary surroundings in which a sizeable section of the population lives. Urban areas in India are almost invariably plagued with insufficient and inefficient sewage facilities. Not a single city in India is fully sewered. Most cities do not have proper arrangements for treating the sewerage waste and it is drained into a nearby river (as in Delhi) or in sea (as in Mumbai, Kolkata and Chennai), thereby polluting the water bodies. Only 35-40 per cent of the urban population has the privilege of sewage system. Most of the cities have old sewerage lines which are not looked after properly. Often sewerage lines break down or they are overflowing.

Table 9.7 Status of Sewerage System in Urban Areas in India

	Class I Cities*	Class II Cities / Towns
Number	414	489
Cities having STPs	112	22
Number of STPs	211	31
Sewage generated (in mld)	26164	2965
Sewage generation in cities having no STPs	11512 (44%)	2822 (95.2%)

Source: Compiled from Central Pollution Control Board Report on Status of Sewage Treatment in India Nov.2005.

•Class I cities: Population above 100,000.

**Class II towns: Population between 50,000 & 100,000.

Of the 3500 towns in India hardly 200 are sewered. The status of sewerage system in class I (population 100,000 and above) and class II cities (population between 50,000 and 100,000) in India is shown in table 9.7.

Urban pollution is part of the high technology-high production problem. The urban cities are out of phase with ecological reality. The trend towards urbanisation has led to the neglect of the countryside in addition to the chain of evils it results in: deforestation, desert expansion, soil erosion, pollution of all forms—all these eventually making pure air and water scarce goods.

However urbanisation is not an evil. There are many who consider increasing migration from rural areas, as a positive development because it relieves rural misery and brings about a flow of money from urban to rural areas. In this sense cities act as reception centres for rural poor and as custodian of culture. The argument is for a cleaner city and for a just and suitable balance in the rural urban population and economic activity. As Barbara Ward, says in her book, "Home of Man", cities will always be needed as repositories and custodians of culture. What is needed therefore is a wiser, saner, happier balance between the rural urban distribution of people and economic activity.

This can be achieved by

1. Developing spatial pattern of urbanisation suited to the socioeconomic conditions of India.
2. Government investment programmes on housing and urban services including pollution control, keeping pace with the requirements of the increasing urban population.
3. Increasing trend in urbanisation can be arrested by resorting to decentralised production—"production by the masses as against mass production" to quote Gandhiji. Government should have a clear policy of industrial location which will encourage dispersal of people. Attention should be paid to investments in villages which can arrest migration from rural to urban areas. Technologies which involve small scale operation and which are less environmentally damaging should be developed and encouraged.
4. An effective urban land policy should be designed to make land available at affordable prices to meet housing needs. The urban land (Ceiling and Regulation) Act (1976) limited the quantity of vacant land in cities that could be owned by an individual. The proliferation of unauthorised lay-outs and mushroom growth of flats should be controlled. Land pooling can be attempted with the help of owners and Government agencies. Restrictions on ownership of houses with provision to prevent benami will solve the shortage in housing. Huge investments in villages may be made to create townships. This can be achieved in collaboration with reputed private establishments.
5. Laws have been framed to prevent air and water pollution in cities. What is needed is strict enforcement of these laws.

Conclusion

Over-urbanisation has today necessitated most of the cities to undertake renewal schemes. Urban renewal involves "renewing the urban life where the process of degeneration or decline is set into motion due to a variety of factors like technological advances, industrialisation, modernisation and their cumulative impact on the settlement pattern and social organisation". Aiming to improve the physical living conditions of decaying city, various measures have been undertaken by the Government in different countries. However all these Government investment programmes can be effectively carried out only with efficient and non-corrupt political and administrative management. Qualitative upgradation of local body administrators with high level technical and financial skill is essential.

Questions

1. What is urbanization? Examine the trend in global urbanization
2. What are the environmental impacts of urbanisatoin.
3. Comment on Urbanisation in India and examine its impact.
4. What is urban heat island?
5. Suggest measure to make urban development more sustainable.

Exercise

1. Download the report on Indian Urban Infrastructure and services from the website given below and prepare an article on profile of India's urban centres.
   http://icrier.org/pdf/FinalReport-hpec.pdf
2. Compare the state of environment in Indian metropolitan cities

10

ENERGY AND ENVIRONMENT

"It is energy that lights the lamp that lets you do your homework, that keeps the heat on in a hospital, that lights the small businesses where most people work. Without energy, there is no economic growth, there is no dynamism, and there is no opportunity."

–Rachel Kyte, World Bank Vice President

Energy is the foundation stone of the global economy and a powerful engine of economic and social development. The development of all countries from that of a subsistence level to what it is today would not have been possible without access to the different forms of energy resources. Without appropriate energy services there can be no true economic development. The energy resource available to the nations determines the level of development and the quality of life in a nation. The magnitude of energy consumed per capita has become one of the indicators of development progress of a country.

Energy is an essential ingredient for almost all human activities: it provides services for cooking and space/water heating, lighting, health, food production and storage, education, mineral extraction, industrial production and transportation. All energy production and consumption has environmental impacts. The exponential increase in the consumption of energy has caused significant environmental impact on the planet, most notable of which is the climate change attributed to the emissions of greenhouse gases and carbon-di-oxide. Other significant environmental impact of energy consumption are: acid rain, which is a threat to the ecosystems of several lakes and rivers; lead contamination of the atmosphere; nuclear wastes from nuclear power plants and the waste heat from thermal power plants.

10.1 Forms of energy

Energy resources have been classified according to different criteria such as based on their renewability or based on conventionality in deriving the energy.

A common classification is to differentiate energy forms into exhaustible/depletable and non-depletable/ renewable energy resource. The distinguishing feature of an exhaustible energy is that, it gets exhausted when used as an input of a production process, that is, the temporal services provided by a given stock of an exhaustible resource are finite. **Renewable** means that a source is not depleted by use – wind is always renewable, while biomass can be renewable if regrowth is matched by consumption. Fossil fuels are non-renewable, as they will eventually be depleted (i.e. run out) as there is no viable way to produce more of them.

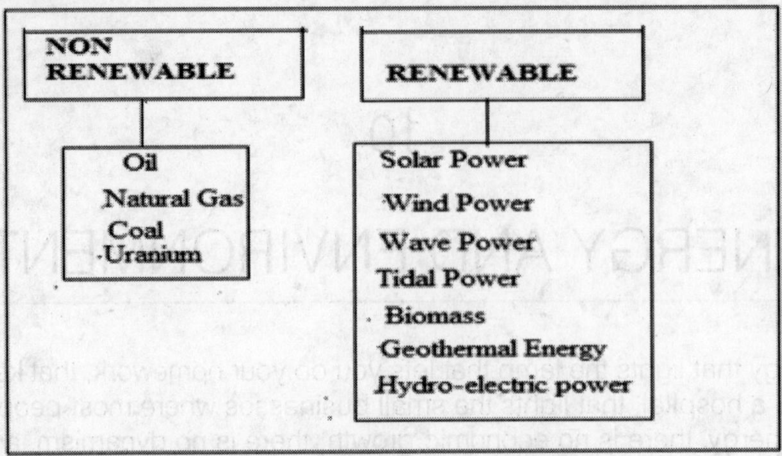

Box 10.1 Classification Energy Sources

Energy Resources are also classified on the basis of its availability as primary or secondary energy sources. **Primary energy** sources are energy as it is available in the natural environment. **Secondary energy** is the energy ready for transport or transmission.

Primary Energy Resources	Secondary Energy Resources
1. Fossil fuels such as coal and natural gas	
2. Nuclear Fuels such as Uranium, Thorium etc.	1.Petrol,diesal, Kerosene Oil
3. Hydro Energy	
4.Solar Energy	2. CNG and LPG
5. Wind Energy	
6. Geothermal Energy	3. Electrical Energy based on coal, diesal gas.
7.Ocean Energy such as tital energy, wave energy	
8.Hydrogen Energy	

Box 10.2 Primary and Secondary Energy Resources

Energy in its primary form can be of different kinds. The main types are Chemical (fossil fuels-coal, oil, natural gas, peat; biomass - wood, agricultural residues, etc.), Potential (water at a certain height), Kinetic (wind, waves), Radiation (sun), Heat (geothermal reservoirs, ocean thermal reservoirs) and Nuclear (uranium). The primary form of energy must generally be converted into secondary or final forms of energy before it can be used. A simple example is that of hydro energy where the primary energy is potential energy stored in the water in a dam. The water is used in a hydro power station, where the potential energy is converted to electricity – the secondary energy. In other words, the potential energy of a waterfall (primary energy) is converted into electricity (secondary energy), which is transmitted and transformed to supply (final) energy to a factory, where it is converted into mechanical energy (useful energy) for productive operations. Important types of secondary energy are electricity and mechanical energy. Chemical energy in the form of refined oil products is also an important secondary energy resource.

Table 10.1 Different Classifications of Energy Sources

Energy Source	Familiarity		Reproducibility		Monetisation	
	Conventional	Non-conventional	Renewable	Non-renewable	Commercial	Non-commercial
Large scale hydro power	*		*		*	
Coal	*			*	*	
Oil and Gas	*			*	*	
Nuclear	*			*	*	
Fuelwood		*	*		*	*
Agri residue		*	*		*	*
Animal dung		*	*		*	*
Industrial waste		*		*	*	
Solar thermal		*	*		*	*
Solar photovoltaic		*	*		*	
Wind		*	*		*	*
Small scale hydro power		*	*		*	*
Biogas		*	*		*	

Source: Adapted from FAO Regional Wood Energy Development Programme in Asia, 1997, "Energy and Environment Basics", pp14

Renewable sources of energy are also known as non-conventional sources of energy and non-renewable sources of energy are known as conventional sources of energy. Conventional (non- renewable) sources of energy are also classified as commercial and non-commercial fuels. **Commercial energy** refers to those energy sources which have to be paid for. While coal, lignite, petroleum products, natural gas and electricity are commercial fuels, agricultural waste, cow dung and fuel wood are non-commercial sources of energy. It is common to place the same energy source in more than one category. This can be understood from Table 10.1.

Most of the energy sources are substitutable to each other since most energy forms can be converted to another - such as coal to electricity, or solid biomass to produce liquid or gaseous fuels of higher calorific value. All forms are ultimately converted into heat. The inter-fuel substitution process enables an economy to substitute its abundantly available resources in the place of the scarce resource.

10.2 Energy Data

During 2000–2012, coal was the source of energy with the largest growth. The use of oil and natural gas also had considerable growth, followed by hydro power and renewable energy. Renewable energy grew at a rate faster than any other time in history during this period, which is due to an increase in international investment in renewable energy. The demand for nuclear energy decreased, possibly due to the accidents at Chernobyl and Three Mile Island.

According to the Energy Information Administration (EIA), the world's total energy consumption in 2008 was 505 quadrillion British Thermal Units (BTUs). 85% of this was derived from fossil fuels. By 2035, the world's energy consumption is projected register an increase of 53% from 2008.

In 2012 approximately 22% of world energy was consumed in North America, 5% was consumed South and Central America, 23% was consumed in Europe and Eurasia, 3% was consumed in Africa, and 40% was consumed in the Asia Pacific region. In 2013, world energy consumption by power source was oil 31.1%, coal 28.9%, natural gas 21.4%, biofuels and waste 10.2%, nuclear 4.8%, hydro 2.4%, and 'other' (solar, wind, geothermal, heat, etc.) sources 1.2%. Oil, coal, and natural gas were the most popular energy fuels.

The report by WEC (World Energy Council), along with "World Energy Resources", in 2013, observed that by 2030 electricity will absorb 44% of primary energy resources for its production and now it is already responsible of 40% of CO_2 emissions resulting from human activities. Global data on energy reveals that 40% of electricity production is from coal, followed by gas with 22.5%, 16% hydroelectric, 13% nuclear, 4% oil, 2.4% wind and other renewable with 2.1%.

Coal has the strongest consumption percentage growth in the last twenty years, since it is used on a large scale in countries like China and India for electricity production while oil has been losing its role as the great leading energy resource. However the share of fossil fuels in total primary energy production is predicted to decrease from 82% in 1993 to 76% in 2020, while that of renewable (excluding hydro power) is expected to increase from 10% to 16% for the same period. The current proven reserves of coal is over 110 years with present energy consumption, while that of gas and conventional oil is 60 years and 56 years respectively.

With respect to conventional oil, the Middle East North Africa (MENA) is enriched with 50%, followed by Latin America (20%) and North America (13%). More than 2/3 of consumption of conventional oil is concentrated in 3 areas: North America (26%), East Asia (22%) and Europe (21%). However when we consider individual nations instead of regions or areas, Venezuela leads the top 5 nations for conventional oil reserves followed by Saudi Arabia, Canada, Iran and Iraq; cumulatively they have 64% of world reserves (World Energy Council, 2013).

The 5 countries with the largest reserves of natural gas are Russia, Iran, Qatar, Turkmenistan and Saudi Arabia. Cumulatively they have 67% of the world reserves.

The hydroelectric plants account for about 15% of the global production of electricity from all sources and have a primary energy market share of a little over 2%.

Due to significant availability of uranium there is no criticality to a possible development of nuclear power. Europe is the continent that holds the highest number of reactors and the maximum installed power (44% of the total), while Asia (China main contributor with 28 reactors) is the continent with the highest number of reactors and power in the implementation phase (46 reactors).However, probability of a serious Fukushima (Japan) like disaster pose challenges to the development of nuclear power.

Biomass which is renewable energy is the most important of all the forms of renewable energy: more than 85% come from woody biomass, about 8% from agricultural products and by-products and approximately 5% from waste of municipalities and industrial processes. The biggest "producers" of bio-energy are China, India, Nigeria and the United States and the largest producers of bio-fuels from wood are India, China, Brazil, Ethiopia and Nigeria.

Renewable energy sources are inexhaustible, that is, naturally replenishing and they restore themselves over short periods of time. Such sources include hydropower, wave or tidal, geothermal, solar, wind and biomass. Nations are increasing the development of renewable energy sources to reduce the reliance on fossil fuels, and to provide energy security and improve environmental quality.

Among renewable energy sources, wind and solar energy are gaining popularity in the recent times. Harnessing energy from sunlight is solar energy. The term solar energy refers to power generation through either photovoltaic cells or thermal--solar systems. Each year, the Earth's surface receives sunlight with an energy content equivalent to ten times more than that stored in all known reserves of coal, oil, natural gas, and uranium combined. The popularity of wind and photovoltaic energy resources is largely due to generous incentives. Solar photovoltaic (PV) is a technology that has seen tremendous growth over the past few years. China, United States, Germany, Spain and India are the first five countries for wind production while Germany and Italy for photovoltaic electricity. Italy with more than 6 percentage of its electricity production from photovoltaic energy is ranked first in the world.

Nearly 93% of India's requirement of commercial energy is being met by fossil fuels, with coal contributing 56%, and oil and natural gas contributing 37%. Hydropower and nuclear power contribute to only 7% of total energy production. The total energy production in India from commercial sources is only 3.5% of total world production.

Even though many sources of energy are available, many regions of the world face energy shortages and energy security is crucial issue discussed at global level. According to Clerici A and G Alimonti , the main drivers in energy sector over the past 20 years are:

- emerging environmental issues but without a common approach to emission reductions
- continued growth in energy consumption, electricity in particular
- explosive increase in renewables, specially, wind and photo voltaic in particular due to generous government subsidies
- impact of Fukushima on nuclear industry
- financial and economic crisis and its impact on energy consumption trends, in particular in industrialized countries;
- increase in oil prices.
- development of shale gas in the United States with a drop in local gas prices which are 1/3 of gas prices in Europe and 1/5 of those in the Far East;
- growing influence of public opinion on energy policies; – rapid spread of information technologies in all sectors.

10.3 Environmental Impact of Various Sources of Energy

Energy is essential for all we do as individuals and as societies. Energy is the backbone for the economic development of a nation. Energy production, use, and distribution also cause some of the most pressing environmental problems.

Energy - Environment interdependence has serious global environmental impact. The current patterns of energy production and use, which have shaped the development process in the past, are environmentally unsustainable. The energy challenge now faced by countries around the world is about providing energy services for sustainable human development. The energy we generate and use affects our environment in many ways. Some energy sources have a greater impact than others. Energy is lost to the environment during any energy transformation, usually as heat. Nothing is completely energy efficient.

Apart from Carbon di oxide (CO_2), Methane (CH_4) and nitrous oxide (N_2O) are powerful greenhouse gases emitted by the energy sector. Methane accounts for nearly 10% of energy sector emissions and originates mainly from oil and gas extraction, transformation and distribution. The balance is nitrous oxide emissions from energy transformation, industry, transport and buildings.

Some of the observations made by the Special Report on Energy and Climate Change by the International Energy Agency published in 2015 include:

- Over the past two-and-a-half decades, global CO_2 emissions increased by more than 50%. Between 2000 and 2014 the average annual rate of increase accelerated to 2.3% mainly due to a rapid rise in CO_2 emissions in power generation in countries in the OECD.

- Even though CO_2 emissions increased almost three-fold in China and two-and-a-half times in India between 1990 and 2014, per-capita emissions in both countries are still below the average level in OECD countries.
- China's per-capita emissions in 2014 reached 6.2 tonnes, matching the level of the European Union, but a third lower than the OECD average. India's per-capita emissions were 1.6 tonnes in 2014, or about 10% of the level in the United States and 25% of the level in China.

10.3.1 Fossil fuels

Worldwide, 90% of the energy powering the turbines that produce electricity comes from burning fossil fuels, i.e., coal, oil, and natural gas. The advantages and disadvantages of fossil fuel as an energy source are:

Fossil fuels, (coal, petroleum and natural gas) are not renewable; hence at some point they will become increasingly costly as they are depleted and the resulting scarcity will present challenges to national energy security. Further, combustion releases air pollutants nitrogen oxides (NO_x) volatile organic compounds (VOCs); sulfur dioxide (SO_2) and CO_2; the gases are responsible for climate change, ozone layer thinning and acid rain. Extraction, transport, refining and use of fossil fuels adversely affect the earth's surface, cause pollution of aquatic systems. Besides, they involve the consumption of large amounts of land and other resources for electricity transmission lines, oil and gas pipelines, road and rail transport of fuels and fuels storage.

Fossil fuel combustion process is the main cause of the CO_2 accumulation in the atmosphere. Due to the increasing consumption of fossil fuels as energy resource the average concentration of CO_2 has reached almost alarming levels and is expected to increase further in the near future. The rate of increase of the CO_2 concentration has accelerated in the last sixty years.

Since 2000, the share of coal has increased from 38% to 44% of energy-related CO_2 emissions; while the share of natural gas stayed flat at 20% that of oil declined from 42% to 35% in 2014. Few countries account for a significant share of energy-related CO_2 emissions. In 2012, three countries – China, United States and India – gave rise to almost half of global CO_2 emissions from fossil-fuel combustion.

The sulfur content of coal ranges from 1% to 5%. Sulfur is converted to sulfur dioxide (SO_2) during burning, which result in acid rain. NO_x, also (results from burning coal) causes acid rain.

Coal mining and processing produce large quantities of waste and air pollutants. Burning coal contributes to water pollution when air pollutants, such as, acids, metals and other particulates, are deposited into water. When air pollutants are deposited on soil, soil becomes acidic. This adversely affects the quality of soil, bringing down its productivity. Surface and underground mining expose sulfur containing rocks to the water and air that oxidizes the sulfur to acid. Ash resulting from burning coal is deposited on soil or in waterways.

Coal also contains radioactive elements, Uranium and Thorium, exposing people living near coal burning power plants to radiation.

To sum up, major disadvantages of coal are:

- Requires expensive air pollution controls (e.g. mercury, sulfur dioxide)
- Significant contributor to acid rain and global warming
- Requires extensive transportation system.

Despite its problems, tremendous reserves of coal exist around the world and its use will continue. The challenge is both to continue to develop clean-coal technologies, *and* to find ways to assure it is used. "Clean coal" technology is being developed to remove harmful materials before they can affect the environment and to make it more energy-efficient.

Petroleum, a non-renewable resource is cleaner than coal, but produces the same air pollutants that arise when coal is burnt. However the carbon content of oil, and thus the amount of CO_2 emitted, is less than coal, but more than natural gas. The recovery, processing and use of petroleum cause adverse environmental effects. Besides, the environmental impact of petroleum in transportation must also be considered. Marine oil spills have devastating effects on aquatic environment. The grounding and breaking up of Torry Canyon in 1967 near Scilly Isles, UK, the Amaco Cadiz on March 17th 1978 on the French coast line and that the *Exxon Valdez oil* spill which occurred in Prince William Sound, Alaska, in 1989, are examples of marine pollution by oil spills. Spills sometime lead to fires or explosions, loss of life, and pollution.

Natural gas, a non-renewable, is said to be cleaner & greener. It generates only about half as much CO_2 per unit of energy as coal, one third less CO_2 than oil. However burning of natural gas produces NO which causes acid rain. A primary component of natural gas is Methane which is a green house gas. The disadvantages of oil & natural gas are:

- Very limited availability.
- Major contributor to global warming.
- Very expensive for energy generation.
- Liquified Natural Gas storage facilities and gas transmission systems have met opposition from environmentalists.

10.3.2 Hydro power

The hydroelectric plants produce nearly 16% of the global production of electricity from all sources. It is reported that hydroelectric potential in North America and Europe is exploited for more than 85%, in South America for 33% and in Asia and Africa for 22% and 7%, respectively. A dam generates little air pollution and depletes few non-renewable resources. Dams are needed to generate electricity, to prevent floods, and to provide water for irrigation. However hydro power has serious environmental impact, particularly if the dam is a large dam. Hydroelectric power plants changes water flow and water temperature harming fish populations, and disturbing plants and animals; Construction of dams results in the relocation of people and animals living near the dam site. The presence of hydroelectric dams changes the migration patterns and hurts fish populations. Hydroelectric plants are capital intensive. Hydroelectric power distorts land use and disturbs ecosystem. The Three Gorges Dam project on the Yangtze River in China is reported to have led to the displacement of one million people, in addition to the devastation of land and ecosystems.

10.3.3 Nuclear Power

Nuclear power is popular because:

- The energy produced per amount of material consumed is the highest available. Uranium-235 is the isotope of uranium that is used in nuclear reactors. Uranium-235 can produce 3.7 million times as much energy as the same amount of coal.
- Costs are competitive with coal, the major source used in the world.
- Uranium, the source material, is abundant.
- Plutonium, a by-product of commercial nuclear plant operation, can also be used as a fuel.
- the amount of waste produced is the least of any major energy production process.

Nuclear power plants produce no air pollution and has no acid rain and climate change impacts, but they do produce byproducts like nuclear waste and spent fuels. Most nuclear waste is low level radio active wastes and special regulations are in place to prevent them from harming the environment. But some spent fuel is highly radioactive and are hence stored in specially designed facilities. In addition to the fuel waste, much of the equipment in the nuclear power plants becomes contaminated with radiation which become radioactive waste after the plant is closed. These wastes remain radioactive for many thousands of years, which does not allow re-use of the contaminated land.

Nuclear power plants use large quantities of water for steam production and for cooling, affecting fish and other aquatic life. Likewise, heavy metals and salts can build up in the water used in the nuclear power plant systems. When water is discharged from the power plant, these pollutants can adversely affect water quality and aquatic life.

The potential for accidental release of radio-active materials and exposure to people, and the problem of long-term disposal of radioactive wastes, are the main environmental concerns of nuclear power. The disadvantages of nuclear power are:

- Requires larger capital cost because of emergency, containment, radioactive waste and storage systems
- Requires resolution of the long-term high level waste storage issue in most countries
- Potential nuclear proliferation issue.

Marquita K Hill (2004) sums up the objections and counter arguments to nuclear power as follows:

- Nuclear reactors cannot be operated safely. Proponents of nuclear power argue that modern nuclear reactors are different from, and much safer than those involved in the 1986 Chernobyl accident in the Ukraine. Plants with advanced reactor designs that take imperfect human operators into account can operate safely.
- Radioactive wastes cannot be safely disposed. Burying of nuclear wastes is highly controversial. Supporters of nuclear power argue that nuclear waste can be can be vitrified and safely stored in a deep underground repository in a stable geological formation.

"Nuclear power might have been less controversial if safety and radioactive waste concerns had been handled early in the history of its use. However, nuclear technology's initial user was the military, who did not consider health, safety, and environmental concerns a priority." (Hill, 2004)

10.3.4 Wind energy is a clean energy source. However the manufacture, transportation, and building of access roads cause environmental problems. Wind energy produces no air or water pollution because no fuel is burned to generate electricity. The most serious environmental impact from wind energy may be its effect on bird and bat mortality. Unless locations are planned to avoid bird migration routes, turbines can result in bird deaths. Wind turbine design has changed dramatically in the last couple of decades to reduce this impact. Noise is sometimes a problem too. Large tracts of land are needed, but the land can be used for crops or trees where surface is not covered by machines and plant structures. Wind energy needs locations with dependable and strong winds. A major problem with wind energy is the transportation of power to customers. The cost of wind energy has fallen greatly over the years.

Wind power can be used in small systems. Wind energy is used to pump water. Modern wind machines are sometimes used to generate electricity for private homes. Wind turbines would fit into urban landscape and are not dependent on large wind farms.

10.3.5 Biomass energy refers to any organic fuel such as wood, crop wastes or other vegetation, and animal dung, or fuel such as charcoal derived from organic material. In terms of usage bioenergy is by far in the first position as "renewable", with a share of about 8% of global resources. Biomass can be used directly to produce electricity, or indirectly to produce biodiesel, ethanol, or methane. Although biomass fuel sources release carbon dioxide when burned, generally they are not considered net releasers because they also remove carbon from the atmosphere during their growth cycle.

10.3.6 Solar power does not directly pollute but pollution is generated when solar panels are manufactured, transported, and maintained. The toxic chemicals used to manufacture PV cells affect workers. To produce large amounts of electric energy, large land areas would be covered with solar panels. Solar power plants are located in areas where sunlight is plentiful, but must be stored and transported to less-sun-rich areas. Therefore new power lines are required over which conflicts arise with reference to area to be designated for the new power lines.

10.3.7 Geothermal energy refers to the heat below the Earth's surface. Hot water and steam available close to the Earth's surface are used to generate electric power. Such geothermal energy can release noxious chemicals along with the steam.

Table 10.2 summarises the overall nature of the impacts.

Table 10.2 Environmental Impact of Various Energy Forms

Energy Source	Energy production	Environmental Impact
Oil, Petroleum	Non renewable	Refining and consuming produce air, water, and solid waste pollutants
Natural Gas	Non renewable	Produces fewer pollutants than oil and coal, and less CO_2
Coal	Non renewable	Produces CO_2 and other air, water and solid waste pollutants
Biomass: Wood and organic waste including societal waste	· Renewable · In terms of timber, it is easily harvested and abundant in certain areas; but it takes a long time to grow a tree.	· Burning emits CO_2 and other pollutants · Loss of habitat when trees are harvested, unless sustainable tree farms are in place.
Hydro-electric	· Renewable · Clean resource with high efficiency · Influenced by climate and geography	Destruction of farmlands, dislocation of people, loss of habitat, alteration of stream flows
Solar Power (photo-voltaic)	· Renewable · High economic cost particularly in terms of start-up · Dependent on climate and geographical location · Need a storage system for the energy to ensure reliability · Not advanced enough for global use	Large land use

Solar Power - (solar thermal)	· Renewable · Central-thermal systems to convert solar energy directly to heat · More competitive economically than photovoltaics · Dependent on climate and geographical location	
Geo-thermal	· Extracts heat from underground masses of hot rock. · Technology is still undeveloped. · Can be geographically dependent	Disrupts natural geyser activity
Wind Power	· Renewable · Unlimited resource that is a very clean process, no pollutants	· Aesthetic issues · Needs lots of land · Possible impacts on birds and their migration patterns · Some noise pollution
Nuclear Fission	· Non renewable resource U-235 (uranium) · Highly technological infrastructure necessary for safe operation · Production of nuclear energy has a high cost due in part to regulations · High water usage for cooling	· Byproduct is highly radioactive and highly toxic · Produces radioactive wastes that have a long lifetime · Disposal solution complex technically and politically · Safety issues in terms of operating a facility with the potential to release radiation to the atmosphere · Public perception problem in terms of radiation, etc.
Nuclear Fusion	· Technology is not yet viable and requires research investment · Technology still not developed enough to make this a viable source	Possibility high for water pollution because of radioactive tritium

Source: Adapted from http://environ.andrew.cmu.edu/m3/s3/11sources.shtml

Conclusion

We need ***every energy source we can get.*** Energy demand has been and will continue to increase. The environmental impacts of the various forms of energy calls for consideration of sustainable energy use. Based on Brundtland Commission's definition of sustainable development sustainable energy may be defined as "any type of energy that can potentially be used well into the future without harming future generations." Such a definition focuses primarily on the issue of permanence. This definition underlines the long-term availability of energy as primary concern. Sustainable energy is the combination of energy savings, energy efficiency measures and technologies, and the use of renewable energy sources with the objective of providing energy security (sufficient, safe, affordable) for present and future generation.

Sustainable energy should be based on these economic, environmental and social dimensions. For this the processing, transportation, distribution and consumption of energy must result in reduction in consumption of non-renewable resources and environmental damage, while providing universal access to energy.

Questions

1. Give the various classifications of energy sources.
2. What are the various environmental impacts of the different types of energy.
3. In the light of the environmental impact of the various energy sources, and the growing demand for energy, what are the energy options for the developing countries. Explain with particular reference to India.

Exercise

Compare the environmental impact of renewable energy resource with that of non- renewable energy giving examples.

11

FORESTS AND ENVIRONMENTAL QUALITY

"We cannot restore—once it is lost—the majesty of a forest whose trees soared upwards 2000 years ago."

—President Lyndon B. Johnson

Life of man and progress of civilisation have been profoundly influenced by the presence or absence of forest or their relative abundance or scarcity. Forests are a renewable resource and they play a vital role in enhancing the quality of environment by influencing the life-support system. In the march of man towards development our civilisation has faced three different stages of forests;

1. civilisation dominated by forests
2. civilisation overcoming forests, and
3. civilisation dominating forests

The two decades after the World War could be placed under the third stage i.e., civilisation dominating forests. These two decades were characterised by growth and progress all over the world. Material progress was achieved at the cost of exploitation of natural resoureces.

11.1 Forest Cover Data (source: UN (FAO) Global Forest Resource Assessment Report, 2015)

In 1990 the world had 4128 million ha of forest; by 2015 this area has decreased to 3999 million ha. This is a change in forest cover from 31.6 percent of global land area in 1990 to 30.6 percent in 2015. Between 1990 to 2015, there was a net loss of some 129 million ha of forest (natural and planted) representing an annual rate of 0.13 percent and a total area about the size of South Africa. Between 2010 and 2015 there was an annual loss of 7.6 million ha and an annual gain of 4.3 million ha per year, resulting in a net annual decrease in forest area of 3.3 million ha per year. The bulk of the world's forest is natural forest, amounting to 93 percent of global forest area or 3.7 billion ha in 2015. From 2010 to 2015, natural forest decreased by a net 6.6 million ha per year.

The biggest forest area loss occurred in the tropics, particularly in South America and Africa, although the rate of loss in those areas has decreased substantially in the past five years. Average per capita forest area declined from 0.8 ha in 1990 to 0.6 ha per person in 2015. As population increases forest land is converted to agriculture and other land uses.

Decrease in forest coverage is an important issue at both national and global level due to its impact on climate change and biodiversity. For example, over the last 25 years global carbon stocks in forest bio-mass decreased by almost 17.4 gigatonnes (Gt). This reduction was mainly driven by conversion of forest areas to other land uses and forest degradation.

11.2 Role of forests

Forests have been a source of life from time immemorial. Forests perform two important functions: the productive function and the protective function. The productive function of forest resources indicates the economic and social utility of forest resources to national economies and forest-dependent local communities. Productive function of the forests include the many products that are extracted from forests, ranging from timber, wood fuel to food (berries, mushrooms, edible plants), fodder and other non-wood forest products. By quantity, industrial round wood and wood fuel are the most important products; among non-wood forest products, food and fodder are the most significant.

Forests play a protective role, for instance in ecosystem conservation, in maintaining clean water, and in reducing the risks of impacts of floods, avalanches, erosion and drought. Protective functions can be local or global and include:

- Influence on climate.
- Protection from wind erosion.
- Coastal protection.
- Protection from avalanches.
- Air-pollution filters.
- Protecting water resources

More specifically the functions of the forests include:

- Forests help us breathe. Forests release the oxygen we need to live and absorb the carbon dioxide we exhale. Just one adult leafy tree can produce as much oxygen in a season as 10 people inhale in a year. Hence forests are referred to as reservoirs of oxygen.
- Forests supply timber, fuel wood, fodder, and a wide range of non-wood products;
- Forests are the natural habitat for bio-diversity and repository of genetic wealth; According to Russel McLendon, a wild life writer, forests cover a third of all land on Earth, providing vital organic infrastructure for some of the planet's most diverse collections of life. Forests provide many animals with shelter from inclement weather, protection from enemies, situation for homes, and materials for nests. Rainforests known as "cradles of diversity support 50 percent of all living organisms on Earth. Tropical forests are home to more than 50 percent of the 10-30 million species on Earth. Forest degradation and fragmentation diminish biodiversity.
- Forests help to maintain the temperature at a lower level and prevent them from rising. A portion of the solar radiation is reflected back into the space by earth's atmosphere. The rest reaches the surface of the earth as not much is absorbed by the atmosphere. The forests present on the earth's surface will reflect a portion of this sun's rays again back into outer space and absorb the rest. This we call the "albedo effect"—a phenomenon that refers to the proportion of sun light that the earth's surface reflects back into space. Forests diminish the daily range of air temperature - forest cover lowers the daily mean temperature in spring and summer and raises it slightly in autumn and winter. Forests lower the daily maximum of air temperature and raise the daily minimum. Trees intercept sunlight and alter the quantity and quality of radiation reaching forest floor compared with that reaching open sites. If forest coverage is thick and wide, the forests would absorb the heat and prevent the rise in temperature.
- The ultra violet rays from the sun are absorbed by the ozone layer. Forests serve as a natural filter of the ultra violet radiation that threatens the health of the people.
- Forests help to minimise the impact of air pollution, water pollution and noise pollution. By maintaining water flow of the rivers, reducing sedimentation in rivers and streams, by reducing

surface runoff of rain water, reducing silting of reservoirs, forests to a great extent protects the habitat from serious water pollution problem. Similarly by its protection against the physical violence of winds, air pollution effects are reduced. Forests maintain CO_2 and O_2 balance in the atmosphere, maintain water sheds in optimum condition and conserve soil.

- Forests increase precipitation. Air of forest is cooler and moist, than air in the open. Forest increases the precipitation of any area by influencing the evaporation of water from the land.
- Forests protect soil. Forest usually reduce the maximum soil temperature and increase the minimum soil temperature with the depth of the soil. The influence of forest vegetation on soil relate to the producing of a new substratum of soil and the changing of soil structure. Forest vegetation assists in the formation of soil by the accumulation of plant remains.
- Forests also act as sinks and sources of carbon. Forests represent 28 percent of the world's biome, and account for nearly 50 percent of the global carbon stocks. Forest have the potential to control climate change through their influence on the global carbon cycle.
- Forests provide a number of ecological and environmental services, such as water purification, erosion control and carbon sequestration. One method by which forests influence human activities, indirectly but strongly, is through the part they play in regulating the water cycle. The presence of dense and uniform woodland, particularly over hilly areas, is a major factor which can guarantee water supply during the dry season and also the best means of preventing floods in drainage basins at other times.
- Forests provide space for recreation and opportunity for ecotourism.

To publicize both the value and plight of woodlands around the world, the United Nations declared March 21 the International Day of Forests in late 2012.

11.3 Effects of Deforestation

Deforestation is the clearing of forest for a non-forested land use such as agriculture, grazing or urban development. NASA observes that if the current rate of deforestation continues, the world's tropical forests will vanish within 100 years – causing unknown effects on global climate and eliminating majority of the species.

Causes for deforestation are classified as direct and indirect causes. Deforestation has arisen from four principal causes, often in combination with each other - clearing forests for agriculture, logging and fuel wood, overgrazing, fire and clearance of land for mining. These are direct causes of deforestation. Urbanisation and industrialization and infrastructure are also directly responsible for loss of forest cover.

There are also few other causes which are indirectly responsible for loss of forests.

- Over population is the main cause of deforestation. Increasing population increases demand for more food and space for accommodation, the provision of which results in more clearing of forests.
- Poverty is another indirect cause. Poor farmers who do not own any land clear trees to meet their livelihood needs. The poor people who live in and around rainforests rely on these ecosystems for their survival. They collect fruit and wood, hunt wildlife and are paid by companies that extract resources from forest lands.
- Exploitation of forest resources of underdeveloped third world countries by industrialised countries. The heavy debt burden of the poor countries compels them to exploit their natural resources including their forest resources to earn foreign exchange for servicing their debts. For example the timber companies of Japan exploited the forests of South East Asian countries in return for infrastructure development aid.

Loss of forests is the price for development in most of the developing countries. The Silent Valley Project, proposed to be built on the Kundhipuzha river in Palghat district would have submerged nearly 850 hectare of virgin tropical ever green forests. Whatever be the cause, this deforestation has serious consequence on the quality of life. Tropical rainforests are estimated to have covered as much as 12% of the land surface on earth. But now they cover less than 5%.

The influence of forests on environment may be localised or far reaching. The climate, rainfall relative humidity, wind, soil, etc. are all influenced by forests. Hence indiscriminate felling of trees or deforestation disturbs ecological balance and deteriorates quality of life. Deforestation shows signs of decrease in several countries but continues at a high rate in others. Globally around 13 million hectares of forest were converted to other uses or lost through natural causes each year between 2000 and 2010 as compared with 16 million hectares per year in the 1990s.

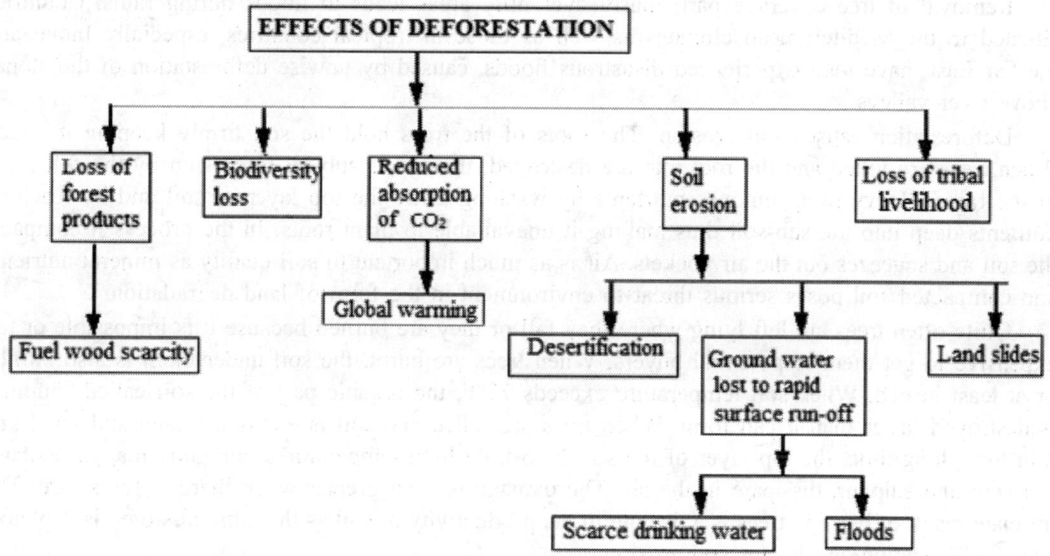

Figure 11.1 Effects of Deforestation

Source:https://saferenvironment.wordpress.com/2008/08/18/effects-of-environmental-degradation/

11.4 Climate and Deforestation

Climate change is arguably the toughest environmental challenge of the 21st century. One of the biggest contributors to climate change is carbon dioxide. The destruction of forests could change the global climate and de-stabilise polar ice caps. In the absence of forests, the heat from solar radiation that strikes the earth's surface but is not absorbed by the atmosphere are reflected back by the earth's surface leading to a rise in atmospheric temperature. The Food and Agriculture Organization of the United Nations (FAO) estimates that about 13 million hectares – an area roughly equivalent to the size of Greece – of the world's forests are cut down and converted to other land uses every year (FAO 2006). Forests have a vital role to play in the fight against global warming.

Forests absorb and store carbon in their trees and soil. But if forests are cleared or disturbed, this carbon is released as carbon dioxide and other greenhouse gases. The tropical rain forests are reservoirs of carbon, which is stored in living vegetation. Releasing this carbon by cutting trees and then burning them or leaving them to decay will add to the concentration of CO_2 in the atmosphere. In the past century the amount of CO_2 in the atmosphere has increased by about fifteen per cent.

Half the increase has occurred since 1958. Since 1860 forest clearing has contributed some 90,000 million to 180,000 million tonnes of carbon to the atmosphere, compared with 150,000 million to 190,000 million tonnes from the burning of coal, oil and natural gas. It is estimated that more than 1.5 billion tons of carbon dioxide are released to the atmosphere due to deforestation, mainly through cutting and burning of forests, every year. If we continue at our current rate of deforestation there will be no more rainforests in 100 years. Forest clearance accounts for nearly fifty per cent of the added CO_2 which traps heat that would otherwise pass through the atmosphere into outer space. This "green house effect" means that the predicted doubling in the atmospheric concentrations of CO_2 will result in an average rise of about 5°F in the earth's atmosphere. The warming will not be uniform around the globe: the North and South Poles are forecast to have temperature increases of as much as 18°F; this may cause some melting of the polar ice packs, raising ocean levels and changing rainfall patterns around the world.

Removal of tree coverage particularly over hilly areas leads to floods during rains. Countries situated in the Mediterranean climates as well as those in tropical countries, especially India, and the Far East, have long experienced disastrous floods, caused by unwise deforestation of the slopes above river valleys.

Deforestation causes soil erosion. The roots of the trees hold the soil firmly keeping it intact. When trees are felled and the root mat are destroyed, the soil is subject to erosion by the full force of the rains. Heavy rain, removes nutrients by washing away the top layer of soil and by leaching nutrients deep into the sub-soil thus making it unavailable to plant roots. In the process it compacts the soil and squeezes out the air pockets. Air is as much important to soil-quality as mineral nutrients and compacted soil poses serious threat to environment in the form of land degradation.

Quite often trees are left lying where they fall or they are burned because it is impossible or too expensive to get them to potential buyers. When trees are burnt, the soil under them is also burned or at least heated. When soil temperature exceeds 75°F, the organic part of the soil called "humus" is destroyed faster than it can form. When trees are felled and soil is exposed to sun and wind and rain for a long time, the top layer of the soil is lost. At high temperatures, the nutrients, particularly nitrogen and sulphur, dissipate in the air. The damage is even greater when there is forest fire. The ultimate result of burning trees is a decline in the productivity of soil as the nutrient stored is depleted. Thus deforestation accelerates soil erosion.

Above all forests are the home of a large variety of animals and birds. Deforestation results in the extinction of some of the species of animals and birds. Animal forms that have been documented and recognised as threatened now amount to over one thousand. Yet it represents only a tiny fraction of the problem. By the end of the century we shall be fortunate if we have not said goodbye to one million of the 5-10 million species that make up the planetary spectrum of species. Deforestation is also responsible for this though not entirely responsible.

It is essential that we recognize the value of the benefits of forests and take necessary measures to prevent deforestation, restore damaged forests, and maintain healthy ecosystems. How forests are managed can affect their future roles in maintaining genetic and taxonomic variation, ecosystem functions and environmental services.

11.5 Situation in India

Forest cover analysis by the Forest Survey of India (FSI) using satellite data, defines forest as an area of more than 1 ha and >10% of tree canopy cover. Based on this definition of forests, deforestation can be defined as the process of change of land use with depletion of tree crown cover to less than 10%.

India is one of the 12 centers of origin and diversity of several plant species in the world. The forests of India are endowed with rich flora and fauna. There are about 45,000 plant species in India which is 12% of the global plant wealth. The animal species are approximately 81,250. There are 92 National Parks and 500 Wildlife Sanctuaries in India. The total extent of protected areas include five designated World Heritage Sites, fourteen Biosphere Reserves, six Ramsar Sites, twenty eight Project Tiger Reserves and nine Elephant Reserves (Forest and Wildlife Statistics, MoEF, 2004). The State of Forests Report of the Forest Survey of India observes that the actual forest cover of India is 633,397 km^2 which is around 19.3% of the geographic area of the country. Only 38 million ha of forests is well stocked. Nearly 10 mln ha of forests are marked for ecological stability, 15 mln ha for production of timber for industry and other uses, 25 mln ha as social forestry to meet the demands for fuel and fodder and 14 mln ha of forests are under protected area network. India has to meet the needs of 16% of the world's population and 19% of world's cattle from 1% of the world's forest resources. Hence forests are under severe pressure in India.

Unfortunately India's forests are being turned into concrete jungles. **Nearly 135 hectares of forest land is being diverted every day to other uses.** The major factors responsible for deforestation in India are: shifting cultivation along with encroachment for agricultural land, mining, quarrying, expansion of settlements, dam construction and illegal logging. Apart from biotic pressure, the following factors contributed to the decline and degradation of forest resources in India (GOI, 1984):

- Increase in human and livestock populations;
- Poor management of forest soils;
- Inadequate scientific and technical inputs;
- Inadequate skills and training of the staff to play their expected new roles;
- Poor investment on forest development;
- Damage caused by mining, irrigation projects, industries, roads and shifting cultivation;

By 1970 the ill-effects of deforestation became serious in the form of fodder and wood-fuel scarcity, soil erosion, flash floods, water scarcity, loss of precious flora and fauna and climate change. Due to scarcity of wood on village common lands, rural women spend around 15-35 hours every week in walking long distances for collecting fuel-wood from interior forests. Deforestation resulted in floods and the damage from floods affected 58 million ha of agricultural land and over 60 million people during the 1980s. The extent of damage had increased by four folds over the earlier two decades.

Due to deforestation nearly 45 % of total geographical surface area, is affected by serious soil erosion. The destruction of vegetation has been the main cause for both soil erosion and flood damage. India's two key ecological zones—the Himalayas and the Western Ghats—are witnessing fast denudation of the country's prime level forests. They can be saved only if tree farmers are encouraged to raise commercial forests.

The Chipko Movement opened the eyes of those who had been blind to the threat to our environment. The Chipko Movement born in a small hilly village of the Uttar Pradesh, in 1973, has successfully focused national and even global attention on the eco-system of the Himalaya. It was not only an attempt at saving trees on the Himalayan slopes but also questioned development based on the ruthless butchery of nature to achieve short-term gains. It challenged the traditional notion that forests mean timber and underlined their role in maintaining the quality of soil, water, and pure air which are the basis of life. Besides such movements, the new policy for forests development adopted at the National and State levels, emphasises the need for the development of community forestry or social forestry in India.

India has a number of legislative measures to protect the forests. The legal framework consists of four main national laws:

- Indian Forest Act, 1927;
- Wildlife (Protection) Act, 1972;
- Forest (Conservation) Act, 1980
- Biological Diversity Act, 2002.

The Indian Forest Act provides the basis for forest administration in the country. The states can also enact their own laws; rules and regulations for administration and management of forests within the overall legal provisions of the central enactments. Most of the states have enacted their own legislations for management of forests. The Forest Conservation Act of 1980 was enacted to prevent the indiscriminate conversion of forest area for non-forest purposes. The role of India's forests in the national economy and ecology was emphasized in the National Forest Policy, 1988, which focused on restoring the ecological balance and preserving the remaining forests. The National Forest Policy lays down three basic and widely accepted objectives of forestry development which are:

1. To ensure regular supply of raw-materials for the forest based industries
2. To protect existing forest cover so as to increase environmental protection
3. To tap the forest resources in such a way as to provide maximum benefits to tribal and other villagers living near forests.

Social forestry was projected with the aim of taking the pressure off the forests and making use of all unused and fallow land. Social forestry was initiated in 1980s to assist rural communities and landless people to meet their livelihood needs for fodder, fuel wood, small timber, fruits, and minor forest produce through community planned and managed nurseries and tree plantations in common lands and non-forest public lands. Social forestry programme implemented tree planting in wastelands, institutional lands and non-forest public and private lands for the supply of forest raw material as well as market products. Many states launched Social Forestry/Community Forestry Programmes during late 1970s and early 1980s under externally aided projects for undertaking afforestation in private and community owned barren and degraded lands with the active co-operation and involvement of local population. Through the social forestry scheme, the government has involved community participation, as part of a drive towards afforestation, and rehabilitating the degraded forest and common lands.

In 1988, the Forest (Conservation) Act, 1980, was amended to facilitate stricter conservation measures. While the Wildlife (Protection) Act governs the conservation of wildlife and related matters within and outside the Protected Area (PA) network, the Biological Diversity Act, 2002 governs the protection and control of biodiversity and biodiversity related traditional knowledge. The 1988 National Forest Policy's goal of bringing a third of the total land area under forest cover has not been achieved.

As a follow-up of the new National Forest Policy 1988, the Ministry of Environment and Forests issued detailed guidelines in June 1990 for people's involvement in forest conservation and management which was termed as Joint Forest Management (JFM). Joint Forest Management was employed initially in the state of Haryana. After the initial successes in West Bengal and Haryana, the JFM schemes received national importance in the legislation of 1988 and thrust in the Guidelines of 1990. JFM involved village communities and voluntary agencies in the protection and development of degraded forests. Till date, of the total 173,000 villages in the forest fringe, JFM has been implemented in 61,000 villages.

In 2002 the National Afforestation Programme was launched to increase the forest cover of the nation. In eight years NAP achieved about 1.69 million ha afforestation.

The Ministry of Environment and Forests launched an Integrated Forest Protection scheme during 10th Five year plan (2002-2007) to provide holistic support to forest protection. The components provided for in the scheme were, Forest Fire Control and Management, Working Plan Preparation/

Survey and Demarcation and Strengthening of Infrastructure for Forest Protection. The scheme has been implemented on sharing basis. The major focus is on:

- introduction of modern tools and technologies in management and protection of forests like GPS and GIS in the preparation of working plans
- strengthening of infrastructure for field level functionaries which include vehicles for mobility and communication
- use of remote sensing technology in detection of forest fires and physical measures to control them.

Since forests constitute the first line of defense against environmental degradation and pollution resulting from economic activity, the 12th Finance Commission provided a grant of Rs 1000 Crores for the first time to be distributed among the states during 2005-10 in accordance with the share accounted for by each state in the total forested acreage in the country. The 13th Finance Commission observed that the grant must be continued because forests provide a variety of services like carbon sequestration, sediment control and soil conservation, ground water recharge, protection from extreme weather events and preservation of biodiversity. The Commission recommended an aggregate grant of Rs 5000 Crores for all the States, which has been accepted by the Government, to be distributed during 2010-15 in five annual installments.

In the 11th Five year plan (2007-12), the scope of the Integrated Forest Protection scheme was broadened and renamed as Intensification of Forest Management with additional components. The additional components include:

- Conservation and Restoration of Unique Vegetation & Ecosystems,
- Control and Eradication of Forest Invasive species
- Preparedness for Bamboo Flowering and
- Protection and Conservation of Sacred Groves

The Ministry of Environment and Forest finalized the Green India Mission (GIM) as a response to climate change impacts. The overarching objective of GIM is to increase forest/tree cover in 5 million ha of land, and improve quality of forest cover in another 5 million ha of lands. The mission proposes to take a holistic view of greening by restoring ecosystems and habitat diversity and enhancing biodiversity. It is clear that "over a period of time forestry management in India has changed from production oriented forestry to protection oriented and finally to conservation oriented forestry. Forest management is now people centric with benefits flowing directly to the communities managing the forests" (Dr V K Bahuguna). It is hoped that such programmes will bridge the gap between man and forests.

Questions

1. Why are forests important?
2. Explain the effects of deforestation.
3. Examine the state of forests in India and the measures taken by Government of India to protect our forests.

Exercise

1. Prepare a note on Global Forest Carbon Mechanism?
2. On a world map and on a map of India mark forest coverage by density with different shades and examine the extent of deforestation and dense forest coverage by different regions.

3. The **dodo bird** inhabited the island of Mauritius in the Indian Ocean, where it lived undisturbed for so long that it lost its need and ability to fly. It lived and nested on the ground and ate fruits that had fallen from trees. A combination of human exploitation and introduced species significantly reduced **dodo bird** populations. Within 100 years of the arrival of humans on Mauritius, the once abundant **dodo bird** was a rare bird. The last **dodo bird** was killed in 1681. Although the **dodo bird** became extinct in 1681, its story is not over. What is more interesting is the effects of its extinction on the ecosystem. A scientist noticed that a certain species of tree was becoming quite rare on Mauritius. In fact, he noticed that all 13 of the remaining trees of this species were about 300 years old. No new trees had germinated since the late 1600s. Now, more than 300 years after one species became extinct, another was to follow as a direct consequence?

   Look for the answer by searching on internet for Dodos. You can start your search from the following site:

   http://www.bagheera.com/inthewild/ext_dodobird.htm

SECTION 3

ECONOMIC DEVELOPMENT AND ENVIRONMENTAL QUALITY

12

ECONOMIC GROWTH AND ENVIRONMENTAL QUALITY

"We clearly have an obligation to safeguard the biosphere. It is our home, which we share with all other known life, each dependent upon the others."

—*Russel H. Peterson*

Environmental protection and economic growth are generally considered as conflicting objectives. The quality of environment emerged as a public cause during the early sixties as a result of some of the outstanding books and articles on environmental crisis. To name a few are: Rachel Carson's "*The Silent Spring*", Barry Commoner's "*The Closing Circle*", the Club of Rome's "*The Limits to Growth*", Goldsmith's "*Blue Print for Survival*" and Boulding's "*The Coming of the Spaceship Earth*". These and few other literary explosions and the almost simultaneous occurrence of several ecological disasters led many to ask: ""Economic growth—at what cost?"

During the last century, the world has seen tremendous performance of economies: acceleration in economic growth that has resulted in spectacular increase in human welfare. This tremendous progress in material welfare has come at a very heavy cost, that of the degradation of our natural environment. The basic life-supporting capital - forests, species, and soils - is being depleted and fresh waters and oceans are being degraded at an accelerating rate. Nearly 40% of the forestcover is lost, groundwater resources are being depleted and contaminated, enormous reductions in biodiversity have already taken place and the stability of the planet's climate is being threatened by global warming. Thus it is obvious that environmental issues have grown in scope and urgency. Eight years after the Earth Summit at Rio, *The Global Environmental Outlook 2000*, a report by the United Nations Environmental Programme (UNEP) reported that the "environmental gains from new technology and policies are being overtaken by the pace and scale of population growth and economic development."

According to the Millennium Ecosystem Assessment (2005):

- Sixty per cent of a group of 24 ecosystems are now degraded or exploited beyond ecological limits.
- World has lost 50 per cent of its wetlands since 1900. More land was converted to cropland in the 30 years after 1950 than in the period 1700-1850
- Forest area has shrunk by about 40 per cent over the past 300 years. The world has lost 50 per cent of its mangrove forests since 1980.Twenty-five countries have completely lost their forests and 29 countries have less than 10 per cent forest cover.

- Loss of biodiversity is reflected in the decline of the world's richest species habitats—tropical forests. Nearly 55 percent of tropical forests have already been destroyed. In 1996, 25 per cent of the world's approximately 4630 mammal species and 11 per cent of the 9675 bird species were at significant risk of total extinction. Today's pace of extinction is generally placed at not less than 5,000 species per year. The current species extinction rate is about 1,000 times higher than the rates that prevailed over the planet's history.
- If present consumption patterns continue, two out of every three persons on Earth will live in water stressed conditions by the year 2025.

An attempt at evaluating the costs of economic growth in terms of environmental deterioration, first and foremost, necessitates the definition of both the terms. While economic growth implies increase in output of goods and services generated by economic activity, environmental deterioration refers to degradative changes in the eco-systems which are habitat of all life on the planet.

12.1 Environmental Impact

Though a few growing economies today challenge unlimited growth, their continued growth of output and population will eventually lead to environmental crisis. Since the amount of habitable space on earth and total stock of renewable and non-renewable resources is limited, the assimilative and absorptive capacities of the earth's air, water and land resources are affected. "Effluents reduce Affluence"—is their claim. Paul Ehrlich identified three factors which are responsible for environmental impact(EI). They are: Population, Resource use per person (affluence) and Environmental Impact (EI) per unit of resource consumed. Thus Environmental Impact (EI) is expressed as:

$$EI = P \times A \times T$$

This relationship gives an estimate of the contribution of the three factors of environmental impact.

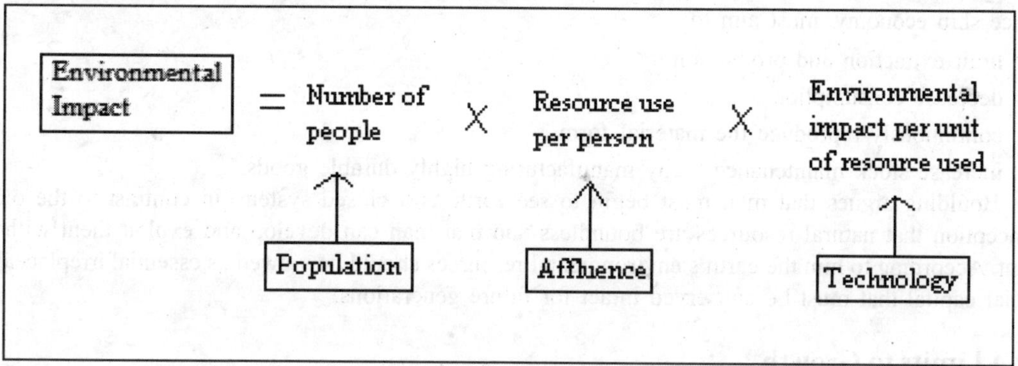

Figure 12.1 Factors Determining Environmental Impact

12.2 Accounting for Environmental Degradation

It is generally held by many economists that sustained economic growth increases human welfare. Keynes saw economic growth as a prerequisite for good life. Basing their arguments on historical and international comparisons, many economists consider economic growth as the necessary means to greater human welfare.

Measurement of economic growth in terms of output of goods and services is considered deficient as it does not take into account the external costs of environmental pollution. Edward F. Denison, in an article titled "Welfare Measurement and the GNP" considers air and water pollution, volume of solid wastes generated etc., as the real costs of economic growth and suggested that the value of deterioration to environment should be deducted from NNP to obtain a better measure of output.

When trees in the forest are cut and sold as timber, the revenue from it is included in GNP but the value of forest lost is ignored. Similarly when a wetland ecosystem is cleared to construct a building or provide a highway, additions are made to GNP but the value of ecosystem services lost is ignored. In the case of oil spillson ocean floor, the cost incurred to remove the oil is included in the GNP but the value of the lost biodiversity is ignored. The goal of greening national income accounting is to provide policy makers with information on the economy – environment interactions so that environmental goals and consequences can be incorporated in to the policy making processes. Greening national income considers inter-generational impacts of today's production activities (Karpagam and GeethaJaikumar, Green Management, 2005) Chapter 22 gives details on greening of national income accounts.

12.3 Boulding's Spaceship Economy

In 1966, Kenneth Boulding, in his classic essay "The Economics of the Coming Spaceship Earth" described the past open economy of apparently illimitable resources, which he called the "cowboy economy". "The closed economy of the future might similarly be called the 'spaceman' economy, in which the earth has become a single spaceship, without unlimited reservoirs of anything, either for extraction or for pollution, and in which, therefore, man must find his place in a cyclical ecological system." (Boulding,1966). The cowboy economy is characterized by reckless and exploitative behaviour of people who are least worried about the quality of environment and nature. The spaceship economy, on the other hand, recognized that the planet has limited supplies of resources and limited capacity to assimilate wastes. This economy needs to adopt strategies that promote economic use of materials, energy and environment, and maximisation of recycling of substances, materials and products. A space ship economy, must aim to:

1. limit extraction and production
2. decrease consumption
3. continuously reproduce the material form.
4. increase stock maintenance – by manufacturing highly durable goods.

Boulding argues that man must begin to see earth as a closed system, in contrast to the older conception that natural resources are boundless and that man can develop and exploit them without limit. According to him the earth's environmental resources should be viewed as essential irreplaceable social capital that must be conserved intact for future generations.

12.4 Limits to Growth

Several economists and philosophers of the earth have prescribed a state of 'no growth' in capital and productive system. Philosophers of the Earth like Prof. Jay Forrester of MIT, Barry Commoner, Paul and Anne Ehrlich, and D.H. Meadows have predicted that the present course of environmental degradation, will, if continued, destroy the capability of the environment to support a reasonably civilised human society. It is to avert this that they prescribed a "no growth" strategy. The "Limits to Growth" model of the Club of Rome supports these arguments through a mathematical model and predicted a collapse of the world as a result of depletion of limited resources. The computerised model developed by the Club of Rome predicted that the existing exponential growth rates of population and economic activity could not continue indefinitely on a planet that had only limited natural resources and limited ability to deal with pollution. The model prescribed that "to circumvent the disaster; we must stop short of the limits imposed by nature on our activities". (Chapter 13 gives an exclusive treatment of the LTG model).

In 1972 the magazine "The Ecologist" devoted an entire issue to 'Growth Vs Environment' debate. Thirty three eminent academicians argued that unlimited economic growth could not continue into the future without serious environmental implications. Later this issue was published as a book titled "Blue Print for Survival". The book stated that "The principal defect of the industrial way of life with its ethos of expansion is that it is not sustainable ... By now it should be clear that the main problems of the environment do not arise from temporary and accidental malfunctions of existing economic and social systems. On the contrary, they are the warning signs of a profound incompatibility between deeply rooted beliefs in continuous growth and the dawning recognition of the earth as a space ship, limited in its resources and vulnerable to thoughtless mishandling".

12.5 Trade-off between Environment and Economic Growth

The arguments against growth have been criticised by those who favour economic growth as a prerequisite for improving the lot of humanity. Pro-growth economists argue that higher levels of industrial development will allow societies to devote additional resources to tackle pollution problem without sacrificing economic growth. Besides, it is argued that only with continued economic growth, the additional resources required to achieve the desired standards of air and water quality can be raised. It is argued that growth properly composed and properly weighted can be complementary with environmental protection. Industrial anti-pollution devices and technology that produces them are part of GNP and faster growth renders polluting agents such as motor cars etc. more rapidly obsolete. Hence both pollution and reduction of pollution may be considered as a function of level of income.

The inevitable trade-off between environmental objectives and growth in the long run is illustrated in figure 12.2. The figure illustrates possible temporal growth path of GNP and of something to be measured by an index of the preservation of the environment (or of reduced pollution).

In figure 12.2, H is high growth path, L is lowgrowth path. Until time T, the high growth strategy sacrifices the environment. But at T and forever thereafter high growth promotes a purer environment. Which path is chosen will depend upon the rate of time discount for environmental purity, compared with that of GNP; since the relative value attached to reducing pollution increases with rising income, the rate of discount for the environment is likely to be lower than that of GNP. Hence those who give priority to environment advocate a higher growth strategy and thereby promote rapid development of anti-pollution techniques, processes and products.

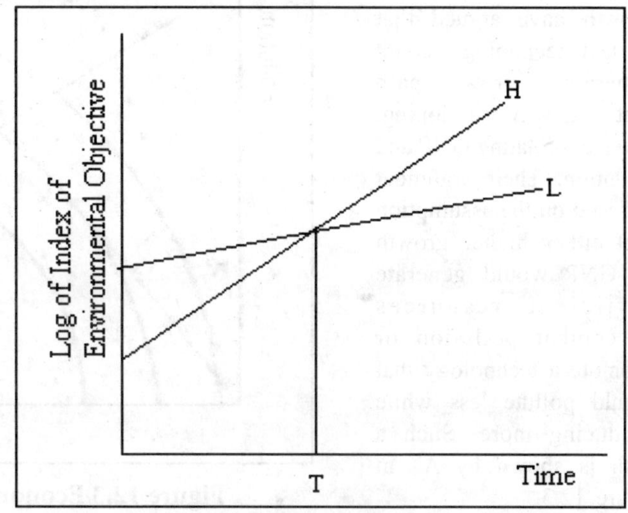

Figure 12.2 Growth Vs Environment Over Time

A similar analysis is presented in figure 12.3, using social indifference curves. In figure 12.3 the function OA and OA' indicate the growth path of GNP and the pollution associated with it. On the X axis is measured GNP (or consumption per capita if the savings rate and population are held constant). The curves W_1, W_2, and W_3 are social indifference curves, and each one shows alternative combinations of GNP and pollution that give the same level of social welfare. Since pollution and social welfare are inversely related, the shape of the indifference curves is different from normal convex indifference curves. The social indifferences curves in figure 12.3 are arranged such that W_2 indicates a higher level of welfare than W_1, and W_3 indicates a higher level of welfare than W_2. This follows the assumption that for any given level of GNP, social welfare is greater, the lower the level of pollution is.

The implication of the growth path OA in the figure 12.3 is that the social welfare increases as the economy proceeds from the origin towards point K on OA, since increase in GNP more than compensates for increase in pollution. This is reflected by the movement in the figure to indifference curves showing higher levels of welfare. Beyond K, or if economy grows faster, economic growth of the type shown by OA, causes a decline in social welfare, i.e., the economy moves to an indifference curve showing lower level of welfare, (e.g., W_2 to W_1, beyond K). The argument may be precisely stated as follows:

If pollution increases at least as fast as GNP and if social preferences are such that social indifference is achieved only if GNP grows faster than increases in pollution, then social welfare will eventually decline.

If the growth path is steeper than OA, as shown by OA', the result is a decline in social welfare earlier than at K. At K', the growth path is tangent to a higher indifference curve W_1, showing lower level of welfare. Thus economic growth beyond a certain level is said to be causing reduction in welfare if accompanying pollution grew faster. It is hence considered by anti-growth theorists that technological growth cannot be relied upon to improve environmental quality. On the other hand supporters of economic growth have argued that in fact technology could generate a growth path that is downward sloping, inversely relating GNP and pollution. Their argument is based on the assumption that either higher growth of GNP would generate sufficient resources to combat pollution or promote a technology that would pollute less while producing more. Such a path is shown by A" in figure 12.3.

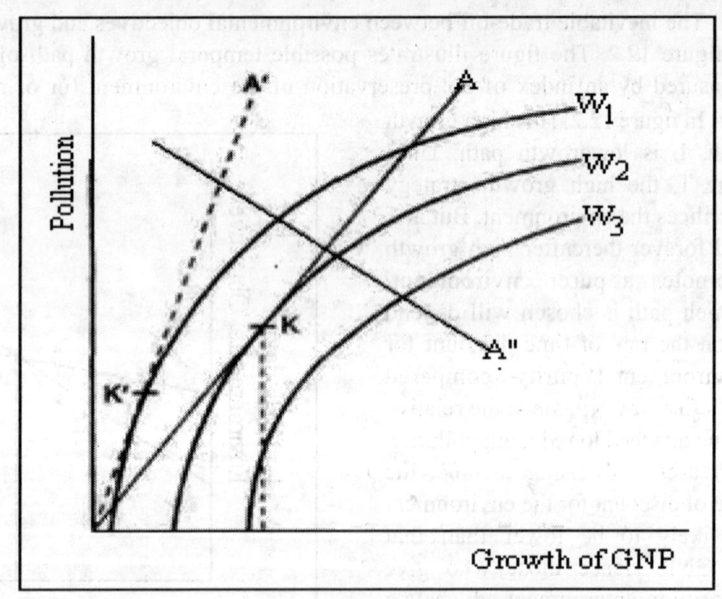

Figure 12.3 Economic Growth Vs Pollution

12.6 Environmental Kuznets Curve (EKC)

The Environmental Kuznets curve (EKC) explains the relationship between economic growth and environmental quality as a country moves on its development path. The EKC suggests that initially as economies grow development is accompanied by environmental degradation. After a certain level of development is reached environmental quality improves with further growth in the income of the economy. Figure 12.4 illustrates an EKC.

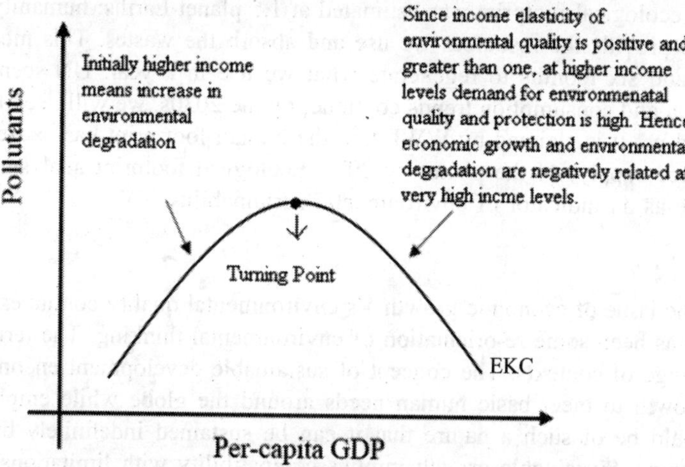

Figure 12.4 Environmental Kuznets Curve

The environmental Kuznets curve is a hypothesized relationship between various indicators of environmental degradation and income per capita. It holds that in the early stages of economic growth,environmental degradation and pollution increase, but beyond some level of per capita income economic growth leads to environmental improvement. The EKC theme was popularized by the World Bank's *World Development Report 1992* (IBRD, 1992), which argued that: "As incomes rise, the demand for improvements in environmental quality will increase, as will the resources available for investment".The EKC takes its name after Simon Kuznets who explained the relationship between income inequality and economic development using an inverted 'U' shaped curve. EKC hypothesis has been applied to various indicators of environmental degradation, such as deforestation, carbon emissions, sulphur and nitrogen oxide emissions and municipal waste. (See chapter 14 for detailed discussion on EKC).

12. 7 Ecological Foot print

The ecological footprint, a concept developed by Mathis Wackernage and Wiliam Rees in 1996 refers to the human demand on the Earth's ecosystem services. It is a standardized measure of demand for ecosystem services with reference to the planet Earth's capacity to regenerate resources and perform its vital functions. It represents the amount of biologically productive land and sea area necessary to supply the resources required by human population and to assimilate the associated waste. Using this, we can estimate how much of

Table 12.1 Ecological footprint of Select Countries (2013) (in global hectares per capita)

Countries	Ecological Foot print
Australia	8.80
Canada	8.75
U S A	8.59
United Kingdom	5.05
China	3.59
India	1.06
Africa	1.39
Asia	2.32
Europe	4.86
World	2.86

Source: http://data.footprintnetwork.org/

the earth it would take to support humanity if everybody followed a given lifestyle. For 2007, humanity's total ecological footprint was estimated at 1.5 planet Earths; humanity uses the equivalent of 1.5 planets to provide the resources we use and absorb the wastes. This means it now takes the Earth one year and six months to regenerate what we use in a year. UN scenarios suggest that if current population and consumption trends continue, by the 2030s, we will need the equivalent of two Earths to support us. It is claimed by WWF that the human foot print has exceeded the bio-capacity (available resource supply) of the planet by 20%. Ecological footprint analysis is now widely used around the globe as an indicator of environmental sustainability.

Conclusion

The debate on the issue of economic growth Vs environmental quality continues till date. Since 1980 however, there has been some re-orientation of environmental thinking. The term 'sustainability' has appeared in a range of contexts. The concept of sustainable development encompasses the necessity of continued growth to meet basic human needs around the globe while emphasising the fact that this growth should be of such a nature that it can be sustained indefinitely by respecting nature's boundary conditions. Sustainable growth implies compatibility with limitations of natural resources and waste absorption capacity of the environment. In a sustainable world, "The environment would be enhanced and global population would be balanced with the planets' carrying capacity. . . . Society, would, at long last, apply its collective intellect and energy to the central task of an intelligent materials policy—making the most of what we already have". Preservation of environmental quality is now the major challenge facing the world just as how labour and social questions were challenges in the classical or neo-classical period in economics. We can no longer believe that "in the long term we shall be dead" for in the long term, the "homo sapiens" depend on environment for its survival. Economic development without environmental considerations can cause serious environmental damage impairing the quality of life of present and future generations. It is time to strike a balance between the demands of the economic development and the need for the protection of the environment. This calls for sustainable development - the meeting of "the needs of the present generation without compromising the ability of future generations to meet their own needs.".

Questions

1. Is economic growth at the cost of environmental quality? Explain using economic theory and empirical evidences
2. Explain the concept of ecological foot print.
3. Examine the views of the anti-growth theorists.

Exercise

1. Through a simple survey, calculate ecological foot print of 5 individuals belonging to different income group, age group and different sex. And make a comparison
2. Read the article "Is Economic Growth the Environment's Best Friend "by Eric Neumayer and summarize the arguments under environmental optimism and environmental pessimism

13

LIMITS TO GROWTH

"It is important to demonstrate that we are, for practical purposes, limited to our own small planet."

—*Paul Ehrlich*

Growth is a recurrent theme in the discussions of life - growth in output, growth in population, growth in the costs of some of 'the better things in life'. Many of the indicators of quality of life are said to possess, explosive character of compounding growth. Compounding growth always and unavoidably becomes explosive in the long run. Compounding growth of a variable is depicted by a geometrical expansion in the magnitude of the variable (2, 4, 8, 16 etc.) as time varies arithmetically (1,2, 3, 4).

Prof. Jay Forrester of MIT, has predicted a deterioration in the quality of life in future. This dire prediction has been supported by many biologists and scientists, like Barry Commoner, Paul and Anne Ehrlich. In fact two recent studies use elaborate computerised models of the world, which trace out paths of future history characterised by a violent collapse of the world system—1. The "World Dynamics" model by Forrester, and 2. The Limits to Growth by the Meadows Team.

Barry Commoner predicted that the present course of environmental degradation, if continued will destroy the capability of the environment to support a reasonably civilised human society. To avert this he prescribed a state of 'no growth' in capital and productive system. These verbal non-mathematical arguments were supported by the complex mathematical model 'Limits to Growth' prepared by the 'Club of Rome' under the leadership of Dennis L. Meadows.

13. 1 Club of Rome

The Club of Rome was a loose-knit group of about seventy-five men from twenty-five nations—the members being eminent scientists, industrialists, economists, sociologists and educators. It is more appropriately, a 'elitist multinational intellectual brotherhood', with about seventy-five members, united by a common conviction that the possibilities of continuous growth have been exhausted and timely action is vital if a planetary collapse is to be averted. The club was originally founded by Aurelio Peccei. In June 1970, the club planned a project entitled "The Predicament of Mankind". Aurelio Peccei Hugo Theimann, Edward Pestel and others had already prepared a list of preliminary goals, a survey of methodologies and a statement of the 'Problematique'—what social and economic forces will accompany the transition of the world from growth to equilibrium. What was lacking was a suitable methodology to deal with the complex interactions of the world economic system. It was at this time that Jay Forrester's *World Dynamics* was published. This world Model I was soon refined and examined in greater details by Meadows and his team of Club of Rome. This Club of Rome model was published in 1972; it predicted that, the collapse of the world, as a result of, depletion of limited resources and increase in the levels of pollution, will not take very long, perhaps only a few decades. The policy implication of the model is that "to circumvent the disaster, we must stop short of the limits imposed by nature on our activities".

13.2 Basic Thesis of the Model

Limits to Growth is a study about the future of our planet and on the predicament of mankind. The basic thesis in the Limits to Growth model is that infinite growth is impossible on a finite planet. The book postulated that exponential growth in *population, industrial output, agricultural and natural resource consumption, and pollution from all these activities* would result in severe constraints on all known global resources by 2050 – 2070. The basic thesis of the Limits to Growth model is summarized as follows, by Mahbub Ul Haq:

Many critical variables in our global society—particularly population and industrial production—have been growing at a constant percentage rate; the absolute increase in each year is becoming extremely large. Such increases will become increasingly unmanageable unless deliberate action is taken to prevent such exponential growth. However, physical resources—cultivable land and non-renewable minerals—and the earth's capacity to absorb pollution are finite. Sooner or later, the exponential growth in population and industrial production will bump into these physical limits and will then plunge downward with a sudden and uncontrollable decline in both population and industrial capacity. Since technological progress cannot expand all physical resources indefinitely, it would be better to establish conscious limits on our future growth rather than to let nature establish them for us in catastrophic fashion.

There are five basic factors that ultimately limit growth in this planet— population, agricultural production, natural resource, industrial production and pollution. According to the Meadows team, continued exponential growth in world's population, industrial output, agricultural and natural resource consumption and pollution from these activities would result in severe constraints on all global resources by 2050 to 2070. The model is built specifically to investigate five major trends of global concern:

- rapid population growth,
- accelerating industrialization
- exponential increase in demand for agricultural output
- depletion of natural resources
- deteriorating environment.

The conclusions of the Meadows team are:

1. If the present growth trends in world population, industrialization, pollution, food production, and resource depletion continue unchanged, the limits to growth on this planet will be reached sometime within the next one hundred years. The most probable result will be a rather sudden and uncontrollable decline in both population and industrial capacity.
2. It is possible to alter these growth trends and to establish a condition of ecological and economic stability that is sustainable far into the future.
3. If the world's people decide to strive for this second outcome rather than the first, the sooner they begin working to attain it, the greater will be their chances of success.

According to Turner, Four key elements are required to understand the LTG Model. These are:

- The presence of positive and negative feed- back loops and the relative strength of these feed back loops.

- The presence of resources such as renewable and non-renewable resources, their recovery potential and the rate of degradation.
- Delays in signals from one part of the world system to another which can have serious consequence on a possible solution which implies inter-temporal effects of adverse environmental degradation.
- The last is treating the world system as a complete system of sub-systems which calls for a holistic approach that requires taking into consideration the impacts on all the sectors simultaneously.

13.3 Factors Affecting Growth in the Model

There are five basic factors that ultimately limit growth in this planet— population, agricultural production, natural resource, industrial production and pollution.

- The limits model postulated in 1972 that world population had been growing exponentially in the last century and that if the present rate of growth continued, this world's population of 3.6 billion in 1972 would double in the next thirty-five years.
- The model in a similar way highlighted the growth of demand for food production;
- Growth in the demand for non-renewable resources like the gold, zinc, lead, tin, uranium, silver and other minerals and renewable resources;
- Industrial growth influenced by rate of investment and depreciation,
- finally the model explained increase in pollution levels depending on capital consumption.

Each of the five factors mentioned in the model, interacts constantly with all the others.

- population cannot grow without food
- food production is increased by growth of capital
- more capital requires more resources
- discarded resources become pollution
- pollution interferes with the growth of both population and food

The model observed that over long time periods each of these factors also feeds back to influence itself.

One of the reasons for the widespread attention paid to the 'Limits to Growth' model was that it derives its conclusion from a computerised global model which incorporates the essential inter-connections between resource-use, population and pollution. In the model the variable 'Quality of Life' is held to depend positively on food supplies and industrial outputs, and negatively on population density and pollution. Food output, industrial output, population and pollution are interlinked in various ways. For example, population growth is positively related to food output but food output is negatively related to pollution levels, which, in turn, is positively related to industrial output. These links are called "feedback mechanisms". The feedback mechanism could be positive or negative. A positive feedback is one where the growth in one variable causes a change in another which causes further growth in initial variables. On the other hand, when the growth in one variable causes changes in another which reduces the growth in the initial variable, it is a negative feedback.

A simplified and slightly modified model of Meadows and Forrester depicting the above inter-relationship is given in figure 13.1 The figure 13.1 highlights the inter-relationships between five limiting factors—shortage of maintainable natural resources, of non-maintainable natural resources of man-made capital assets, level of environmental pollution and size of population. In the figure solid lines represent positive and broken lines represent negative feedback. Thus in the figure, output per head Q/N is assumed to be higher.

- Higher is the amount of maintainable natural resources per head, or L/N

- Higher is the amount of remaining stock of non-maintainable (exhaustible) natural resources per head, E/N
- Higher is the amount of man-made capital assets per head K/N,
- More advanced in the state of technology (T), and
- Lower is the level of pollution

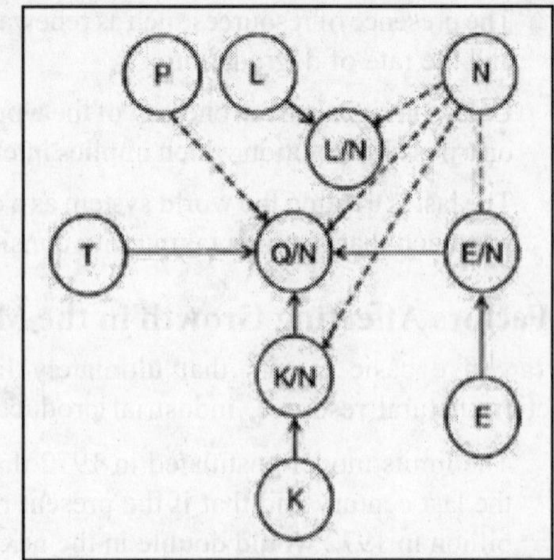

Figure 13.1 A Simplified Model of Variables Limiting Economic Growth

Q – Total output of goods and services; N – Population; L - A unit of land E - amount of exhaustible resources; K - Capital resources; T - State of technical knowledge; P - amount of Environmental Pollution.

13.4 Predictions of the Model

The model predicted that if the present growth trends in world population, industrialization, pollution, food production, and resource depletion continue unchanged, the limits to growth on this planet will be reached sometime within the next one hundred years. There are some basic truths which Prof. Meadows emphasised through their work.

- There must be an end sooner or later to the exponential growth of population and output and the limit to such a growth may come upon us unexpectedly if we are not careful.
- The ultimate limit to growth may become effective either because of the exhaustion of non-maintainable natural resources or because of pressure upon the limited supply of maintainable natural resources or because of the chocking effects of excessive environmental pollution.

The results of the model were arrived through computer simulation, which assumes some mathematical relationship to be true and uses the computer to determine what sort of future it implies.

The authors describe the process:

". . . the collapse occurs because of non-renewable resources depletion. The industrial capital stock grows to a level that requires an enormous input of resources. In the very process of that growth, it depletes a large fraction of the resource reserves available. . . . Finally investment cannot keep up with the depreciation and the industrial base collapses taking with it the services and agricultural systems, which have become dependent on industrial inputs. . . . Population finally decreases when the death rate is driven upward by lack of food and health services'. Hence Forrester and Meadows concluded that if there is no major change in the present system, population and industrial growth will certainly stop within the next century at the latest. Their prescription calls for a transition to a world of Zero Economic Growth."

13.5 Criticisms

1. The assumption on non-renewable resources has been criticized by Mahbub Ul Haq. He criticised the model's assumption that reserve of the non-renewable resources was finite and would increase only by five times over the next one hundred years. The model suggests that mankind faces a final curtain about one hundred years from now through depletion of non-renewable resources. However, the figures on reserves of non-renewable resources

show increase in the reserves of some resources. Further, the pessimism of the assumption of non-renewable resources becomes even more evident if one considers that the concept of resources itself is a dynamic one. Many things become resources over a period of time. The expansion of the last one hundred years has mainly been rendered possible with the new resources of petroleum, aluminium and atomic and other sources of energy. For example, there exists a vast potential for exploiting resources on the sea bed. Reserves of nodular materials—distributed over the ocean floor, are estimated to be sufficient to sustain a mining rate of four hundred million tonnes a year virtually for an unlimited period of time. If only one hundred million tonnes of nodules are recovered every year—it would add to the annual production of copper, nickel, manganese and cobalt to the extent of roughly one-fourth, three times, six times and twelve times respectively compared to current world production levels. Thus the generalisation of the 'limits model about complete disappearance of all renewable resources, at a particular point of time, in the future, is a figment of imagination. The problem is not one of expecting natural resources to accommodate forever our current patterns of growth, production and consumption. Clearly they will not. However, as resources become scarce, they tend to get recycled and reused thus paving the way for the efficient use of resources. Hence, they will last long enough to allow us time to make deliberate adjustments in the way we use them so that resource-needs can be met indefinitely.'

2. Role of technological improvement and input substitution ignored: A major criticism of the LTG model has been the omission of technological improvement and input substitution. It has been pointed out that the model assumes a fixed stock of exhaustible, non-renewable resources. The on-going production activities are said to result in irretrievable loss of these resources. But continuing technological improvements which facilitates more effective use of the same fixed stock of resources and the scope of input substitution, seriously undercut the no-growth argument. Prof. William Nordhaus, who made a study of the Forrester-Meadows Model, refers to it as 'iron law of resource use'. To make the model more realistic, Nordhaus allowed for substitution among inputs in the process of production. Similarly the model assumed that population, capital stock and pollution would grow at exponential ratio, but the technology to fight pollution would not grow at exponential rate. This assumption made the model inherently unstable.

Turning to the issue of population growth, the LTG model predicts that there is an optimal size of population and any excessive population above this optimum size can become destructive. It assumed in 1972, that population will continue to grow exponentially to double itself in another thirty-five years. But empirical studies suggest a 'demographic transition' during the process of economic growth, as a result of growing affluence that dampens the rate of new births.

While the limits-model speaks of continued economic growth as impossible, the critics of the model have established it as a possibility, but some economists argue that continued economic growth is undesirable. This argument implies a choice. We can either follow a continued economic growth or reach a state of zero economic growth. It is argued that continued economic growth involves high social and cultural costs and results in general degradation of the quality of life. Perhaps that is why continued economic growth is considered as undesirable.

The assumptions regarding pollution are criticised as the weakest part of the model, as one devoid of any scientific basis. The model claims that pollution rises at the same speed as the growth of capital stock and further assumes that the earth's capacity to absorb pollutants is four times the present annual level and that pollution levels beyond certain limits will start affecting human mortality. While it may be true that accumulating pollution levels will deteriorate quality of life and health, there is little evidence to show that life itself will be destroyed. What is more, the authors do not consider that higher levels of industrial development will allow societies to devote additional resources to taking care of the pollution problem without sacrificing continued economic growth. Further, it is only with continued economic growth, that the additional resources, required to achieve the desired standards of air and water quality, can be raised. Some economists say that 'Zero Economic Growth' itself makes demand on resources. Hence ZEG merely postpones a collapse, which is done even by a negative growth. Any rate of economic activity produces an eventual collapse.

The role of price mechanism is not considered by the LTG model. As resources become scarcer, price will rise and new technology will be stimulated along with search for new materials and substitutes. However, this does not invalidate LTG thesis because the exponentially increasing impact of growth nullifies any of the adaptive behaviour we might expect from the market system.

Critics have exposed faults in the mathematics and underlying assumption. Many critics have criticised the limits model for using arbitrary numbers. They argue that it makes little sense to test for the sensitivity of the model or to changes in parameter value, if the initial parameter value is arbitrarily chosen. It is further pointed out that the nature of resource estimates in LTG model is dubious. The reserve estimates of resources have been revised over time and are likely to change again in our own life time—hence the model based on such old estimates cannot yield proper results.

13.6 Policy Implications

A major policy conclusion from the model is the prescription of a Zero Growth Rate—both in population and material production. The model did not consider the choices open to society; even if physical limits to growth were conceded. First, there is the choice between development and defense —it is said that an 'environment quality' conscious society could devote less to defense which consumes a major share of world resources and generates a high pollution —and more to development. Secondly, there is the choice of patterns of growth—a less resource consuming different pattern of consumption could be chosen. Finally, it has been suggested that the rich nations could stop growing and the developing nations can grow without creating pressures on global physical limits.

A second major policy concern is the world income distribution. The model's prescription that the collapse of the world can be avoided by zero economic growth implies the possibility of massive redistribution of income. For, if present world income distribution is freezed, zero economic growth will not save the world. "It would only bring about a confrontation between the haves and the 'have-not's". It is said that the question of distribution of income was recognised by the limits model but the model did not discuss as to how such a massive redistribution of income can be effected in a stagnant world.

13.7 Update on the Limit to Growth Model

On the 20th anniversary of the publication of *Limits to Growth*, the team updated *Limits* in a book called *Beyond the Limits*. *Beyond the Limits* argued that in many areas the model had expanded the demands on the planet's resources and sinks, beyond what could be sustained over time. The main challenge identified in *Beyond the Limits* was how to move the world back into sustainable territory.

In a new study, *Limits to Growth: The 30Year Update*, the authors are far more pessimistic than they were in 1972 and conclude that humanity is dangerously in a state of overshoot. Some of the signs of such an overshoot are:

- Sea level has risen 1020 cm since 1900. Most nonpolar glaciers are retreating, and the extent and thickness of Arctic sea ice is decreasing in summer.
- The gap between rich and poor, is widening. In 1998 more than 45 percent of the globe's people had to live on incomes averaging $2 a day or less; while, the richest one fifth of the world's population has 85 percent of the global GNP.
- Around 75 percent of the world's oceanic fisheries were fished at or beyond capacity (FAO estimate , 2002). The North Atlantic cod have been almost pushed to biological extinction.
- Nearly 38 percent, or nearly 1.4 billion acres, of currently used agricultural land has been degraded.

They point out that "we are drawing on the world's resources faster than they can be restored, and we are releasing wastes and pollutants faster than the Earth can absorb them or render them harmless. They are leading us toward global environmental and economic collapse —but there may still be time to address these problems and soften their impact." They warn that much must change if the world is to avoid the serious consequences of overshoot in the 21st century.

Conclusion

When *The Limits to Growth* was first published in 1972, the model was attacked by many who didn't understand or misrepresented its assertions, dismissing it as an exaggeration. But the happenings in the last 30 years only validate the book's warnings. In the word of Mathew Simmons, the noted energy economist, the most incredible aspect of the book is the accuracy of the basic trend extrapolation concerns after thirty years. He adds that there is nothing in the book which has so far been even vaguely invalidated and states that the chilling warnings of how powerful exponential growth rate can be are right on the track. In the words of Mathew Simmons:

"The most amazing aspect of the book is how accurate many of the basic trend extrapolations ... still are some 30 years later." Thirty years ago, it seemed unimaginable that humanity could expand its numbers and economy enough to alter the Earth's natural systems. But experience with the global climate system and the stratospheric ozone layer have proved them wrong. Simmons points out that the LtG "was never a doomsday book. Rather it was hoped that it would trigger a change in the flow of human trends to avoid such a doomsday."

To conclude it is clear that the appropriate response to environmental problems is not to prevent the expansion of the economy, but rather to provide a powerful set of incentives to reduce those activities that degrade the environment. With incentives as a basic part of the economic structure, the inevitable catastrophe envisioned may be avoided. Continued economic growth and the associated increases in standards of living are consistent with improvements in environmental quality, if producers and consumers economise on their use of environmental resources. Economists today prescribe a policy of 'sustainable growth' for global equilibrium, from an ecological and economic point of view.

Questions

1. Explain the prognosis of the limits to growth model. How far due to agree with the model. Justify your stand.
2. What are the criticisms to the LTG model.

Exercise

Read the book A Synopsis: Limits to Growth: The 30-Year Update by Meadows, Jorgen Randers, and Dennis Meadows or its synopsis downloadble from the website:

http://donellameadows.org/archives/a-synopsis-limits-to-growth-the-30-year-update/

Using data on ecological foot prints , and carrying capacity , comment on the truth of the LTG model.

14

ENVIRONMENTAL KUZNETS CURVE

Without adequate environmental protection, development is undermined. Without development, resources will be inadequate for needed investments and environmental protection will fail. In short, promoting development and protecting the environment are complementary.

-The World Development Report ,1992

Economic growth that provides us with crucial inputs, outputs and amenities can also impair the earth's ability to support life. Many economists and environmentalists emphasize that economic development is necessarily at the cost of environment. Some of the books and articles that support this view are: the Limits to Growth by the Club of Rome, Costs of Economic Growth by Mishan, Barry Commoner's "The Closing Circle", "Silent Spring" by Rachel Carson, Goldsmith's "Blue Print for Survival" and Boulding's "The Coming of the Spaceship Earth". These works contend that continued and reckless economic growth would result in an environmental catastrophe that would hamper future prospects of economic development. Environmental degradation can cause irreversible damage once certain ecological thresholds have been crossed. Thus economic growth comes with a price tag - environmental degradation.

14.1 Growth Vs Environment

The anti-growth theorists strongly feel that the world may not be able to sustain economic growth indefinitely without running into resource constraints or without polluting valuable natural resources. They argue that environmental degradation will eventually halt economic growth. Increase in the volume of economic activities requires larger inputs of resources and generates larger quantities of wastes. Daly observed that increased extraction of natural resources, accumulation of waste and concentration of pollutants will eventually exceed the carrying capacity of the biosphere, degrade environmental quality and lead to a decline in human welfare, despite rising incomes.

Those who support economic growth, however, argue that economic growth is necessary to ensure environmental improvement. Beckerman (1992) observed that "in the end, the best – and probably the only way to attain a decent environment in most countries is to become rich". The World Bank, in its 1992 World Development Report, reported that "economic growth is essential for environmental stewardship".

Relationship between economic growth and environmental quality is not the same along a country's development path. During the process of economic development, initially the quality of the environment deteriorates as pollution emissions increase, and then after some time the environmental quality improves again as an economy achieves higher levels of income and development. Many research articles on environment – development linkages published during the 1990s emphasized that "environmental pressure increases faster than income in the early stage of development and slows down relative to GDP growth in higher income levels. This systematic relationship between income change and environmental quality has been called the Environmental Kuznets Curve (EKC)" (Dinda, 2004).

14.2 The EKC Concept

The EKC hypothesizes that environmental degradation will initially increase with rising levels of income per capita and, upon reaching an income turning point, will start to decrease. Stern pointed out that the environmental Kuznets curve (EKC) is a hypothesized relationship between various indicators of environmental degradation and income per capita. Research studies show that the environmental impact indicator is an inverted U-shaped function of income per capita. The EKC concept was first proposed and tested by Grossman and Krueger in the early 1990s in their study of the potential impacts of NAFTA. The term "Environmental Kuznets Curve" was coined by Seldon and Song (1994) based on an earlier works by Grossman and Krueger (1992), Shafik and Bandyopadhyay (1992) and Panayotou (1993). A large number of studies have tested the existence of EKC for various pollutants.

In the early stages of economic development, natural resource stock is abundant and wastes are less because of low economic activity. As economy develops by promoting industrialization, resource depletion and waste production accelerate and environmental degradation increases. At higher levels of economic development, the production process of the economy becomes more information based and the service sector is boosted. This, combined with improvements in technology and increased demand for environmental quality, results in a steady decline of environmental degradation. After a certain level of per capita income is reached, pollution is negatively linked with the process of economic growth and further economic development improves the quality of environment. This relationship between environmental degradation and per capita income of an economy is captured by the EKC.

14.3 EKC and the I = PAT Equation

In the IPAT, an environmental impact I is expressed as a product of factors – population, *P*, "affluence" (GDP per capita), A and "technology," T.

$$I = P \times A \times T$$

In the I = P.A.T equation, *P* multiplied by *A* is just GDP. Therefore the technology factor *T* is the ratio of the environmental impact to GDP (I / GDP). The Environmental Kuznets Curve hypothesis says that T (Technology) is a function of A (Affluence) that increases at small values of *A* and declines at high values of *A*. Eric Kemp-Benedict observes that any functional form of an environmental Kuznets curve must reflect this.

The IPAT equation and the EKC are in a sense both looking at the same issue - limits to growth; but the EKC approach is optimistic. The advocates of the IPAT equation argued that the combined growth in population, affluence and technology would have to be limited in order to preserve the environment. Thus the IPAT equation implied that continued economic growth is impossible. EKC does not imply this and is hence different from the IPAT equation. This is based on two arguments: first, the technology can serve to offset the detrimental effects of rising population and affluence. Secondly, the IPAT model does not include any behavioral response to detrimental environmental degradation in the form of prices and policy changes. The turning point of the U shaped EKC and the falling portion of the EKC are due to (1) technological improvements made possible by rising GNP and (2) policy responses to environmental degradation. This makes the EKC different from the IPAT equation.

14.4 Shape of the EKC

EKC hypothesizes that environmental degradation will initially increase with per capita income and upon reaching an income turning point, will start to decrease. EKC is a bell shaped curve – inverted 'U' shape.

The EKC is so called after Simon Kuznets who in 1995 predicted that as capita income increases, income inequality also increases at first and then starts declining after reaching the turning point. Kuznets represented this relationship between income per capita and income inequality by a bell-shaped curve which came to be popularly known as the Kuznets Curve. In 1990s it was suggested that the level of environmental degradation and per capita income follows the same inverted- U-shaped relationship as does income inequality and per capita income in the original Kuznets Curve.

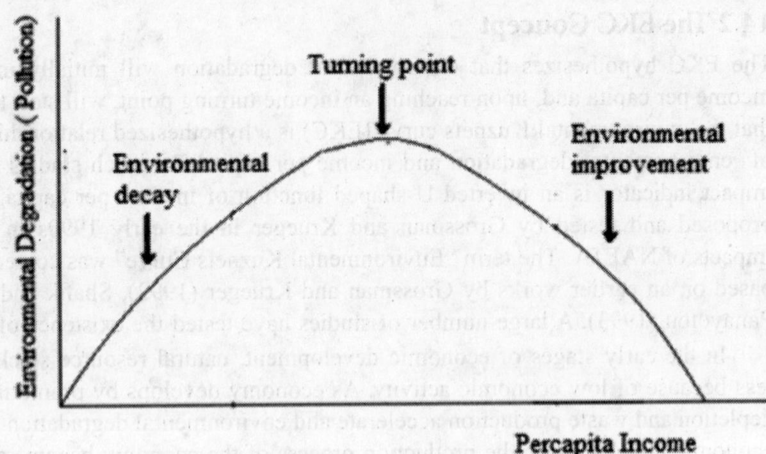

Figure 14.1 Environmental Kuznets Curve

The inverted-U-shaped relationship between economic growth and an indicator of environmental degradation came to be known as the EKC due to its resemblance to Kuznets' inverted U relationship between income inequality and economic development.

14.5 The Three Effects

Several effects are given for explaining the shape of the EKC. These are:

- Scale Effect
- Composition Effect
- Technological Effect
- Income effect

The scale effect implies that increased scale of production may place greater stress on the environment. Assuming that technology does not change, more output requires more input and results in more wastes. Thus as the scale of economic activity increases to meet the growing demand, there is an increase in environmental degradation which is termed as scale effect. Graphically, the scale effect is a monotonically increasing function of income since the larger the scale of economic activity, higher is the level of pollution, when there is no change in the structure of the economy and technology.

The Composition or structural effect refers to changes in the composition of economic activity - that accompanies economic growth. As economy grows the composition of economic activity changes and the resulting environmental effects can be positive or negative depending on the kind of change in the composition of economic activity. Hence the changing share of industry and agriculture and the service sector in GDP represent structural change. Initially at low levels of development, economic growth results in a shift from agriculture to industrialization which increases pollution levels. At high levels of development, the shift is from industries to service sector, and as a result, pollution decreases. Hence the change in the share of industry in GDP represents structural change. Initially as share of industry rises pollution increases and later as share of industry decreases pollution decreases. This is composition effect and it is represented as an inverted U (non- monotonic) function of GDP.

Technology effect refers to the change in environmental quality arising from a switch to more environmentally sustainable production techniques. Due to technology effect countries switch over to a green (less polluting clean) technology instead of 'brown'(polluting and resource consuming) technology. The technology effect is determined by the combined influence of incomes and a producers' response to market and institutional incentives.

Income effect: Most of the EKC models have emphasized the role of income elasticity of demand for environmental quality. Environmental quality is a luxury good. The demand for environmental quality is greater at high income. The income elasticity of demand for environmental quality is positive and greater than 1. The consumers with higher incomes are willing to spend more for green products and demand government action for environmental protection. This is reflected through defensive expenditures and choice of less environmentally damaging products.

Dinda (2004) explains this as follows:

"Poor people have little demand for environmental quality; however, as a society becomes richer, its members may intensify their demands for a healthier and cleaner environment. The consumers with higher incomes are not only willing to spend more for green products but also create pressure for environmental protection and regulations. In most cases where emissions have declined with rising income, the reductions have been due to local and national institutional reforms, such as environmental legislation and market-based incentives to reduce environmental degradation".

Expressed in simple terms, at low income levels, pollution is high because pollution abatement technology is not available and pollution abatement is not a priority for people. At high income levels, environmental awareness makes people demand better environmental quality and stricter pollution control policy from government; further at high income levels better techniques of pollution abatement are available.

Initially as the economy is devoting all its resources and efforts for development and higher growth rate, pollution increases with growth (scale effect) and hence the EKC is rising upwards. Soon with the achievement of a moderately higher growth rate, the economy's structure changes and hence the share of less polluting industries in GDP - service sector - increases (composition effect). Finally when economy is going through high growth, environmental awareness is high and there is demand from people for the adoption of environmentally friendly technologies and environmental regulation. As a result pollution decreases and EKC slopes downwards (technology or abatement effect).

One of the main contributors to the work on the Environmental Kuznets Curve is Stern. Stern points out that there are both **proximate and underlying factors** that explain the shape of the EKC. While the scale effect, the composition effect and technology effect are proximate causes, environmental regulation, awareness and education are underlying causes.

14.6 Existence and Turning Point of the EKC

The EKC shows that economic growth, per se, is not, a threat to the environment. The underlying reasoning is that a country cannot invest in abatement until they have reached a certain level, a turning point, of income. The EKC helps one to know where a country is in terms of environmental protection. The turning point of an EKC where environmental quality improves with rising per capita income is relevant for policy decisions. The estimated value of the turning point can guide the policy makers in knowing how long it will take for the economy to reach these turning points under the existing growth rate. The important information the EKC provides for policy makers is: at which level of income there is a turning point in environmental degradation. Adoption of proper policies can change the steepness of the EKC and thereby lower the turning point. Further early implementation of appropriate policies will help in reaching the turning point earlier.

Table 14.1 lists select pollutants and the estimated turning point. Shafik (1994), Selden and Song (1994), Grossman and Krueger (1995) and Cole *et al.* (1997) are most widely cited studies. EKC has been tested for almost all pollutants.SO_2, SPM, CO, NOx, Lead and VOC. Studies revealed turning points and even the shape of the EKC varies widely between studies. A brief note on select studies is given below:

Grossman and Krueger (1991) reported the existence of an EKC relationship for ambient levels of sulfur dioxide and dark matter (smoke). The turning point was observed in the range of about $4,000 to $5,000 of per capita income using a purchasing power parity measure (approximately equal to $6,200 to $8,200 in 2001 U.S. dollars) . For SPM the turning point was observed at lower levels of income.

Shafik and Bandopadhyay (1992) estimated the relationship between economic growth and several key indicators of environmental quality reported in the World Bank's cross-country time-series data sets. The results for sulfur dioxide, suspended particulate matter, and fecal coliform showed the existence of an EKC . The turning-point incomes in 1985 US dollars for these pollutants were observed to be $3,700, $3,300 and $1,400 respectively. (In 2001 U. S. dollars, the turning points would be about $6,100, $5,400, and $2,300).

Selden and Song (1994) examined EKC for SO_2, SPM, oxides of nitrogen and carbon monoxide. They tested for the existence of an EKC relationship for four major pollutants in developed countries with respect to per capita income. Their results supported the existence of an EKC relationship for all four air pollutants. They found turning points of $8,700 for SO_2, $11,200 for NOx, $10,300 for SPM, and $5,600 for Carbon monoxide.

Grossman and Krueger (1995) made use of the data from Global Environment Monitoring System's Air Project and Water Project for some of the important pollutants and found an EKC relationship for some of the indicators selected for the analysis. They focused on river basins. They estimated turning-point incomes (in 1985.U S. dollars) for 11 indicators which is shown in table 14.1.

Table 14.1 Turning point for Select Pollutants - Grossman Kruger 1995 Study Result

Pollutant	EKC Turning Point	
	1985 US $	2003 US $ (approximate)
Arsenic	4900	8300
BOD	7623	12800
Cadmium	5000	8400
COD	7853	13300
DO	2703	4500
Fecal Coliform	7955	13500
Nitrates	2000	3400
Lead	10,500	17, 700
Smoke	6200	10500
SO_2	4100	6900
Total coliform	3000	5000

Source: 1. Grossman and Krueger (1995) and 2. Yandle Bruce, Maya Vijayaraghavan, and Madhusudan Bhattarai (2002)

Cole, Rayner, and Bates (1997) tested EKC using cross-country panel data sets. The environmental indicators used in this analysis are: carbon dioxide, carbonated fluorocarbons (CFCs) and halons, methane, nitrogen dioxide, sulfur dioxide, suspended particulates, carbon monoxide, nitrates, municipal waste, energy consumption and traffic volumes. Mostly data covered was for OECD countries. The study found the turning point of CO and NO_2 emissions to be around $9,900 and $14,700, respectively They concluded that "meaningful EKCs exist only for local air pollutants, while indicators with a more global, more indirect, environmental impact either increase with income or else have high turning points with large standard errors".

Studies reveal three shapes of EKC: (a) monotonically increasing (b) inverted 'U' shaped (c) 'N' shaped. From various research studies it is reported that sulfur dioxide (SO_2) and oxides of nitrogen (NOx) usually conform with the EKC relationship, whereas the stock pollutants such as waste and carbon dioxide (CO_2) often exhibit the monotonically rising relationship. Christoph Martin Lieb (2003) observed that EKC is monotonically rising both for stock and global pollutants.

The shape of the EKC is sensitive to:

- **the time period chosen:** Harbaugh et al. (2000) extended the data base of the 1991 study by Grossman and Krueger by another 10 years, and found that the estimated pollution-income relationship turned into an inverted-S shape.
- **the choice of the countries in the sample:** Stern and Common (2001) enlarged the database of an earlier study by Seldon and Song (that included 22 OECD countries) by including 73 countries, most of which are developing countries and concluded that the "turning point of the EKC becomes quite higher when the data of developing countries are included or separately estimated".
- **Environmental measurements:** measures of environmental degradation may be classified as emission of the pollutants and environmental concentrations of pollutants. While the former is a flow measurement the latter is a stock measurement. It is easier to obtain an inverted-U curve for concentration than for emission indicators as concentration is a more direct environmental quality indicator.

The turning point is dependent on:

- whether the pollution indicators reflect the average environment situation of a whole country or
- whether they merely illustrate the situation in urban areas.
- Whether the area covered is residential area or commercial area – Dinda observes that the turning point of the EKC in residential areas proved much higher than in areas with intense commercial activity.

Of late many studies are reporting 'n' shaped or upward sloping (monotonically increasing) curve. The 'N' shaped income- pollutant relationship implies that pollution will increase indefinitely beyond a particular level of income at which the second turning point takes place.

Monotonically increasing income emission relationship is particularly true of CO_2. An EKC relationship is not sufficiently supported in the case of CO_2 emissions. Majority of studies show evidence of a monotonically rising curve for CO_2.

14.7 Policy Relevance of EKC

In 1997 Panayotou concluded that the quality of policies and institutions in a country can significantly reduce environmental degradation at low-income levels and speed up improvements at higher-income levels. His study, based on data from 30 developed and developing countries for the period 1982–94 showed that policies such as more secure property rights and better enforcement of contracts and effective environmental regulations can help flatten the EKC and reduce the environmental price of higher economic growth, as illustrated in Figure 14.2.

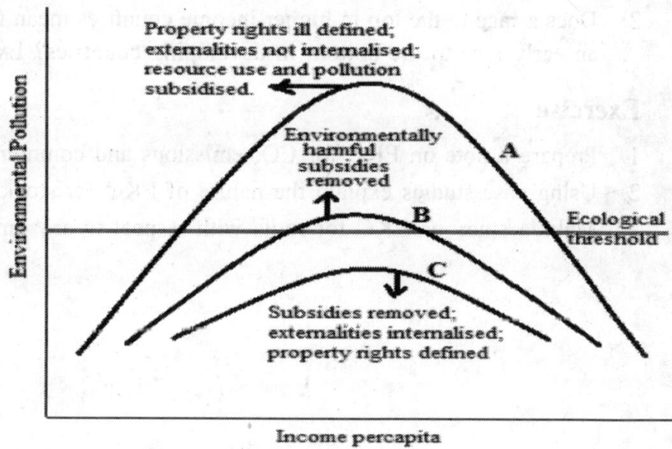

Figure 14.2 The Income – Environment Relationship Under Different Policy Scenarios

Source: Panayotou, 2003

The following observations can be made figure 14.2:

- The height or degree of convexity of the EKC reflects the environmental price of economic growth : the steeper the rising portion, the higher the sacrifice in terms of environmental quality for every increase in per capita income.
- The higher the EKC curve (EKC A and B in figure14.2) greater and more critical are the environmental impacts before the peak is reached.
- A deep EKC (EKC A) is neither environmentally nor economically optimal.

The following measure will flatten the EKC.

1. Definition and enforcement of property rights.
2. Stricter regulations and their implementation.
3. Tax on pollution and removal of environmentally harmful subsidies.

In the words of Panayotou: "better policies such as more secure property rights, better enforcement of contracts, and of effective environmental regulations can help flatten the EKC and reduce the environmental price of economic growth. Faster economic growth and higher population density (beyond a certain point) do increase moderately the environmental price of economic growth but better policies can easily offset these effects and make economic growth more environmentally friendly and sustainable (by flattening the EKC as not to violate any ecological thresholds)."

Developing countries and underdeveloped countries should consider these points while designing development policies.

Conclusion:

EKC highlights an inverted-U shaped relationship between environmental degradation and per capita income. Those who oppose economic growth focus on the scale and industrialization effects and ignore the abatement effect of higher incomes. The technology effect is ignored. Advocates of economic growth highlight the technological possibilities for pollution abatement and resource efficient production methods made possible by economic growth. All the three effects should be considered with equal importance. This will show the true dimension of the issue and help in the formulation of appropriate policy intervention in the right direction.

Question

1. Explain the EKC and account for the turning point.
2. Does a race to the top in higher-income countries mean that dirty industries are exported, causing an early race to the bottom in developing countries? Examine using EKC.

Exercise

1. Prepare a note on EKC for CO_2 emissions and comment on the nature of the curve.
2. Using case studies explain the nature of EKC for stock and flow pollutants .
3. Make a study on EKC for India with respect to any environmental quality variable.

15

ECONOMICS OF SUSTAINABLE DEVELOPMENT

"Reconciling our economic rules and practices with the dictates of environmental sustainability is now much more than a purely academic interest, it is essential for human survival."

—Sandra Postel

The Millennium Ecosystem Assessment Synthesis Report_(2005) made two important observations: "Over the past 50 years, humans have changed ecosystems more rapidly and extensively than in any comparable period of time in human history, largely to meet rapidly growing demands for food, fresh water, timber, fiber and fuel. This has resulted in a substantial and largely irreversible loss in the diversity of life on Earth"

"The changes that have been made to ecosystems have contributed to substantial net gains in human wellbeing and economic development, but these gains have been achieved at growing costs in the form of the degradation of many ecosystem services, increased risks of nonlinear changes, and the exacerbation of poverty for some groups of people. These problems, unless addressed, will substantially diminish the benefits that future generations obtain from ecosystems."

Economic progress has come at the expense of weakened biological diversity and compromised natural systems. What is needed now is a change in the production methods and consumption behavior to one that is environmentally sustainable. In other words, what is needed is sustainable development – development that lasts.

15.1 Definitions of Sustainable Development

The term sustainable development was brought into common use by the World Commission on Environment and Development in its seminal report called "Our Common Future". Despite a wide acceptance of the concept of sustainable development, no single definition is yet available which everybody accepts. Most of the definitions are built upon the view expressed by the Brundtland commission which defines sustainable development as "Development that meets the needs of the present generation without compromising the ability of future generations to meet their own needs". This definition contains three concepts that require explanation. They are: needs, development and future generation. Development is a qualitative concept, incorporating notions of improvement and progress and includes cultural, social and economic dimensions. Development is often confused with growth. Growth in contrast to development denotes, expansion of the economy in quantitative terms.

The use of the concept "needs" in the definition is linked to the distribution of resources. Elsewhere in the Brundtland report, sustainability is defined as: meeting the basic needs of all and extending to all, the opportunity to satisfy their aspirations for a better life. Economic growth has converted luxuries to need for some people while for the poor even the basic necessities are not affordable. Meeting the needs of all, therefore involves heavy environmental costs. It means redistributing resources and hence is a moral issue. Edward Barbier defines sustainable development as one which is directly concerned with increasing the material standard of living of the poor at the grassroot level which could be quantitatively measured in-terms of increased food, real income, educational services, health care, sanitation, water supply etc. In more specific terms sustainable development aims at reducing the absolute poverty of the world's poor by providing lasting and secure livelihoods that minimise resource depletion, environmental degradation, cultural disruption and social instability. Sustainable development is in this sense a development that meets the basic needs of all, particularly the poor majority, for employment, food, energy, water and housing and ensures growth of agriculture, manufacture, power and services to meet these needs.

The Brundtland definition emphasises on protecting the future generation. As emphasised by most environmentalists, we have, a moral obligation to handover the planet in good order to future generation, i.e., the present generation should bequeath a better environment to the future generation. The present generation should promote a development that enhances the natural and built environment in ways that are compatible with:

- Conservation of natural assets, offsetting any unavoidable reduction by a compensating increase so that the 'stock' does not diminish.
- Preservation of the regenerative capacity of world's natural ecosystem.
- Achieving greater social equality.
- Avoiding the imposition of added costs or risks on succeeding generations.

The intergenerational' aspect has been emphasised by few other definition too. To Tietenberg, sustainability principle involves the use of all resources in a manner which respects the needs of future generations.

An OECD "Insights" by Strange and Bayley (2008) observes that "Sustainable development is about integration: developing in a way that benefits the widest possible range of sectors, across borders and even between generations. In other words, our decisions should take into consideration potential impact on society, the environment and the economy, while keeping in mind that: our actions will have impacts elsewhere and our actions will have an impact on the future". According to Mutofa K Tolba (of UNEP), the concept of sustainable development implies:

- Help for the very poor because they are left with no option other than to destroy their environment.
- Idea of self-reliant development, within natural resource constraint.
- The idea of cost effective development, using differing economic criteria to the traditional approach; i.e., to say, development should not degrade environmental quality, nor should it reduce productivity in the long run.
- The great issues of health control, appropriate technologies, self-reliance and food, clean water and shelter for all.
- People centred initiatives are needed; human beings in other words, are the resources in the concept.

Winpenny J.T. makes the inter-generational aspect even more explicit when he says: "Sustainable development is **that** which leaves our total patrimony, including natural environmental assets, intact over a particular period. We should bequeath to future generations the same capital, embodying opportunities for potential welfare that we currently enjoy". Sustainable development, hence, rejects all "policies and practices that support current living standards by depleting the productive base, including natural resources and leaves future generation with poorer prospects and greater risk than our own". The inter-generational aspect in the definition involves 'ethical norms' pertaining to the right of future generation.

David Pearce, defines sustainable development as a vector of desirable social objectives such as an increase in real income per capita, an improvement in health and nutrition; educational achievement; access **to** resources; a fairer distribution of income and increase in basic freedom and adds that the elements to be included in the vector are open to ethical debate.

There is a plethora of definitions of the concept of sustainable development. A satisfactory definition of the concept has become the Holy Grail of environmental economics. (See box 15.1). However, all these definitions have a common focus: that sustainable development means improving the quality of human life while living within the carrying capacity of supporting eco-systems.

"Sustainable development is meeting the needs of present without compromising the ability of future generations to meet their needs."

-World Commission on Environment and Developmen,1987

Sustainable development – development that is likely to achieve lasting satisfaction of human needs and improvement of the quality of human life".

—Robert Allen, "How to Save the World".

"Our standard definition of sustainable development will be non-declining per capita utility— because of its self-evident appeal as a criterion for inter-generational equity".

—John Pezzey, 'Economic analysis of sustainable Growth and Sustainable Development, World Bank, Environment Department, Working Paper No. 15.

"We summarise the necessary conditions (for sustainable development) as "constancy of the natural capital stock. More strictly the requirements as for non-negative changes in the stock of natural resources such as soil and soil quality, ground/ and their quality, land biomass, water biomass and the waste assimilation capacity of receiving environment".

—David Pearce, Edward Barbier, Anil Markandya, *in* "Sustainable Development and Cost Benefit Analysis".

"The core idea of sustainability, then, is the concept that current decisions should not impair the prospects for maintaining or improving future living standards".

—Robert Repetto, "World Enough and Time".

Sustainable Development is development which allows all future generations to have a potential average quality of life at least as high as the average quality of life of the current generation." In this definition quality of life is a measure of the average well-being of the members of a generation and depends on traditional material consumption as well as on leisure environmental quality, etc.

—Economics of sustainable development—A Report from working group.

"Sustainable development is a social construct, referring to the long-term evolution of a hugely complex system – the human population and economy embedded within the eco-systems and bio-geo-chemical flow of the planet."

-Meadows, 1998.

BOX 15.1 Select Definitions of Sustainable Development

Although the evolution of sustainable development as the new development paradigm is the result of public pressure, the concept, as such, is not new. As early as 1849, the concept of 'sustainability' has been used by all those working on forest management. Similarly the concept of sustainability, has been frequently used in fishery economics literature and in agriculture. Sustainability is implied in Hicksian writings (1968) when he defines a person's income as the maximum amount he can spend during the week and still expect to be better off at the end of the week. Obviously Hicksian definition emphasises "Sustainable consumption" which is the focus of some of the many definitions we have today.

15.2 Components of Sustainability

There are three basic components of sustainable development: economic, social and the environment component. The three components are interdependent. The objective of sustainable development, according to Edward Barbier, is to maximise the goals in the three systems balancing the trade-offs and setting priorities among various goals.

The economic component of sustainability requires that societies pursue growth paths that generate optimal flow of income while maintaining their basic stock of man made capital, human capital and natural capital. Economic sustainability also requires internalising all costs including the environmental costs associated with production and consumption. There are three goals of an economic system which should be pursued in a sustainable way:

- increasing production of goods and services
- satisfying basic needs or reducing poverty
- improving equity

These goals must be achieved, holding the stock of capital constant and internalising all costs.

The social dimension of sustainable development is built on the twin principles of justice and equity. For a development path to be sustainable over long-period of time, wealth, resources and opportunity should be equitably shared. All citizens should have access to minimum standards of security, human rights, and social benefits such as food, health, education, shelter, and opportunities of self- development. Social sustainability is based on the concept that future generations should have the same or greater quality of life benefits as the current generation do. Failing to put emphasis on the social part of decision or action will gradually result in the collapse of the system.

Social equity implies equal opportunities to all for education and for making productive contribution to society. These have to be ensured to achieve the social goals of (a) cultural diversity (b) social justice (c) gender equality (d) public participation.

The environment component requires sustainable resource use, efficient sink function and maintenance of stock of natural capital i.e., the environment should be able to perform its three functions efficiently and uninterrupted so that ecological stability and resilience are not affected. Environmental sustainability requires proper management of our natural resources and underlines that our impacts on the environment must be minimised. Promotion of habitat restoration and preservation are also included in environmental sustainability. Environmental sustainability implies that the populations, biodiversity, and overall functionality of ecosystems are maintained over an extended period of time. Unnecessary disturbances to the environment should be avoided whenever possible.

All the three components are interdependent. The integration of the three components imply:

- **Economic Growth and Equity** –an integrated approach in order to foster responsible long-term growth while ensuring that no nation or community is left behind.

- **Conserving Natural Resources and the Environment** – To conserve our environmental heritage and natural resources for future generations.
- **Social Development** – ensure that the rich fabric of cultural and social diversity, respect the rights of workers, empower all members of the society, to play a role in determining their futures.

Table 15.1 lists the key components of sustainable development given by the World Commission on Environment and Development (1987).

Table 15.1 Components of Sustainable Development

Component	Goal
Ecological limits and equitable standards	Encourage consumption that is ecologically possible for all
Economic activity and equitable resource allocation	Ensure economic growth that allows all people to meet their needs
Population control	Prevent population from exceeding the productive potential of the ecosystem
Resource Conservation	Protect all natural Systems
Carrying capacity and sustainable yield	Identify the productive potential of the ecosystem
Resource retention	Reduce the rate of depletion for the non- renewable resources
Species diversification	Conserve and protect plant and animal species
Adverse impact minimisation	Prevent damage to the ecosystem caused by pollution
Community control	Prevent the exploitation and degradation of ecosystems
Broad national/ international framework	Jointly manage the biosphere
Economic viability	Pursue economic well-being given the government policies that limit growth
Environmental Quality	Make environmental quality a corporate goal
Environmental audit	Track the progress of environmental management Systems

Source: World Commission on Environment and Development. 1987. Our common future. Oxford University Press, U.K.

As development becomes sustainable the three systems converge as shown in figure 15.1.

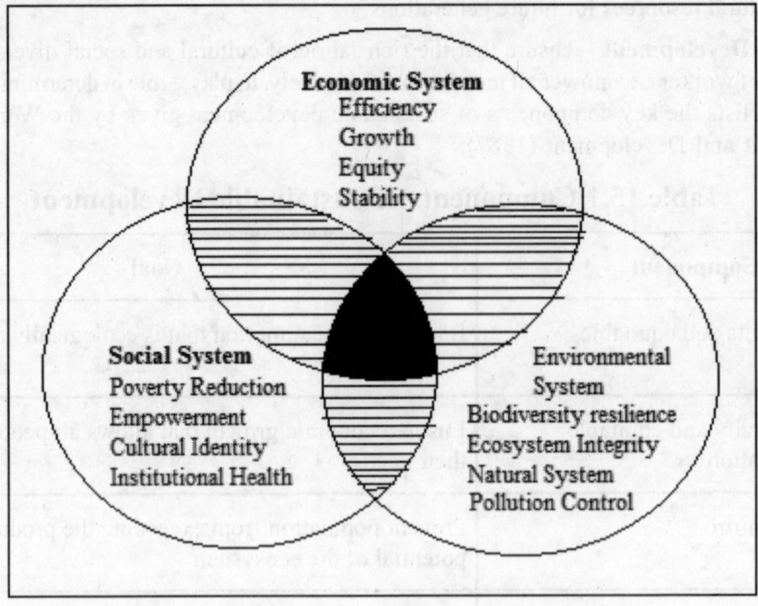

Figure 15.1 Components of Sustainability

Sustainability aims to achieve a harmony, or balance, in the interactions of the three systems, which is represented by the checked area in the diagram. As the diagram shows, the area in which the interests of all three systems converge – the shaded area in figure 15.1- is small relative to the size of each system.

15.3 Models of Sustainable Development

Sustainable development requires the recognition of the interdependencies among environmental, social, and economic systems in our world. There are many models of sustainable development which facilitate a better understanding of concepts of sustainable development. The models of sustainability help in educating policymakers and the public in general, in bringing about sustainable development. The models are:

- The Three Pillars Basic Model
- The Egg of Sustainability Model
- AtKisson's Pyramid Model
- The Prism Model of Sustainability
- The Amoeba Model

15.3.1 The Three Pillars Basic Model: The Principle of Three Pillars of Sustainability holds that to solve the sustainability problem completely, all the three pillars of sustainability must be sustainable. The three pillars are social, environmental (ecological), and economic sustainability. This model is called 'three pillars' or 'three circles model'. The three inter-locking circles in figure 15.1 explain the model. The convergence of the three circles (systems) implies the triangle of environmental (conservation), economic (growth), and social (equity) dimensions. This is the dark black area in figure 15.1 In the model,

- Environmental sustainability refers to the ability to continue indefinitely the harvesting of renewable and non- renewable resources, and keep pollution within the assimilating capacity of the environment.
- Economic sustainability is the ability to support a defined level of economic production indefinitely.
- Social sustainability is the ability of a social system, such as a country, to function at a defined level of social well-being indefinitely.

The three components /pillars – social, economic and environmental- already explained in section 15.2 is illustrated the form of pillars in figure 15.2.

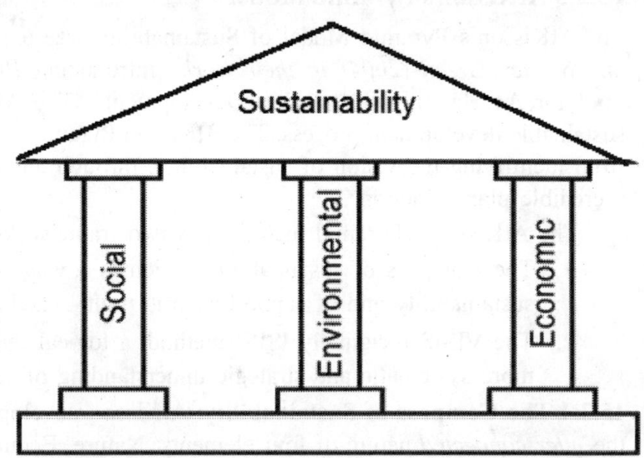

Figure 15.2 The Three Pillars of Sustainability

15.3.2 The Egg of Sustainability Model

The 'Egg of Sustainability' model was designed in 1994 by the International Union for the Conservation of Nature, IUCN. The International Development Research Center (IDRC 1997) replaced the graphics of three pillars or interlocking circles of society, economy, and the environment with the 'Egg of Sustainability'. The *Egg of Sustainability* explains the relationship between people and ecosystem as one circle inside another, like the yolk of an egg. Just as an egg is good only if both the white and yolk are good, so a society is well and sustainable only if both, people and the eco-system, are well.

The model holds that human beings can prosper only if they adapt themselves to the limits of environmental carrying capacity. Hence ecosystem is placed at the centre of the egg (figure 15.3) implying that without ecosystem wellbeing social and economic well-being won't be possible.

Thus the model is in line with the IUCN principle:

Sustainable development = human well-being + ecosystem well-being

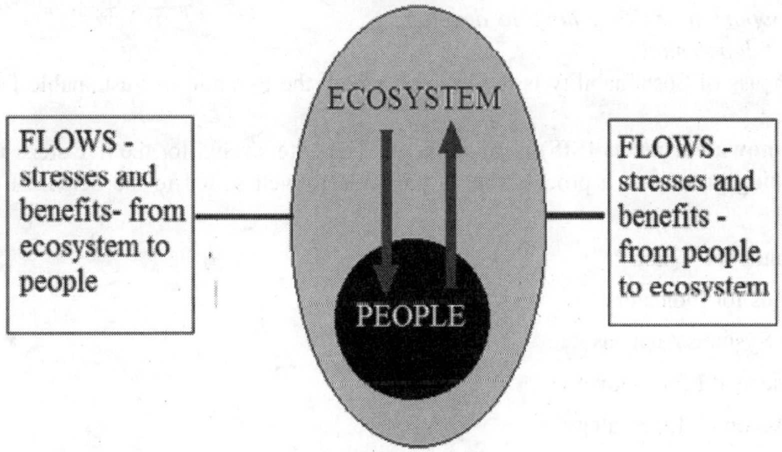

Figure 15.3 The Egg of Sustainability

15.3.3 AtKisson's Pyramid Model

The AtKisson's Pyramid Model of Sustainability was explained by *Alan AtKisson, R. Lee Hatcher, and Sydney Green (2004) in their work* "Introducing *Pyramid*: A Versatile Process and Planning Tool for Accelerating Sustainable Development". The AtKisson's Pyramid is a blue print for the sustainable development process. The AtKisson Pyramid process supports and accelerates the progress from identifying the vision of sustainability, through analysis and brainstorming and agreements on a credible plan of action.

The AtKisson's Pyramid incorporates two frameworks:

1. The Compass of sustainability which is a way of representing the different dimensions of sustainability and of supporting true multi-stakeholder engagement.
2. The VISIS (originally ISIS) method, a logical thinking process that helps groups develop a more systematic and strategic understanding of sustainable development.

15.3.4 The Compass of Sustainability: AtKisson developed the Compass of Sustainability to stress the *inter-connected* nature of four elements: Nature, Economy, Society, and well-being of all human beings. All must be healthy for sustainability to be realized. A regular compass is used to find out direction –North, East, South and West. Retaining the first letter, the sustainability compass replaces the directions with Nature, Economy, Society and Well-being of Individuals.

Briefly, the four points of the sustainability compass - Nature, Economy, Society, and Well-Being of human beings mean:

- **Nature** *refers to the ecological systems and natural resources.*
- **Economy** *is the process by which resources are put to work to produce the things and services that humans want and need.*
- **Society** *is the collective and institutional dimension of human civilization, including everything from governments to social norms regarding equity and opportunity.*
- **Well-Being** *is to satisfaction and happiness of individual people -- their health, their primary relationships, and the opportunities they have to develop their full potential.*

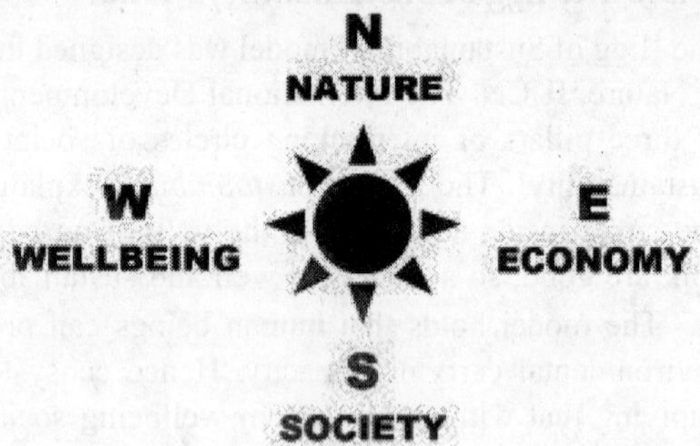

Figure 15.4. The Compass of Sustainability

Source: Atkisson Inc.

The Compass of Sustainability is the base on which the Pyramid of Sustainable Development is built.

VISIS (known earlier as ISIS) is an acronym. The letters stand for the five steps in a sequential strategic thinking process -- a process that is particularly well suited to the demands of sustainable development.

- V stands for Vision
- I stands for Indicators
- S for Systems Analysis
- The second I for Innovation
- The second S for Strategy

By following the VISIS method, the user stands a better chance of managing limited resources wisely, and successfully creating a change in the target entity, a change in the direction of sustainability.

The Pyramid combines the five steps into a structured group process to provide training, planning, or general decision-support for more sustainable outcomes [Figure 15.5].

*The Compass defines what sustainability is; and the Pyramid supports users through the process of implementing Sustainable Development. T*he Pyramid process involves working through five "Levels," corresponding to the five steps in the ISIS method.

The five steps in the model include:

- Level 1: Indicators- Measuring the trend
- Level 2: Systems- Making the connections
- Level 3: Innovations- Ideas that Make a Difference
- Level 4: Strategies: From Idea to Reality
- Level 5: Agreements: From Workshop to Real World

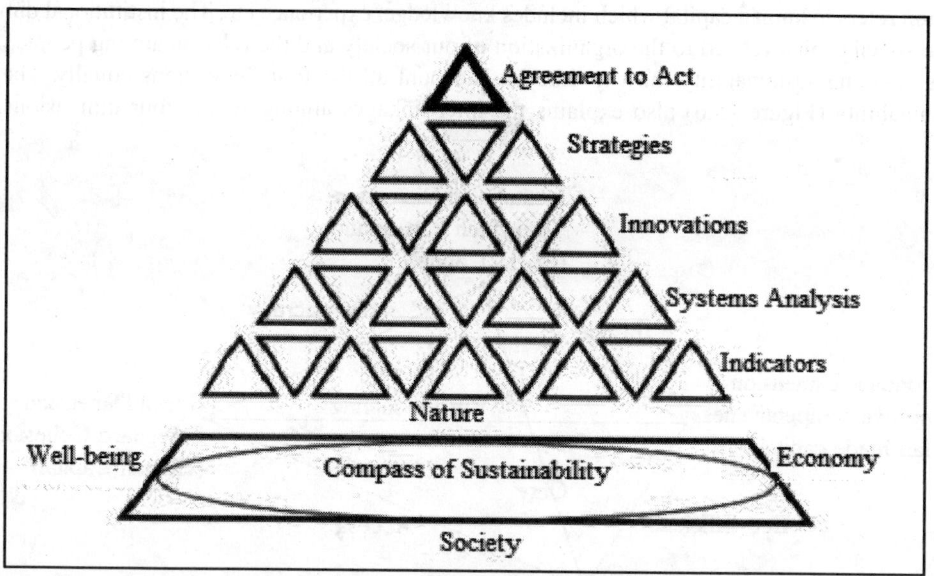

Figure 15.5 Pyramid of Sustainability

The Pyramid process *supports* and *accelerates* a group's progress on the sustainable development journey, starting with the vision of sustainability, through analysis and brainstorming, through to consensus on a credible and meaningful plan of action.

Pyramids help create action - for sustainability. Nearly two hundred to and three hundred Pyramids have been created so far, in over 20 countries. Some examples of the kinds of projects Pyramid processes have already helped to create are:

- The development of the "Lighthouse Project" concept for the Baltic Sea Region — now, there are a dozen such projects helping to promote sustainability around Europe's northern sea
- The creation of a center for sustainable design in the city of Townsville, Australia (this helped the city win its bid to host the World Ecotourism Summit)
- "Green office", "eco-school", and village development projects in many parts of Southeast Asia

Pyramid can help any organization to make sustainability a meaningful reality through a disciplined "building-up" process of information gathering, systems analysis, innovative thinking, strategic planning, and consensus.

15.3.5 The Prism Model of Sustainability

The 'prism of sustainable development' was developed by the Wuppertal school. This model defines sustainable development in terms of four components – economy, environment, society and institution. The model stipulates four dimensions:

- Economic dimension (man-made capital)
- Environmental dimension (natural capital),
- Social dimension (human capital)
- Institutional dimension (social capital).

The economic dimension stands for man-made capital such as building and roads. The environmental dimension includes natural capital comprising of non-renewable and renewable resources. The social dimension refers to human capital which includes knowledge, experience etc. The institutional dimension refers to social capital related to the organization of our society and the relation among people. Action towards attaining sustainability must to take into account all the four dimensions equally. The Prism of Sustainability (Figure 15.6) also explains the inter-linkages among all the four dimensions.

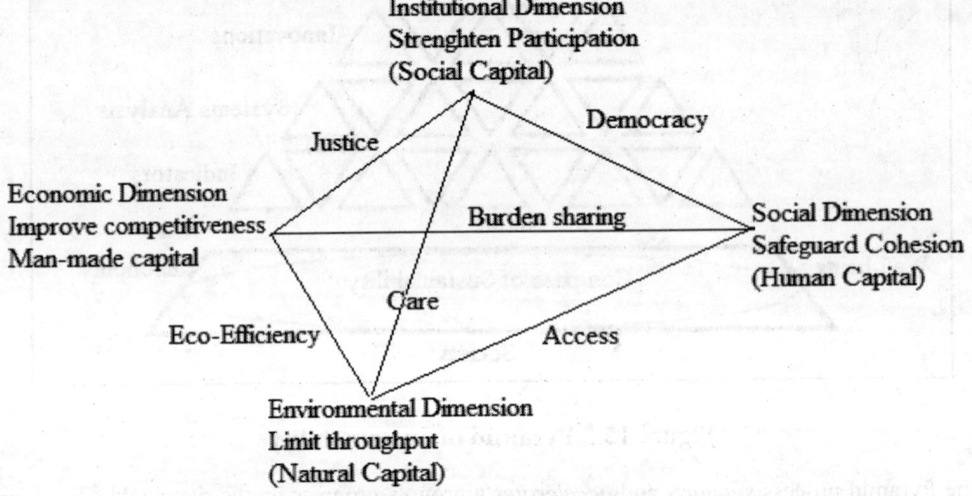

Figure 15.6 The Prism of Sustainable Development

15.3.6 The Amoeba Model

The Amoeba Model is used to visually assess a system's condition relative to an optimal condition. AMOEBA, in the Dutch language, stands for 'general method of ecosystem description and assessment'. It is a visual tool, originally designed to capture the sustainability of marine ecosystems. It helps to develop quantitative and verifiable ecological objectives, which can be used to assess the sustainability of ecosystems.

The development of an AMOEBA involves setting a reference condition that represents the natural state of a given ecosystem. This natural state is assumed to be sustainable: the further the system departs from this state, the less sustainable it becomes. The model is illustrated by a circle in which circle's circumference depicts the reference situation. The various indicators are marked in and around the circle. Lines (rays) are drawn from the centre to the indicator. Each ray is a dimension of sustainability of the ecosystem being studied. Actual situations are points on these rays that will not normally lie on the circumference.

This type of model allows simultaneous assessment of different indicators, and easy comparison between components of the system. The AMOEBA approach provides integrated information for environmental policy-making, aiming at sustainable development.

The AMOEBA approach developed by Ten Brink (1991) combines several indicators into one overall picture in order to simplify ecological information. The AMOEBA was originally developed for the Dutch Water Management Plan. Sixty indicator species were selected to represent the ecological situation in the North Sea and pre-industrial values from 1930 were used as the reference condition.

Kellett et al. (2005) explain the use of the AMOEBA model for assessing sustainability of tidal ecosystems. The AMOEBA in Figure 15.7 presents the sustainability of a coastal tidal ecosystem. The various species of the coastal tidal ecosystem considered here are: seagrass, tiger prawns, sand worms, and mangroves. The reference condition, depicted by the circle, is the optimal population size of each species in an ecosystem in a natural state. At the point of intersection of the circle and an AMOEBA arm, the reference condition has been met or exceeded.

In figure 15.7, if an arm falls short of the circle, the respective population size is too small. If an arm extends beyond the circle, the population size is too large. The tidal ecosystem is not sustainable since excepting tiger prawn, the rest of the species' population size is either smaller than the optimal size (sea grass and mangroves) or larger than the optimal size (sand worms). For tiger prawn the population size is optimum. This type of model allows simultaneous assessment of different indicators, and easy comparison between components of the system.

Bell & Morse 1999 proposed a modified version of the AMOEBA for sustainability analysis replacing the reference conditions with threshold ranges.

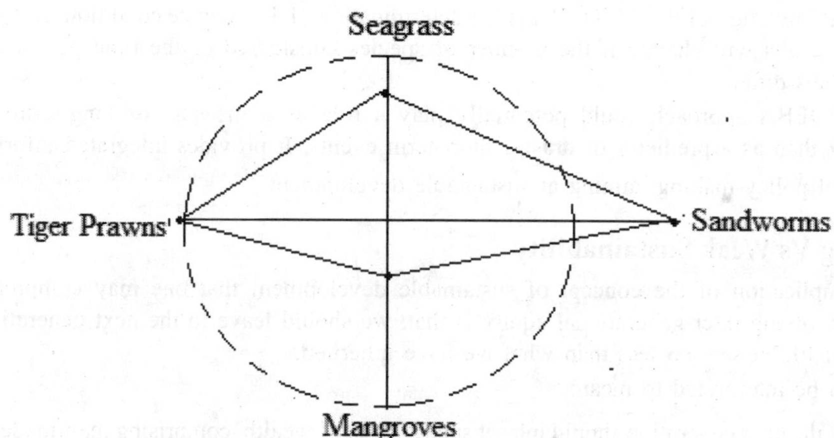

Figure 15.7 Simple AMOEBA for a Tidal Ecosystem

Source: Kellett et al.,2005, Copyright CSIRO Australia downloaded from http://www.clw.csiro.au/publications/technical2005/tr1-05.pdf

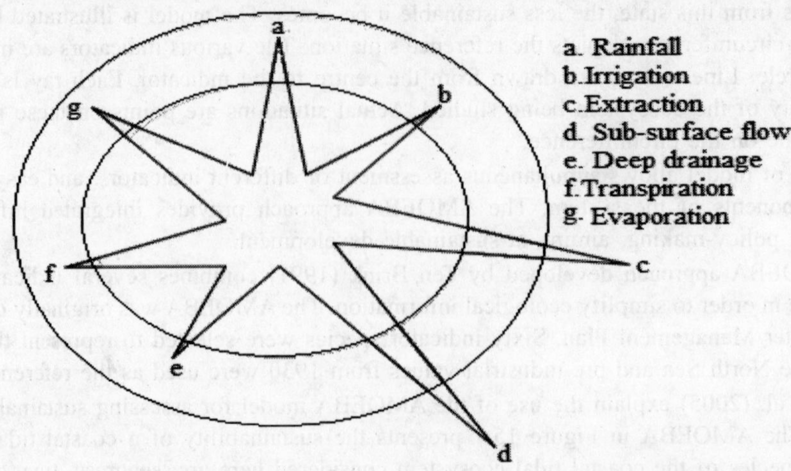

Figure 15.8 AMOEBA for Water Balance Indicators of an Irrigation System

Source: Kellett et al., 2005, Copyright CSIRO Australia downloaded from http://www.clw.csiro.au/publications/technical2005/tr1-05.pdf

In Figure 15.8 there are two circles instead of one - the inner circle depicts the lowest acceptable value for a SI and the outer circle depicts the highest acceptable value for the SI. The zone between the concentric circles is depicted as sustainable, while the area outside this zone is unsustainable

The Figure 15.8 is an AMOEBA figure for an imaginary irrigation system, in which seven water balance indicators are given. In this case, the extraction of ground water [c] is higher than the highest recommended value and hence may result in falling water tables and increased cost of pumping. However since the value of sub-surface ground water flow [d] is greater than highest recommended level, over all water balance is likely to be sustainable depending on the values of other indicators.

The main limitation of the AMOEBA is the determination of a reference condition. It is questioned whether the results will change if the number of species considered or the time period chosen for reference values differs.

The AMOEBA approach could potentially play a role as a measure of long-term ecosystem health, rather than as a predictor of drastic short-term events. It provides integrated information for environmental policy-making, aiming at sustainable development.

15.4 Strong Vs Weak Sustainability

The basic implication of the concept of sustainable development that one may comprehend from definitions involving inter-generational equity is that, we should leave to the next generation a stock of 'quality of life' assets no less than what we have inherited.

This can be interpreted to mean:

- That the next generation should inherit such a stock of wealth, comprising man-made assets and environmental assets.
- That the next generation should inherit a stock of environmental assets which is not less than that inherited by the previous generation.
- That the components of the inherited stock should be man-made assets, natural assets and human assets.

The first interpretation stresses both man-made and natural. The second emphasises on natural capital only and the third includes human capital besides natural and man-made capital. Based on the classification of capital, sustainability of development process may be verified. The conflict here is whether sustainability rule should be defined in terms of natural capital alone or in terms of aggregate capital stock, where aggregate capital stock includes:

- Man made capital (K_M) consisting of machines, buildings, roads etc.
- Human capital (K_H) comprising of the stock of knowledge and skills.
- Natural capital (K_N) that includes all renewable and non-renewable resources or any natural asset yielding a flow of ecological services with economic values over time.

Modern expositions of economic growth would add another type of capital, *social capital* (K_S). Social capital concerns the relationships between individuals, and between individuals and institutions.

Defining sustainable development as a situation where well-being for a given population is not declining, or preferably is increasing over time, Pearce et al state that this requires each generation to pass on, an undiminished stock of total capital to the next generation, thus under lining the inter-generational fairness requirement. Two rules are drawn with respect to inter-generational fairness and sustainability:

1. Sustainable development requires non-declining total wealth
2. Sustainable development requires non-declining **natural** wealth.

The first rule given above represents the idea of weak sustainability, and the second rule represents the idea of strong sustainability.

15.4.1 Weak Sustainability

The weak sustainability rule implies that all forms of capital are substitutable for each other. Based on this rule, Pearce has proposed a constant capital stock rule as a criterion for sustainability. An essential condition for sustainability is that a nation's stock of capital should not decline through time. According to Pearce and Atkinson, "The condition for sustainable development, therefore, amounts to each generation leaving the next generation a stock of productive capacity, in the form of capital assets and technology, that is capable of sustaining utility or well-being per capita than that enjoyed by the current generation". This may be expressed as:

$$dK/dt \geq 0, \text{ where } K = K_M + K_H + K_N$$

The equation given above implies that the change in the real value of aggregate assets at a point in time, *dK*/*dt*, must be at least zero in the aggregate. That is, changes in the value of the three components of the overall stock, *K*, can be traded off for each other. In other words, if some part of natural capital, K_N, is depleted then this is consistent with sustainability as long as *adequate* investment is made in other forms of wealth; e.g. assets such as buildings, roads etc which form man-made capital.

An implicit assumption in the constant capital rule (CCR) is that all forms of capital are substitutable for each other. This **weak sustainability (WS) rule,** implies that any one form of capital can be depleted provided 'proceeds' are reinvested in other forms of capital.

The weak sustainability rule implies that we can pass on less environment so long as we offset this loss by increasing the stock of roads and machinery or other man made physical capital. Weak sustainability rule will hold if there is perfect substitutability between different forms of capital. WS requires that the depletion of any form of capital is compensated by investment in some other form of capital. It is not consistent with decreasing capital stocks and 'consuming' the proceeds. For example, where a non-renewable asset such as a stock of oil is being mined, WS requires that some portion of the revenues of this mining activity be invested in alternative assets. (Atkinson et al, 1997)

15.4.2 Strong Sustainability Rule

Table 15.2 Weak and Strong Sustainability

Form of sustainabilty	Requirement
Weak Sustainability (WS)	dK/dt ≥ 0, where $K = K_M + K_H + K_N$
Strong Sustainabilty (SS)	dK/dt ≥ 0 and *dKN/dt* ≥ 0

Source: Pearce and Atkinson (modified)

The **strong sustainability (SS) rule** requires that the nations stock of natural capital is non-declining. It implies that natural capital stock cannot be substituted for man-made capital. This means that natural capital and man-made capital are complements. Herman Daly, explains through appropriate examples strict complementarity of natural and man-made capital and says that the shortage of one will severely limit the productivity of the other. The complementarity of natural resources and man-made capital is obvious from the fact that timber production is now limited by remaining forests' and not by the 'capacity of saw mills' and similarly 'fish catch is limited by fish population and not fishing boats'. Supporters of SS argue that certain functions of the environment cannot be duplicated by humans or human made capital. For example ecological assets and ecosystem that perform life support services cannot be replaced. In short, they are *critical natural capital* and hence cannot be substituted at all.

The supporters of strict complementarity of natural and man-made capital insist on *strong sustainability* (SS) *test.* What SS requires *in addition to* WS is that the stocks of K_N should not decline. Strong sustainability which requires constancy of natural capital stock, i.e., non-negative changes in the stock of natural resources and environmental quality, implies that environment should not be degraded further but improvements would be welcome. SS refers to the separate protection of the different natural capital forms. This implies that the value of natural capital should not decline and assumes unlimited replacements within natural capital. For example, rents from oil extraction could be partly invested in future energy provision.

Strong sustainability holds that certain elements of natural capital are "critical" due to their unique contribution to human well-being. These critical elements play a vital role in the functioning of an ecosystem. Thus the term 'critical natural capital' was coined. Critical natural capital refers to the particular configuration of natural capital that provides a particular set of critical ecosystem services. Critical natural capital highlights the need to maintain the ecological functioning of natural systems above certain thresholds of degradation. (Pelen et al, 2015)

In the book Blue Print for a Green Economy, Pearce et al provide four reasons why strong sustainability rule is superior to weak sustainability rule. These are (i) lack of sufficient substitutability (ii) irreversibility (iii) uncertainty and (iv) intra-generational equity. In general the supporters of strong sustainability give several reasons to justify the non-substitutability of natural capital.

Firstly, while destruction of manufactured capital is rarely irreversible, that of natural capital is almost always irreversible; besides, while manufactured capital is reproducible natural capital is not so always.

The irreversibility and uncertainty of natural capital makes natural capital unique and precious and underlines the need for its protection and preservation.

Secondly, the strong sustainability test is supported for realising social objectives besides economic efficiency argument which says that decline in natural capital below the safe minimum stock will result in unacceptable large social cost. The Brundtland report states:

"If needs are to be met on a sustainable basis, the earth's natural resource base must be conserved and enhanced." The social objectives that could be realised through strong sustainability test are:

- Justice in respect of socially disadvantaged

- Justice between generations
- Justice to nature
- Resilience to external shocks such as climatic variation and to stresses such as international indebtedness. The strong and weak sustainability test requires measuring depreciation of natural capital which is difficult and complex.

Thirdly the contribution of natural capital to human well-being is multidimensional. There are four ecosystem services that natural capital makes to human wellbeing: security, basic materials for a good life (includes consumption and production), health, and good social relations. These ecosystem services provided by natural capital play an important role in determining the economic activities of human beings and their welfare. Hence natural capital is complementary and not a substitute to manufactured capital as well as to human and social capital.

Fourthly intra-generational and inter-generational equity support SS rule. Arguing for inter-generational equity UNDP observes: "Today's generation cannot ask future generations to breathe polluted air in exchange for a greater capacity to produce goods and services. That would restrict the freedom of future generations to choose clean air over more goods and services". Hence conserving natural capital for the sake of future generation, i.e., intergenerational equity, is important. Intra-generational equity argument supports SS rule on grounds that the poor are often more adversely affected by adverse environmental quality than the rich.

Table 15.3 Main Differences between Weak and Strong Sustainability

	Strong Sustainability	Weak Sustainability
Key Idea	The substitutability of natural capital by other types of capital is severly restricted.	Natural capital and other types of capital are perfectly substitutable
Consequences	Certain human actions result in irreversible consequences	Technological innovation and monetary compensation for environmental degradation
Sustainability issue	Conserving the irreplaceable 'stocks' of critical natural capital for the sake of future generation	The total value of aggregate stock of capital should be atleat maintained or ideally increased for future generartion
Key concept	Critical natural capital	Optimal allocation of resources

Source: Adapted from Pelenc, Jérôme, Jérôme Ballet, and Tom Dedeurwaerdere, 2015

Sustainable development is an equity issue than an efficiency issue. This is not to undermine the importance of efficiency in the use of resources which is vital for achieving sustainability. However as economic efficiency is a necessary condition for sustainable development but not a sufficient condition, sustainable development is guaranteed only if intergenerational and intra generational equity is assured by the development policies pursued. Equity requirements are sufficient conditions. Thus sustainable development requires efficient management of resources for providing a decent quality of life for both the present and future generations.

15.5 Theoretical Approaches to Sustainable Development

Section 15.4 distinguished between weak and strong sustainability. While weak sustainability assumed perfect substitutability between natural capital and other forms of capital (such as physical or manmade capital and human capital), strong sustainability assumed that natural capital and other forms of capital are complements or only marginally substitutable. SS is known as ecological sustainability. Theoretical approaches to sustainable development are based on the rules of WS and SS. There are many rules or approaches for operationalising SD. They are:

- The Hartwick – Solow Approach or the Neo Classical Approach
- Ecological Economics Approach
- Pearce – Atkinson Approach / Genuine Savings Approach
- Safe Minimum Standards Approach

15.5.1 The Neo Classical Approach - Hartwick Solow Approach

The neo-classical view, or weak sustainability view, is the mainstream economists' view of sustainable development. From a neoclassical point of view sustainability is defined as the maximization of human welfare over time.

The Hartwick-Solow approach to sustainable development, represents the neo-classical perspective on the economics of sustainable development. Hartwick defined sustainability in terms of non-declining consumption over time. In 1974 Solow defined sustainable state as one which satisfies some relevant criterion of inter-generational equity. He argued that the undiscounted utility of per capita consumption should be constant over infinite time. But due to difficulties in sustaining a constant level of undiscounted utility of per capita consumption, sustainability is better interpreted in terms of consumption rather than utility.

In 1977 John Hartwick proposed a rule for ensuring non-declining consumption through time, for economies making use of a non-renewable resource in its economic process. He showed that, as long as the stock of capital did not decline overtime, non – declining consumption is possible. As the stock of oil, a type of natural capital runs down, the stock of man- made capital is built up in replacement. Hartwick's Rule states that if the rents (the surplus of revenues over production cost) derived from exhaustible resource extraction are saved and then invested entirely in reproducible capital (man-made or human capital), then under certain conditions, the levels of output and consumption will remain constant over time. That is, if, stock of natural capital is declining and if the stock of man-made and human capital is increasing in such a way that total capital stock is held constant, then consumption path will be non- declining. Here non-declining consumption path depends on the substitution possibilities of the inputs in the production process. If the Hartwick rule is followed & if resources are extracted efficiently then it is possible for the economy to have positive & constant consumption through time.

In the Hartwick model natural resource does not act as a constraint to growth. Man-made capital and natural capital are assumed to be perfect substitutes for each other. Thus non-declining natural capital is not a compulsory requirement for sustainability. The emphasis is on constant capital stock, where capital stock is total capital stock comprising of human, man-made and natural capital. Keeping natural capital constant is not required. Hence the Hartwick-Solow approach is viewed as being equivalent to weak sustainability.

The S-H criterion does not specify the minimum consumption level as requirement for sustainability; this implies that an economy can be sustainable even if 'living standards are abysmally low, provided they do not get any lower'. If there is a minimum level of consumption required to enable a decent living standard by any human being, such a minimum level of consumption must be identified to check the sustainability of the development path. Any consumption level which is lower than the minimum level required for decent living is not sustainable (Perman, et al, 2003). Sustainable development therefore requires that two conditions are satisfied:

- Non declining level of consumption through time
- The non-declining level of consumption must be above the minimum level of consumption required for a decent level of living.

Assumptions of the Hartwick- Solow Approach

The Hartwick- Solow approach assumes perfect substitutability between natural and manufactured capital. Accordingly, two inputs - exhaustible resource & physical capital - must be substitutable for one another; as the exhaustible resource is depleted, the physical capital stock is accumulated & the latter substitutes for the former in the production process in such a way that output does not diminish. Given the tremendous growth in man-made capital, world over now, susbtitutabilty assumption implies that the decline in non-renewable resources is not a problem since the decline in natural capital will be offset or compensated by the huge increase in man-made capital.

Secondly, in the Hartwick-Slolow approach price distortions due to environmental externalities are either simply ignored or assumed to be corrected without much difficulty.

Lastly, the approach assumed a positive discount rate. Present income or consumption is valued more by people than future income or consumption since future is uncertain, due to which people tend to discount futre benefits and costs. The idea of discounting future benefits and costs is an ethical issue because any decision made on the basis of the prevailing discount rate by the current generation will affect the welfare of the future generation.

If these assumptions hold Hartwick rule will promote sustainable development.

Limitations of Hartwick- Solow Approach:

1. Natural resource & man-made resource, are not substitutes but are complements. Increasing output requires increasing the use of both types of inputs in most cases. This limits operationality of Hartwick's rule.
2. It ignores the inter-linkages between the economic system and the natural ecosystem.
3. The H-S approach does not recognize the fact that beyond a certain threshold, the scale of human economic activities could cause irreversible damage to the natural environment thus ignoring the nature of the uncertainly associated with long term natural resource management. This could have a serious impact on the the quality of human life.
4. The assumption of positive discount rate is criticized. A positive discount rate that encourages people to consume more at present than in the future, is detrimental to the welfare of the future generation. If intergenerational equity is to be achieved, low discount rates or an alternative sustainability rule needs to be adopted.
5. H-S Approach ignores the impact of externalities on price.

15.5.2 Ecological Economics Approach

Ecological Economics approach (EE) recognizes the linkages between ecological & economic systems.

It is based on the premise that natural & human capital are not substitutes but are complements. According to this approach the limiting factor for economic development is natural capital. Fish have become limited, rather than fishing boats. Timber is limited by remaining forests, not by saw mills; petroleum is limited by geological deposits and atmospheric capacity to absorb CO_2, not by refining capacity. For this reason, the EE approach held that natural capital is the limiting factor to future economic growth. Due to this emphasis on natural capital and the argument that the stock of natural capital must bc constant, the ecological economics approach is referred to as strong sustainability criterion. Strong sustainability means treating natural capital (Kn) separately --on the assumption that we cannot substitute man-made capital for it. Strong sustainability holds man-made capital cannot, replace the ecosystem services particularly the life-support services, like protection from UV radiation and climate regulation.

In a deeper sense the EE approach is based on inter-generational equity. If stock of natural capital must be held constant , what is the stock level at which it must be held constant – at the existing level or at the level consistent with maintaining the critical function of natural capital (such as regulation of atmospheric composition) or at a level in between these two? The supporters of strong sustainability argue that the ideal size at which natural capital must be held constant is that level which would ensure, at the minimum, that, future generation will be left no worse-off than current generation.

In its extreme version the ecological economics approach implies that the natural capital must not be used at all. This is implied in the definition of sustainable development given by the UNESCO which asserts that:

"Every generation should leave water, air and soil resources as pure and unpolluted as when it came on earth. Each generation should leave undiminished all the species of animals it found on earth".

This is a very strong version of sustainability which is not feasible since any economic activity is bound to have some adverse effect on the environment.

Another view of sustainability by economists holds that the rule for sustainability is to prevent reductions in the level of natural capital below some constant value. If the constant level is the current level of natural capital, then it would require banning all the projects and policies having a negative impact on natural capital. If this cannot be done, then, as suggested by Pearce et al, *reductions in natural capital from specified projects / policies can be offset by investments in projects / policies which generate environmental benefits that would add to the stock of natural capital.*

Thus the rule for sustainability involves either a weak or a strong **sustainability constraint.** The weak constraint to the sustainability rule requires that the discounted sum of environmental costs must be not greater than the discounted sum of offsetting benefits **over the time period** considered. The strong constraint on the other hand requires that environmental costs are not greater than environmental benefits in **each period**.

The EE approach stresses the importance of the issue of scale. Scale, here refers to the size of a human economic system relative to global natural ecosystem. Ecological economists believe that at present the impact of the activities of the economic sub-system causes significant stress on the limited capacity of the natural ecosystem. The alarming increase in the rate of generation of toxic waste, the rapid acceleration of deforestation in the tropical rain forests, rapid trend of specie extinction, increasing evidence of stratospheric ozone depletion & global warming are all examples of this. The EE approach, underlines the recognition of biophysical limits to economic growth because the growth of economic sub-system is bounded by a finite & non-growing ecological sphere .

The ecological economics approach to sustainable development mainly comprises of the views of Herman Daly and Common and Perrings. While Daly explains sustainable development in terms of the laws of Thermodynamics using the concept of Steady State Economy, Common and Perrings define sustainability in terms of maintenance of ecosystem resilience.

Herman Daly's Steady State Economy (SSE)

Herman Daly argued for the idea of the 'steady-state economy'. Daly's arguments are based on the laws of thermodynamics, and his steady-state economy is similar to Boulding's 'Spaceship Earth', considered in section 12.3 in Chapter 12. According to Daly a steady- state economy is "one that develops qualitatively (by improvement in science, technology, and ethics) without growing quantitatively in physical dimensions;". His steady state economy refers to an "economy with constant stocks of people and artefacts, maintained at some desired, sufficient levels by low rates of maintenance 'throughput', that is, by the lowest feasible flows of matter and energy from the first stage of production (depletion of low entropy materials from the environment) to the last stage of consumption (pollution of the environment with high entropy wastes and exotic materials)." Daly's concept of Steady State Economy proposes three principles:

1. Stock of producers' and consumers' goods and human population is to be maintained at a level that is sufficient for a good life and sustainable for a long future.
2. The final benefit of all economic activity, is to be maximized, given the constant stock.
3. The rate of throughput, which is the entropic physical flow of matter and energy from nature to human economy and back to nature's sink as wastes is to be minimized, given the constant stock.

Daly's rule for sustainability says: "Never reduce the stock of natural capital below a level that generates a sustainable yield unless good substitutes are currently available for the services generated". Daly developed three **"operational principles" or management rules** under which constant natural capital stock could be maintained. These rules are:

1. For a renewable resource, the rate of harvesting should not exceed the rate of regeneration.
2. For non-renewable resources, part of the net receipts should be invested into a renewable substitute at a rate such that by the time the non-renewable resource is economically depleted, the substitute can fully assume the former role. The investment in renewable substitutes must be sufficient to make possible the same amount of consumption that the non-renewable resource permitted before exhaustion.
3. Ecological services that are required in order to maintain life shall be conserved, and waste and pollution levels are to be maintained within the natural assimilation capacity;

Daly's rule emphasizes that natural capital without good substitutes should be protected regardless of the cost of doing so. In other words, under the presumption that future generation will benefit from preserving resources, the Daly's rule requires that the current generation must make potentially large sacrifices for the sake of the posterity. To satisfy Daly's conditions a substantial reduction in resource consumption and emissions of pollutants is a must.

Common & Perrings Approach

Common and Perrings, supporters of ecological economics, have suggested that the economic perspective of 'Hartwick-Solow sustainability' needs to be complemented by an ecological approach of 'Holling-sustainability' which is based the resilience and stability of ecosystems.

Supporters of ecological economics hold that sustainability should be defined in terms of the maintenance of ecosystem resilience. The EE approach to sustainability is based on two important concepts: Stability & Resilience. Resilience is the propensity of the ecosystem to retain its organizational structure & function in essentially the same way following a significant disturbance. Resilience is a property of ecosystems rather than that of an individual population. It is the potential to 'bounce-back' in response to any disturbance like forest fires, floods etc. Stability on the other hand is the propensity of a population to return to some kind of equilibrium following a disturbance.

The concept of resilience in ecological systems was first introduced by the Canadian ecologist C S Holling. For example "a forest ecosystem, may recover from a pest infestation through an increase in the population of predators that control the pest, an expansion of species unaffected by the pest, or possibly a development of pest resistance in affected species" (Jonathan M Harris). The patterns of response may vary but the integrity of the ecosystem will be preserved.

While stability is a property relating to the populations comprising an ecosystem, resilience is a property of the ecosystem. A resilient ecosystem need not imply that all populations within the system are stable; it is quite possible that a disturbance can result in a species disappearing even though the ecosystem as a whole continuous to function in broadly the same way & so is resilient. On the other hand, individual population can only be stable if the ecosystem is resilient.

The Common-Perrings model of SD, combines ecological concepts of stability & resilience with economic efficiency. Commons & Perrings define a system as being ecologically & economically sustainable if it is resilient. Any behavior which reduces the system's resilience is potentially unsustainable behaviour. Common and Perrings showed that an inter-temporally efficient development path will not be ecologically sustainable, if the resilience of the ecosystem is adversely affected. To preserve ecological stability consistent with inter-temporal efficiency, economic-environment interactions should be organised in such a way that the disturbances from such activities will not pose a threat to the system's resilience.

The two approaches to sustainability – the neo classical approach and the ecological economics approach differ on two distinct aspects. First, in ecological economics approach, nature is the ultimate source of wealth. Thus EE is ecocentric in approach with focus on nature where as the -neo classical economic approach is basically anthropocentric, with focus on man. Secondly, EE considers natural & human capital as complements where as the neo-classical approach considers them as substitutes.

15.5.3 Pearce and Atkinson's Sustainability Index - Real Savings Approach

The notion of Genuine Savings was first devised by Pearce and Atkinson (1993) using an empirical application of the Hartwick rule. According to this test, if all savings are reinvested in the two forms of capital, man-made capital and natural capital, then the aggregate capital stock will not be falling, and a constant consumption stream can be maintained. Using this Pearce and Atkinson developed a sustainability index or indicator of the form:

$$Z = \frac{S}{Y} - \frac{d_M K_M}{Y} - \frac{d_N K_N}{Y}$$

where 'S' is gross savings

Y is income

d_M is depreciation on man made capital

d_N is depreciation in natural capital

The above indicator assumes that $d_H = 0$, i.e., knowledge and skills do not depreciate. Sustainability condition is that the value of net change in total capital stock must be equal to or greater than zero. Net capital accumulation K is expressed as:

$$K = S - d_K$$

Assuming that $d_H = 0$, d_K is expressed in terms of d_M and d_N. Hence $K = S - d_M K_M - d_N K_N$. Dividing through by Y,

$$\frac{K}{Y} = \frac{S}{Y} - \frac{d_M K_M}{Y} - \frac{d_N K_N}{Y}$$

In terms of sustainability indicator Z

$$\frac{K}{Y} \text{ is replaced by } Z$$

Hence,

$$Z = \frac{S}{Y} - \frac{d_M K_M}{Y} - \frac{d_N K_N}{Y}$$

'Z' score is equivalent to the real savings ratio after all sources of capital usage are taken into account and the value of $Z \geq 0$ to ensure sustainability. This is a weak sustainability indicator. The strong sustainability indicator based on 'strict complementarity' of K_M and K_N, takes the form:

$$\frac{d_N K_N}{Y} \leq 0$$

i.e., stock of natural capital should be non-declining. A positive value for $d_N K_N/Y$ is unsustainable. Pearce and others applied the weak sustainability test for 22 countries. In this approach Pearce and Atkinson showed that an economy is sustainable if it saves more than the depreciation on its man-made and natural capital, i.e Z is greater or equal to zero.

Table 15.4 gives the results of the weak sustainability test. The results of the test showed that many countries were unable to pass even the weak sustainability test. The results revealed that a relatively high positive savings ratio does not guarantee clearing the weak sustainability test. Mexico, Indonesia and Nigeria, inspite of a high S/Y value of 24, 20 and 15, have Z values of 0 and -2 and -5 respectively.

It is also clear from table 15.4 that the United Kingdom is only marginally sustainable (Z = 0) because of pollution damages and rents that accrued due to exploitation of North Sea oil and natural gas discoveries, which resulted in decline in savings. Netherlands, Japan and Germany pass the weak sustainability test with Z scores of + 14, +17 and + 10 respectively. This is because of low d_N/Y, and high S/Y. The weak sustainability test is however a static test where Z values are for just one period. Table 15.4 reveals that all the countries for which the strong sustainability test ($\frac{d_N K_N}{Y} \leq 0$) was applied failed to pass the test. Column 3 in table 15.4 has positive values for all countries included and by SS rule a positive value for $d_N K_N/Y$ is unsustainable.

Table 15.4 Test for Weak Sustainable Development

	S/Y	d_M/Y	d_N/Y	Z
Sustainable Economies				
1. Brazil	**20**	**7**	10	+ 3
2. Costa Rica	**26**	**3**	8	**+ 15**
3. Czechoslovakia	**30**	10	7	**+ 13**
4. Finland	**28**	15	2	**+ 11**
5. Germany	**26**	12	4	**+ 10**
6. Hungary	**26**	10	5	**+ 11**
7. Japan	**33**	14	2	**+ 17**
8. Netherlands	**25**	**10**	1	**+ 14**
9. Poland	**30**	11	3	**+ 16**
10. United Slates	**18**	12	3	**+ 13**
11. Zimbabwe	**24**	10	5	**+9**
Marginally Sustainable				
12. Mexico	**24**	12	12	**0**
13. Philippines	**15**	11	4	**0**
14. UK	**18**	12	6	**0**
Unsustainable				
15. Ethiopia	**3**	1	**9**	**-7**
16. Indonesia	**20**	5	17	**-2**
17. Madagascar	**8**	1	16	**-9**
18. Mali	**-4**	4	**6**	**-14**
19. Nigeria	**15**	3	**17**	**-5**

15.5.4 World Bank's Genuine Savings Methodology

World Bank has devised a genuine savings indicator to assess an economy's sustainability. Genuine Savings (GS) is a measure of how a nation's total capital stock changes every year. Genuine savings represent "…the value of the net change in the whole range of assets that are important for development: produced assets, natural resources, environmental quality, human resources, and foreign assets". GS measures the true rate of saving in an economy after taking into account investments in human capital, depletion of natural resources and damages caused by pollution. GS is based on the concept of green national accounts. It is an indicator that helps policy makers to track the progress of the economy towards sustainable development.

Four adjustments are made to standard measure of gross savings of the economy to derive the Adjusted Net Savings (ANS) or Genuine Savings (GS). These are:

(i) consumption of fixed capital is deducted to obtain net national saving;
Gross national saving – Consumption of fixed capital = Net National Saving

(ii) current public expenditure on education is added to account for investment in human capital;

(iii) deduction of the value of depletion of natural resources.

(iv) deductions are made for pollution damages, including lost welfare in the form of damages to human health.

GS is expressed as:

GS or Adjusted Net Savings = Net National Saving + Education Expenditure – Energy depletion – Mineral depletion – Net forest depletion – Damage from carbon dioxide emissions – Damage from particulate emissions,

where Net National Savings = Gross National Savings – Consumption of Fixed Capital. The indicator is measured in percentage by dividing ANS by Gross National Income (GNI).

Positive savings allow wealth to grow over time. If an economy's adjusted net savings or GS is positive, economic theory suggests that the present value of wellbeing is increasing and ensures that the future generations enjoy at least as many opportunities as current generations. On the otherhand, persistently negative adjusted net saving indicates that an economy is on an unsustainable path.

Hamilton and Clemens (1999) have shown empirically that the levels of saving are negative in a wide range of countries when the environment and natural resources are included in the savings measure. Cross-country estimates of the GS indicator show that genuine savings is persistently negative for Sub-Saharan Africa and Middle East and North Africa due to the heavy resource dependence of these economies. Countries with less dependence on natural resources such as the high-income OECD countries showed high positive values.

The World Bank regularly publishes a comparatively comprehensive GS measurement exercise for over 150 countries. Due to international variations in data availability, the World Bank focused its valuation efforts on three areas of natural capital depletion: the valuation of resource rents with respect to non-renewable resources, the depletion of forests beyond replacement levels, and the marginal costs of carbon dioxide emissions. (Brown, et al, 2003)

According to the World Bank, the Genuine savings approach has the following advantages:

- It presents resource and environmental issues within a framework that finance and development planning ministries can understand.
- It reinforces the need to boost domestic savings, and hence the need for sound macroeconomic policies.
- It highlights the fiscal aspects of environment and natural resource management, since collecting resource royalties and charging pollution taxes are basic ways to ensure efficient use of environmental resources.

Calculation of GS has the following limitations:

- Lack of data for some resources such as ground water, land degradation, fish stocks, diamonds, and certain other minerals.
- Lack of agreed methodology for some ecosystem services for example, placing a value on biodiversity.
- Measurement errors

15.5.5 Safe Minimum Standards Approach

Safe Minimum Standards attempts to eliminate risk of catastrophic outcomes in the management of natural resources. The concept of the safe minimum standard was introduced by Ciriacy-Wantrup (1952) in order to include explicitly uncertainty and irreversibility into the appraisal of natural resource utilisation. The SMS Approach to sustainability holds that if there is a possibility that an action will trigger unacceptable consequences, then that action should not be taken. The method was applied to issues such as water quality, agricultural land use, and to endangered species. Ciriacy-Wantrup regarded the safe minimum standard as a form of insurance policy against possible large future losses. In situations where the human impact on natural environment are regarded uncertain but may be large and irreversible the proposed action or project must be rejected. SMS suggests that natural capital and human capital are not substitutes and hence sustainability warrants the maintenance of non-declining natural capital. Kaivo-oja et al (2001) in their article "Advanced sustainability analysis" define the SMS rule as: prevent all reductions in natural capital stock below the safe minimum standards identified for each component of this stock unless social opportunity cost of doing so are " unacceptably" high. According to the SMS approach deciding to conserve today is shown to be the risk-minimising way to proceed."

SMS is considered as a hybrid between neo classical approach and the ecological economics approach to sustainability. It does not reject the basic tenet of the standard economics approach that natural capital and man-made capital are substitutes and at the same time it collaborates with the ecological economics approach that nature in some ways imposes limit on factor substitution.

SMS is recommended when a cost benefit analysis cannot be undertaken because of fundamental uncertainty about the value of natural capital. SMS is generally equivalent to a social rule that delivers minimum regrets.

15.6 Realising Sustainable Development

Herman Daly has listed few general principles of sustainable development, as a first step towards operationality of the concept.

The main (first) principle, is to limit the human scale to a level which is within the carrying capacity of the environment. The carrying capacity of the environment is like a 'plimsoll line' of the ship which is the load limit mark for the ship. In the absence of such a plimsoll line for the economy, human scale grows beyond the carrying capacity and deviates from the path of sustainable development. For sustainable development, population and per capita resource use must be limited since scale of macro economy relative to ecosystem is defined as population times per capita resource use.

Secondly, technological progress should be through put efficiency increasing rather than throughput quantity increasing.

Thirdly, renewable resources should be exploited on a profit maximising sustainable yield basis and in general not be driven to extinction, i.e., harvesting rate should not exceed regeneration rate.

Fourth, for non-renewable resource, rate of depletion should not exceed rate of creation of renewable substitutes. Besides these market failure related to resource pricing and property rights should be corrected.

Ralph Rookwood has given ten general 'Rules of conduct' for sustainable development in his article "Making it Happen". They are:

Rule 1 Fundamental changes in attitude—a change from activities and processes that abuse the natural world to alternatives that respect its limitation.

Rule 2 Facilitating innovation and replicating best practice, that are environmentally beneficial.

Rule 3 Establishing sustainability indices for measuring improvements in sustainability and adopting specific targets at national, regional and local levels—to which action programmes and monitoring can be geared.

Rule 4 Maximising scope for initiative for increased action at all levels, through:

- Community involvement
- Decentralisation
- Positive incentives
- Removal of fiscal and institutional barriers.
- The creation of policy and administrative frameworks conducive to the achievement of sustainability objectives.

Rule 5 Redefining growth in terms of "Quality of life" to give a composite index which will indicate whether the total national output is expanding in conformity with sustainability principles.

Rule 6 Redefining costs and profitability to reflect externalities and other environmentally damaging practices to promote investment decisions compatible with sustainability criteria.

Rule 7 Adopting long term objectives for buildings and urban areas compatible with sustainable development criteria.

Rule 8 Long term continuity in the implementation of environmental policies to achieve sustainable development.

Rule 9 Setting up a single national body, responsible for preparing a coherent set of national objectives for waste recycling, pollution control and non-renewable resources substitution, designing environmental performance standards, environmental capacity limits and requirements for environmental impact assessments.

Rule 10 Diversionary principle to be followed for long term survival. i.e., the money should be diverted from activities that are environmentally damaging to those which are environmentally friendly and which would promote sustainable development. A good example is diversion of money from waste disposal to waste reduction. Besides a special environmental conversion assistance fund should be established for providing grants or loan to those business units who cannot afford conversion to energy efficient clean technology.

Conclusion

A lot has been said and written about sustainable development. The concept today has become just a 'cliche'. Many feel that it is just another catch phrase like appropriate technology of 1970s. But environmentally sound process of economic development is the need of the day and this need has promoted the concept of sustainable development as a new development paradigm. Sustainable development is a practical guide to the survival of humanity in general. It aims at bringing together man, nature and development for a better future.

Questions

1. Give the various definitions of sustainable development and interpret them.
2. Distinguish between weak and strong sustainability
3. What are the various models of sustainable development
4. Compare neo-classical approach of sustainable development with the Ecological economics Approach
5. Is Safe Minimum Standards Approach a better option than the other Approaches. Give an example where it can be used.

Exercise

1. Go to the following websites and make a study on Genuine Savings indicator for various countries/ regions /groups and make a comparative study on the sustainability of development in these countries/ regions (geographic) / groups (by income) studied.
   http://documents.worldbank.org/curated/en/908161468740713285/Genuine-saving-as-a-sustainability-indicator
   http://siteresources.worldbank.org/EXTSDNET/Resources/Little-Green-Data-Book-2013.pdf

SECTION 4

WELFARE ECONOMICS AND ENVIRONMENTAL ECONOMICS

16

Paretian Welfare Economics

"Environmental values are economic values; it is in principle just as important, in the interests of economic efficiency and therefore economic welfare, to conserve our limited natural resources, to make wise and sparing use of our limited clean air, water and living space, as it is to economise in the use of labour and capital."

—*Alfred Kahn*

Economists see environmental problems as problems of human welfare. The environment renders valuable services to human beings as a supplier of renewable and non-renewable resources, as a sink for waste from production and consumption activities of the economic agents, and by maintaining ecological balance. The crucial fact about these functions is that they are not priced because of absence of market for these services. As a result, the functions and services of the environment have either no prices or have non-optimal prices which in turns leads to overuse or overexploitation of these functions and misallocation of resources. Therefore environmental problems are basically problems of non-optimal pricing and misallocation of resources, which is the subject matter of welfare economics. Welfare economics tries to assess what an "optimal" configuration of an economy is in terms of prices and quantities of inputs and output, i.e., it explains conditions required for optimal resource allocation, optimal pricing, etc.

This chapter explains some of the basic concepts in welfare economics that are essential for a better understanding of economics of environmental issues.

16.1 Welfare Economics – Pareto Optimum and Pareto Efficiency Conditions

Welfare economics is the economic theory of measuring and promoting social welfare. Welfare economics explains how a competitive equilibrium maximises welfare. It explains the obstacles to maximization of welfare and deals with policy measures to correct for such obstacles and achieve welfare maximization.

The First Theorem of Welfare Economics establishes that a competitive equilibrium is for the common good. It states that the market equilibrium of an ideal market system yields an efficient (Pareto optimal) allocation of resources. A situation is said to be **Pareto optimal** if there is no feasible alternative that makes everyone better off. In other words, Pareto Optimum refers to a situation in which it is not possible to make any one individual better off, through policy changes, without making atleast another individual worse off.

Pareto efficiency refers to an allocation of resources from which it is not possible to find another allocation that would make any consumer better off without making someone else worse off. The concept of Pareto Optimality or Efficiency is important for two reasons. Firstly, to study how a competitive market economy allocates resources. Secondly, to understand how economic policy might help an economy to achieve efficiency when there are deviations from the optimum state.

There are three necessary conditions that must be satisfied for an allocation of resource to be efficient - production efficiency, consumption efficiency and product mix efficiency. The three conditions are stated in terms of marginal rates of substitution (MRS), marginal rates of technical substitution (MRTS) and marginal rates of product transformation (MRPT).

Let us consider an economy in which there are two persons A and B, two goods X and Y, produced with the help of two inputs labour (L) and capital (K). The productive inputs, are available in fixed quantities. It is assumed that there is perfect competition in both product and factor market. It is assumed that both X and Y are private goods and the production and consumption of these do not involve any externalities. Given these assumptions, the conditions required for Pareto optimality can be explained. There are three conditions that must be satisfied for resource allocation to be Pareto optimal or Pareto efficient. They are:

BOX 16.1 Conditions for Pareto Efficiency

Efficiency in Consumption : $MRS^A_{XY} = MRS^B_{XY}$

$$\left[\frac{MU_X}{MU_Y}\right]^A = \left[\frac{MU_X}{MU_Y}\right]^B$$

Efficiency in Production : $MRTS^X_{LK} = MRTS^Y_{LK}$

$$\left[\frac{MP_L}{MP_K}\right]^X = \left[\frac{MP_L}{MP_K}\right]^Y$$

Efficiency in Product Mix : $MRPT_{XY} = MRS_{XY}$

$$\frac{MC_X}{MC_Y} = \frac{MU_X}{MU_Y}$$

1. Efficiency in consumption.
2. Efficiency in production.
3. Efficiency in product mix.

16. 2 Efficiency in Consumption

The rule for efficiency in consumption requires the equality of Marginal rate of substitution (between the two goods x and y) for the two consumers and is expressed as

$$MRS^A_{XY} = MRS^B_{XY}$$

$$MRS_{xy} = \frac{MUx}{MUy}$$

Hence the condition for efficiency in consumption is:

$$\left[\frac{MU_X}{MU_Y}\right]^A = \left[\frac{MU_X}{MU_Y}\right]^B$$

If this condition is not met, then the two consumers can exchange commodities at the margin in such a way that both gain and neither suffer, i.e., mutual beneficial exchange will be possible. Only when the ratios of marginal utilities are equal, exchanges will not be mutually beneficial, i.e., a Pareto improvement is not possible. (A gain to one or more persons without any one else suffering is known as Pareto Improvement). Efficiency conditions can be illustrated using the Edgeworth Box Diagram.

Figure 16.1 shows individual A's indifference map in the normal way, while individual B's indifference map is superimposed on A's indifference map by turning B's map upside down, thus forming a box. This is the Edgeworth box, named after its inventor, the Oxford economist, F.Y. Edgeworth. The size of the box is determined by quantities of good X and good Y available in the economy.

In figure 16.1, south-west corner is A's origin Ox, and units of X for A are measured left to right on the horizontal axis, while units of Y to A are measured bottom to top on the vertical axis. The preferences of A for X and Y are shown by the four indifference curves labeled A_1, A_2, A_3, A_4. Any move north-east yields greater utility to A i.e., A will be on a higher indifference curve. For B, the origin is $0'_B$, north-east corner in the figure 16.1. For B increased quantities of X are measured from $0'_B$ and increased quantities of Y are measured bottom to top from the origin $0'_B$. Since B's indifference map is placed upside down on A's map, B's indifference curves are concave to A's axes. Any change that results in a move towards 0_A, will increase B's welfare, placing him on a higher indifference curve.

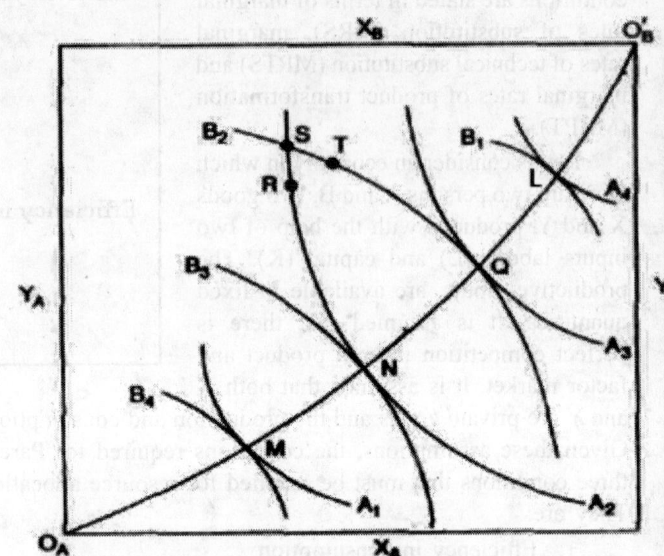

Figure 16.1 Efficiency in Consumption – Edgeworth Box Diagram

The line connecting the points of tangency of the two sets of indifference curves is called as the "contract curve". At the points of tangency, i.e., on the contract curve, the slopes of A's and B's indifference curve are equal. Since the slope of an indifference curve is the marginal rate of substitution (MRS), it can be said that contract curve is the locus of points where $MRS^A = MRS^B$. Since the contract curve is not a straight line, MRS will vary along its length.

The exchange of X and Y between A and B can be explained using the indifference maps of A and B within the Edgeworth box given in figure 16.1 Suppose initially they are at S, a move from **S to N**, will improve B's utility, taking B to a higher indifference curve, while A would be no worse off. Similarly a move from **S to Q** will benefit A without harming B. However, when exchanges result in a movement along the contract curve; improvement to both is no longer possible, since any movement along the contract curve is a gain in utility to one person and a loss to the other. Any movement north-east is a gain for A and a loss for B. A and B will reach a point on the contract curve through bargaining and exchange of goods. Where this point will be, will depend on the bargaining skills of A and B.

But once they are on the contract curve, they are on an efficient point, since all points on the contract curve are Pareto efficient or Pareto optimal. Thus efficiency in consumption is illustrated by points on the contract curve inside the Edgeworth box for consumption. In figure 16.1, points such as M, N, Q and L are Pareto efficient while R, S, and T are inefficient.

At all points on the contract curve,

$$MRS^{A}_{XY} = MRS^{B}_{XY}$$

16. 3 Efficiency in Production

The rule for efficiency in production is similar to that for consumption. If production should be efficient, then there should be equality of marginal rate of technical substitution between the inputs, i.e,

$$MRTS^{X}_{LK} = MRTS^{Y}_{LK}$$

Since MRTS = MP_L/MP_K (slope of an isoquant), the condition for efficiency in production may be rewritten as

$$\left[\frac{MP_L}{MP_K}\right]^X = \left[\frac{MP_L}{MP_K}\right]^Y$$

Production efficiency may be illustrated using an Edgeworth box for production.

The analysis is similar to consumption Edgeworth box, except that on the horizontal axis we measure input labour and on the vertical axis we measure capital instead of X and Y and isoquants replace indifference curves. The two producers employ homogenous inputs. Any point inside production Edgeworth box is a point in "input space". The dimensions of the box signify that there are fixed quantities of labour and capital available to the two producers (firms). It is assumed that one of them produces X and the other produces Y. As in the case of consumption efficiency, efficiency in production requires that a point on the production contract curve is attained. In figure 16.2, a production Edgeworth box is illustrated. Points such as K, M, N, Q and L are Pareto efficient while R, S, and T are inefficient. At all points on the contract curve.

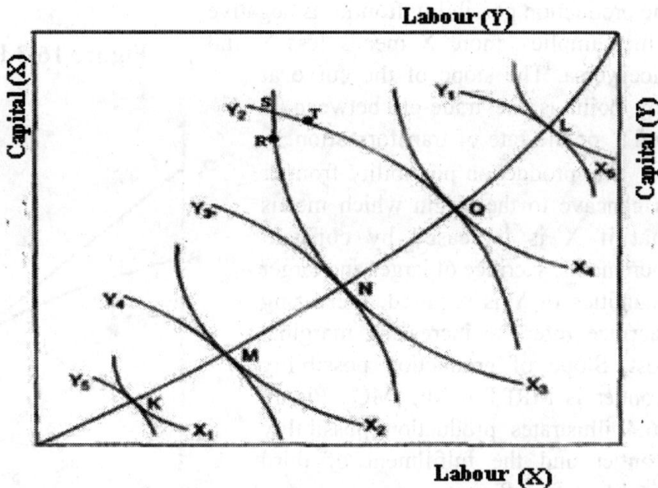

Figure 16.2 Efficiency in Production – Edgeworth Box Diagram

$$MRTS^{X}_{LK} = MRTS^{Y}_{LK}$$

16. 4 Efficiency in Product Mix

This is given by the condition, $\mathbf{MRPT_{XY} = MRS_{XY}}$.

MRPT is the marginal rate of product transformation given by the slope of the product transformation curve or production possibility frontier. Production possibility frontier can be derived from the Edgeworth box of production. The points K, M, N, Q, and L on the contract curve in figure 16.2 within the Edgeworth box of production may be transformed from input space to output space to derive the production possibility frontier. In figure 16.3, X-axis measures quantity of commodity X while Y-axis measures quantity of commodity Y. Points K', M', N', Q', and L' in the figure correspond to the points K, M, N, Q, and L in figure 16.2.

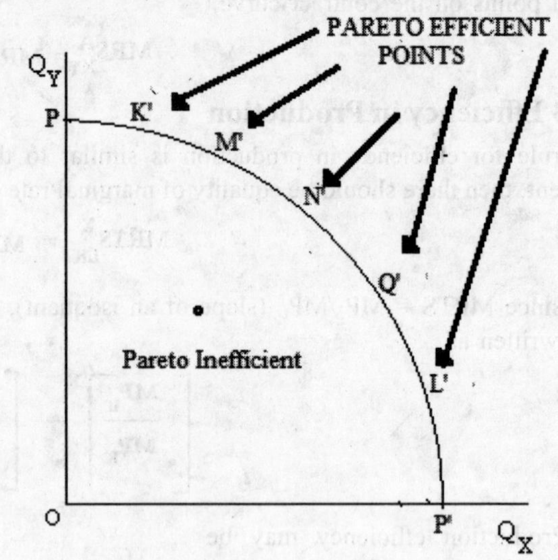

Figure 16.3 Production Possibility Frontier

The production possibility frontier expresses the maximum quantities of X and Y that can be produced with the resources available. All points on the curve are efficient. Points inside the frontier are inefficient combinations of X and Y while points outside the frontier are unattainable. The slope of the production possibility frontier is negative which implies: more X means less Y and vice versa. The slope of the curve at any point is the trade-off between X and Y or the rate of transformation.

The production possibility frontier is concave to the origin which means that if X is increased by constant increments, sacrifice of larger and larger quantities of Y is required. Increasing sacrifice refers to increasing marginal cost. Slope of production possibility frontier is MRPT = MC_x/MC_y. Figure 16.4 illustrates production possibility frontier and the fulfillment of third condition for efficiency.

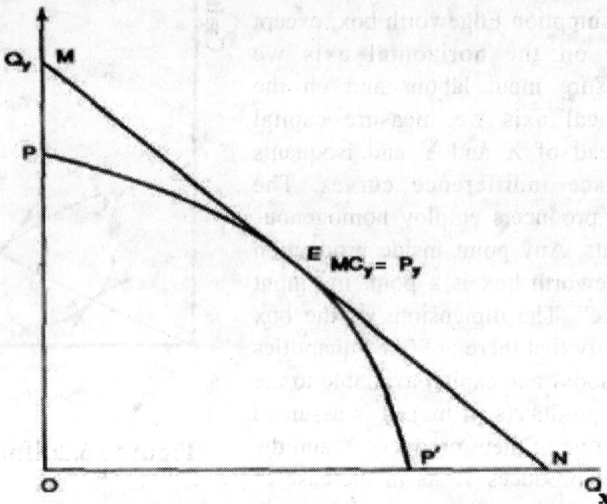

Figure 16.4 Efficiency in Product Mix

In figure 16.4, PP' is the production possibility frontier, MN is the price line. At E, slope of the production possibility frontier is equal to the slope of the price line. The third rule of efficiency is:

$$MRPT_{XY} = MRS^A_{XY} = MRS^B_{XY} \quad \text{---------------- (1)}$$

Where MRS_{XY} = MUx/MUy

Therefore (1) may be expressed as:

$$MRPT_{XY} = \left[\frac{MU_X}{MU_Y}\right]^A = \left[\frac{MU_X}{MU_Y}\right]^B \quad \text{------------------------(2)}$$

At equilibrium, consumers maximise satisfaction by equating MU ratio to price ratio, i.e., when consumers are in equilibrium,

$$\left[\frac{MU_X}{MU_Y}\right]^A = \frac{P_X}{P_Y} \text{ ---------------------- (3)}$$

Therefore

$$\left[\frac{MU_X}{MU_Y}\right]^A = \frac{P_X}{P_Y} = \left[\frac{MU_X}{MU_Y}\right]^B$$

Hence substituting P_x/P_Y for MUx/MU_Y in (2)

$$MRPT_{XY} = P_x/P_y$$

Since

$$MRPT_{XY} = MC_x/MC_y$$

$$MC_x/MC_y = P_x/P_y$$

OR

MC =P

Thus at E, the third condition for efficiency is satisfied since P_X/P_Y is the slope of the price line and MC_X/MC_Y is the slope of the production possibility frontier.

We establish then that a Pareto optimum price is equal to the marginal cost everywhere. Under perfect competition long run equilibrium ensures that MC = P. Hence perfect competition assures Pareto Optimum. Thus the three rules for efficiency can be summed up in one fundamental theorem. "Every competitive equilibrium is a Pareto Optimum. And every Pareto Optimum is a competitive equilibrium".

Questions

Define Pareto Optimum and explain the Pareto Efficiency conditions.

Exercise

Show that Perfect competition ensures Pareto Optimality

17

MARKET FAILURE

Market power and externalities are examples of a general phenomenon called market failure—the inability of some unregulated markets to allocate resources efficiently.

—N Gregory Mankiw

A market failure is a situation where free markets fail to allocate resources efficiently. Price mechanism fails to account for all the costs and benefits involved. As a result market will not provide the socially optimum supply of the good. The good will be either over produced or under produced. Market failures have negative effects on the economy because an optimal allocation of resources is not attained. In other words, the social costs of producing the good or service are not minimized, and this results in a waste of some resources.

17.1 Causes of Market Failure

Market fails to yield optimum results when one or few or all of the following factors are present.

1. Presence of imperfect competition, which gives monopoly power to the seller.
2. Presence of incomplete information
3. Presence of public goods
4. Presence of externality

The first two of the four factors, namely, presence of imperfectly competitive markets and incomplete information, are structural factors.

17.1.1 Existence of Market Power

The competitive forces which generate efficiency require that no single firm or producer controls a large share of the market. If a single firm controls a large share of the market and becomes dominant it will gain monopoly power. Such a monopoly power will result in higher price and lower quantity than in a competitive market.

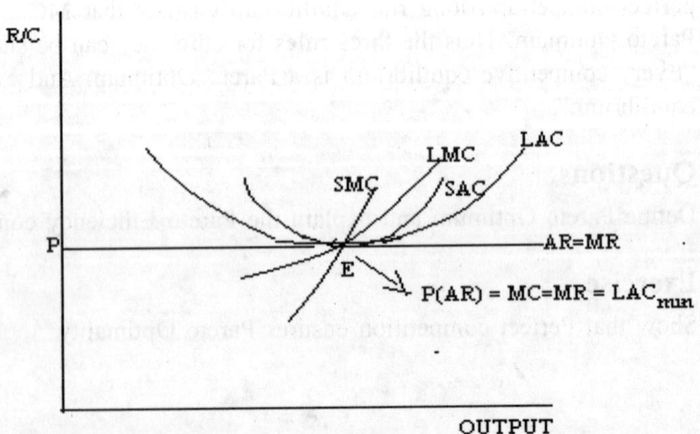

Figure 17.1 Efficiency under Perfect Competition

Perfectly competitive market achieves efficiency in the long run. When firms under perfect competition are in equilibrium in the long run both allocative and productive efficiency are ensured. This is shown in figure 17.1.

The allocative efficiency of the competitive firm is reflected by the equality of price to marginal cost (P=MC) at the long run equilibrium position of the firm. At equilibrium not only is MC equal to MR, but MC is also equal to AR (Price) which implies allocative efficiency. At equilibrium, LAC is at its minimum. This is shown by tangency of LAC to MR (=AR) at minimum point. This ensures productive efficiency. This result is possible only under competitive conditions where each firm is one of a very large number of firms producing and selling homogeneous product. Hence firms accept the price determined by the market forces of supply and demand. Firms are price takers and have no monopoly power.

Presence of imperfect competition increases the monopoly power of the seller. Under conditions of imperfect competition, firms gain monopoly power by controlling a considerable portion of the market. Factors such as product differentiation, few sellers, imperfect and incomplete knowledge of the market conditions among buyers give monopoly power to sellers. Hence the AR curve of the firm slopes downward with MR below it. As a result at equilibrium given by MC = MR condition, price (AR) is greater than MC (P> MC). Thus there is ***allocative inefficiency***. Since AR is downward sloping, the plant is not fully utilised at equilibrium and there is excess capacity. The inefficient outcome due to monopoly power under imperfect competition is illustrated in figure 17.2.

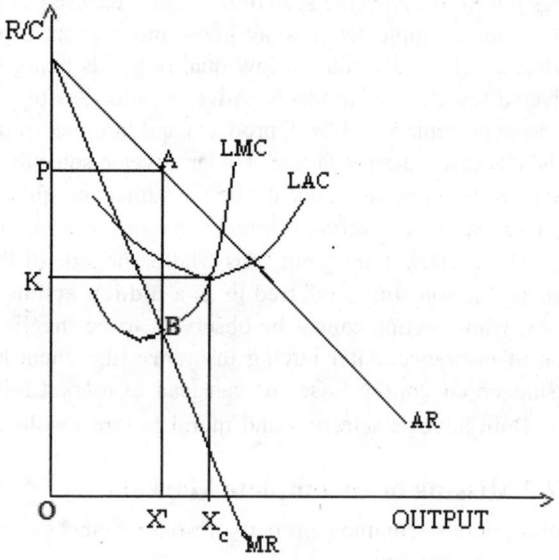

Figure 17.2 Inefficiency Under Imperfect Competition.

Figure 17.2 illustrates inefficiency under imperfectly competitive conditions. In the figure, output of the imperfectly competitive firm is equal to OX'. Price is equal to OP=X'A. Marginal Cost at equilibrium is equal to X'B. Figure 17.2 clearly shows that:

a. P> MC (X'A.>X'B)

b. Presence of excess capacity at equilibrium to the extent of $X'X_c$

17. 1. 2 Presence of Incomplete Information

Incomplete information is the second source of market failure. Competition will result in efficient outcome only if all participating agents – producers and consumers have all the required information about the market forces. Under perfect competition it is assumed that all producers have access to the information regarding technology and factors of production while consumers have the complete information on what is available at what price in the market. Price / quality information is available to all consumers which enables them to make the right choice. However in the real world complete information about the market forces is not available to all producers and consumers. There is asymmetry information – this is particularly true of quality of inputs and outputs available in the market. Information asymmetry refers to the fact that the buyer and the seller of a commodity may have different amounts of information about that commodity's attributes.

Consumers overestimate or underestimate quality, due to lack of information; producers lack incentives to provide information since there is a gain in producer's surplus when information is incomplete. Accurate information would lead to a lower surplus for the producer. If consumers underestimate quality due to lack of information, there will be 'under-consumption' and producers would have an incentive to provide information since accurate information would lead to a gain in producer's surplus.

Information asymmetry and adverse selection was first pioneered by George Akerlof in his article "The Market for Lemons: Quality Uncertainty and the Market Mechanism". Asymmetric information can lead to two consequences – adverse selection and moral hazard. Adverse selection is a situation where one party in a transaction knows something about its own characteristic that the other party does not know. Adverse selection is often referred to as a **hidden information** problem in a market, where for example sellers may know more about a product than a buyer (Estrin and Laidler,1995). Adverse selection results in low quality goods being sold more than high quality goods. There is an adverse selection of products. Adverse selection represents market failure since 'good' products are under-represented, and 'bad' products and 'are over-represented, in the market. The externality between products cause market failure. Under adverse selection, therefore, sellers of high-quality products will have an incentive to *signal* to the consumer the quality of their product. This may take the form of: *reputation*, *standardization*, *informative advertising*, and offering *warranties* in the event of defects.

Moral Hazard are "situations where one side of the market can't observe the actions of the other side and is sometimes referred to as a **hidden action** problem"(Varian,1990). This may then lead the party, whose action cannot be observed, to be 'negligent', or to not take 'due care'. Best example is that of insurance. After buying insurance, the client has less of an incentive to reduce risk, because insurance covers the loss; this can lead to market failure.

Both adverse selection and moral hazard result in market failure.

17.2 Missing or Incomplete Markets

Public goods, common property resources and externalities represent cases of missing markets or incomplete markets.

17.2.1 Public goods

There are two important features of public goods:

- Non-excludability
- Non- rivalry

Non- excludability implies that no individual can be excluded from the consumption of the good once it is provided. The benefits derived from public goods cannot be confined solely to those who have paid for it. Indeed non-payers can enjoy the benefits of consumption at zero cost. This is termed as the **'free-rider'** problem.

Non-rivalry on the other hand means that the consumption of the good by one person will not prevent others from enjoying the good.

Examples of public good include street lights, light house, defense of a country, etc.

Due to the features of non-excludability and non-rivalry of the public goods, the **private sector** will not be willing to and able to provide public goods. Hence they are provided by the Government. For public goods MC = 0. Allocative efficiency requires that P = MC. In the case of public goods, since MC= 0, allocative efficiency implies that P=MC=0. Therefore public goods have to be provided at no charge. It is for this reason that public goods are mostly provided by the government. Private firms will not provide public goods since they cannot charge for consumption. Due to the features of non-excludability and non-rivalry, the condition for efficient allocation of public goods hence differs from that of private goods. In the case of private goods, for optimum allocation, the condition is:

$$MRPT_{XY} = MRS^{A}_{XY} = MRS^{B}_{XY}$$

The efficiency condition for public goods is:

$$MRPT_{XY} = MRS^{A}_{XY} + MRS^{B}_{XY}$$

For a detailed discussion on public goods see chapter 20, section 20.2

17.2.2 Externalities

Externalities are the spill-over effects, or 'third-party' effects, of production or consumption for which no appropriate compensation is paid. Externality is defined as the cost or benefit imposed by the production and consumption activities of firms and households, respectively, on the rest of the society towards which no payment (compensation) is made. Externalities could be positive or negative.

Table 17.1 Positive and Negative Externalities

Positive externalities	Negative externalities
Occur when society benefits from the consumption or production of a commodity or service	Occur when costs are imposed on society from the consumption or production of a commodity or service
Example: Education, vaccination etc.	Example: Pollution, smoking etc.

- When there are external costs of production, marginal social cost will be greater than Marginal private cost. MSC > MPC. MSC = MPC + MEC where MSC is Marginal Social Cost; MPC is Marginal Private Cost and MEC is Marginal External Cost. Ignoring MEC will result in over production of output.
- When there are external cost of consumption, marginal social benefit less than the marginal private benefit. (MSB < MPB) This leads to the good or service being over-consumed relative to the social optimum.
- Consumers can create externalities when they purchase and consume goods and services.
  1. Pollution from cars and motorbikes
  2. Litter on streets and in public places
  3. Noise pollution generated by neighbor playing stereo loudly.
- When there are external benefits of production marginal social cost will be less than marginal private cost. MSC < MPC.
- When there are external benefits of consumption marginal social benefit is greater than marginal private benefits. (MSB>MB)

Externalities cause market failure if the price mechanism does not take into account the full social costs and social benefits of production and consumption.

17.3 Correction of Market Failure

There are various measures to correct market failure such as indirect taxation, subsidies, tradable pollution permits, extension of property rights, regulation and minimum prices.

Direct Provision: A common method used by governments to address the market failure of public goods is direct provision. That is, governments oversee the production of public goods and/or their distribution to the public. This alternative is most obvious with national defense.

Regulation: A second noted method is government regulation commonly used to address instances of market failures due to market imperfection, externalities, and imperfect information. For example, the price charged by a firm with significant monopoly power might be regulated by government. Or government might restrict the amount of pollution emissions from a particular productive activity. Regulations requiring sellers to provide information to buyers is a means of addressing the market failure of imperfect information. Governments enforce laws that limit the quantity of a harmful good produced or banning its production, combined with harsh penalties for violators of the legal limits.

Economic instruments: . These include taxes, and subsidies. Many countries have a tax on pollution. Subsidies are used to correct market failure caused by externalities; For example in the case of pollution which is a negative production externality, subsidies are used to cover partially or totally the cost of pollution control equipment. Pollution permits are also used to correct market failure due to pollution. While pollution permits are popular in USA, pollution taxes are common in European countries. Section 6 discusses the various instruments available to correct market failure caused by negative production externality (Pollution).

Government intervention

Apart from regulation, Government can play an important role in correcting market failures. Few such measures are:

- pricing policy that set price equal to marginal cost or fixing a price ceiling.
- government investment programmes on education that will improve the knowledge of the people. This would create awareness among consumers about the market, about pollution related health issues etc.
- government investment in pollution treatment programmes.

No single measure can solve the issue of market failure and restore efficiency. What is needed is policy mix of all the instruments in accordance with the factor causing market failure. All these measures can only yield a second best situation. The first best is not having an instance market failure.

Questions

1. Define market failure .Explain the various types of market failure.
2. Suggest measures to correct market failure.

Exercise

Is traffic congestion a consumption or production externality" Explain your stand.

18

CONSUMER'S SURPLUS AND PRODUCER'S SURPLUS

Let every individual and institution now think and act as a responsible trustee of Earth, seeking choices in ecology, economics and ethics that will provide a sustainable future, eliminate pollution, poverty and violence, awaken the wonder of life and foster peaceful progress in the human adventure.

— John McConnell, founder of International Earth Day

The doctrine of consumer's surplus was originally stated by the French engineer-economist J.A. Dupuit in1844. He tried to measure the amount of consumer's surplus that would accrue to people as a result of the construction of a bridge across a river.

18.1 Marshall's Concept of Consumer's Surplus

The concept of consumer surplus gained prominence after Marshall's "Principles of Economics". Marshall defined consumer surplus as the excess of price which the consumer would be willing to pay for the good (potential price) rather than go without the thing, over that which he actually does pay (actual price)'. It is the difference between the potential price and the actual price. Marshall used the triangular area under the demand curve to represent consumer's surplus. In figure 18.1 consumer's surplus is measured by the area APB and OP is the price of the good.

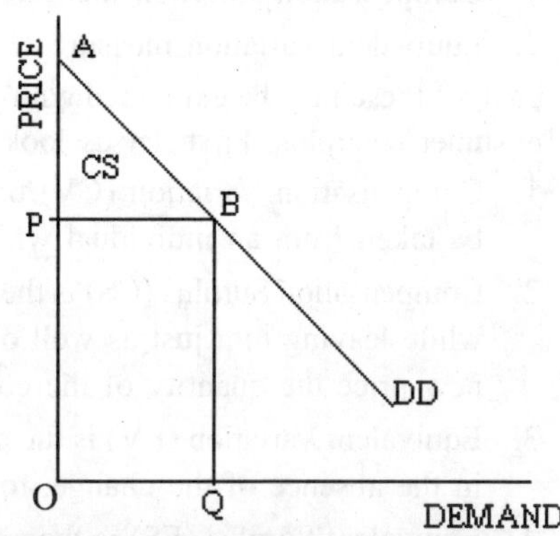

Figure 18.1 Consumer's Surplus Using Demand Curve

18.2 Marshall's Concept of Consumer's Surplus Using Indifference Curves

Marshall's definition of consumer surplus may be illustrated using indifference map as shown in figure 18.2. The Y axis represents the amount of money and the X axis the quantity of the commodity X. Price of the commodity is given by the slope of the line AB. At this price the consumer will buy ON of X by spending AL (= FP) since I_2 is the highest indifference curve attainable with the budget line AB. ON of X is available to the consumer at point R on I_1 also. Points R and A are on the same indifference curve I_1. Point A represents a combination of all income and no X, while point R represents a combination of ON of X and OK of income (since the consumer will have to spend AK to buy ON of X). The consumer is indifferent between A and R. That is, the consumer is willing to pay as much as AK for ON (quantity of commodity) for an all -or-none offer. But he spends only AL to buy ON of X. Marshall's definition of consumer surplus is the difference between the maximum amount that the consumer is willing to pay and the amount actually paid. In figure 18.2, consumers surplus is equal to AK - AL = LK. (or FR= FP = PR).

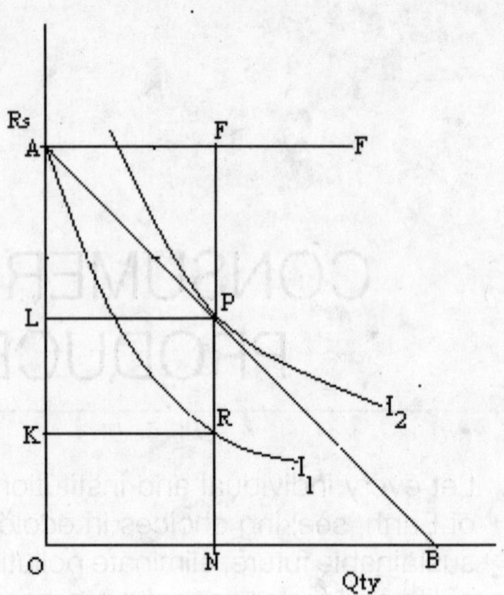

Figure 18.2 Consumer's Surplus Using Indifference Curves

18.3 Hicksian Four Measures of Consumer's Surplus

The above measures refer to the surplus satisfaction of a consumer when he is able to buy a good at a given price in comparison to the case where the good is not available. Actually consumer surplus arises whenever there is a change in price. In an attempt to avoid the cardinal measures of utility, and to explain consumer's surplus with reference to price changes, Hicks introduced the concept of compensation variation.

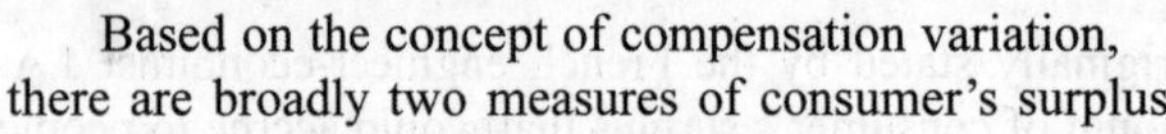

Based on the concept of compensation variation, there are broadly two measures of consumer's surplus.

1. Compensation variation measure.
2. Equivalent variation measure.

Each of these may be explained with and without quantity constraint. Thus there are four measures of Consumer's surplus. First, let us look at the definition of the four measures of consume surplus:

1. Compensation Variation (CV) of a change in price is the amount of compensation that can be taken from an individual while leaving him just as well off as *before* the change;
2. Compensation Surplus (CS) is the amount of compensation that can be taken from the individual while leaving him just as well off as before the change if he were constrained to buy at the new price the quantity of the commodity he would buy in the absence of compensation;
3. Equivalent Variation (EV) is the amount of compensation that has to be given to the individual, in the absence of the change, to make him as well off as he would be with the change;
4. Equivalent Surplus (ES) is the amount of compensation that has to be given to the individual, in the absence of the change, to make him as well off as he would be with the change if he were constrained to buy at the old price the quantity of the commodity he would buy in the absence of compensation.

18.4 Compensation Variation Measure of Consumer's Surplus

Compensation variation measure, also known as the *willingness to pay* measure, refers to the maximum sum of money which the consumer would be willing to pay for the privilege of buying at a lower price, which when paid leaves the consumer in his initial level of welfare. This is the *price compensation variation* [CV_p] measure of consumer's surplus. If this measure constrains the consumer to buy the amount of goods at the new equilibrium, then the measure is known as quantity compensation variation measure [CV_q]. The two measures are illustrated in figure 18.3. In figure 18.3, the distance CV_p

measures price compensation variation. Original price ratio is represented by PL and the consumer is initially in equilibrium at E_1. With a price fall the new price line is PL' and E_3 is the new equilibrium of the consumer. CV_p is the maximum sum of money that can be taken from the consumer after a fall in the price of the commodity X, while leaving him just well off as he was before the fall in the price of the commodity X. After the removal of the amount PM the consumer's equilibrium is defined at E_2. CV_p is equal to PM = E_3K. However if the consumer is constrained to buy the quantity associated with the equilibrium E_3, then consumer surplus is equal to E_3R. This is Quantity Compensation Measure - CV_q. It is clear from the figure 18.3 that $CV_p > CV_q$ ($E_3K > E_3R$). Thus we have two measures of consumer's gain—price compensation variation and quantity compensation variation—in moving from E_1 to E_3. These measures relate to sums of money which when paid will leave the consumer in his initial welfare position. I_1

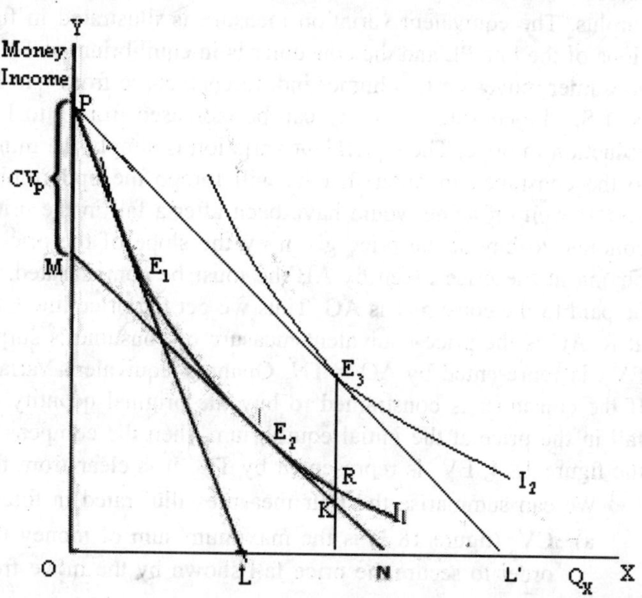

Figure18.3 Price and Quantity Compensation Variation Measures of Consumer Surplus

18.5 Equivalent Variation Measure of Consumer's Surplus

The equivalent variation measures would leave the consumer in his subsequent welfare position after paying compensation. Equivalent Variation measure, also known as the <u>*Willingness to Accept*</u> measure, refers to the minimum sum of money that the consumer would be willing to accept for foregoing the opportunity of buying at a lower price, which when paid leaves the consumer in the higher level of level of welfare

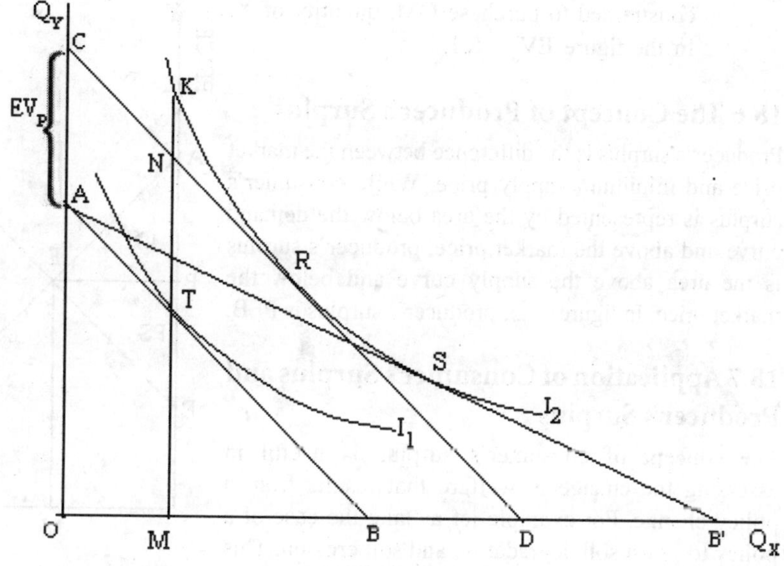

Figure 18.4 Equivalent Variation Measure of Consumer's Surplus

associated with the price change. This is the *price equivalent variation* [EV_p] measure of consumer's surplus. The equivalent variation measure is illustrated in figure18.4. Initially the price of X is the slope of the line PL and the consumer is in equilibrium at T. If the price of the commodity X falls, the consumer moves on to a higher indifference curve from I_1 to I_2. The new equilibrium of the consumer is at S. The consumer's utility can be increased from I_1 to I_2, by increasing his income, instead of a reduction in price. The equivalent variation is simply the minimum sum of money that must be given to the consumer, in order that he will forego the opportunity of buying at a lower price, to make him as well off as he would have been after a fall in the price of X. In order that the consumer will continue to buy at the price given by the slope of the price line AB and forego the opportunity of buying at the price given by AB',he must be compensated. The minimum sum of money that must be paid to the consumer is AC. Thus we get the price line CD. On CD the consumer's equilibrium is at R. AC is the price equivalent measure of consumer's surplus. In Figure18.4, the price equivalent, EV_p, is represented by AC = TN. Quantity equivalent Variation EV_q involves a quantity constraint. If the consumer is constrained to buy the original quantity of X, OM, that he was buying before a fall in the price at the initial equilibrium, then the compensation that must be paid to him is KT. In the figure 18.4, EV_q is represented by TK. It is clear from the figure that $EV_q > EV_p$, ie., TK > TN.

We can summarise the four measures illustrated in figures 18.3 and 18.4.

a) CV_p (figure 18.3) is the maximum sum of money the consumer would be willing to pay in order to secure the price fall shown by the move from PL to PL'. In this figure, CV_p = MP.

b) CV_q (figure 18.3) is the maximum sum the consumer would be willing to pay to secure the price fall assuming he is constrained to buy the quantity of X at E_1. In this figure, CV_q = RE_3.

c) EV_p (figure 18.4) is minimum sum that the consumer is willing to receive in order to forego the benefit of the price fall shown by the move from AB to AB'. In the figure drawn, EV_p = AC.

d) EV_q (figure 18.4) is the minimum sum that the consumer is willing to receive in order to forego the price fall, assuming that he is constrained to purchase OM, quantity of X. In the figure EV_q = KT.

18.6 The Concept of Producer's Surplus

Producer's surplus is the difference between the market price and minimum supply price. While consumer's surplus is represented by the area below the demand curve and above the market price, producer's surplus is the area above the supply curve and below the market price. In figure 18.5, producer's surplus is PEB.

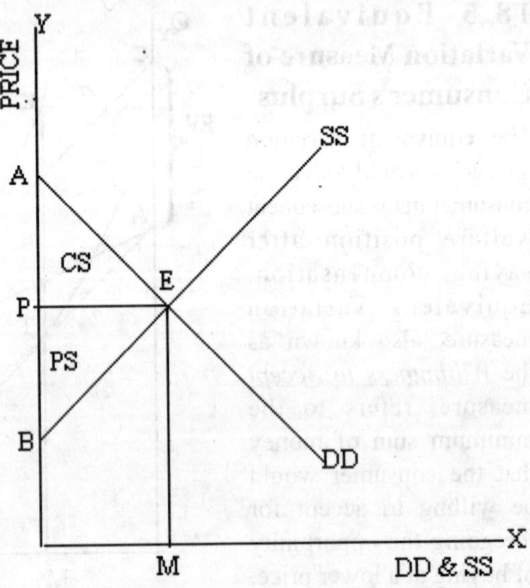

Figure 18.5 Consumer's Surplus and Producer's Surplus

18.7 Application of Consumer's Surplus and Producer's Surplus

The concept of consumer's surplus is useful in assessing the change in welfare that results from a policy change. For example let us take the case of a policy to arrest soil degradation and soil erosion. This measure will increase crop yields. The benefits from increase in crop yield to the society can be assessed by measuring consumer's and producer's surplus from the increase in crop yield. An increase in crop yield shifts the supply curve to the right or downwards .

In figure 18.6 before a policy change is initiated to control soil degradation, consumer's surplus is PAE and producer's surplus is PBE. Thus the total surplus before a policy change to reduce soil degradation is BAE. As a result of the policy the supply curve for crop yield shifts to SS' position and the new consumer's surplus is P_1AC and producer's surplus after the change in policy is P_1BC. Total surplus after the policy change is BAC. It is clear from figure 18.6 that there is a change in total surplus given by the difference between BAC and BAE. This is shown by the area BEC in figure 18.6.

The concept of consumer's surplus is applied by the contingent valuation method, a benefit evaluation method, employed to evaluate benefits from programmes to protect the environment.

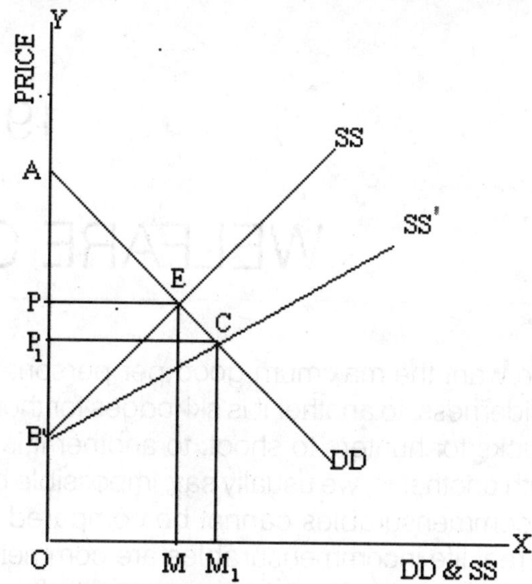

Figure18.6 Impact of Policy Change on Consumer's and Producer's Surplus

Questions

1. Differentiate between Marshall's and Hicksian concept of consumer's surplus
2. Explain the Equivalent variation and compensation variation measures of consumer's surplus.
3. What is producer's surplus.

Exercise

Give real life examples of the concept of consumer's surplus and producers surplus related to environmental programme.

19

WELFARE CRITERIA

We want the maximum good per person; but what is good? To one person it is wilderness, to another it is ski lodges for thousands. To one it is estuaries to nourish ducks for hunters to shoot; to another it is a factory land. Comparing one good with another is, we usually say, impossible because goods are incommensurable. Incommensurables cannot be compared.... Theoretically this may be true; but in real life incommensurables are commensurable. Only a criterion of judgment and a system of weighting are needed....

—Hardin 1968:1244

An important concept in welfare economics, enriching the theoretical tool kit of environmental economics, relates to the different criteria for ranking improvement in welfare due to a policy change. How do we decide whether a given policy measure is an improvement, (increase in welfare) compared to some initial situation, for at least one individual, while at the same time not worsening any other person's position? Different theoretical approaches are available for assessing the welfare implications of a policy change.

19.1 Pareto Improvement Criterion

A simpler approach to decide whether a given policy measure is an improvement or not, is the Pareto criterion for social change which may be stated as follows: A movement from one situation to another improves social welfare if and only if no individual receives a lower utility from the new situation and at least one receives greater utility. By this criterion, a policy change is socially desirable if everyone is made better off (the weak Pareto criterion) or at least some are made better off while no one is made worse off (the strong Pareto criterion). The Pareto criterion is illustrated in figure 19.1.

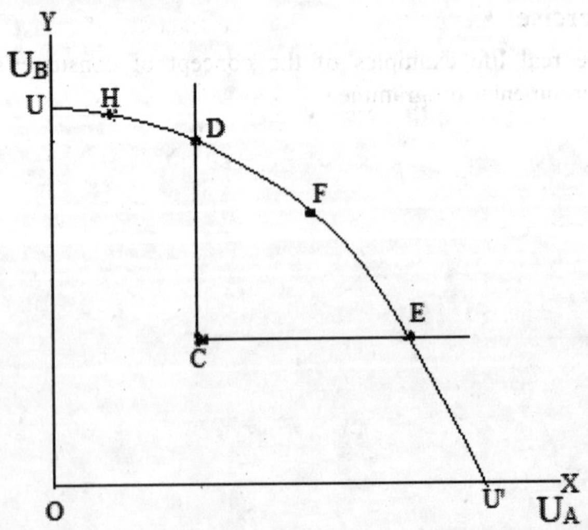

Figure 19.1 Pareto Improvement Criterion explained using Utility Possibility Frontier

The explanation of Pareto improvement criteria begins by assuming that there are two individuals A and B consuming a given bundle of commodities X and Y. The curve labeled UU' is the Utility Possibility Frontier (UPF) for the two individuals A and B. The UPF is derived from the contract cure within the Edgeworth Box of consumption, for the individuals. Since it is derived from the contract curve which is a locus of optimum consumption points, all points on UPF are also Pareto optimum. A's utility is represented on the horizontal axis and B's utility on the vertical axis. The Paretian criterion shows that any policy change which causes a movement from C to point F on the UPF UU' is an improvement because it makes both individuals better off thereby maximising their welfares. Likewise, a movement from C to D or E on the UU' curve is an improvement for it makes at least one person better off without making the other worse off. Movement from C to D makes B better off without affecting A and movement from C to E makes A better off without making B worse off. Movement to any point within the segment DE implies that either A or B or both A and B will benefit from the policy change. But any point outside the segment DE is not a Pareto improvement. For instance, any movement from C to H increases B's welfare at the expense of A's welfare.

The Pareto criterion is indeed weak. According to this criterion, we can evaluate changes that improve or deteriorate welfare of all households. Nothing can be said about a policy change which makes some better off and others worse off. Any project that makes every one better off passes Pareto test, while any project which makes anyone worse off is rejected by this test. Unfortunately, most projects have both gainers and losers. Pareto criterion cannot be applied to evaluate projects which benefit some and harm others. For such cases, welfare economics has another criterion namely the compensation criterion.

19.2 The Compensation Criterion or the Kaldor – Hicks Criterion

Compensation principle was developed by Nicholas Kaldor in his paper "Welfare Propositions of Economics and Interpersonal Comparisons of Utility", 1939. Kaldor held that if the gainers from the change could more than compensate the losers and yet be better off themselves, then the policy change is an improvement. Kaldor does not require that the losers should actually be compensated. Rather he requires that the gainers should be able potentially to compensate the losers out of their gains. Hicks presents the same criterion in a little different way thus:

"If A is made so much better off by the change that he could compensate B for his loss, and still have something left over, then the reorganisation is unequivocal improvement".

The Kaldor - Hicks criterion can be explained using the utility possibility frontier. Figure 19.2 explains Kaldor – Hicks Compensation Criterion. UU' is the utility possibility curve which represents the various combinations of utilities obtained by individuals A and B. A downward movement on the utility possibility curve UU', increases the utility of A and decreases that of B, while an upward movement increases the utility of B and decreases the utility of A.Starting from an initial point M inside the utility possibility curve UU', if a change in policy results in a movement from M to M', on the utility possibility curve UU', utility of individual B increases while the utility of A decreases. This implies that as a result of the policy change, B is better off while A is worse off than before.

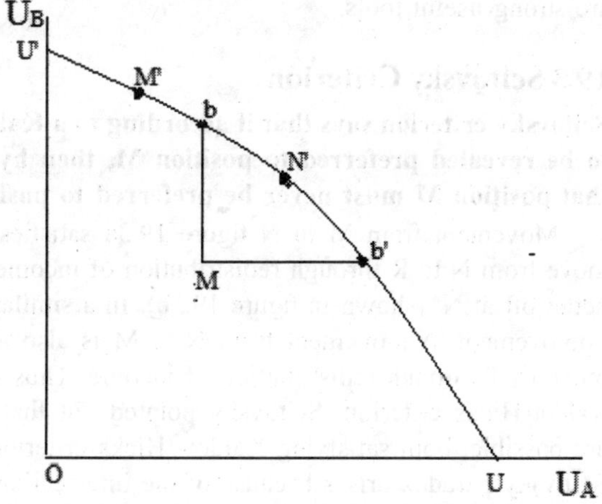

Figure 19.2 Kaldor Hicks Criterion

Such a policy change which benefits some and adversely affects others cannot be evaluated using the Pareto Criterion. The criterion proposed by Kaldor and Hicks enables us to say whether or not social welfare has increased as a result of movement from M to M'. According to Kaldor-Hicks criterion, if individual B who gains with the movement from M to M' could compensate individual A who is the loser and still be better off than before, then the policy change and the resulting movement from M to M' is an improvement.

In Figure 19.2 it can be seen that the utility possibility curve UU'passes through points b, N' and b'. If individual B compensates A for the loss suffered, they can move from position M' to the position b or N, or b' depending on the amount of compensation . At these points either one of them (with out affecting the other) or both are better off than at M.

A simple test for an improvement of welfare according to the Kaldor-Hicks criterion is that the initial bundle should lie below the utility possibility curve representing the new bundle. Thus a move from M to M' satisfies the Kaldor – Hicks criterion for the reason that M lies below the utility possibility curve UU_1' of the final bundle M'.

An important feature of the Kaldor Hicks criterion is that the compensation is only hypothetical or potential and no compensation is paid actually. If compensation is actually paid the criterion becomes Pareto criterion.

To further illustrate the Kaldor criterion, let us consider a proposed project, say, construction of a dam across a river. Initial situation 'R' is one in which the river is kept in its original state with the accompanying unemployment in the region. The altered state S' is one with a hydro electric plant in the river valley which implies, lower environmental quality, as valuable ecosystem is lost when the river is dammed. Alternative S is desirable if and only if the losers (those who want to preserve the environment) can be compensated for their loss of utility by those who gain from the project. In other words, the project is desirable if gainers can compensate the losers, hypothetically.

This requires that each individual who is against the project be asked to state the sum he is willing to pay to keep the valley in its natural state. Let this sum be M_G. Similarly, each supporter of the project be asked how much he is willing to accept (or receive) if state R is chosen. Let this sum be M_L. If $M_G > M_L$, the project may be considered desirable.

The compensation criteria are useful in decision-making involving trade-off. Most policy changes, such as introducing an effluent tax or building a new road involve trade off—some gain and some loss. For analysing the effects of such policy changes, compensation criteria and social welfare functions are strong useful tools.

19.3 Scitovsky Criterion

Scitovsky criterion says that if according to a Kaldor-Hicks welfare criterion position N is shown to be revealed preferred to position M, then by the same principle it should also be ensured that position M must never be preferred to position N.

Movement from M to N figure 19.3a satisfies Kaldor-Hicks criterion because it is possible to move from N to R through redistribution of income from gainers to losers, with both A and B being better off at N' (shown in figure 19.3b). In a similar way the reverse movement also proves to be an improvement. A movement from N to M is also an welfare improvement because it is possible to move to T through redistribution of income. Thus the reverse movement from N to M also satisfies Kaldor-Hicks criterion. Scitovsky pointed out that a paradox arises since to and from movements are possible, both satisfying Kaldor- Hicks criterion. This came to be known as Scitovsky Paradox. Scitivsky paradox arises because of the intersection of the two Utility Possibility Frontiers, with the points M and N located on two different UPFs but both within the cross – point of intersection of the UPFs (figure 19.3a).

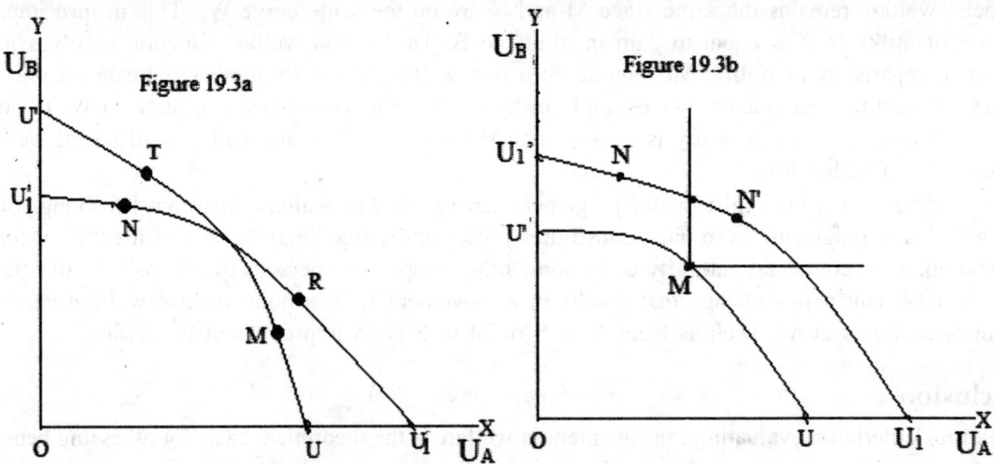

Figure 19.3a and 19.3b Scitovsky Criterion

Scitovsky removed the inconsistency in the Kaldor-icks criterion through his Double criterion, according to which:

(a) **gainers of a policy change are able to compensate the losers to accept the change;** (b) **losers of the policy change cannot persuade gainers to remain in the original situation**. This is possible only when the two utility possibility curves are one above the other and do not intersect each other. The Scitovsky criterion is illustrated in Figure 19.3b.

19.4 Bergson Samuelson Criterion

The various criteria discussed are certainly useful in assessing improvement in welfare arising from policy changes but are restricted in application due to the assumptions. Pareto criterion is limited in its scope since it ignores interpersonal comparisons of utility. Externalities and market imperfections hamper applying the Pareto criterion. Kaldor-Hicks and Scitovsky criteria are limited due to the assumption that only potential compensation is required. To overcome these restrictions, Bergson and Samuelson introduced the welfare function. Social welfare function is a function of the utility levels of all individuals in the society. It is expressed as:

$$W = W(U_1, U_2, U_3, \ldots U_N)$$

where W is Social Welfare, and U_1, U_2, $U_3 \ldots U_N$ are ordinal utility indices of utility of the individuals in the society. Social welfare functions are based on explicit value judgments and incorporate inter-personal comparisons of utility. The social welfare function is illustrated using social indifference curves which are also called welfare frontiers. A social indifference curve or welfare frontier is a collection of combinations of utilities of the two individuals A and B. All combinations on a given social indifference curve represent the same level of welfare. A movement from point M to point N on a given social welfare curve in figure 19.4 implies that B's utility increases but A's utility decreases but

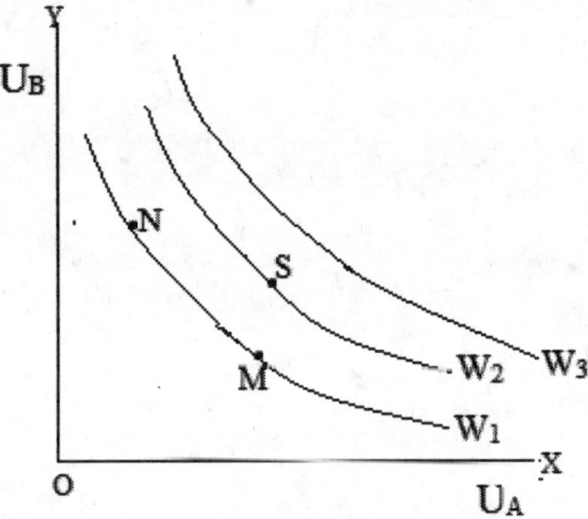

Figure 19.4 Bergson Samuelson Social Welfare Function

the social welfare remains the same since M and N are on the same curve W_1. This in turn implies that loss of utility to A is equal to gain in utility to B. Thus social welfare function involves inter personal comparisons of utility. Movement from one welfare curve to another indicate changes in welfare for both the individuals. For example in figure 19.4 movement from point N on W_1 to point S on W_2, means A's gain in utility is greater than B's loss of utility and still overall social welfare has moved to a higher level.

According to Bergson explicit value judgements are required to evaluate situations involving policy changes. "These judgments as to what constitutes justice and virtue" may be that of the "legislator,or by some other governmental authority or by some other unspecified persons or groups". As illustrated in figure 19.4, any policy change that results in a movement from a point on one welfare curve to a point on a higher curve, such as from N to S or M to S is an improvement in welfare.

Conclusion

The various criteria for evaluating improvement in welfare is the theoretical basis for assessing benefits from environmental resources and their functions and for decision making under situations of conflict between development projects and conservation and protection of environment.

Question

1. Explain the various criteria for evaluating welfare changes arising from policy changes.

Exercise

1. There are people who want to preserve forests for its intrinsic value. There are others who want the forest land or building a factory. How do you compare welfare in such cases? Do you think the theoretical principles of welfare criteria are applicable here?

SECTION 5

ENVIRONMENTAL ECONOMICS

20

ECONOMICS OF POLLUTION

"We are going to make little real progress in solving the problem of pollution until we recognise it for what primarily it is; an economic problem, which must be understood in economic terms."

—*Prof Larry Ruff*

Environmental Economics mainly builds its theoretical foundation on welfare economics. The production and consumption of economic goods imposes a significant cost on the society. Environmental economics analyses rules for the efficient use of the environment. Economic activity draws heavily on the three functions of the environment: supply of renewable and non-renewable resource, waste assimilation and maintenance of biodiversity. The three economic functions of the environment are inter-related and efficient use of the first two functions is a fundamental requirement for the environment to perform its third function. A misuse of the first two functions results in environmental crisis.

Environmental functions have both a qualitative and quantitative dimension. The adverse effects of our actions on the quality of environment are explained *by economics of pollution.* The effects of our actions on the quantity of environmental resources available for future use are explained by economics of resource use or *resource economics.* This chapter will analyse theoretical issues related to pollution focusing on:

a. Pollution as an externality.
b. Second best theorem.
c. Environmental quality as a public good.

20.1 Economics of Pollution

Economists consider pollution to be an externality. Externalities result when firms and households do **not appropriate the full** costs or benefits of their productive or consumptive **activities. Externality** may be defined as the cost or benefit imposed by the production and consumption activities of firms and households respectively on the rest of the society towards which no compensation or payment is made. The definition makes it clear that externalities arise from both production and consumption activities and that their impact could be beneficial (positive) or adverse (negative).

The concept of externality can be traced back to Alfred Marshall's ideas on external economies. Marshall introduced the concept of external economies, which contains the key to the economic analysis of production. Marshall defined external economies to include only the benefits enjoyed by producers. In 1920, A.C. Pigou pointed out that externalities involved both benefits and costs. He explained negative externalities through his classic illustration of damages to woodlands caused by sparks from railway engines—thus leading the discussions that considered pollution as an externality. In 1950, K.W. Kapp presented the first substantial discussion of externalities and social costs in his book "The Social Cost of Private Enterprise" in which he analysed all external costs arising from production processes in the form of air and water pollution.

Externalities can be classified as:

1. Positive or beneficial consumption externality (e.g., vaccination against an infectious disease).
2. Positive or beneficial production externality (e.g., pollination of blossom in an orchard arising from proximity to beehives).
3. Negative or adverse consumption externalities (e.g., noise pollution from a loud music system).
4. Negative or adverse production externalities (e.g., effluents and emissions from factories).

Externalities have also been classified as pecuniary externalities and real or technological externalities. Technological externalities alter the production function (utility function) of a third party not involved in the production (consumption) process that generates the externality. Pollution of air and water are examples of real or technological externalities. Pecuniary externalities, on the other hand, are reflected in market prices. They arise due to changes in the price of some input or output in the economy. Pecuniary externalities do not cause distortions in the efficient allocation of resources while real or technological economies require efficiency conditions to be redefined.

Pollution is a negative externality. Most environmental problems come under the category of negative externalities. They represent the costs of production and consumption decisions which are not borne by the agents involved in the transactions. The discharge of organic and inorganic effluents into a river by a firm will lower the quality of the river water. The DO—Dissolved Oxygen content of water in the river will be lowered, thus making the water unfit for drinking purposes. Besides, the reduced oxygen content will even bring down the number of fish in the river, affecting the income of the fishing industry. The factory discharging the untreated effluent into the river does not compensate the people affected by the deterioration in the quality of water. They are hence *external cost to the* firm that causes the pollution. The firm will price its products on the basis of the cost it bears in making them: Wages, rent, material inputs and so on. These private costs will not include the cost arising due to the effluent discharged , since this is not paid by the firm. Pollution is thus an externality-cost falling on third parties.

The firm actually has an economic incentive to pollute. It is cheaper to pollute the river than it is to treat the effluent before discharging it in to the river. So long as the firm is not legally prevented from doing so, a rational firm will pollute and not treat its effluent/emissions.

The presence of such externalities in economic theory is an instance of *market failure.* While the market system appears to be highly efficient at using priced resources like labour, land, raw materials, etc., it fails to guide firms towards the efficient use of unpriced environmental resources. This market failure arises because, firms take into account, only the market price of the resources it uses for its decision making. The assimilative capacity of the environment that the firm uses when it discharges emissions into air or effluents into the water is an unpriced environmental service which the firm does not incorporate into its decision making analysis. Because of such external effects, markets fail to allocate resources efficiently. In our analysis of efficient resource allocation in chapter 16, we assumed that production and consumption activities do not involve external effects. But negative externalities in the form of air and water pollution are pervasive and inevitable in the modern industrial economies. In such cases, efficiency conditions need to be modified to account for externalities. Even a competitive market economy cannot allocate resources efficiently by equating price ratio to marginal private cost ratio, if production and consumption activities generate external costs. In such an economy if we are to have output and price levels that are socially efficient, we must include in our calculations both private cost and external cost, i.e., the cost that is relevant for 'efficient' outcomes of P and Q is marginal social cost and not marginal private cost and Marginal Social Cost = Marginal Private Cost + Marginal External Cost. i.e.,

MSC = MPC + MEC

In the absence of externalities, socially optimal output is reached when P = MPC, where MPC = marginal private cost. In the presence of externalities, marginal external cost should be added to marginal private cost.

MEC may be defined as the additional cost imposed on third parties from the production of an additional unit of output. Optimal output, when externalities are present is determined by equality of price to MSC. **The presence of externalities lead to over production of a good relative to the socially optimal level.** This is illustrated in figure 20.1.

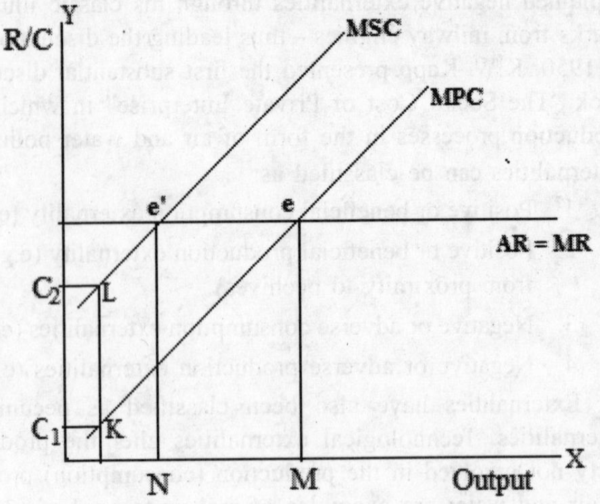

Figure 20.1 Effect of External cost on Firm's Output

Figure 20.1 has been drawn on a crucial assumption that marginal external cost is constant per unit of output. The vertical distance between MPC and MSC, is MEC and it is the same throughout, implying that MEC per unit of output is constant. In reality, with increase in the level of output, there will be an increase in external cost also. The MPC curve represents marginal private cost. It includes all incremental cost to the firm, of labour, material and capital. The AR = MR line shows the price level determined by the demand and the supply of the product and passed on to the firm. The firm being one among many, in a perfectly competitive market, cannot alter the market price. The firm's equilibrium, defined by MC= MR condition is at point 'e' which yields an output level of OM. However, production by the firm causes pollution; the cost due to the discharge of pollution by the firm is called as external cost. The external cost is added to private cost to arrive at social cost (private cost + external cost = social cost) which is taken into consideration for defining the equilibrium when there is externality. From the society's point of view, for social optimum to exist, the firm should account for this external cost also. In figure 20.1 the external cost is the distance between the MSC and MPC. There is an external cost of C_1C_2 (KL) per unit of output. Ideally the 'price = marginal cost' should occur at e', at which P = MSC. The output corresponding to this equilibrium e' is ON. Thus there is difference between socially optimal output level and private optimal output level (NM). **There is an exaggeration or overproduction of the firm's output when externalities are not accounted for by the firm.** The society would be better off with ON units of output. The resources used to produce NM units of output have greater value in other employments. There is an **over production** of this good equal to NM units which means that some other good or goods is being under produced or not produced at all.

The above analysis can be extended to a whole industry. For this we need to derive the supply curve. Horizontal summation of MPC schedules gives the private supply curve PSS and horizontal summation of MSC curves gives the social supply curve SSS in the figure 20.2. The SSS curve lies above PSS curve reflecting the difference between MSC and MPC. The vertical distance between SSS and PSS curves gives the aggregate external cost imposed on the society by all the firms in the industry.

The SSS and PSS curves together with the industry demand curve in figure 20.2 help us to analyse the full effects of external diseconomies on price and resource allocation. The market demand curve intersects the private supply curve PSS curve at E_1, resulting in price OP_1, and output OM_1. However, if the firms account for external costs, SSS curve is the relevant supply curve. The Market demand curve intersecting SSS curve, yields an output OM_2 and price OP_2.

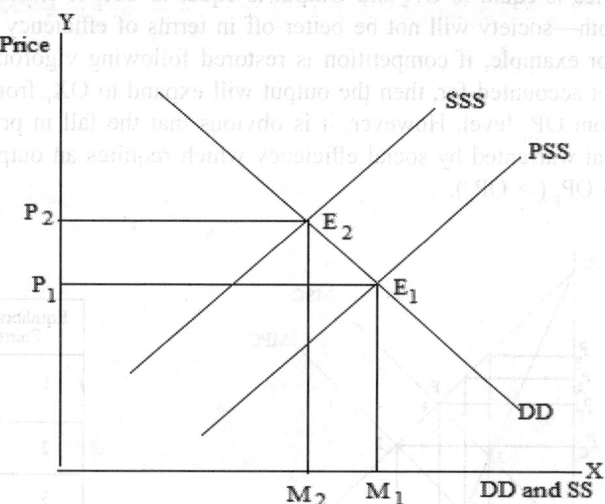

Figure 20.2 Effect of Externality on Industry

Comparing this price output level, with the price and the output, when externalities are not accounted for, we can say that private market leads to too high an output ($OM_1 > OM_2$) at too low a price, ($P_1 < P_2$). Over production due to externalities is M_2M_1 units of output. This means that some other industries are producing less. Society as a whole would be better off if this industry behaved as if SSS and not PSS is the supply curve. Thus, in the presence of externalities, market mechanism fails to allocate resources efficiently.

20.2 Problem of Second Best

The problem of attaining an efficient allocation of resources becomes still more complex once we consider the effects of such externalities on price and output in an imperfectly competitive market. The presence of externalities and imperfection simultaneously, a real world situation, distorts efficiency in a more serious way than when only one is present. On the one hand, externalities cause price to fall below marginal social cost of production and the resulting output is high compared to a situation where production costs and external costs are covered by the firm. On the other hand, imperfect competition results in a price above marginal cost (P > MC) whereas under perfect competition (P = MC). Hence when the competition is imperfect, price is higher and output lower than under perfect competition. The two effects thus work in opposite directions and will tend to offset each other. In theory, either effect could dominate the other. However, to determine which effect is stronger, is an empirical problem.

Let us assume that the imperfection in the market takes the form of monopoly, i.e., there is only one producer of the product. The monopolist's equilibrium is given by the equality of MPC with MR. This results in an output OX_A at a price P_A in figure 20.3.

Figure 20.3 has been drawn on the assumption that external costs per unit of output remains constant at all levels of output. Thus the vertical distance between MSC and MPC will give MEC. The figure illustrates two distortions from efficiency.

1. Degree of monopoly power.
2. External cost.

Correction of both the problems is necessary in order to restore efficiency. Economists call such a situation as the problem of second best; such an equilibrium where both the problems are corrected is shown at point F in the figure where AR curve cuts MSC curve. At this Second Best equilibrium, price is equal to OP_F and Output is equal to OX_F. If either one of the distortions is corrected but not both—society will not be better off in terms of efficiency than if the situation remained uncorrected. For example, if competition is restored following vigorous anti-trust campaign, but externalities are not accounted for, then the output will expand to OX_C from OX_A and the price will fall to OP_C level, from OP_A level. However, it is obvious that the fall in price and an increase in output is more than that warranted by social efficiency which requires an output level of OX_F ($< OX_C$) and a price equal to OP_F ($> OP_C$).

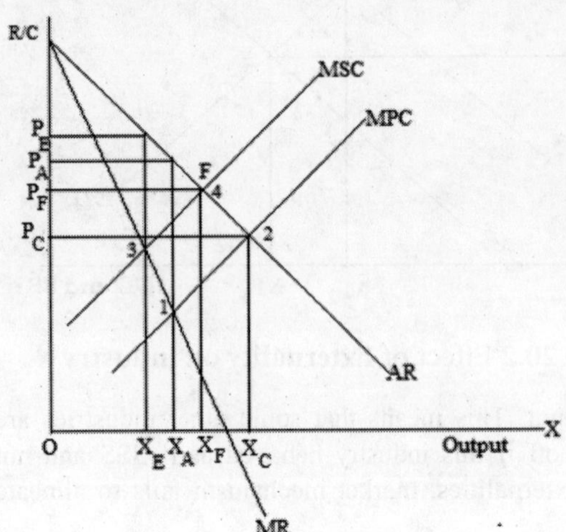

Equilibrium Point	Equilibrium Condition	Price	Output
1	MPC = MR	P_A	X_A
2	MPC = AR	P_C	X_C
3	MSC = MR	P_E	X_E
4	MSC = AR SECOND BEST	P_F	X_F

Figure 20.3 The Second Best Theorem

Alternatively, if competition is not restored but externalities are internalised, by means of an effluent tax equal in amount to external cost per unit of output, then monopolist would take into consideration MSC curve for determining his equilibrium price and output. Accordingly his equilibrium is defined at the point of equality of MR with MSC. This results in a price of P_E and an output level of OX_E. This output is lower than the monopoly output ($OX_E < OX_A$) and price is higher than monopoly price ($P_E > P_A$). OX_E is less than the socially optimum output ($OX_E < OX_F$) and OP_E is greater than the socially optimum price ($P_E > P_F$). Thus when an industry is characterised by monopoly and

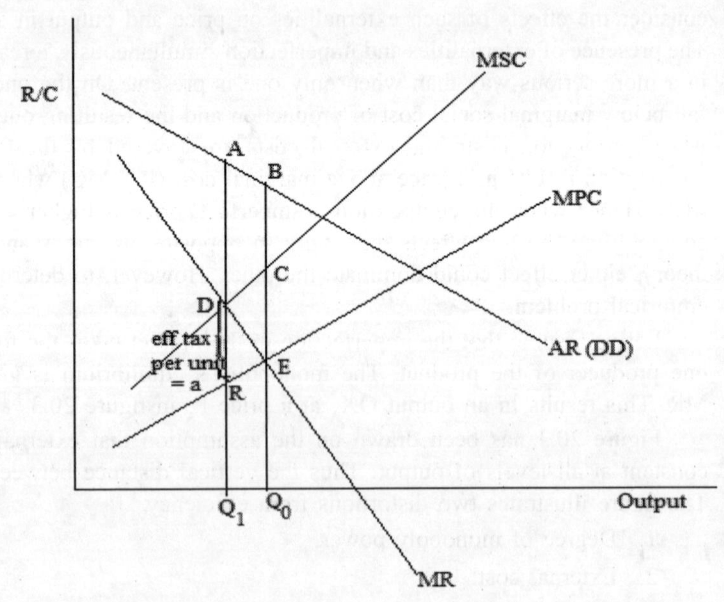

Figure 20.4 Welfare Loss when Externality is Internalised by an Effluent Tax Imposed on the Monopolist

externalities, it is always desirable to correct for both the distortions. It cannot be presumed that a more efficient outcome than the one existing will result if at least one is corrected. Both problems must be jointly treated to achieve improvements in resource allocation. Piecemeal attempts will not restore efficiency.

In fact it can be shown, that if we try to correct for one deficiency— (pollution) in a market where there exists another deficiency— (monopoly)—the result will be a further welfare loss. This is illustrated in figure 20.4. In figure 20.4, we relax the assumption of constant MEC. Hence the vertical distance between MSC and MPC increases with output. In figure 20.4 BE is difference between price and marginal private cost at the original profit maximising output level Q_0. This difference is greater than the difference between MSC and MPC (BE > CE). If the monopolist is compelled to internalise the externality, through the payment of an effluent tax, he will then equate MSC to MR, assuming that the tax is equal to MEC. The equilibrium after tax is at D and accordingly output of the monopolist decreases to Q_1 This decrease in production reduces total welfare by $Q_1AB\ Q_0$ while the social cost for this production is only $Q_1DC\ Q_0$. Hence there is a net loss to society ABCD.

20.3 Solutions to Externality

The preceding analysis indicate that the existence of technological externalities cause the most perplexing problems. Many solutions have been suggested to this problem; a detailed discussion of each of these will be taken exclusively in a later chapter. A brief mention of the different solutions is given below.

Basically in all the available literature on the problem of technological externalities we can find at least seven solutions to this problem. They are:

1. **Total prohibition** of the action that causes to pollution.
2. **Direct Regulation** which takes three forms:
    a. Effluent/Emission Standard which includes setting a ceiling to the level of the quantity of effluent/emission discharged into water or air. For example, in the case of air pollution Government would have to specify just how much smoke a factory could emit.
    b. Ambient Standard which is a never exceed limit for a pollutant or minimum desired level of any component or indicator of the ambient environment (Example: DO in water should not fall below 100 ppm)
    c. Technological Standard which is specification of a particular pollution equipment to be installed, such as an electro static precipitator; this also includes stipulating the height of the chimney.
3. **Market based instruments** (MBIs) such as **taxes and subsidies**: Here the idea is to encourage activities that contribute to common good and discourage those that deviate from common good. Accordingly a polluter may be required to pay a tax for every unit of waste discharged. A subsidy on the other hand would require payment of a financial incentive for every unit of pollution abated. Subsidy could also be in the form of a payment to the firm to cover in part or full the cost of the required pollution control equipment.
4. MBIs also include the sale of **pollution permits** which require the establishment of a system of marketable licenses. Each license would give its owner the right to pollute up to a specified amount in a given place during a particular period of time. These licenses could be bought and sold in an organised market.
5. **Voluntary action** such as non-mandatory investment in pollution control equipment by firms that decide to be socially responsible or voluntary separation of solid wastes by consumers who can deliver them to collection centers for recycling.

6. **Direct investments** by the Government on sewage plants, effluent treatment plants etc.
7. **Restoration of property rights** is also suggested by many who strongly believe that "common property" nature of the resources is responsible for the damages imposed on them. The advocates of this measure believe that restoration of private property ownership will serve as an incentive for preservation and conservation of resources.

Thus there is a whole menu of measures which can effectively deal with problems created by technological externalities. None of these is perfect. Nor does any one solution dominate the other as 'the best'. What is best for dealing with one type of externalities may not be so for another. The merit of the tool also depends on the time, location, etc. Hence a policy mix of the various tools after appropriately weighing the pros and cons of each measure is required.

20.4 Environmental Quality as a Public Good

We saw in Chapter 17 that the efficiency conditions for securing a Pareto optimum require modification in the presence of *public goods.* In this section we analyse the problem arising due to the "public goods nature" of the environmental quality. Public goods can be contrasted with private goods. A private good can be attributed to a specific individual. Individuals compete against each other in using the good and potential users can be excluded. There is *rivalry and exclusiveness* in the use of a private good. Rivalry implies that the consumption of the good or service by one person reduces the availability or utility of the good or service to another person, that is, consumption by an individual excludes all other consumers. E*xcludability* means that the use of the good is restricted to those who pay for it and those who are entitled to it. Those who do not pay for it can be prevented from accessing and using it. A public good has exactly opposite features. Its consumption is non-rival, i.e. the consumption or use of the good or service by one person does not reduce the availability or utility of the good or service to another person.

Provision of a public good to any one individual (A) entails its provision to every other individual (B), whether he wants it or not. Non-rivalry implies that additional consumption of the good does not add anything to the costs of production. Consumption of the good by one individual does not reduce the quantity available to others. For example, an additional truck on a fly over or bridge does not add to the cost of providing the bridge. Individual cannot be excluded from using the public good, once it is provided.

Non-excludability implies that no one can be prevented from accessing because of non-payment; it is extremely expensive to exclude or it is not practical to exclude people who do not pay for a good from the benefit of receiving the good. Property rights cannot be attributed to individuals for any public good; It could be because of physical impossibility to implement exclusion or controlling access would be inordinately expensive or cumbersome or socially unacceptable. On account of features of non-rivalry and non-excludability, provision of a public good ensures that each individual consumes the same amount of it. The classic textbook examples of public goods are light houses and national defence systems. The consumption of these services by any individual does not reduce the amount available to others and no one can be excluded from the benefits of these services, once it is provided. In the case of public goods the market mechanism fails, either completely or in part and this market failure is corrected by the government making a direct provision of the good.

Environmental quality is considered to be a public good that must be consumed in equal amounts by all. This is because private property rights cannot be defined for environmental quality: exclusion is not possible and rivalry in consumption does not exist. It is therefore clear that very many environmental resource and services come under the classification of public goods, like the benefits from biological diversities, the services of wilderness resources, the climate regulation mechanism of earth's atmosphere etc. As a result of features of non-rivalry and non-excludability the probability of markets existing to provide these public goods is extremely low. Even if a private market were to exist the outcome would not be efficient.

Characteristics of the good	Excludable	Non-Excludable
Rivalry	Private goods possess the features of both rivalry and excludability. Any good which an individual has purchased and is therefore rightfully the owner of it. Could be a book, a pen or a car.	Common Property Resource/ Common Goods are largely available to all but are limited in supply; therefore they are non-excludable but rivalry in use. Such goods are likely to result in tragedy of Commons situation. Example: Ocean fishery
Non-Rivalry	Club or Toll goods are excludable, but non-rivalry in use. Examples include subscriptions to cable TV, access to private parks.	Public goods are both non-rivalrous and non-excludable. Examples include light house, national defense etc.

BOX 20.1 Classification of Goods

The distinctive features of a public good makes its demand curve the vertical summation of the individual curves while for the private good it is the horizontal summation of individual demand curves. This is because, at any time, the quantity available of a public good is:

$$X_{PU} = X^A_{PU} = X^B_{PU} = X^C_{PU} = \text{------} = X^N_{PU}$$

While for a private good, it is:

$$X_{PR} = X^A_{PR} + X^B_{PR} + X^C_{PR} + \text{-------} + X^N_{PR}$$

where A, B,... N are individuals.

Figures 20.5a and 20.5b illustrate the demand curves for private and public goods respectively. As illustrated in figure 20.5, the total demand for a private good of an economy is added horizontally. In figure 20.5a we add quantities. In the figure, D_AD and D_BD' are the demand curves of the two individuals A and B. The downward slope of the curve accounts for the inverse relationship between price and quantity. Curve D_BED^* is the aggregate demand curve of the two individuals. D_BED^* is obtained by adding up the quantities each individual will buy for each price level, i.e., horizontally adding D_AD and D_BD'. For example if the price is P_1, A's demand for the good is P_1A and B's demand for the good is P_1B. Adding P_1A and P_1B we get P_1Q. Similarly at price P_2, A's demand is P_2C and B's demand is P_2D and market or aggregate demand is $P_2C + P_2D = P_2Q'$. The curve D_BED^* is the market or aggregate demand curve for the private good.

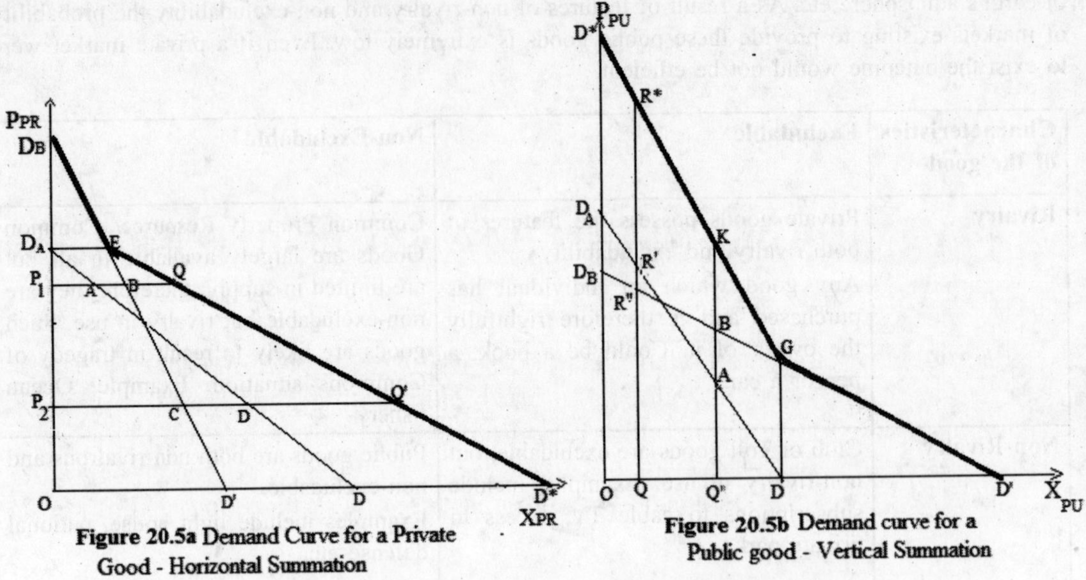

Figure 20.5a Demand Curve for a Private Good - Horizontal Summation

Figure 20.5b Demand curve for a Public good - Vertical Summation

Figure 20.5 Demand Curves for Private and Public Goods

In the case of a public good, both A and B consume the same quantities, but they differ in how much they are willing to pay for any quantity. Hence we cannot add quantities. Instead, we sum the individual evaluation of the public good. In the figure, D_AD and D_BD' are the demand curves of the two individuals A and B for the public good. We add their demand curves D_AD and D_BD' vertically to derive the aggregate demand curve for the public good. For example, for quantity OQ, individual A is willing to pay QR' and B is willing to pay QR". Adding QR' to QR" gives the point R* on the aggregate demand curve for the public good. Similarly, for quantity OQ' A is willing to pay Q'A and B is willing to pay Q'B. Adding the two sums we get the aggregate willingness to pay for OQ'. Sum of Q'A + Q'B gives another point- point K - on the aggregate demand curve for the public good . The curve D*GD' reflects the aggregate willingness of individuals A and B to pay for each and every quantity of the public good. The bold curve D*GD' is the aggregate demand curve for the public good.

20.5 Optimal Provision of Public Good

The conditions to be satisfied for Pareto optimum in an economy providing public and private goods differs from that in an economy providing private goods alone. In an economy containing private goods alone, for optimality, MRS of all individuals should be equal which in turn should be equal to MRPT, i.e., in an economy with two private goods X and Y and two individuals A and B, for Pareto optimal allocation of resources,

$$MRPT_{XY} = MRS^A_{XY} = MRS^B_{XY}$$

On the other hand, in an economy containing public and private goods the social rates of marginal substitutions between public and private goods must be equal to the sum of individual marginal rates of substitution (Samuelson 1954), i.e.,

$$MRPT_{XY} = MRS^A_{XY} + MRS^B_{XY}$$

In such an economy the sum of MRS is equal to MRPT while in private goods economy the MRS of each individual is equal to that of the others and also equal to MRT. Figure 20.6 shows the implication of this equivalence.

In figure 20.6 MC_{PU} is the marginal cost of providing the public good, assumed to increase as more is provided, i.e., provision of an additional unit costs more; if it refers to removal of smoke, then the removal of an additional percentage of smoke may be said to be possible at additional cost only. The curves MV_1 and MV_2 in figure 20.6 are the marginal valuation curves. They are derived from individual's indifference curves which show his preferences between public and private goods. MV_1, refers to the marginal valuation curve for individual 1 and MV_2 refers to the marginal valuation curve for the individual 2. Further MV_1, and MV_2 measure MRS between public and private goods for the two individuals. Since MV_1, and MV_2 measure MRS the diagram can be used directly to illustrate Pareto optimal provision of goods in the economy. In the figure MRPT reflected in the MC curve. Since each unit of public good is consumed by each consumer, aggregate marginal valuation curve is derived by vertical summation of MV curves. For example the value placed on OMth unit of the public good by individual 1 is ab and by individual 2 is ac, resulting in an aggregate marginal value of ad (ad = ab + ac). The intersection of the aggregate marginal valuation curve with the marginal cost curves gives the optimal quantity of public good. This occurs at point Z in figure 20.6, corresponding to which X* units of the good is provided. This quantity satisfies the optimality condition, for at Z,

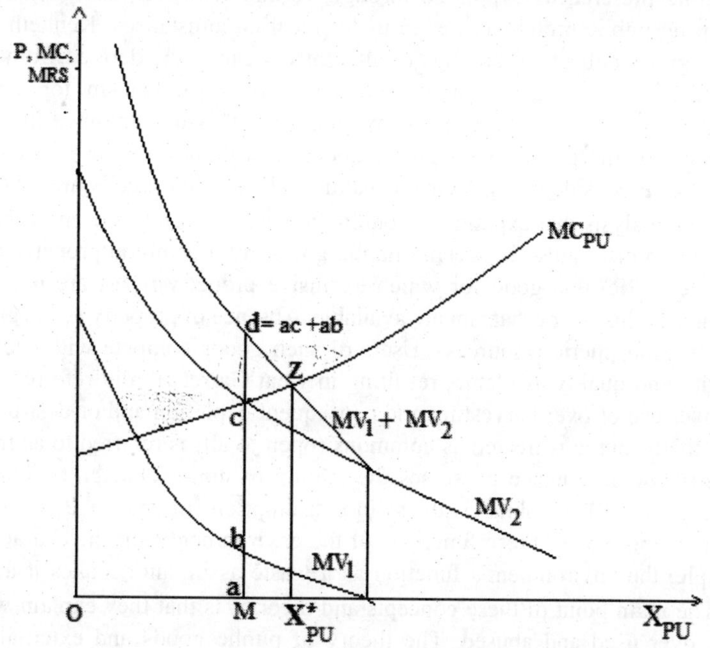

Figure 20.6 Optimal Provision of a Public Good

$$MC = MRS_1 + MRS_2$$

However the very characteristic feature of public good makes the estimation of marginal valuation and demand curve for the public good difficult. Because of the features of non-rivalry and non-excludability, there is a tendency on the part of the individuals to either over state or under-state their preferences. Since the benefits of a public good, like the installation of a drinking water treatment plant , is enjoyed by all, regardless of whether they have indicated their willingness to pay for the treated water, there are people who either under-state their valuation or never reveal it. Such people will enjoy the benefits of the programme as 'a free rider'. If individuals believe that their valuation will affect their tax or the cost of the programme then they would understate it. On the other hand if they find their valuation of the public good will not affect their tax burden, they will over-state their true valuation of the public good. Hence government must resort to rough approximations based on public preferences expressed through voting. However, voting is deficient as a mechanism for measuring public preferences even under ideal circumstances. Kenneth Arrow has demonstrated that unambiguous collective rankings of alternatives cannot be derived from the aggregation of individual rankings. Voting, hence, cannot be counted as a mechanism for determining public interest on environmental issues. There are many such crucial issues involved in the provision of public goods. Financing of the provision of public goods, distribution of the cost among the beneficiaries are all issues to be considered in decision making when public goods are provided.

Any analysis that explains the public goods approach to the environmental problem is incomplete if it fails to distinguish between a public good and a common property resource. A common property resource (CPR) is a good for which exclusive property rights are not defined for historical reasons although exclusion mechanism are available. Absence of property rights gives open access to such goods (earth's atmospheric resources). Users of such goods compete with each other virtually affecting the quantity and quality available, resulting in what Garret Hardin referred to as "Tragedy of commons". The over use or over harvesting and consequent depletion and/or destruction of a resource that results when the resource is treated as commons (open to all) is referred to as tragedy of commons. Common property resource hence possesses the feature of non-excludability, like a public good, but unlike a public good CPR exhibits rivalness in consumption. In chapter 2, we discussed the functions of the environment. Not all these functions of the environment bear the characteristics of a public good. For example, the environment's function as a waste assimilator makes it a CPR, but not a public good.

The main point of these concepts and theories is that they explain why environmental issues tend to be over used and abused. The theory of public goods and externalities explain why individuals are induced to use environmental resources liberally but not so induced when it is a question of contributing to protect the resources. What is required is collective action. We have to make collective decisions about the appropriate use of our environment failing which we can never hope to recover from our current state.

Question

1. Define an externality. Give a note on different types of externality with examples.
2. Explain the impact of pollution on the efficiency of market.
3. Explain the second best theorem
4. Why is environmental quality considered as a public good. What are the conditions for the optimal provision of a public good.

Exercise

1. Describe a free rider situation that had adverse environmental impact. Suggest a measure that would remove free rider problem.
2. State atleast three acitivities that you do which have positive and negative effect on others. Give reasons for undertaking such activities which impact others. Are there rules that prevent or promote such activities. If so state them.

21

NATURAL RESOURCE ECONOMICS

> "Natural resources—the ultimate supply factor—will act either as a serious constraint or as a vibrant sustaining contributor to growth."
>
> —*Robert D. Hamrin*

The term "natural resources" refers to those "economic factors in production or consumption which owe their origin and existence to natural phenomena or to processes that occur automatically in nature". Natural resources possess two important features namely, either their stock is fixed or the stock of the resource is subject to a biological growth rate. This chapter explains the determination of optimum rate of harvest for both types of natural resource - one which has a fixed stock and one which grows.

21.1 Classification of Natural Resources

Natural resources are classified commonly as renewable and non-renewable resources. Renewable resources are those which may be used without depletion. Renewable resources are therefore referred to as flow resources. Solar energy is a renewable energy which may be tapped without affecting the flow available in future. Fisheries and forests are also renewable resources but they have a biological growth rate; their stock will not get exhausted as long as their biological growth rate is greater than the rate of harvest of the resource. However, whenever the rate of harvest exceeds the biological growth rate of the resource, depletion of the resource is unavoidable.

Table 21.1 Classification of Resources

Type	Renewability	Example
Flow or Renewable Resources	Less susceptible to human modification →	Solar Energy
	More susceptible to human modification →	Soil, Forest, Fish
Fund or stock or non-renewable resources	More Recyclable →	Metals
	Less or not recyclable →	Fossil Fuel

Non-renewable or exhaustible resources, are depleted by use. Their stock size is given. Examples include fossil fuels and mineral resources. However due to recycling and innovative technologies available, it is possible to extend the use of non-renewable resources. Table 21.1 presents a classification of resources.

21.2 Evolution of Resource Economics – A Brief Summary

Any attempt to trace the history of natural resource economics begins with references to writings of the economists belonging to the classical school on resource scarcity.Adam Smith believed in the generosity of nature and ruled out the role of absolute scarcity of resources. However he hinted at the possibility of a stationery state that would eventually arise inspite of an increased productivity in agriculture due to the distributional and social impacts from the relative scarcity of agricultural output. Smith failed to consider the role of technology. Barnett and Morse in their work titled "Scarcity and Economic Growth—The Economics of Natural Resource Availability" (1963) observed that while Malthus emphasised on absolute scarcity, Ricardo spoke of relative scarcity. The Malthusian theory assumed that the stock of agricultural land was absolutely limited. Beyond this limit, continuing population growth would require increasing intensity of cultivation and would eventually result in diminishing marginal returns. Ricardo on the other hand pointed out to relative scarcity arising due to decline in quality of land. Ricardian concept of scarcity does not imply absolute limit to resource availability. There was always another land of lower quality available to be used up. Ricardo hinted at a temporary scarcity of a particular stock of resources, but held that it does not necessarily lead to an absolute constraint on growth.

Mill's analysis of natural resource scarcity provided an important link between classical and contemporary views. Mill focused his attention on non-renewable resources and said that scarcity of non-renewable resources would be a constraint on economic growth irrespective of population problem. He supported Ricardo's relative scarcity approach to natural resource scarcity. He stated that continued exploitation of earth's natural resources will force society to consider stationary state as a desirable outcome. Mill felt that for the sake of posterity, people ought to be content to be stationary, "long before necessity compels them to it".

Jevon's views on natural resource scarcity are drawn from his *The Coal Question* (1909). Jevons wrote extensively on the exhaustibility of non-renewable resources, particularly coal. Jevons considered exhaustibility of coal as the most important threat to sustained economic growth. Jevons, while focusing exclusive attention on the impact of exhaustibility of coal on Britain's economic growth, ruled out the possibilities of the replacement of coal by substitutes like petroleum. He was equally pessimistic about the impact of technological change on reducing mining costs and increasing effective reserves. He rejected the view that technological innovation induced by rise in prices of scarce resources would alleviate the constraint on economic growth imposed by the scarcity of exhaustible resources.

Alfred Marshall rejected the notion that scarcity of resources would constrain economic growth. He emphasised the role played by the 'growth of organisation and knowledge' and the accompanying innovations in preventing scarcity. This increased strength from organisation, held Marshall, would ward off the constraints on economic growth from diminishing returns in agriculture. Marshall's views reflect the transition from the pessimistic view of the earlier economists to a new optimistic view of natural resource scarcity.

A.C. Pigou was one of the earliest economists to point out that our preference for present needs and pleasures will hurt the future generation yet to be born. He strongly argued that individuals distribute their resources between present and future on the basis of wholly irrational preferences. Human beings regard costs and benefits in future as being of less importance than costs and benefits now. Hence they act with selfishness, consuming maximum resources now giving importance to present benefits than to future benefits. Such selfishness, will result in depletion of resources and future benefits will be sacrificed for smaller present ones. Pigou cited the examples of fishing operations conducted with disregard to breeding season causing extinction of certain species and extensive farming operation that reduce the fertility of soil. Pigou recommended that governments should control use of exhaustible resources through the legislation.

The modern contemporary view on natural resource scarcity is best expressed by Harold Hotelling in his article entitled "The Economics of Exhaustible Resources" published in 1931, where he wrote; "contemplation of the world's disappearing supplies of minerals, forests and other exhaustible assets has led to demand for regulation of their exploitation. The feeling that these products are now too cheap for the good of future generations, that they are being selfishly exploited at too rapid a rate and that in the consequence of their excessive cheapness, they are being produced and consumed wastefully, has given rise to the conservation movement".

Hotelling also supported the Ricardian view of relative scarcity. He said that such relative scarcity of economically useful resources would be reflected in market price which will increase the production of the required resources—either from newly discovered reserves or by application of technology that will promote substitution. This is in line with Marshall's views. Highlighting the need for conserving resources, Hotelling used the concept of present value maximisation to analyse what maximises the present value of the stream of benefits that consumers enjoy, from the stock of natural resources.

In the study "Scarcity and Growth: The Economics of Natural Resource Scarcity" published in 1963, Harold Barnett and Chandler Morse accepted Ricardian relative scarcity as a possibility but indicated that it will be overcome by the march of science. Barnett and Morse observed "Nature imposed particular scarcities but not inescapable general scarcity". In their view natural resource scarcity would lead to a rise in the market price of that resource which will provoke search for substitutes, explore recycling possibilities and discovery of new reserves. These would mitigate the scarcity and the constraint it imposes on economic growth.

It is clear that the concern about increasing scarcity of resource is not new. First of all, a distinction should be made between absolute scarcity and relative scarcity. Absolute scarcity exists where insufficient physical quantities of the resource are available to meet the demand for it, i.e., supply of the resource is insufficient to meet the demand. Relative scarcity, on the other hand exists when the physical quantities of the resource are sufficient to meet the demand, but problem arise over quality of supplies; poorer grades of the resource may be available to meet the demand, but cost of extraction will be higher.

There are three important indicators of resource scarcity:

1. A rising marginal resource extraction cost.
2. Marginal exploration and discovery costs.
3. Real market price indicators.

However technological advances will open up possibilities for exploring and discovering new deposits. In addition markets will react to the rising price/cost signal by encouraging substitution, new ways of using resources, recycling and efficient use of resources.

Partha Das Gupta (1993) examines various possibilities, that will certainly postpone if not prevent resource exhaustibility. They are:

1. Development of new materials such as synthetic fibres.
2. Technological developments which increase productivity of extraction activities.
3. Technological advancements like aerial photograph that make exploration activities easier and cheaper.
4. Technological advancements that will promote efficient use of resources.
5. Improvements in recycling technology.
6. Substitution of low grade resource reserves for high grade deposits that are getting exhausted.

The conventional views do not include in their analysis physical principles like: the laws of thermodynamics, which would change the emphasis from the conventional relative scarcity issue to an absolute scarcity issue. More recent studies point out that absolute scarcity of resources coupled with growing population and its increased consumption would be a major constraint on economic activity. Natural resources and physical environment constitute the fundamental foundation upon which all economic activity is constructed.

21.3 Theories of Natural Resource Use

The growing concern about the increasing scarcity of fossil fuels and other raw materials has provided us with various theories and models of natural resource use. In majority of these works the emphasis has been on the optimal use of exhaustible and renewable resources. The theories which emphasised only on relative scarcity of natural resources held the optimistic view that market forces would dictate optimal rate of exploitation effectively and automatically the economic system will adapt itself in the long run to natural resource scarcity constraint.

To facilitate a clearer understanding of the theoretical models of resource depletion, a brief note on the logic of inter-temporal choice is essential. The analysis of inter-temporal choice treats one unit of a commodity consumed in the current period (t_0) and one unit of the same commodity consumed at a later period (t_1) as entirely two different commodities. The analysis is analogous to the constrained choice between alternative commodities in the traditional static consumer demand theory. However it differs from the traditional static theory of consumer behavior in the choice facing the consumer. While in the traditional theory the consumer faces choice between two goods in the same period, in the inter temporal choice theory, the consumer's choice is of the same good in two different periods of time. Indifference curves can be used to express relative preferences between consumption in the two time periods.

The slope of such indifference curves—being the marginal rate of substitution of current for future consumption—will reflect the rate at which future consumption will be sacrificed for current consumption. The slope of the indifference curve is - (1 + d) where 'd' is the marginal rate of time preference proper. Since individuals are assumed to prefer present consumption to future use, the value of future commodity flows should be discounted, to make them comparable with current period quantities.

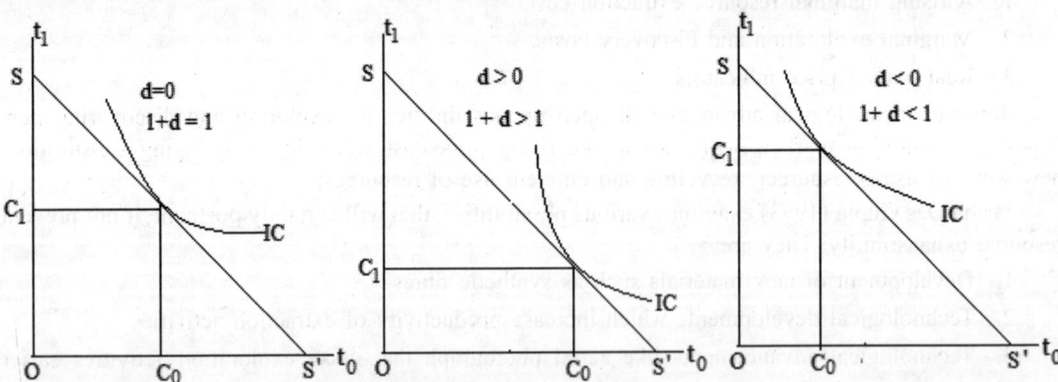

Figures 21.1a, 1b & 1c Inter-temporal Allocation of Fixed Resources Stock Under Different Levels of Social Time Preference

The figures 21.1a, 21.1b and 21.1c illustrate a simple approach to the determination of optimal natural resource use. In the illustration SS' denotes the resource constraint line. There is a given stock of resources OS, which can all be either consumed now (t_0) or preserved entirely for future

(t_1). Joining these two extreme consumption possibilities we get SS' line. On this, we superimpose, the society's indifference map between current and future consumption.

Figure 21.1a, the slope of the indifference curve 1 + d = 1, since marginal rate of time preference 'd' is equal to zero. Hence the stock would be equally allocated between two time periods. OC_0 consumed now and C_0S preserved to be consumed in future. Future consumption will be OC_1. In 21.1b the indifference curve reflects a positive rate of time preference (d > 0 and 1 + d > 1). When 'd' >0, it results in high level of extraction of resources in the current period (OC_0). In figure 21.1.C, marginal rate of time preference is negative, that is, 'd' is less than zero (d< 0) ; hence current consumption is low and maximum is preserved for future. Only OC_0 is consumed now and C_0S is preserved to facilitate a high level of consumption of OC_1, in future. In this case, 1 + d < 1.

21.4 Discounting

The rate of time preference 'd' in section 21.3 plays a crucial role in determining the rate of depletion of a resource. Time preference leads us to the phenomenon of discounting. Economic analysis assumes that a cost or benefit of Re. 1 means more at present than in the future. This lowering of importance of future gains and losses is known as discounting. The procedure by which we find, the present value of future benefits (costs) is known as discounting. Discount rates are mostly positive because:

1. People always prefer present over future (impatience). This is pure *time preference.*
2. Capital is productive (i.e.), one rupee worth capital today will generate goods and services worth more than a rupee in future. Hence an entrepreneur would be willing to pay more than one rupee to acquire one rupee worth of resources today. This argument is known as *marginal productivity of capital* argument while the first argument is called pure time preference argument.
3. Discount rates may also be based on opportunity cost of capital. (i.e.), on the returns of the next best investment of a similar risk that is foregone.

Discounting future benefits and costs is questioned when applied to policy making related to environmental resources. The emission of chlorofluorocarbons (CFCs) that damage the ozone layer, global warming caused by increasing concentration of greenhouse gases have serious catastrophic consequences on future generations. As these effects spread far into the future, discounting will make the present value of such damages considerably smaller than actual damages done. Similarly where the benefits of a project such as afforestation, accrue to people 50 or 100 year hence, discounting will lower the value of such benefits and pose the risk of such projects being rejected. Discounting affects the rate at which we use up natural resources. Higher the rate at which future is discounted, faster the resources are likely to be depleted, leaving less for future generation. Hence many feel that discounting future benefits and costs, contain an in-built bias against future generation. Environmentalists object to discounting, saying that discounting is inconsistent with the philosophy **of preservation** and conservation and sustainability. Yet discounting is a **valuable** guiding principle in the management of resources.

21.5 Renewable Resources

A renewable resource is one which has the capacity to regenerate itself, i.e., its stock is not fixed. Even though over extraction exceeding the levels of regeneration will affect the available stocks, the economics of renewable resources depends, crucially on their population dynamics. Examples include fish stocks, trees etc.

Figures 21.2 shows the population dynamics of a hypothetical renewable resource, say that of fish. The figure shows the size or cumulative growth of the stock of the resource as a function of time. Initially the fish population increases at increasing rate for some time. Soon the increase in the population of the fish is too high to be supported by the ecosystem; the fish compete for food and the rate of growth slows down, and eventually reaches the maximum level S_{max} the ecosystem's carrying capacity.

The cumulative growth curve at first increases by larger increments and later by smaller increments. He curve has a vertical intercept showing that there is a critical minimum level of population required for further additions to stock. This level is called as S_{min}. If the size of the stock of the resource (fish), goes below this, the resource or specie will become extinct.

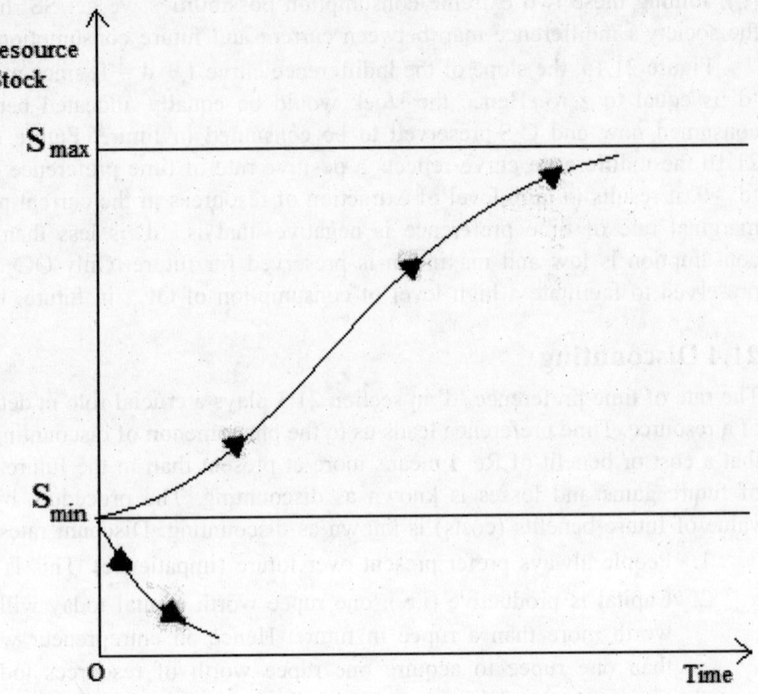

Figure 21. 2 Growth of a Renewable Resource Over Time

The theory of optimum extraction of renewable resources begins with the concept of growth function of a renewable resource. The growth function of a renewable resource is a function of the size of the stock itself, given the ecological characteristic of the ecosystem. This type of growth where the growth depends on the stock size is known as 'density dependent growth'. Let us refer to this biological growth as 'G' which may be expressed as:

$$G = G\ (S)$$

where 'S' is stock size, in the given period. In figure 21.3 the biological growth function of a renewable resource (fish) is illustrated. It is a logistic growth function. Logistic growth is one example of density dependent growth where the growth rate of the resource depends on the size of the stock of the resource. This concept was first applied to fisheries by Schaefer in 1957.

Figure 21.3 shows the growth in the resource stock on the vertical axis and the level of stock on the horizontal axis. The growth function illustrates the relationship between the stock size of the resource and the associated rate of change in the stock size of the resource due to biological growth. Here growth refers to the net annual increment to the stock level. The growth function shows that there is a maximum size to which the resource can grow. The stock size of the resource exceeds this maximum stock size only under extra ordinarily conditions, favourable for the growth of the resource.

It can be seen in figure 21.3 that with increase in stock size from zero the growth of the resource rises, and reaches a maximum. The stock size at which the maximum growth is reached is called as the maximum sustainable yield (MSY). After reaching maximum the growth of the resource registers a decline. The slope at any point of the growth–stock curve is given by dG/dS.

S_{MAX} is the maximum stock size given the environmental conditions. If there is a change in any of the environmental factors of the ecosystem, such as change in the temperature of water (if it is a specie in the river ecosystem), then the stock size will change.

Maximum Sustainable Yield (MSY) is the largest perpetual yield that could be obtained from the resource. The stock size associated with it is denoted as S_{MSY}. It is the most we can take from the resource on a sustainable basis, without reducing its long term stock. Besides MSY and S_{MAX}, figure 21.3, illustrate another concept S_{MIN}. S_{MIN} is the critical level of the stock which is essential for the survival of a specie. If the stock (or population) falls below S_{MIN}, reproduction will be less than natural mortality and the species may gradually become extinct. The biological growth rate G is zero, when the stock size is equal to zero and when it is maximum - S_{MAX}. For all in between values the growth is positive. Figure 21.3 is drawn on the assumption that S_{MIN} is equal to zero.

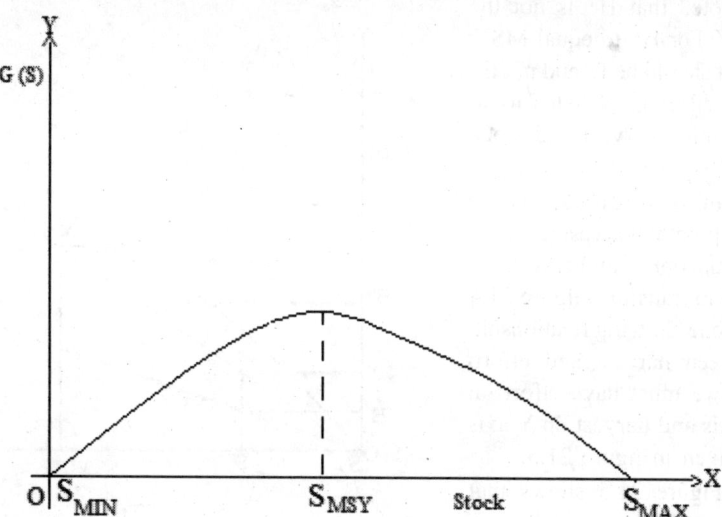

Figure 21.3 Logistic Growth Curve of a Renewable Resource

If the rate of harvest is set equal to MSY, the resource will survive for ever and we can get the maximum from it in each period. However MSY does not correspond to the optimum harvest rates. We need to introduce rate of harvesting and the costs and revenue related to harvesting the resource, to determine the optimum yield. The level of harvest or exploitation or yield depends on 'effort'. Effort refers to the resources and time devoted to harvesting the resource and is expressed as

$$E = H / S$$

where 'S' is the stock and H is the actual harvest. For example if the stock size of the fish population in a pond is 200 fish and 100 are caught (harvested), then E = 100/200 = ½.Greater the effort, greater the harvest. In figure 21.4, with an effort E_1 harvest will be H' for a stock of S', which increases to H" with the effort E_2. The above expression may be rewritten as: H = (E) * (S). In our example, E= (1/2) and S = (200) Therefore H = 1/2 * 200 = 100.

Having defined H, rate of harvest can be introduced in figure 21.3 which is illustrated in figure 21.4. Figure 21.4 shows how choice of the effort level will determine harvest and stock level. An effort level of E_1 corresponds to a harvest H* and stock S*, where E_1 cuts the growth curve, i.e., where effort is equal to rate of growth of the resource (at point M in the figure). With this effort E_1, if harvest is greater than H*, it implies that harvest is greater than sustainable yield and the stock will fall and eventually in the long-run lead to the extinction of the species. Sustainable yield is where harvest equal growth rate. Harvest levels lower than H* implies that harvest is less than sustainable yield and hence the stock will grow.

A harvest level below *H** along E_1 such as H' implies that the harvest is less than the rate of regeneration of the resource (biological growth) and hence the stock will grow to S* again. It should be noted that H* is not the MSY. For H* to equal MSY, effort should be E_2 and not E_1. This effort level helps us to determine harvest and stock level.

In figure 21.4 H* is not the optimum harvest level. To find the optimum harvest, we need to transform figure 21.4 into one showing relationship between harvest and effort, i.e., we must have effort on X axis and harvest on Y axis as given in figure 21.5.

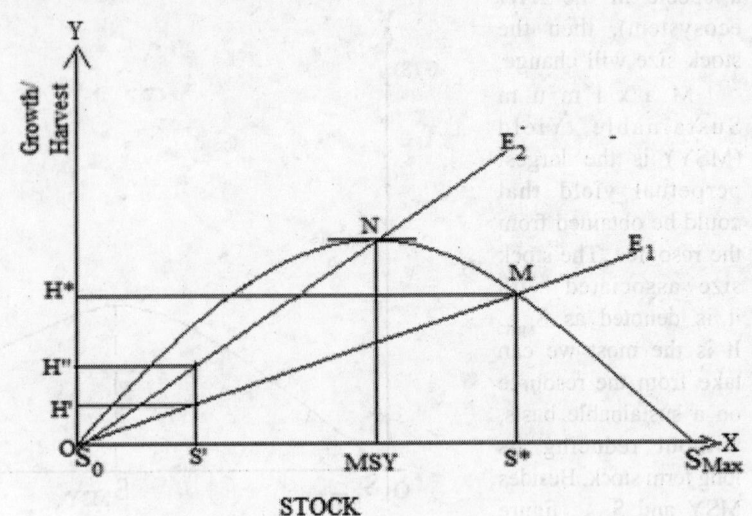

Figure 21.4 Effort—Growth Relationship

Figure 21.5 shows that effort and resource stocks are inversely related—as effort increases stock decreases and vice versa. S_{MAX} in figure 21.4, corresponds to zero effort (E_0) in figure 21.5 and zero (or S_0) in figure 21.4 corresponds to E_{Max} in figure 21.5. An increase in fishing efforts is a movement from left to right in the figure . This movement will cause resource stock to shrink. Interms of stock of the resource, the movement is from right to left.

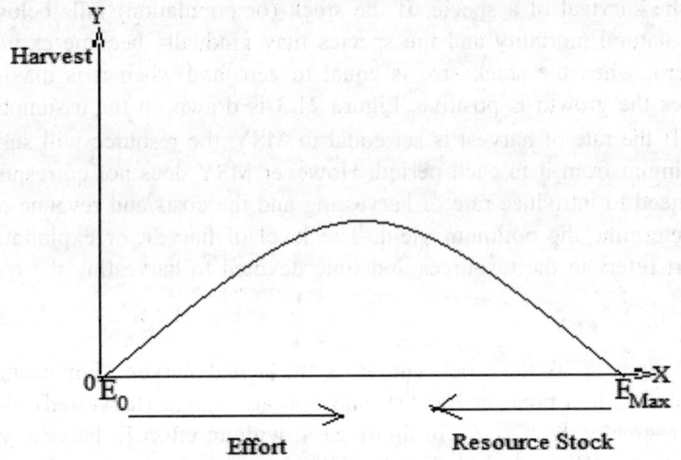

Figure 21.5 Effort - Harvest Curve

The effort harvest curve in figure 21.5 enables us to introduce TR and TC into our analysis. The optimum harvest level requires the following assumptions to be made:

- The price of the resource (fish) is constant
- the marginal cost of extracting the resource (marginal cost of fishing) is constant; and
- the amount of harvest (*H*) per unit of effort *E put in* is proportional to the size of the resource stock. (that is, the smaller the stock size of the resource the lesser will be resource extracted (or harvested).

Total cost of extraction of a resource will include the wages, equipment and fuel cost and reward for risk taken by the entrepreneur etc. Since MC of extracting the resource is assumed to be constant,

TC increases at a constant rate and is shown as a linear function in figure 21.6. Due to the assumption that price of the resource remains constant, TR = Amount harvested and the harvest curve becomes the TR curve (since TR from harvest = Price x Quantity harvested). Optimum sustainable yield corresponds to level where marginal cost of harvesting is equal to marginal revenue from harvesting. The MC = MR principle is the same as in any other economic sector. This means that slope of TR = slope of TC since MC is the slope of TC and MR is slope of TR. This occurs where the distance between TR and TC is maximum. At point E in figure 21.6, the relevant cost function is TC_1.

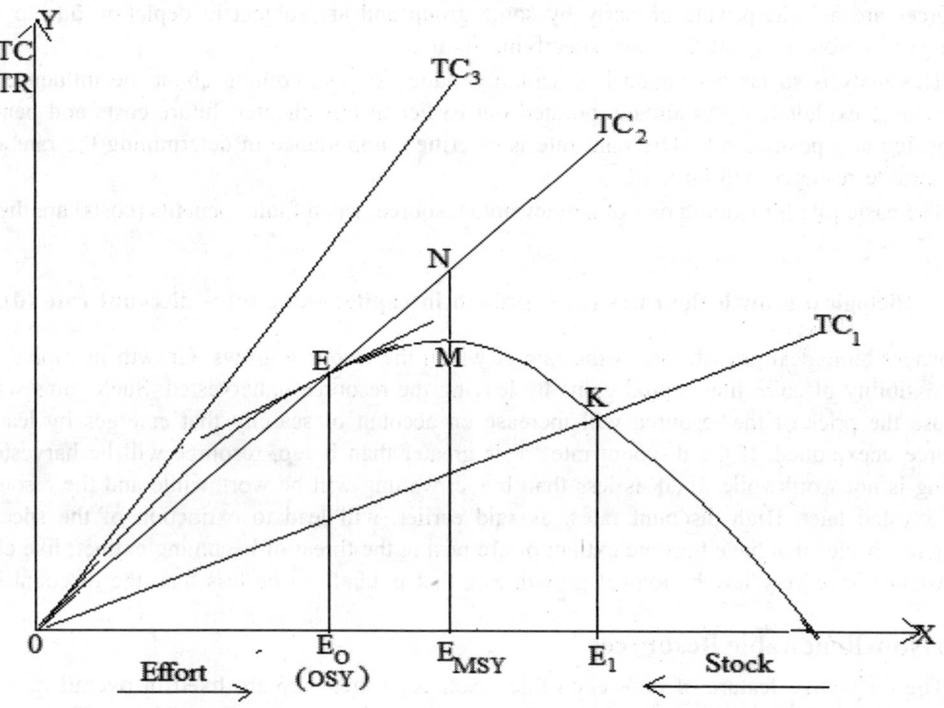

Effort Figure 21.6 Optimum Sustainable Yield

In figure 21.6 fishing effort on either side of E_0 is sub-optimal. To the right of E_0, MC > MR and to the left of E_0, MC < MR. E_0 gives the profit maximising level of harvest. Several observation may be made about Eo.

- The profit maximising equilibrium E_O or the OSY does not correspond to MSY, E_{MSY}-
- If the cost of harvesting is very high, i.e., if the price of effort is very high, the profit maximising solutions will be nearer to the origin. If the cost is very high, with TC lying above TR at all points, then no exploitation will take place (TC_3 in figure 21.6). If cost is zero, cost curve coincides with X axis and MSY will coincide with OSY.

If the resource is an open access resource, profit maximisation will attract entry, which will dissipate extra profits of solution at E, and the open access solution is at K where TC curve cuts TR curve. Obviously, where there is open access to the resource, stock (measured right to left in the Figure 21.6) at equilibrium is less than at optimal solution ($E_1 < E_0$) and open access does not coincide with MSY, unless by chance TC cuts TR at the maximum. For open access to lead to extinction of the specie effort should be costless or rate of harvesting should be greater than rate of regeneration of the resource (h > g). An open access resource is characterized by rivalry in exploitation; any person who has the capability and desire to harvest or extract the resource can use it. As a result its extraction results negative externalities. It is the open access resources that are subject to a "Tragedy of Commons Situation" explained by Hardin. Such open access resources are different form Common Property Resources for which the rights to exploit the resources are held by persons in common with others. The rights are defined in different ways – it could permit unlimited exploitation by the group members or it may specify rules for use by each member. (Robert Wade, 1987). Common property resources are accessible to the whole community or village but no individual has exclusive ownership or property rights since there are certain rights defined with reference to its use. Common property resources are held as private property by some group and are subject to depletion due to weak or absence of enforcement of the rules specifying its use.

The analysis so far developed is essentially static—it says nothing about the influence of time on resource exploitation. As already pointed out earlier in this chapter, future costs and benefits are discounted at a positive rate. Discount rate is of critical importance in determining the rate at which a renewable resource will be used.

The basic rule for exploitation of a renewable resource, when future benefits (costs) are discounted is :

Biological growth the rates (b) + growth in capital value (c) = discount rate (d),

where biological growth rate is the rate at which the resource grows. Growth in capital value is the possibility of collecting capital gains by leaving the resource unharvested. Such gains will occur because the price of the resource will increase on account of scarcity that emerges by leaving the resource unexploited. If the discount rate 'd' is greater than b + c, resource will be harvested now; waiting is not worthwhile. If 'd' is less than b + c, waiting will be worthwhile and the resource will be harvested later. High discount rates, as said earlier, will lead to extinction of the species. For example, species that have become extinct or are posing the threat of becoming extinct, like elephants and whales have very low biological growth rate that is likely to be less than the discount rate.

21.6 Non-Renewable Resources

The distinctive feature of non-renewable resource is that they are fixed in overall quantity and therefore the more we extract, the less will be available for the future generation. Thus there is an opportunity cost involved. This opportunity cost is referred to as "user cost" which is the fundamental concept underlying the theory of optimum extraction of an exhaustible resource.

The fundamental rule for harvesting a renewable resource is stated as:

Biological growth rate + growth in capital value = discount rate.
(b) (c) (d)

For exhaustible resources, there is no growth function. Hence b = 0. Therefore the basic rule for optimally using a non-renewable resource with costless extraction is:

growth in capital value (c) = discount rate(d).

This is the fundamental principle of economics of exhaustible resource use. It says that the resource should be extracted in such a way that the rate of growth of price of the extracted resource should be equal to the rate of discount. This fundamental rule is known as Hotelling rule. In 1931 Harrold Hotelling explained rules for optional rate of depletion of exhaustible resources in his classic article, "The Economics of Exhaustible Resources" in the *"Journal of Political Economy"*. In simple terms, Hotelling's rule implies that in equilibrium the resource rent (the net price), defined as the difference between the market price of the resource and marginal extraction costs, must increase at a rate equal to the rate of interest. If extraction costs are assumed to be equal to zero, the price of the extracted resource is the same as price of resource in the ground. If extraction costs are positive, price of the extracted resource, will be greater than price of the resource in the ground. Price of the resource in the ground is known as royalty or rent or user cost.

With positive user cost, price of the extracted resource at any time t is given as P = C + R, where C is extraction cost and R, is 'royalty', also referred to as rent or as marginal user cost.

Therefore optimal price P* = MEC + MUC,

where MEC is marginal extraction cost and MUC is marginal user cost. Optimal use and pricing of an exhaustible resource may be explained using a simple model which is illustrated in figure 21.7.

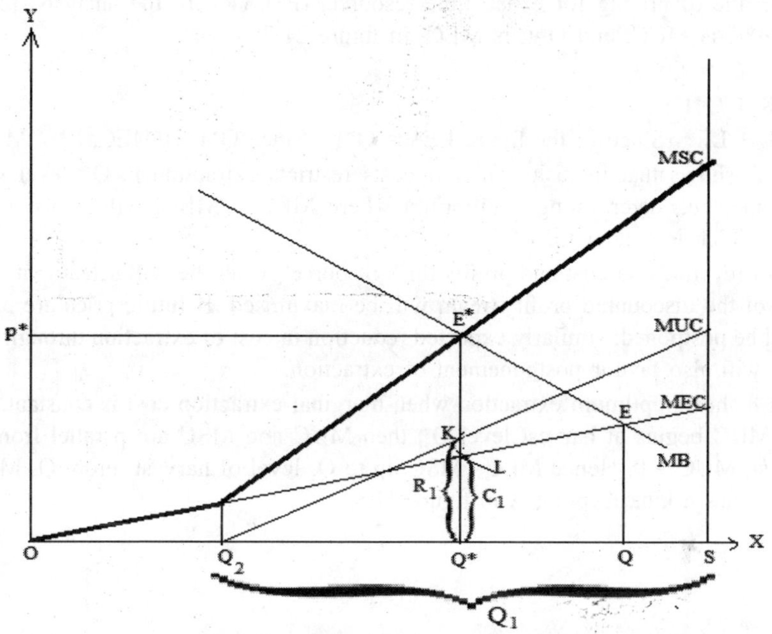

Figure 21.7 Optimum Use of Non Renewable Resource

In the model marginal extraction cost (MEC) is the cost incurred to extract or harvest an additional unit of the resource. Marginal user cost on the other hand arises from fixity of the resource stock. Since total availability of the resources is fixed, its current consumption comes at the expense of future benefits, i.e., it involves an opportunity cost.

In figure 21.7, Q_1 represents the maximum that would be demanded in future. Initially let us assume that the fixed stock of the resource is S and the stock is in excess of the maximum quantity that would be demanded in future. Hence present consumption is made from this surplus stock over future consumption. Therefore present consumption will not rob the society of future benefit from this resource i.e., initial consumption is made out of the difference between S and Q_1. Let this difference between S and Q_1 be Q_2. When resource extraction exceeds Q_2, current consumption beyond Q_2 will progressively rob society of benefits it would have enjoyed, if those resources were available for future consumption. These future benefits foregone by current consumption is termed "user cost" or opportunity cost. User cost of each successive unit—marginal user cost— of current consumption is the discounted value of future consumption foregone.

In figure 21.7, the demand curve for future resource use (MSB) is downward sloping. Each successive unit of current consumption incurs a progressively greater loss of future consumption; marginal user cost curve is upward sloping. The user cost is seen by many as an externality—a cost (loss of benefit) imposed on third parties (future generation) by the production and consumption acts of present generation. The real cost to the society hence of consuming a unit of resource in the current period is MSC, the sum of marginal extraction cost and marginal user cost.

$$MSC = MUC + MEC$$

MSC is upward sloping since MEC and MUC are upward sloping. Optimal use and pricing of the resource is at E, where the MBC curve for the resource intersects the MSC curve at E*. At such an equilibrium, the resource is priced P* and Q* units are extracted in the current period. Since MUC represents present discounted value of future consumption of the resource, pricing is in line with the basic rule of pricing for exhaustible resource, (P=C+R). In the analysis, for an extraction level of Q*, Q*K is MUC, and Q*L is MEC. In figure 21.7,

R_1 = Q*K, C_1 = Q*L

P* = Q*K + Q*L

P* = Q*L + LE* (Since in the figure LE* = Q*K; Since Q*L is MEC, P* - MEC =MUC)

Figure 21.7 shows that inclusion of user costs restricts extraction to Q* level while failure to include the same, i.e., determining equilibrium where MEC = MBC, will imply a larger level of extraction (Q) which is greater than Q*.

In terms of revenue and cost and profits for a resource owner, he will select that rate of at which present value of the discounted profit stream will be maximised. If future price are expected to rise, extraction will be postponed; similarly expected reduction in cost of extraction through a technological breakthrough, will also favour postponement of extraction.

Figure 21.8 shows optimum extraction when marginal extraction cost is constant. When MEC is constant and MUC begins at harvest level Q_2, then MUC and MSC are parallel from Q_2. Up to Q_2 level of harvest, MUC = 0. Hence MEC= MSC up to Q_2 level of harvest. From Q_2 MUC is positive. Therefore MSC has a kink at point A in figure 21.8.

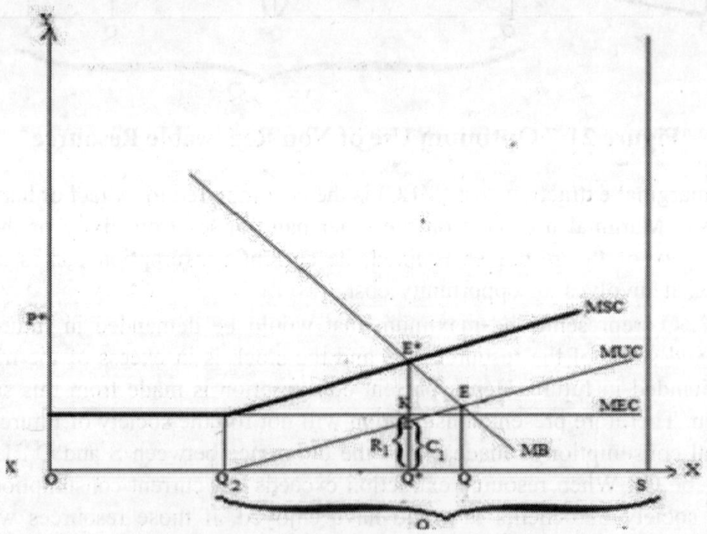

Figure 21.8 : Optimum Extraction of Exhaustible Resource when MEC is Constant.

To conclude, the various rules explained in the chapter for optimal extraction of renewable and non- renewable resources may be summarised as follows: For a renewable resource, marginal cost of extraction must equal marginal revenue from extraction for profit maximising extraction in anygiven time period. Over a time period, however, for a renewable resource, discount rate should be equal to biological growth rate of the resource and capital gain from leaving the resource exploited. In the case of non-renewable resources, the rule for optimum extraction of the resource requires that the discount rate is equal to the rate of growth of price of the extracted resource. This is the Hotelling rule for the exploitation of the non renewable resource when the cost of extraction is zero. With positive costs, the rule is P = C + R (i.e.) the resource should be managed such that its price is equal to marginal extraction cost and royalty on the marginal unit of resource. Royalty is also referred to as the user cost. Failing to take "user cost" will lead to over exploitation of resources.

21.7 Conservation of Resources

If our future generations should inherit a rich resource base, we must conserve our resources. Conservation is defined by Gifford Pinchot as "the use of natural resources for the greatest good of the greatest number for the longest time". To him conservation implies both development and protection of resources. A more meaningful and precise definition of resource conservation simply means consuming less virgin natural resources than we otherwise would. More broadly, conservation can be defined as the process of prolonging the useful life of resources, either by preserving or by reusing and recycling.

The Global 2000 report prepared by the US Government in 1980 reports:

"If present trend continue, the world in 2000 will be more crowded, more polluted, less stable ecologically, more vulnerable to disruption than the world we live in now. Serious stresses involving population, resources and environment are clearly visible ahead".

There is no doubt that the rapidly growing world population is straining the earth's carrying capacity today. We are not only running out of non-renewable resources but are also faced with the destruction of renewable resources system's capacity to regenerate. Over fishing has extensively damaged many oceanic fisheries. Nearly 6 million hectares of land per year are lost to desertification: at this rate world's desert area is expected to expand almost twenty per cent by 2000. Over grazing, destructive cropping pattern and felling of trees for fuel are reasons for desertification. The Global 2000 report has further projected that if the present trend continues, there could be a forty per cent decline in both forest cover and stock of commercial size wood in less developed regions by 2000. The trends for non-fuel minerals also show steady increases in demand and consumption. The global demand for most non-fuel mineral commodities is projected to increase three to five per cent annually, slightly more than doubling by 2000. Hence if we are to maintain and rejuvenate our resources we need to become conservation minded.

Methods of Conservation

Several methods/strategies have been suggested by conservationists, some of which are being followed in an attempt to conserve resources. The first line of defense towards protecting our resources is waste reduction. Resource conservation basically means reduction of the amounts of solid wastes that are generated besides reduction of overall resource consumption and utilisation of recovered resources. Waste reduction is advocated as a principal means of conserving resources because a reduction in wastes implies more economical and efficient use of resources. Waste reduction can be achieved by redesigning industrial processes and by locating plants in such a way that the residues of one plant, can whenever and wherever possible be effectively used as raw-materials by another industry. Waste reduction reduces environmental impacts and energy demands besides conserving natural resources. Further it provides a check on the ever increasing costs of waste management.

Waste reduction techniques are the key components of an efficient management program. They do not require complex capital intensive technology . A firm can reduce waste through four important strategies: managing inventory, modifying production processes, reducing waste volume, and recovering waste. In general waste reduction can be achieved through several ways:

1. increasing the durability of products
2. utilising material substitution
3. recycling and
4. marketability of industrial wastes.

Increasing the durability of products means designing products for longer use and designing them for easy and economical repair or manufacture. The replacement of unbreakable containers in the place of brittle/breakable containers is an example. Increasing the durability of the product, otherwise called as 'product life extension', does not merely mean making it tougher or stronger. It involves designing problem and marketing problem. As pointed out by a Canadian research team: "the design problem is to ensure that replacement of worn parts is simple: the marketing problem is to make parts available". It further pointed out that if products are not durable, they should be repairable and durability meant "either better materials or easily replaceable parts or both". Increase in durability will reduce wastes generated and promote preservation of our natural resources.

The process of **material substitution** as a mean of conserving resources depends on technology. The transistor for example, requires one millionth of the materials needed to make the vacuum tube it replaces. Similarly commercial satellites, solid state electronics, microfilm facilities have reduced material requirements in communications industry. Aluminum is being extensively substituted for tin, particularly in the production of metal cans and containers. Similarly plastics are being used for insulation and anti-corrosive purposes where lead and zinc were originally used.

Substitution that would make possible more efficient energy use, will promote conservation of energy. Some have even suggested substitution of labour or capital for energy.

However, material substitution possibilities is also limited by certain conditions. It is possible that all raw-materials including the substitutable materials will be depleted at the same time. Secondly, substitution may involve time lags. The time required for effective substitution is a crucial factor. Equally important is the interval required for diffusion of the substitute technology in all processes of the industry. It has been reported by an international review of this question that the total time required for effective substitution has been of the order of 25 to 30 years when diffusion time is included. Besides time factors, side effects of substitute materials in the form of more pollution also may pose problems. Aluminum smelters, for example, may involve more pollution than tin which they replace.

Thus while material substitution is an effective technique for resource conservation, it is limited by pollution impacts, time lag, and by the ability to manage the substitution process.

Marketability of industrial wastes is also suggested as an alternative for recycling. The recycled wastes of an industry may find a market as an input in another industry. A number of companies are today re-using their wastes in their own production process after treating them or they are marketing them. The sugar industry today has found a permanent market for its by-product bagasse in the paper manufacturing industry. This strategy of marketing the wastes, can be compared to the market solution to externality problem, in which firms exploit the possibilities of earnings revenue while accounting for its external costs.

Recycling

Recycling is the most popular method practiced today for conserving resources. Recycling simply means extending the life of a resource. It is the re-use of a given input or output. For example, from the effluents of distilleries manufacturing alcohol, methane is separated by a chemical process which is then recycled in the production process as fuel for boiler. The residual liquid of the effluent after separation of methane, contains nitrogen, phosphate and potassium and is canalised in cane fields and has resulted in considerable increases in cane yield.

Production activities of the society draw raw materials from the environment and transform them in to final products. This transformation of input into output which we call as production function includes a crucial action – that of discharging residuals into the environment. Consumption activity also discharges residuals into the environment. The Law of Conservation of Matter and Energy, explained in chapter 2 brought out the fact that all materials taken from the environment for production and consumption must end up in some form in the environment which acts as a sink for the residues. Due to the scarcity of virgin material excessive extraction and use of these material needs attention. It is necessary to recycle the used materials. This can be expressed interms of a simple equation known as the simple Mass Balance Equation.

$$\mathbf{TM = VM + RM}$$

where

TM - Total materials used by an economy; VM - Virgin materials

RM - Recyclable materials

Recycling is important for the following reasons:

1. Protects and conserves natural resources.
2. Saves energy and promotes energy conservation
3. Limits waste accumulation in landfills and reduces the amount of waste sent to landfills and incinerators
4. Prevents pollution by reducing the need to collect new raw materials.
5. Reduces greenhouse gas emissions that contribute to global climate change.
6. Helps to protect the environment for future generations.

Optimum Recycling

Optimum recycling minimizes the net social cost of waste management. Recycling is considered economically efficient if marginal cost of recycling is equal to the marginal benefit from recycling. Here marginal cost of recycling is the cost incurred to recycle an additional unit of waste residual. Costs include costs incurred for the separation of recyclable materials, costs associated with processes involved in recycling and other external costs resulting from recycling.The benefits of recycling essentially arise from the extension in the life of the recycled resource, the reduced pollution impact and the reduced demand for land for dumping

The private costs of recycling includes the amount spent on labour, trucks, machinery, land and other administrative expenses to store , process and transport the recycled material. There are also external costs such as pollution from the use of incinerator, pollution from trucks that carry both waste to be recycled material etc. Research studies reveal that that all external costs could range between $15 – 20 per tonne while that of incineration alone could be between $20 per tonne and $ 39 per tonne.

Adding the external costs to the private cost of operating the recycling plant gives the total social cost of recycling. The revenue from the sale of recycled materials is the economic value of providing recycled materials. To this, external benefit from recycling such as avoided health and environmental damages from waste disposal must be added to arrive at social benefit of recycling. Social benefit of recycling and the social cost of recycling are the two crucial cost concepts that determine the optimum recycling. From the total social costs we get the marginal cost which can be used for determining the optimum recycling.

Empirical evidence suggests that recovering and re-using industrial wastes is both technically feasible and economically attractive. However, recycling is not a costless exercise. Optimal level of recycling is at the point at which extra costs of recycling outweighs extra benefit, that is, when $MB_R = MC_R$. Optimum recycling is shown in figure 21.9

At point E in figure 21.9 $MB_R = MC_R$. Hence the corresponding amount of recycling OR* is optimum. Corresponding to the equality of marginal cost and marginal benefit of recycling, TC from the various processes of recycling will be minimum.

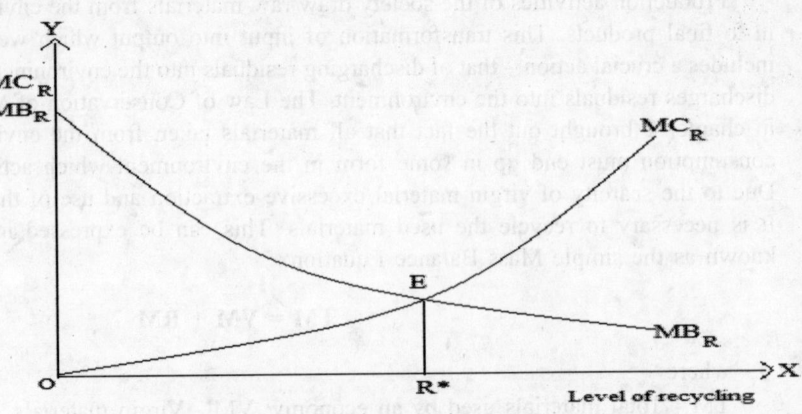

Figure 21.9 Optimum Recycling

Facts on Recycling

- Recycling one tonne of paper saves 682.5 gallons of oil 7000 gallons of water and 3.3 cubic yards of land fill space. Further recycling of one tonne of paper saves 17 trees and 4000 kw of energy.
- Recycling a single plastic bottle can conserve enough energy to light a 60 W bulb for up to 6 hours.
- Recycling one aluminum can saves enough energy to listen to a full album on one's iPod.
- Recycling one ton of plastic can save up to 2,000 gallons of gasoline.
- Recycling one tin saves enough energy to run a TV for 2 hours
- We generate 21.5 million tons of food waste each year. If we compost that food, it would reduce the same amount of greenhouse gas as taking 2 million cars off the road.
- In 2010, paper recycling had increased over 89% since 1990.
- A glass container can go from a recycling bin to a store shelf in as few as 30 days.
- Nearly 60 to 70% of waste found in dustbins can be recycled and reused and close to 50% of the same waste can be composted.
- Recycling aluminum is 95% more efficient than creating aluminum.

Recycling Facts of Countries

- Switzerland has the highest recycling rate in the world with over 52% of its waste getting recycled. Austria comes in a close second with a recycling rate of 49.7%. Switzerland recycles over 167 metric tons of paper per 1,000 people each year, making it the world leader in paper recycling.
- The U.S. recycles 31.5% of its waste, making it 7th in the world for recycling.
- The average home in Germany has at least five distinct color-coded bins for different kinds of wastes. These include bins for packaging, paper, glass, compost, and trash.
- Recycling rates in Australia are high with 95% of Australian households partaking in recycling programs.
- In Finland, 9 out of 10 plastic bottles are returned for recycling and almost 100% of glass bottles are also recycled.

- China is the world leader in reusing aluminum, with 99.5% of it's aluminum waste being recycled.
- Japan recycles 76% of its plastic, making it top in the world for plastic recycling.
- Nearly 1/5th of the waste produced in Greece is plastic and only 1% of that plastic is recycled.
- Recycling rates in South Africa are on the rise with 40% of glass waste being recycled in 2013, which is a 230% rise from six years prior!

There are a number of other measures which supplement those already mentioned. Developing and using products requiring less material per unit of product (like smaller automobiles), substituting re-usable products for single use disposable products, increasing the number of times the items are re-used and reducing the number of units of products consumed per year per household are some of the measures in practice.

Conclusion

Conservation of renewable resources like forests, fisheries etc. require a careful and well-designed Government policy. Appropriate land use policy measure, a good forest policy and efficient use of alternative energy sources can to a great extent ameliorate misuse of renewable resources. What is required is a holistic approach to resource management. Land that grows trees for timber also provides habitat for wild life besides storing and filtering water. It may also contain deposits of precious metals. Hence resources cannot be managed with blinders; the damage inflicted on a resource have devastating effect on one or few more resources. When it comes to resources, we must consider them all together. Only an integrated and holistic approach will lead to optimal use of resources.

Questions

1. Classify resources and explain the evolution of economics of natural resources.
2. Bring out the role of time preference in natural resource economics.
3. Is optimum sustainable yield (OSY) of renewable resources the same as maximum sustainable yield (MSY)? Explain using a diagram.
4. Explain the model for optimum harvesting of non-renewable resources.
5. What are the methods of conserving resources.
6. What is recycling of wastes. Explain the economic significance of recycling.

Exercise

- Is relative price of a natural resource a good indicator of change in its scarcity? Justify your stand
- Distinguish between CPRs and OARs (Open Access Resource) and give examples. Is definition of property rights a solution for efficient management of these resources.

22

ACCOUNTING FOR ENVIRONMENT

"To defend and improve the environment for present and future generationshas become an imperative goal for mankind."

—The Declaration of the UN Conference on Human Environment, Stockholm (1972).

The national income and product accounts measure economic growth of a nation. The conventional system of national accounts is based upon the System of National Accounts (SNA) designed by the United Nation's statistical office. Economic accounts of most countries are calculated using the standard format (SNA) developed by the United Nations Statistical Division (UNSD). However this is not any more considered as an appropriate and complete indicator of a country's economic performance on grounds that it omits non-market activities, such as unpaid work and the value of leisure time. The failure to account for environmental degradation and depletion of natural resources is also questioned.

Gross National Product (GNP) is the total monetary value of all finished goods and service in an economy in one year. It is the basis upon which countries are ranked from rich to poor. GNP is regarded as an indicator of the health of an economy—a rising GNP indicating that the country's health is improving and a falling GNP indicating a deterioration in the economy's health. GNP's popularity as an economic indicator continued unchallenged so long as the environmental side effects of production and consumption activities were negligible and insignificant. But today economic activities result in significant damages to the environment, which impose considerable costs on both existing as well as on future generation. The particular way we measure GNP and GDP and other measures based on GNP or GDP, fails to consider many issues that are very important for accurate economic assessments and valid policy making. In its annual report on world development indicators, the world bank observes:

"GNP per capita does not by itself constitute or measure welfare or success in development. It does not distinguish between aims and ultimate uses of a given product, nor does it say whether it merely offsets some natural or other obstacle or harms or contributes to welfare". Salah El Serafy and Ernst Lutz of Work Bank argue that income accounting based on SNA "produce readings of levels of activity and growth over time that can lead to faulty policy advice. Such readings frequently exaggerate income and thus encourage consumption and promote habits of behaviour that cannot be sustained over the longer time".

A country's economic book keeping consists of income accounts and capital accounts. While income accounts produce the GNP figure, capital accounts track changes in wealth. As lumber factories, textile mills, office buildings and other artifacts become old and fall into disrepair, a subtraction is made from the capital accounts to reflect their depreciation in value. However no similar subtraction is made for the deterioration of forests, soils, air quality and other natural endowments. When trees are cut and sold for timbers, the revenue from it is counted as income and reflected in GNP. But no deduction is made for the deterioration of the forest - destruction of a natural asset. This will give an inflated figure of income and wealth. The country with such inflated levels of GNP will be considered better off than it really is and will be ranked higher on performance scale. In the words of Robert Repetto of Yale University, this failure to account for natural resource destruction that occurs in the process of income generation, makes GNP, "a false beacon, and can draw those who steer by it onto the rocks". Such omissions will make the country an ecological bankrupt, even though its GNP is increasing.

22.1 Shortcoming of Traditional National Income Accounting with Reference to Environmental Issues

The deficiency in the ability of the current national income accounting framework to account for environment arises mainly because of the inconsistent treatment of natural and manmade capital. There are three specific short comings.

First, failure to account for depreciation of natural resources; the conventional national accounts system measures a nation's wealth in terms of man-made capital only and ignores natural capital. Though these natural capital (e.g., exploitable forests, fishing stocks and minerals and other assets such as fresh air, water and the like) are valued highly by the society, they are not included in balance sheets. Although national accounts make, allowance for the depletion of man-made capital in arriving at an estimate of NNP or national income, they fail to record the depreciation (depletion) of natural capital.

Secondly, failure to include environmental defensive expenditure; Environmental defensive expenditure are those expenses on goods and services to mitigate environmental damage. In other words, defensive expenditure refers to expenditure incurred to restore environmental assets. They are also known as restoration costs. The expenditure incurred to restore environmental assets are included in national income and show up as income generating activities. No allowance is made for the corresponding environmental damages. Such expenditures, referred to as 'defensive expenditures' are 'regrettable necessities". This leads to overestimation of national income. Environmentalists feel that they should be regarded as the costs of consuming other goods and services rather than as benefits. Private firms deduct such defensive expenditures from final value added. In contrast national income accounting considers such defensive expenditure as productive contributions to national output, if they are incurred by public sector or households. It is held that such defensive expenditures should be deducted from GNP in its current form.

Thirdly, failure to account for the environmental damages in the form of pollution of water and air, degradation of soil etc resulting from economic activities of production and consumption is questioned. If a wetland is drained so as to make way for a sports complex the SNA would record the latter as an investment and ignore the former. It is suggested that adjustments must be made in national income to include such degradation of natural resources.

Forests provide the best example of the distortion arising out of the failure of national income accounting. Commercial felling of trees at rates, greater than their regeneration, increases current income levels, but, at the expense of decline in capital assets. Developing economies, dependent on primary resources such as timber, minerals and agricultural crops will be affected most, if national income accounting excludes environmental factors.

The treatment of natural capital in national income accounting differs from that of produced capital in three important ways:

1. While additions to stock of man-made or produced capital structure and equipment is included in accounting entries, there is no entry for additions to stock of natural resources .
2. Contribution of natural resources to current production is omitted while the value added by produced capital is included.
3. While depreciation of man- made capital is deducted from GNP to arrive at national income figure, no such deduction is made for depreciation of natural capital.

Economists at the World Resource Institute have examined how an environmentally adjusted accounting method will result in a GNP figure much lower than one given by conventional accounting method. They calculated depreciation for just three resources—forests, soil and petroleum—for Indonesia and found that average annual growth for Indonesia's GNP dropped from 7.1 per cent in 1971 to 4 per cent in 1984.

Similarly, a failure to deduct for damages to environment (pollution) while including defensive expenditures as income has serious consequences. The Alaskan oil spill of March 1989, the most environmentally damaging accident in the US history recorded a rise in GNP, since the 'cleanup' costs of $2 billion was added to income. Thus expenditure for mitigating pollution (waste treatment and health care) show up as income generating activities in national income accounts despite the fact that people incur there expenses only reluctantly. The US would have been much better off, had the Alaskan oil spill never happened but GNP in conventional terms suggests otherwise. It is therefore obvious that the damage to the environment's ability to perform its functions has very serious economic and social welfare consequences. But our conventional accounting methods fail to acknowledge this fact.

El Serafy and Lutz argue that omission of environmental degradation in accounting will not reflect sustainable income. Sustainable income is the maximum that can be consumed in a given period without reducing the amount of consumption available in a future period. Failure to measure sustainable income will affect development and growth. Of all the different concepts related to GNP, NNP or national income is (see Box 22.1) considered to be relatively more sustainable because it deducts capital depreciation from GNP. But GDP and GNP are more widely used because of difficulties associated with measurement of capital depreciation. Inspite of the difficulties in the measurement of capital consumption, environmentalists hold that allowances for capital consumption or depletion should not be confined to manmade capital alone, but should also be applied to natural capital such as forests, fishing stocks etc. Only when such adjustments are made will accounting reflect sustainable income or true income.

BOX 22.1 National Income/GNP Concepts

GNP: The market value of all finished goods and services produced during a given period of time in a given economy.

NNP: GNP - Depreciation

Depreciation: Capital consumption allowance — provision made for the use of physical capital.

The idea of 'sustainable income' has its origin in Sir John Hick's definition of income as the maximum value which a person can consume during a period and still be as well off at the end of the period as at the beginning. To Hicks "The purpose of income calculation in practical affairs is to give people an indication of the amount which they can consume without impoverishing themselves". (Value and capital: John R. Hicks—2nd edition, OUP, 1946) Extending this to the national income, true income refers to the maximum amount a nation can consume without depleting the stock of assets available for future. This requires allowance for depreciation and hence constitutes the difference between GNP and national income. Based on the same principle, environmentalists argue that, GNP should be adjusted for depletion of natural capital also; otherwise income will be overstated. Natural resource stocks are part of national wealth and hence ignoring their depletion is equivalent to considering the reductions in national wealth as increases in national income.

22.2 Adjustments to National Income to Incorporate Environmental Degradation

Environmentalists argue for three kinds of adjustments to national income to reflect the impact of income generation activities on environment. These are, as noted already, adjustments for depletion of natural capital, adjustment for environmental degradation and adjustment for defensive expenditure. Adjustment for depletion of natural capital requires that stocks of natural resources such as oil and gas reserves, stock of fish, forests etc. should be treated in the same way as stock of manmade capital. Therefore a reduction should be made for the depletion of natural capital. Under the conventional system, NNP would be defined as:

$$NNP = GNP - D_M$$

where "D_M' is depreciation of manmade capital. If accounting is attempted for depletion for natural capital,

$$NNP = GNP - D_M - D_N$$

where D_N is depletion of natural capital.

There are two ways of calculating D_N:

- Depreciation method.
- User cost method.

In the depreciation method, depletion is valued as that part of receipts from the sales of resource which can be uniquely attributed to that resource. Assuming zero extraction costs, whole receipts R, would be attributed to depletion of the resource. Hence environmentally adjusted GNP, referred to as ENP, would be:

$$ENP = GNP - D_M - R$$

With positive costs of extraction, 'R' will include a cost element; (like wages, rent, etc.). Depletion then, will be less than R. On the other hand the user cost method provides for deduction in GDP and GNP by redefining R'. The user cost method is based on the principle that, 'R' the receipts from sale of a natural resource comprises of two elements: capital consumption or user cost ('U') and income 'M'. The recognition that the ownership of a natural resource confers an income advantage to its owner, makes all the difference. The relative shares of the two elements—'U' and 'M' in R depends upon the level of reserves, current rate extraction and choice of discount rate to apply to future flows of income from sales. In the user cost method R is defined as net receipts from sales, i.e., gross revenue from sales of the resource less purchase of current goods and services required to extract the resource.

The depreciation method estimates of income are significantly greater than estimates arrived at using the user cost method. This is because, in depreciation method depletion is expressed as:

D = R — Costs of extraction, whereas, in user cost method, D = R - M - Costs of extraction.

There is an additional income element to be subtracted and hence the residual estimate of depletion is less. In the user cost method GNP and GDP would be redefined to exclude the user cost depletion estimates. Hence income estimates using this method will be less than that using conventional measures.

Environmental degradation occurs when the quality of natural environment declines, caused by pollution of air, water, etc. Such degradation should be accounted for in the same way as depletion of mineral resources discussed above. However practical problems of valuing the effects of such degradation are more severe than in the case of mineral resources: Deviation from an accepted environmental standard defined by the environmental authority is usually considered, for measuring degradation. Cost of restoring prescribed quality/standards will give an estimate of environmental degradation. Definition of 'environmental standard' however poses problems.

While estimates of depletion of natural mineral resources may be obtained using replacement cost metnod or restoration cost method, degradation of environmental quality may be estimated using willingness to pay method. These methods are discussed later in the chapter on valuation of benefits. Environmentalists argue that in addition to depreciation of manmade capital and depletion of natural resources, costs of environmental degradation should be deducted from GNP/GDP to arrive at a sustainable national product.

In the conventional standard approach to national income accounting, defensive expenditures are treated as any other form of consumption and show up as income generating activities. They are directly or indirectly included in GDP. Environmentalist argue that such defensive expenditures should be excluded from or atleast deducted from GDP so that we come closer to sustainable income. If defensive expenditures are not under taken then the result is environmental degradation—depletion of natural capital. Identification and measurement of such expenditures pose problems. As El Serafy and Lutz point out, "it does not make sense to incorporate expenditures incurred to redress some or all of the negative consequences of production or consumption activities in the stream of income generated by economic activity".

Lutz and El Serafy have given two approaches for a better accounting of defensive expenditure—one is to treat such expenditures as intermediate, rather than as final expenditure. The other is to treat even such resources as air, water and the like, as natural capital which get depleted over time. Hence they may be included in accounting in the same way as other natural (mineral) resources are included. Many economists have raised the question; why "defensive environmental expenditure" should be treated differently from other forms of defensive expenditures, like expenditure on armed forces. An increase in GDP caused by increased military expenditure or increased expenditure on environmental protection may not add to welfare. But that does not call for a redefinition GDP/GNP. It only reflects the limitation of GDP as a measure of welfare.

The practical, conceptual and theoretical limitations of attempting to measure depletion of natural capital and identification of defensive expenditures are indeed overwhelming. However, such an environmentally adjusted GNP and NNP will provide a more useful guide to economic performance and therefore to policy than the conventionally defined GNP and NNP.

The United Nations Statistical Office (UNSO) and the World Bank have developed a System for Environmentally Adjusted Economic Accounts (SEEA). This is an attempt to integrate environmental data with the existing national accounts information while maintaining basic national income accounting concepts. Through this an Environmentally adjusted Net Domestic Product (EDP) and an Environmentally adjusted Net Income (ENI) are calculated. In calculating SEEA, environmental assets (such as soil, wildlands and bio diversity) are added to productive assets as stores of wealth, provided they are linked to economic activities of consumption and production. Similarly additional costs related to environment are included in SEEA. Such costs include:

- Imputed charges for the depletion of minerals and other natural resources.
- Costs of degradation of land, water, air, that result from production and consumption activities. Such costs are deducted from GDP to arrive at EDP.

To arrive at ENI, the following five items should be subtracted from EDP

- Environment protection expenditure of government and households.
- Environmental effects on health and other aspects of human capital.
- Environmental costs of house hold and government consumption activities.
- Environmental damage from capital goods that are discarded and
- Negative environmental effects in the country caused by production activities in other countries and negative environmental effects transferred abroad.

Norway, France and the United States are the few countries to have attempted environmental and resource accounting earlier than other countries. China's Green GDP for 2004, showed economic losses due to environmental damage at about 3% of national income.

The World Bank has developed a measure of national income known as the "adjusted Net National Savings" measure. This measure helps in assessing how a country manages its natural resources and environmental quality and also assess whether a country is saving for the future or causing depletion that may make future generations worse off. This measure is explained in Chapter 15 in section 15.5.4.

22.3 Greening India's National Income

India's National Accounts Statistics (NAS) has made a beginning in greening its national income, by incorporating environmental considerations in estimating GDP and other aggregates such as Gross Capital Formation and Gross Fixed Capital Formation. Box 22.2 gives a list of some measures that have already been initiated

Gross Domestic Product (GDP) includes:

- value added in the electricity, gas & water supply sector through transmission and distribution of electric energy, manufacture of gas in gas works including gobar gas and distribution through mains to household, industrial, commercial and other users, production of LPG, and collection, purification and distribution of water excluding the operation of irrigation system.
- the value of minerals extracted (where minerals can occur in nature as solids, liquids or gases and in underground and surface mines) and income from quarries and oil wells with all supplementary operations (not depletion of minerals).
- the value of timber, fuelwood and non-timber forest products extracted from forests (to the extent that data are available on quantities and prices).
- the value of natural growth of cultivated assets for certain crops.
- output of dung manure.

Gross Capital Formation (GCF) includes:

- capital transfers from the Government to corporations for the purposes of water supply.
- capital investment made by household sector in bio-gas plants and wind energy systems.
- capital expenditure incurred (estimated) in installation of wind energy systems (windmills,
- aero-generators and wind turbines) and unit prices of installation capacities.
- outlays on improvement of land and development or extension of mining sites, timber tracts and plantations.

Gross Fixed Capital Formation (GFCF) includes:

- estimates of improvement of land, irrigation works, flood control projects, laying of new orchards and plantations, forestry & logging and fishing.
- estimates of extraction of both major and minor minerals with respect to public sector, non-departmental enterprises, private corporate sector, and household sector.

Change in Stocks (CIS) includes:

- estimates of produced/unsold stocks of major and minor minerals (but not depletion of minerals).
- estimates in the agriculture sector for all the three institutional units
- estimates of electricity, gas and water supply, only for public and private sectors
- changes in unsold timber extracted .

Source: *Reproduced from "Green National Income in India – A Framework" Ministry of Statistics and Programme Implementation, Government of India, 2013.*

Box 22.2 Environmental considerations currently included in India's National Accounts

The Report on "Green National Income in India – A Framework" prepared by the Expert Group Commissioned by Ministry of Statistics and Programme Implementation, Government of India (2013) under the Chairmanship of Partha Dasgupta, made the following observations on India's efforts at Greening its National Income:

- In India GDP does not account for depreciation of natural capital stock resulting from economic exploitation and environmental degradation.
- India's GDP underestimates the value of natural resources even when their use is monetized. Non-monetized environmental goods and services are not reflected in the national accounts.
- The contribution of other forest services such as carbon or hydrological services, is completely excluded.
- Changes in stock of ground water are currently not accounted for.
- GDP ignores non-monetized degradation of environmental quality and includes monetized social costs associated with attempts to improve quality. For example, the effects of air and water quality on health are ignored or included as consumption expenditure when they lead to the purchase of medical services.
- GDP increases when expenditures are made on pollution abatement. This is a distortion because environmental protection expenditures are actually social costs of maintaining environmental quality (i.e., defensive expenditures).
- Lastly, the national accounts are not yet able to examine fully the distributional implications of changes in natural or environmental goods and services.

The impact of environmental degradation on India's economic growth during the decade 1980-1990, has been analysed by the National Environmental Engineering Research Institute (NEERI). The results of the analysis reveal that during this period India's GDP increased by Rs 202,354 crores or by 5.66 per cent a year on an average. But when one takes into account the degradation of environment, one gets a very different picture, since the cost in terms of environmental damage to the economy, for the same period was Rs 333,652 crores adjusting for this cost in GDP, yields a negative growth rate of -5.73 percent.

In 2003 the Green Indian States Trust (GIST) released a series of environmentally adjusted accounts under the Green Accounting for Indian States Project. The loss of forest ecological services (i.e. soil erosion prevention, flood control and ground water augmentation) over three years (2001-03) due to declining dense forests was estimated at an astounding 1.1 per cent of GDP

Conclusion

Even the improved estimates of national income and GNP, are considered insufficient to determine whether or not human welfare is improving. GNP is no longer appreciated as an indicator of welfare. Instead, the Human Development Index (HDI) developed by the United Nations Development Programme and derived from 3 factors—life expectancy, literacy and purchasing power—is more useful for ranking and comparing countries on the basis of human development. Economist Herman Daly and Theologian John Cobb, have developed an Index of Sustainable Economic Welfare (ISEW). This index accounts for air and water pollution, cropland and wetland losses and other forms of environmental deterioration. It also includes costs of commuting and car accidents besides accounting for income inequality. Economic performance must be assessed using a variety of indicators and these indicators may move in opposite directions, making it difficult to say whether a society is better off or worse off. Yet the use of all these indicators with appropriate weights can alone give a meaningful assessment of economic performance of a nation.

Questions

1. Why is it important to include issues related to environmental degradation in national income accounting.
2. What are the ways by which environmental issues can be incorporated in national income. How does it affect national income estimate. Give specific examples.

Exercise

Download the Report on "Green National Income in India – A Framework" prepared by the Expert Group Commissioned by Ministry of Statistics and Programme Implementation, Government of India (2013) and give a write up on India's efforts and prospects in greening national income.
Website for the report:
http://mospi.nic.in/sites/default/files/publication_reports/Green_National_Accouts_in_India_1may13.pdf

23

THE ENVIRONMENT AND INTERNATIONAL TRADE

"Progress' as defined by our modern economic system, is not only perpetuating environmental deterioration, but accelerating it."

—*Sandra Postel*

Trade provides access to economic resources in other countries, so that economies can have access to goods and resources that cannot be found or produced in their regions. Trade helps some countries to add to its domestic production level of certain goods, bridging the gap between its production level and needs. Through trade, the economic-base of a country can be altered or enlarged.

According to economic theories of international trade - the theories of international specialisation and comparative advantage - trade is central to economic growth, increased world production and an efficient distribution of resources. Over the last few decades there has been a growing support for free trade, justified on grounds that free trade will improve economic welfare. The question is whether this move towards free trade will make it more difficult for the countries to protect the environmental resources they value. The relationship between trade and environment needs to be analysed on two grounds: one impact of trade on environment and two, impact of environmental policy on trade. While the former is explained in terms of trade- environment linkages the later is explained in terms of multilateral agreements and the role played by international institutions.

23.1 Trade – Environment linkages

Trade and trade liberlisation have four important effects on environment and development:

- product effects
- technology effects
- scale effects
- structural effects

Product effect refers to effects of the traded product on the environment. This could be positive or negative. Product effect is positive when trade promotes use of goods and technologies that protect environment. An example would be the solar and wind power technology. When trade facilitates movement of goods that are not environmentally friendly, then product effect is negative. Examples include trade of toxic and hazardous waste material from developed nations to underdeveloped and developing nations for reuse as cheap inputs. The trade of such goods and their movement also pose the threat of spillage.

Technology effect is similar to product effect. It refers to the technology involved in the production of the goods traded. Technology effects are positive when trade reduces the pollution intensity of the product. Trade is likely to promote environmentally harmful technology also.

Scale effects refer to cost efficiency of production facilitated by trade. Trade can increase efficiency, producing more goods with the same given set of natural resources, labour, machines and technology. Efficiency in production generated by import of cost efficient technology enable a country to produce goods with less resources and thus generate positive environmental effects. However it also true that the increased output from scale effect will increase negative environmental impact as pollution and resource use increase with increase in output. Growth in trade increases scale of output in all sectors which in turn adds to environmental degradation.

Structural effects

Structural effect refers to the change in the composition of goods produced by the nation. If due to trade, the composition of the economy changes so that the share of less polluting sectors in the GDP of the nation increases then trade will result in environmental improvements. Often firms importing input are responsible for a change in composition towards greener goods. Firms can insist that they will buy only from suppliers whose products are ISO 14000 certified. Ford and GM, the two prominent automobile manufacturers in the US, declared that they will buy only from suppliers that are certified as following the ISO 14001 environmental management system.

On the contrary if due to trade, the composition of the economy changes so that the share of polluting sectors in the GDP of the nation increases then trade will result in environmental damages. Trade may result in the creation of a sectoral composition that increases pollution and resource depletion.

While the four effects mentioned above are mostly associated with positive environmental benefits from trade , it is pointed out that trade liberalization is likely to speed up environmental pollution and deplete resources if the country specializes in the making of pollution intensive or resource intensive goods. The export of leather and leather products by Indian tanneries have resulted in lot of negative environment related trade effects for India. It can be summed up that liberalized trade has the potential for both positive and negative environmental impacts.

Trade's effect on the environment depends on the context---what regulatory and other restrictions apply to the production and use of traded items, how stringently regulations are enforced, and how trade-generated revenues are used. The standard economic position is that environmental considerations do not undermine the case for free trade. The debate on the impact of trade on environment focuses on how the principles and practice of world trade can be reconciled with the need to protect the environment. Environmental controls are regarded by the proponents of trade liberalisation as one more category of trade barriers. "Compliance with anti-pollution standards may increase the cost of exportation and importation, injure trade balances, and even deny products to nations which believe they need them". (Sriboonruang, Satien, Environmental Implication of International Relations).

World trade has promoted patterns of consumption that not only harms local ecology but also will lead to levels of consumption that cannot be sustained by earth's resources. Trade changes what we consume and consumption today has become heavily environmentally destructive. One example is the trade in frogs' legs. In 1977, Bangladesh had been supplying restaurants in Europe and the US, "the much favoured hind limbs of frog". At that time there were approximately one billion frogs in the country, far behind the world's requirement of 6500 tonnes of legs a year. By 1988, more than 50 million frogs were being exported by Bangladesh mostly to the

US. Frog exports peaked at $10.5 million a year but research showed that the 'real' price of the trade was phenomenal. Frogs are insectivorous and each frog can eat more than its weight (about 200 gm). An acre of paddy field can be kept insect free by just less than 50 frogs. Frogs protect crop and are natural biological control agents: frog wastes too is a fine organic fertiliser. Indeed, it was during this period of flourishing 'frog' trade that use of pesticides in Bangladesh increased. Bangladesh imported more than $89 million of pesticides. By 1989, Bangladesh was importing an extra 25 per cent of pesticides a year to cope with its frog loss. Government figures reveal that it was spending $30 million a year to earn $10 million. The irony is that some of the very same companies that were importing the chemicals, were exporting frogs' legs to the west. The trade was stopped only when Friends of the Earth helped the Bangladesh government realise that the export of frogs legs was an 'economic and environmental suicide.' A temporary export ban was imposed and extended further later. This had immediate effects. Imports of pesticides by Bangladesh Governments declined by 40 per cent and frog numbers are on the increase. Inspite of the ban, illegal trade is still said to be taking place; exports of frogs' legs from Bangladesh and India with companies labeling the frogs as 'frozen food'.

Source: The Guardian: 17 June 1994, p. 16

BOX 23.1 Trade, Consumption Patterns and Environment

Supporters of unrestricted trade are for fewer import and export controls. The liberal economists and the proponents of trade liberation argue that the link between trade and environmental protection is only indirect. According to such liberal economists, if environmental regulations are implemented at national level, then trade will be environment neutral. In the absence of an environmental policy, trade may magnify the environmental impacts of production and consumption activities, but trade is not the direct cause of such activities. In fact, the proponents of free trade argue that trade promotes the technology needed to protect the environment.

Defenders of free trade argue that free trade will accelerate economic growth which in turn will promote a cleaner environment. They base their argument on the Environmental Kuznets Curve (EKC) hypothesis according which nations will shift to less-polluting production methods after passing through a "dirty" stage of development.

It is held that world trade and environmental protection are mutually supportive. There can be no trade without sustainable use of natural resources, while environmental protection requires the wealth and technology trade can generate.

The environmentalists on the other hand argue that the current trading system does not take sufficient account of environmental issues. It is argued by environmentalists that liberalised trade will promote consumption and production patterns that cannot be sustained (see box 23.1). It is argued that countries which liberalise trade will lose their right to determine their own environmental standards, since free trade is characterised by harmonised international system. Further it is argued that liberalised trade hurts the environment through the "race to the bottom" in environmental standards as nations reduce environmental standards in order to attract foreign capital and to gain competitive advantage.

23.2 Economic Theory of Trade and Environment

The economic analysis of environmental issues distinguishes three different types of situation with regard to trade and environment. They are:

- Situations in which any environmental damage arising from a country's economic activity is confined within its frontiers, but the goods produced by the polluting activities are traded in international markets and can be produced in any number of different countries. An example of this situation is the pollution of the river Palar (Tamil Nadu, India) caused by tanneries exporting leather to the world market. Another example is that of pollution of River Bhavani, by the export oriented hosiery units of Tirupur, near Coimbatore, caused by the textile mills at Erode, Tamil Nadu.

- The second situation is one where the economic activity in one country causes damages to the other, i.e., pollution is not a local or national problem as in the first situation, but an international or trans national problem, as pollutants are transported by air/water to other countries. This situation includes besides pollution of rivers that runs through few countries, pollution of oceans and of the global atmosphere. Acid rain is an outstanding example of the second situation. These two situations are known as unidirectional international externalities or unidirectional environmental spill over.
- The third situation resembles the second, except that there is no material flow involved, i.e., there is an activity causing damage to environment—even though the damage does not travel beyond boundaries, it affects people in other countries who care for the environment. An apt example would be forest clearing for agriculture by country A, that depletes its wild life and results in species' extinction. People in country B who care about wild life and species diversity in A, will be affected by the forest clearance in country A. If the inhabitants of B are not concerned about the environmental damage occurring in A, then this situation is similar to the first situation involving no trans-boundary damage flow.

The first situation explained above may be explained using a simple trade model. The model is explained through figure 23.1.

In figure 23.1 MPC is the private marginal cost for an industry that produces primarily for exports. The production of the product involves externality, i.e., the industry discharges its effluents into a river and pollutes the river, but pays no compensation to those using the river. The inclusion of externality generates the marginal social cost curve MSC. The country's own demand curve for the product is represented by the usual demand curve DD. The world price level determines the domestic price which is P_0 in the figure. Given P_0 price output for home consumption is Q_0. If external costs are not considered the production volume is Q_2. Hence Q_2Q_0 will be exported. If the industry is compelled to internalise the externality, then its optimum output will be Q_1 and hence Q_1Q_0 will be exported. Thus there will be a reduction in exports if externality is internalised.

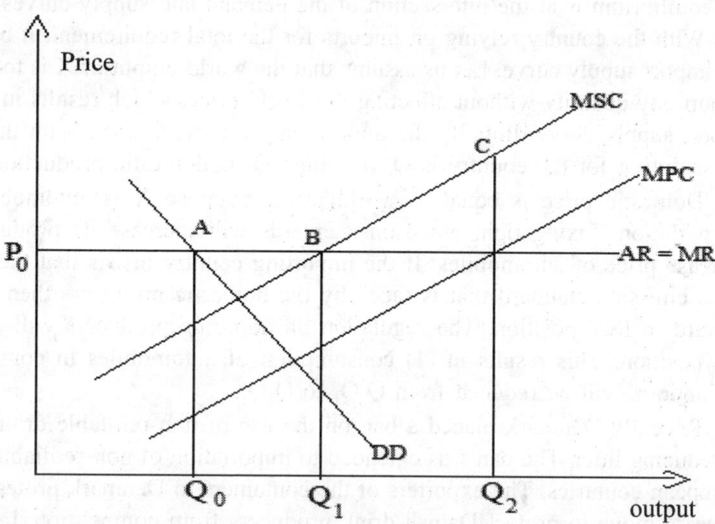

Figure 23.1 Effects of Externality on Domestic Production and Imports

In the absence of transnational pollution, a global optimum may be obtained with free trade, if each country pursues that environmental care policy which is optimal for that country. It is held that tariffs and import restrictions against countries with lower environmental standard will lead to a distortion in the optima division of labour anc a welfare loss for all Efficiency in internationa allocation merely requires that the countries follow an optimal policy and the means they use to achieve it are immaterial. Figure 23.2 explains the impac of environmental regulatior on imports. The figure considers a country, A, tha relies upon imports for a large part of its supply o good X. Demand curve DD is the demand for the product while SS is the supply curve of domestic producers. Without imports

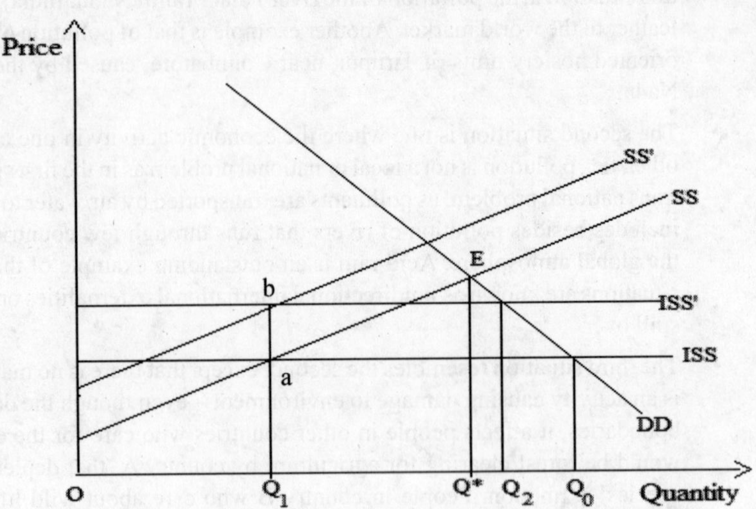

Figure 23.2 Effects of Environmental Regulation on Domestic Production and Imports

the equilibrium is at the intersection of the demand and supply curves at E resulting in a quantity of Q*. With the country relying on imports for the total requirement, it becomes necessary to introduce the import supply curve. Let us assume that the world output of X is too large. Hence country A could import any quantity without affecting the world price, which results in a perfectly elastic (horizontal) import supply curve. Initially the import supply curve is ISS. With the addition of imports the total consumption for the country is Q_0 of which Q_1 is domestic production and hence Q_1Q_0 is imported.

Domestic price is equal to world price. Suppose X is automobiles, the use of which causes air pollution. Fixing tight emission standards will increase its production cost, which in turn will increase price of automobiles. If the importing country insists that the imported car should meet the same emission standard that is faced by the domestic producers then import supply curve will shift upward to ISS' position. The regulation on domestic producers will shift domestic supply curve to SS' position. This results in (1) consumption of automobiles in country A declines from Q_0 to Q_2 (2) imports will be reduced from Q_0Q_1 to Q_2Q_1.

Recently Denmark placed a ban on the use of non-refillable drink containers with the objective of reducing litter. The ban was extended to importation of non-refillable containers from neighbouring European countries. The exporters of the containers to Denmark protested against the ban saying that it was a move to protect Danish drink producers from competition, but the European court gave the verdict in favour of Denmark.

When the production processes of a commodity that is imported creates pollution problem, the matter is not as clear as in the case of automobiles where pollution is the result of consumption. The importing country cannot legally put a tariff on an imported good, the production of which involves pollution. There is nothing that guarantees a uniform regulation in all the countries producing this good, unless multi-lateral agreements are signed by countries to reduce pollution from production of goods that are traded. The same is true of reciprocal externalities.

Externalities are reciprocal when consumption and production activities in any two countries A and B, has spill-over effects on each other's utility. Let us suppose that the consumption of good X, say fossil fuels, results in pollution that affect citizens of both the countries. The situation of reciprocal externality—externality that spills over national boundaries is illustrated in figure 23.3. In the figure,

NMD represents National Marginal Damage—that is, pollution from the use of an additional unit of fossil fuels. NMB is National Marginal Benefit curve, i.e., benefit from consuming an additional unit of fossil fuel. If the countries A and B acted independently without any cooperation, then, country A, for instance will emit OM pollution or equivalently undertake MP unit of abatement. On the other hand, if countries cooperate towards the goal of joint maximisation of welfare, then each country will consume fossil fuel upto the point where marginal benefit from an additional unit of fossil fuel consumed is equal to total marginal damage of pollution, represented by the curve TMD in figure 23.3.

The efficient level of pollution is OM* and M*P is pollution abated. It should be noted that pollution under cooperation is lower than when firms act independently (OM* < OM) and abatement is higher with cooperative behaviour (M*P > MP). For a fully efficient abatement a pollution tax of T* is required. It has two components: (1) the amount 'bc' which is on the pollution, affecting the country of origin of the pollutant and the amount 'ab' which is on the damage affecting other countries. Such an efficient outcome is however difficult in real world and the inefficient non-cooperative outcome (MP abatement) is most likely to happen.

Yet another issue in environment trade debate is the claim made by many that environmental regulations/standards are opted by many countries to protect themselves against international competition. In 1991, the United States forced a ban on imports of Mexican Tuna on grounds that the Mexican fishermen were using methods that killed too many dolphins. This move by the US was questioned, saying that it was a move to protect the US tuna companies from foreign competition. The dispute committee of GATT (General Agreement on Trade and Tariff) ruled that the US ban on Mexican tuna was contrary to international trade rules. Under GATT rules, countries cannot discriminate between products on the basis of production process.

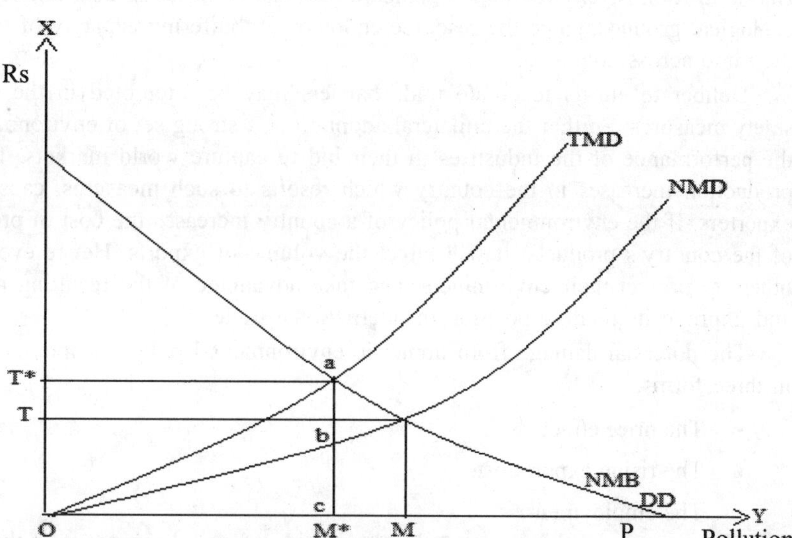

Figure 23.3 National and Global Efficient Levels for a Reciprocal Externality

23.3 Role of Unilateral Measures

William J. Baumol and Wallace E. Oates recommend unilateral measures by the victimised countries if it is impossible to resolve environmental problems jointly. They have prescribed trade restrictions where transnational environmental damages are severe. The aggrieved country, for example, can impose a duty on imports from the offending country, particularly a duty on the goods, the production of which is the source of pollution. If the pollutee nation is only an insignificant importer of the goods, then this measure may not yield results. If, however, a number of nations decide to impose such a duty— acting independently and simultaneously—then the results will be rewarding. Such duties will force the polluting country to force its firms to control emission and thus open up path for bilateral negotiations and agreements. However, there are two rules to be catered to, during the operation of such a system of duties, to prevent their misuse. They are:

i. A country that imposes trade restrictions on a polluting nation would be required to specify the conditions under which the restriction would be dropped, i.e., they could be expected to specify acceptable pollution levels from the offending country. Once the standards have been met, the restrictions could automatically be dropped;

ii. The polluting standards imposed should not be more restrictive than those which it imposes on its own industries.

23.4 Trade, Environmental Policy and Economic Relationships

Differences in national standards of pollution control have considerable impact on international trade. It could make pollution intensive industry to concentrate in countries where environmental regulations are weak. This is known as the pollution haven effect. Further differences in environmental regulations among countries may lead to a distortion in cost of production and to artificial trade barriers. Harmonization of environmental standards across countries is also not supported on economic and ecological grounds, since the resource endowment, buffering capacity of the local ecosystem are not the same across countries.

Deliberate efforts to create trade barriers may be attempted in the disguise of environmental safety measures. Further the unilateral adoption of a strong set of environmental measures will impair the performance of the industries in their bid to capture world markets. This is because the cost of production increases in the country which resorts to such measures, causing a serious detriment to exporters. If the environmental policy of a country increases the cost of production (and hence price) of the country's products, it will affect the volume of exports. Hence every country would wait for others to protect their environment, and take advantage of the resulting reductions in relative costs and improve its relative position in international trade.

The potential damage from domestic environmental policy in international trade is said to arise in three forms:

- The price effect,
- The rising export costs
- The employment.

The second and third are essentially considered as a by-product of the first. The price effects of environmental programmes refer to the rise in price as a result of the increased cost of protecting the environment from the pollution created by the domestic industries. For example, it has been estimated that for a number of industrial countries, strong environmental programmes will increase export prices from 3.5 per cent to 9 per cent. Such a price rise may be significant. But their effect on a country's competitive position in international markets, is comparable to perhaps one or two years of regular inflationary price increase. This inflation is not disadvantageous if it is universal and proceeds at an equal pace in all countries. However, the rate of inflation is seldom the same in all countries.

Many economists feel that rising export costs reduce a country's net revenues from international trade only if the quantity sold falls by a larger proportion than rise in price. If the proportionate increase in price is greater than the proportionate decrease in exports, the country, in fact, will experience an increase in revenue. Hence its balance of payments may actually improve.

The impact of domestic environmental programmes on the balance of payments of a country depends on:

- The nature of controls and their impact on costs.
- The effect of such controls on the price of domestic products and price effects.
- The price elasticity of demand for exports of the nation in question.

Similarly it has been argued that the unemployment problem resulting from reductions in exports may be offset by the tax, expenditure and other monetary policies of the government. Besides, the industries producing equipments for protection of environment will generate some employment opportunities., the evolution of international monetary system may itself resolve any balance of payments' problem posed by the environmental programmes.

23.5 Multi-lateral Agreements

Transnational environmental issues, with trade implication are often resolved through International Agreements. Many such agreements have been signed in the last few decades. The first such trade related international environmental treaty is **Phylloxera Agreement of 1878,** which restricted trade in grapevines to prevent the spread of pests that damage vineyards. Similarly in 1906 the **Berne Convention** banned the use of white phosphorus in matches on grounds that phosphorus caused serious occupational disease called called phosyjaw in which the jaws of the victim dissolved into pus causing severe pain and disfiguring to the patient. The Convention required each country to pass laws prohibiting the use of white phosphorus in matches. The prohibition /regulation of the use of white phosphorus was implemented in national laws over the next few years and its industrial use ceased.

Most of these agreements emphasise on stringent controls on pollution, similar to those controlling polluters within national boundaries, i.e., non-discrimination against firms in other countries. According to a report by the International Institute for Sustainable Development and the United Nations Environmental Programme, since the 1972 Stockholm Conference, an extraordinary number of international environmental agreements have been concluded. There are several hundred international agreements that govern some aspects of the environment. In 2009 the United Nations Environment Programme (UNEP) identified over 280 Multilateral Environmental Agreements (MEAs) which are completely dedicated to environmental protection and also cover trade related specific issues. Box 23.2 lists some of the important MEAs. A brief note on select MEAs are given below.

- Convention on International Trade in Endangered Species of Wild Fauna and Flora (CITES), 1975
- Vienna Convention for the Protection of the Ozone Layer, 1985
  - Montreal Protocol on Substances that Deplete the Stratospheric Ozone Layer, 1987
- Basel Convention on the Control of Transboundary Movement of Hazardous Wastes and their Disposal, 1992
- Convention on Biological Diversity (CBD), 1992
  - Cartagena Protocol on Biosafety, 2003
  - Nagoya–Kuala Lumpur Supplementary Protocol on Liability and Redress, 2010*
  - Nagoya Protocol on Access to Genetic Resources and Equitable Sharing of Benefits Arising from their Utilization to the Convention on Biological Diversity, 2014
- UN Framework Convention on Climate Change, 1992
  - Kyoto Protocol to the UN Framework Convention on Climate Change, 1997
- Rotterdam Convention on the Prior Informed Consent Procedure for Certain Hazardous Chemicals and Pesticides in International Trade,2004
- Stockholm Convention on Persistent Organic Pollutants, 2001
- Minamata Convention on Mercury, 2013

Source: *International Institute for Sustainable Development & United Nations Environment Programme. (2014). Trade and Green Economy: A Handbook. Published by the International Institute for Sustainable Development, Geneva.*

Box 23.2 Select International Agreements to Protect Environment

Convention on International Trade in Endangered Species of Wild Fauna and Flora (CITES), an international agreement between governments, was drawn up in 1973 and entered into force in 1975. The aim of CITES is to ensure that international trade in specimens of wild animals and plants does not threaten their survival. CITES seeks to regulate trade in certain species and their parts, as well as products made from such species by making various types of restrictions – ranging from a general prohibition on commercial trade to a partial licensing system. CITES has been ratified by 183 members.

Vienna Convention for the Protection of the Ozone Layer, 1985 and the Montreal Protocol on Substances that Deplete the Stratospheric Ozone Layer, 1987

In 1981, UNEP acted on a proposal to develop a global convention on the ozone layer. The protocol to the Vienna Convention, the Montreal Protocol on Substances that Deplete the Ozone Layer (the Protocol), was adopted in September 1987 and set out a framework for reducing the production and consumption of ozone-depleting substances (ODS) and binding commitments for ratifying parties. The Montreal Protocol entered into force in January 1989 and, as of August 2008, has been ratified by 193 countries. The Montreal Protocol bans all trade in the ozone depleting substances and trade in products containing controlled substances between parties and non-parties.

Basel Convention on the Control of Transboundary Movement of Hazardous Wastes and their Disposal, 1992

The Basel Convention resulted from the concern of developing countries that they could become the dumping ground for hazardous wastes of the developed nations. The Basel Convention covers hazardous wastes that are explosive, flammable, poisonous, infectious, corrosive, toxic, or eco-toxic. The Convention provided for the reductions of hazardous waste generation and the promotion of environmentally sound management of hazardous wastes wherever the place of disposal.

Trade related provisions in the Protocol relate to the rule that restricts the Parties to the Protocol to only export a hazardous waste to another party that has not banned its import and that has provided prior consent to the import in writing. Further Parties to the Protocol are prohibited from importing from or export to a non-party, unless there is an agreement or arrangement in place that does not deviate from the provisions of the Convention.

Convention on Biological Diversity (CBD), 1992

The Convention on Biological Diversity (CBD) entered into force on 29 December 1993. It has 3 main objectives:

- The conservation of biological diversity
- The sustainable use of the components of biological diversity
- The fair and equitable sharing of the benefits arising out of the utilization of genetic resources.

The Cartagena Protocol on Biosafety (CPB) ***to the Convention on Biological Diversity*** is an international agreement. The Cartagena Protocol aims to ensure the safe handling, transport and use of living modified organisms (LMOs). It was adopted on 29 January 2000 and entered into force on 11 September 2003.

Trade related dimension of CBD and CPB are found in the WTO Agreement on Trade-Related Aspects of Intellectual Property Rights (TRIPS). The Protocol provides for restriction of import of specific LMOs by parties to the Protocol.

Nagoya Protocol on Access to Genetic Resources and Equitable Sharing of Benefits Arising from their Utilization to the Convention on Biological Diversity is an international agreement which aims at sharing the benefits arising from the utilization of genetic resources in a fair and equitable way. It entered into force on 12 October 2014. The trade dimension of the Protocol relates to the Nagoya Protocol's relationship with the WTO TRIPS Agreement.

UN Framework Convention on Climate Change, 1992

The Un Framework Convention on Climate Change (UNFCCC) is an intergovernmental treaty developed to address the problem of climate change. It was one of the key outcomes of the Rio Earth Summit in 1992. In 1997, the Convention was strengthened with the Kyoto Protocol, which obligated the developed countries to legally binding obligations to cut their emissions by 5.2% below 1990 levels by 2008-2012 in aggregate.

The Kyoto Protocol, 1997

The Kyoto Protocol obliges developed nations to cut their emissions of greenhouse gases by an average of about 5% for the period 2008-2012 compared with 1990 levels. The Protocol came into force as a legally-binding document on 16 February 2005. Developing countries are not required to reduce emission levels unless developed countries provided funds and technology.

The Protocol's first commitment period started in 2008 and ended in 2012. By the end of the first commitment period in 2012 a total of 192 countries had ratified the protocol. A second commitment period was agreed in 2012, through the Doha Amendment to the protocol, in which 37 countries have binding targets.

The UNFCCC and the Kyoto Protocol do not explicitly or specifically contain any trade restrictive measures. But it is expected that the parties will adopt domestic policies and measures with significant trade implications in their activities taken to reduce GHG emissions,

The Rotterdam Convention on the Prior Informed Consent Procedure for Certain Hazardous Chemicals and Pesticides in International Trade, is a MEA that provides obligations on the imports and exports of select hazardous chemicals. It was adopted in response to dramatic growth in chemicals trade and came into force on 24 February 2004. To date it has143 Parties. The Convention promotes shared responsibility between exporting and importing countries in protecting human health and the environment from the harmful effects of hazardous chemicals and provides for the exchange of information about potentially hazardous chemicals that may be exported and imported.

Stockholm Convention on Persistent Organic Pollutants, 2001 The Stockholm Convention is a global treaty to protect human health and the environment from persistent organic pollutants (POPs). POPs are chemicals that remain intact in the environment for long periods. The Stockholm Convention focused on eliminating or reducing releases of 12 POPs, the so-called "Dirty Dozen". The main aims of the Stockholm Convention are:

- Eliminate dangerous POPs, starting with the 12 worst
- Support the transition to safer alternatives
- Target additional POPs for action
- Cleanup old stockpiles and equipment containing POPs
- Work together for a POPs-free future

Over 150 countries signed the Convention and it entered into force, on 17 May 2004.

Minamata Convention on Mercury, 2013 addresses **specific human activities which are contributing to widespread mercury pollution.** The Convention is named after the **Japanese city of Minamata**, which came to be known world over due to a tragedy involving methyl mercury from industrial wastewater from a chemical factory discharged into Minamata Bay. The agreement's objective is to reduce global mercury pollution over the coming decades. The Convention **was adopted by delegates from over 140 countries in January 2013, after three years of negotiation.** The convention addresses trade in mercury as one of the issues.

Table 23.1 gives a summary of details on trade –environment linkages in MEAs.

Table 23.1 Trade-Environment Linkages in Multilateral Agreements

Multilateral Agreement	Salient Feature	Trade-Environment Linkage
Convention on International Trade in Endangered Species of Wild Fauna and Flora (CITES) 1975	To ensure that international trade in specimens of wild animals and plants does not threaten their survival.	Regulates trade in certain species and their parts, as well as products made from such species by making various types of restrictions – ranging from a general prohibition on commercial trade to a partial licensing system
Montreal Protocol on Substances that Deplete the Stratospheric Ozone Layer, 1987	Ban on the production and consumption of certain chemicals (listed by the Protocol) which deplete the stratospheric ozone layer.	Bans trade in products containing ozone depleting substances between parties and non-parties.
Basel Convention on the Control of Transboundary Movement of Hazardous Wastes and their Disposal, 1992.	Provides for the reductions of hazardous waste generation and for the promotion of environmentally sound management of hazardous wastes wherever the place of disposal is.	Controls export of hazardous waste to another party by Parties to the Protocol and restricts importing from or export to a non-party. The import or export of hazardous wastes not allowed if wastes will not be treated in an environmentally sound manner at their destination.
The Rotterdam Convention, (2004) on the Prior Informed Consent Procedure for Certain Hazardous Chemicals and Pesticides.	Provides for control of imports and exports of select hazardous chemicals.	Provides for a national decision-making process on export and import of chemicals. Parties can decide which of the chemicals listed in the Convention they wish to agree to import.
The Cartagena Protocol on Biosafety (CPB) *to the Convention on Biological Diversity* (2003)	Aims to ensure the safe handling, transport and use of living modified organisms (LMOs).	LMOs released intentionally into the environment are subject to an advance informed agreement procedure and those intended for direct use as food, feed or processing are to be accompanied by documents identifying them.
Minamata Convention on Mercury (2013)	Addresses **specific human activities which are contributing to widespread mercury pollution.**	Parties may export mercury only if the importing party has given its written consent for the transaction and commits to storing and using of imported mercury in ways allowed by the Convention. The Minamata Convention also regulates trade with non-parties.

Stockholm Convention on Persistent Organic Pollutants (POPS), 2004.	Aims to protect human health and the environment from substances that persist in the environment and accumulate in the food chain disrupting hormonal functions in animals and humans.	Establishes an international regime for the control of certain substances that persist in POPs.

23.6 GATT and Environment

GATT (General Agreement on Trade and Tariff) is the main international institution governing trade, and was established in the 1940s.Its purpose is to set out a list of rules and procedures to be followed by nations in their international trade relationships. The main objective of GATT is to promote free trade by removing barriers to trade in the form of tariffs and quotas on imports. There is also a provision in GATT that outlaws non-tariff barriers such as excessive inspection requirements, excessive product specifications and the like. One of the central intentions of GATT implies that there should be no discrimination against foreign producers in relation to domestic producers, that is, trade without discrimination, in which each member nation opened its markets equally to every other.

GATT played a major role in the enormous expansion of world trade in the second half of the 20th century. By the time GATT was replaced by the World Trade Organisation (WTO) in 1995, 125 nations were signatories to its agreements, which had become a code of conduct governing 90 percent of world trade. WTO adopted its principles and the trade agreements reached under its umbrella.

Environment was first mentioned only in the TBT agreement (Technical Barriers to Trade). GATT rules are in principle, binding. There are many exceptions which can cause the main regulations in GATT rules to be set aside. Article XX of GATT allows countries to sidestep the normal trading rules, if required, to (1) protect human, animal or plant life or health, or (2) to conserve exhaustible natural resources, on condition that such measures do not discriminate between sources of imports or constitute disguised protection on international trade.

However, when such trade restriction are set to achieve the protection of human, animal or plant life or health and for 'conserving the natural resources' there should not be any unjustifiable discrimination between countries where the same conditions prevail.

GATT rules, in principle, regulate only trade of products and goods and do not cover production processes. This implies that measures against imports, based on how the goods are manufactured, are not permitted.

Prior to the Stockholm Conference, the growing concern on the implications of environmental protection policies on international trade, gave rise to the establishment of the Group on Environmental Measures and International Trade (known as the EMIT Group). The growing volume of international trade flows between 1971 and 1991, once again brought to world attention the impact of environmental policies on trade and trade on environment. As a result the Tokyo Round established the Agreement on Technical Barriers to Trade (TBT), also known as the "Standards Code". TBT called for non-discrimination in the preparation, adoption and application of technical standards and regulations. During the Uruguay Round, the TBT Agreement was modified to incorporate environment in the following:

- General Agreement on Trade in Services
- Agreements on Agriculture
- Sanitary and Phytosanitary Measures (SPS)
- Subsidies and Countervailing Measures
- Trade-related Aspects of Intellectual Property Rights (TRIPS).

Following these developments, the EMIT Group studied the effects of the environmental protection measures on international trade and trade provisions contained in multilateral environmental. After the Marrakech Agreement, the EMIT Group became the Committee on Trade and the Environment-CTE.

The GATT completed eight rounds of multilateral trade negotiations. The eigth round is the Uruguay Round (the 8th round) which concluded in Marrakesh in 1994 and provided for the establishment of the WTO in 1995.

23.7 WTO and Environment

The World Trade Organization came into existence on January 1, 1995 as a result of the Uruguay Round trade negotiations (1987-1994) and has now 153 members. The WTO incorporated all the elements of GATT and aims at lowering the trade barriers and promoting fair trade. The preamble to the WTO agreement states:

> "relations in the field of trade and economic endeavour should be conducted with a view to raising standards of living, ensuring full employment and a large and steadily growing volume of real income and effective demand, and expanding the production of and trade in goods and services, while allowing for the optimal use of the world's resources in accordance with the objective of sustainable development, seeking both to protect and preserve the environment and to enhance the means for doing so in a manner consistent with their respective needs and concerns at different levels of economic development".

Thus the concept of sustainable development is incorporated as a principle to guide the interpretation of the WTO Agreements.

Functions of WTO are:

- Administering trade agreements.
- Acting as a forum for trade negotiations.
- Settling interstate trade disputes.
- Reviewing national trade policies.
- Assisting developing countries in trade related policy issues through technical assistance and training programmes.
- Cooperating with other international organisations.

Until the beginning of the 1990s, the WTO was concerned only with issues related to market access. However following environment related disputes of "ecological dumping" and disputes such as the tuna-dolphin conflict between Mexico and the USA, WTO was compelled to take note of environmental disputes / issues arising from trade practices. The Committee on Trade and Environment (CTE) created in 1995 under the WTO attempts at bringing environment and sustainable development issues into the mainstream of WTO work.

The most important provisions as far as environmental issues are concerned are Article XX of the GATT and the Agreements on Sanitary and Phytosanitary Measures and the Agreement on Technical Barriers to Trade.

Article XX of GATT permits WTO members to take the following measures:

- measures 'necessary to protect human, animal, or plant life or health
- measures 'relating to the conservation of exhaustible natural resources

But these measures are allowed only if such measures do not lead to any discrimination between countries where similar conditions prevail and should not cause disguised restriction on international trade. Any country that wants to apply this article must " first demonstrate that the measure it intends to apply is necessary to protect the environment and, second, that the measure is the most efficient way of accomplishing this objective".(Cordero Paula et al,2008)

In addition, Article XX clarified the following points with reference to the application of this measure: (Cordero Paula et al,2008)

- a country cannot require another to adopt specific technologies or environmental measures; it must allow different technologies and/or measures that have the same final effect.
- when a measure is applied to other countries the differences in the conditions prevailing in those other countries must be taken into consideration.
- before promulgating a trade measure countries must try to negotiate with the exporting country or countries.
- foreign countries affected by trade measures must be allowed the necessary time to make the appropriate adjustments.
- foreign countries or producers must have access to a fair and transparent process, to appeals procedure and to appropriate guarantees so that the application of the measure can be reconsidered.

The **Agreement on Technical Barriers to Trade (TBT)** was designed to reduce the scope for countries to use technical standards as disguised barriers to trade. Technical standards with restrictive trade effects are permitted for the following four purposes:

- for the protection of the environment
- for national security requirements
- for the prevention of deceptive practices and
- for the protection of human health and safety and animal and plant health and life.

However national treatment and non-discrimination must apply when technical standards are adopted as mandatory regulations.

Agreement on Sanitary and Phytosanitary Measures (SPS) was negotiated in the Uruguay Round prevent countries from using the quarantine provisions to secure economic protection rather than to protect health and safety. The SPS provides that when restrictions on trade are applied they must be based on internationally established guidelines. If any member applies any other standard then it requires scientific evidence backed by and risk assessment procedures to protect public health. The agreement allows governments to implement measures in pursuit of objectives relating to human, animal and plant life or health. The SPS Agreement sought to ensure that SPS measures are not misused for protectionist purposes and not for creating barriers to international trade.

There is an argument that WTO did not give importance to environmental issues arising from trade. The purpose of the WTO is to promote unrestricted free trade and to help countries to benefit from open trading system. If it is to be used as an instrument to achieve environmental purposes, then similar considerations will have to be given to other areas of public policy such as health and human rights. That would defeat the primary objective of WTO. The existing WTO provisions and agreements permit countries sufficient flexibility to raise their domestic environmental standards and impose certain trade restrictions in cases where its own environment is adversely affected provided it does not lead to discrimination and trade barriers.

Doha Declaration: In November 2001 the Fourth Ministerial Conference was held in Doha in which negotiations were initiated to clarify the relationship between the multilateral trade systems and the environment. The Doha declaration incorporated the issue of impact of environmental measures on market access especially in developing countries which feared that their products would be eliminated from international trade due to environmental measures adopted by developed nations. The Doha

Conference further discussed issues related to the provisions of the Agreement on Trade-related Aspects of Intellectual Property Rights, eco-labeling requirements, fisheries subsidies and technical assistance and environmental reviews.

The Doha Round of negotiations did not yield much result since developing countries did not agree on the issues of agricultural subsidy and market access for industrial goods. However this does not mean that environmental negotiations have come to a standstill; environmental issues are addressed in the bilateral and multi-lateral agreements like the North American Free Trade Agreement (NAFTA), Convention on International Trade in Endangered Species (CITES), and the Kyoto Protocol.

Conclusion

Trade is an integral part of today's economic structure. Expanded global trade will bring benefits in terms of increased efficiency, technology transfer, and the import and export of sustainably produced products. Introducing sustainability into trade policy will require institutional changes at global, regional, and local levels. Future trade agreements must take environmental sustainability more explicitly into account.

Questions

1. What are trade related environmental issues. Give examples.
2. Bring out the trade, environmental policy and economic linkages.
3. Explain the economic theory of trade – environment relationship.
4. Bringout the significance of multilateral agreements to minimize environmental impact of trade.
5. Bring out the role of WTO in trade related environmental issues.

Exercise

1. Is harmonization of environmental standards a solution to trade related environmental issues? Will differences in environmental policies lead to "eco-dumping" or "pollution havens.
2. Discuss merits of the WTO ruling in the Tuna-Dolphin case between the US and Mexico.
3. Should trade in toxic wastes be banned or can it serve a useful function?
4. From the website given below download the book: Trade and Green Economy by IISD and UNEP and make a note on multilateral agreements and their implications to international trade . Are multi-lateral Agreements sufficient to solve environmental issues arising from international trade. http://www.unep.org/sites/unep.org.greeneconomy/files/publications/Trade-GE-Handbook-FINAL-FULL-WEB.pdf

SECTION 6

ENVIRONMENTAL POLICY

24

ENVIRONMENTAL POLICY – AN INTRODUCTION

> "It has become a recognised fact that civilised society is still intensively 'working' on transforming our planet, ...into a desert, annihilating life. Everyone understands that it is time to stop this disruptive process, but we are not hurrying with the decisive initiatives."
>
> —*Prof M.A. Markov*

Since the last few decades, the exploitation of environmental goods and services has been increasing at an alarming rate that we are almost at the brink of an environmental crisis. This is evident from the following facts on environmental degradation available from various sources such as "The World Counts", "Do Something.org" :

- The World's population is already over 7 billion; by 2025 the figure will touch 8 billion and will most probably surpass 9 billion by 2045.
- Increasing population is already generating heavy pressure on planet Earth. We already need 1.5 planets for our resource needs and for the disposal of wastes. If nothing is done to arrest this growth in population and consumption and waste generation trends, we will need 2 Earths by 2030.
- Every year, we extract an estimated 55 billion tons of fossil energy, minerals, metals and bio-mass from the Earth.
- We have a garbage island floating in our ocean, mostly comprised of plastics - the size of India, Europe and Mexico combined!
- Over 1 million seabirds and 100,000 sea mammals are killed by pollution every year.
- Water pollution causes approximately 14,000 deaths per day, mostly due to contamination of drinking water by untreated sewage in developing countries.
- For every one of the 6 billion people on Earth, nearly four tons of carbon dioxide is spewed into the air annually.

These alarming facts on environmental degradation have compelled governments to think in terms of designing an environmental policy to address the issue of environmental degradation. It was only in 1969 that the 'need to look at natural environment as a policy issue' was exposed by a U N Report (Zylicz Tomasz, 2010). More popularly known as the U Thant Report, this report, did not give any specific guideline regarding the formulation of an environmental policy. The United Nations Conference on the Human Environment in Stockholm in 1972 is a response to the U Thant

Report. After this Conference, many governments established exclusive departments, in charge of environmental protection. The Conference called upon Governments to take measures for the preservation and improvement of the human environment, for the benefit of all the people and for their posterity. More specifically Principle 11 of the Conference proceeding states:

> The environmental policies of all States should enhance and not adversely affect the present or future development potential of developing countries, nor should they hamper the attainment of better living conditions for all, and appropriate steps should be taken by States and international organizations with a view to reaching agreement on meeting the possible national and international economic consequences resulting from the application of environmental measures. [United Nations 1972]

The Stockholm Conference provoked nations to design an appropriate environmental policy. Since then nations have adopted various policy instruments for protecting the environment. The Rio Conference further strengthened the need for protecting the environment and promoting sustainable development through effective environmental policy measures and principles. It spelt out the need for endorsing the polluter pays principle and the precautionary principle in the environmental protection policy. Principles 15 and 16 of the Rio Declaration on Environment and Development implied the application of the two principles.

Principle 15

In order to protect the environment, the **precautionary approach** shall be widely applied by States according to their capabilities. Where there are threats of serious or irreversible damage, lack of full scientific certainty shall not be used as a reason for postponing cost-effective measures to prevent environmental degradation.

Principle 16

National authorities should endeavour to promote the internalization of environmental costs and **the use of economic instruments**, taking into account the approach that the **polluter should, in principle, bear the cost of pollution,** with due regard to the public interest and without distorting international trade and investment.

Source: Report of the United Nations Conference on Environment and Development(UNCED)

Downloaded from:

http://www.un.org/documents/ga/conf151/aconf15126-1annex1.htm

Box 24.1 Principles 15 and 16 of the Rio Declaration on Environment and Development

24.1 Economic Foundations of Environmental Policy

Designing an environmental policy first of all requires an understanding of the fact that environmental degradation arises due to two reasons:

- Government failure
- Market failure

Government failure is 'imperfection in government performance' (Orbach, Barak, 2013). It is argued that government failure occurs when government intervention causes a more inefficient allocation of goods and resources than would occur without that intervention, that is when government has created inefficiencies because it should not have intervened in the first place or when it could have solved a given problem or set of problems more efficiently by generating greater net benefits. Government failure also occurs whenever the government performs inadequately, that is, when it fails to intervene or does not sufficiently intervene (Orbach, Barak, 2013).Weimer and Vining (2004) distinguish between passive government failure and active government failure. Passive government failure refers to situations where government inaction results in Pareto inferior outcomes - failure of government to intervene. Active government failure on the other hand refers to situations where government action results in outcomes worse than if government had done nothing.

Market failure is defined by Bator (1958) as the failure of a system of price -market institutions to stop "undesirable" activities. Theoretically a market failure can be defined as an equilibrium allocation of resources that is not Pareto optimal—which may be due to market power, natural monopoly, imperfect information, externalities, or public goods. Market failure means failure to achieve Pareto Optimality.

The presence of market failure is evidence that there must also be government failure: the failure to correct market failure (Weimer and Vining, 2004). Connolly and Munro observe that "just as a market failure is not a failure to bring a particular or favored solution into existence at desired prices but is rather a problem which prevents the market from operating efficiently, a government failure is not a failure of the government to bring about a particular solution but is rather a systemic problem which prevents an efficient government solution to a problem" (Connolly, S. & Munro, A. 1999). "

The neo-classical theory explains that under perfectly competitive conditions resources will be efficiently allocated by the market. The theory also asserted that market failures arising from imperfections in market conditions must be corrected by the government. When government fails to intervene efficiently it is government failure. Pollution of any form is an instance of market failure and the failure of the government to define property rights or effectively impose environmental standards results in pollution; this is an instance of government failure. Designing and implementing an environmental policy efficiently is the solution for both market failure and government failure.

24.2 Optimum Pollution or Zero Pollution

What is the level of pollution expected to be achieved from the application of an efficient environmental policy? Is it zero pollution or optimum pollution? In other words, "how much of pollution is to be reduced?" Ecologists say that pollution should be reduced to a level within the assimilative capacity of the environment. Assimilative capacity refers to the ability of the **environment** to absorb and carry wastes without adverse effects on the environment or on users of its resources. When assimilative capacity is exceeded, the result is pollution. Reduction of pollution to the assimilative level has both costs and benefits. Hence economic theory recommends that pollution be reduced to an optimum level, which is a level of pollution at which marginal cost of pollution reduction is equal to marginal benefit from pollution reduction. Zero pollution is justified only when a total ban is imposed on the pollutant due to its severe adverse effects on human welfare and health of flora and fauna.

Law of Thermodyanamics explains that pollution is an inevitable by-product of any economic activity. As long as the wastes discharged are within the assimilative capacity of the environment, pollution is not an economic problem. Pollution becomes an economic problem only when it exceeds the natural absorptive capacity of the environment since it makes the absorptive function of the environment limited and there is trade-off between environmental quality and pollution. As pollution increases environmental quality decreases justifying the economic basis for environmental protection. Economics applies the principle of efficiency to environmental protection and holds that pollution should be controlled to that level at which total costs of pollution is minimized. Pollution corresponding to this minimum cost is termed as optimum pollution.

Costs arising due to pollution are referred to as waste disposal cost by Prof. Dales. Waste disposal costs may be defined as the sum of pollution control cost and pollution damage costs.

Pollution control costs are those costs incurred either by firms or individuals in the private sector or by the Government to control pollution that results from some production and consumption activities and costs incurred to prevent pollution from happening. Pollution Control costs includes both pollution treatment or abatement costs and pollution prevention costs. While the former is incurred after pollution occurs the latter is incurred before pollution occurs.Examples of these concepts of cost include:

- costs incurred by a local Government to treat its sewage before dumping it into a river are pollution prevention costs. costs incurred by a firm to install an electro-static precipitator or increase stack height that would minimise the residues emitted to the atmosphere is also pollution prevention cost.
- Public and private expenditures on various clean-up programmes. These are typically pollution treatment or abatement costs.

Pollution causes welfare damages. Such damages are both real and pecuniary. Observable deterioration of physical assets and properties are pecuniary damages while a deterioration of the health of living beings is a 'real cost'. Both air and water pollution pose health hazards and increase the medical expenses to the society to maintain a given standard of health. Besides, both damage properties, and bring down the value of property. Air pollution may cause paints to peel and impose additional painting costs on the owners of the building. Such explicit money costs of maintenance of physical assets will increase with increase in pollution. But there are certain welfare costs of pollution damage which cannot be directly measured. At most we can measure them by finding out the sum of money needed to pay to avoid such a damage. In sum, waste disposal cost is the sum of pollution control cost and pollution damage cost.

Total Waste Disposal Cost = Total Pollution Control Cost + Total Pollution Damage Cost. Since Pollution Control Cost includes Pollution Abatement Cost and Pollution Prevention Costs, Waste Disposal cost may be expressed as:

Total Waste Disposal Cost = Pollution Prevention Costs +Total Pollution Abatement Cost + Total Pollution Damage Cost.

Figures 24.1a and 24.1b illustrate TPAC and TPDC curves.

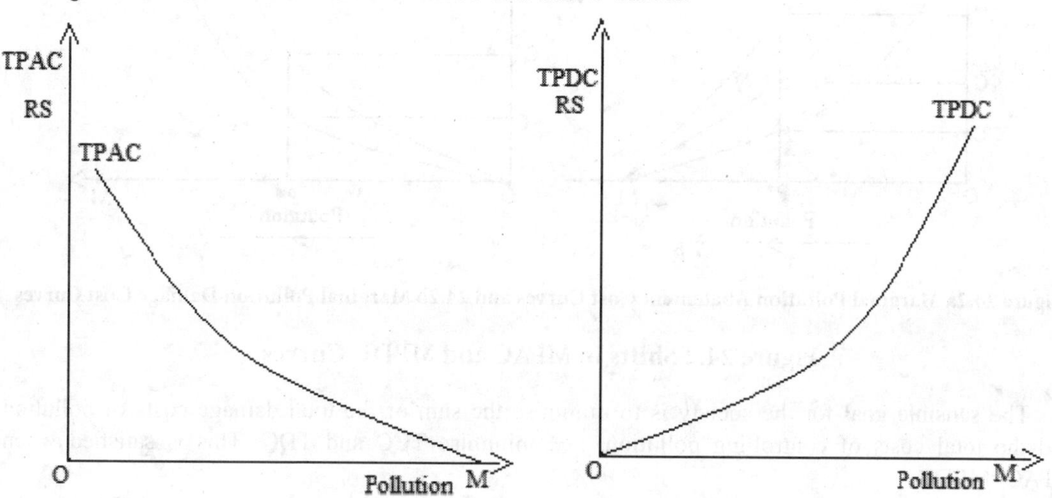

Figure 24.1a Total Pollution Abatement Cost Curve Figure 24.1b Total Pollution Damge Cost Curve

Figure 24.1 Pollution Cost Curves

Economic theory holds that total cost should be minimized for efficient pollution reduction, that is, Total Pollution Control Cost (TPCC) should be minimized. TPCC is minimized when Marginal Pollution Abatement Cost (MPAC) is equal to Marginal Pollution Damage Cost (MSDC).

MPAC is the cost incurred to treat or control an additional unit of pollution and is the slope of TPAC. MPAC increases with reduction in pollution. This is because reduction of additional units of pollution requires mare sophisticated technology which is very expansive. MPAC is the slope of TPAC. The position of MPAC depends on technology. With an improved technology, MPAC shifts downwards.In figure 24.2a, MPAC is the original marginal pollution abatement cost curve. With an improved technology the MPAC curve shifts downwards to MPAC' position while with an inferior technology the MPAC would be MPAC". Accordingly cost of controlling pollution to P* level is the highest with MPAC" (OC") and lowest for MPAC'(OC') and clearly OC" > OC'. MPAC curve is also interpreted as the demand curve for pollution opportunities.

MPDC is the cost to the society from an additional unit of pollution. Damage costs reflect the externalities. MPDC is the slope of TPDC. It is the rate of change in TPDC and hence the slope of TPDC. Slope of the marginal damage cost curve is influenced by the nature of the pollutant and shift of MPDC is due to change in weather conditions, location of pollution, changes in people's preference for environmental quality, change in the assimilative capacity of the environment, changes in population, etc.

In figure 24.2 MPDC is for a rural area and MPDC' is for an urban town where the impact is severe. In figure 24.2b the damage cost from OP* of pollution is OC with the damage function MPDC and OC' (>OC) if the damage function is MPDC'. It can be seen that the damage costs are higher in urban areas than in rural areas for any given level of pollution.

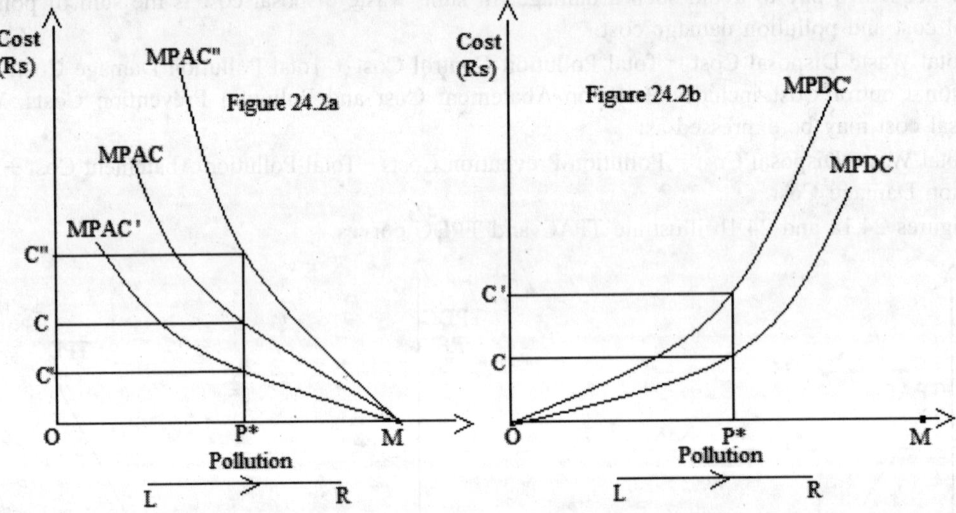

Figure 24.2a Marginal Pollution Abatement Cost Curves and 24.2b Marginal Pollution Damage Cost Curves

Figure 24.2 Shifts in MPAC and MPDC Curves

The sensible goal for the society is to minimise the sum of the total damage costs of pollution and the total costs of controlling pollution, i.e., minimise TCC and TDC. This is satisfied when MPAC=MPDC.

Figure 24.3 shows the optimum level of pollution by locating the minimum point of TPCC curve. The minimum does not coincide with the inter-section point of TPAC and TPDC. But it corresponds to the intersection point MPAC and MPDC. In the figure, optimum pollution is at P*. Further reduction in pollution will cost more than it is worth and when the pollution level exceeds P* extra cost to society of additional pollution is greater than the cost of preventing it. In figure 24.3, the lower

* MPAC curve is also interpreted as the demand curve for pollution opportunities.

panel consists of MPAC and MPDC. The cost of allowing pollution to increase from P* to K is much greater than the cost of preventing it. For example, if pollution level is OK, marginal cost of controlling it is KL and marginal damage cost to society is KM and KM > KL. To the left of P*, cost of pollution control is greater than the cost to society of pollution. At G, marginal control cost is GH and Marginal damage cost of pollution to society is GJ and GH > GJ. Only at P*, MPAC = MPDC and total costs are minimum. P* is the optimum level of pollution. In figure 24.3 area marked 'b' is the total damage costs (TPDC) caused by a pollution level of P* while the area marked 'a' is the total abatement cost (TPAC) of reducing pollution to P* level. The sum of a + b is the total costs from P* level of pollution. At P* level of pollution, sum of total abatement cost and total damage cost are minimized. However at P* level of pollution, TPAC and TPDC are not equal to each other (area 'a' is not equal to the area 'b'). The condition for optimum pollution specifies the equality of MPAC and MPDC and not the equality of TPAC and TPDC.

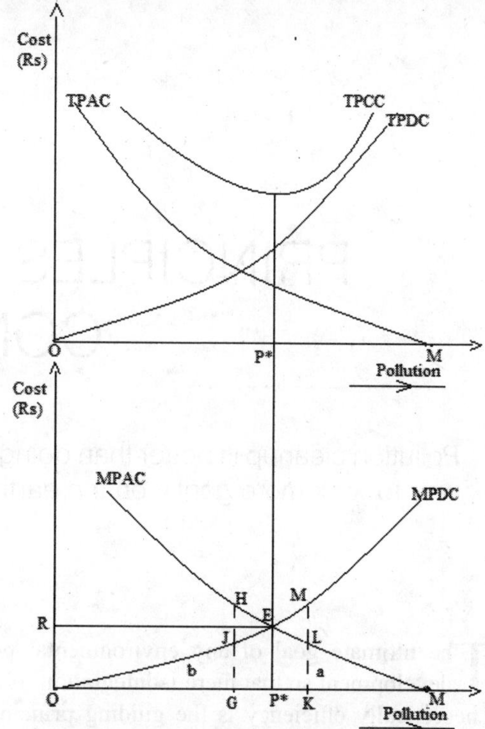

Figure 24.3 Optimum Pollution

Conclusion

The concept of optimum pollution is very useful in designing the appropriate policy for pollution control provided accurate information on damage costs and pollution abatement cost is available. While it is easy to get information on abatement costs, measuring damage costs imposes challenges. However if such information is available and if the optimum level of pollution is known, then designing an effective and efficient environmental policy with appropriate standards for various pollutant and an appropriate effluent/ emission tax will be easier and the government will be able to choose the right policy mix for controlling pollution.

Questions

1. Can optimum level of pollution be equal to zero? Justify your answer
2. What is the condition for Optimum pollution level?
3. In the case of pollutants like the green house gases or pesticides (like DDT), what is the optimum level of pollution.
4. Account for the shifts in MPAC and MPDC and show the impact on optimum pollution when the two curves shift.

Exercise

Analyse the possible change in optimum pollution when
MAPC shifts downwards
MPAC shifts upwards
MPDC shifts upwards
MPDC shifts downwards.
Account for the shifts in MPAC and MPDC.

25
PRINCIPLES OF POLLUTION CONTROL

Pollution cleanup is better than doing nothing, but pollution prevention is the best way to walk more gently on the earth.

—*(Miller 1993:15)*

The ultimate goal of any environmental policy is to put the nation on the path of sustainable development so that there is integration of economics and ecology in decision making at all levels. Theoretically efficiency is the guiding principle of an environmental policy. Actual implementation of the policy is guided by many simple rules. Two such rules relate to:

- Polluter Pays Principle
- Precautionary Principle

25.1 Polluter Pays Principle

The concept of Polluter Pays Principle can be traced to Plato's writings. Plato wrote; "If anyone intentionally spoils the water of another…let him not only pay for damages, but purify the stream or cistern which contains the water.Kautilya,the Indian Philosopher wrote in his Arthasastra (Study of Economics) about different levels of financial penalties harming the environment. He prescribed that compensation must be paid in the case of damage to "the ploughing or seeds in another's field—channels or a field under water". He prescribed that the compensation had to be in accordance with the extent of damage. Gradually the Polluter Pays Principle was recognized as a policy instrument of pollution control at national and international levels.

The Polluter Pays Principle (PPP) as a policy instrument was first clearly formulated by the OECD Secretariat in 1972. It states that whoever is responsible for damage to the environment should bear the costs associated with it. Under the 1972 and 1974 OECD Recommendations, the Polluter-Pays Principle means that the polluter should bear the "costs of pollution prevention and control measures", where costs of pollution prevention and control measures refers to "measures decided by public authorities to ensure that the environment is in an acceptable state". This implies that the polluter has to bear the cost of measures he is legally bound to take to protect the environment.

The basic principle of PPP is that the price of goods and service should reflect the total cost. The PPP aims at correcting improper cost allocation. Improper cost allocation refers to the external cost (pollution) resulting from production and consumption activities which are not reflected in the product price. These are costs on the society and are known as externalities. Failure to incorporate these costs results in over production and is an instance of market failure. Making the producer of the externality bear the cost - internalize the externality – is the basis of PPP. Many interpret PPP as implying that the polluter must pay for:

- The cost of pollution abatement
- The cost of environment recovery
- Compensation costs for victims of damages resulting from pollution.

The intention of the PPP was to make the polluter to 'limit their pollution and bear the cost of measures taken to that end'. Many misinterpret it as a principle that permits polluters to pollute.

There are two interpretations of the principle: the weak PPP and the strong PPP. The weak or standard definition of PPP does not require polluters to bear the additional costs of accidental damages. The OECD Guiding Principles states that the PPP should " ….not be accompanied by subsidies that would create significant distortions in international trade and investment." This is referred to as the weak or standard PPP. However there were exceptions to this such as assistance for R&D on methods of pollution abatement. Further polluter did not have to pay for residual damages. Hence this is referred to as weak or standard PPP.

In 2001, the OECD stated that "... the polluter should be held responsible for environmental damage caused and bear the expenses of carrying out pollution prevention measures or paying for damaging the state of the environment where the consumptive or productive activities causing the environmental damage are not covered by property rights." This version of the PPP is referred to as the extended or **strong PPP** in the literature. Khan M R distinguishes between weak and strong PPP as follows "Weak form prohibits government subsidies for pollution abatement, to ensure that product prices reflect costs of pollution control. Strong form calls for governments to assure internalization of all environmental costs, including residual damage, in the form of liability and compensation. This means the strong form subsumes the weak form plus the principle of equity".

Accidental Pollution: In 1989 PPP was extended by OECD to include the cost of accidental pollution. The 1989 recommendation implies that neither the risk nor the consequences of accidental pollution should be paid from the public funds but should be borne by the polluter. Accident prevention will be more effective when the polluter has to bear the cost of all operations made necessary by an accident (cleaning, rehabilitation).The Recommendation of the Council concerning the Application of the Polluter-Pays Principle to Accidental Pollution states that: "In matters of accidental pollution risks, the Polluter-Pays Principle implies that the operator of a hazardous installation should bear the cost of reasonable measures to prevent and control accidental pollution from that installation which are introduced by public authorities in Member countries in conformity with domestic law prior to the occurrence of an accident in order to protect human health or the environment".

Principle 16 of the Rio Declaration in 1992, reaffirmed the PPP and said: "National authorities should endeavor to promote the internalization of environmental costs and the use of economic instruments, taking into account the approach that the polluter should, in principle, bear the cost of pollution, with due regard to the public interest and without distorting international trade and investment."

PPP has been extended in recent years from pollution control at the source towards control of product impacts during their whole life cycle.

The European Commission strengthened the PPP through five important principles :

- the PPP to force those creating pollution to pay the costs of meeting socially acceptable environmental quality standards.
- the prevention or precaution principle, which explicitly recognizes the existence of uncertainty and seeks to avoid irreversible damages via the imposition of a safety margin into policy; it also seeks to prevent waste generation at source as well as retaining some 'end-of-pipe' measures.

- economic efficiency/cost effectiveness principle applying both to the setting of standards & design of the policy instruments for attaining them.
- the subsidiarity principle to assign environmental decision and enforcement to the lowest level of government, capable of handling it without significant residual externalities.
- The legal efficiency principle to preclude the passage of regulations that cannot be realistically enforced.

There are four merits attributed to the PPP by Bugge:

- economically, it promotes efficiency;
- legally, it promotes justice;
- it promotes harmonization of international environmental policies;
- it defines how to allocate costs within a country.

The 'polluter pays' principle is incorporated in the environmental policy of most of the nations. The various policy instruments in use which are based on PPP are:

- Command-and-control approaches when it applies the PPP and imposes sanctions on polluters, requiring them to pay compensation to victims of pollution.
- Market-based instruments such as a pollution tax and tradable pollution permits
- Product labelling

In 2010 India established a "green" court in line with the PPP to make polluters pay for the damages resulting from production, becoming the third country in the world after Australia and New Zealand to set up such a tribunal. India has applied the PPP to give remedial relief to check and control environmental degradation. The Supreme Court applied the Polluter Pays Principle in the *Vellore Citizens Welfare Forum* case and directed polluting tanneries for payment of compensation to the affected persons and also for payment of cost for restoring the damaged ecology.

Justice Kuldip Singh, who delivered the judgment of the Court, observed:

The "Polluter Pays Principle" as interpreted by this Court means that the absolute liability for harm to the environment extends not only to compensate the victims of pollution but also the cost of restoring the environmental degradation. Remediation of the damaged environment is part of the process of "Sustainable Development" and as such the polluter is liable to pay the cost to the individual sufferers as well as the cost of reversing the damaged ecology.

25.2 The Precautionary Principle

The pervasiveness of increasingly unpredictable and uncertain catastrophic risks from human actions on environment and human health such as those posed by Climate change underlined the need for developing a **second** tool to protect the environment: the Precautionary Principle (PP). The Precautionary Principle was introduced by the Rio Declaration on Environment and Development in 1992 in the United Nations Conference on Environment and Development (the "Earth Summit"). The Declaration included Precaution as one of 27 principles to guide environmental and development policies. The term 'precautionary principle' has its origin in the German word *Vorsorgeprinzip*, meaning foresight.

The Precautionary Principle states that whenever there is risk of severe damage to humans and/ or the environment, absence of scientific conclusive proof is not a reason for inaction. It is a 'better-safe – than – sorry' approach, in contrast to the traditional 'wait and watch' approach to environmental protection. It is a logical extension of words of wisdom that guide daily life, such as: "an ounce of prevention is worth a pound of cure" 'prevention is better than cure" look before you leap'; It challenges us to prevent harm before it occurs. When there is uncertainty regarding the impacts of an activity, the precautionary principle advocates action to anticipate and avert environmental harm. According to an UNESCO report (2005) the PP is "is a strategy to cope with scientific uncertainties in the assessment and management of risks. It is about the wisdom of action under uncertainty".

Principle 15 of the Rio Declaration on Environment and Development (or Agenda 21) of 1992, recommended that the precautionary approach shall be widely applied by all countries in accordance with their capabilities. (Box 24.1 in Chapter 24). Principle 15 states:

"In order to protect the environment, the precautionary approach shall be widely applied by States according to their capabilities. Where there are threats of serious or irreversible damage, lack of full scientific certainty shall not be used as a reason for postponing cost-effective measures to prevent environmental degradation".

The crucial terms in this definition that need special explanation are (K S Kavikumar) :

1. **lack of full scientific certainty:** As stated in the definition 'lack of full scientific certainty' may not be cited as reason for inaction but any other development priority such as poverty eradication may get more priority than environmental issues in underdeveloped nations (penguin Vs poverty argument).
2. **cost-effective measure** simply means that the costs of proposed actions must be assessed and compared.
3. **'applied by States according to their capabilities'** means that technological and economic capabilities of the nations must be borne in mind while applying the principle.

The participants of the Wingspread Conference in the United States defined the principle as: "When an activity raises threats of harm to human health or the environment, precautionary measures should be taken even if some cause and effect relationships are not fully established scientifically. The process of applying the precautionary principle must be open, informed and democratic and must include potentially affected parties. It must also involve an examination of the full range of alternatives, including no action. In this context the proponent of an activity, rather than the public, should bear the burden of proof." While the Rio declaration recommended the application of the PP whenever there are of "threats of serious or irreversible damage", the Wingspread Conference definition recommends its applications whenever "activity raises threats of harm to human health or the environment". While the Rio Declaration insists on cost effective regulatory measures, the Wingspread definition does not mention anything about costs.

The Wingspread Conference definition brought together the four elements of precaution:

- prompt action even in the face of scientific uncertainty,
- burden of proof and persuasion on proponents
- transparency
- assessment of alternatives.

The "Late Lessons from Early Warnings" Report (Harremoës et al., 2001) gives examples of cases where a precautionary approach could have saved lives and resources. The case of the asbestos (Box 25.1) clearly shows the relevance of the PP.

Asbestos is the main cause of mesothelioma, a fatal disease with a very long incubation time. Lack of full scientific proof of harm contributed to long delay before action was taken. The early warnings of 1898–1906 were not followed up by any kind of precautionary action to reduce exposure to asbestos. A Dutch study estimated that in 1965 when the mesothelioma hypothesis was plausible but unproven, if a ban had been imposed, it would have saved the country some 34,000 victims and Euro 19 billion in building costs (clean up) and compensation costs. It is estimated that in the European Union (EU) alone, some 250,000 – 400,000 deaths will occur over the next 35 years, as a consequence of exposure to asbestos in the past.

Timeline of Ban on Asbestos

1898 UK Factory Inspector warns of harmful and 'evil' effects of asbestos dust

1906 French factory report of 50 deaths in female asbestos textile workers and recommendation for controls

1911'Reasonable grounds' for suspicion, from experiments on rats, that asbestos dust is harmful

1911 &1917 UK Factory Department finds insufficient evidence to justify further actions

1930 UK Merewether report finds 66% of long-term workers in Rochdale factory with asbestosis

1931 UK Asbestos Regulations specify dust control in manufacturing only and compensation for asbestosis, but this is poorly implemented

1935-49 Lung cancer cases reported in asbestos manufacturing workers 1955 Research by Richard Doll (UK) establishes high lung cancer risk in Rochdale asbestos workers.

1959-64 Mesothelioma cancer identified in workers, neighborhood 'bystanders' and the public in South Africa, the United Kingdom, and the United States, amongst others

1998-99 EU and France ban all forms of asbestos

2000-01 WTO upholds EU/French bans against Canadian appeal

Source: Modified from UNESCO/COMEST 2005 "The Precautionary Principle"

COMEST: World Commission on the Ethics of Scientific Knowledge and Technology

Box 25.1 Need for Precautionary Principle - the case of Asbestos

The European Union Communication defines PP as:

"The precautionary principle applies where scientific evidence is insufficient, inconclusive or uncertain and preliminary scientific evaluation indicates that there are reasonable grounds for concern that the potentially dangerous effects on the environment, human, animal or plant health may be inconsistent with the high level of protection chosen by the EU".

The various definitions agree on certain key elements though the wordings may differ. Some of the common points of the various definitions, listed by UNESCO, (2005) are:

- The PP applies when there exists considerable scientific uncertainties about causality, magnitude, probability, and nature of harm;
- Some form of *scientific analysis* is mandatory; a mere fantasy or crude speculation is not enough to trigger the PP. Grounds for concern that can trigger the PP are limited to those concerns that are plausible or scientifically tenable.
- Application of the PP is limited to those hazards that are *unacceptable*;
- Interventions are required before possible harm occurs, or before certainty about such harm can be achieved, thus doing away with "wait and see" strategy.
- Interventions should be proportional to the chosen level of protection and the magnitude of possible harm.

The UNESCO has given a working definition of the PP which is as follows:

"When human activities may lead to morally unacceptable harm that is scientifically plausible but uncertain, actions shall be taken to avoid or diminish that harm. Morally unacceptable harm refers to harm to humans or the environment that is

- threatening to human life or health, or
- serious and effectively irreversible, or

- inequitable to present or future generations, or
- imposed without adequate consideration of the human rights of those affected".

In this definition 'actions' refer to "interventions that are undertaken before harm occurs that seek to avoid or diminish the harm".

25.2.1 Steps of Precautionary approach

The steps involved in the application of the Precautionary Principle include the following Tickner J et al(1999) :

1. Identification, description and understanding the problem or threat. This involves asking the following questions: How big is the problem? How far could it extend in space and time? What is the potential scale of the threat - Global, regional, national or local? How serious could the effects be? Is the threat reversible?
2. Describing what is known and what is unknown. This necessitates finding answers to questions such as: Are we dealing with something that is unknowable, or about which we are totally ignorant? What would it take to reduce the uncertainties?
3. Identifying alternatives to the activity or product. The problem is to be restated to describe the purpose of the activity. For example it could be the introduction of a pesticide for better pest management. In this case, all the alternate methods of pest management which are safer for environment and to the health of the people must be examined.
4. Course of Action must be determined: which means finding out the level of precaution needed – whether the proposed activity should be stopped (ban the new pesticide) or look for alternatives or ask for modifications to reduce the negative impacts?
5. Monitoring the performance of the proposed activity and those undertaking the activity should bear the cost of monitoring, but it should be conducted by an independent party.

25.2.2 Components of Precautionary Approach

Joel Tickner et al (1999) observe that a precautionary approach to environmental decision making involves many components. Some of these are:

- **Setting Goals:** The precautionary principle encourages planning based on well-defined goals rather than on future scenarios and risk calculations that may be plagued by error and bias.
- **Seeking out and evaluating alternatives**: Rather than asking what level of contamination is safe or economically optimal, the precautionary approach asks how to reduce or eliminate the hazard and considers all possible means of achieving that goal, including forgoing the proposed activity.
- **Shifting burdens of proof**: Proponents of an activity should prove that their activity will not cause undue harm to human health or ecosystems.
- Developing more democratic and thorough decision-making criteria and methods.

25.2.3 Limitations of PP

The following points have been raised as limitations of the PP.

1. First of all there are too may definitions of the principle which differ with reference to evaluation of uncertainty, severity of consequences considered and how the costs and risks of precautionary measures are considered.
2. The principle does not specify how much of precaution is needed in any given situation.

3. It is pointed out that the precaution Principle will hamper development and innovation of technology since the burden of proof is on the product/ service before it comes into market.
4. Some critics of the PP argue that the principle is subjective based on value judgement or and not based on actual facts. This makes it susceptible to abuse by policymakers who will assume power because of ambiguity and subjectivity in the principle.

Inspite of the limitations it cannot be denied that the PP is a marked shift from post damage control (civil liability as a curative tool) to a pre-damage control (anticipatory measures) of risks. The precautionary principle goes beyond regulation "to provide a way of thinking, acting, planning, and making decisions about human activities that pose the threat— however uncertain—of serious, cumulative, or irreversible harm. It not only provides a framework for a more effective regulatory system, it is also a motivating belief and an overarching principle"(Carolyn et al, 2000).

25.2.4 Precautionary Principle in some of the International Treaties

Apart from the 1992 Rio Declaration whichsaid that the precautionary approach shall be widely applied by States according to their capabilities in order to protect the environment (See above) the following are some of the international agreements that incorporate the principle.

The Montreal Protocol on Substances that Deplete the Ozone Layer, 1987, one of the first international environmental agreements to embody the Precautionary Principle provided for precautionary measures to be taken in controlling CFCsto protect the ozone layer.

Framework Convention on Climate Change, 1992, urged signatories to take precautionary measures to anticipate, prevent, or minimize the causes of climate change and mitigate its adverse effects.

Cartagena Protocol on Biosafety – CBD - (2000) focused on the precautionary principle in the negotiation of the CBD on the trade of living genetically modified organisms (LMOs). The Protocol emphasized that the development, handling, transport, use, transfer and release of living modified organisms are based on Precautionary principle, undertaken in a manner that prevents or reduces the risks to biological diversity or human health. The Protocol reaffirmed in several places that lack of scientific certainty shall not prevent States from taking action to avert potential risks.

Convention on International Trade in Endangered Species of Wild Fauna and Flora (CITES, Washington, 1973), incorporated the precautionary principle into criteria governing the listing of species in the CITES Appendices and stated that Species listed in Appendix I may not be commercially traded, and trade in species included in Appendix II is regulated by a permit system. The precautionary principle was to be the basis for decision making with reference to:

- which species should be placed in the Appendices
- transfer of species from Appendix I to Appendix II.

It was specified that in the case of scientific uncertainty, Parties should act "in the best interests of the species".

Conclusion

The Polluter Pays Principle and the Precautionary Principle are incorporated in both national environmental policy and global environmental treaties. While the polluter pays principle is a curative approach to pollution control, the precautionary principle is a preventive approach to pollution control. The two Principles will strengthen the environmental policy and make it more effective and help nations to achieve sustainable development.

Questions

1. Polluter Pays Principle is a curative action while the Precautionary Principleis a prevention principle – Explain through appropriate case studies.
2. "Precautionary Principle would divert the attention of the regulators and the regulated community from known or plausible hazards to speculative and ill-founded ones resulting in dangers to environment hazards" - Do you agree? Justify your stand.

Exercise

1. Take the case of the tanneries in Tamilnadu, India and comment on the effectiveness of the application of Polluter Pays Principle and Precautionary Principle.
2. In the case of a development project such as building a dam or a nuclear power plant how will justify them in the light of the Precautionary Principle.

26

ENVIRONMENTAL POLICY TOOLS – COMMAND AND CONTROL

It is simply economically impossible to require controls that even approach zero emissions.

—*Barry Commoner*

Environmental protection has emerged as a major issue on the nation's policy agenda, thanks to the Stockholm Convention and the Rio Summit, resulting in significant increases in the scope and number of environmental regulations which have undoubtedly yielded huge benefits to the society. In Chapter 24 we saw that environmental problems are essentially instances of market failure and government failure. Economists suggest market based instruments such as tax on pollution for'internalising the externality'. Further the public good characteristics possessed by environmental quality require authoritative intervention by the government. Thus the two prominent and popular policy tools available to control pollution are: Direct Regulation and Market Based Instruments. More than these it is important to involve people to participate in promoting improvement in environmental quality.

26.1 Environmental Policy Instruments

To control pollution effectively and efficiently, the government can use some or all of the following steps:

1. specify the amount of pollution that each source is allowed to discharge;
2. specify the action to be adopted by the source of pollution to control pollution , such as specifying the pollution control technology to be adopted;
3. liability rules, a mechanism for compensating victims of pollution that causes harm to human health and the environment.
4. impose a tax on emissions / effluent to discourage releases to the environment;
5. introduce a subsidy for treating and reducing the pollution it creates;
6. create market for the externality through marketable pollution permits;
7. public reporting of emissions or risks to human health and the environment by the polluter;
8. encourage action from individuals to be friendly with environment.

The various measures mentioned above are "policy instruments". The first three measures listed above come under the category Direct Regulation; the measures 4 – 6 are called by economist as market based instrument; seventh and eighth encourage public involvement.

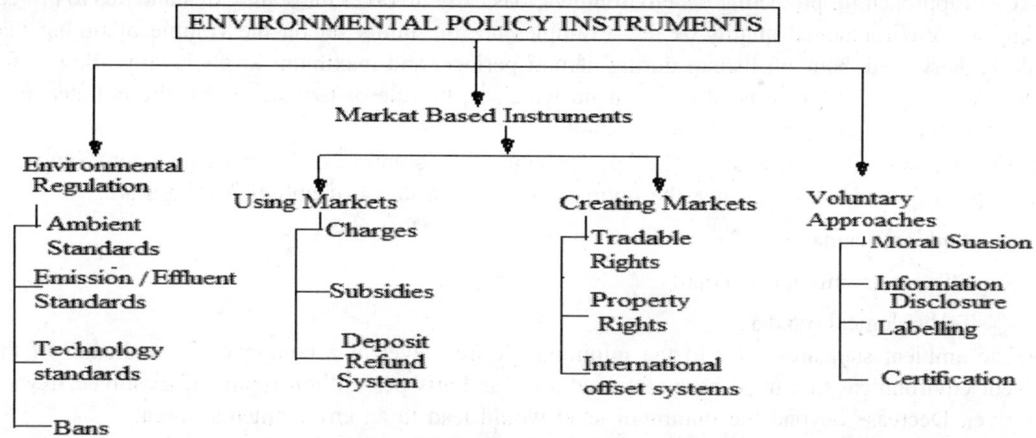

Figure 26.1 Classification of Environmental Policy Instrument

Source: Environment Policy Division, SIDA 2003, Instruments of Environmental Policy (modified)based on World Bank (1997)

World Bank has classified environmental policy instruments under four categories, namely: (a) Using markets (b) Creating markets (c) Environmental regulations (d) Engaging the public

No nation can dependent on any single policy measure but a combination of the various measures is needed for efficient and effective control of pollution. This chapter discusses the role of Direct Control as a pollution control policy instrument and examines the advantages and limitations of using the tool.

The Environmental policy Committee of OECD recommended that the choice of environmental policy instruments can be made against five sets of criteria:

i) Environmental effectiveness: This refers to permanent incentive to pollution abatement, technical innovation, and product substitution.

ii) Economic efficiency: This requires that the cost of complying with the environmental requirements is minimised.

iii) Equity or distributive consequences of the policy tool, referring to the distribution of burden of costs among firms and the tax burden on consumers of the product.

iv) Administrative feasibility and cost: This relates in particular to the ease and cost of monitoring discharges and the number of target groups involved and also upon the nature of existing legal and institutional settings.

v) Acceptability: The regulatory measure and economic instruments imposed must be acceptable to the target group.

26.2. Direct Regulation or Command and Control

In general Command and Control refers to specific guidelines or regulations prescribed by a government or its agency to the affected party on how to comply with its mandatory requirement. Individuals responsible for the environmental harm do not voluntarily come forward to clean the mess they create. This gave rise to interference by the government directly by using its coercive power to regulate pollution creating activities or indirectly through policy measures that would alter the behaviour of individuals and internalize the external costs imposed on the society. In most countries direct regulation is the first step towards control of pollution. Direct Regulation is also known as Command and Control, (CAC).

CAC approach for protecting the environment, basically involves the setting of standards to protect or improve environmental quality. A few examples are the limits set on the volume of timber that could be harvested, bans on fishing during certain periods, and maximum levels legally allowed for pollution emissions. It consists of a command which is the rule or regulation that the polluter must adhere to and a control enforcing the standard.

The standard is a mandated level of performance that is enforced through legislation. There are three types of standards to achieve the optimum or efficient level of pollution. These are:

- Ambient standard
- Effluent or emission standard
- Technological standard

The ambient standards refer to the minimum desired level of a component or indicator of the ambient environment that must be maintained such as Parts per million (ppm) of dissolved oxygen in a river. Decrease beyond the minimum level would lead to an environmental threat.

Emission / Effluent standard refers to the maximum permissible level of the pollutant such as permissible level of SO_2 or NO_x that can be emitted in the atmosphere or BOD level in water. It is a never exceed limit for any pollutant. The ambient standards and the emission standards are performance related. They are in essence imposition of legal ceilings on the amount any polluter is permitted to emit/discharge. For example, in India, Minimum National Standards (MINAS) for waste water discharges and emission standards for several industries have been fixed by the Central Board for Prevention and Control of Water Pollution and Air Pollution.

Technological standards specify how a particular activity must be carried on—for example, direct control may require industries to install an electrostatic precipitator (ESP) or scrubbers to capture some of the emissions of the polluting firm or installation of an effluent treatment plant. In some of the western countries, direct regulations prohibit backyard incinerators or the use of high sulphur coal. Direct control may also specify the stack height of the polluting firm. Standards could also be product standards or input standards specifying the characteristics for the pollution creating product and input.

The first two types of direct control, prescribing a standard for the environmental media or fixing a ceiling on the quantity of effluents/ emissions requires that it should be possible to measure the volume of emissions discharged by the polluter. Such metering of emissions is complex and error prone. It is difficult to get accurate values of wastes discharged. Under such circumstances the second method of direct control that instructs the firms to use a particular pollution control device is more useful.

26.2.1 Setting the Standard

Setting the standard – ambient standard or emission standard poses the question of the level at which the standard should be prescribed. Economic theory holds that the standard is set to achieve efficient level of pollution which is given by the equality of marginal pollution damage cost with marginal pollution abatement cost curve. Figure 26.2 defines efficient level of pollution as P* given by the point e* at which MPDC = MPAC. In the figure MPDC is positive only from e' level of pollution implying that up to e' level, pollution is within the assimilative capacity of the environment and hence does not impose a cost on the society or does not become an externality. Pollution becomes an externality only when it is a cost on the society, which is when it exceeds the absorptive capacity of the environment.

Therefore it is suggested that the standard may be set on the basis of a threshold level which is based on zero level of risk from pollution - at e' in figure 26.2. But defining such a threshold level is difficult. For many pollutants there may not be any threshold level, i.e., the marginal damage function is positive from the first unit of pollutant. In such cases the standard which equates both damage cost and abatement cost yields an efficient emission level. In the case of highly toxic pollutants a total ban is the only appropriate measure.

The next issue in setting the standard is whether standards should be uniform or vary across firms. MPAC varies among firms. There are firms which can control pollution at lower costs than other firms in the industry. When there are such differences in the pollution abatement costs, uniform standards will violate the conditions of both equity and efficiency.

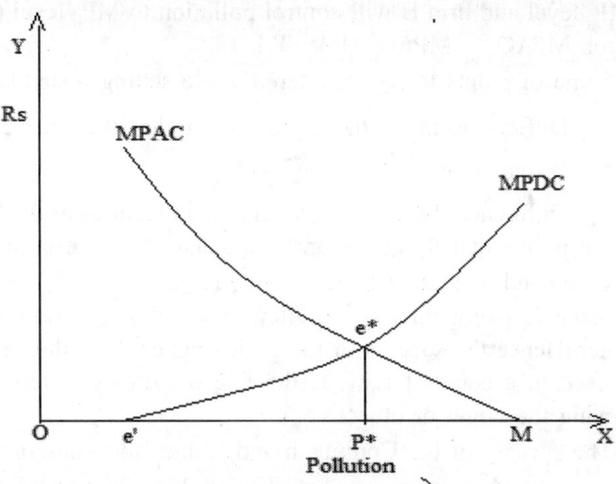

Figure 26.2 Emission Standards

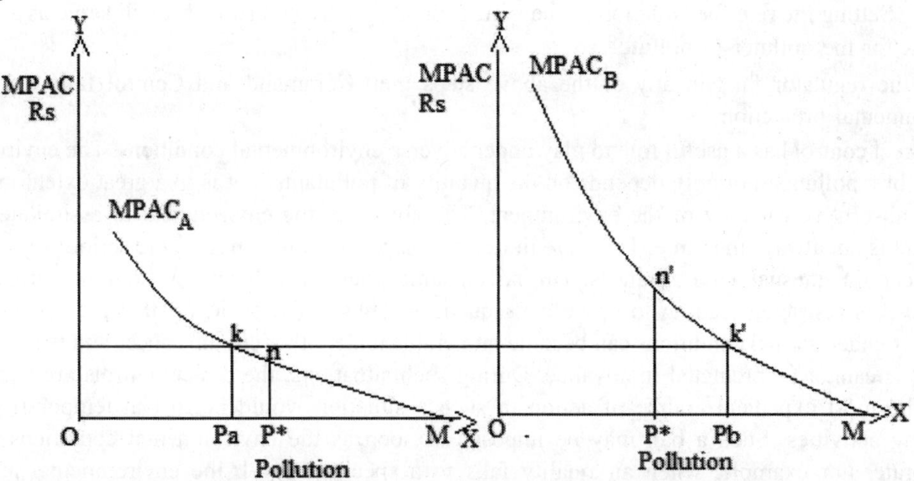

Figure 26.3 Standards when MPAC differs among firms

Equity requires that the financial burden of controlling pollution is distributed among firms in accordance with their pollution abatement cost. That is, those firms with a lower MPAC should control more pollution than firms with higher MPAC. For example there are two firms A and B and both A and B are required to reduce pollution by MP*. If $MPAC_A < MPAC_B$, then firm A will be able to control pollution without strain but firm B will find it difficult. In such a situation, setting the standard at the level of pollution at which $MPAC_A = MPAC_B$ will give an equitable solution than setting a uniform standard in accordance with the MPAC = MPDC rule. When cost of controlling pollution differs among firms, setting the standard in accordance with the MPAC of all firms will not only yield an equitable pollution control, but also result in an efficient pollution control. This is illustrated in figure 26.3.

In figure 26.3 the MPAC of the two firms are $MPAC_A$ and $MPAC_B$. It can be seen that $MPAC_A$ is flatter than $MPAC_B$. If both the firms are required to control pollution by MP* (uniform reduction) the firm A's MPAC is P*n and firm B's MPAC is P*n' and clearly P*n' is greater than P*n. Instead if differences in cost are taken into consideration, then firm A with lower cost will control pollution to MP_a level and firm B will control pollution to MP_b level ($MP_a > MP_b$) and at this level of pollution control, $MPAC_A = MPAC_B$ ($P_a k = P_b k'$).

Some of points to be considered while setting a standard are:

- Differences in weather conditions in the different locations.
- Differences in population levels
- Differences based on rural and urban features of the location.

Yet policy makers prefer uniform standards since implementing it will be easier.

Command and control regulations, requires that if polluters deviate from the specified standard, they have to pay a fine. This policy tool views pollution as an illegal act and hence penalizes the polluter. Hence the success of the policy depends on the penalty imposed on the polluter if his guilt is proved in a court of Law. If the fine or penalty is too low, then the policy will not succeed in achieving the target or objective.

The success of the Command and Control depends on:

a. Monitoring the firms for any possible violation of the pollution laws so that the polluter can be identified.
b. Proving and establishing the guilt of the polluter in the Court of Law.
c. Setting the fine for violation of the regulation at a high level so that it will serve as a deterrent for the polluter to pollute.

If the regulator fails in any of the above steps then Command and Control fails as a tool of environmental protection.

Direct control has a useful role to play under adverse environmental conditions. The environmental impact of a pollutant not only depends on the quantity of pollutants, but is to a great extent influenced by the absorptive capacity of the environment. The ability of the environment to assimilate a given pollutant is not always the same. There are times when a pollutant may have more serious repercussions under certain unusual circumstances. During an atmospheric inversion for example, dispersion of pollutants is restricted leading to grave consequences. Thus emission levels that are acceptable and harmless under normal conditions can become intolerable under other circumstances and these abnormal situations cannot be predicted in advance. During such situations, the direct controls are very useful, since the most expedient course of action in such a situation would be to ban temporarily certain polluting activities. Such a ban may be imposed as soon as the environmental conditions begin to deteriorate. For example, when air quality falls to a specified level, the environmental authorities may invoke temporary bans on burning trash.

Direct Control is particularly significant in cases of pollution involving highly hazardous pollutants. In the case of pollutants like cyanide, even a small quantity of which has adverse impacts on the health of human beings and animals and other living organisms , direct control should be used to totally prohibit the discharge altogether. In such cases where the pollutant is so highly toxic that concern over their impact outweighs any economic consideration, a total ban is the solution.

Command and Control is preferred when the MPAC is uniform across firms in the polluting industry and when information on MPAC of all firms is available to the regulator.

However exclusive reliance on direct control has not been reliable and successful in practice. It has been criticised on grounds that it does not provoke and promote incentive to innovate equipments that will control pollution more efficiently. Further, direct controls can be effective only when the fine it imposes on the polluter, for non-compliance with the regulation, is sufficiently high. Due to higher cost of compliance and high information requirement command and control is unpopular.

Industries oppose C&C on two grounds:

1. Interference from government that specifies the technology of pollution control
2. High cost of meeting the standard.

Regulators complain that they have to constantly learn about technological developments in the various industries.

Inspite of the various limitations observed by the polluting firm, administrators and environmentalists, C & C is still an important part of the environmental policy in almost all the countries. Countries which have included market based instruments like a tax or pollution permits or any other policy tool, have command and control as an integral part of their environmental policy mix.

26.3 Liability Rules are based on the faith that if polluters are made liable for the damages they cause, they will have an incentive to limit pollution. Liability mechanisms are a part of both civil and common-law systems. The liability rules provide incentive for socially responsible behavior by polluters through **legal liability** for environmental damages or the consequences arising from any environmental damage. Liability rules include payments made under civil laws as compensation for the damages resulting from pollution activity. If the polluter knows that he is liable to pay compensation for the damage arising out of his action, he will minimize risks. Liability rules assess and recover damages **ex post** which makes it different from other instruments. As long as the compensation to be paid by the polluting firm is higher than the benefits from non-compliance, liability rules will be effective. The legal system of the country should be well developed for liability rules to operate. Liability rules has been imposed for damage to coral reefs and compensation paid for restoration and clean-up and for loss in tourism revenues work effectively.

Example of liability rule (USEPA, 2005)

On June 2, 2000 a truck traveling from the Yanacocha gold mine in the Peruvian Andes spilled 151 kg of mercury between the villages of Choropampa and Magdalena. The residents of the villages who were not informed about the hazards of mercury collected mercury believing it to be valuable. Soon many were affected and hospitalized. Newmont, one of the major partners of the mine with 51% share, paid a fine of 1.74 million soles (approximately $500,000) to the Peruvian government and agreed for the following:

- to provide health insurance for five years for individuals with symptoms of mercury poisoning;
- to construct a number of public works projects in the affected area;
- to respond to the recommendations of the Compliance Advisor Ombudsman (CAO).

The total cost to the firm for these was stated as nearly $10 million in the company's financial statements for 2000 (USEPA, 2005).

Conclusion

Command and Control and liability rules rely on the existence of a well framed legal system and an established judiciary. Lack of adequate evidence and loop holes in laws will make both ineffective. Hence exclusive reliance on these is not sufficient to protect the environment. Direct Regulation must be complemented with economic instruments which are discussed in chapters 27 and 28.

Questions

1. Which of the following is desirable?
   (a) High standards and weak enforcement
   (b) relatively lower standards and strict enforcement
2. Justify the case of varying standards for pollutants.
3. Examine the salient features of C& C in India for either air pollution or water pollution.

Exercise

Prepare a case study on liability rules.

27

POLLUTION CONTROL: MARKET USING INSTRUMENTS

If anyone intentionally spoils the water of another ... let him not only pay damages, but purify the stream or cistern which contains the water..."

—*Plato*

The general objective of an environmental policy is to achieve sustainable development. More specifically the objectives include conservation of resources and minimizing the wastes generated in production and consumption activities well within assimilative capacity of the environment. The failure of the regulatory approach to achieve the goals set for environmental protection has compelled the governments to look for alternative policy tools which are more effective and cheaper. Supporting Economic instruments, Agenda 21 states that environmental regulation cannot alone deal with the problems of environment. Prices, markets and governmental fiscal and economic policies play a complementary role in shaping attitudes and behaviour towards the environment. (UNCED: Agenda 21, Chapter 8).

27.1 Meaning and significance of Market Based Instruments (MBIs)

Economists advocate a set of market based instruments to internalize the external costs. Market Based Instruments are defined as policy tools 'that encourage behaviour through market signals rather than through explicit directives'. UNEP (2009) states that if a tool affects the cost or price in the market, then it is a market-based economic instrument. MBIs are also referred to as "price incentives" or "economic instruments" (EIs) since they provide incentives to firms and consumers to include environmental concerns in their decision making. The UNEP mentions three important principles that support MBIs:

Polluter Pays Principle according to which the polluter should pay for the damages to the environment arising from his production/ consumption activities (see Chapter 25). It requires that the external costs generated by pollution are internalized and reflected in the market price and output of the goods and services.

The User or Beneficiary Principle is an extension of the PPP which says that if an action provides a benefit, those who receive the benefit should pay for the cost of providing that benefit. For example those who benefit from the aesthetics of a recreation park must pay for the maintenance of the aesthetics of the park.

The "full-cost recovery principle": According to this principle the costs of environmental services should be fully recovered from the entity benefiting from the service. This principle implies that consumers should pay the full cost of electricity, water supply, wastewater treatment and waste services.

27.2 Evolution and Components of MBIs

The concept of using taxation to correct negative externalities, such as pollution, is generally credited to A C Pigou (1920). Hence pollution taxes are sometimes referred to as Pigouvian taxes. A Pigouvian tax intends to correct inefficient market outcomes caused by externalities. Pigou suggested a per-unit tax on goods generating negative externalities such as pollution and said that it should be equal to the marginal externality at the socially efficient quantity. Such a tax will internalize the externality. Pigou suggested further that the revenue from such a tax maybe utilized for creating positive externalities, such as installing a common effluent treatment plant or any environment clean up programme.

Ronald Coase (1960) ruled out the need for government intervention in the form of regulation or taxes. Coase felt that environmental externalities are not the consequence of market failures but rather of a failure of regulation. Arguing that environmental degradation is the result of absence of well- defined property rights, he suggested that markets can potentially solve externalities if property rights are clearly defined and negotiations between parties concerned is feasible.

Dales (1968) endorsed Coasean view when he suggested that an actual market in property rights is the solution to pollution problems. He dismissed Pigouvian tax on grounds of information required to set an optimal tax. The concept of transferable property rights evolved from the writings of Coase and Dales.

Baumol (1972) argued that Pigovian taxes are most effective but felt that implementation of such a tax would be difficult. Instead he suggested an environmental charges-standards approach.

The Polluter Pays Principle formulated by the OECD Secretariat in 1972 laid the foundations for the use of market based instruments, particularly, the use of pollution tax and charges. The PPP stated that the price of goods and service should fully reflect the total cost where the total cost includes the costs arising due to pollution apart from production costs.

In 1992, the use of economic instruments to control pollution was strongly recommended by the United Nations Conference on Environment and Development (UNCED) held at Rio de Janerio, which identified "making effective use of economic instruments and market and other incentives" as one of the programmes. The objectives of this programme as given in Agenda 21 are:

1. To incorporate environmental costs in the decisions of producers and consumers, to reverse the tendency to treat environment as a "free good" and to pass these costs on to other parts of society, other countries or to future generations.
2. To move more fully towards the integration of social and environmental costs into economic activities, so that prices will appropriately reflect the relative scarcity and total value of resources and contribute towards the prevention of environment degradation.
3. To include, wherever appropriate, the use of market principles in the framing of economic instruments and policies to pursue sustainable development. (UNCED: Agenda 21, Chapter 8)

Market based instruments include a number of options such as:

- pricing mechanisms consisting of fees, charges and taxes.
- subsidy systems, including grants, low-interest loans, favorable tax treatment etc.
- deposit-refund systems to encourage recycling or the proper disposal of the product
- Pollution permits
- performance bonds

The Market based instruments give the polluter an incentive to reduce pollution to the permissible level in a cost efficient way. World Bank classifies MBIs as Market Using MBIs and Market Creating MBIs. While charges, subsidies and refundable deposits are components of market using MBIs, tradable permits and international offset systems are market creating MBIs. In this chapter we will see features and examples of Market using instruments.

27.3. Market Using Instruments: Charges

A charge is a price paid for the use of the environment in general. Charges control pollution by imposing a fee on the polluters. There are various types of charges - such as effluent or emission charge, user charge, product charge and administration charge.

A user charge is a fee paid for the use of natural resources or for the disposal of pollutants; In general it is a charge paid for a specific environmental service provided to the charge payer. Example: treating waste water or disposing of wastes. Water use fee is an example of a user charge for the use of the natural resource – water.

A **product charge** is a fee imposed on products that have environmentally harmful effects, during manufacturing, consumption or disposal, on the environment. Tax on leaded petrol, pesticides and batteries are examples. Some countries have tax on sulphur content of products and CFC tax.

An Effluent/ Emission Charge is imposed by the government on the effluents /emissions released into the environment and are based on the quality and quantity of the effluent/emission discharge.

Administrative charges are "fees that should be paid to cover the expenses made by the controlling authorities for control, authorization and related administration" (Grossman,1999).

27.3.1 Pollution Tax / Charge

A pollution tax is used to correct the misallocation of resources when social costs are different from private costs and are generally based on the estimated damage. It is also known as an externality tax. An example is a tax on sulphur di oxide emissions. The higher the level of wastes discharged by a firm, the higher will be the tax bill for the firm and a firm can reduce its tax bill by treating its wastes and thus reducing its pollution load. The residual charge or waste disposal tax are forms of pollution tax.

Effluent or Residual Charges of a fixed amount per unit of waste, is imposed on all sources of a given kind of waste. An effluent charge is the price that the polluters have to pay for the opportunity to discharge wastes into environment.

If the polluters are not subject to any effluent charge, i.e., if they do not have to pay at all for the discharge of the firm's wastes, then it means that the price for the opportunity of polluting is zero. Hence the supply curve for pollution opportunities will coincide with X axis when there is no effluent charge. On the other hand if the firm is subject to an effluent charge of say Rupees ten per unit of waste it discharges, then the supply curve will move upwards to the position shown in figure 27.1

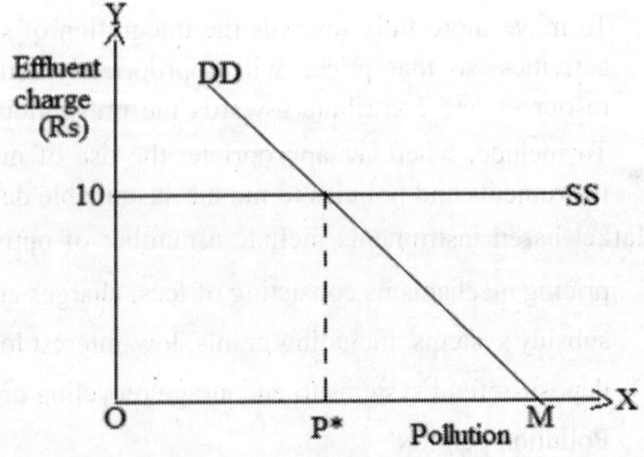

Figure 27.1 Effluent Charge and Level of Pollution

In figure 27.1, on X axis is measured levels of pollution. Left to right is prevailing pollution level and right to left is pollution controlled. DD is the demand curve for pollution opportunities. It can also be seen as marginal pollution abatement cost curve. It slopes downwards from left to right, showing that if price for pollution removal (effluent charge) is set at a sufficiently high level, polluters will be careful about the amount of pollution they cause. When the price for pollution opportunity is zero, the level of pollution is OM. When an effluent charge of Rupees ten is imposed, the equilibrium quantity of pollution, given by the intersection of the demand curve and supply curve for pollution opportunities reduce from OM to OP*. Thus it can be seen that a pollution tax reduces the level of pollution.

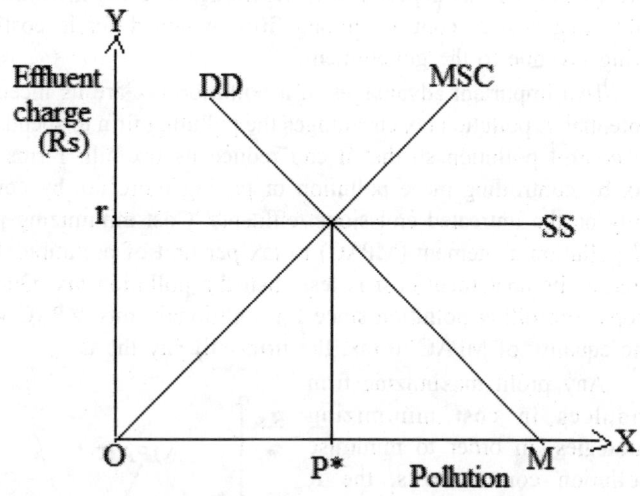

Figure 27.2 Optimal Effluent Charge

However, optimal reduction of pollution will require a residual charge given by the intersection of the demand curve for pollution opportunities and the supply curve for pollution opportunities and the marginal social cost curve should pass through the point of intersection as shown in figure 27.2. In the figure the optimal effluent charge is 'r' at which OP* units of wastes (pollutant) are discharged by the polluter.

Arguments in favour of pollution tax: Pollution charges are considered to be more effective and more reliable than direct controls. They are automatic, certain and promote incentives to innovate cheaper costs of pollution control (because it will reduce pollution control cost for the firm). Besides a pollution tax is hailed by economists as the least cost method for achieving pollution control. A pollution charge gives incentives to firms to reduce pollution.

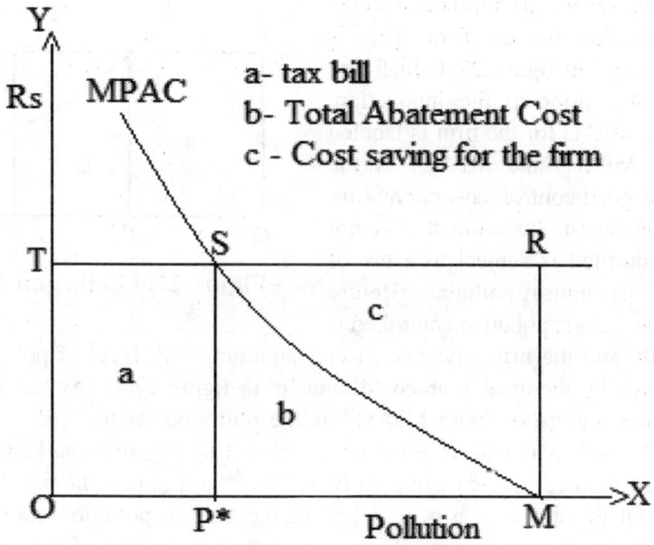

Figure 27.3 Cost Saving Feature of a Pollution Tax

Figure 27.3 explains that the pollution tax is cost saving for the firm. In the absence of any tax or an emission charge, the total emission of the firm is OM. If an emission charge of OT is levied, then the firm will emit only OP* and reduce emissions by MP*. For this the firm incurs abatement cost and the total abatement cost to the firms is the area marked 'b' in figure 27.3. The firm has to pay the charge on OP* of emissions which is shown by the area 'a' in the figure. Total cost to the firm is given by the sum of abatement cost and tax bill. This is the area 'a' + 'b' in the figure. If the firm does not take any effort to control pollution, it will have to pay on the total pollution OM. This corresponds to the area OTRM in figure 27.3 which is a +b +c. The burden to the firm is higher by the area 'c'; in other words, by controlling pollution to OP* level the firm saves and the savings to the firm is given by the area 'c'. Pollution charges possess many advantages such as dependability, flexibility to firms in controlling pollution, economy, and equity in allocating cost of controls among firms which differ in costs of controlling pollution. Besides they bring revenue to the government.

Two important advantages of a pollution tax are its incentive to innovate and its revenue raising potential. A pollution tax encourages the polluting firm to spend on cost minimizing improved technology to control pollution so that it can reduce its tax bill. Firms always have the option of paying less tax by controlling more pollution or paying more tax by controlling less pollution, since the tax is only on the untreated emissions /effluents. Cost minimizing firms always compare the marginal cost of pollution abatement (MPAC) to tax per unit of pollution. The firm chooses to control pollution as long as its abatement cost is less than the pollution tax. Once the MPAC is equal to the tax rate it stops controlling pollution since for additional units MPAC will be greater than tax rate. So beyond the equality of MPAC to tax, the firm will pay the tax.

Any profit maximizing firm indulges in cost minimizing strategies. In order to minimise pollution control costs, the R and D department of the firm constantly works on innovation of newer technologies that can reduce pollution control cost. This results in substantial cost reduction for the firm. This is shown in figure 27.4. In figure 27.4 , prior to the innovation, the MPAC for the firm is labeled as MPAC' and MPAC'' is the marginal control cost curve after innovation. Pollution that is not controlled is subject to a tax of 'T' per unit of pollution. Before innovation , pollution controlled is MP' and the firm pays tax on the remaining OP' level of pollution. Total control cost to the firm is given by the areas marked 'd' and 'e' in figure 27.4. Tax bill is equal to the area marked a + b+ c. After innovation, with MPAC'' as the pollution control cost curve, pollution controlled increases to MP'' and total cost of pollution controlled is the areas marked b + d. Tax bill post innovation is the area marked 'a'. We can clearly see that there is a reduction in tax bill by the areas marked b and c. Of this the area b is absorbed as increase in pollution control cost for controlling the additional P'P'' level of pollution. There is a reduction in cost of controlling MP' level of pollution which is depicted by the area 'e' in figure 27.4. Therefore total cost saving to the firm is areas marked c and e. Hence a pollution tax encourages firms to innovate new pollution control techniques which yields substantial reduction in both tax bill and control cost for the firm.

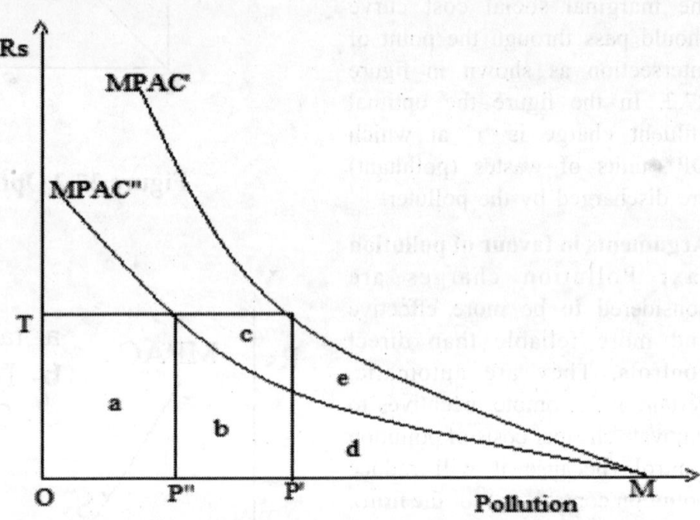

Figure 27.4 Pollution Tax and Incentive to Innovate

A pollution tax brings revenue to the treasury. Environmental taxes not only correct the distortion caused by pollution but also raise revenue which is a major advantage over other instruments. The revenue from environmental taxes can be used to reduce other taxes, to reduce the budget deficit, to pay for public goods or to address distributional goals. This is referred to as the Double Dividend Effect. The first dividend is the removal of distortion caused by the externality pollution. The second dividend is the efficiency gain resulting from a cut in the tax rate of a pre-existing distortionary tax such as the income tax. The second dividend is also known as the "revenue recycling effect" because the revenue raised from environmental taxes can be put a variety of uses as mentioned already.

Arguments against a pollution tax:

In spite of the merits claimed in favour of an effluent tax, there are three objections to a pollution tax. The first of these comes from the industrialists who sometimes say that a residual charge would impose an 'unfair double burden' on the industry. The industrialists argue that they will have to pay the tax and at the same time incur expenditure on installing pollution abatement equipment. But in reality this is not so. The firms install pollution control equipment only if it is cheaper than paying pollution tax. The firms always have the option of paying the tax or reducing pollution by installing the equipment to control pollution. This is explained using figure 27.3.Once a charge is imposed on effluents or emissions discharged by firms, the firms will start controlling pollution to reduce its tax bill. Being a cost minimizer, the firm constantly compares cost of pollution abatement to the tax bill and controls pollution as long as it is cheaper than paying tax. In figure 27.3, the firm treats pollution by MP* level since for treating pollution to MP*, abatement cost is lower than tax. Beyond P* level of pollution, abatement cost is higher than tax. The firms obviously choose the less costlier of the two. Hence those who support pollution tax, say that a tax is far from being a double burden.

Secondly, consumers object to a pollution tax on grounds that the industry would pass on atleast a portion of the burden of charge on them in the form of higher product prices. This aspect is illustrated in figure 27.5.

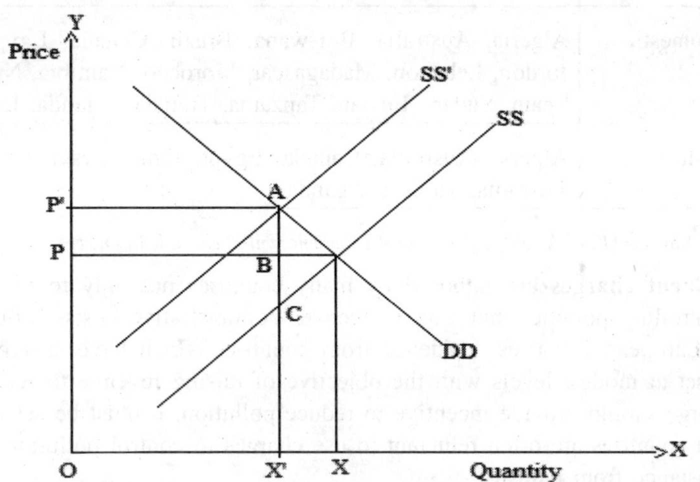

Figure 27.5 Effect of a Pollution Tax on Firm's Price and Output

A pollution tax results in the upward shift of the supply curve which, intersecting with the demand curve DD, results in price OP'. The vertical distance between the two supply curves—the original pre-tax supply curve SS and the supply SS' curve after the imposition of the tax, is the burden of the tax per unit of output. At X' level of output, 'AC' is the tax. However at the new higher price level OP', the producer will pass on at least a part of this burden to the consumers. Price difference is equal to PP', which is equal to AB; the burden on consumers is BA and the burden on producer is the remaining portion of the tax which is BC. When the tax burden is AC, the firm bears only BC and remaining BA is borne by consumers of the final product. The extent of tax burden passed on to the consumers depends on the elasticity of demand and supply curves.

A third objection to a pollution tax is from environmentalists, who consider it as a license to pollute. The environmentalists claim that the polluters should pay compensation to the victims and not taxes to the Government.

27.3.2 Experience with Pollution Taxes/ Charges

Fees, charges and taxes are the most commonly used economic instrument to control pollution and protect the environment. In many countries the revenue raised from such a charge is used for administering the implementation of the charge and some countries also use the funds for pollution control investment by the government. Evidence available on the use of economic instruments also show that user charge such as water use charge is imposed in most of the countries for the cost of treating and delivering water to atleast one of the three sectors: agricultural, industrial and households. Most countries do not impose user charge on water used in agriculture. Empirical evidence shows that in general industry pays the highest fees, followed by households, and agricultural users typically pay the lowest rates. Table 27.1 gives details on the application of user charges.

Table 27.1 Incremental Water Use Charges in Select Countries

Sector	Select Countries which have imposed water user charge
Agriculture	Algeria, Australia, Brazil, Canada, France, Israel, Namibia, Portugal, Spain, Tunisia, United States.
Domestic	Algeria, Australia, Botswana, Brazil, Canada, Egypt, France, India, Israel, Italy, Jordon, Lebanon, Madagascar, Morocco, Namibia, New Zealand, Pakistan, Portugal, Spain, Sudan, Taiwan, Tanzania, Tunisia, Uganda, United States, United Kingdom.
Industry	Algeria, Australia, Canada, Egypt, India, Israel, Pakistan, Portugal, Spain, Sudan, Tanzania, Tunisia, Uganda.

Source: *US EPA, 2004 International Experience with Economic Incentives for Protecting the Environment (modified)*

Effluent charges are imposed by many countries not only to provide incentives to polluters for controlling pollution but also to recover administrative costs. Effluent charges are more common in European countries. Evidence from countries which have an effluent charge shows that the fee is set at modest levels with the objective of raising revenue to recover administrative costs. If the charge should provide incentive to reduce pollution, it must be set at high rates. It is also observed that countries are often reluctant to use charges to control pollution for political reasons and due to resistance from industries.

Water Pollution Charge in the European Union

Effluent charges on direct discharges of effluents exist in seven Member States of the European Union - Belgium, Denmark, France, Germany, the Netherlands, Spain, and the United Kingdom. Many other States are preparing to introduce a charge. Denmark, Germany and Spain collect charges only for direct discharges into surface waters. Direct discharges include discharges from agriculture, industries, sewage treatment plants, landfills domestic sewage from treatment facilities and rain water discharge. Belgium, the Netherlands, and France apply the same economic instrument in charging for direct discharges and indirect discharges.

In **the Netherlands (the Dutch)** wastewater charges have been levied since 1971. For discharge into state waters, effluent charge is imposed and collected by the Water Management Authority, Central

Government, referred to as '*Rijkswaterstaat'*, whereas for discharges into the non-state surface waters and sewerage systems, the regional Water Boards impose and collect the charges. Effluent charges are imposed on both direct and indirect discharges. Pollution load is expressed in pollution units (p.u.). The parameters considered for calculating the charge are COD, Nitrogen, phosphorous, heavy metals, sulphate and chloride. For the large polluters the charge is directly linked to the quantity of pollutants they discharge. It is not so for small polluters and households.

Charges are calculated by multiplying the pollution load expressed in pollution units (p.u.) by the unit tariff . There is a flat rate for discharges in to state waters. In 2000, for discharges in to state waters the rate was about € 32/p.u. For discharges into regional waters, the rates differ between water boards and are higher than for state waters, which was around € 39.03 in 1999. (Hansen Wenke et al 2001)

The maximum assessment for households is 3 p.u. for discharges into state waters, which can be reduced to 1p.u. for one-person households on request. Small business units, producing less than 5 p.u, are also charged for 3 p.u. which may reduced to 1 p.u. for businesses discharging 1 p.u. or less (Henk Warmer & Ronald van Dokkum, 2002).

The pollution level decreased substantially after the imposition of the charges. The success of the charge in Netherlands is mainly due to the high level of the charge and transparency of the charge program. The Dutch charges are reported to be eight times those of France and 16 times those of Germany in per capita terms. Panayotou (1994) hails the Dutch system as "the most relevant, not only because it has been very effective and administratively inexpensive but because it takes monitoring and enforcement difficulties into account, differentiating between large, medium, and small firms and households".

Columbia's Discharge Fee system for water effluents is a model of a well-functioning, economic-incentive pollution control program in a developing country. Many of Colombia's most important water bodies are severely polluted by both the domestic sector and industries, the former contributing to a greater share of water pollution in Columbia. Industrial pollution is totally uncontrolled. Lack of access to sewer system, lack of sewage treatment plants and sparingly or non-operated waste water treatment plants by the municipalities are responsible for the high organic pollution load (less than 1% of municipal waste water was treated) in the water bodies of the country. Very few industries treated their effluents. Major polluters are manufacturers of beverages and alcohol, industrial chemicals, and paper products. (Blackman Allen, 2007).

In Columbia regional environmental regulatory authorities are responsible for pollution control in the country. The jurisdiction of the regional authorities is determined solely by the ecological considerations. The command-and-control water pollution control policies designed by the environment ministries and enforced by the regional boards required dischargers to obtain permits to meet effluent standards. Weak and poor monitoring and poor enforcement of command and control by the regional authorities, due to corruption and lack of infrastructure required for monitoring compliance resulted in violation of environmental standards. As a result, most of Colombia's rivers such as the Bogotá, Cali, Cauca, and Medellín, were severely polluted.

Colombia's environmental Legislation was reformed in 1993 to provide for the introduction of a national discharge fee to be imposed on polluters. In just three years after implementing the pollution charges, industrial wastes in 12 of the largest urban centers reduced by 15% to 20% and agricultural wastes in key banana and coffee-producing areas reduced by 25%.The new incentive based discharge fee gave polluters flexibility in meeting water pollution standards. Polluters had to pay for the right to pollute but had the freedom to choose their method of pollution control in a cost minimizing way. The pollution discharge fee was imposed on municipal authorities too which made them set up water treatment plants to treat the organic wastes.

The waste water discharge fee's success is also attributed to the "the incentives it created for regulatory authorities to improve permitting, monitoring, and enforcement". The Colombian pollution fee has emerged as a model for developing-world communities where pollution is threatening the health of the people in a critical way. Thomas Black-Arbeláez, a Colombian-American economist (backed by his experience with American pollution control policies) and the architect of the discharge fee programme observes: "We've found that market-based instruments like this can really work in reducing water contamination. They force people to be more innovative and they produce a more efficient allocation of resources." In the opinion of David Wheeler of the World Bank "the Colombian experiment is without question the most promising we've seen in the developing world".

China's Pollution Levy: In 1982, the Chinese environmental policy included a pollution levy and stated that "in cases where the discharge of pollutants exceed the limits set by the state, a compensation fee shall be charged according to the quantities and concentration of the pollutants released". While levy rate and structure was designed by the Central government, the local Environmental Bureaus were responsible for the collection of the levy. Pollution levy covered air emissions, effluents, solid waste, noise and radioactive substances. Until 1993 the levy applied only to the portion of discharges that exceeded the standards set by the regulator. From 1993 this changed to include all discharges for water and from 1998 for SO_2. The levy was very low in magnitude compared to the incremental control cost of pollution denying any incentive effect for the polluter. In 1996, around four billion Yuan were collected from half a million polluting firms. A major portion of the revenue, more than 75%, from the levy is returned to the polluting enterprises to finance their pollution control investments. The balance is for environmental management at the local and regional level. The Chinese levy is therefore a good example of a hybrid policy with substantial subsidy component. The levy returned to the polluting enterprises serve as an incentive to invest on pollution control. The revenue form the pollution levy has shown a rising trend from 7.31 billion Yuan in 2003 to 188.9 billion Yuan in 2012. China is replacing its pollution levy with an environmental tax system with a broad base, covering a vast range of pollutants.

Malaysia's standard cum two tier charge system: The decision by the Malaysian government to promote production of palm oil for exports ended up as an environmental tragedy in the country. During 1975-1985, crude palm oil production rose from 1.3 million tones to 4.1 million tones making it the country's second largest earner of foreign exchange. This came at the cost of environmental quality.

The level of pollution from effluent discharge became a major problem in the 1970s. By mid-1977, 42 rivers in Malaysia were severely polluted, primarily due to the impact of the disposal of untreated effluents into the rivers. It is reported that in 1975 the pollution from the palm oil mills was equivalent to pollution generated by a population of more than 10 million people. The palm oil mills discharged the effluents in the rivers without any treatment making all the 42 rivers of Malaysia unfit to live for any aquatic organisms. Daily discharge alone increased by more than 300% from 1965 to 1977. The situation compelled the Malaysian Government to control pollution from the palm oil industry and protect the rivers through the Environmental Quality Act (EQA). The Act threatened to withhold operating licenses from the worst polluters which compelled the palm oil producers to adopt pollution control technologies. The DOE soon adopted a new policy strategy and combined command and control with a two tier effluent charge system. The annual license fee of the palm oil mill was linked with its projected BOD load. The palm oil mills were instructed to reduce the BOD load of the effluent.

A licensing system was introduced to control the pollution load being discharged into rivers and onto land. The licensing system consisted of effluent standards and effluent charges. Progressively stringent effluent standards were imposed on the palm oil industry. The licensing system was implemented in four stages. The phasing of standards for BOD over four years helped palm oil producers to learn and adopt efficient and effective technology to reduce the pollution load and conform with the standards prescribed. The palm oil mills were given one year to install treatment facilities after which they were required to reduce their wastewater discharges, biological oxygen demand (BOD) concentration from 25,000 mg/l untreated effluent to 5,000 mg/l in 1978/79, to 500 mg/l by 1981, and to 100 mg/l by 1984 onward. After a year of low effluent fee on the BOD, to help the firms to adapt to the licensing system, compliance with the BOD standard became mandatory. From the second year, a much stricter BOD standard (100 mg/l in 1984 onward) and higher effluent charges were imposed on the palm oil mills. The charges imposed were MR100 (US$40) per ton for biological oxygen demand loads above the standard and MR10 per ton for biological oxygen demand loads equal to or less than the standard. Besides, the polluters were required to pay a non-refundable flat fee of MR100 as annual license-processing fee. The mills that succeeded in reducing the biological oxygen demand were rewarded by being charged at a lower rate. The policy achieved remarkable results: The palm oil industry has made steady progress towards meeting the target of 100 mg/l biological oxygen demand. The mills' average daily discharges fell from about 220 tons to 125 tons. From 1977 to 1989 BOD load in the rivers decreased significantly by more than 95%. The policy was clearly effective in reducing pollution and improving the quality of Malaysia's rivers. More interestingly the policy measure did not result in loss of competitiveness for the palm oil mills. The gradual imposing of the licensing system and the regulation allowed the firms to adjust to the stringent rules. Some of the enterprises even developed commercial byproducts such as animal feed fertilisers and biogas from the effluent and avoided the cost of treatment as well as the pollution charges. (Markandya, A. and A. Shibli, 1995, and Kathuria and Kahn, 2002)

27.4 Market Using Instruments - Subsidies

Subsidies: The OECD defines a subsidy as: "any measure that keeps prices for consumers below market levels, or for producers above market levels, or that reduces costs for consumers and producers."

With reference to environment, there are pro-environmental subsidies and environmentally harmful subsidies. While pro-environmental subsidies promote environmentally friendly production and consumption, environmentally harmful subsidies have negative impact on the environment. In this section, we focus exclusively on pro-environmental subsidies which will be referred to as 'environmental subsidies'.

An environmental subsidy is the mirror image of a pollution tax. While a tax penalises the polluter, a subsidy gives incentives for environmentally friendly actions.Subsidies act as a reward for reducing emissions. The regulating authority pays to the polluter a subsidy for each unit of pollution reduction, starting from a base level. Instead of imposing charges on polluting firms, the subsidy approach offers cash payments to firms for reducing emissions.

With a cash subsidy on controlled emissions, polluters control pollution as long as the subsidy is greater than the marginal cost of pollution. The advocates of subsidies say that financial inducement can be just as effective when it takes the form of a reward for good behaviour than in the form of penalty (tax). Subsidies can take the form of grants, low-interest loans, tax holidays, favorable tax treatment, and preferential procurement policies for products or be somewhat indirect, such as in adjusted depreciation schedules.

Subsidies mostly take one of the following two forms:

- Partial payment of the cost of installation of some sort of pollution control equipment.
- The offer of a fixed reward for every reduction in emissions from some base level, usually some amount that the polluter used to emit in the past.

Subsidies cover a part of the investment on pollution control equipment. A subsidy to help to pay the cost of control equipment can be effective when the firm is considering the purchase of the equipment but is not able to do it because of the high cost. For example, the wastes from a firm may be recycled and put to valuable uses but the prohibitively high cost of a recycling plant may prevent the firm from doing so. In such cases subsidies come to the rescue of the polluter. But where the polluter gains nothing from the purchase of control equipment, a partial subsidy merely reduces the cost for the polluter — a cost that he did not want to incur at all. The subsidy covers only a partial payment of the cost of the equipment and the other` part of the cost of the equipment is borne by the firm.

Based on the Review of Subsides in Sweden (2003) and other reports subsidies may be classified as:

- Resource related subsidies which includes mainly subsidies to agricultural sector for promoting environmentally friendly agricultural practices such as organic farming. Subsidies for promoting resource conservation practices and technologies also come under this category.
- Energy related subsidies include subsidies that promote energy efficiency, energy conservation, energy research particularly those related to bio energy technology, and subsidy for solar and wind energy plants installation.
- Transport-related subsidies includes subsidies towards production of energy efficient vehicles, infra- structure subsidies, fuel tax exemptions and rebates.
- Pollution-reducing subsidies such as subsidies to set up effluent treatment plants and to promote use of pollution control technology.

27.4.1Subsidy vs. Tax

There are a number of crucial differences between a tax and a subsidy. In the first place, while effluent charges clearly reduce the net profits of a business, subsidies increase them. Hence it is being misused. It is being used to keep alive a polluting enterprise that would otherwise have been unprofitable. A tax discourages the production of commodities, the production of which causes pollution, whereas a subsidy encourages such outputs to expand. Thus a subsidy that is intended to reduce pollution actually increases it by causing expansion in the firm's output. This is illustrated in figure 27.6.

In figure 27.6, the supply curve shifts upward from SS to SS' position due to a tax on polluting output. The new equilibrium is at E' resulting in an output OX' which is less than the pre-tax output level OX. On the other hand a subsidy for reduction in the volume of polluting output reduces costs and shifts the supply curve downward to SS" position. As a result the new equilibrium is at E" which results in an output OX" greater than OX. It is argued that the reduction in cost brought about by subsidies will increase profits and attract entry by new firms. Thus subsidies add to the output and net profits of the firm while a pollution tax decreases it. The expansion in output by existing firms and entry

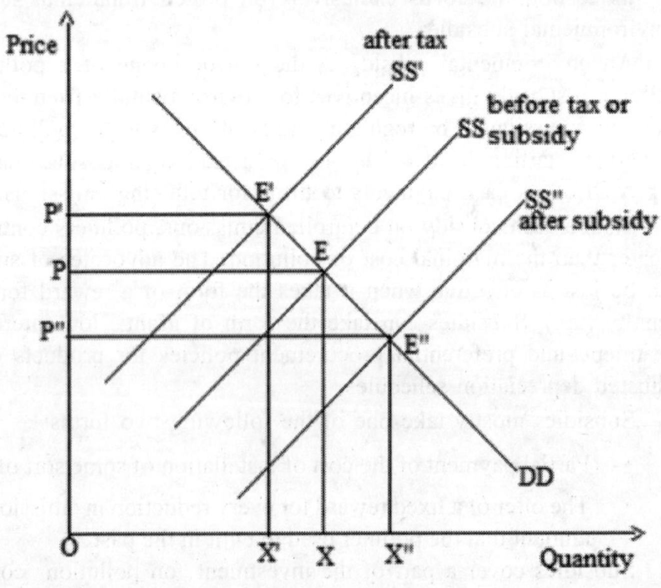

Figure 27.6 Impact of Tax and Subsidy on Price and Output

by new firms increases pollution thus defeating the very purpose for which the subsidy is given.

In the case of a pollution tax, the government "punishes" the firm (polluter) by imposing a charge for polluting the environment but in the case of the subsidy, the government encourages the firm for its environmentally friendly behaviour.

The effect of taxes and subsidies on output and price is illustrated in figure 27.6. While a tax decreases the quantity of the polluting output, a subsidy tends to increase it.

Secondly, the enforcement of subsidy scheme poses administrative problem - when subsidy is paid for every reduction in pollution beyond a certain level, it is necessary that a bench mark must be established from which reductions are to be measured. The environmental authority must determine some hypothetical normal level of emissions for each polluter to serve as the point of reference. This level must be acceptable to all producers. Effluent charge does not pose such administrative problems.

Finally a tax on pollution generates revenue while a subsidy is a demand for revenue from public treasury. Thus an effluent charge confers the incidental benefit of revenue generation. A subsidy in the form of tax concessions (write-off) to firms installing pollution control equipment, reduces the choice the firm can have among the alternative means available for pollution control.

In the case of the pollution tax the polluter is punished by the government with a charge on pollution, where as a subsidy, "encourages" the firm to improve its behaviour. In the long run a subsidy reduces the average cost of production, while the tax increases the average cost of production.

A firm with costs above the market price may still be able to operate if they receive a subsidy, which is not the case with a tax. A subsidy based on quantity of emissions reduced, produces the same effect as a tax for an individual polluter. In both cases, the more he emits, the worse off he is financially, because he either receives a smaller subsidy or a higher tax bill.

Critics say that subsidies are likely to encourage consumption of scarce resources and argue that investment in purification equipment is not always the most effective way to combat pollution.

27.4.2 Environmental Subsidies in Select Countries

In **Sweden**, most of the environmentally motivating subsidies are energy and resource related subsidies. Subsides for environmentally motivated investments are given for speeding up Sweden's transition to ecologically sustainable society. Investment subsidy for an ecological restructuring was given to encourage an eco-cycle adaptation of buildings and technological infrastructure. Investment subsidies are given for investments in wind power and bio-fuel fired combined heat and power production and for solar heat establishments in houses, apartments and premises. Besides, subsidies are given for maintaining biodiversity and for sanitation and restoration of polluted areas. Grants are given for converting electrically heated residential buildings to district heating or to another form of heating.

The **Yugoslavian** government exempts pollution control equipment from custom duties and also provides subsidies, in the form of reduced interest rates to new technologies that reduce pollution.

Turkey provides subsidized credit for relocation of polluting plants. For example, leather tanneries relocating to the Maltepe Industrial Zone north of Izmir, are entitled to subsidized interest rates of 35 percent for general loans and 22 percent for construction and infrastructure investment. This is a clear incentive as interest costs in 1988 and 1989 accounted for 20 percent of total investment expenditures. In addition the federal government offers a 40 percent tax deduction on investment for the tanneries relocating to another industrial zone during the first two years of estate construction (1988 and 1989) and a 7 percent reimbursement on investment for small and medium-scale tanneries (Kosmo 1989).

Subsidies for reforestation activities are common in many countries. Belgium, Finland, the United Kingdom, Portugal, Turkey and Japan give either tax exemption or subsidies for reforestation or for planting of trees or land restoration activities etc. Subsidies for the use of renewable energy sources, for energy saving measures, for recycling wastes are popular in Denmark, Netherlands and Switzerland. Resource conservation measures such as use of renewable energy, and energy saving activities are encouraged in Denmark. Energy saving improvements qualify for deductions from taxable income in Switzerland. Table 27.2 gives information on environmental subsidies in select Asian countries.

Table 27.2 Environmental Subsidies in Select Asian Countries

Country	Details about Subsidy
Indonesia	Tariff reduction for imported waste water treatment equipment
Korea	Low interest loans and income tax deductions for Purchase of energy saving equipment. Corporate Income tax deduction of 10% to firms producing energy saving equipment and pollution control equipment and 3% deduction to firms importing such equipment.
P R China	Reductions and exemptions from tariffs and customs duties for pollution control equipments
Thailand	a) Pollution control equipment not produced in Thailand is exempt from import duties, and foreign specialists working on pollution control activities are exempt from income taxes. b) Partial grants and low interest loans are made available from the Environment Fund to local administrations and private businesses required to set up treatment facilities. Other subsidies include the reduction of import duties to no greater than 10 per cent for equipment used for any treatment facilities.
Taiwan	Corporate income tax deduction on pollution control equipment.
Phillipines	Tax exemptions for pollution control equipment. Exemptions of up to 100% of import duties and local taxes are given on anti-pollution devices for industries covered by the Investment Priorities Plan. The Environmental Code enacted in 1977 allowed (a) exemption to the extent of fifty (50) per cent of tariff duties and compensating tax for the importation of pollution control equipment, devices, spare parts and accessories for a period of five (5) years from the date of implementation of the Decree. The decree also provided for deductions equivalent to fifty (50) per cent of the expenses actually incurred on research projects undertaken to develop technologies for the manufacture of pollution control equipment which have been proven effective and commercially reproducible, from the taxable income of the person or firm actually undertaking such projects
Indonesia,Korea, Thailand, Taiwan and P R China	Soft loans on pollution control. Firms can borrow for pollution control equipment and clean technology at favorable interest rates and other loan terms

Source: Modified based on information from USEPA 2004 : "International Experiences with Economic Incentives for Protecting Environment and WHO/UNEP 1997 (Water Pollution Control - A Guide to the Use of Water Quality Management Principles, Chapter 6).

A number of countries such as Belgium, Finland, Spain, Portugal, Turkey, Japan, UK and India subsidize reforestation activities.

In **India** environment promoting subsidies are provided for the following activities: sewerage and sanitation, soil and water conservation, fisheries, forestry and wild life, agriculture research and education, Special Areas Development Programme, flood control and drainage, non-conventional sources of energy, ecology and environment.

In 2008-09 the subsidies to the above mentioned heads amounted to Rs 5231.67 crores. The Government of India also provides for:

- Rebate on the cess payable upon installation treatment plant of sewage or trade effluent
- Customs or Excise Duties and Sales Tax Rebate
- A higher rate of depreciation for pollution control equipment
- Concession in profit tax for investments in pollution control equipment

27.5 Refundable Deposits and Environmental Performance Bonds

"Environmental performance bonds and deposit refund systems are economic instruments that aim to shift responsibility for controlling pollution, monitoring, and enforcement to individual producers and consumers who are charged in advance for the potential damage" (Panayotou, 1995) .

The deposit-refund system is a combination of a product charge (the deposit) and a subsidy for recycling or proper disposal (the refund). Deposit-refund systems require a monetary deposit (charge / fee) at the time of sale of a product which is returned when the item is returned at the end of its useful life. The fees are partly used to subsidize the administrative costs associated with the return, recycling and reuse of the products. Deposit-refund systems shifts the responsibility for controlling environmental degradation to the producers and consumers of polluting products. The fee or deposits gives them the incentives to return the byproducts of their production and consumption activities for recycling or safe disposal. The main objectives of a deposit refund scheme are to:

- discourage illegal or improper disposal.
- divert recyclable items from the waste stream

Deposit systems are commonly applied to beverage containers, lead-acid batteries, and tires, car batteries and vehicle hulks, to plastics and hazardous materials.

One serious limitation of deposit-refund systems is the additional cost incurred in collecting and refunding deposits on the return of the containers or used products and the additional costs involved in collecting and returning used products for disposal. But these costs are partially offset by the interest earned on deposits, unclaimed deposits, and sales of collected used products.

The share of the deposit fee in the total product cost must be sufficiently high for the deposit refund system to be effective. Return rates are high if the deposit fee is high and low if the deposit fee is low. For example Norway and Sweden have refundable deposit system for car hulks. In Norway, the deposit in 1988 was ECU 130 per vehicle, while in Sweden it was only ECU 42. Hence while more than 90% of disused cars were returned in Norway, in Sweden a much smaller percentage of disused cars was returned. Similarly a doubling of the deposit on aluminum beverage cans in 1987 by Sweden, increased the return of the cans to nearly 80% from the previous return level of 60% to 70%.

Norway, Sweden and Finland have a well-functioning deposit refund system on beverage containers, coexisting with a product charge on non-renewable products. The rate of return of containers is 90% for beer and soft drinks and 70 - 80% for wine and liquor.

Germany has a single use deposit system for bottles since 2003, known popularly as the 'Pfand'. Pfand refers to a portion of the price on the bottles that a consumer can get back on returning it to the counter. Most of the super markets have a reverse vending machine which scan Pfand returns and print a receipt for the total value of the refund. Pfand can be collected in any retail store and not necessarily at the store where the drink (or water) was purchased.

Table 27.3 Deposit Refund Systems

Product Subject to Refundable Deposits	Country
Specified Beverage container – PET bottles and Glass Bottles.	Australia, Austria, Belgium, Brazil, Chile, Canada, Czech Republic Colombia, Denmark, Ecuador, Finland, Hungary, Italy, Iceland, Korea, Japan, Mexico, Netherlands, Norway, Poland, Sri Lanka, Sweden, Turkey, Switzerland, Taiwan, United States, Venezuela
Batteries –Lead acid batteries, car batteries, lead accumulators, N-CD batteries	US (some states), Mexico, Korea, Denmark, Netherlands
Scrap Autos, car hulks	Norway, Sweden, Finland
Small chemical container	Denmark
Waste management households (glass and plastic, car batteries)	Sri Lanka Mexico, Colombia, Ecuador, Jamaica, Venezuela, Taiwan, Korea
Packaging Wastes	France, Germany
Refrigerators, Fluorescent light bulbs	Austria
Air conditioners, Washing machines, Television and lubricants,tyres	South Korea

Source: OECD, 1999 and Karpagam M and GeethaJaikumar 2010.

South Korea has one of the most extensive deposit systems covering a variety of items such as packaged paper, metal cans, glass and PET bottles, batteries, tires, lubricating oils, televisions, and washing machines.

Robert Solow and Edwin Mills have suggested the method of using a refundable deposit for pollution in cases where it is not possible to monitor, observe and detect environmental damage. For example it may not be possible to detect whether an oil tanker has dumped its wastes in the sea. In such cases they recommend that potential offenders should be required to leave an appropriate deposit with the environmental authorities which can pay an interest on all such deposits. The funds may be used by the environmental authorities for its environmental protection activities but must be refunded to the polluter in case he ceases his activities that cause pollution. For example, in the case of oil tankers, the owners of oil tankers are required to pay to an international authority a deposit sufficient to cover the cost of clearing up oil spills and compensation for any damage. The owners of the oil tanker should prove regularly that they had disposed the cargo and wastes properly. The owners would be refunded their deposits in the event of sale of the ship. Such a scheme of refundable deposits makes socially undesirable activities, unprofitable to the individual. This technique has been found to be very useful in the encouragement of recycling or reuse.

The main advantage of the deposit refund mechanism to control pollution is its potential to reduce littering problems and divert wastes to landfills. Deposit refund systems provide a monetary incentive to the consumer to return the product or package, and an infrastructure for its collection and recycling.

Deposit refund schemes cost effective schemes since they do not involve any monitoring costs and collection costs. They reflect polluter pays principle. However if the refunds are too low, the public may not have an incentive to participate in the scheme.

Kaseke (2004) observes that deposit refund system may result in deposit fraud in the form of false invoices, misrepresentation of goods, faulty classification of products, altering of import specifications, and smuggling from third world countries. Further, a high deposit provides an incentive for entrepreneurs from neighbouring jurisdictions to bring bottles, cans, etc. across the boundary to collect the deposit.

Performance Bonds

Performance bonds are charges for potential pollution. They are fees imposed on companies that extract certain natural resources, such as timber, coal, oil and gas. Amount deposited as the performance bond is refunded when the payer fulfills certain obligations. In this sense performance bonds are similar deposit-refund system. Very often the governments have to spend huge amounts on cleaning up the mess created by polluting firms and restoring the degraded environment. Performance bonds and deposit refund system help in reducing the financial commitment of the government for restoring the degraded environment.

According to Panayotou, environmental bonds ensure the following:

- resource extracting companies and potential polluters take adequate measures to minimize the environmental damage caused by their activities;
- they undertake clean up of residual damage and restoration of damaged environment in the most cost efficient manner;
- adequate funds are available for the clean-up of waste and restoration of damaged environments by anyone who fails to comply.

Performance bonds are commonly used in: mining companies to reclaim mining sites, timber harvesting firms to comply with harvesting regulations and in construction industry to perform construction activities in compliance with the prevailing rules. In the case of timber harvesting performance bonds help in avoiding logging and encourage regeneration.

In Indonesia mine operators are required to give reclamation guarantee clearly stating the value of the potential environmental damage likely to result from the mining operation. The guarantee amount which is based on the cost of reclamation is returned by the government upon satisfactory performance by the mining firm.

Performance bonds have lower monitoring and enforcement costs than charges or pollution tax but the administration cost of performance bonds may be high as it requires a financial institution that will manage and reinvest the funds, pay interest, assess performance, and dispose the bond accordingly.

Conclusion

MBIs that use markets, discussed in this chapter, are preferred by many for their efficiency and flexibility. The instruments that come under this category such as taxes, charges, subsidies etc, enable firms to control pollution efficiently and give them freedom in their efforts to control pollution. The market using instruments are not replacements to command and control but they complement the prevailing regulation to control pollution.

Questions

1. Define and classify market using instruments?
2. Explain the rationale for a pollution tax/ charge. Discuss its merits and limitations.
3. Compare a pollution tax with a pollution subsidy.
4. Explain the significance of refundable deposits as a market using instrument and give examples.

Exercise

- Prepare a literature study on the use of market using instruments.
- Make a study of the use of MBIs by the European nations.

28

POLLUTION CONTROL - MARKET CREATING INSTRUMENTS

What mankind must know is that human beings cannot live without Mother Earth, but the planet can live without humans.

—*Evo Morales*

One of the most important reasons for environmental issues is the absence of markets for environmental resources. Creation of markets for environmental resources is pointed out as an effective solution for internalizing the externality. An important way in which markets are created for environmental resources is by definition of property rights and issuing tradable pollution rights.

28.1 Definition of Property Rights

Ronald Coase argued that environmental degradation is the result of absence of well- defined property rights; he suggested that markets can potentially solve externalities if property rights are clearly defined and negotiations between parties concerned is feasible. Dales (1968) endorsed Coasean view and suggested that an actual market in property rights is the solution to pollution problems. He dismissed Pigouvian tax on grounds of information required to set an optimal tax. Transferable pollution permits evolved from the writings of Coase and Dales.

Definition of property rights for resources provides a fundamental incentive for better resource management. Allocation of property rights is a method that protects the environmental resources by putting them into the hands of private individual who consequently have a financial stake in their preservation. Society's resources are often in far greater danger when they are held as common resources, since "everybody's property is no one's property". Anyone who exploits them suffers only minimum loss. As a result such common property resources are over consumed or exploited. Hardin's Tragedy of Commons is an example of this (Box 4.1in chapter 4). Hence it is suggested that if exclusive property rights are defined for such resources, the public good, environmental quality, can be transformed into a private good and optimal environmental allocation will be reached. In the absence of well defined property rights for resources, market fails to allocate environmental resources efficiently among its various uses. Hence lack of adequate property rights can be treated as a cause for market failure. Definition of property rights will result in the emergence of markets for environmental resources, correct the market failure and determine scarcity prices for the resources. Government intervention is required to assign environmental property titles. With property rights adequately defined, market will find the correct allocation.

A property right can be defined as a set of rules specifying the use of scarce resources and goods. The set of rules include obligation and rights. Prof. Dales has distinguished four types of property rights.

- First is **exclusive property rights** that cover the right of disposal and the right to destroy the resources, notably the right of sale. Even such exclusive property rights are controlled by a set of rules which protect other individuals or maintain economic values. For example, city zoning laws.
- Second is status or **functional ownership**, which refers to a set of rules limited to a specific person or status. In such cases the right to use an object or to receive a service is not transferable.
- Third is the **right to use** a public utility (such as a highway) or a public good (a national park) relate to a specific use.
- Fourth is common property resource with **no exclusion** defined.

Historically the property rights have not been defined for the use of environment and have hence resulted in their misuse. J. Burton, in his "Externalities, Property Rights and Public Policy: Private Property Rights to Prevent the Spoliation of Nature" points out that the growing desert of the Sahel region in Africa is due to the non-existence of property rights. It is reported that parts of northern Africa were the granery of the Roman Empire. In the Sixth Century, the Arabs changed the property rights into a common property pasture system, which resulted in the degradation of the land.

28.2 Coase Theorem

Any account on the property rights approach is incomplete without the mention of the celebrated Coase Theorem which states that in the absence of transaction costs, bargaining among different users of the environment will result in a Pareto optimal allocation of environment when exclusive (transferable) property rights to the environment are defined. The resulting allocation is independent of the initial distribution of property titles. The Coase Theorem is illustrated in figure 28.1

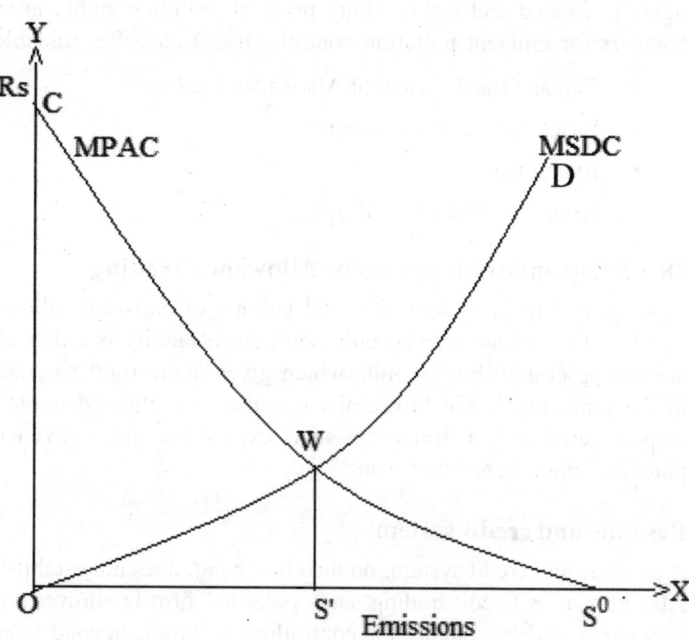

Figure 28.1Coase Solution without Transaction Cost

In figure 28.1, we are considering only two individuals—a polluter and a pollutee. The damage per unit of pollutant to the pollutee is given by OD and the marginal abatement cost to the polluter is S°C. If exclusive property rights to the environment is given to the pollutee, he will withstand the pollution so long as the polluter pays a compensation that lies above his marginal damage curve. But the polluter is willing to offer a compensation that is below his marginal abatement costs. The bargaining position of the polluter and pollutee is on S°C and OD respectively. The result of the bargaining process between the two is at W at which S°S' of pollution is abated and an optimal environmental quality of OS' is maintained. If on the other hand, initial property right was with polluter, he would have to be compensated by the pollutee for reducing his emissions. The polluter will be willing to abate pollution only if the compensation was greater than his marginal abatement cost curve S°C and the pollutee will be willing to pay a compensation that is below the marginal damage curve. The bargaining process results in an optimal solution, again at W. The Coase Theorem thus shows that optimal environmental allocation is independent of the initial distribution of property rights.

The property rights approach can work only when the damage to the natural resources comes from a few sources that are easily identified; where private owners themselves cause environmental deterioration, this solution is not applicable. The most important point is that, it may have adverse effect on distribution of wealth. If conversion of society's resources into private property is made on the basis of 'to the highest bidder' principle, it will have serious consequences.

28.3 Market Creating Instruments – Pollution Permits

A Pollution Permit is a market based policy instrument and is also known as tradable or transferable permit. Rights to pure air are allocated to the firms leading to a trade between the firms which need more permits and firms which have surplus permits. Thus the approach is based on the allocation of property rights and the creation of a market that did not exist earlier.

Under this policy tool, the owner of a permit has the right to emit or pollute a certain amount specified in the permit. Permits work by creating a market, where, rights to pollute may be traded among firms. If rights to pollute, in the form of permits to pollute are traded, a market for pollution rights is created and the resulting price of pollution rights in such a market provides incentives to polluters for efficient pollution control. OECD classifies tradable permits in to four categories.

- Cap and trade system or Allowance Trading
- Baseline and credit system
- Averaging
- Usage or Abstraction Rights

28.3.1 Cap and trade system or Allowance Trading

In a cap and trade system, the total volume of emissions allowed from all firms is first determined which is the ceiling on total emissions. Each facility is either allocated permits or participates in an auction process to buy permits which gives it the right to emit a portion of total permissible level of the pollutant. If the firm emits less than the allowed quota given in the permits, it can sell its surplus permits. If a firm's emissions exceed the quota given in the permits it holds, then it must purchase more from other firms.

Baseline and credit system

A baseline and credit system, on the other hand, does not establish any fixed ceiling on total emissions. Also known as Credit trading, each polluting firm is allowed to emit a base level of emissions. The firm earns tradable credits for controlling pollution beyond what is specified in one's permit. If the firm's emissions are below the base level, it can sell the surplus credits. If it emits above the base level, it must purchase credits to comply with its emissions requirements. The credit worthiness of the activity is certified by the regulator who recommends that the credit can be transferred. No extra credit will be given to a firm for any control of pollution which it would have done anyway.

Averaging In this the regulator sets the average limit values of emissions for an entire range of similar products produced by firms in the same industry. The firms must comply with the average limit value – they have the option to exceed these limit values for some of the products they sell, provided that these excess emissions are offset by lower than average levels of emissions for other products. If for any firm, the emissions are lower than average limit value prescribed, it can transfer its unused permits to another firm whose average performance is poorer than that prescribed.

Usage or Abstraction rights aim to formally regulate access to common resources in order to prevent Hardin's tragedy like outcome. Transferable fishing rights is an example of such an approach.

28.3.2 Permit Market

Tradable pollution permits achieve a desired level of pollution control at an optimal cost to society if the permit market is active.In a simple application of the instrument, the environmental authority determines the maximum amount of a specific type of pollution per unit of time that is within safe limits—that is consistent with the community's environmental objective—and then issues a batch of permits authorising (altogether) just that amount of pollution. Each permit could give its owner the "right" to pollute up to a specified amount in a given place during a particular period of time. These permits are offered for sale in an organised market where its price is determined by its supply and demand. The supply curve would be a vertical line since the total number of permits issued at any time is fixed, while the demand curve is downward sloping.The situation is explained using figure 28.2 In the figure,the initial equilibrium price is OP at which OQ number of permits are issued. In the absence of a price for permits, the firms would demand OQ' number of permits. Over the years when population increases or with economic growth, the demand for pollution permits increase from D' to D", resulting in higher equilibrium price OP'.

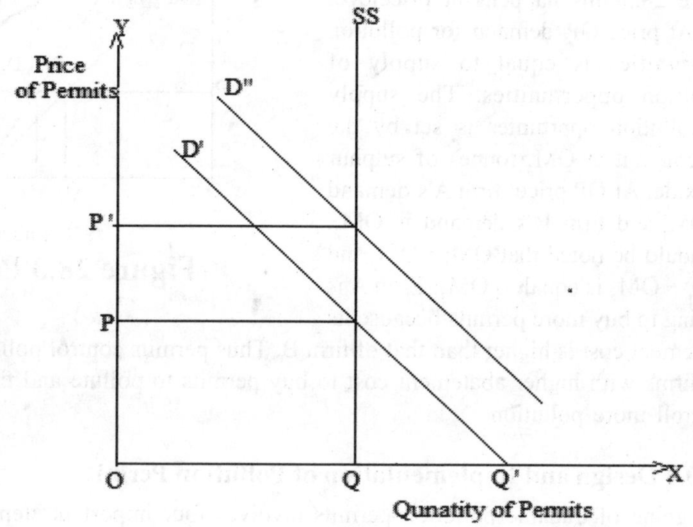

Figure 28.2 Determination of Price of Pollution Permits

28.3.3 The Working of a Pollution Permit

Since permits are transferable, polluting firms can buy and sell (trade) permits at a price determined by the market place.

The working of a pollution permit is explained using figure 28.3 using an example consisting of two firms A and B, each polluting M tonnes of SO_2 per day. Total pollution is therefore 2M. It is assumed that initially there is neither regulation nor any economic instrument in use. The marginal pollution abatement cost of firm A is higher than that of firm B.

The government decides to limit pollution to a level less than 2M, say to OM_3 tonnes of SO_2 and issues permits to limit pollution to OM_3 level. The supply is fixed at the level OM_3 and hence the supply curve is parallel to Y axis, that is, vertical at $Q = OM_3$. The marginal pollution abatement cost curve is the firm's demand curve for pollution opportunities. The aggregate demand curve is the horizontal summation of the demand curves of the two firms. It is kinked at point K in figure 28.3.

In the described situation, the firms together want to pollute 2M tonnes of pollution but the permissible limit set by the government is OM_3 which is lower than 2M.There is thus exccess demand which pushes up the price. The increase in price continues till demand for pollution opprtunities is equal to supply of pollution opportunities. In figure 28.3 this happens at pricelevel OP. At price OP, demand for pollution opprtunities is equal to supply of pollution opportunities. The supply of pollution opprtunies is set by the governemnt at OM_3 tonnes of sulphur di oxide. At OP price, firm A's demand is OM_1 and firm B's demand is OM_2. It should be noted that $OM_1 > OM_2$ and $OM_1 + OM_2$ is equal to OM_3. Firm A is willing to buy more permits because its abatement cost is higher than that of firm B. Thus permits control pollution efficiently giving incentive for firms with higher abatement cost to buy permits to pollute and firms with lower abatement costs controll more pollution.

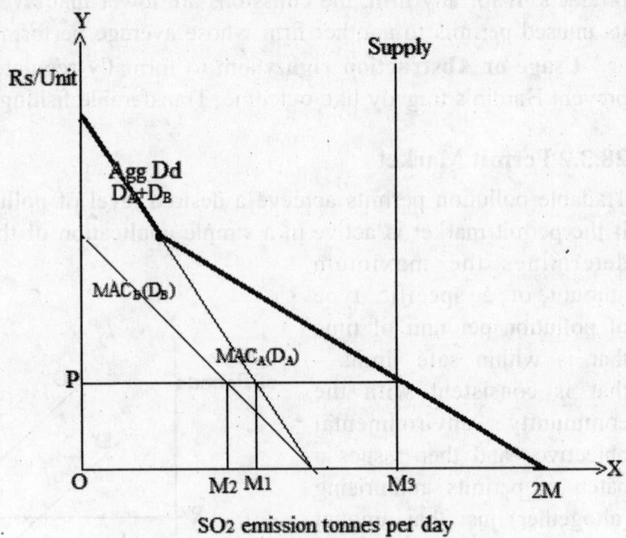

Figure 28.3 Pollution Market

28.3.4 Design and Implementation of Pollution Permit

Designing of tradable pollution permits involves four important steps (Revesz, R L et al, 2000). **First** step is the identification of the pollutant to be regulated and the region to be covered by the permit scheme.

Second step is the determination of the acceptable level of aggregate emissions level in a given time period. Based on this aggregate level, number of emission permits is decided. Each permit authorises the holder to emit a fixed amount of the regulated pollutant.

Third step involves the definition of the 'bundle of rights' for each permit. This involves: specifying the date of expiry of the permit, whether the permits can be eliminated by the government before the date of expiry and whether unused permits can be retained for use at a later date.

The **fourth** step is determining the **method of allocating the permits**. The two common methods of allocation are: **grandfathering and auctioning**. In the grandfathering option, permits are distributed among the polluting firms in accordance with previous emission history either without any charge or for some pre-determined charge. Alternatively if the government decides to auction the permits among the polluting firms, the rules for trading the permits in the market will be specified by the government.

28.3.5 Conditions for Success of the Permit System

OECD (1991) observed that the pollution permit system works effectively only if the following conditions are fulfilled:

- The number of pollution sources is large enough to establish a well-functioning market.
- The sources of pollution are well defined.
- The amount of pollution generated by each source is easily computed.

- There are differences in the marginal costs of pollution control among the various sources.
- There is potential for technical innovation.

The success of the pollution permit scheme depends on the ability to measure and monitor accurately the aggregate emissions discharged; this information is important for the decision on number of permits to be issued. Accurate measurement of emissions is necessary to check the polluting firm's compliance to rules of the system. The determination of the overall permissible level of emissions or environmental standard in general, is mostly based on some method of valuation which poses problems of subjectivity and choice of discount rate etc. This limits the precision of the defined permissible level of aggregate pollution.

Choice of the appropriate method of allocation –grandfathering or auctioning is important. The Permit must be carefully designed to avoid distributional consequences that are likely to arise if permits are distributed on an ad hoc basis or if they are auctioned. Many critics feel that the grandfathering allocation option involve equity considerations.

The nature of the pollutant involved, its volume and impact must be rightly assessed. Further the spatial and temporal impact of the pollutant must also be known with certainty for permits to be effective. The rules must be clearly specified regarding the geographical and time limit of the permit. If these conditions are met and if there is adequate competition in the market for permits then tradable permits will complement other existing pollution control instruments in controlling pollution efficiently.

28.3.6 Advantages of Permits

The pollution permits work in many ways like a tax. It is dependable, and permanent. Since polluters pay for the amount they pollute, it is also equitable. It generates revenue to the government like a tax. It does not specify the way in which pollution should be abated and hence does not interfere with private decisions. Pollution permits also promote least cost method of abating pollution.

The main advantages of pollution permit are its cost effectiveness and its least interference in the decision making of the firms. A permit system reduces the total costs of meeting a predetermined environmental standard, thus making it cost effective. Since the low cost firm gets the option of abating the emissions and the high cost firm has the option of buying the permits, the burden of pollution control is fairly distributed; that is, use of permits promotes equity .

Baumol and Oates point out that pollution permits besides sharing the virtues of the tax approach, have at least two clear advantages over the tax approach which are given below:

It reduces the uncertainty about the quantity that will be emitted into the community. Under a tax rate, the quantity of emissions depend on the response of the polluting firm to the tax rate imposed. On the other hand, in the case of pollution permits, the ceiling on emissions is determined in advance by the environmental authority which enforces this ceiling by issuing a specified number of permits that would allow only that total quantity of emissions already decided.

If a new firm enters the industry or if an additional plant is set by an existing firm, the increased demand for permits will push up the price of permits which may make incurring abatement cost cheaper for some firms and they will be willing to sell permits. The new firms and the expanding firms can buy permits from existing firms which are willing to sell. While this process goes on, the quantity of pollution will remain constant. This is a distinct advantage of permits in a dynamic economy.

Secondly, pollution permits are invulnerable to inflation, and works effectively even as population and industrial activity increase. This is because, their price will automatically increase following increases in population and industrial activity. Similarly when the impact of pollution varies between location, number of permits issued in each location can be varied depending on the impact of pollution. For example, in an area more vulnerable to pollution, fewer permits may be sold by decision.

Yet another distinct advantage of permits is that it provides for purchase of permits by third parties such as an environmental group which is more concerned in lowering pollution than an average individual. The permits purchased by these groups are not exercised and not available to polluting firms. This is a clear positive externality on the rest of society.

28.3.7 Disadvantages of Permits

The principal disadvantages of transferable emission permits are:

- The idea of permits to pollute has been questioned on moral and ethical grounds.
- The choice of the method for allocating the permits among potential users could have significant equity implications.
- Permits are ineffective when the number of participants is few.
- It is pointed out that permits can be purchased by existing firms for the purpose of deterring entrants.
- It is observed that a tradable emission permit regime is likely to result in the formation of "hot spots" of pollution – that is, locations at which the damage caused by pollutants is particularly severe. In the words of Ackerman and Stewart (1985) the tradable permit system "could allow the creation of relatively high concentrations of particular pollutants in small areas within the larger pollution control region".

28.3.8 Experience with Tradable Permits

The United States was the first country to apply tradable pollution permits for controlling pollution. The first trading of permitted rights to pollute began in the 1970s as a mechanism to meet ambient air quality standards. To increase flexibility and efficiency the US permit system has four important programmes - emission netting, offsets, bubbles and banking.

Offsets permitted the entry of new sources in an area where National prescribed standards are not met (a non- attainment area), provided the emissions of the existing source is reduced by atleast as much as what the new source would contribute.

Bubble allows a firm to combine the limits for several different sources into one combined limit and to determine the firm's compliance based on that aggregate limit instead of from each source individually. The term 'bubble' was used to refer to an imaginary bubble over a source such as a refinery that had several emission points each with its own emission limit.

Netting allowed large new sources and major modifications by existing sources to be exempted from certain review procedures if existing emissions elsewhere in the same facility was reduced by sufficient quantity.

Netting and Bubble allowed trading of emission reductions among different sources within a firm, as long as the combined emissions under the "bubble" are within the prescribed level.

Banking allowed firms to accumulate emission credits for future use or sale if they are able to reduce emissions below the prescribed level.

Some of the major areas where pollution permits are applied in the US include :

- the U.S. Environmental Protection Agency's (EPA's) Emissions Trading Program that includes trading of emission rights of pollutants regulated under the Clean Air Act for improving local air quality through the control of volatile organic compounds (VOCs), CO, SO_2, particulates, and NOx.

- the phasedown of leaded gasoline in the United States
- U.S. heavy duty motor vehicle engine emissions trading
- water quality permit trading

The most important application of the tradable permit system in the United States is the one that regulates SO_2 emissions, the primary cause of **acid rain**. This was introduced in 1990 with the objective of reducing sulfur dioxide and nitrogen oxide emissions by 10 million tons and 2 million tons, respectively, from 1980 levels. Phase 1 of the programme which was initiated in 1995, covered electric utilities and coal fired power plants east of the Mississippi River that generated very high emission levels of SO_2 The second Phase of the programme which began in the year 2000 included almost all electric power generating units. It is reported that the SO_2 trading market resulted in cost saving of nearly $1 billion per annum relative to costs under the command and control approach. The programme yielded large welfare effects, particularly positive health effects from reduction in local SO_2 and particulate emissions. Stavins (1991) reports that large companies such as Amco, Dupont, and 3M have traded emission credits and a relatively active market for such trades has developed in the US. Due to the flexible options under the programme, the US firms have been able to save nearly between $5 and $12 billion in compliance costs. Experts feel that emission trading in the US has produced improvement in air quality achievable under a command and control regime but at a much lower cost (Panayatou, 2005).

Table 28.1 Permit Programmes in the US

Programme	Traded commodity	Period of operation
Emission trading under CAA	Criteria pollutants	1974 - present
Lead Gasoline Phasedown	Rights for lead in gasoline among refineries	1982 -1987
Water Quality Trading	Point- non-point sources of nitrogen and phosphorous	1984 -1986
CFC Trading for Ozone Protection	Production rights for some CFCs based on depletion potential	1987 - present
Heavy Duty Engine Trading	Averaging, banking,and trading of credits for NOx andparticulate emissions	1992 - present
Acid Rain Reduction	SO_2 emission reduction credits;Mainly among electric utilities	1995 - present
RECLAIM Programme	SO_2, NO_2 emission among stationary sources	1994 - present

Source: Stavins (2002) - Modified

RECLAIM (Regional Clean Air Incentives Market) is the world's first comprehensive emissions market programme for reducing air pollution. It is a "cap and trade" permits program implemented in the Los Angeles River Basin in the US to reduce emissions of SO_X and NO_X annually by the amounts necessary to achieve the AQMP (Air Quality Management Plan) targets: meeting air quality standards for SOx and NOx emissions by 2003 and meeting the goals for reducing ROG (Reactive Organic Gases) emissions by 2010. More specifically the target was to reduce SO_2 emissions by 75% and NO_2 emissions by 60% by 2003. RECLAIM applied the bubble concept and sought to regulate total emissions in the bubble. RECLAIM includes over 350 participants in its NOx market and about 40 participants in its SO_2 market. As of the end of 2001, RTC permits for over 300,000 tons of NOX and over 100,000 tons of SO_2 had been traded. Most of the trading has occurred within firms and RECLAIM markets have been active.

Table 28.1 gives information on tradable permits program in the US. Tradable Permit Programs are gaining popularity in many countries. Some of the countries which have an operating permit system are: Canada, Germany, Chile, China, Mexico, Singapore, the Netherlands, Australia, and New Zealand. Many countries have started to design programs in tradable greenhouse gas emission credits.

28.4 Environmental Offsets

Environmental offsets are actions taken by developers to compensate for the adverse impacts of their developments on the environment. More precisely environmental offsets refer to 'actions taken outside a development site that compensate for the impacts of that development - including direct, indirect or consequential impacts'. The central idea of an offset program is that developers "offset" environmental impacts at a development site by undertaking equivalent environmental improvements at a second, nearby, site. The offsets are undertaken by the developers or through purchase of environmental "credits" by the developer from a "offset bank". The offset bank is a business or government agency that specializes in generating these credits.

The offset programme is based on the principle of making the polluting firm to indulge in environmentally beneficial activities which would offset the environmentally damaging consequences of its production activities.

Environmental offsets are economic instruments and are based on polluter pays principle. An environmental offset programme is a falen of core regulation that ranges form of a command and control system to a cap and trade system *(Hahn & Richards, 2013)*. The objective is to internalize the external cost arising from development projects that cause adverse impact on the society. The objective of any environmental offset is "No Net Loss". Sometimes the offset programme will result in net environmental improvements if developers of the project are required to achieve environmental improvements greater than the negative impacts generated by their project.

An environmental offset programme provides for the compensation of the environmental impacts at one site through activities at another site. For example if the effluent discharge by a firm damaged a river ecosystem in an area then the firm would be required to spend on some ecosystem beneficial service like maintain a tree coverage in a forest or maintain an wetland in another area.

An offset is the final step of the mitigation hierarchy. Any mitigation effort at the site of the project to mitigate the negative environmental impact of the project has three important steps.

1. Avoiding the negative consequences
2. Minimising the negative consequences
3. Restoring environmental quality

Environmental offsets are to be applied only after all reasonable and appropriate efforts have been made - first to **avoid** adverse impacts, then to **minimise** the unavoidable impacts, and finally to **restore** the environmental quality. After these initial steps have been taken, finally offset principle is applied to meet the environmental objective of a scheme.

International offset refers to offsets in the case of global environmental issues. Carbon offsets and biodiversity offsets are popular examples. Carbon offsets are the most discussed example.

28.4.1 Biodiversity offsets

OECD defines biodiversity offsets as "measurable conservation outcomes that result from actions designed to compensate for significant, residual biodiversity loss from development projects". They are based on the principle that the negative impact on biodiversity from development can be compensated, if sufficient habitat can be established or protected elsewhere.

Environmental offset schemes are the most popular in the United States, particularly the wetland mitigation banking. A mitigation bank is operated by insisting that if developments cause wetland impacts that cannot be mitigated on-site then wetland offset at a secondary site is approved. A mitigation bank is a wetland , stream or other aquatic resources area that has been restored or preserved as a compensation for the adverse impact to aquatic resource. The physical area in hectares that has been restored or enhanced or preserved is the bank site.

USBPA reports that in 2001 nearly 219 wetland mitigation banks were operating in the United States. Nearly 139,000 acres were included in the 219 approved banks that provide a combination of wetland restoration, creation, enhancement, and/or preservation. An additional 95 banks were under review with approval pending as of December 2001, that included an additional 8000 acres.

Offset schemes are also used in Australia, Brazil, Canada, European Union member states, Mexico, Switzerland, and Uganda.

28.4.2 Carbon offsets

A carbon offset is a reduction in emissions of carbon di oxide or greenhouse gases made in order to compensate for or offset an emission made elsewhere.It is a credit for greenhouse reductions achieved by one party that can be purchased and used to compensate (offset) the emissions of another party. Carbon offsets are typically measured in tonnes of CO_2equivalents (or CO_2e). Credits are given in the form of a certificate representing the reduction of one metric ton (2,205 lbs) of carbon dioxide emissions, the principal cause of climate change. One carbon offset represents the reduction of one metric ton of carbon dioxide or its equivalent in other greenhouse gases. (Miner. M, 2012)

For example wind energy companies often sell carbon offsets. The wind energy company benefits because the carbon offsets it sells make such projects more economically viable. The buyers of the offsets benefit because they can claim that their purchase resulted in new non-polluting energy, which they can use to mitigate their own greenhouse gas emissions. The buyers may also save money as it may be less expensive for them to purchase offsets than to eliminate their own emissions.

Purchase of carbon offsets imply that funds are generated for projects that reduce **greenhouse gas** (GHG) emissions. Carbon offsets helps in the reduction of global greenhouse gas emissions.

To reduce global warming, greenhouse gas emissions must be reduced by about 60-80 percent below current global levels. Carbon offset projects can help meet this challenge. There are various types of carbon offset projects which result in the reduction of greenhouse gas emissions.

- Renewable energy projects-such as solar and wind energy which reduce emissions by reducing the dependence on of fossil-fired energy sources.
- Energy efficiency projects, such as low-energy consuming bulbs and industrial processes that reduce CO_2emissions by using less energy to accomplish the same tasks.
- Greenhouse gas capture projects which capture methane from agriculture or landfills.

- Bio-sequestration projects which increase forest coverage and enhance the biological uptake of CO_2

The carbon trade came about in response to the Kyoto Protocol which was signed in Kyoto, Japan, by some 180 countries in December 1997. The Kyoto Protocol called for the 38 industrialised countries worldwide to reduce their greenhouse gas emissions between the years 2008 -2012 to levels that are lower than those of 1990.

There are two markets for carbon offsets – one which is large exists in order to achieve compliance with Kyoto Protocol. In this larger market, companies and governments buy carbon offsets in order to comply with upper limit (caps) on the total amount of carbon dioxide they are allowed to emit. In 2006, about $5.5 billion of carbon offsets were purchased in the compliance market, representing about 1.6 billion metric tons of CO_2e reductions. The other is a smaller market where individuals, companies and governments voluntarily purchase offsets to mitigate their greenhouse gas emissions from transportation, electricity use and other sources. For example an individual can buy carbon offsets to compensate for the greenhouse gas emissions generated from his consumption or production activity. In 2008, $705 million of carbon offsets were purchased in the smaller voluntary market representing about 123.4 million metric tonnes of CO_2e reductions. (Mark Miner, 2012)

Offsets are seen as important policy tool to promote environmental protection and achieve sustainable development.

Conclusion

Definition of property rights and creation of markets for environmental resources and services have a very important role in protecting the environment. There is clearly an increasing trend in the use of these instruments. The contribution of these instruments towards efficiency and equity in environmental protection is an important point in favour of these instruments.

Questions

1. Explain Coase theorem and bring out its policy implications.
2. What are pollution permits. How does a permit market work?
3. Bringout the advantages and limitations of a permit market.
4. What are offsets in permit programme. Give an example.

Exercise

Prepare a case study on carbon or biodiversity offset permit programme

Prepare a literature study on the use of tradable pollution permits.

29

COMPARISON OF POLLUTION CONTROL POLICY INSTRUMENTS

The quicker we humans learn that saving open space and wildlife is critical to our welfare and quality of life, maybe we'll start thinking of doing something about it.

—Jim Fowler

Continuous improvement in the quality of environment requires perception, economic strength and research along with policies and administration geared to achieve the right aims. The basic objective in the use of any method of controlling pollution is to achieve it at least cost. In the last three chapters we have seen the features and working of various environmental policy instruments such as: command and control, environmental taxes, tradable pollution permits, subsidies, refundable deposits etc.The economists are often not in agreement as to which of the various tools is most effective. To many economists, the problem in using the various tools is basically the problem of choosing the best policy instrument in order to reach the set target. Baumol and Oates suggest the following criteria for a meaningful appraisal of the different pollution control policy instruments.

1. *Dependability*, a test of the reliability of the tool in achieving its objective—whether its effectiveness is automatic or ruled by a number of unpredictable elements.
2. *Permanence* which refers to the length of period during which the policy tool is effective—whether it is effective only so long as there is public concern or is effective even when other issues have captured the attention of the public.
3. *Adaptability to economic growth* questions the flexibility of policy instruments to adjust to normal expansion in economic activities and population growth.
4. *Equity* refers to the fair distribution of the financial burden of the programme among individuals and firms.
5. *Incentives for maximum* effort examines whether the instrument offers adequate incentives to achieve this desired environmental quality.
6. *Economy* relates to therelative costs involved in the use of the various policy tools to improve the quality of the environment. It takes into consideration the issue of achieving the targeted quality in environment at the least cost.
7. Political attractiveness is concerned with the popularity of the policy tool with the legislators and voters.
8. Minimal interference with private decisions requires that the chosen policy instrument should give a choice among different methods to achieve the end and not give specific instruction for reducing pollution.

NO instrument passes all the criteria. A policy that is favourable with regard to some criteria may be unfavourable with regard to others, making the appraisal of a choice very difficult. An attempt is made in this chapter to compare effluent charge and direct regulation on the basis of the above criteria.

29.1 Dependability

One chief weakness in the use of direct control has been the problem of enforcement. Polluters have often been able to avoid or delay, meeting the required standards, by resorting to litigation. Direct controls treat environmentally damaging activities as illegal acts; an environmental tax, on the other hand, considers them as normal consequences of economic activity and hence are to be controlled by procedures that are routine and regular. The use of effluent charge, for example, requires only metering of the level of effluents or emissions. Under direct control on the other hand, the violators of the regulation must be first caught in act, prosecuted and found guilty before he or she is fined. If any of these steps fail, the violators escape from the grip of the regulation. Sometimes the fines under direct control are so low that regulation becomes ineffective.

29.2 Permanence and Adaptability to Growth

The direct controls draws its support from public enthusiasm and hence is effective only so long as there is public concern. But public support changes with time and hence the effectiveness of direct control is transitory. Fiscal incentives on the other hand require no reinforcement once instituted. It is a common belief that "nothing is certain but death and taxes". A tax on a toxic effluent is routine and permanent and exerts a continuous and definite influence on managerial decisions.

This 'permanence' of a polluting tax makes it least adaptable to expansion in economic activity (economic growth) and population growth. Once levied, a tax bill continues in a routine fashion. Hence what was substantial ten years ago, may become relatively modest in the current period, reducing the efficacy of the instrument. But pollution continues to increase with economic activity and population. One way to remove this weakness is to base the tax on the price of the final products the polluters produce so that it will increase with inflation and growth or tradable pollution permits may be used which deals effectively with growth and inflation.

29.3 Equity

Equity, as stated already, refers to the distribution of financial burden among the polluting firms. Apparently direct controls pose to be more equitable than an effluent charge or subsidy but this is merely an illusion. Let us take the example of a regulation that would require all polluters of a particular lake or river to reduce pollution by fifty per cent. The direct control appears to be non-discriminatory since it would require all polluters, irrespective of their cost of controlling pollution, to reduce their discharge by fifty per cent. However, the costs of controlling pollution are not uniform. Some firms are able to control pollution at a lower cost while others find it expensive. Hence requiring such firms with differences in costs of abating pollution, to reduce pollution by the same extent, is far from being equitable. From this perspective, an effluent fee is more equitable than regulatory approach requiring uniform reduction in waste. A tax solution will ensure that those who find it cheaper to reduce pollution will do most of the pollution control while those who find it expensive will do less pollution control. Pollution will be reduced by each firm up to the point at which the effluent charge is equal to the marginal cost of pollution control as shown in the figure 29.1.

Figure 29.1 illustrates two firms A and B, producing the same level of pollution M with different marginal costs of pollution control. Firm A has more favourable marginal abatement costs than firm B. If a tax OT is imposed on the two pollution firms, given their marginal pollution abatement cost curve, firm A will control more pollution than firm B. Firm A will reduce pollution to MP_A and firm

B will reduce pollution to MP_B (where $MP_A + MP_B = MP^*$). If instead both firms are required to reduce pollution to MP, (such that 2MP = MP*) then the extra cost of control to firm B is greater than the reduction in costs of control to firm A (RN > KL). Thus an effluent charge has allocative advantage. However this allocative advantage of a pollution tax is only a part—the less important part of equity issue. The ultimate question in equity issue is "who bears the cost". It is said that a substantial part of the cost is borne by the buyers of the polluter's product, who are either rich or poor. Whether the product of the polluter is consumed more by rich or by poor should be known to make any comparison of the different policy tools on equity issue.

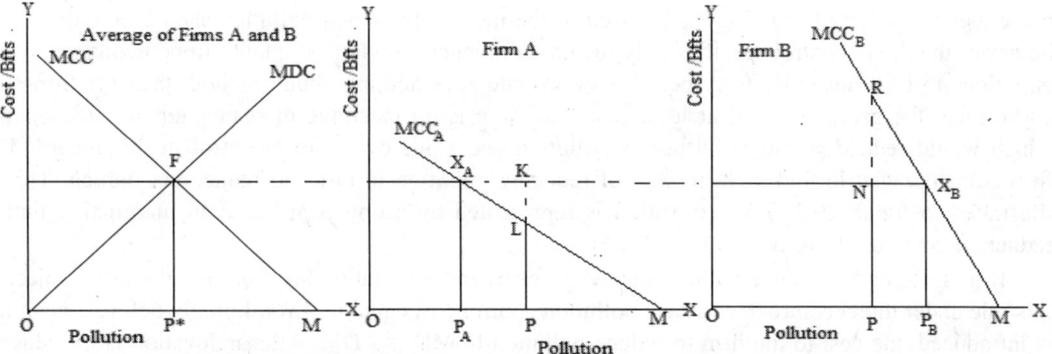

Figure 29.1 Allocative Advantages of a Pollution Tax

29.4 Economy

A pollution tax is said to be more economical and efficient than direct control. The pollution tax achieves environmental goal at the least cost to the society. Taking the example of two firms A and B, which emit the same quantity of effluents initially and the cost of controlling pollution for which are Rupees five per unit and Rupees fifteen per unit respectively, we can show that a pollution tax will achieve reduction of pollution by a given amount at a lower cost than direct control. If each firm is required to reduce pollution by fifty per cent under direct control, then the average cost of pollution control is Rs. 10. But if instead a tax of Rs. 6/unit is levied, entire pollution abatement would be by firm A, since the cost of pollution control for firm A (Rs. 5/unit) is lower than effluent tax. Hence, firm A will control pollution and avoid tax altogether while firm B will pay the tax and maintain its level of discharges. Thus the cost incurred here to control pollution is only Rs. 5/unit.

In terms of figure 29.1, the extra cost to firm B under direct control that requires uniform cut in emissions is RN which is greater than KL which is the reduction in costs of control to firm A when a tax of Rs 6 per unit is imposed and it can be seen that RN > KL. Thus a pollution tax achieves environmental goal at the least cost to the society.

29.5 Inducement to Maximum Effort

The pricing technique offers continuing incentives to the polluter to reduce pollution. Every reduction in pollution, however small it might be, say even by one per cent, reduces tax bill. Under direct control there is no such incentive. If the firm is required to reduce pollution to fifty per cent of pre-control level then a discharge equal to 49.6 per cent is legal while a discharge equal to 51 per cent is declared illegal. Not only is this absurd, it also reduces scope to reduce pollution beyond fifty per cent even if the firm can reduce pollution by a considerable amount with a negligible additional outlay. The firm has no incentive to reduce pollution beyond fifty per cent, however low the additional cost may be.

29.6 Minimal Interference with Private Decision

The pricing technique neither assigns quota nor gives any instruction to the polluting firm about the kind of pollution control technology to be employed. The freedom that firms have in choosing any technology it desires to control pollution, gives greater scope of innovation. Direct regulation on the other hand prescribes standards & technology to be used for pollution control.

29.7 Incentive to Innovate

The direct controls do not offer incentives to innovate in pollution control technology because it prescribes the precise technology to be used or the method by which pollution should be reduced. If, however, the direct control specifies only the environmental standard or quality to be maintained (say, emissions to be reduced by forty per cent or so) and says nothing about method, then the firm may try to meet the given standard at least cost, but there is no incentive to search for new technology which would reduce pollution further. A pollution tax, gains over direct control in this regard. The firm is encouraged to find a cheap way of reducing pollution in order to reduce tax burden. This is illustrated in figure 29.2. The innovation is represented by a downward shift in marginal pollution reduction cost curve, from MPAC to MPAC'.

If it is decided to reduce pollution by MD, (or permit a pollution level of OD),the firm subject to this rule under direct controls, will save pollution control cost equal to AMF. Initially before innovation is introduced, the cost to the firm to reduce pollution to MD is ADM. After innovation is introduced, the cost, incurred to reduce pollution is FDM. Thus the reduction in cost is AMF.

However, under an effluent fee system, a firm will react to the same innovation by increasing its level of control to MG, the efficient level given an effluent fee of E. Before innovation is introduced, expenditure to the firm is MDA plus an effluent tax bill of OEAD. After innovation, the expenditure to the firm is MGH plus an effluent tax bill of OEGH. The pollution control cost in the case of a pollution tax is MGH. It can be seen in figure 29.2 that the area MGH excludes AFM of the cost incurred before innovation but has an additional area GDHF. The area FDM is a cost component in both the situations - before and after innovation. At the same time there is a decrease in the tax bill, which is equal to HGDA. Deduction of GDHF (increase in cost after innovation) from HGDA (reduction in tax bill after innovation) gives the difference HAF. Already MFA is reduction in cost after innovation. Adding reductions in cost and tax bill after innovation we get AFH + AFM = AMFH or AMH. Thus as a result of innovation there is a total savings of AMH and it is clear that the savings from a given innovation are greater under effluent fee than under regulation (AMH > AMF). Also under the effluent fee, more pollution is reduced MG > MD.

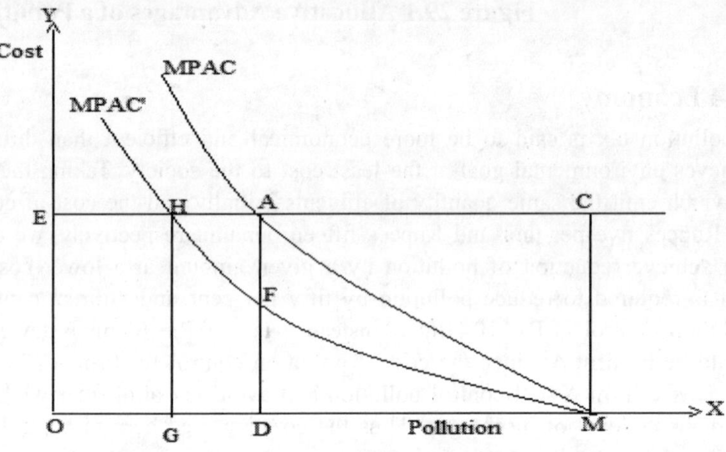

Figure 29.2 The Incentive to Innovate of a Pollution Tax

29.8 Political Acceptability

Pollution taxes bring revenue to the treasury while at the same time maintaining quality of life. This is more than enough to make it politically acceptable, particularly in the context of growing fiscal pressures and the huge investment costs to be incurred to control pollution. However, on the basis of the above arguments one should not be misled to believe that effluent fee is a foolproof system. Martindale (1976) has pointed out, four major disadvantages of a pollution tax: complexity, uncertainty, insensitivity and expense.

A pollution tax according to Martindale, cannot be effective in dealing with emissions from complex industrial process. It cannot deal with cases requiring variety of standards operating in different locations for different pollutants. The more complex and flexible the requirements of pollution controls are, the less appropriate a pollution tax is.

29.9 Uncertainty

The magnitude of the effects of a pollution tax is uncertain. Whether the pollution tax will achieve the desired environmental quality is doubtful. Even if it is known, raising the tax rate (in case it is inadequate) to meet the desired level of environmental quality will take time.

A more serious difficulty in applying a tax for pollution control is with reference to the inflexibility and insensitivity of the pollution tax. A given level of emissions is frequently more harmful in one location than in another. Similarly air pollutants from a factory may be more dangerous to community, if the factory is located on the windward side of the town. Inflexibility of tax rates over time can also be highly disadvantageous. A given emission may cause more damage at some times than another. Damage from effluents discharged into a river will pose greater threats during drought, since the capability of the river to absorb and disperse pollution is low during a period of drought. If the tax rate is raised sufficiently high to deal with such differences, it may become costlier and restrictive during normal periods. Some economists have suggested peak-load pricing to avoid this insensitivity. Under peak-load pricing, it is suggested that effluents that reduce dissolved oxygen may be subject to a higher tax rate during summer, giving allowance for the river's lower absorption capacity and to a lower rate during winter.

A pollution tax is said to be ineffective during inflationary periods and population growth (already noted). To avoid these the pollution tax will have to be revised regularly. The main disadvantage arising with a pollution tax is the monitoring and measurement of level of emissions/ effluents. In many cases the costs of monitoring and administrative costs exceed that of a standards/enforcement system. Common (1977) suggested a tax on inputs rather than on emissions to overcome this problem. He suggested that a tax on sulphur content of the oil will effectively reduce sulphur dioxide emissions. Such a tax will encourage substitution of cleaner inputs in the place of sulphur which will decrease SO_2 emissions.

Firms still are opposed to taxes because it is not easily escaped once enacted, whereas direct control offers scope for violation. James Buchanan and Gordon Tullock point out that the opposition to taxes from the business community may be because of the reduction in profits, it brings about, whereas direct control may even increase profitability. The direct controls by imposing output restriction and preventing entry of new firms into polluting industries to reduce pollution, may result in rise in prices and profits.

A pollution tax is said to be actually more expensive to a discharger than a standards/enforcement system. This is illustrated in figure 29.3.

The MPAC curve in the figure is the marginal pollution control cost curve. It slopes upwards right to left, from point B. It begins at the level of pollution that would exist if there was no control–OB. As control increases and pollution is reduced, MPAC increases at an increasing rate as higher levels of control are reached. If it is decided to reduce pollution to OD, (by BD) then an effluent charge of OE (AD) will be the efficient rate. With this effluent charge the total cost to the polluting firm to control pollution will be areas (1) (2) in the figure. This includes a tax bill of OEAD + a control cost of ABD. Under the regulatory approach on the other hand, with a pollution level set at OD, the firm will incur a cost of ABD represented by area (1). Thus an effluent tax generates more expense for the polluter than does an equivalent regulation. Nevertheless it is said that if the pollution tax is equivalent to the external costs of pollution, then the increased price reflects the true cost of production. The tax is said to internalise the externality and is hence supported. Also implementation of regulation is weak and insufficient in many countries. Further it is argued that the firm actually reduces its total tax liability by incurring control cost. In the absence of any control activity the firm's tax bill will be areas (1), (2) and (3), that is OECB. By exercising its option to control and pay tax for the uncontrolled pollution the firm saves ABC or area marked (3) in figure 29.3. Hence Tax on pollution is economical for the firm when it controls pollution.

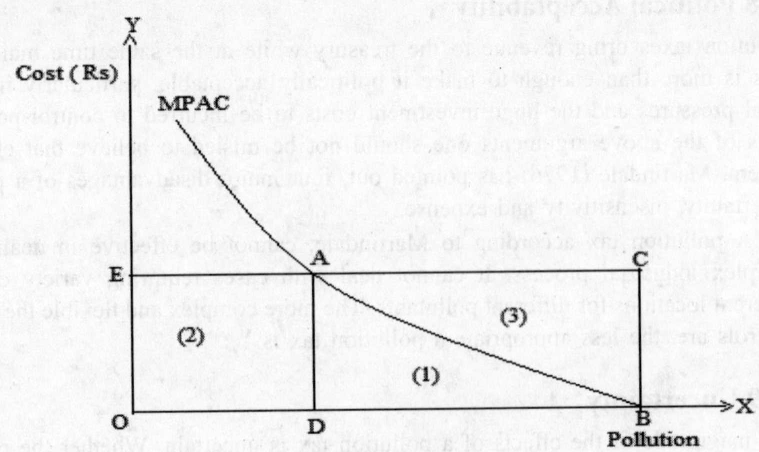

Figure 29.3 Relative Expenses to a Polluter under a Pollution Tax and Regulation

Conclusion

The case for and against pollution tax and a comparison of it with direct control is a complex one. There is no perfect instrument and there is no obvious choice among the different instruments of pollution control. The advantages and disadvantages of each of these depend on the type of pollutant, number and size of polluters, identification of source of pollution, cost and ease of measuring pollution and enforcement costs. To choose the appropriate policy mix we should consider efficiency, practicality and political acceptability. Obviously there are trade-offs involved and a compromise is inevitable.

Question

Compare a pollution tax with command and control.

Exercise

Take the case of a country where both regulation and MBIs are effectively used and analyse their complementarity.

30

ENVIRONMENTAL PROTECTION – VOLUNTARY PARTICIPATION

"People everywhere are offended by pollution. They sense intuitively that we have pressed beyond limits we should not have exceeded. They want to clean up the world, make it a better place, be good trustees of the earth for future generations."

—*James GustaveSpeth*

Voluntary Participation includes such policies as moral suasion which involves the community in environmentally friendly pursuits, voluntary agreements, the information provision and product labeling. These measures are many times successful in achieving a specific environmental objective where regulation or economic instruments are inadequate.

30.1 Moral Suasion

Moral suasion or voluntarism by the people is based on the belief that ultimately nature will be protected from man, when and only when, the public realise their moral responsibilities towards nature. Voluntary trash recycling programmes, voluntary use of unleaded and low lead gasoline, sale of auto emission control kits, energy saving programmes are some of the popular voluntary programmes. Moral suasion is non-mandatory investment in pollution control equipment by firms that decide to act in a manner that meets their social responsibilities. Voluntaristic response is the basis for car-pooling programmes, garbage/trash disposal programmes etc. However, the success of these programmes to control pollution is to a great extent influenced by strength of the population willing to participate in such programmes. It is said that only around five per cent of the population are reliable group of citizens whose conscience move them to participate in voluntarily programmes. Hence where the problem of pollution is high and substantial improvement in environmental quality is posing a problem, direct controls and price incentives are more effective and reliable. Voluntarism is mostly ineffective in cases of reducing pollution from industries. The firms that cause pollution seldom come forward voluntarily to either install a pollution control equipment or treat its discharges before releasing them. This is because of the pressure of competition they face. Every firm is constantly trying to not only produce at least cost but to prevent its cost from exceeding those of its rivals. Under such circumstances, voluntary steps to cut back emissions will only add to its cost. Even if a morally and socially responsible firm was to consider such a move, namely, install an expensive equipment that would reduce emissions, it would not do so, as along as even one of its rival firms was going to continue business without emission control. A firm, willing to take such a risk will soon find itself driven out of business.

It is pointed out that the reports by firms of their growing accomplishments in pollution control activities, is in reality an exaggeration of the actual magnitudes of achievements. Some firms are also said to be using voluntarism as a diversionary tactics. In order to avoid an effluent charge or the restrictions that direct controls may impose, firms are often found, supporting voluntary programmes like voluntary recycling etc. Despite these limitations, voluntary programmes have useful roles.

Firstly, where the fiscal processes of a country fails to generate enough funds for the maintenance of environmental quality, voluntary programmes can be relied upon. This is the state in majority of the low income and lower-middle income group countries, where public activities like schools and hospitals are subject to under financing to such an extent that financing of environmental protection is assigned the lowest priority. In such countries the community may be forced to rely on voluntary personnel to carry out environmental cleanup programmes.

Secondly, voluntarism can be helpful in instances where the activities that damage the environment have to be detected and monitored i.e., where polluters have to be identified and level of pollution has to be metered. Both direct controls and effluent charge require detection and monitoring of the activities that cause damage, to the environment. If we do not know how much waste a plant discharges into a waterway, we cannot determine, how much it should be taxed or even whether there has been a violation of the legal standards underlying a programme of direct controls. There are instances where any systematic surveillance is extremely difficult. An example is the littering by picnickers and campers in a picnic spot. The isolation and dispersion of these persons and the unpredictability of their movements make policing difficult; Here only two solutions exist:

a. an appeal to the conscience of the people who visit such places. Today we see several 'litter free zones' in the city in places frequented by people with appeals 'not to litter'.
b. imposition of disproportionately heavy penalties upon a few people who happen to be caught is an example to others is indeed found to be an efficient solution but many people consider it as totally unfair.

Hence in cases where policing is difficult, voluntarism appears to be the only acceptable alternative.

A third and potentially important role for voluntary measures arises when there are sudden and unexpected episodes of pollution perhaps due to a gasleak or so. A sudden and unexpected atmospheric inversion over a city that aggravates the pollution to life threatening levels requires instantaneous remedial measures. Relying on the government alone during such periods of emergency will delay action and aggravate the situation. In such brief but serious emergencies where there had been no advance preparation, and when there is no time to plan and enact a systematic programme, there is no better substitute for voluntary compliance. During such episodes in which dangerous concentrations of pollutants are involved, the authorities appeal to the public to avoid activities that would aggravate the problem. The role played by the voluntary groups during Bhopal tragedy in relief works is a are clear evidence to this merit of voluntary programmes.

Moral suasion, has an important role to play in the protection of environmental quality particularly in brief unexpected emergencies or where effective surveillance is impossible.

30.2 Voluntary Agreements

One of the |most striking developments in environmental policy area, of the 1990s is the "voluntary Agreements " to pollution abatement. In this approach firms make commitments to improve their environmental performance beyond legal requirements. Börkey et al classify voluntary agreements into four categories. These are:

1. **Unilateral Commitments** set by the industry acting independently without any involvement of a public authority. They are emissions reduction agreements among firms, with no involvement from government. One example of such a unilateral arrangement is the Responsible Care

initiative undertaken by the Canadian Chemical Producers' Association in response to the threat of more stringent regulations. Decline in public confidence in the chemical industry is also a reason for the Responsible Care scheme. The programme aimed at improving the firm's performance in safety and environmental protection through appropriate rules. Over seventy companies have agreed to it. The participating firms agreed to submit their plants to regular verification of compliance by an external committee which comprised of industry experts and community representatives. The results of this verification are made public.However a study by King and Lenox (2000) observed that Responsible Care "was essentially a form of greenwash, distracting regulators from passing new legislation while allowing members to get away with worse performance than otherwise". In 2013 Gamper-Ravindran and Finger endorsed the findings of King and Lenox after a more sophisticated research. ISO 14001 is sometimes considered as an industry self-regulation programme.

2. **Negotiated Agreements** involve commitments of environmental protection developed through bargaining between a public authority and industry. They are frequently signed at the national level between an industry sector and a public authority, although agreements with individual firms are also possible. Negotiated agreements have been used extensively in the Netherlands, Germany, and Japan. Among developing countries Negotiated Agreements are popular in Chile, Columbia and Mexico.
3. **Public Voluntary Programmes** in which participating firms agree to standards that have been developed by public bodies such as environmental agencies. This programme invites firms to set goals and undertake abatement efforts, in exchange for technical assistance, an opportunity to share information with fellow participants, and public recognition. Examples are the US program 33/50 and the Eco-Audit and Auditing Scheme (EMAS) implemented by the European Union. However PVPs are criticized for 'slowing the passage of more meaningful mandatory regulations by creating an illusion of environmental progress' (Lyon, 2013).
4. Private agreements reached through direct bargaining between stakeholders; polluters and pollutes. They are contracts between a firm (or group of firms) and victims of pollution by these firms. The contract stipulates the undertaking of an environmental managementprogramme and/or the setting of a pollution control equipment. An example is the Swedish "6E model" (Ecology, Emissions, Efficiency, Economy, Energy and Ergonomics). The 6E model aimed at improving both the external and working environment.

Voluntary approaches may be developed by single firms as well as by coalitions of firms. For example, many large firms in OECD countries have developed a company environmental plan where they commit to go beyond compliance of laws governing waste recycling, and energy and material consumption.

Voluntary agreements may take place at local, national , regional or global level. In Japan there are about 30 000 local negotiated agreements. An example of a global Voluntary Agreement programme is the agreement signed between the International Federation of Building and Wood Workers and IKEA which concerns working conditions, the natural environment and health and safety for workers at enterprises throughout the world that manufacture and supply goods for the Swedish company. It covers almost one million employees in 70 countries (Webb and Morrison, 1999).

Agreements could be binding or non-binding . Agreements are binding if sanctions in the case of non compliance are specified, which may be enforced through law. Binding agreements are hence more effective. Non-binding agreements do not provide for sanctions in the case of non-compliance with conditions specified in the agreement. If environmental targets are specified by the party (parties) to the agreement, the voluntary approach is target based. On the other hand if the parties to the agreement agree to comply with and implement select targets set by the regulation processes of the government, the approach is implementation based. Whatever be the type of the voluntary agreement, all voluntary approaches are essentially non –legislative commitments for pollution control. Firms are not compelled to be a part of voluntary agreement. Even though the immediate effects of voluntary agreements have not been promising, they are considered useful when other instruments are not effective in controlling pollution.

30.3 Information Disclosure

Environmental information disclosure empowers the civil societies to monitor both the government environmental agency and polluters. It allows enterprises to understand their environmental performance through reporting and disclosing to the public and thus take action to improve it. Active information disclosure refers to any information released by the government to the public as required by legislation; and passive disclosure refers to any information released upon the request of the public.

The U.S. Toxic Release Inventory program of 1988 is first information disclosure programme. Among the developing countries, the first large scale programme of public disclosure of information on polluting firms is Indonesia's Programme for Pollution Control Evaluation and Rating referred to as PROPER.

Indonesia's Programme for Pollution Control Evaluation and Rating referred to as PROPER

During the 90s Indonesia witnessed impressive growth rates and was one of the miracle economies of Asia. Industrial production, income and employment generation and poverty reduction were impressive. The manufacturing sector boom benefited millions of Indonesians in terms of income and employment but caused severe pollution problems and natural resource degradation. The government realized that the manufacturing sector needed strong incentive based policies to persuade them to control pollution. The limited scope and lack of resources of the Ministry for Population and the Environment (MoPE) made it clear that it was time to move from advocacy to accountability.

In the early 1990's industrial pollution accounted for 25 per cent to 50 per cent of the total pollution load in the rivers of Java, Indonesia's main island. The pollution load of the rivers posed serious health problems for the population and was a threat to the coral reef diversity of the island. As a result environmental activism became strong and created pressure for the government. This compelled the Malaysian Government to create an environmental agency for enforcing regulations on behalf of the government and thus the National Environmental Impact and Management Agency (BAPEDAL) was established in November 1990. In June 1995, the Ministry of Environment, Government of Indonesia launched the Program for Pollution Control, Evaluation and Rating - PROPER - as a motivating force for environmental improvement. It used public disclosure, environmental awards and reputational incentives for motivating the manufacturing firms to be more environmentally conscious. PROPER rates factories on the basis their compliance with national standards for waste water discharge. The Public are informed about the ratings through the media. The program's objective is to:

- promote and enforce compliance with pollution control standards,
- encourage pollution reduction, introduce the concept of "clean technology
- promote an environmental management system through the use of incentives and transparency.

The introduction of the PROPER program marked the beginning of the "third wave" in environmental protection in the developing world.

PROPER scheme targeted major industrial water polluters and evaluated the efforts of company's environmental regulations relating to water pollution control. It ranked participating companies interms of a five-color code, in which each participating company was assigned a color according to its environmental status. The five colours and the performance of the companies is given in Table 30.1.

Table 30.1 Ranking Codes of PROPER

Colour	Rank
Gold	Best
Green	Excellent
Blue	Good
Red	Unsatisfactory
Black	Worst

Thus companies with no pollution control effort were marked black and firms that met international standards of environmental excellence were ranked gold . Major polluters of the rivers were chosen first for ranking. In June1995, 187 plants were informed of their ranking and told that their rank would be made public in December 1995. New companies were gradually added to the programme. In July 1997, 270 companies were covered by the programme. Of the 270, none qualified for gold, 14 companies with excellent performance qualified for green. While 135 companies which just met regulations were given blue, performance of 116 companies was unsatisfactory and 5 companies the worst performance came under the code Black. Though participation was compulsory for the major polluters selected by the programme administrators, companies could also volunteer to be included. An increase in the overall compliance with the effluent standard from 33% to 50% was reported within the first few years. Due to the Asian financial crisis in 1997 there was a set- back in the application of PROPER and the PROPER programme became inactive from 1997 to 2001. However the programme was reinstated in 2002 with the passing of two important Ministerial Decrees with greater level of institutionalization'. By 2010 the total number of companies in the program reached 690. (S.Afrah, H. Garcia & Thomas Sterner, 2011)

30.4 Product Labelling /Ecolabelling

Product labeling is a declaration of environmental performance of the product. It is more popularly known as ecolabelling. It refers to a label which identifies overall environmental preference of a product based on life-cycle considerations. The eco-label is granted by an independent third party, not influenced by the company which seeks certification. Ecolabels inform us about the environmental impacts from producing or using a product. They help in greening consumer's purchase decisions. There are many different labelling programs, run by governments, private companies and non-governmental organisations. Ecolabels are also often differentiated on the basis of the organisation issuing the label. Ecolabels are discussed in detail chapter 35.

30.5 Certification

Environmental certification is a systematic framework to manage the immediate and long term environmental impacts of a firm's products, services and processes. ISO 14000 series is a voluntary approach to environmental regulation. This most popular certification is done by the International Standards Organisation at Geneva. Environmental certification by ISO is a series of certification referred to as ISO 14000. The ISO 14000 family of standards provides practical tools for companies and organizations of all kinds looking to manage their environmental responsibilities such as:

- minimise their environmental footprint
- diminish the risk of pollution incidents
- provides operational improvements
- ensure compliance with relevant environmental legislation, and
- develop their business in a sustainable manner

The current version of ISO 14001 is ISO 14001:2015 which was published in September 2015. There are more than 300,000 certifications to ISO 14001 in more than 170 countries around the world.

Any company or firm applying for ISO14000 certification must first put in practice Environmental Management Standard (EMS) which according to ISO is a "part of the overall management system, that includes organizational structure, planning activities, responsibilities, practices, procedures, processes, and resources for developing, implementing, achieving, and maintaining the environmental policy"

ISO 14001 sets out the criteria for an EMS. According to ISO 14000 note on Environmental Management, ISO 14000 does not state requirements for environmental performance, but provides a framework that a company or organization can follow to set up an effective EMS. ISO 14001 assures the company management and employees as well as external stakeholders that environmental impact is being measured and improved.

Chapter 35 discusses environmental certification in detail.

Conclusion

Exclusive reliance on voluntary initiatives is insufficient to achieve an acceptable level of industry-wide compliance. The results of a KPMG Ethics survey of 1000 corporations show that that 58% of those who said they had a code did not have anyone designated to be responsible for ethics within the company.

Yet it is true that voluntary approaches are reflection of good citizenship. All stake holders must account for environmental issues. Industries, firms, public agencies, and individuals are part of the problem. Hence it makes sense to include all of them as part of the solution and encourage environmentally conscious citizens. Certainly voluntary approaches are not substitutes for other instruments. They should be seen as complements to the policy and regulatory frameworks.

Questions

1. Bringout the role of voluntarisn by firms in environmental protection.

Exercise

Prepare a detailed study on the PROPER scheme.

SECTION 7

COST - BENEFIT ANALISIS

31

COST BENEFIT ANALYSIS –AN INTRODUCTION

"As the carpet of increased choice is being unrolled before us by the foot, it is simultaneously being rolled up behind us by the yard."

—*E J. Mishan*

Cost benefit analysis is the systematic appraisal of all benefits and all costs of a contemplated course of action in comparison with alternative courses of action. It is a technique which has developed over last two decades in order to provide information for social decision making. It is based on the criterion that all the costs and benefits of a particular action should be considered, to whomsoever in society they may accrue. It differs in this respect from financial appraisal techniques, which take into account only those costs and benefits falling on the decision-makers. Cost-benefit analysis, is usually a tool of the Government, rather than of the individual person or firm, since the latter are influenced in their decision only by cost and benefits affecting them directly. In sum, it is a social decision-making machinery, involving an attempt to evaluate all the major costs and benefits arising from a contemplated course of action. Cost Benefit Analysis (CBA) brings greater objectivity into the decision making.

CBA is used to assess efficiency of projects, programs and policies worldwide. It is widely applied in protecting environmental resources. CBA is applied whenever and wherever any proposed action involves environmentally adverse impacts such as construction of huge dams, clearing forests for highways, power projects with environmental side effects etc.

31.1 Steps in Cost Benefit Analysis

The benefit-cost criterion to undertake a given course of action is that the additional benefits to be derived from taking the action should exceed the corresponding additional costs. In simpler terms, this criterion means that a course of action be undertaken only if the sum of all the expected advantages outweighs the sum of all the expected disadvantages. The undertaking of a cost-benefit study can be divided into a number of steps.

The **first step** relates to the identification of the alternatives to be assessed and this may involve either the undertaking of a 'project' or no action at all; or a choice between different projects. Should the project be undertaken or not? The answer to the question is:

Proceed if $E(B) > E(C)$. Do not proceed if $E(B) < E(C)$

That is, if the present value of the expected benefits exceed expected costs then the project may be undertaken. If costs exceed benefits then the project is to be rejected. In this stage it is also important to identify who are likely to be affected by the policy and the relevant time period.

The **second step** concerns the optimal scale of the policy or project. If the project consists of building a dam, CBA can say something about whether it should be a small or medium or large dam. If what is to be evaluated is a policy of improving environmental quality, then CBA will help in identifying the optimal or desirable level of environmental quality. Optimal scale is given by the equality of the marginal social benefits to the marginal costs of the project. It must be determined if it is a single government project which will undergo CBA, or are there several competing projects. If the policy evaluated has no alternative, and is a statutory obligation, *i.e.* adoption of the policy or programme is required by law (mandatory) then no CBA is required. But if the under taking of the project is questioned, then CBA is done to prove that benefits outweigh the cost.

If there are several competing alternate projects then all the competing projects must be identified. CBA helps in identifying the project with the highest net benefit. For example if there are three mutually exclusive projects that cost the same, they are evaluated with reference to a benchmark, which normally is the current situation. If the three projects cost the same, the one with the highest net benefits will be chosen.

Third step is the identification of all the impacts.

Fourth step is the prediction of all the consequences – both, positive and negative - associated with the project. Consequences from alternatives should also be assessed. For example, in the case of a proposal for the construction of a dam, the benefits of irrigation facilities it creates should be weighed against the direct financial costs to construct the dam and the costs in terms of deforestation and displacement of people that the dam is likely to create.

The **fifth** step involves the task of establishing or attributing values for the costs and benefits at the time they occur. The cost and benefits of the project must be expressed in money terms.

Discounting the benefits and costs is the **sixth** step. The costs and benefits of the project when it is implemented must be discounted to reflect their present value. Discounting is the opposite of compounding interest on an investment. Discounting facilitates inter-temporal comparisons, when costs and benefits occur at different points in time. The basic idea is that, future costs and benefits are worth less today. A benefit is more valuable in the present than in future. Hence future benefits must be discounted to arrive at their present value. Discounting is based on the observation that people's preference for present is more than that of the future. For example Rs100 received today is worth more than Rs100 received next year. If Rs 100 is deposited in the bank today at 5% interest , it will grow to Rs105 next year. This means that in order to get Rs100 next year one should deposit Rs 95 today. Therefore the present value of Rs 100 available next year at 5% discount rate is Rs 95 today. Larger the discount rate, the smaller is the present value if time interval is also longer. This hold true of costs also. All future costs and benefits should be discounted to reflect their present values.

CBA makes recommendations based on the Net Present Value (NPV). NPV is the sum of the present value of the benefits minus the sum of present value of the costs. : if the discounted benefits are greater than discounted costs the policy or project should be accepted. In other words, if NPV > 0, the project should be accepted.

Seventh step of a cost-benefit analysis is applying the sensitivity analysis to deal with uncertainty. This involves recalculating NPV by changing values of select parameters and find out for which value of these parameters NPV is very sensitive. This exercise yields different answers which may be used to answer questions related to uncertainty.

The **eighth** and the final step is the presentation of the information synthesized in the earlier steps with recommendation for the project with highest rate of return.

31.2 Theoretical foundation of Cost Benefit Analysis

Cost Benefit Analysis is firmly based on concepts in welfare economics such as Pareto Efficiency, Pareto improvement, Kaldor –Hicks Compensation Criterion, Consumer's surplus and Producer's surplus. These are discussed in detail in this book in Chapters 16, 18 and 19 in Section 4 which explain Welfare Economics.

The concept of highest net present value in a CBA is explained through the use of two concepts of consumers surplus – willingness to pay (WTP) and willingness to accept (WTA).

The concept of consumer's surplus, explained interms of willingness to pay and willingness to accept, is used in evaluating consumer's preferences and benefits. The concepts of WTP and WTA are nothing but Hicksian compensating and equivalent variations measures of consumer's surplus.

CBA makes recommendations based on **economic surplus or net economic benefits** generated by a *project.* If the economic surplus is measured in terms of money, WTP is the measure of benefit. This implies that the benefit to an individual is measured by the maximum sum of money that the individual is willing to pay in return for the benefit. Similarly, WTA is the minimum amount of money that the individual would be willing to accept as compensation for the cost incurred to him.

Robert Sugden defines Economic surplus as the surplus that results whenever a person pays less than her WTP for the benefit she receives and/ or when she is paid more than her WTA as compensation when sheincurs a cost.The difference between actual payment and WTP, or between WTA and actual compensation is termed as surplus. The focus of a CBA is the *total* economic surplus generated, i.e. the net sum of the surpluses generated for all individuals. CBA approves a project if and only if they generate positive net surplus.

Pareto efficiency is defined as a situation where it is no more possible to make anyone individual better off without making another individual worse off. This is a difficult condition to be achieved in the real world; yet theoretically it is the best defining condition for allocative efficiency. Cost benefit analysis is based on the concept of efficiency for arriving at its recommendations for decision making.

The concept of **Paretian improvement** refers to situations where a policy change improves some people's welfare without making anyone else worse off. Paretion improvement is a social desirable outcome but it is difficult to be achieved in the real world situation. Hence Kaldor and Hicks suggested that a change is considered to be socially beneficial if the gainers from the policy could compensate the losers and enjoy benefits after such a compensation. In the Kaldor –Hicks criterion gainers need not actually compensate the losers, but it is enough if they are able to compensate.

Any public policy or programme will have favorable effects on some people and unfavorable effects on others, i.e., there are both beneficiaries and losers for any and every government policy or programme. Cost benefit analysis would recommend the policy if benefits are greater than costs (B> C). This implies that the economic surplus permits gainers to compensate the losers. Compensation of losers by gainers potentially is possible. This is potential Pareto improvement situation.

If actual compensation is made then the criterion becomes Pareto improvement criterion. Hence Kaldor Hicks criterion explains that it must be at least theoretically possible to compensate the losers who had to sacrifice something and still make someone better off when the policy is implemented. The concept of net present value implies the same. Cost benefit analysis suggests that only policies that have positive net present benefits are to be adopted.

The welfare economic foundations of a CBA are thus well established through the concepts of Paretian efficiency, welfare improvement criteria and in the measures of consumer's surplus.

31.3 Rules of CBA

The objective of CBA is to achieve maximum economic efficiency which requires that B> C.

The most basic criterion for accepting a project compares costs and benefits to ensure that the net present value (NPV) of benefits is positive:

$$NPV = \sum_{t=0}^{T} (B_t - C_t)/(1 + r)^t$$

where Bt and Ct are the benefits and costs in year t, r is the discount rate, and T is the time horizon.

Two simple rules govern the choice of projects using CBA.

Rule 1: If there is no budget constraint or any other constraint, adopt all projects that have positive net benefits (i.e., NPV).

Rule 2: If there are constraints which limit the number of projects you can choose; then choose the combination of projects that maximizes net benefits (i.e., NPV).

Corollary of these rules is: never adopt a project with negative net benefits.

Additional guidelines

In the single project choice situation, adopt the project if the NPV > 0. If NPV is negative, reject the project. If the situation is choosing one project from a number of mutually exclusive alternatives, then choose that project in which net benefits are maximum.

Choice of appropriate scale

If the situation requires the choice of an appropriate scale of operation of the project on hand, then economic theory suggests that marginal rules must be applied.

The project may be continued until MC=MB at which point net benefits are maximized. For example if the project on hand is environmental improvement through pollution reduction then reduce pollution up to the point where marginal cost of pollution reduction is equal to the marginal benefit from pollution reduction. Benefit cost ratio (B/C) is often used to compare mutually exclusive projects and those projects where B/C > 1 are adopted.

Other Criteria Used in CBA

CBA uses few other criteria for project selection or rejection. Two such criteria are:

- Internal Rate of Return Criterion and (IRR)
- Benefit Cost Ratio Criterion (BCR)

Internal Rate of Return is the rate of discount which reduces NPV to zero. If IRR > rate of discount, the project is acceptable, since if IRR > r, NPV > 0. According to this criterion.

$$NPV = \sum_{t=0}^{T} (B_t - C_t)/(1 + IRR)^t = 0$$

In the Benefit /Cost ratio, if B/C >1, NPV is greater than one then the project is to be accepted. Each of these criteria has both merits and limitations. However NPV is the most popular and commonly used criterion.

31.4 A Simple Cost Benefit Analysis

Cost benefit analysis helps us to compare the benefits (which represent demand) with cost (which represent supply). To justify the expenditure of scarce resources on improvements in environmental quality, it is necessary to show that the improvements in environmental quality are more valuable than the goods and services foregone, when resources are spent to control pollution rather than produce goods and services.

A very simple illustration of a benefit—cost analysis in this section involves the marginal benefit = marginal cost (MB = MC) principle to decide on the appropriate level of improvement in environmental quality by reducing pollution. It is assumed for simplicity that Marginal Control Cost (MCC) is constant. That is, it is assumed that each additional rupee spent on the programme results in one more unit of output of pollution abatement, i.e., if the first rupee spent helps in removing four per cent of the pollution, then every rupee spent on pollution control will remove four per cent of pollution. Assuming further that the Government has full knowledge of the exact quantitative dimensions of costs and benefits, the efficient level of pollution control is OB in the figure 31.1.

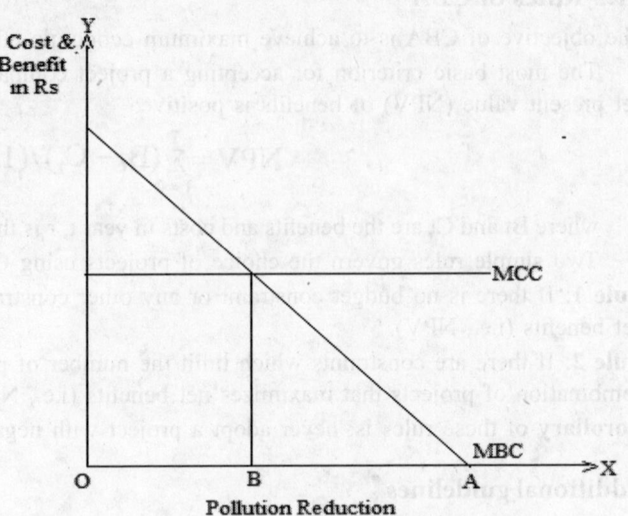

Figure 31.1 Efficient Level of Pollution Reduction

In Figure 31.1, on the X axis is measured levels of pollution reduction. As we move from origin to A level of pollution decreases since pollution reduction increases. At A, pollution is zero. On the Y axis is measured costs for and benefits from removal of pollution in Rupees.

The MBC schedule which reflects the marginal benefit from control of pollution is downward sloping indicating that the first few units of pollution removed are more significant to the public than the subsequent reductions in pollution. This assumption is plausible in that the reduction of first few units of pollution lessen health hazards while, the removal of last units would only mean reductions in annoyance and increments in aesthetic values. MBC is the demand curve for less pollution because it represents the sum of the amounts each household is willing to pay to remove an additional unit of pollutant at a particular level of

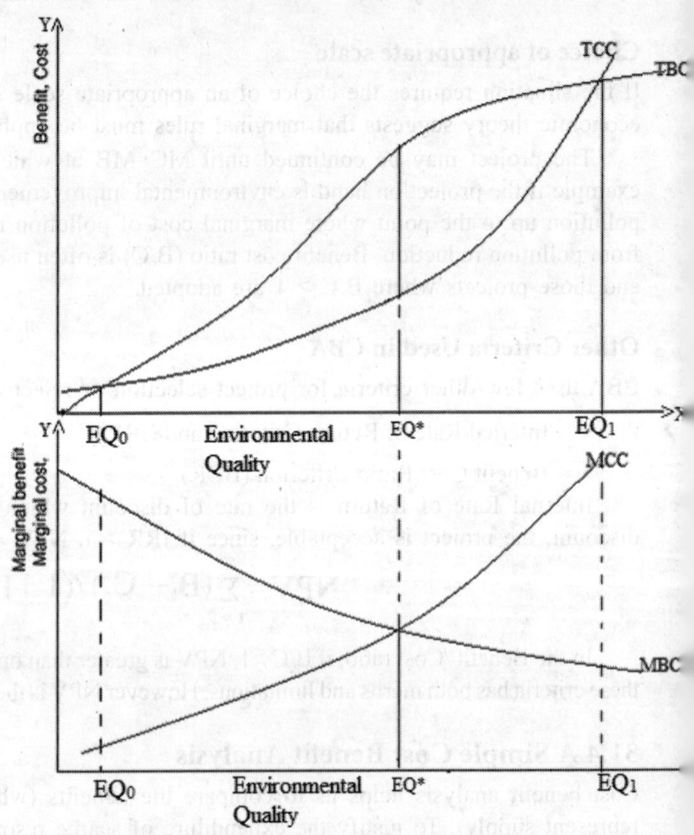

Figure 31.2 Efficient Level of Environmental Quality

concentration of the pollutant and this amount declines with the removal of every additional unit of pollution.

The efficient or optimal level of output (pollution reduction) is OB at which MBC = MCC. At levels of output below OB, i.e., removal of pollution below OB, MBC> MCC for reductions beyond OB, MCC > MBC. Hence the efficient level of reduction in pollution is OB. Clearly OA, representing zero pollution is not possible and economical because the opportunity cost of resources employed in pollution abatement is higher than benefits of pollution removed.

The assumption of constant marginal cost should be relaxed for a more realistic and complete analysis of an efficient level of pollution control. This would mean a rising MCC as shown in figure 31.2 where environmental quality (and not levels of pollution) is measured on the X axis. Once we allow MCC to rise, the analysis has to be modified.

In the figure 31.2 TCC and MCC reflect the costs of controlling emissions and improving environmental quality. Two criteria may be used to find the efficient level of environmental quality. First TBC must be greater than TCC. This would mean any environmental quality between EQ_0 and EQ_1. To find out the unique solution, a second condition should be satisfied: namely MBC = MCC. That is slope of TBC (which is MBC) is equal to the slope of TCC (which is equal to MCC). This occurs where MBC and MCC intersect. In Figure 31.2 this is shown by the environmental quality level EQ*.To the left of EQ*, MBC > MCC.To the right of EQ*, MCC > MBC.An alternative approach to evaluate a project is to consider equality of TBC and TCC. This is equivalent to having a benefit cost ratio of one to one. In many public debates people assume that a benefit cost ratio of one to one is the correct criterion. This means equality of TBC to TCC which in our diagrams points to two levels of environmental quality, EQ_0 and EQ_1. But we have already seen that both EQ_0 and EQ_1, are inefficient since in the former MBC > MCC and in the latter MCC > MBC.

31. 5 Limitations of Cost Benefit Analysis

CBA is a useful technique for the evaluation of projects where market information is either deficient or absent. However there are several objections to the use of CBA for assessing environmental impacts.

1. Problems in attaching valuations to costs and benefits: Some costs have a significant impact on the environment and some are likely to change over time. The value attached to the any particular specie is very significant for some and nothing for some others. Benefits from certain projects are felt by generations much away from the time of implementation. Such costs and benefits are not included or given adequate coverage in a CBA.
2. The CBA may not cover everyone affected. There may be positive and negative third party effects (externalities) which are likely to be omitted in a CBA.
3. CBA gives priority to efficient decision making but ignores the equity aspect. Often the beneficiaries (gainers) of a project are different from the victims (losers) of the project. Since only potential compensation of losers by the gainers is considered by the CBA, the equity issue is ignored and therefore questioned.
4. Measuring benefits poses a very big challenge in a CBA, particularly, when it is with respect to placing a value on environmental assets and ecosystem services. Similarly valuing human life when the CBA is applied to health projects is a serious challenge. Additionally evaluation of benefits using Willingness to pay method makes CBA very subjective.
5. Measurement errors such as those related to discounting in the case of future cost and benefits, measuring indirect impacts are serious issues in a CBA. The use of discounting underestimates future harms and the irreversibility of environmental problems

6. Omission of certain costs and benefits which are not directly and immediately felt and double counting of certain costs and benefits pose the problem of under estimation of costs and overvaluation of net benefits.

Scott Farrow and Michael Toman (1999) list some of the most important recommendations for doing aeffective and meaningful cost benefit analysis. These include the following:

- A clear statement of the problem to be addressed by regulation.
- A logical and consistent definition of baseline conditions.
- Identification and at least some assessment of a range of alternatives, not just one preferred or "mandatory" alternative.
- Providing information on the real "drivers" of benefits and costs in their natural units of measurement such as: sickness cases avoided, recreational visits, tons of pollution emitted, etc.
- Treatment of benefits and costs with attention to direct and indirect effects and monetization of benefits and costs to the greatest extent possible using consistent valuation rules.
- Incidence of benefits and costs must be viewed in the light of their implications for equity concerns.
- Evidence that data used in the analysis is credible.
- Assessment of potential uncertainties in the analysis by using sensitivity analysis.
- Consistent and logical procedures for discounting benefits and costs.
- Presentation of the analysis in a standardized format and as transparently as possible.

Conclusion

Despite various measurement and conceptual problems, it is argued that CBA is better than other ways of including the environment in project appraisal. It gives a comprehensive picture of pros and cons of a project and a guideline for accepting or rejecting a project.

Questions

Illustrate and explain the theoretically efficient level of environmental improvement given by the MC = MB rule.

1. What are the various criteria applied in a CBA?
2. What are the limitations of a CBA? Suggest measures to make CBA a more reliable tool.

Exercise

1. List the direct and indirect cost and benefits associated with a project to construct a four lane road near a forest in a rural area without much transport facility.

32

ECONOMIC VALUATION OF ENVIRONMENTAL BENEFITS

Placing a value on environmental services is an important issue in environmental economics. Such evaluations are significant for more than one reason: firstly, such valuations signal the growing scarcity of the environmental resources. Secondly, valuation of benefits aids in any kind of decision making on projects involving a conflict between development and conservation. Thirdly, such valuations help the decision makers to include non-quantifiable, subjective variables in decision making so that the true economic worth of the project is considered for decision making. Finally such valuations help in adopting the appropriate policy mix for decision making.

The value of any good or service is determined by the demand and supply for the goods. The area under the demand curve gives the willingness of the consumers to pay for the goods, while, from the supply curve, we can get information about the cost of supplying the goods. Opportunity cost of supplying goods or services can also be identified from the SS curve. The concepts of willingness to pay and the opportunity cost are crucial to the estimation of benefits from environmental protection activities.

32.1 Components of Total Economic Value

The value of environmental resources arises from their contribution to people's welfare. The concept of *total economic value* (TEV) of an environmental resource is defined as "the sum of the values of all service flows that natural capital generates both now and in the future – appropriately discounted" (Pascual et al., 2010). The total economic value of environmental services is broadly classified as use value and non-use value. **Use value** is defined as the value derived from the actual use of an environmental resource ;examples include hunting, fishing, bird watching etc. Use value is further classified as direct use value and indirect use value. The products from the trees in the forests available for various uses such as the timber for furniture, barks, leaves and flowers for medicines, fruits for consumption are examples of direct use of an environmental resource. Direct use value includes the consumptive uses of the resource (fuel wood collection) non-consumptive uses (hiking).

***Indirect use values* or functional values**, derive from "the natural interaction between different ecological systems and processes' (Barbier 1998); In other words, indirect use values may be described as the benefits individuals experience, indirectly, as a consequence of the primary ecological function of a given resource (Torras,2000). Forests provide lot of indirect benefits such as defense against soil erosion, flood control, or carbon sequestration. The benefits from the ecosystem functions such as protection of watershed and prevention of soil erosion by forests are examples of indirect uses of the environmental resources.

Apart from use value, natural resources may also possess **non-use value** which are unrelated to any actual, direct or indirect use. *Non-use values* have two components, namely existence value and bequest value. While **existence value** refers to the psychological benefits that people derive from the mere knowledge that the resource exists, **bequest** value arises from the desire to preserve natural capital in order to pass it on to future generations. A person might be willing to pay to protect the rain forests in Kerala, simply because he or she values the fact that it exists. This is existence value.

There is another important component of total economic value, referred to as option value. **Option value** is the value that people place on having the option to enjoy something in the future, although they may not currently use it. For example a person may wish to see the Amazonian rain forests some time in future.

Option value refers to the benefits derived by an individual from the option of preserving the use of a particular resource when the individual is either uncertain about future use or faces uncertainty about the availability of that resource in the future. This is like an insurance value (CesareDosi,2000). Figure 32.1 gives the components of total economic value.

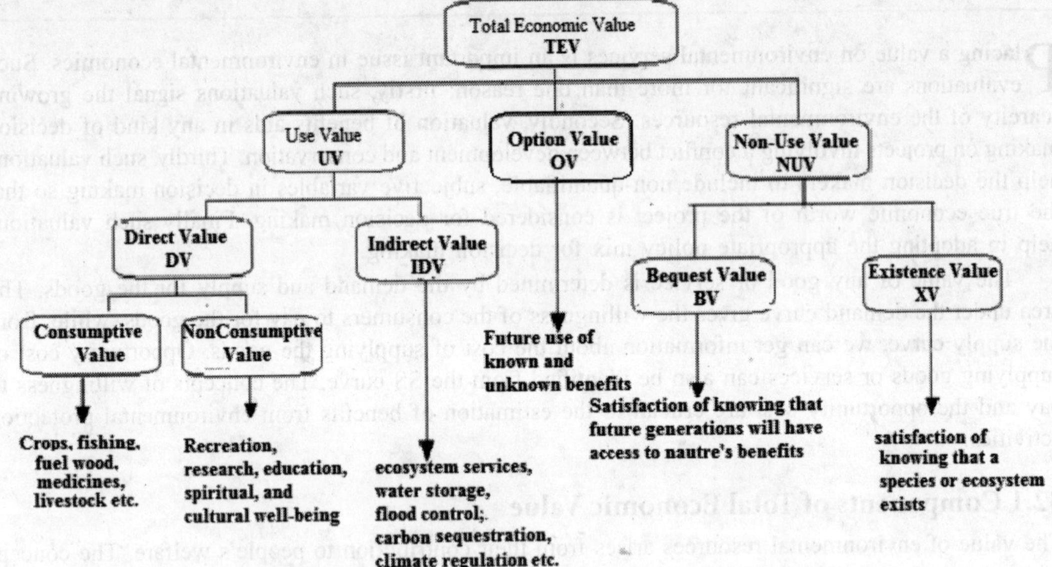

Figure 32.1 Taxonomy of Total Economic Value

Source: Modified from Pearce and Moran,1994 (IUCN Publication)and Pascual et al (2010)

TEV may therefore be expressed as:

TEV = UV + NUV + OV, which may be expressed as:

TEV = DV + IDV + BV + XV + OV

32.2 Techniques for Valuation of Environmental Benefits

There are numerous methods available for the evaluation of non- market goods such as environmental goods and services. Munasinghe (1992) gives a classification of the various valuation techniques on the basis of the type of market. According to Professor Munasinghe environmental benefits may be measured using market information directly by observing the environmental impact on production, health etc. If direct information is not available, indirect information from proxy market may be used. If market does not exist, information from constructed markets may be used to evaluate environmental benefits.

Valuation techniques are mainly classified on the basis of two important observations:

- Whether valuation is to be based on observed economic behavior (revealed preference) or whether valuation is to be based on responses to survey questions (stated preference).
- Whether monetary estimates of values are observed directly (market prices) or inferred through some indirect method (surrogate market)

Besides there also few cost based methods and conventional market based approaches.

Based on these considerations and other practical issues evaluation of environmental benefits may be classified as shown in figure 32.2.

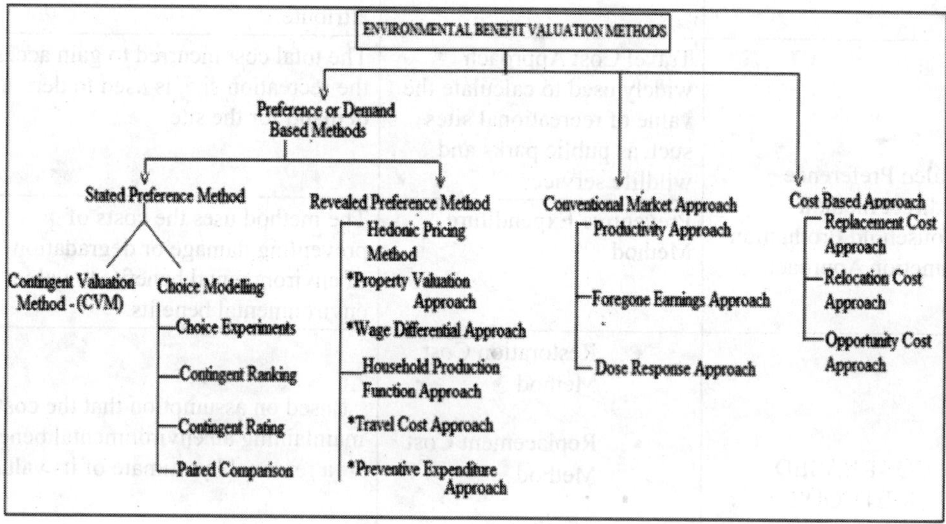

Figure 32.2 Methods to Value Environmental Benefits

Pearce and Turner classify the available techniques as direct and indirect techniques. While direct techniques are environmental demand curve approach, indirect techniques are 'non-demand approaches'. Direct techniques directly measure the monetary value of environmental services by deriving its demand curve. This may be done by asking individuals to express their preferences or by identifying a surrogate market –the market for a complementary goods in the 'household's production function' in order to infer individuals' preferences. The *travel-cost method*, the *hedonic price method*, and the *contingent valuation* belong to direct approach.

The indirect techniques do not value the environmental commodity via a demand curve but instead is based on a 'dose-response' relationship between environmental degradation and its impact. The production function methods (factor income or productivity approach) and cost based methods are indirect methods. Table 32.1 gives a brief note on the various methods.

Table 32.1 Methods to Evaluate Environmental Benefits – A Summary

Method	Basis	Definition
Stated Preference	Contingent Valuation Method: survey: using questionnaire	Uses questionnaires to ask people their WTP or WTA with respect to any environmental good or service.
	Choice Modelling: Survey using questionnaire	Respondents consider various given options by balancing (trading off) the various attributes.

Revealed Preference indirect method -Hedonic method	Property Valuation Method	The value of an environmental amenity is obtained from property markets. Change in the value of property due to an environmental attribute is the criterion for measuring benefit.
	Wage Differential Method	Differences in wages reflect the working conditions and hence it is possible to isolate the value of the relevant environmental amenity or attribute.
Revealed Preference indirect method - Household Production Function Approach	Travel Cost Approach widely used to calculate the value of recreational sites such as public parks and wildlife services.	The total cost incurred to gain access to the recreation site, is used to derive the demand for the site.
	Preventive Expenditure Method	The method uses the costs of preventing damage or degradation of environmental benefits to value environmental benefits.
COST BASED METHODS	• Restoration Cost Method • Replacement Cost Method • Avoided Cost Method	Based on assumption that the cost of maintaining an environmental benefit is a reasonable estimate of its value.

Source: Based on Pascual U, et al 2010. " Economics of valuing ecosystem services and biodiversity".

32.3 Direct Methods

The direct techniques measure the monetary value of environmental services. Direct method is an attempt to elicit preferences directly by the use of survey and experimental techniques, such as the contingent valuation method or the delphi method. In this, respondents are asked to directly state or reveal their strength of preference for a proposed change. Individual or personal valuations, contingent on a hypothetical market are sought. The direct methods based on surveys are useful in valuing the benefits of improvement in environmental quality when indirect methods are inadequate. They are particularly useful in valuing benefits from a programme to preserve a specie or a historical monument.

As already pointed out, direct methods assess the value of the environmental good or service by deriving its demand curve. Demand curve is derived either by asking individuals to express their preferences or by taking into consideration the preferences for a related good which is a complement of the environmental good or service, the value of which is being assessed. Direct methods are further classified as stated preference method and revealed preference method.

Stated preference methods: Stated preference approaches construct a market for the environmental good or service. This is done by asking individuals to state their willingness to pay for some change in the provision of an environmental good. It consists of surveys where respondents are directly asked what value they attach to non-marketable environmental services, and to express their preferences towards changes in service flows. This approach is used to estimate both use and non-use values.

Revealed preference methods: This method involves inferring an implicit value for a non-marketed good from the observable prices of the marketed goods and services which are either substitutes or complements for the environmental good under consideration. In this the value of the natural resource under consideration is revealed by related market behaviour and market prices. Revealed preference techniques derive the value for the environmental good or service by observing individual choices in related markets. This method is applicable for measuring use values alone.

32.3.1 Stated Preference Method

As said earlier stated preference methods consists of directly asking individuals to state the value they attach to unmarketable environmental services and to express their preferences towards changes in service flows. This approach is used to estimate both use value and non-use value. The main types of stated preference techniques are:

(a) **Contingent valuation method (CV)** which uses questionnaires to ask people how much they would be willing to pay to improve the provision of an ecosystem service, or alternatively, how much they would be willing to accept for its loss or degradation.

(b) **Choice modeling (CM)** in which respondents are given a choice between several options, each consisting of various attributes, one of which is either a price or subsidy. Respondents are then asked to consider all the options by balancing (trading off) the various attributes.

32.3.1.1Contingent Valuation Method

The CV method aims to construct a hypothetical market for a good or service and elicits from individual respondents, their Willingness to Pay (WTP) for the good or service under consideration, contingent on the market constructed. CVs are widely used to estimate the benefits of environmental resources for which no market exits. The aim of CV is to elicit valuations, which are close to those that would be revealed if an actual market existed. This technique directly assesses WTP or WTA for a particular environmental outcome in a carefully constructed hypothetical or simulated market. The method involves directly asking individuals the value they attach to environmental attributes; they are asked to directly state their preferences towards environmental changes. In some cases, people are asked for the amount of compensation they would be willing to accept to give up specific environmental services. It is called "contingent" valuation, because people are asked to state their willingness to pay, *contingent* on a specific description (hypothetical) of the environmental service. The method involves providing a description of the existing situation and the possible changes to the environment. Then respondents are directly asked about how much they are willing to pay (WTP) or willing to accept (WTA) to prevent the proposed change in the environment.

The theoretical basis for contingent valuation approach is micro economic welfare theory which explains how individuals maximize their utility subject to an income constraint or minimize their expenditure subject to utility constraint. CV methods elicits information through a survey from the respondent on the maximum willingness-to-pay (WTP) to obtain a desired good not currently possessed, or minimum compensation (WTA) required to give up a good that is currently in the possession of the respondent. The process estimates the respondents' consumer surplus for the environmental good. The link between welfare economics and CV is quite direct: CV traces out the willingness to pay of economic agents for a proposed change in a good.

The most prominent example of the CV method is the natural resource damage assessment after the Exxon Valdez oil spill in 1989. On 24th March 1989, the Exxon Valdez oil spill occurred in Alaska and the State of Alaska sued the company for the loss of passive-use values. In the words of Carson *et al.* (2003), "*the Exxon Valdez represented the quintessential case in which, to ignore passive use values, was to effectively say that resources that the public had chosen to set aside and not develop could be harmed at little or no cost to the responsible party*". The economists who estimated the damages from the oil spill reported a lower bound estimate on willingness to pay amounting to $2.8 billion to prevent another oil spill similar to the Valdez.

Contingent Valuation Method (CVM) was used by Bob Davis in 1963 to estimate the benefits of outdoor recreation activities. CVM is the only direct method that can be applied for determining both user and non-user value. The CVM tries to identify the value of the benefits that people derive from any environmental programme such as, an air quality improvement programme or the preservation of a species threatened to become extinct. The CVM basically involves asking a number of individuals the maximum sum they are willing to pay to have the benefit or the minimum sum they are willing to accept to forego the benefit. The concept of willingness to pay and willingness to accept are derived from Hicksian measures of consumer's surplus—compensation variation measure and equivalent variation measure. The compensation variation measure of consumer's surplus given by Sir John Hicks, defines consumer's surplus as the maximum sum the individual is willing to pay for the privilege of buying at a lower price and retain his initial level of welfare. Equivalent variation on the other hand, measures consumer's surplus as the minimum sum the consumer is willing to accept for foregoing the opportunity of buying at a lower price such that he gets the subsequent level of higher welfare, facilitated by the price fall (See Chapter 18 for detailed note on Hicksian measures of consumer's surplus). The theoretical basis of these concepts is in fact responsible for the marked differences between what people are willing to pay and what people are willing to accept.

Methodology of calculating WTP/WTA

Calculation of WTP/WTA involves several steps which are discussed below.

Step 1: The first step is **setting up the hypothetical market**. This step involves identification and description of the environmental quality characteristics to be evaluated. For example it could be improving the quality of water in a river that is likely to increase the use of the river water for fishing, conducting water games and the use of the river site for recreation. The step identifies respondents to be approached, including sampling procedures used to select respondents.

First step requires that the following points are considered:

- Discussion with stakeholders to define the environmental good to be valued.
- Decision on the nature of the market. This involves decision regarding environmental good or service to be valued and the improvement in it to be made.
- Determine the quantity and quality of information on the environmental good under consideration.
- Determination of who will pay for the environmental good and who will benefit from it.
- Decide on the sampling method : whether to use convenience sample, representative or stratified sample.

Step 2: The second step is designing and application of a survey questionnaire: This step in turn requires that the following points are considered :

- Decision of mode of administering the questionnaire: whether it will be a face-to-face, or by mail, telephone, internet, groups. In-person interviews are considered to be the most effective because it is often easier to explain the required background information to respondents in person, and people are more likely to complete a long survey when they are interviewed in person. In some cases, visual aids such as videos or color photographs may be presented to help respondents understand the conditions of the scenario that they are being asked to value.
- Surveyor must consider inducements or incentives to increase the response rate.
- Whether interview will be conducted by the researchers themselves or through hired private companies. Results would be more reliable if the research is conducted by the researcher personally.

Designing the questionnaire in order to make people reveal the maximum willingness to pay is a crucial part of the CVM. The questionnaire should comprise of:

- A clear statement of the environmental feature or amenity that people are asked to evaluate.
- A set of questions that will describe the respondent in economically relevant ways like income, residential address, age, use of related goods, etc.
- Questions to elicit willingness to pay (or willingness to accept) from individuals. The willingness-to-pay question should also define a way in which payment would be made (a general tax, a voluntary donation or an entrance fee). For example, a question can be formulated in the following way: 'Are you willing to pay as entrance fee (Rs --) if the river site is converted into a recreation site and the river water made available for games, swimming, fishing and boating or would you prefer to pay an annual donation for the same?"

The respondents will be provided information on: when the service will be available, how the respondent will be expected to pay for it, how much others will contribute, the institutions that will be responsible for the delivery of service and the quality and reliability of the services. The objective of the questionnaire is to elicit from the respondents their estimate of the worth of the environmental good or service. In economic terms, they are asked to reveal the maximum amount they would be willing to pay rather than go without the environmental factor in question.

In addition it is important to consider the following points:

- determine whether a willingness-to- pay (WTP) or a willingness-to-accept (WTA) scenario is presented.
- Determine an appropriate payment vehicle (tax, donation, price).
- Choose elicitation method (e.g. dichotomous choice vs. open-ended elicitation method).

Step 3: Implementing the survey for obtaining bids: In this step, the survey is done to obtain the WTP/WTA of the respondents. The survey follows either a simple bidding game or an iterative procedure. There are several broad ways in which WTP/WTA is calculated:

- The first is the open ended format Here the respondent is asked: "what is your maximum willingness to pay or minimum willingness to accept for a certain environmental quality". The responses are averaged and extrapolated to arrive at an aggregate willingness to pay and aggregate willingness to accept.
- The second one is the bidding game format which uses an iterative [repetitive] procedure. In this the interviewer starts with a certain sum and asks whether the WTP is equal or more than that. If it is more, he increases the sum quoted and if it is less he decreases the sum. This process is carried on till the desired sum is reached. The last accepted sum is the respondents' maximum willingness to pay.
- The most widely used approach for eliciting information about the respondent's WTP is the so-called **dichotomous-choice format** developed by Bishop and Heberlein in which the respondent is asked if he would pay Rs X (in the form of an entry fee or taxation or donation) to obtain the environmental attribute or quality under consideration. The answer in the form of 'yes' or 'no' (for and against) is recorded and no further question is asked. The chosen amount is the bid value. WTP is greater than the bid amount if the respondent is in favour of the programme and WTP is less than the bid amount if the respondent votes against the plan. Mean WTP can be calculated by forming broad intervals around the respondent's WTP amount. The main drawback of this format is that it leads to a qualitative dependent variable and reveals little about individuals' WTP since the individual just says "YES" or "No". In the improved version of this method, the dichotomous choice questions are continued with follow up questions. For example, if the

respondent's answered initially that he was not willing to pay Rs 20 for the proposed project, then the bid amount may be reduced to Rs 10. If the respondent says 'YES' the second time, then his WTP falls between Rs 10 and Rs 20. The bid amount offered in the second round will be lower than that in the initial round if the respondent's answer was 'NO' in the first round. It will be greater than that offered in the initial round if the answer is 'YES' initially. The response to these two questions generates a series of Yes/Yes, Yes/No, No/Yes, and No/No answers …. The responses are regressed on the bid amount, demographic characteristics of the respondent, and other relevant variables. The results of this regression model can then be used to monetize the average and median economic benefits of the environmental change considered in the survey. The dichotomous choice methods have been widely used to elicit WTP for water quality improvement.

- A fourth approach is the **payment card method**. This method was first developed by **Mitchell and Carson** as an alternative to the bidding game. This method specifies the increase or decrease in the value of the environmental good to be provided in quantitative terms. The method provides substantial details about the institutional structure of the hypothetical market. The approach is either an open-ended or a closed-ended format. The open-ended format provides an exact monetary amount for WTP by the respondent, which is a point on the demand curve. The closed-ended format provides a yes or no answer to a question specifying both the precise amount of a non-market good to be gained or lost and the precise amount of money to be paid or received. The interviewer lists a number of possible WTP values on a card and asks the respondent to pick the amount on the card that best represents his willingness to pay. The amount chosen by the respondent is his WTP. Cameron and Huppert observe that the chosen amount is a lower bound for the respondent's WTP.

Step 4 Analysis of results and estimating the bid curve: Most CV studies estimate a bid function. On the basis of information available from the questionnaire, a general willingness to pay can be derived which is likely to be of the following form:

$$WTP_i = f(Q_i, Y_i, T_i, S_i)$$

where Q_i is the quantity/quality of the attribute, Y_i is the income, T_i is an index of tastes and S_i is an index of socio economic factors.

Two points are to be noted here:

- If open ended elicitation method is used simple mean can be used to calculate WTP / WTA.
- If dichotomous choice method is used expected value of WTP /WTA is to be estimated.

Estimating the bid curve: A bid curve can be estimated based on the bid equation using WTP /WTA amounts as dependent variables and the variables on the right side of the equation as the independent variables. In the simple open ended CVM surveys WTP bids can be regressed against Q, Y, T and S. Bid curves are particularly useful to explain and test the sensitivity of WTP to variations in Q. In the dichotomous choice format bid curves are logit- probit functions and they predict the probability of a YES response to a particular offer price.

Step 5 Aggregating the data: In this step the mean WTP/WTA bids are converted to a population total figure. Calculating the mean for the total population from the sample mean values requires that the sample mean is multiplied by the number of households in the population N. Here the population could be the local population or regional population or national population. However if the sample is a biased reflection of the relevant population, then appropriate adjustments must be made for the same. If the benefits are to be aggregated over a time period then an appropriate discount value must be applied to express the present value of future benefits.

Assessment of CV method: The application of the CV approach to the valuation of environmental benefits has grown intensely over the last three decades. Improved versions of the CVM are in use to overcome the challenge of validity and reliability of results. Many studies point out to the existence of 'biases' in the administration of the method. Survey methods are subject to a number of biases which are explained below:

- **Hypothetical bias**: The most serious limitation of CVM is that it is hypothetical in nature. People face a hypothetical situation and hence their responses may not reflect their real preference or actual willingness to pay. People may not know enough about their real preferences to be able to give their valid responses and even if they know their preferences, they may have incentives to misrepresent them to the investigator. If the respondents feel that their answers may be useful in determining the price of the good, they may understate their preference. Similarly individuals may also over state their preferences, if it would benefit them in any way. Hypothetical bias is the difference between stated WTP in a hypothetical market situation and the actual payment behavior that can be observed in the actual market. The difference can go in either direction – positive or negative. Respondents who do not take the hypothetical situation seriously provide unrealistic responses because they do not actually have to pay the amounts of money they assign to resources. The bias can be minimized if respondents are provided with more information about the project.
- **Information bias**, arising from the inadequate information or misleading information furnished by the interviewer. The WTP values may be understated or exaggerated due to:
  - Information about the characteristics of the good.
  - Information about substitutes and complements.
  - Information on relative expenditure.
  - Information on the behavior of others.

  Many studies show that reliability of WTP is higher when more information is provided. To overcome information bias and to arrive at reliable WTP values "full unbiased" information should be provided.
- **Strategic bias**, arising from the individual's desire to influence the outcome of the study, for his or her personal benefit. The strategic bias depends on what respondents feel will be done with their answers, thus causing them to conceal their real preferences. Respondents might exaggerate their WTP if they favor the policy, or understate their WTP. For example, a respondent who is against a user fee or a tax may understate his willingness to pay to avoid the same.
- **Starting point bias** in which respondents are influenced by the values listed in the survey. Starting-point bias occurs when the selected value influences the observed final bids. The starting value informs the respondent about expected or reasonable bids and thus influences the final bid outcome. This problem is greater, the less familiar the respondent is with the object to be valued, and the valuation procedure.
- **Payment Vehicle bias** is influenced by the type of payment method mentioned in the survey, such as taxes or donations. When respondents are asked their WTP, they are informed that their payment could be either an increase in user charge or an entry fee or a donation or a tax. The WTP is influenced by the payment method quoted. This difference in WTP, dependent on the method of payment, is known as payment vehicle bias.
- **Sampling bias occurs** when those selected as respondents do not represent the larger population.

Embedding effect is said to occur when the values of resulting WTP differ according to whether the good is valued exclusively or is a part of package of goods. It is possible that the expressed values might apply to more attributes or features than for the attribute for which the benefit is being evaluated. Kahneman and Knetsch (1992) distinguished between two different kinds of embedding effects – perfect embedding and regular embedding. Perfect embedding occurs when the value /WTP of a specific good is almost the same as that of a more inclusive good. Regular embedding, on the other hand, occurs when the WTP for a good is assigned a lower value when it is inferred as part of a collection of goods/ features than if the particular good is evaluated on its own. It is difficult to identify the value of a particular thing when it is embedded in a collection of similar things. For example, a research study by Svedsater (2000) observed that the WTP of respondents for limiting global warming was nearly £161 when it was the only attribute which respondents had to value and nearly £60 when respondents were asked to attach values to three other environmental concerns (Rain forests, endangered animals and air pollution) along with global warming. This happens when the values for the other three concerns are embedded into the value placed on global warming. To overcome the embedding effects, the researcher must carefully clarify the attribute to be valued and add follow-up questions.

WTP and WTA differences

Survey methods value non-market environmental goods by eliciting from respondents their maximum WTP for the proposed environmental improvement or alternatively respondents could be asked to state the minimum amount they would be willing to accept (WTA) to forgo the environmental improvement (or accept the continuing environmental damage) .For example if the issue considered is cleaning a lake to improve the quality of its water, the two questions posed to the respondent are:

- What is the maximum amount of money you would pay for the restoration of water quality in the river? Answer to this question yields hypothetical WTP.
- What is the minimum payment you would accept as compensation if the lake water continues to be polluted? Answer to this question yields hypothetical WTA

It is common for one to think that there should be no difference between WTP and WTA. But empirical studies reveal that willingness to pay is atleast one third to one fifth lesser than the willingness to accept. Obviously the loss of something that we already have is more significant to us than the gain of something that we are yet to possess. A study by Bishop and Heberlin, to evaluate the significance of wild fowl to hunters, in Wisconsin, revealed that the willingness to pay was $21 while the willingness to accept was $101.

Some economists attribute the difference between WTP and WTA to income effect and hence feel that it is very small. But many studies point out that the differences between WTA and WTP could be arbitrarily large depending on the degree of substitutability between the non-market good and other ordinary market commodities. A study by Hammack and Brown showed that the waterfowl hunters were willing pay only $247 more to continue hunting while their WTA for giving up the opportunity was $1044. A 1994 study by MacDonald and Bowker on industrial plant odour showed that the WTP of the respondents was $105 while WTA was $735. Based on these studies it is inferred that the ratio of WTA to WTP ranges from 2.1 to 5.1. Horowitz and McConnell (2002) observed from their review of 45 studies that the mean WTA/WTP ratio in the 45 studies they reviewed is 7.17.

The difference between WTP and WTA are attributed to economic and psychological reasons. While economists include income effect and availability of substitutes as major factors causing a disparity between WTA and WTP, endowment effect is the major psychological factor causing the disparity.

1. **Income effect:** Payment for a obtaining good is constrained by income but a compensation for giving up a good is not constrained by income. Though economic theory implies that with small income effect WTA must be equal to WTP, the income constraint is stronger higher the income elasticity of good. When the income effect is stronger the difference between WTP and WTA will be higher with WTA exceeding WTP.
2. **Availability of substitutes:** Goods lacking good substitutes may have divergent WTA and WTP values even if income effects are modest.

The CV method was first used by **Robert K Davis** in 1963 to estimate benefits of hunting and outdoor recreation in a Maine Backwoods area. Knetsch and Davis (1966) used contingent valuation method to study the recreation value of Maine Woods. Ronald Ridker (1967) used the CV method in several studies of air pollution benefits.

Bishop and Heberlein (1979) evaluated outdoor recreation with the CV approach using two distinct experiments in their study of goose hunting in central Wisconsin and derived an estimate of the average consumer surplus (CS) from a hunting permit.

Carson and Mitchel (1993) estimated the national benefits of controlling fresh water pollution to meet the requirements of the Clean Water Act of 1972 and observed that the mean WTP of the people for improving and maintaining a water quality to facilitate boating, fishing and swimming were $106, $80 and $89 respectively.

Kramer and Mercer's (1997) study of the value of tropical rain forest protection surveyed a random sample of 1200 United States residents in 1992 and asked their willingness to donate to a United Nations fund to increase the world's rain forests preserved in their natural state from 5% to 10%. They concluded that Americans are willing to make a one-time donation of $21 to $32 per household. When extrapolated to the population of households this range became $1.9 to $2.8 billion.

The World Bank used contingent valuation studies to estimate WTP for piped water connections in Kerala, India (Singh *et. al.*, 1993).

Jordon and Elnagheeb (1993) estimated WTP for improvement s in drinking water quality and reported that the aggregate WTP for all of Georgia was estimated to be about $111.5 million per year for public water users and $42.3 million per year for private well owners.

Tapovang and Kruavan (2000) estimated WTP of Residents of Banghok for improving water quality in the River Chao Phraya through financing a central waste water treatment facility and concluded that the WTP of the residents was 100.81 baht and 115.03 baht per month for improving the water quality to facilitate fishing and swimming respectively.

Kim and Cho (2002) determined how much consumers would be willing to pay to reduce copper in their drinking water in nine counties Minnesota using the payment-card model and the aggregate WTP for all nine counties was estimated to range from $1.66 to $2.38 million.

A study by Phuong D.M., Gopalakrishnan C, (2003), used CVM to the valuation of the rural water resources in the Mekong Delta, Vietnam, showed that the loss of value of the rural water resources due to pesticide contamination in the Mekong Delta is about US$251 million.

Zhang (2011) estimated willingness to pay (WTP) for water quality improvements, and its influencing factors of residents in the Lake Tai area in China and observed that respondents would prefer to pay 141 CNY per household a year, approximately 0.70% of their annual per capita disposable income, as an environmental fee to improve water quality in Lake Tai.

Box 32.1 Select CVM studies

3. **Endowment effect** arises from the notion that a thing in the possession of an individual is more valuable to him than when it is not. In the CVM the endowment effect keeps the estimates of willingness to pay low while estimates of willingness to accept are kept high by the endowment effect since WTP means the responder has to part with some of his income already in his possession and hence he/ she will be willing to pay a lower amount only. WTA makes addition to the income of the respondent and hence he will give a higher amount as his response. This widens the gap between WTA and WTP.

Besides these effects it has been noted that the more the good differs from an ordinary market good, the higher is the ratio of WTA/WTP (Horowitz and McConnell, 2002). Thus in the case of public goods in general, and environmental goods and services in particular the difference between WTA and WTP is accounted for. Uncertainty in the characteristics or quality of the good is also found to enhance the difference between WTP and WTA (Isik, 2004).

In 1993 the National Oceanic and Atmospheric Administration commissioned a Blue Ribbon Panel to answer the question 'Is CV a valid method for determining the lost economic value from natural resource damages?' The panel included many prominent economists, including two Nobel Prize winners, Kenneth Arrow and Robert Solow. The members of the NOAA Blue Ribbon Panel concluded that the CV method can produce reliable estimates of the lost value from natural resource damages provided researchers meet a high standard of proof. The panel established a set of guidelines for CV studies to follow in order to gain reliability. The CVM is today used extensively to elicit values of benefits from the improvement in environmental quality. It is the only method that can be employed to measure both use value and non-use value of the environmental goods/service.

32. 3.1.2 Stated Preference Method – Choice Modelling

Choice modelling (CM) is a stated preference valuation method that has its origin in conjoint analysis. It is used to estimate non-market environmental benefits and costs. CM is based on the notion that any good can be described in terms of its **attributes**, or **characteristics**. For example, a lake can be described in terms of its attributes such as water quality, depth, boating, swimming and other recreational facilities, fishing opportunities, scope for supply of drinking water etc. When attributes are different the good gets differentiated. CM proceeds on the basis of changes in the attributes.

In this method, respondents are given a choice between several alternatives or options, each consisting of various attributes, one of which is either a price or subsidy. Choice modeling questionnaires are similar to contingent valuation questionnaires in that they contain background information about the good or service, an elicitation question, and debrief questions. The main difference between the two methods is in the form of the elicitation question. In choice modeling questionnaires, respondents are presented with a series of choice sets, each containing usually three or more alternative goods. An alternative is a combination of several attributes, each attribute having a value. The attributes used are common across all alternatives. Their levels vary from one alternative to another. One of the alternatives in each choice set will be business as usual scenario. Respondents are asked to choose their preferred alternative from each choice set.Each alternative includes a money indicator such as a price or tax as an attribute. The main difference between CM and CVM is that the former asks for rankings or ratings while CVM asks for values. (WERF, 2008, and J. Mogas).

CM conveys the following information:

- the attributes that are significant determinants of the values people place on non-market goods;
- the implied ranking of these attributes amongst the relevant population.
- the value of changing more than one of the attributes at the same time.

There are four types of CM

- Choice Experiments
- Contingent Ranking
- Contingent Rating
- Paired Comparisons

In **choice experiments** respondents choose from a set of alternatives where one is the statusquo. Generally the number of attributes is restricted to 4 - 6 for an efficient working of the model. For example if there are two alternatives A and B, each having four attributes (one of which is a money value), the respondent is required to state their choice of A or B or neither. Choice of "neither" implies that the choice sets are in no way better or worse than the status quo scenario. The attributes in each alternative differs in terms of quantity and could be an improvement (positive) or otherwise (negative).

In **contingent ranking,**respondents rank alternatives in terms of their preferences with the most preferred alternative taking the rank 1, next best taking the rank 2 and so on.

In **contingent rating** respondent is asked to rate each alternative on a scale. The scale could be between 1 to 10 with 1 being most preferred and 10 being least preferred.

In **pairwise comparison** respondents indicate how strongly they prefer any alternative over another one. Alternatives are compared in pairs. Respondents are asked to indicate the strength of their preference on a numeric scale. This a relative score and it tells us how an alternative compares with others.

32. 3.1.3 Delphi Method

The Delphi technique is a unique version of the survey technique that attempts to place a value on a particular good through the direct questioning of experts. The technique was developed by Dalkey&Helmer of the KANE corporation in 1963. The technique consists of asking a group of experts to place their values on several goods. These values of the experts along with their explanations are circulated, and the experts are asked to reconsider their estimates and make new judgements. Through successive rounds, values are hoped to come closer until, they cluster tightly around a mean value. Throughout this process the identity of any expert is not revealed to the others and group is not assembled face to face. The accuracy of the Delphi survey results depend on quality of experts involved and their ability to reflect societal values.

32.4 Revealed Preference Methods

Revealed preference techniques are based on the observation of individual choices in the existing markets that are related to the environmental good or service, value of which is being measured. It is based on the notion that the choice of the economic agents "reveals" their preferences. They are also **known as Surrogate Market Approach** since they derive value for environmental goods and services from the market for private good and services which are related to the environmental good, the value of which we want to measure. The goods or services bought and sold in these surrogate markets are either complements or substitutes of the environmental commodities. The purchase of the private good by the individuals reveal their preferences for both the private marketed good and the environmental good.

The two main methods within this approach are:

- Hedonic Pricing Method which includes Property Valuation Approach and Wage Differential Approach
- Household Production Function method that includes Travel Cost Approach and Preventive Expenditure Method.

32.4.1 Hedonic Approach

The Hedonic Pricing Approach (HPM) attempts to estimate an *implicit price* for environmental attributes by looking at real markets in which those characteristics are explicitly traded. It tries to measure the value of a non-marketed environmental service as a measurable component ('attribute' or 'characteristic') of a marketed good. That is, it uses the information about the demand for a marketed commodity to derive the value of the non-marketed environmental good or service. Property value approach and wage differential approach are examples of surrogate market approach.

Property Valuation Method (PVM) uses the price of substitute or complimentary goods to value any environmental benefit. PVM proceeds by estimating an *implicit price for the* environmental characteristics, by looking at real markets in which those characteristics are effectively traded.

PVM evaluates the contribution of environmental attributes of housing - the attributes such as air quality, proximity to parks, quality of drinking water available, greenery in the area etc. Since these environmental attributes are not directly traded in markets, they are embedded in the market value of a house. Thus "clean air" and "aesthetic view" are effectively traded in the property market - purchasers of houses and land do consider these environmental dimensions as characteristics of property.

The Property Value Approach seeks to find the relationship between the level of environmental services (such as noise level or air pollution) and the price of the property. Property value approach has been used to value such things as noise levels around airports, earthquake risks, urban air quality and amenity value of forests. The value of a house, for example, is affected by many variables such as size, construction, location and quality of its environment. When variables such as size, construction and locational advantages (in terms of proximity to hospitals, schools, shop, etc.) are controlled, the price difference between similar units helps to determine the implicit price for the environmental amenity. A house constructed in a less congested, less polluted area with a beautiful view is an example. The information gathered from consequent variations in house prices may be used as a surrogate for measuring the value of the unpriced variable, namely environmental quality.

The basic assumption in this method is that the purchasers of the property will reveal their attitude to a bundle of attributes (structural, environmental and aesthetic) by their willingness to pay. In reality, the price of houses reflect a very large range of attributes—like the type of construction, number of rooms and size and location of the property. For example, assuming that individuals have all relevant information with respect to these attributes, the price of a house can be taken to be a function of its structure, neighbourhood environmental quality characteristics. If P is the price of housing, the function can be written as

$$P_H = f\ (Si,\ Ni,\ ENVi)$$

where Si represents the various characteristics for the 'i'th housing unit such as size, number of rooms, age and type of construction, presence of garden, garage etc. Ni represents a set of neighbourhood characteristics for the 'i'th house like security, and proximity to school, hospital, park, shops, work place, etc., and ENVi is the quality of environment at the 'i'th site which includes factors such as proximity to parks, water quality, air quality, waste management facilities, noise level in the area etc. If observation on prices and characteristics are available, and if non-environmental attributes are controlled, the difference in price of the property can be attributed to differences environmental characteristics. The function can be estimated by a multivariate analysis. The implicit price of the given environmental characteristics is obtained by partially differentiating the equation.

The implicit price can be used as a measure of the benefits of the marginal increase in Qi [such as an improvement in air quality]. The information gained from the above process may be used for estimating the demand curve for environmental quality. In this method it is important to identify how much of price difference is due to difference in environmental quality between properties. Once the hedonic price equation has been specified, the environmental price, i.e. the value of a marginal change in the environmental characteristic, is obtained by partially differentiating the above equation with respect to ENV

$$P_{ENV} = \delta P_H / \delta ENV$$

Using regression analysis, the proportion of change in the value of the property that is due to changes in environmental attributes can be identified.

A study of the effects of air pollution on housing units in Boston with respect to three income groups revealed that households were willing to pay more for marginal improvements in nitrogen oxide levels, keeping in mind the higher initial level of pollution. The study also revealed that households with higher incomes were willing to pay more for a given improvement.

The property value approach places great demand on data and may therefore be of limited use in developing countries. With greater availability of data on the property market, the method may become more meaningful. The method is subject to omitted variable bias. The analyst must identify and include all the independent variables in the hedonic price equation; omission of any variable will result in a biased estimate of implicit price.

Some of the independent variables in the hedonic price equation may be clearly correlated with each other. For example, if a house is located in an industrial estate, with an increase in air pollution, there may be an increase in noise pollution too. Similarly, for a property located in a flood prone area, with an increase in the probability of floods, the probability of water borne diseases also increases. Such a multicoilinearity will lead to an imprecise estimate of the demand curve.

Choice of the best functional form that has a good interpretative predictive power also poses problem in the use of property value approach. Besides this method will not give an accurate estimation if it fails to consider expected changes in environmental quality around the property site. If these limitations are overcome, property value approach can be effectively used to value environmental benefits.

32.4.2 Wage Differential Method: The wage differential method is very similar to property value approach. It rests on the theory that in a perfectly competitive market, demand for labour is determined by the value of its marginal product and the supply of labour. A higher wage rate is required to induce workers to undertake risky occupations—the risk may be due to health, pollution or to life through accidents. Differences in wage levels for similar jobs may be considered as a function of differences in attributes of the job, relating to work and living conditions. If the relationship between wage levels and attributes can be estimated, then implicit price can be determined. Several empirical studies conclude that the reason for higher wages in cities are due to a worker's willingness to 'work and live' in cities with higher levels of environmental and health amenities. This method is also known as wage risk premium method because it values changes in morbidity and mortality arising from environmental hazards. The method, like any other hedonic method, uses multiple regression to relate wages to the factors which influence them, like risk of accidents, pollution, etc. The method may be theoretically sound but labourmarkets do not behave as required by the method. Assumption of perfect competition in labour markets is far from reality. It is difficult to identify and measure all the attributes that affect labour supply and wages on account of requirement of thorough and extensive data. It is particularly difficult to apply this method to labour markets in developing countries and underdeveloped countries, where the poor have no choice about the quality of their working conditions.

32.5 Household Production Function Approach

When the household's production function is identified in its utility maximising pursuits, the revealed preference method is also called as the household production function approach. The travel cost approach and the preventive expenditure method are two popular household production methods that are basically hedonic.

32.5.1 Travel Cost Method: Travel Cost Method, (TCM), is considered to be one of the oldest non-market valuation methods. It was suggested by Harold Hotelling in 1947, but was formally introduced and popularised by Wood and Trice and Clawson and Knetsch. TCM is frequently used in outdoor recreation modelling. The cost of consuming environmental goods are specifically used as a proxy for their price: in other words, the time and money spent travelling to a free or low cost recreation site indicates the consumer's true valuation of that site. The costs incurred to visit a recreational site reflects the recreational value of that site. Hence, the cost of consumption is used to estimate the true economic value of an existing recreation site, even if no admission charge is levied. Travel cost depends upon several variables like distance cost, time cost and entrance fee, if any. The total travel cost includes:

TTC = TRC + AC, where TTC is total travel cost, TRC is transportation cost and AC is Accession Cost. If there is no entry fee, accession cost is zero. Travel cost includes distance cost and time cost which vary among individuals. The further away the potential users of the recreation site are, the less is their expected use of the site.

Travel cost method can be used to evaluate benefit of recreation sites using one of the following:

- a simple zonal travel cost approach, using data collected from visitors
- an individual travel cost approach, using a more detailed survey of visitors.

The method proceeds by eliciting information of travel cost from the visitors to the recreation site through a questionnaire.The method in its simplest form requires three important questions to be asked to a sample of visitors to the recreation site apart from other questions to elicit the demographic profile of the respondents. The three questions are:

1. How far do you have to travel to visit the site?
2. How often do you visit this site?
3. How much do you spend to travel to this site?

In the individual travel cost approach, survey data collected from individual visitors is used in the statistical analysis and is hence a complicated method.

The zonal travel cost method is the simplest and least expensive approach. It is applied by collecting information on the number of visits to the site from different distances. A set of zones surrounding the site are defined by concentric circles around the site, or by geographic or administrative divisions. Zoning by concentric circle around the site will zone respondents into areas that are equidistant. On the other hand, in zoning by geographic divisions method, distance will differ. By zoning the respondents in to areas that are equidistant from the site, a visitation rate, i.e., visitors per thousand population can be found. Visitation rate per thousand in each zone is the total visits per year from the zone, divided by the zone's population in thousands.

The distance travelled is translated into a cost that includes travel cost and other related recreational expenditure. From this a Trip Generating Function [TGF] is evolved which predicts the number of visits undertaken by the individual in any particular zone around the site. Once a TGF has been estimated the impact of an increase in fee on the number of visits from each zone can be studied. The travel cost is used as a proxy for the price of recreation and visitation rate is taken as the proxy for the quantity of recreation. Using **regression technique**, the equation that relates visits per capita to travel costs and other important variables can be estimated. Using the results of the regression analysis, the demand curve for the site can be derived for each zone. The demand curve is expressed as:

$$VR = f(C + X)$$

where VR is visitation rate, C is cost of visiting the site and X is other factors influencing the decision to visit.

The area below the calculated demand curve and above the cost curve is used as an estimate of the consumers' surplus for the present users of the site from any particular zone. Thus consumers' surplus is estimated for all zones, and is added together to estimate the total valuation of the recreation site by all users.

TCM poses certain problems in the computation of the demand curve. These are:

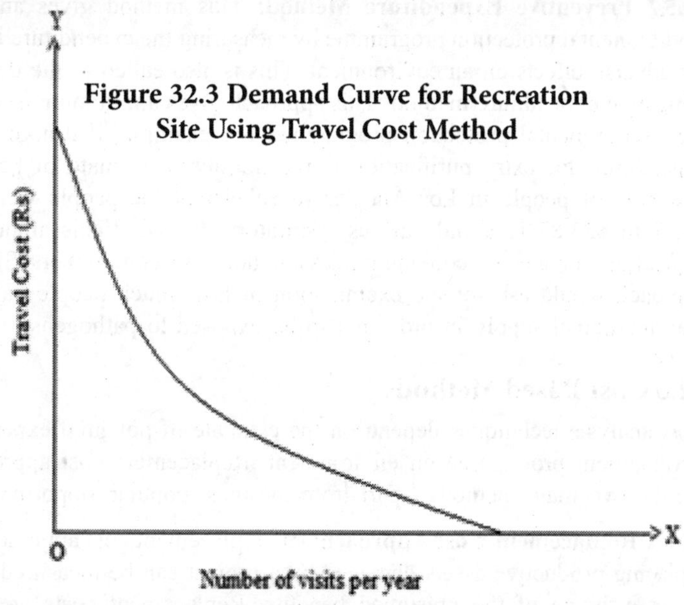

Figure 32.3 Demand Curve for Recreation Site Using Travel Cost Method

1. Choice of the dependent variable: TCM poses the problem of exercising options regarding the choice between using data on either visits from a given zone or visits made by a given individual.
2. The TCM method requires that a distinction is made between meanderers, i.e., those for whom the visits to the site is only a part of the purpose of their journey, and purposeful visitors—those for whom a visit to the site in question is the only purpose of their visit. The presence of meanderers will not give a precise value.
3. The method captures only use value and ignores existence and bequest values. Besides these, TCM also poses statistical problems.

Apart from the limitations in deriving the demand curve, the travel cost method is limited in its scope of application because it requires user participation. It cannot be used to measure non-use values. It cannot be used to measure values to on-site environmental features and functions and off-site values supported by the site. Further defining and measuring the opportunity cost of time, or the value of time spent traveling, can pose serious problems.

However the method is based on actual behavior - what people actually do and not on what people say they would do in a hypothetical situation. The method is relatively inexpensive to apply.

Blackwell Boyd in 2007 calculated the value for recreational visit to surf beaches within the local urban setting of Mooloolaba beach, Sunshine Coast, Queensland, using individual travel cost model and found that the consumer surplus measures per person per visit are $12.99 for the entire sample, $11.86 for a visitor, and $2.39 for a resident and the annual estimates were calculated as $862 million for the entire sample, $153 million for residents and $205 million for visitors.

Mike Raybould and Mr Neil Lazarow (2008) made a survey of a survey of Gold Coast City residents use and attitudes toward Gold Coast ocean beach and foreshore areas. Using a crude travel cost model it is estimated that average travel costs per adult beach visit were between $0.50 and $2.30.

Assessing the recreational value provided by Yuelu Mountain Park in China applying travel cost method, in 2008, Tiantian Tang estimated a consumer surplus of € 0.75 per trip for local individual and € 64.52 per trip for non-local individual; the annual access value of Yuelu Mountain Park was calculated to be € 20.43 million

Box 32.2 TCM - Select Case Studies

32.5.2 Preventive Expenditure Method: This method gives an estimation of the benefit of the environmental protection programme by measuring the expenditure incurred for eradicating or reducing the adverse effects on an environment. This is also called as the defensive expenditure method or the mitigative expenditure method. This approach gives a minimum estimate of the benefits received from the environmental protection programme. For example, if drinking water is polluted, the additional expenditure for extra purification is the minimum estimate of benefits. A study done in 1986, for a sample of people in Los Angeles revealed that the people were willing to pay anything around \$0.97 to \$23.87 to avoid various respiratory diseases. This amount was expressed in the form of expenditure on electric cooking ranges and home air-conditioners. Similarly, the preventive expenditure approach would ask for the examination of how much people pay to get water from sources other than municipal supply in order not to be exposed to pathogens.

32.6 Cost Based Methods

Cost analysis techniques depend on the estimate of potential expenditure to value the impact of any development programme on environment. Replacement cost approach and relocation cost approach are the two main methods, apart from the most popular, opportunity cost approach.

32.6.1 Replacement Cost Approach: The replacement cost approach assumes that the cost incurred in replacing productive assets damaged by a project can be measured and these costs can be interpreted as an estimate of the presumed benefits. Replacement costs are true costs of replacement if the damage has actually occurred. The method gives a minimum estimate of the presumed benefit from the environmental protection programme. An example of this method is the cost of replacing trees damaged by water pollution. This method was applied to assess the benefits from soil conservation programme in upland agricultural areas in Korea. The cost of physically replacing lost soil and nutrients was taken as a measure of the potential benefits of preventing soil erosion and nutrient loss. The study showed that the economic benefits of the proposed steps to prevent soil erosion were greater than the replacement costs and thus justified the preventive measures.

32.6.2 Relocation Costs: This is a variant of the replacement cost technique. In this, the actual cost of relocating a physical facility because of changes in environmental quality are used to evaluate the potential benefits of an environmental improvement programme. For example, in the case of a stream into which effluents are discharged, the cost of relocating the domestic water supply unit, if the polluted stream had a domestic water supply unit in the downstream, will reveal the benefits from pollution reduction.

32.6.3 Opportunity Cost Method: The opportunity cost method is the main principle in the evaluation of cost and benefits. Most of the resources have alternative uses in the economy and cost of using them is the alternative use that is foregone. For example, steel used in constructing transport facility is unavailable for use in constructing a petro chemical plant. In a properly operating market system, the prices of goods supplied will reflect the opportunity cost of all resources used in production. Thus the opportunity cost method uses the market data to calculate the cost of preserving benefits. What economic benefits must be given up when a resource is not exploited is the criterion for the evaluation of benefits. Benefits from preserving land for a national park instead of cutting the trees for timber is the value of the timber foregone. In Newzealand, the opportunity cost approach was used by environmental groups to persuade the government to save indigenous forests. In the U.S.A., the proposed damming of Hells Canyon for hydro-electric power generation would have irrevocably altered a unique wilderness area. Based on the opportunity cost of preserving Hells Canyon, seen as the difference between the cost of hydro-electric power and the next cheapest power source, Krutilla and Fisher concluded that generating power from a nuclear plant rather than the hydro source was worth the cost.

The opportunity cost approach forms an integral part of any cost benefit analysis. It is relatively quick and easy to handle and provides valuable information. It is very useful when the net social benefits of a proposed action cannot be measured. Under such circumstances, the social opportunity cost is used to evaluate the net social benefit of the proposed action.

32.7 Conventional Market Approach

Conventional market approach to measuring benefits relies on the use of the actual market price of the product, the production of which has consequences on environment. This approach takes the form of productivity approach and foregone income approach.

32.7.1 Productivity Approach: In this method, environmental factor is viewed as a factor of production. Changes in environmental quality lead to changes in productivity which in turn will affect the price of the product through a change in output. These changes can be observed and measured. For example, a reduction in soil erosion may increase rice/paddy yields. Comparison of rice output with and without soil conservation scheme shows the difference in productivity arising from soil conservation. Similarly, improvement in the water quality by reducing salinity may improve the crop productivity.

In programmes like soil conservation or water quality improvement, change in the output multiplied by the price of the output gives an estimate of the benefit of the programme. Thus in productivity approach, a change in the environmental factor is said to influence the production function and hence the supply of marketable goods from the given resources. The value of changes estimated through the market price of the goods is hence used as measure of the benefit or loss resulting from a change in environmental quality.

32.7.2 Human Capital or Foregone Earnings Approach: This method uses human productivity measured in terms of foregone earnings to evaluate benefits of an environmental programme. The lost earnings and medical costs that result from the environmental damage caused by a project and comparable savings that would accrue from preventing that damage is the standard of valuation. The earnings lost and cost of health care due to a deterioration in environmental quality are examined. This method is more applicable when the illness is of a relatively short period and does not have long term negative effects. An example of this method is the reduction in diarrhea due to an improvement in water quality—the reduction in the incidence of diarrhea will reduce absenteeism from work and improve productivity.

The foregone earnings approach requires the fulfillment of the following conditions:

1. The etiology of the disease [cause and effect] must be clearly identifiable.
2. The illness must be of short duration, not life threatening and without major long term effects.
3. The precise economic value of earnings and medical care should be known. If the disease is chronic and its effect is debilitating, but not completely disabling, valuation is complicated. This is the case when the victim functions at less than full potential although seeming to be healthy.

32.7.3 Dose Response Method: Dose response method evolves a functional relationship between the pollutant and the effects. It is also known as the production function approach.The dose response function for a given segment of population is an estimate of the relationship between levels of one or more residuals to which the population segment has been exposed and the effects of such exposure. Regression analysis has been used to estimate dose response relationships for both acute and chronic effects. The dose response function thus shows the relationship between human health and exposure to pollution of various types. The dose response function is also used to assess the damage to properties and flora and fauna, caused by pollution. The total effect on health, properties and flora and fauna caused by exposure to pollution is analysed and a value is placed on this. The dose response function is mainly used as a tool in productivity approach and foregone income approach.

32.8 Benefit Transfer Method

Beginning from 1980s researchers are seen using a method known as the benefit transfer method for quicker and less costly estimation of environmental benefits.The benefit transfer method estimates economic values for environmental goods and services by making use of available information from similar studies already completed in another location and/or context. Smith V K, van Houtven, G. and Pattanayak, S.K (2002) define it as the "…practice of adapting value estimates from past research to assess the value of a similar, but separate, change in a different resource." In other words, this method uses values from preexisting research studies that were estimated for sites with similar characteristics and in similar contexts for application into existing policy decisions. Benefit transfers are most often used when there is lack of time, funding, data availability or other constraints to do a primary data survey. The method uses not only the WTP/WTA results of the pre- existing studies but also uses existing valuation functions and models. Although the method has been in use since 1980s, the use of benefit transfer method became popular from 1990s.

There are two categories of benefit transfer approach:

- unit transfer
- benefit function transfer

Unit value transfers use a single value from an earlier study of a similar site and require demographic and physical characteristics of the two sites to be very similar. In this if adjustments are made in the transferred unit values to reflect differences in site characteristics, then it is referred to as adjusted unit benefit transfer.

Benefit function transfers use an average of values from previous studies and apply them to the environmental good/service for which values are to be estimated (Navrud, S.; Ready, R, 2007). This approach uses functions and parameter values from earlier studies which have been estimated by applying the relevant valuation technique. There are three crucial steps to be followed before Benefit transfer method is applied. They are:

- Identifying the environmental good or service to be valued
- Identifying similar and appropriate existing studies
- Assessing the relevance and applicability of the existing studies.

Once the environmental good or service to be valued has been identified the following steps are crucial. Identifying similar studies is very crucial. Appropriate and similar studies should be chosen and their relevance should be assessed before using them. Using inappropriate studies will result in transfer errors. Transfer errors refer to the difference between resulting estimates and actual values. Since estimates are based on values from earlier studies, it is important to verify the appropriateness of the studies used.

Benefit transfer method is hailed as a practical, timely and cost effective approach to estimate the value of environmental goods and services if cautiously applied to avoid transfer errors.

Conclusion

Measuring environmental of benefits can be made by using any of the appropriate methods. Such valuations are becoming very crucial to decision making in environmental management. The policy makers and courts rely a lot on the information provided by such benefit valuations. With environmental audit and E.I.A becoming compulsory in many countries, benefits valuations are required for better policy formulations. Newer techniques are being developed to uncover values that were previously not considered for evaluation. The accuracy of the results, however, depend on the proper use of the appropriate method.

Questions

1. Explain why it is difficult to estimate the value people place on environmental goods, the benefits they receive from cleaner air and other services of nature.
2. What are the various components of economic value of an environmental resource? Give examples.
3. Explain the theoretical foundations of the valuation methods.
4. Account for the difference between WTP and WTA and give examples of research studies on the difference between the two.
5. Classify the various methods available to measure environmental benefits.
6. Explain the designing of a CVM
7. What are the limitations of CVM
8. Given an account on the Choice modeling approach to evaluating environmental benefits.
9. Explain the hedonic methods.
10. How are environmental benefits measured using household production function method?
11. Write a note on the various cost based methods
12. Explain the use of conventional market based methods to measure environmental benefits.
13. What is benefit transfer method?

Exercise

1. Describe how you will proceed with a CVM survey for a policy to clean a polluted water body in your state/ region/country.
2. Consider any recreation site in your district/state of residence and do a TCM and give the results. Also test for comparability of your results with CVM.
3. Try to isolate the increase in property value due to environmental features in your district area.
4. Locate from the website prominent research articles on benefit valuation for air or water quality improvement or any such environmental programme, which may be used for applying the benefit transfer method. Justify the selection.

33

ENVIRONMENTAL IMPACT ASSESSMENT

"The purpose of Environmental Impact Assessment (EIA) is to give environment its due place in the decision making process by clearly evaluating the environmental consequences of a proposed activity before any action is taken."

—The UN Economic Commission for Europe (1987).

Environmental Impact Assessment [EIA] refers to the evaluation of the effects of a major project on a man-made natural environment. It is a decision making tool that predicts both the beneficial and adverse environmental consequences of policies, programmes, plans and projects. The EIA proposes measures to mitigate adverse effects and predicts whether there will be significant adverse environmental effects, even after the mitigation is implemented. EIA compares the various alternatives for a project and seeks to identify the one which represents the best combination of economic and environmental costs and benefits. The increasing scale, complexity, uncertainty and risks of the major development projects have culminated in the use of EIA, thanks to the public awareness of and activism against environmental effects of mega projects.

33.1 Evolution of EIA

Early attempts as project assessment relied on technical feasibility studies and cost benefit analysis. The CBA placed a monetary value upon non-economic variables such as marine ecosystems or the social and health impacts of pollution. On account of its failure to incorporate temporal changes such as changes in price level, discount rate and interest rate, CBA often yielded inflated measure of benefits. Omission of unforeseen harmful impacts that reduce predicted benefits of the project has been a serious limitation of the CBA, besides its failure to consider distributional aspects of costs and benefits. The omission of secondary benefits of the projects on environment can lead to serious consequences if the project is implemented. The Aswan dam on River Nile in Egypt is a monumental example of all that can go wrong with large dams. Egypt's Aswan dam caused a dramatic increase in the waterborne disease, schistomiasis. The perennial irrigation projects fed by the Aswan dam have resulted in widespread salinisation. Prior to the dam, annual floods in Nile helped to washout the accumulated salts. With the construction of dam, the salts accumulated on land and thus nearly 35 per cent of irrigated land was affected on account of the reduced silt load of the Nile. Before the construction of the dam, Nile deposited 100 million tonnes a year of organically rich sediment on nearly 10,000 sq km of land. Today it deposits just a few tonnes a year, the remaining being trapped behind the dam. The reduction of silt has resulted in coastal erosion and as a consequence, sandine shoals catch has decreased from 15000 tonnes a year prior to the dam, to 500 tonnes a year after the dam. Due to its detrimental secondary effects such as loss of agricultural productivity, and a reduction in Mediterranean fishing industry, the Aswan dam failed to be the promised "source of everlasting prosperity". The limitations of the CBA, provoked the need for an alternative tool to evaluate development projects. The EI A thus began as an alternative to CBA for social accounting.

EIA is one of the successful policy innovations of the 20th Century for environmental protection and for achieving sustainable development. EIA was introduced in the U.S.A. following the enactment of the National Environmental Policy Act [NEPA] by the United States Congress in 1969. It is only after mid 1980s that EIA gained popularity among policy makers throughout the world. In 1989, the World Bank adopted EIA for major development projects, and insisted that the borrower country had to undertake the EIA under the Bank's supervision. It is currently practiced in more than 100 countries. Today EIA has evolved as a management tool—a planning aid—that helps in identifying, predicting, assessing impacts on environment from proposed development projects. It is a valuable mechanism that aids in promoting sustainable development.

33.2 Definition of EIA

EIA is an "anticipatory, participatory, integrative environmental management tool which has the ultimate objective of providing decision makers with an indication of the likely consequences of their decisions relating to new projects or new programmes, plans or policies". EIA ensures that the likely effects of new development on the environment are fully understood and taken into account before the development is allowed to go ahead. As the U.K. department of environment puts it, an EIA,

"is essentially a technique for drawing together, in a systematic way, expert qualitative assessment of a project's environmental effects and presenting the results in a way which enables the importance of the predicted effects and scope for modifying or mitigating them, to be properly evaluated by the relevant decision making body, before a decision is taken."

EIA can be broadly defined as the systematic identification and evaluation of the potential impacts (effects) of proposed projects, plans, programmes or legislative actions relative to the physical, chemical, biological, cultural and socio-economic components of the total environment (Canter, 1996).

EIA helps the decision makers to identify the likely effects at an early stage and to improve the quality of project planning and decision making. It is a process used to predict the environmental consequences of proposed major development projects, to identify and plan for appropriate measures to reduce adverse impacts.

The EIA is both a science and art. It is a science in terms of its methodologies and techniques employed to identify, predict and evaluate the environmental impacts of development programmes. It becomes an art when it is used to influence decision making. The significance of EIA has been summarised by Calwell as follows:

- EIA is a means to a larger end—the protection and improvement of environmental quality.
- It is not just a single technique or method but a procedure that uses many approaches to evaluate environmental impacts.
- It is interdisciplinary.
- It is an integral part of project planning and not just an appendage.
- EIA does not make decisions but its findings should be considered in policy and decision making.

33.3 Objectives of EIA

The long term aim of EIA is to promote sustainable development by ensuring that development proposals do not undermine vital functions of the environment and the livelihood of people who depend on them. The immediate aim of EIA is to identify all possible environmental effects and risks of development proposals and consider them in the decision making process. In general, the objective of the environmental impact assessment is to prevent situations of environmental deterioration, to establish appropriate measures for reducing human impacts to acceptable levels, and to protect environmental quality. Specific objectives of EIA include:

- To ensure that environmental considerations are explicitly addressed and incorporated into the decision making process at every stage of planning a development project or programme;
- To predict, anticipate and avoid, minimize or offset the significant adverse effects – environmental, economic, social, cultural effects - of development proposals;
- To protect the productivity and capacity of natural systems and the ecological processes which maintain their functions; and
- To promote development that is sustainable and optimizes resource use and management opportunities

33.4 Principles of EIA

International Association for Impact Assessment (1995) and others have developed certain guiding principles of EIA. These basic principles are:

1. ***Purposive***: The EIA process should help in decision making and result in appropriate levels of environmental protection and human wellbeing.
2. ***Inclusive:*** The EIA process should include adequate participation of all stakeholders. The process should involve interested and affected public, and their inputs and concerns should be addressed explicitly in the documentation and decision making.
3. ***Practical:*** EIA should result in output and information that are acceptable and implementable.
4. ***Efficient***: The process should impose the minimum cost burdens in terms of time and finance on proponents and participants consistent with the objectives of EIA.
5. ***Certainty***: The process and timing of assessment should be agreed in advance and followed by all participants.
6. ***Credible*** - The process should be carried out with professionalism, rigor, fairness, objectivity, impartiality and balance, and be subject to independent checks and verification.
7. ***Adaptive***: EIA should be adjusted to the realities, issues and circumstances of the proposals under review without compromising the integrity of the process. Flexibility is desirable in terms of the form of EIA process, issues to be addressed, process time-frames and degree of public participation.
8. ***Systematic***: The process should result in full consideration of all relevant information on the affected environment, of proposed alternatives and their impacts, and of the measures necessary to monitor and investigate residual effects.
9. ***Accountability:*** Decision makers within government need to be able to provide clear and detailed reasons for their decisions to all stakeholders.
10. ***Interdisciplinary*** - the process should ensure that the appropriate techniques and experts in the relevant bio-physical and socio-economic disciplines are employed, including use of traditional knowledge as relevant.
11. ***Focused***: The process should concentrate on significant environmental effects and key issues that are necessary and important for decision making.

12. ***Integrated***: The process should include relationships of social, economic, ecological, and bio-physical aspects.
13. ***Transparent***: EIA should be clear, easily understood and an open process, with early notification procedure, access to documentation and a public record of decisions taken and reasons for them.
14. ***Relevant***: The process should provide sufficient reliable and usable information for decision making.

33.5 The EIA Process

An EIA attempts to answer the following questions:

1. What will happen as a result of the project?
2. What will be the extent of the changes?
3. Do the changes matter?
4. What can be done about them?
5. How can decision makers be informed of what needs to be done?

EIA is an attempt to answer these questions. There are eight steps in a well conducted EIA. These are:

1. Screening	5. Reporting
2. Scoping	6. Review of EIA
3. Impact Analysis	7. Decision Making
4. Mitigation	8. Post Monitoring

The figure 33.1 is a schematic representation of the EIA process

1. **Screening:** Screening clarifies whether a project requires an EIA or not. Where a detailed EIA is not warranted, the resources may be utilised elsewhere. Hence the first step is screening. When the project is at the conceptual level, screening is done to clear a project, comparing it with similar projects in the past. Screening categorises the project proposals into the following three categories:
   (a) Project clearly requiring an EIA.
   (b) Project not requiring an EIA.
   (c) Project for which application of an EIA is not clear.

   If the project does not require EIA, environmental clearance is given without EIA. When it is not clear whether an EIA should be done or not, then a Rapid Assessment is suggested. Rapid assessment identifies the impact based on existing data and/or on the basis of minimum data collected and predicts the magnitude of impacts and evaluates their importance to decision makers and helps to decide whether a detailed EIA is required or not. If no significant impacts are shown in the rapid assessment exercise (referred to as FONSI—Finding of No Significant Impact), then the project is cleared without a detailed EIA. If rapid assessment calls for full EIA, the next step is organising the EIA study, which requires forming the team, identifying the key decision makers who will plan, finance, permit and control the proposed projects, besides studying extensively the laws and regulations that will affect these decisions. Guidelines for whether or not an EIA is required are country specific depending on the laws or norms in operation. Legislation often specifies the criteria for screening and full EIA.
2. **Scoping:** Once it is decided that a formal EIA is required and the team and coordinator have been organized, the next stage is scoping. Scoping is essential for focusing the available resources on

the relevant issues. This stage identifies issues that have a significant impact on the environment and hence need to be probed further. The choice of such primary issues will depend on the magnitude of impact, geographic extent, significance to decision makers etc. Besides defining the boundary and time limit of the study, scoping involves public participation. specific primary issues will depend on the magnitude of impacts, geographical extent, significance to decision makers, etc. Besides defining the boundary and time limit of the study, scoping involves public participation. Identification of the significant issues is based on the views from public, special interest groups and decision makers. Final part of scoping is the preparation of the terms of reference (TOR) and getting its approval by the decision makers. TOR is a written document that specifies the requirements governing EIA implementation, consultations to be held, data to be procured, methodology to be used etc. Approval of TOR takes the EIA to the next crucial step of impact analysis. Scoping is an ongoing exercise throughout the course of the project. Tools such as checklist, matrices, networks and consultations are used extensively during scoping.

3. **Impact analysis:** This step is considered to be the heart of the EIA. This stage of EIA identifies and predicts the likely environmental and social impact of the proposed project evaluates their significance and suggest measures to prevent, and reduce the impacts. Thus there are three steps in impact analysis.

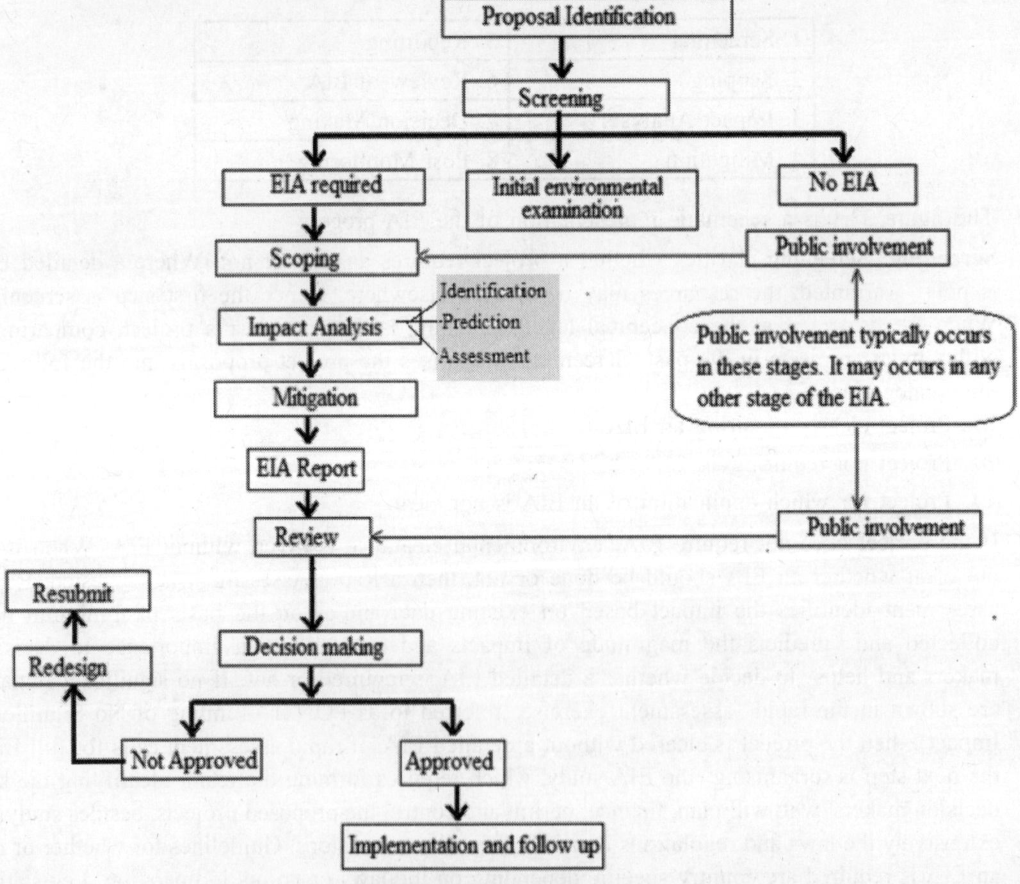

Figure33.1 EIA Process

Source: *The manual in perspective, EIA Training Resource Manual, United Nations Environment Programme, 2002, p114; from CSE (2006) in Understanding EIA - Industry & Environment Unit, Centre for Science & Environment downloaded from http:// www.cseindia.org/node/383*

First step, identification, that answers the first question 'what will happen as a result of the project', helps to assess in detail the most important impacts with the aid of check lists, matrices, networks, and simulation.

The second step, namely, **prediction,** answers the second question, "What will be the extent of the changes?" by quantifying the impacts through mathematical models, physical models, socio-cultural models, economic models and experiments.

The third step is assessment of the impacts. This step seeks to answer the question 'do the changes matter?' This step **assesses** the predicted adverse impacts by comparing it with laws, regulations, or accepted standards or by reference to pre-set criteria, or on the basis of acceptance to local community or public in general. Evaluations involve consultations with relevant decision makers. Prediction and assessment of the impacts requires:

- **Description of existing environment** through the collection of all pertinent environmental data relating to the project site for all seasons.
- **Procurement of relevant by laws through the** assemblage of relevant standards, regulations and bylaws to know the permissible level and quantity of impact.

4. **Mitigation:** If evaluation warrants mitigation for the impacts, the study team, may suggest the following **mitigation** steps:
   - technical/scientific measures : Change of project site, production process, raw materials, etc.
   - legally-mandated measures : introduction of pollution controls, waste treatment, monitoring pollutants, effluents, etc.
   - social acceptability measures: Restoration of damaged resources, compensation to affected persons, etc.

This step provides answer to the fourth question "What can be done about them?" This stage involves consultation with stakeholders and decision makers etc. In this stage, an action plan for impacts and mitigation, called Environmental Management Plan (EMP) is prepared.

According to Ogola (2007), the objectives of mitigation, are to:

- find better alternatives and ways of doing things;
- enhance the environmental and social benefits of a project
- avoid, minimise or remedy adverse impacts; and
- ensure that residual adverse impacts are kept within acceptable levels

5. **Reporting:** Finally EIA study team **documents the EIA process and presents it to the decision makers.** This answers the question "How can decision makers be informed of what needs to be done". The report focuses on major environmental and natural resources as well as issues that need specific attention along with the action plan and a description of the proposed development project. A summary of the EIA for the general public is also presented. The report has visual aids to impart clarity and precision to the information presented in the report. "In addition to summarizing the impacts of the alternatives under study this report must include a section on follow up action required to enable implementation of proposals and to monitor long-term impacts. The purpose of an EIA is not to reach a decision but to present the consequences of different choices of actions and to make recommendations to a decision maker. Recommendations are a crucial part of the Environmental Impact Statement"(FAO).

The EIA thus tells the decision makers all they need to know about the project, its impact, and the final report is referred to as **Environmental Impact Statement (EIS).** Most national environmental laws have specified what the content of EIS should have. The EIS contains:

- Executive Summary of the EIA findings in 2 to 5 pages.
- Description of the Proposed Project in detail
- A summary of the EIA methodology, including the limits of the study and the reasons for them.
- A summary of the baseline data providing an overall picture of present conditions and physical, biological and ecological trends. The consequences of the "no-action" option should be described.
- Significant Environmental Impacts
- Socio-economic analysis of Project Impacts
- Identification and Analysis of Alternatives
- Mitigation Action/Mitigation Management Plan
- Environmental Management Plan
- Monitoring Program
- Knowledge gaps
- Public Involvement
- List of References
- Appendices including
  * Reference documents, photographs, unpublished data
  * Terms of Reference
  * Consulting team composition
  * Notes of Public Consultation sessions

The quality of the executive summary is particularly important as some decision-makers may read this part of the report alone. The executive summary must include the most important impacts, particularly those that are unavoidable and irreversible, the key mitigating measures, proposed monitoring and supervision requirements, and the recommendations of the report.

6. **Review:** Review is done to check the EIA for adequacy and relevance. The process begins with selecting the reviewers who may be experts or the decision maker himself may be the reviewer besides defining the review criteria and scaling of reviews. The reviewing is done by various methods like checklists, expert opinion, public review etc. In reviewing, reviewer sets a scale of reviewing and gives the project a final rating between A to F, with A 'denoting' well performed and F standing for unsatisfactory and B to E imply: from satisfactory to insufficient. The reviewer is expected to submit:
   - A brief summary of the strengths and weaknesses of report
   - Any needs for further study
   - Any terms/conditions that should apply if proposal is granted.
7. **Decision making:** In this penultimate stage reviewers decide whether to allow the project to proceed and establish the terms and conditions for its implementation. The decision makers based on their knowledge and experience and on the basis of the EIA report and the review of the EIA report, decide on the course of action. It is not mandatory for the decision maker to approve the project based on the review and the EIA report. After careful scrutiny by the decision makers, the project either gets the environmental clearance or is asked to be resubmitted after making corrections wherever found inadequate and ineffective. Once the environmental clearance is given by the decision makers,the proponent is bound to follow the EMP (Environmental Management Plan). The project can be started after clearance is issued.

8. **Follow up and Monitoring:** Once the project is commissioned, monitoring begins. Follow up is done to monitor, manage and audit the impacts of project implementation. This is done to:
   a. ensure that impacts do not exceed legal standards
   b. check the implementation of measures described in the EIA report
   c. to provide early warning of potential damages.

The last stage of an EIA is an **Environmental Audit** which is normally done after the completion of the project. The audit will determine whether the recommendations of the EIA were incorporated during the implementation of the project. It will identify gaps, if any, between actual impacts and predicted impacts. Ideally auditing will determine:

1. the accuracy of the original predictions
2. degree of deviation from original predictions
3. possible reasons for deviation and
4. efficacy of the remediation measures.

Information generated from the audit will be useful for future EIAs.

33.6 Methodology of EIA for Identification and Prediction of Impacts

Seven principal methods are used for impact identification, prediction, and evaluation. They are:

- Adhoc approach
- Check lists
- Interaction matrices.
- Overlay mapping,
- Networks
- Simulation Modelling
- Geographical Information System

Ad Hoc Approach: This is the oldest and crudest approach to EIA. This method facilitates qualitative assessment of the total impact and identifies the broad areas of the possible impacts. An example of an ad hoc method is a team of experts assembled for a short time to conduct an EIA. Each expert's conclusions are based on a unique combination of experience, training and intuition. These conclusions are assembled into a report. Sometimes this is the only required or possible approach. This method lacks in quantification and precision.

Checklist: Checklists are more formalized version of ad hoc approaches - specific areas of impact are listed and instructions are supplied for impact identification and evaluation. In the check list methodology, listing of features, affected by a project may be a ***simple check list*** of potentially affected factors without any guide line or information on the measurement of various factors or it could be a ***descriptive checklist*** which includes measurement and predictive technique for each factor. Besides there is also the ***scaling checklist*** which provides a criterion for evaluation of impacts in the form of a subjective ranking or scaling, besides providing for measurement and predictive techniques. Checklist is good technique in the initial stages of assessment and for guidance on the available alternatives. But checklists conceal interactions and can be generated or may even end up with double counting.

Interaction Matrix: Matrices are two-dimensional tables used to identify impacts arising from the interaction between project activities and specific environmental components. They are a display of project activities along one axis with appropriate environmental factor along other axis. When a given action is expected to cause a change in environmental factors, this is noted in the cell that is at the interaction point of the corresponding row and column in the matrix. The impact is noted using numerical score or using symbols. There are different types of matrices.

- Simple matrices
- Stepped matrices
- Weighted matrices
- Advanced network matrices.

Simple matrices are organised to cross reference the different phases of a project (e.g. construction, operation and decommissioning) against elements of the environment.

Stepped matrices consider how the various activities of a project relate to the environmental resource or parameter. It shows resources against functions of the environment. This approach therefore shows how the impact of an action on a resource causes, in turn changes, on another resource.

Weighted matrices attach weights to the impacts and hence magnitude of impacts can be measured quantitatively. By introducing weighting into a matrix it allows the ranking of impacts. However since weights are subjectively determined, errors are bound to arise. Hence criteria for choosing the weights must be given and justified.

Advanced network matrices use matrix to identify the activities of the project and their impact on environment and use network method to consider the relationship between the two in depth.

Leopold matrix: This is based on a horizontal list of development actions and a vertical list of environmental characteristics The Leopold matrix provides a systematic checking of each development action concerned with the project against a listing of environmental factors. In a Leopold matrix the columns of the matrix correspond to project actions (for example, flow alteration) while the rows represent environmental conditions (for example, water temperature). The impact associated with the action columns and the environmental condition row is described in terms of its magnitude and significance.

In the Leopold Matrix the interaction in terms of its magnitude (M) is described in the upper section and the importance (I) in the lower section of each box. The matrix describes the magnitude of an impact by numerical scale by assigning a numerical value from one to ten. The value, ten represents the largest magnitude and the value, one represents the lowest magnitude: values near five represent impacts of intermediate magnitude. The scale of importance also ranges from one to ten. The higher the value, the higher the importance; the lower the value, the lower the importance. Plus (+) or minus (-) is used to show whether an impact is beneficial or adverse.

Project Actions / Environmental conditions	1	2	3	4	5
A		3 / 2			-9 / 6
B		4 / 4	-6 / 5	4 / 2	-7 / 5

Table 33.1 A Simple example of a Leopold Matrix

Source: Chieng,S. Environmental Impact Assessment (modified)

The Leopold matrix lists 100 possible project actions within ten general categories on the horizontal axis and lists 88 environmental factors within four general categories. To use the matrix, the analyst will first have to check all the activities associated with the project. As a second step, all the environmental factors are examined and a slash may be marked in those cells where an impact is possible for the corresponding activity. The magnitude and importance of the impact may then be assessed using an appropriate scale. The appropriate cell is scored for magnitude and importance of the impact. A positive or negative sign is used to donate beneficial or harmful impacts. Rows total reflect the total impact of all project actions on one environmental component while columns total reflect the impact of one project action on all components of the environment. The matrix total gives the total environmental impact.

The matrix approach is reasonably flexible with scope to increase or decrease actions and corresponding environmental component. The matrix can also be employed to identify impacts at every stage of the proposed development activity. The major use of matrices is to indicate cause and effect by listing activities along the horizontal axis and environmental parameters along the vertical axis. This helps in comparing the impacts of both individual components of projects as well as major alternatives. Thus an interaction matrix serves both as a check list and as a summary of impact assessment and is the ideal tool for rapid impact assessment. However a matrix conceals secondary effects and gives scope for double counting, like checklists. Further they do not explicitly represent spatial or temporal considerations, and they do not adequately address synergistic impacts.

Overlay Mapping: Overlay mapping pioneered by McHarg in 1969, is an approach based on principles of land capabilities mapping. In this, the features of the existing environment is super imposed on the base map of the area with the aid of transparent sheets and the impacts are distinguished as high or medium through dark or light shading respectively and low impact attributes are not shaded. Overlay mapping thus provides a powerful visual representation of potential impacts. However, overlay mapping cannot distinguish between direct and indirect effects and cannot reflect synergistic effects arising from two or more factors.

Networks: Networks illustrate the cause-effect relationship of project activities and environmental characteristics. Networks are directional diagrams designed to link secondary and tertiary impacts to primary impacts. There are three steps in a network diagram. First step is to identify the first order or primary impacts on environment from the project. Second step is to identify the secondary changes. The changes in environmental components arising from primary impacts on environment are secondary changes. Identifying tertiary impacts is the third step. The changes in environmental components arising from secondary impacts are referred to as tertiary impacts. Identifying such tertiary impacts and further impacts continue till all impacts are identified and the network diagram is completed. The network diagram thus helps in understanding and exploring the environmental components that produce further impacts which are ignored by other approaches.

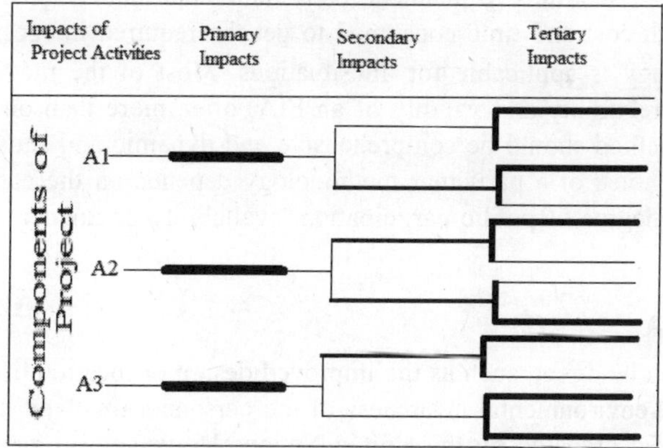

Figure 33.2 A Simple Conceptual General Model of a Network Diagram

There are different types of networks, such as sequence diagrams, directed diagrams or impact trees. The networks can be used to show both temporal and spatial flows of impacts. The merit of a network is its inclusion of indirect impacts that may arise from a project and its provision of visual representation of these impacts. However networks are rarely used because of the higher cost imposed by the informational constraint. Similar to networks is the *systems diagram* method except for the difference that a systems diagram links environmental components on the basis of energy flows between these components.

Simulation Modeling: Simulation modeling involves the integration of standard modeling approaches in natural and social sciences with the help of computers and other highly sophisticated technical aids. Environmentalists developed a rigorous mathematical approach to management of natural resources known as the Adaptive environmental assessment and management (AEAM). The purpose of this method is to produce a tool to predict environmental effects. In this method, small work group of experts design a mathematical model of the proposed project. The interdisciplinary team consisting of scientists, decisionmakers and economists,interact with expertise in modeling techniques through several modelling workshops and predict impacts and evaluate alternatives. In the working group a consensus has to be reached upon important properties and correlations in the systems modelled. The modellers make a mathematical model based upon the result of the working group. The model is evaluated by the working group and it may be refined if necessary.

Models are used to describe, explain and predict the features of environmental systems. Simulation modeling is very useful when considerable uncertainty exists with respect to the dynamic inter relationship between variables and when data is not easily available.

Geographical Information System

GIS is a set of computerized tools for collecting, storing, retrieving, transforming, and displaying spatial data. GIS combines maps with computer graphics and databases. GIS is regarded as the high-tech equivalent of a map. A GIS based map contains a lot of information and are used in diverse applications; from locating telephone wires and street lights in a street to displaying the extent of deforestation in the Brazilian rain forests and the thinning of a glacier in Iceland. A significant application of GIS is the construction of real world models based on digital data. GIS models help in analyzing the trends, identifying the factors causing the trends observed and also help in finding alternative paths to solve the issues. Using GIS we can identify the extent and of deforestation, intensity of deforestation in any specific area and based on this study the impact of this on rainfall and water table etc. GIS is a useful tool for displaying and visualizing trends and patterns in spatial data sets. GIS provides visual aids to planners, consultants and managers. However, the use of GIS is inhibited by this high cost and time consumed to get the required images.

No one methodology is applicable for all situations. Most of the methods fail to evaluate all the impact. To ensure reliability and validity of an EIA, often more than one method is used in the process. The chosen method should be comprehensive and dynamic and should respond to legal and policy requirements. Choice of a particular methodology depends on the nature of alternative being assessed, the role and degree of public participation, availability of finance and other administrative constraints.

33.7 Benefits of EIA

The benefits of EIA can be direct, such as the improved design or location of a project; or it could be indirect, such as better environmental awareness of the personnel involved in the project. According to a EIA course material prepared by the United Nations University, in general the benefits of EIA include:

- Better environmental planning and design of a proposal.
- Improved technology, which lowers waste outputs or an environmentally optimum location for a project.
- EIA helps to protect our environment from haphazard development activities and helps in achieving sustainable development.
- Reducing risks and impacts on the environment and people, and thereby avoid associated costs of remedial treatment or compensation for damage.
- Ensuring compliance with environmental standards. Compliance with environmental standards reduces damage to the environment and disruption to communities. It also avoids the likelihood of penalties, fines and loss of trust and credibility.
- Savings in capital and operating costs since EIA can avoid the undue costs of unanticipated impacts. An "anticipate and avoid" approach is much cheaper than "react and cure" approach.
- Reduced time costs of approvals of development applications. Since EIA helps in taking into account all environmental concerns properly before submission for project approval, delays due to demand for additional information by decision makers or alterations to project such as specific mitigation measures are avoided.
- Increased accountability and transparency during the development process.
- Increased project acceptance by the public due to a transparent EIA process, with provision of opportunities for public involvement of people who are likely to be affected by the project.

33.8 Limitations of EIA

The benefits of EIA in terms of reduced environmental impacts of the project can be reaped only if the required environmental policy and criteria are applied in other contexts also. Since EIA does not provide a final decision and since EIA procedures cannot be expected to stop a proposal, EIA is considered as only an aid to the decision-making process, and **not a decision making tool in itself**. The limited power of EIA may greatly reduce its value. EIA suffers from the following limitations:

- EIA should be undertaken at the policy and planning level rather than at the project level.
- Range of possible alternatives in EIA is often small.
- EIA reports are too academic, bureaucratic and lengthy.
- Time limitation, manpower limitation makes EIA very complicated and time consuming.
- In actual practice, EIA ends immediately after project clearance; no follow up action is taken.
- It does not incorporate the strategies of preventive environmental intervention.

The success of a EIA depends on the availability of resources—both financial and physical resources. Qualified multidisciplinary staff trained in environmental science, engineering, economics, sociology, cultural anthropology and planning with analytical capability for research work play a crucial role in shaping the recommendations of EIA. Besides the availability of these personnel, information and time are significant factors too. Technical guidelines for carrying out various phases of EIA, especially, screening, scoping, prediction, evaluation, and information about environment should be freely available. Though a preliminary assessment may take just 2 to 10 months to be completed, a full EIA may take between 3 months to 2 years. An EIA costs only 1 per cent of the project proposal, which is a relatively small price to pay to prevent costly unforeseen problems, to promote sustainable development and to prevent potentially adverse environment catastrophes.

EIAs are being carried out for various development projects now. For example, the Sepang International Airport on a 10,000 hectares site, 60 kms south of Kuala Lumpur, the 6000 MW thermal power stations of China Light And Power Co. Ltd. at Hong Kong, and the Chemical Complex in Spain in its rural area have involved detailed EIAs requiring study of key issues, like, air quality, water quality, and other ecological impacts.

33.9 EIA in India

EIA was first introduced as a regulatory requirement in 1994. However it can be said that the seeds were sown for including in environmental policy as early as 1976 -77 when the planning Commission asked the Department of Science and Technology to examine the river valley projects from an environmental angle. This was subsequently extended to cover those projects which required the approval of Public Investment Board. The Government of India enacted the Environment (Protection) Act in May 1986. To achieve the objectives of the Act, it was decided to make EIA statutory. After following the legal procedure a notification was issued on January 27th 1994 which made environmental clearance mandatory for the expansion or modernisation of any activity or for setting up new projects . Since 1994, 12 amendments have been made to the 1994 EIA notification.

The MoEF (Ministry of Environment and Forests) notified new EIA legislation in September 2006. The notification makes it mandatory for various projects such as mining, thermal power plants, river valley, infrastructure (road, highways, ports, harbor and airports) and industries including very small electro plating or foundry units to get environmental clearance. Unlike the 1994 EIA notification, the new legislation had put the onus of clearing projects on the concerned state government depending on the size and/or capacity of projects. Where state level authorities have not been constituted, clearance is to be provided by the MoEF. Further the notification provided for addressing all relevant environmental concerns for the preparation of the EIA report, public consultation and appraisal of projects based on public consultation and final EIA report).

Certain activities permissible under the Coastal Regulation Zone Act, 1991 also require environmental clearance. Additionally, donor agencies operating in India like the World Bank and the Asian Development Bank (ADB) have a different set of requirements for giving environmental clearance to projects that are funded by them. Apart from this, any project located in a critically polluted area, within a radius of 15 kilometers of the boundary of reserved forests, ecologically sensitive areas, has to obtain environmental clearance directly from the Central Government irrespective of its project categorization. Ecologically sensitive areas include national parks, sanctuaries, biosphere reserves; Three significant changes were initiated through the 2006 amendment to make the appraisal process more streamlined, transparent, and independent of politicking.

First, the decentralization of regulatory functions to State level Environment Impact Assessment Agencies (SEIAA). SEIAAs were to oversee smaller scale projects and the MOEF would continue to regulate larger scale projects Second, although the final regulatory approval would be decided by the MOEF or the concerned SEIAA, they in turn were to base their approvals on the recommendations of the State Expert Appraisal Committee (SEAC) and the Expert Appraisal Committee (EAC) functioning in the MOEF.

Third, the State Pollution Control Boards (SPCB) or the Union Territory Pollution Control Committee (UTPCC) were given the responsibility for conducting the public hearing, taking responsibility away from the project proponents.

The amendments to EIA notifications of December 2009 exempts from environmental clearance process the biomass based power plants up to 15 MW, power plants based on non-hazardous municipal solid waste and power plants based on waste heat recovery boilers without using auxiliary fuel. The EIA process is now well established and EC has been provided to over 2850 development projects till date. Yet there are constraints such as : deficiencies in screening and scoping; inadequate public participation; weak monitoring; insufficient baseline data; insufficient allocation of resources (time and money); lack of expertise with EIA consultants and professionals; sound legal provisions but weak administrative set up (J.K. Panigrahi, S. Amirapu,2012). This can be improved to a large extent by strengthening the implementation of environmental legislation and improving public participation in environmental impact assessments.

Conclusion

The EIA is a proven management tool used extensively by Governments and NGOs for project planning and approval. The main aim of EIA is to improve decisions on development by increasing its quality and scope of information on the likely impacts of the project under consideration. EIAs are implemented mostly for development projects such as highways, power projects etc. Many countries have made EIA compulsory for any project likely to affect environmental quality. The Government of India has also issued guidelines and checklists for undertaking an EIA for power projects, and location of harbour, mining, land fills, etc.

Questions

1. Which type of project usually requires an EIA?
2. What are the key objectives of EIA review?
3. Explain the preparation of an EIA report?
4. What are the benefits of EIA.
5. What are the popular methods used in the preparation of EIA.

Exercise

1. Describe the evolution of EIA and the EIA process in India
2. Summarise a case study of EIA process in India prepared for any development project.

SECTION 8

CORPORATE ENVIRONMENTAL MANAGEMENT

34

SUSTAINABLE INDUSTRIALISATION

"The Earth isn't dying, it's being killed, and those who are killing it have names and addresses."

– Utah Philips"

Historically, rapid industrialisation has taken place only by tampering with the functions of the environment, the cumulative effects of which have today resulted in environmental crisis. The Business Council for Sustainable Development stated in its report to the UNCED, "We cannot continue in our present methods of using energy, managing forests, farming, protecting plant and animal species, managing urban growth and producing industrial goods". In line with this realisation, many governments and companies are attempting to define and implement sustainable economies and businesses, by experimenting with rational sustainability plans, life cycle analysis and industrial ecology. This chapter seeks to explore corporate social responsibility towards the environment and discusses the role industries can play in the development of sustainable societies.

Corporate environmental responsibility is embedded in the concepts of ecocentric management and sustainable development. There are three popular positions on the broad issue of corporate environmental responsibility:

First is the belief that the only responsibility of business is to make profit and hence the negative effects (pollution) of production can be handled using appropriate economic incentives and disincentives. This attitude is nothing but reliance on free markets.

Secondly, many believe that corporations are responsible for environmental side effects and hence should be made accountable for the damages through **regulation** and **voluntary corporate actions.** i.e., those who support this view advocate corporate reformation.

Finally, it is believed that modem business enterprises are the root cause of environmental crises. They are designed to exploit the natural environment and convert the environmental resources into market valued commodities. It is therefore the responsibility of the public to reject the environmentally destructive industrialization process being pursued now. The advocates of this view call for a radical transformation of the economy, of the corporate enterprises and of our life styles in particular.

34.1 Production Paradigms

The industrialisation process since the advent of the industrial revolution has witnessed at least three paradigms in production systems.

- Craft production system
- Mass production system
- Lean production system

1. Craft Production System: The original industrial revolution in the United Kingdom relied on the craft production system which is based on a blend of the traditional skills of artisans with new sources of power. Under the craft production system, industrial goods were largely made to order and products lacked standardisation. Each item was unique, varying from one another in terms of size and shape. Hence the use of raw materials per unit of output was not "efficient".

2. Mass Production System came into use in the early years of the 20th century; it provided for reaping of maximum economies of scale associated with large batch sizes. The mass production system churning out large batches of products, allowed production processes to be optimised and also helped to reduce the amount of raw material inputs, added advantage to their production .

3. **Lean Production System:** Lean production is about doing more with less: less time, less inventory, less space, less labor and less money. "Lean manufacturing", is a commitment to eliminating waste, simplifying procedures and speeding up production.

Craft -- highly skilled workers use simple flexible tools to make customized products.

Mass -- narrowly skilled professionals design products made by unskilled or semi skilled workers -- standardized products in very high volume - extra workers, extra supplies, extra space to assure smooth production (to keep expensive machines working)

Lean -- combines advantages of craft and mass production, avoiding the high cost of craft and the rigidity of mass production - employs teams of multi skilled workers at all levels - uses highly flexible, increasingly automated machinery to produce volumes of products in enormous variety- uses less of everything compared to mass production (elimination of waste) – waste minimisation philosophy.

Box 34.1 Paradigms of Production System

Lean production originated in Japan in the post war period. With the lean production system, firms were able to develop new models more frequently, make design changes more quickly and adapt to production changes within the factory with less disruption. While mass production refers to a manufacturing process in which products are manufactured on a mass scale, lean production refers to a manufacturing process in which items are produced based on current demand trends. With mass production process the idea is to manufacture the maximum number of products in one lot. A lean production process focuses on producing as per the latest market demand.

A lean production system would help to achieve the following benefits:

- Waste reduction by 80%
- Production cost reduction by 50%
- Manufacturing cycle time decreased by 50%
- Labor reduction by 50% while maintaining or increasing throughput
- Inventory reduction by 80% while increasing customer service levels
- Capacity in current facilities increase by 50%
- Higher quality and higher profits
- Higher system flexibility in reacting to changes in requirements improved.

Thus industrialisation has witnessed three paradigms in the past and now a fourth paradigm – sustainable industrialization - has emerged from the need to integrate environmental sustainability into the production system. In response to pressures on business to become more **sustainable** the new environmental management paradigm has emerged.

34.2 Sustainable Industrialisation

Sustainable industrialisation requires integrating environmental considerations at every stage of decision-making in the supply chain of the product, from resource extraction to disposal of the product – a cradle to grave approach. The product goes through five stages in the following sequence before it becomes a waste:

Material Extraction—Primary Processing—Design and Manufacture—Distribution—Use—Disposal

Every transformation generates environmental impacts which should be considered by the management/decision makers. This calls for an eco-centric approach to production rather than an anthropocentric approach.

From the experience of business corporations that have benefited from sustainable practices, one can theorise that sustainable industrialisation means:

- Adapting practices that build concern for the Earth into the whole apparatus of business, industry and commerce, by consciously avoiding environmental damage, monitoring environmental impacts and having consultations with local communities and the public at large.
- Introducing processes that minimise the use of raw materials and energy, reduce waste and prevent pollution.
- Making products that are "eco friendly" with minimum impact on people and the earth.

Sustainable industrialization commits companies to the following:

1. Shift from anthropocentrism to ecocentrism
2. Realisation that pollution = inefficiency
3. Awareness that pollution prevention pays
4. Acceptance of polluter pays principle
5. Adoption of Precautionary Principle
6. Full cost pricing – internalizing the externality

1.Shift from Anthropocentrism to Ecocentrism: Ecocentric management is opposed to the anthropocentric attitude that pervades corporations today. Ecocentric management rests on the holistic view that the human community, is an integral part of nature and is based on the faith that the humans are not separate from nature. Ecocentrism rejects the idea that nature is simply a resource to be used for human welfare. Nature has a right to exist and function normally. Ecocentrism recognises this right and status of nature and uses it with care and responsibility, by eliminating environmental damage and promoting a life style that is in harmony with nature. Ecocentric management of business enterprises is therefore the first step towards sustainable industrialisation.

2. **Realisation that pollution = inefficiency:** Companies have mostly realised that pollution is also a symptom of inefficiency, since wastes generated from production is Non-Product Output. Pollution is the result of inefficient resource use. Realisation of this by the firms is important for achieving sustainable industrialization. By innovating new technologies which will reduce wastes and promote reuse and recycling of wastes, companies become more efficient since better utilization of resources improves productivity of resources and reuse and recycling of wastes will reduce cost on raw materials. Thus not only does the firm become more efficient but also promotes conservation of resources.

3. **Awareness that pollution prevention pays**: Modern business corporation have realised that "greening" is, in fact, rewarding and hence there has been a shift from 'polluter pay principle' to 'pollution preservation pays'. Even though green consciousness will impose cost on companies, it gives opportunity for enterprise and invention, industrial world has ever seen. Many case studies reveal that corporate improvements in environmental performance have yielded economic benefits.

As pointed out by Business Council for sustainable Development, "Many of the waste reduction and environmentally positive programmes in business are economically viable and are providing positive rates of return in relatively short term periods". Sometimes the benefit comes in the form of straight cost reduction. A leading example is the 3M in company in the United States. In 1975, the head of the 3M's environmental department developed a programme called pollution prevention pays as the first integrated intra company approach for pollution prevention. The plan created incentives for reducing wastes by modifying manufacturing methods. By reformulating production processes, redesigning equipment and recovering waste for reuse or recycling, 3M was able to save \$537 mln. During the 15 year period it reduced its air pollution 120 thousand tonnes, its waste water by 1 bln gallons, its solid waste by 400 thousand tonnes. More than three thousand separate initiatives have contributed to the cause. The 3M company aimed at achieving zero emissions. Now known as the 3P plus, the plan requires the incorporation of environmental issues at all levels of business planning and is used as a factor in employer business reviews. The 3M program is an example of making money while preventing wastes which is the first step for the corporate world to become environmentally responsible.

Foron, a German refrigeration company used a mixture of propane and butane as cooling agents instead of the Ozone depleting CFCs. The company which was at the verge of bankruptcy soon became a dominant firm with its increased market share which compelled other refrigeration companies to adopt the same technology. In Japan legislation requires that all manufacturers label parts as to their recyclability, besides requiring manufactures to establish resource recovery centers. Japanese products are also designed for disassembly. Their new washing machines can be completely disassembled with a single screw driver.The experience of Germany and Japan proves the obvious: that manufacturers look for eco- friendly alternatives when there is regulation and fine. In many cases such fines compel the firms to innovate clean technologies which turn out to be rewarding through a reduction in cost or an improvement in product quality.

The sugar industry in India is an interesting example in terms of reuse of waste. Solid waste from sugar industry (bagasse) serves as a good raw material for pulp and paper industry. Many sugar mills use—bagasse as a substitute for coal in the boiler house for raising steam. Press mud, a filtered waste from sugarcane juice is used as manure by farmers. Press mud is also used to produce bio-gas. Ugar Sugar Works Ltd., in Karnataka uses press mud to supply bio-gas to 120 families residing near the factory. Similarly spent wash, a bio degradable waste from distilleries is also used to generate bio-gas. Thus firms have realised today that pollution prevention pays: that there are considerable resources productivity benefits and product benefits from environmental improvements. Material savings resulting from more complete processing, better utilisation of byproducts, lower energy consumption and reduced material storage are the benefits for the production processes which make products more safe and qualitative, paving the way for higher product resale and scrap value. In India, Harihar Polyfibres implemented 200 projects at its pulp mill between 1983-89 arriving at resource efficiency while its production increased by 20 per cent in this period, energy consumption fell by 60 per cent, chemical consumption by 55 per cent and effluent load by 60 per cent.

An evaluation of 500 industrial case studies in the UK and USA show that companies that reduce waste and prevent pollution by adopting clean technologies have benefited from:

a. Lower cost of raw materials.
b. Lower energy costs.
c. Lower waste disposal costs.
d. Reduced liability for clean-up of contamination caused.
e. Few regulatory complications.
f. Lower operational and maintenance cost.
g. Lower employee, public and environmental risk and lower expense both at present and in future.
h. Better employee morale, productivity and product quality.

In the 500 cases studied, wastes were reduced by 85 per cent to 100 per cent, the pay-back period ranged from one month to 3 years.Thus it is clear that sustainable industrialisation requires the firms to expand their production functions, by including "environmental" services as a separate variable. This will alter their cost function. Initially it may increase cost but as experience of some firms have shown, within a payback period of 2-3 years, obvious cost reductions result. Such an environmentally benign production functions or 'clean' production function will alter the demand functions for the product in favour of companies that resort to such measures. So in the long run, "sustainable industrialisation" benefits the firms, industries and economies at large.

Thus it has been proved that green investments yield net financial as well as environmental gains and can be justified in terms of financial as well as environmental gains. The cost reduction through energy and input efficiency achieved by firms that have included environmental consideration in their process reveal clearly that these steps will in fact give a competitive edge to these firms over other firms by:

a. Giving them comparative cost advantage over other firms who have not adopted green technologies or techniques and
b. By increasing their market share since consumers are increasingly concerned about environmental issues. This automatically makes these industries sustainable.

4. Acceptance of Polluter Pays Principle

The polluter-pays principle stipulates that the person or firm who imposes damages on the environment through production and consumption activities must bear the cost of such damage. Since pollution is often an externality, internalizing the externality through a tax induces the polluting firm to internalize the full social cost of his activity thereby reducing pollution to optimal level.

5. Adoption of Precautionary Principle

According to the Precautionary Principle, if there are reasonable scientific grounds for believing that a new process or product may not be safe, it should not be introduced until we have convincing evidence that the risks are small and are outweighed by the benefits. In the case of existing technologies the principle holds that when new evidence appears suggesting that the existing technology is more dangerous than we had thought, then the use of the existing technology should be limited till we get a better assessment of the risk. Examples include the case of CFCs, lead in petrol and GMOs (Genetically Modified Organisms). The technology or the product will be withdrawn or banned if the dangers are proved beyond doubt. The requirement is to demonstrate beyond reasonable doubt, that what is being proposed is safe. (Saunders, P, 2000).Commitment to the principle is a progressive step towards environmental protection by companies.

6. Full Cost Pricing

Environmental full-cost accounting (EFCA) is defined as a method of accounting that recognizes the direct and indirect economic, environmental, health and social costs of a project or action. It is also known as true-cost accounting (TCA). *It is also referred to as "triple bottom line" since such costs are considered in terms of three dimensions - environmental, economic and social impacts.* Environmental full cost accounting goes beyond the direct costs. It includes indirect costs, including externalities. Externality is an extra cost on third parties. For example, sulphur-di-oxide emissions from burning fuels in electric utilities and from other *industrial* sources impose health cost on the people besides being responsible for acid rain which in turn reduces agricultural yield. Full cost pricing includes the monetary estimates of such costs, though there are practical difficulties in measuring them. Besides the damage cost from pollution, the economic and environmental costs of using natural resources and the environmental and social costs of altering previously undisturbed land for the building of a project are also indirect costs. Since these costs are external to the firm, in the sense that the firm does not normally take these into consideration in its price – output decisions they are known as external cost by economists. If these indirect costs are taken into consideration by firms for decision making, then sustainable industrialization can be achieved.

Besides these requirements, sustainable industrialisation requires the adoption of high environmental performance standards backed up by economic incentives. To achieve these Governments must enforce national environmental laws, regulations and pricing techniques that would promote more efficient resource use, environmentally friendly products and minimise wastes, besides promoting energy efficiency. When companies face environmental regulations and pricing techniques, they look for a new technology with respect to *what it takes, what it makes, and what it wastes.*

Industries should have a choice on how they meet environmental standards. This will promote innovation of new efficient clean technologies. The adoption of the **Polluter Pays Principle,** and the **Precautionary Principle** should ensure that best technology available to meet the standards is employed by the firms to prevent and control pollution. Industries favour self-regulation and feel that the best form of regulation is "no regulation". But the environmental record of many sectors of industry needs to improve and win public confidence on this. The more the industries show that they are environmentally conscious, the more the government's role can be limited in setting standards, fines and taxes. The broad guidelines for sustainable industrial processes are:

- Use of low and no waste technologies.
- Transformation of as much waste material as possible into the marketable product.
- Increasing the life of the products, i.e., producing more durable products.
- Upgrade used products by making components available.
- Recovering components and recycling materials when products cease to be useful.
- Using toxic chemicals only as a last resort.
- Practicing a **"cradle to grave"** approach to integrated waste management, i.e., from acquiring raw materials to transforming them into manufactured usable goods and by managing wastes at every stage, economically.

Robert Frosch and Nicholas Gallopoulos introduced the term *industrial ecology* which provides a positive means for corporations to address environmental needs. The concept of industrial ecology calls for a large scale integrated management tool that considers industrial activities within natural eco system. Kalundborg, in Denmark, exemplifies industrial ecology concept and inter-company greenings (for a detailed discussion see Chapter 35).

34.3 Challenges to Companies

Business enterprises invoke the Darwinian maxim of *'survival of the fittest'* to defend their competitive actions and their ecologically unfriendly methods of production. To business enterprises, running a business with a conscience is like driving with breaks on. Green policies impose an extra cost on the firms. Companies investing on pollution control equipment will have less to spend on developing new products. Management time spent on greening decisions regarding the firm's input, product and waste management is not available for corporate growth. Growth of a business enterprise is measured in terms of scale and profits. Hence industries can become greener, only slowly. It appears that the businesses are unaware of the economic benefits of "greening" their production processes and need a "command-and-control" strategy or public pressure or pollution tax that would put them on a "sustainable industrialisation path".

Germany has passed a legislation that requires 80 per cent recycling of all materials. Resistance of manufacturer to this legislation compelled government to give them a choice.

a. compliance to the law or

b. sur-tax on all package

Faced with this option, 600 German companies formed a private corporation that would help them to recycle their packages. The companies had to pay a fee for participating in this system which varied depending on type and size of packaging. Inspite of the fee companies were willing to participate in this on account of the strict laws limiting the amount of packaging that can be thrown away. Eventually the fee was passed on to the consumers. The system has made Germany a leader in recycling. Similarly German Auto Industry has also designed a plant to recycle old cars. Newer cars are being designed with disassembly in mind. Parts are bar coded to identify types of materials and instructions on reuse. Component materials are being reduced and designs modified to yield 100 per cent reusability.

Environmentalists strongly feel that the manufactures of the product should also be responsible for the product when it becomes a waste. The problem of throw-away society can be placed on the shoulders of the creator of the waste. The efforts of Procter & Gamble and Kimberly-Clark prove good examples for this. They have taken two product initiatives to address environmental concerns. First, through their super absorbent diapers which would reduce the volume of waste for disposal to half. Second a pilot program designed to collect diapers and reclaim the plastic. Both firms have instituted composting programmes. Biodegradable diapers are also being marketed. Fast food restaurants, like McDonald and Burger King are replacing non-biodegradable polystyrene containers with paper.

34.4 Business Charter for Sustainable Development

In 1991, the International Chamber of Commerce (ICC)launched its first Business Charter for Sustainable Development, which was subsequently updated in 2000 and 2015. The 2015 Charter was emphasised in a more holistic manner the economic, societal and environmental dimensions of sustainable development in the context of present day's global realities.The charter recommends a strategic framework to help companies place sustainability at the heart of their operations. The eight principles recommend companies to work in harmony with existing practices, national and international guidelines and standards on all aspects of sustainability. The Charter highlights sustainable development as a business priority.

Conclusion

Business enterprises today face a great challenge: that of promoting a path of sustainable industrialisation. This calls for an 'ecocentric' management at every level of decision making. Such sustainable business practices will lead to a sustainable development and will play a vital role in preserving the earth's finite resources. As industries commit themselves to sustainability, **action** is needed to coordinate the objectives of industries, government and environmental movements. To achieve this:

a. The ecological context within which industries should operate should be discussed thoroughly with experts from industries,government and environmental organisation;
b. Regional and local communities should be consulted on the pattern of industrialisation that best suits their region;
c. New clean technologies that will reduce pressure on environment should be developed;
d. Environmental monitoring and auditing should become mandatory for industries.

Question

What are the various production paradigms?

What are the principles that companies must adopt for achieving sustainable industrialization? Why are firms reluctant to adopt green technology?

Exercise

1. Do a small survey of just 20 to 25 firms and check how far they are committed to sustainable industrialization.
2. From the website of International chamber of commerce make a detailed note on the Eight Principles of the 2015 Business Charter for Sustainable Development.

35

CORPORATE STRATEGIES FOR ENVIRONMENTAL MANAGEMENT

Socialism collapsed because it did not allow prices to tell the economic truth. Capitalism may collapse because it does not allow prices to tell the ecological truth."

– Oystein Dahle, former Vice President, Exxon, Norway

Increased environmental pressure in the last few decades have brought about changes in corporate strategies. Companies exploit the vital environmental functions in all their activities. They consume energy and natural resources, pollute air and water, and generate hazardous and other solid wastes. Many times firms are responsible for major accidents – example is the industrial accident in Bhopal in India, in which tonnes of Methyl Iso Cyanide (MIC) were emitted into the air killing thousands of people. The increased environmental pressure from various stake holders has compelled industries to green their decision making and strategies. Further companies have also realized that being green improves efficiency and gives cost advantages. The realization that firms are as much a part of the solution as a part of the problem is vital for greening corporate strategies.

There are five reasons why business enterprises incorporate environmental management in decision making. These are:

- growing environmental awareness
- precautionary principle – seeking to avoid problems of non-compliance with environmental regulation and pressures from public and environmental litigation costs;
- compliance – simply doing what environmental laws and rules specify and what public opinion demands.
- eco-efficiency – green to be cost efficient.
- proactive – go beyond the requirements of law and giving priority to environmental management by incorporating environmental concerns in all activities of the firm.

35.1 Theories of Corporate Environmental Response

The emergence of environmental issues and the awareness about them pose a serious challenge to firms. There are three stages in a company's environmental response. From an initial 'no environmental response' attitude, company gradually graduates to "compliance forced response" and finally to 'beyond compliance' behaviour after the realisation that pollution prevention pays. In this approach companies are seen to be moving through a stage of 'no environmental response' to 'active environmental response' gradually. Topfer (1985) distinguishes among four types of environmental performance by firms- resistant, passive, reactive and innovative. Resistant firms see environmental issues as a hindrance to growth and hence are against any environmental regulation: passive companies ignore environment since they feel their impacts are negligible: reactive firms comply with environmental regulations and innovative firms go beyond mere compliance with environmental regulation. Petulla (1987) classified firm's response to environmental management as: crisis oriented, cost oriented and enlightened.

Hunt and Auster (1990) describe a five stage 'environmental development continuum', in which at the lower end is 'no protection against environmental risks' and at the other end is the 'proactive environmental management'. Companies that did little or nothing about environmental risks were termed as beginners or fire fighters and placed at the lower end of the continuum and the companies moved along the continuum as their contribution to protect environmental risks improved. Companies with maximum commitment to environmental management are the "proactive" companies and this requires change in attitude and behavior of the companies towards environmental management.

Simpson (1991) categorised corporate responses to environmental pressures into three main groups;

- the`**Why Mes'**, initiate action to green their production methods only after their involvement in an accident with serious environmental impacts.
- the `**Smart Movers'** refer to companies that adopt environmentally friendly methods of production to gain competitive advantage.
- the`**Enthusiasts'** refer to companies that incorporate environmental management in their business strategies beyond mere compliance.

Steger's Generic Environmental Strategies Model argued that in response to regulation, consumer preferences and technological improvements, companies became proactive towards environmental improvement and indulged in environmental improvement activities to exploit the potential competitive advantage. His model explains four categories of corporate environmental strategies: **indifference, offensive, defensive and innovative**. The firm's choice of a strategy is determined by two factors: market opportunities for environmental protection and environmental risk. When both environmental risks and market opportunities for environmental improvement are low companies are indifferent. Companies are offensive when faced with small environmental risks but large market opportunities for environmental improvement. In this situation companies benefit through corporate greening strategies. When environmental risks are large but market opportunities for environmental improvement are small, companies adopt defensive strategy which implies that their intention was just to comply with regulations. Innovative strategy is employed by the firm when both risks and market opportunities are large.

Roome's Strategic Options Model identifies five environmental strategies of companies , namely, non-compliance, compliance, compliance- plus, commercial and environmental excellence and leading edge. While the first three are based on compliance level of the firm with reference to environmental regulations the last two refer to proactive companies that exploit environmental protection opportunities for competitive advantage. Table 35.1 gives Roome's strategic option Model:

Table 35.1.Roome's Strategic Options Model

Strategies	Meaning
Non-compliance	Implies non-compliance with environmental regulation due to cost constraints etc.
Compliance	The firm opts to comply with regulation.
Compliance Plus	Firm goes beyond compliance and take a pro-active approach to environmental management
Commercial and Environmental Excellence	Firm realises that "environmental management is good management" and act accordingly.
Leading Edge	The firm becomes a role model for others and leads them in proactive environmental response

Welford classified environmental response of the small and medium sized enterprises by categorizing the small and medium enterprises into four groups – Ostrich, Laggard, Thinkers, and Doers. Ostrich refers to enterprises which do not recognize the environmental challenges faced by them and assume that the negative impact of their actions on the environment are negligible; They assume that their competitors also feel the same. (The meaning of the term Ostrich is one who tries to avoid disagreeable situations by refusing to face them). Laggards are aware of the environmental impacts of their actions but are unable to take any protective measure due to cost constraint and lack of required inputs. Thinkers are firms which realize that action needs to be taken to correct for environmental damages but wait for others to lead. Doers are the proactive enterprises who plan and incorporate environmental strategies in their decision making.

The various environmental responses of companies discussed so far are:

- Ostrich
- Resistant
- Why Me
- Indifference/Non-compliance/ Laggard
- Thinkers
- Offensive/ smart movers
- Defensive/Compliance
- Compliance Plus/ Doers
- Commercial and environmental excellence
- Leading Edge/ Innovative / Enthusiasts

The various models on corporate environmental response provide a framework for companies to identify where they are in the continuum of corporate environmental strategies – whether the firm is a beginner or a proactivist. Dodge and Welford have developed a scale for assessing the environmental performance of the firms. Known as the ROAST scale, the scale classifies companies on the basis of their environmental performance into five categories. The five categories begin with **resistant companies** and ends with **transcendent firms**. The five point ROAST scale is explained in table 35.2

Table 35.2 Dodge and Welford's Environmental Performance Scale

R	Stage 1 Resistant	Companies are resistant to environmental values and totally unresponsive to environmental initiatives.
O	Stage 2 Observe and Comply	Companies comply with environmental laws eventhough they are unwilling to do so or they lack the ability to comply. The environmental responses of the companies are the result of legislation or court decisions.
A	Stage 3 Accommodate	Beginning of voluntary action - Proactive and responsive behavior of companies seen to emerge. Actions are no longer entirely based upon compliance -
S	Stage 4 Seize and Preempt	Companies voluntarily seize and preempt its actions with environmental concerns - companies respond to external stakeholders.
T	Stage 5 Transcend	Firm's environmental values, attitudes, beliefs and culture, exhibit a total support for the environment. Companies act in a way which is fully consistent with sustainable development

Source: Welford, 1996

Based on the various categories of corporate environmental 'response', Hilson (2000) mentions five distinct stages of corporate environmental management that can be included in this continuum:

- Resistant Environmental Management
- Compliant Environmental Management
- Transitional Environmental Management
- Accommodative Environmental Management
- Proactive Environmental Management.

Companies move from a stage of resistant environmental management to one of proactive environmental management gradually with the development of the economy. These five stages form steps in Corporate Environmental and Social Performance Spectrum. Very few third world companies are in the"Resistant Environmental Management" stage. In such countries environmental regulations are weak and penalties for non-compliance are insufficient to provoke an improvement in the environmental behavior of firms.

Companies in most of the developing nations are in the stage of Transitional Environmental Management which implies that they are gradually moving from a state of non-compliance and environmentally resistant attitude and behavior to a more environmentally responsible behavior.

Companies in almost all developed nations are in the stage of Accommodative or Proactive Environmental Management. Accommodative environmental behavior was made possible by a number of factors: industrial accidents such as the Bhopal tragedy in India, the chemical oil spill in in the River Rhine, the Chernobyl disaster in Russia. These widely reported and highly discussed accidents helped in bringing about a change in the environmental philosophy and values of firms.

Proactive environmental behavior is reflected when firm's environmental management strategies extend far beyond compliance with regulations and commit themselves to continuous environmental improvement. Firm's actions for environmental management are anticipatory. Such companies invest heavily on R & D for pollution control technologies and for manufacturing durable recyclable products. Companies aim at achieving eco-efficiency and sustainable development.

Today companies regard environmental management as a strategic tool for gaining competitive advantage. Having accepted that environmentally responsible behavior is here to stay and that it benefits the firm in the long run, firms are now taking a proactive approach to environmental concerns. Firms feel that by moving beyond compliance and being proactive in anticipation of future changes in environmental regulations, a win-win situation can be achieved.

35.2 Tools of Corporate Environmental Management

The long-term goal of environmental management is to consider environmental aspects in all aspects of a firm's production : product design, the entire manufacturing process, marketing, product delivery and use and consumer service and post-consumer product disposition. Companies which shifted to accommodative and proactive environmental behavior have adopted a series of environmental management tools and strategies. Some of these are:

- Adoption of Environmental Management System
- Environmental Performance auditing
- Environmental Accounting
- Life cycle Assessment – cradle to grave approach
- Environmental marketing or Green marketing and Ecolabelling
- ISO's Standards
- Industrial Ecology

35.2.1 Environmental Management System (EMS): An Environmental Management System (EMS) is a structured framework for managing an organisation's significant environmental impacts. It is a set of processes and practices that helps the organisation to reduce its environmental impacts and become eco-efficient in its operations. It provides a process through which organisations can engage with all its stake holders - employees, customers, clients and input suppliers, insurers and the government and implement environmentally friendly processes. An EMS defines the company's goals for environmental performance and gives a plan for achieving those goals. An EMS helps an organization achieve its environmental goals through systematic, planned and documented manner. An EMS helps the firm to incorporate environmental administration in its every day operations, as well as long term practices.

In order to implement an EMS, a company must identify the significant effects relevant to its business. For maximum effectiveness, an EMS is built into the existing management structure. Adopting an EMS can help an organisation to:

- Manage and improve its environmental performance by helping it to increase resource and energy efficiency and reducing wastes;
- Comply with environmental laws and regulations;
- Generate financial savings through eco-efficient practices;
- Improve its reputation and image with stakeholders;

An EMS follows a PDCA cycle, (Plan - Do - Check – Act). Implementation of an environmental management system requires the following steps to be completed by an organisation:

- Definition and development of an environmental policy that reflects its commitments;
- Identification of actual and potential environmental impacts;
- Identification of relevant legal and other requirements;
- Establishment of environmental objectives, targets and programs;
- Monitoring and measurement of the progress to achieve its objectives;
- Reviewing the progress of the EMS and improving environmental performance;
- Continuous improvement of the organisation's environmental performance.

The EMS and environmental performance are programmed to run in a continuous improvement cycle as outlined in Figure 35.1

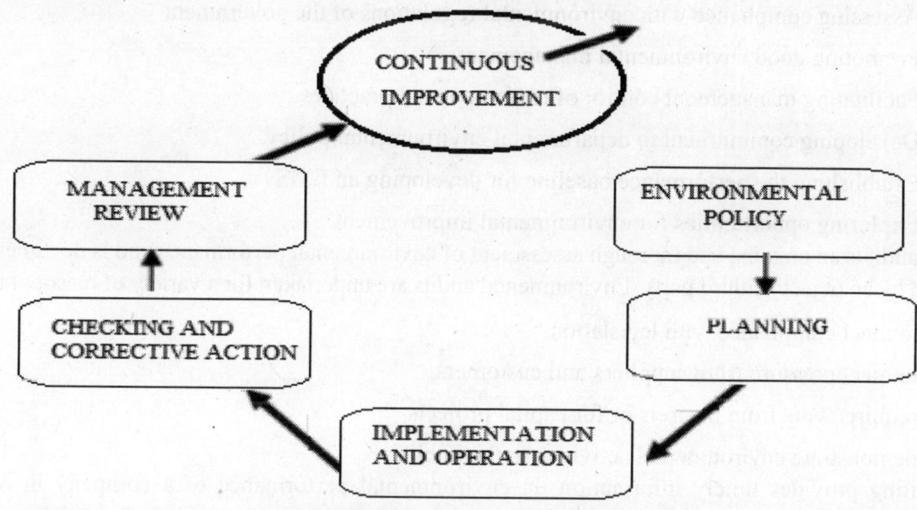

Figure 35.1 Steps in an EMS

An EMS helps a company achieve its environmental goals continuously through consistent greening of its operations. The EMS itself does not define any specified level of environmental performance to be achieved; Targets and goals will differ from company to company and hence each company's EMS is tailored to the company's business and goals. An EMS is a continuous improvement process.

Environmental Management Systems offer a number of benefits to the organization adopting it.

- Improved environmental performance of the organization which results in real cost savings - direct efficiencies in energy, water, waste, purchasing and transport.
- Management of environmental risk.
- Ensuring compliance with environmental regulation – reduces regulatory fines, fees and tax payments.
- Enhance employee morale
- Improves stakeholder relationship - to key clients, regulators and the public.
- Improved corporate reputation which is a pre-requisite for doing business
- Increased market share, revenue and improved competitive advantage

With the continuous support of the top management, the EMS will evolve into a perfect system improving the environmental performance of the organization. The introduction of life-cycle assessment in procurement processes, ISO 14000 certification and other national and international certifications and opting to get products eco-labelled are characteristics of an evolved EMS.

35.2.2 Environmental Performance Auditing

Environmental auditing is a management tool to evaluate environmental performance of the company, to check its compliance with environmental regulation, and to assess whether the system in use is effective in managing environmental improvement. The International Standards Organisation defines an environmental audit as "a systematic, documented verification process of objectively obtaining and evaluating evidence to determine whether specific environmental activities, events, conditions, management systems, or information about these matters conform with audit criteria, and communicating the results of this process to the client".

Environmental audit is a systematic, documented, periodic and objective evaluation of the company's environmental performance in relation to:

- Assessing compliance with environmental regulations of the government.
- Promoting good environmental management.
- Facilitating management control of environmental practices.
- Developing commitment to departmental environmental policy.
- Establishing the performance baseline for developing an EMS.
- Exploring opportunities for environmental improvement.

The audit is an ongoing and thorough assessment of environmental performance and is documented. It is verified by an objective third party. Environmental audits are undertaken for a variety of reasons such as:

- to meet compliance with legislation,
- to meet pressure from suppliers and customers,
- requirements from insurers or for capital projects,
- demonstrate environmental activities to the public.

Auditing provides timely information on environmental performance of a company in relation to goals and objectives. It verifies that activities of the company ensure continued compliance with the environmental legislations in force.

There are three phases in an environmental audit:

- Pre audit
- Audit
- Post audit

The activities of the pre audit stage are:

- Planning the scope of the audit and defining the overall goals, objectives, and priorities.
- Selection of the audit team.
- A study of the industry and the company to be audited.
- Involving the workforce.

Actual audit – second phase of the audit – includes:

- review of company's records and documents relevant to environmental management.
- examining the company's environmental policy.
- interviews with management and select employees at all levels of operation.
- site inspection to collect information about the plant, working practices etc.

Post audit – Third Phase

- evaluation of findings.
- reporting of findings and recommendations.
- preparation of an action plan.
- follow up.

Benefits of an environmental audit: The benefits of environmental audit vary from company to company. However the commonly attributed benefits of an environmental audit include:

- ensuring compliance, not only with laws, regulations and standards, but also with company policies and the requirements of an EMS standard; This helps to prevent fires & litigations.
- provide baseline information to enable organisations to evaluate and manage environmental change, threat and risk;
- enable anticipation of environmental risks and plan responses;
- support the implementation and management of integrated pollution control procedures;
- more efficient resource use and financial savings.
- improve public image
- improve overall quality

35.2.3 Environmental Management Accounting (EMA): Environmental accounting is the practice of using traditional accounting and finance principles to calculate the costs that business decisions will have on the environment (J K Henderson). It is the generation and analysis of both financial and non-financial information in order to support internal environmental management processes. It provides reports for generating environmental information to help make management decisions on pricing, controlling overhead costs and capital budgeting.

EMA is broadly defined by the United Nations Expert Working Group as the identification, collection, analysis, dissemination, and use of information related to:

- physical flow information on materials, energy and water and waste flows
- monetary information related to costs and revenue necessary for environmental decision-making within an organisation.

Accountants involved in environmental management accounting need specific skills to:

- understand the environmental costs of products and services and allocate them properly so that they can be managed and prices are set at an appropriate level

- include all relevant environmental costs in the investment appraisal of projects.

EMA places particular emphasis on accounting for environmental costs. Environmental costs are mostly not included in the accounting of the firm. They are therefore hidden costs. Therefore pricing of the product will not include these costs. By ignoring these costs the firm will be producing more than what it should actually produce and sell them at a lower price. Lower price of the product increases demand for polluting products. Accounting for these costs will enable firms to apply full cost pricing – setting a price that includes environmental costs also. Besides it will enable firms to choose the right volume of production. Helps the firm to isolate the environmental costs from total costs which in turn helps in

- Pricing according to recalculated costs;
- profit margins of products defined in accordance with the recalculated costs;
- make changes in processes or products in order to reduce environmental costs;
- saving money and improving control.

Environmental costs are no longer a minor cost item that can be pooled together with other costs. By identifying and controlling environmental costs, EMA helps environmental managers justify cleaner production projects and improve environmental performance of the company. EMA integrates corporate environmental policy with business policies, and paves the path for sustainable business.

35.2.4 Life Cycle Assessment (LCA): Also known as cradle to grave approach, this approach is a "product management system that helps enterprises to minimize the environmental and social burdens associated with their product or product portfolio during its entire life cycle". ISO 14000 defines LCA as "a technique for assessing environmental aspects and potential impacts associated with the product." The approach examines every significant environmental impact of a product from the extraction and use of raw materials through to the final disposal of the product and its decomposition. Life cycle analysis helps in tracing the environmental impact of the products and services throughout their life (from cradle to grave). It makes a 'cradle to grave' look at a product's life considering the environmental impacts at every stage of the product. This in turn helps in making appropriate changes in production processes and product designs and features so that environmental impact of the product is minimized.A schematic illustration of a product life cycle is shown below:

Raw material →Production →Use →Disposal

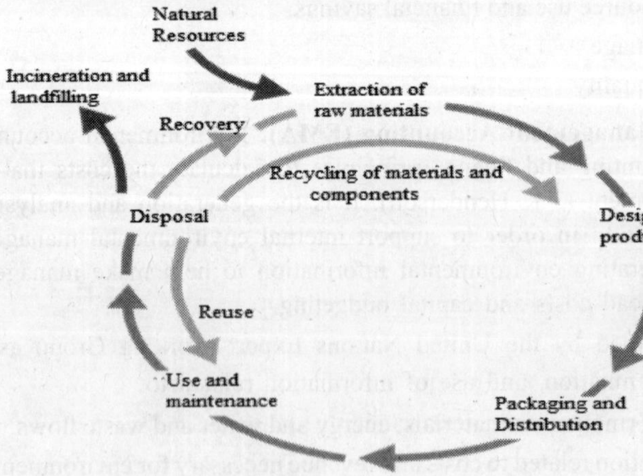

Natural Resources
Incineration and landfilling
Extraction of raw materials
Recovery
Recycling of materials and components
Disposal
Design and production
Reuse
Use and maintenance
Packaging and Distribution

Figure 35.2 A typical Product Life Cycle

Source: UNEP/SETAC. Life Cycle Management: A Business Guide to Sustainability. Paris, 2007. Reproduced in http://www.lifecycleinitiative.org/starting-life-cycle-thinking/what-is-life-cycle-thinking/

The assessment process includes identifying and quantifying energy and materials used in the production processes of the product and wastes released to the environment during the production processes, assessing their environmental impact and examining opportunities for improvement.

The goal of LCA is to compare the full range of environmental damages attributable to products so that the least burdensome one can be chosen. The approach can be applied to assess and improve the environmental performance of a single product or to assess and improve the environmental performance of a company.

LCA is conducted according to internationally recognized ISO 14040.There are four phases in an LCA study according to ISO 14044 :2006 standard:

- *Goal and scope* which defines the intended use of the LCA, specifies system boundaries and selects the functional unit; this stage sets out the context of the study and explains how and to whom the results are to be communicated.
- *Inventory analysis creates a* record of flows from and to nature for a product system. This phase makes an objective, data-based process of quantifying energy and raw materials requirements, air and water pollutants, solid waste, and other environmental discharges incurred throughout the life cycle of a product, process, or activity.These data are related to the functional unit defined already in the goal and scope stage.
- *Impact assessment* evaluates the significance of potential environmental impacts based on the LCI flow results. The impact assessment addresses both ecological and human health impacts, besides including social and economic impacts
- *Interpretation of the results:* The results from the inventory analysis and impact assessment are summarized during the interpretation phase. According to ISO 14040:2006, the interpretation of the results should include:
    * identification of significant issues based on the results of the inventory assessment and impact assessment phases of an LCA;
    * evaluation of the study considering completeness, sensitivity and consistency checks;
    * conclusions, limitations and recommendations.

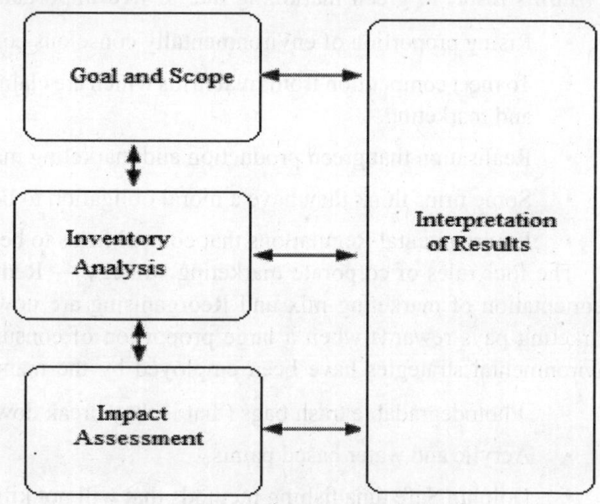

Figure 35.3 LCA Phases

Recommendations include opportunities to reduce or mitigate the environmental impact throughout the whole life cycle of a product (or process or activity) such as changes in product design, raw material usage, production processes, use of the product and waste management. The various phases illustrated in Figure 35.3 are interdependent.

The life cycle assessment (LCA) allows one to examine the full extent of environmental and economic effects assignable to products and processes which helps in making more informed decisions. By performing life cycle analyses, manufacturers can assess the environmental impacts of their products or processes. This helps them to make necessary corrections to decrease the environmental impacts and innovate technology to make efficient and environmentally friendly production.

35.2.5 Environmental marketing or Green marketing

Environmental or Green marketing is the marketing of products that are environmentally safe. It is a new marketing approach that promotes "reconsumption", the ability to use and reuse goods in whole or in parts. Developing products that can be "reconsumed" over generations (life cycle usage) has become the task of the marketers. Consumer sensitivity to environmental issues does not always turn into purchase behaviour. Marketing strategies should achieve this.

Environmental marketing refers to the satisfaction of consumer needs, wants, and desires in concurrence with the preservation and conservation of the natural environment. Walter Coddington defines *environmental marketing* as "marketing activities that recognize environmental stewardship as a business development responsibility and business growth responsibility."

Green marketing focuses on purchasing behaviour alteration or non-purchasing conservation activity. Terms often used by firms in their marketing strategies are: Degradable, Biodegradable, Photogradable, Compostable, Recyclable, Refillable, Ozone Friendly, Enviro Friendly, Recycled Contents.

According to M J Polonsky there is a misconception that green marketing refers solely to the promotion or advertising of products with environmental characteristics. Terms like Phosphate Free, Recyclable, Refillable, Ozone Friendly, and Environmentally Friendly are no doubt attributes of green marketing. However green marketing is a much broader concept. It can be applied to consumer goods, industrial goods and even services. Green marketing includes a broad range of activities such as product modification, changes to the production process, packaging changes, as well as modifying advertising. According to Polonsky, environmental marketing refers to all activities of production that generate minimal detrimental impact on the environment.

Firms resort to green marketing due to five important reasons:

- Rising proportion of environmentally conscious consumers.
- To meet competition from rival firms which are claiming environmentally responsible production and marketing.
- Realisation that green production and marketing may be cost efficient.
- Some firms think they have a moral obligation to be more socially responsible
- Environmental Regulations that compel firms to be more responsible.

The four rules of corporate marketing strategy — Reduction of consumer needs, Reconsumption, Reorientation of marketing mix and Reorganising are now oriented towards green marketing. Green marketing pays rewards when a large proportion of consumers are "ecologically conscious". Several environmental strategies have been employed by the manufacturers. Examples are:

- Photodegradable trash bags (that is they break down when exposed to light.
- Acrylic and water based paints.
- Dolphin Safe tuna fishing methods that will not kill dolphins.
- Less phosphate containing detergent.
- Recycled paper.

Firms marketing environmentally friendly goods will have a competitive advantage over firms marketing goods which are not environmentally friendly. Few examples of firms which have included environmentally friendly marketing strategies are: (Polonsky MJ 1994)

- McDonald's replaced its clam shell packaging with waxed paper because of increased consumer concern relating to polystyrene production and Ozone depletion
- Xerox introduced a "high quality" recycled photocopier paper in an attempt to satisfy the demands of firms for less environmentally harmful products.
- Tuna manufacturers modified their fishing techniques in order to prevent death of dolphins.

Products, the production and consumption of which impose no environmentally adverse effects are called as green products. Green products possess the following features:

- Recyclable, reusable and bio-degradable
- Contain no toxic chemical
- Made of approved natural and non-toxic ingredients only
- Manufacturing does not leave adverse impact on the environment
- Not tested on animals
- Have eco-friendly packaging, that is bio-degradable or reusable packages

Green marketing will promote sustainable industrialization if the claims of the firms are genuine. Very often green marketing claims turnout to be mere advertising campaigns by big corporate polluters. Companies also indulge in *"green washing"*, by which is meant, making claims that lack real merit or misrepresent facts about environmental performance. Such attitude of firms will only make consumers doubt even genuine claims. Monitoring Institutions and ecolabels from recognized institutions have come to being for sorting fact from fiction.

Ecolabelling

Ecolabels are seals of approval given to products that are deemed to have fewer impacts on the environment than functionally or competitively similar products (OECD,1991). Ecolabelling indicates to the customer that a product has certain environmentally friendly benefits.

The theoretical foundation for ecolables is Stigler's work on economics of information. Economics of information holds that consumers (or buyers of any product) spend considerable time, energy and money in finding information on the price of the product they want to buy Thus there is a search cost. Nelson and Akerlof extended the theory of information to include search for information on quality of the product also. Infact consumers are keener on obtaining relevant and reliable information on quality of the product because there are some goods (credence goods) where the quality attributes of the good cannot be assessed by the consumer even after spending considerably on search costs. Environmental attributes of good come under this category. There is asymmetry of information on the environmental friendliness of a product. The buyer is not able to assess the environmental attribute and friendiliness of the product. In such cases labeling by producers provide relevant information of the product attribute and help them to make informed choice. Ecolabelling narrows this information gap. If the information provided by producers through labeling must be acceptable as trustworthy, it requires third party certification, that is, certification by an organization or team, other than the producers, distributors and sellers of the labelled products.

There are various types of ecolabels. It is common to distinguish between first party and third party ecolables.

The international Standard Organisation (ISO) has distinguished between three types of eco labeling schemes. Table 35. 3 gives the ISO classification of ecolables.

Table 35.3 ISO Classification of Ecolables

Type 1	Voluntary, multiple –criteria, third party programme that awards a license that authorizes the use of environmental labels on products indicating overall environmental preference of a product within a particular product category based on life cycle considerations.
Type 2	Informative environmental self-declaration claims
Type 3	Voluntary programme that provide quantified environmental data of a product under pre-set categories of parameters, set by qualified third party and based on life cycle assessment and verified by that or another qualified third party.

Source: ISO Geneva

Eco-labels are affixed by designated institutions – government or voluntary private - to products that pass eco-friendly criteria based on the product's life cycle impact on the environment. Ecolabelling schemes are usually self-financing, with licence fee covering administrative costs. Products are awarded an eco-label after proper assessment and verification by an independent third party and are guaranteed to meet certain environmental performance requirements. A committee of judges determines or suggests which product categories are eligible for labelling. Manufactures must submit products for consideration and if successful, sign a contract for a specified period of time, paying a fee for the label.

Eco-labels are voluntary but are mostly backed by the national government and administered by an independent body. Compliance with eco-label requirements is voluntary, but industries will benefit both domestically and internationally by demonstrating good environmental performance. Having aecolable gives competitive advantage to firms. Ecolabels also help consumers to select products and services with less impact on the environment.

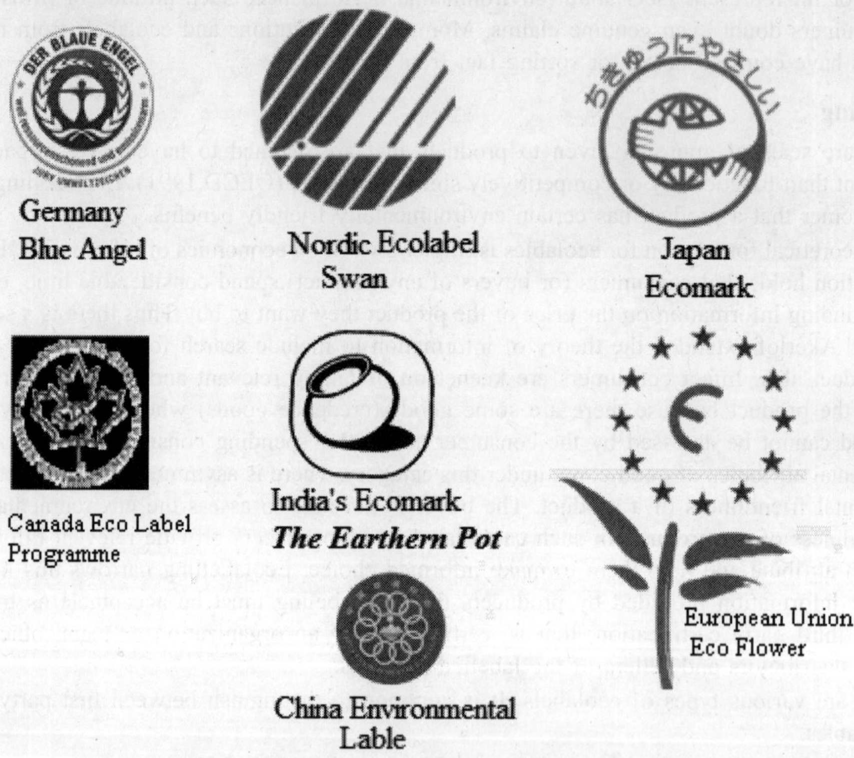

Figure 35.4 Select Ecolabels

According to Gallastegui (2002) successful ecolabeling efforts face a variety of challenges.

- First, the criteria or standards must be selected objectively.
- Second, specific definitions must be made throughout the process. Product boundaries must be clearly delineated, as no two goods are perfect substitutes.
- Third, objective design of the certification process is necessary for the present and the future. The design team needs to define not only the certification process itself, but also the method and time frame by which standards can be updated. This is important so that the certification itself doesn't become arbitrary.
- Finally, a market analysis is necessary to gauge demand and market share for labeled goods

Many governments have launched an ecolabelling program as a means for promoting better consumer information and guiding consumers' choice towards environmental protection. Ecolabelling schemes are available in many countries. Germany was the first country to issue such labels. Canada, Japan, Norway, Sweden, Finland, France, Portugal, Australia, New Zealand also have such schemes.

The Government of India launched the eco-labelling scheme known as `Ecomark' in 1991 for easy identification of environment-friendly products. The criteria follows a cradle-to-grave approach, i.e. from raw material extraction, to manufacturing, and to disposal. The Ecomark label is awarded to consumer goods that meet the specified environmental criteria and the quality requirements of Indian Standards.

35.2.6 ISO 14000

ISO 14000 was adopted by the International Organization for Standardization (ISO), as an approach to improved environmental performance. The ISO standards reflect global consensus on good environmental practice. The family of ISO 14000 is the world's most recognized EMS framework that helps organizations manage the environmental impact of their activities and to demonstrate sound environmental management. ISO 14001 is flexible enough to be applied to any sized organization in both the private and public sectors. ISO offers a broad spectrum of standards to deal with specific environmental challenges. It has developed more than 350 International Standards for monitoring various environmental issues such as the quality of air, water and soil, as well as noise pollution and radiation. The standards set by ISO help organisations to take a pro-active approach to environmental issues.

ISO 14000 does not focus on environmental outcomes (such as pollution reduction) but focuses only on the environmental aspects of an organisation's processes and products and services. This implies that these standards do not fix environmental targets to be achieved by the organisations but prescribe a system that will help the organization to achieve its own environmental objectives and targets.ISO14000 involves a third party audit.

ISO 14001 is the corner stone standard of the ISO 14000 series. ISO 14000 was first published in 1996 and specifies the actual requirements for an environmental management system. It applies to those environmental aspects over which the organization has control. Other standards in the series include the following:

- ISO 14004 provides guidance on the development and implementation of environmental management systems.
- ISO 14011 provides specific guidance on auditing an environmental management system (now superseded by ISO 19011)
- ISO 14012 provides guidance on qualification criteria for environmental auditors and lead auditors (now superseded by ISO 19011)
- ISO 14013/5 provides audit program review and assessment material.
- ISO 14020 through ISO 14024 Environmental Labeling
- ISO 14030 , ISO 14032 Environmental Performance Evaluation
- ISO 14040 through ISO 14043 Life Cycle Assessment
- ISO 14050 Terms and Definitions

Benefits of ISO 14000

Adherence to the ISO 14000 standard provides significant economic benefits to the organisations, such as:

- better conformance to environmental regulations,
- more efficient use of resources and energy

- improved process efficiency ;
- reduced waste generation and disposal costs
- better corporate image among the consumers in the market
- increased returns
- Market extension for the company's product/ service
- Framework for continuous improvement of the organisation's environmental performance.

The situation today is that organisations which do not opt for ISO 14000 will find it difficult to expand their markets and sustain in future. The organizations that realize the value of the natural environment as an input supplier are assured of a bright future. ISO 14000 assist organisations to improve their market and returns.

35.2.7 Industrial Ecology

Industrial ecology conceptualises industry as a man-made ecosystem that operates in a similar way to natural ecosystems, where the waste or by product of one process is used as an input into another process. In an industrial ecosystem no waste would leave the industrial system or negatively impact natural systems. Industrial ecology "deals with flow of resources through the economic system" (Ramesh Ramaswamy, 2004). *The concept of industrial ecology owes its origin to the concept of industrial ecosystem developed* by Robert Frosch and Nicholas Gallopoulos, in their important article "Strategies for Manufacturing" in the journal *Scientific American* in September 1989. According to Frosch and Gallopoulos "the traditional model of industrial activity - in which individual manufacturing processes take in raw materials and generate products to be sold plus waste to be disposed of - should be transformed into a more integrated model: an industrial ecosystem. In such a system the consumption of energy and materials is optimized, waste generation is minimized and the effluents of one process...serve as the raw material for another process." According to Patel (1992) industrial ecology is based on the "cradle-to-grave"production philosophy, but adds that, in an ideal circumstance there is no grave."

There are a number of definitions of industrial ecology. The common traits of the concept of industrial ecology from the various definitions as enumerated by Andy Garner and G A. Keoleian,(1995) are:

- a systems view of the interactions between industrial and ecological systems
- the study of material and energy flows and transformations
- a multidisciplinary approach
- an orientation toward the future
- a change **from linear (open) processes to cyclical (closed) processes**, so the waste from one industry is used as an input for another
- an effort to reduce the industrial systems' environmental impacts on ecological systems
- an emphasis on harmoniously integrating industrial activity into ecological systems
- the idea of making industrial systems emulate more efficient and sustainable natural systems.

The major principles of industrial ecology as defined by Tibbs (1992) are:

- Create industrial ecosystems - view waste as a resource; create partnerships with other industries to trade by-products which are used as inputs to other processes.
- Balance industrial inputs and outputs to natural levels - manage the environmental-industrial interface; increase knowledge of ecosystem behavior and apply it to industries. Learn and apply how and when industry can interact with natural ecosystems and the limitations.

- Dematerialisation of industrial output - use less virgin materials and energy by becoming more resource efficient; reuse materials or substitute more environmentally friendly materials; do more with less.
- Improve the efficiency of industrial processes - redesign products, processes, equipment; reuse materials to conserve resources.
- Energy use - incorporate energy supply within the industrial ecology; use alternative sources of energy that have less or no impact upon the environment.
- Align policies with the industrial ecology concept - incorporate environment and economics into organisational, national and international policies; internalize the externalities; use economic instruments to encourage a move towards industrial ecology; use a more appropriate discount rate; use a more comprehensive index to measure a nation's wealth rather than GNP.

Frosch R A and Gallopoulos compared the industrial ecosystem to a biological ecosystem and observed that "much could be gained if the industrial system were to mimic the best features of the biological analogue". This is possible if each process and network of processes are viewed as a "dependent and inter related part of a larger whole".

Case study:The Kalundborg Industrial Ecosystem

One of the popular examples of industrial ecology is that of Kalundborg, a small industrial zone 120km west of Copenhagen in Denmark. The unplanned industrial park at Kalundborg began as a single power station and developed into a cluster of companies which rely on each other for material inputs. The core participants are:

- Asnaes, Denmark's largest a 1,500 megawatt coal fired power plant;
- An oil refinery owned by Statoil, Denmark's largest refinery with a capacity of 3.2 million tonnes/year
- Novo Nordisk, an international biotechnological company, that produces pharmaceuticals and industrial enzymes.
- Gyproc, Scandinavia's largest plasterboard manufacturer, making 14 million square meters of gypsum wall board annually.
- The city of Kalundborg, which distributes water, electricity and district heating to around 20,000 people.

The participants exchange materials and energy for mutual benefit, such that by-products from one business can be used as low-cost inputs by the others. There was no initial planning of the overall network. Gyproc initiated the symbiosis by locating its facility in Kalundborg to take advantage of the fuel gas available from Statoil.

Originally, the motivation behind the clustering of industries at Kalundborg was cost minimization and seeking marketing of unwanted by-products. Gradually the participants realized that they were generating environmental benefits as well. The project has enabled its participants to achieve substantial cost savings and to improve their resource efficiency. International Institute of Sustainable Development (2013) observes that the project began in 1972 and that by 1994, 16 contracts had been negotiated. It further notes that the estimated savings totalled US $10 million a year, yielding an average pay-back time of six years.

The system involves both energy flows and material flows among the participants.

Energy flows include:

a. The refinery Statoil, supplies excess gas to Gyproc. Surplus gas from the Statoil refinery, which used to be flared off, is delivered to Gyproc as a low-cost energy source. Gyproc has recorded a 90-95% saving in oil consumption after switching to gas supplied by the adjacent refinery.

b. The power station, Asnaes, supplies the city with steam for the district heating system of the town besides supplying steam to Novo Nordisk and Statoil. While the Statoil refinery receives 40% of its steam requirements, Novo Nordisk receives all of its steam requirements from Asnaes. The power plant also supplies heat to its own fish farm.

c. Since 1981, the town of Kalundborg has eliminated the use of 3,500 oil-fired domestic heating systems by distributing heat from the power plant through a network of underground pipes.

d. The power plant uses treated waste water from Statoil refinery for some of its cooling needs. By doing so, it reduces the withdrawals of fresh water from Lake Tissø. The resulting byproduct is hot salt water, a small portion of which they now beneficially supply to the fish farm's 57 ponds.

e. From 1992, Statoil built a sulphur recovery unit to reduce sulphur di oxide emissions in order to comply with regulations. The surplus clean gas from Statoil was used by the power plant in the place of coal.

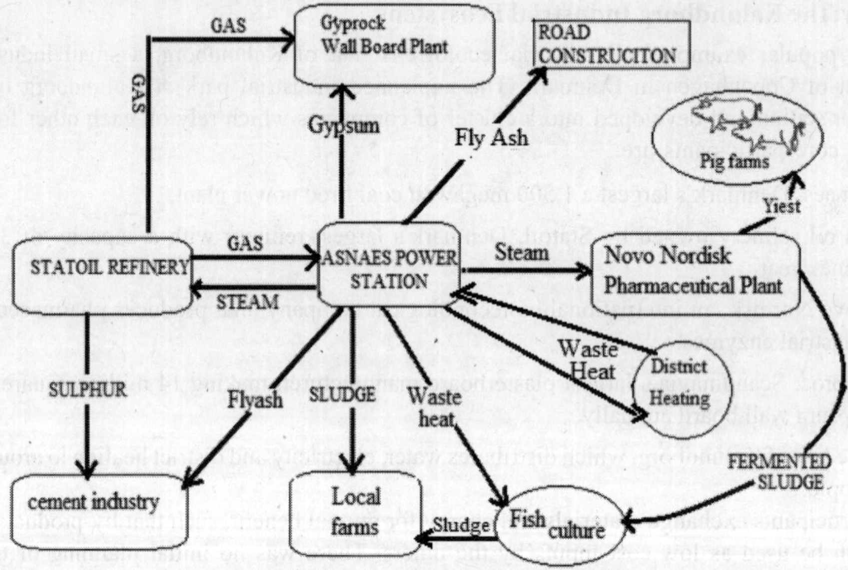

Figure 35. 5 Industrial linkages at Kalundborg

***The figure is neither drawn to scale nor is it an accurate depiction of the location of the participants.**

Material flows include:

a. Sludge from Novo Nordisk's processes and from the fish farm's water treatment plant is supplied to nearby farms as fertilizer. Industrial enzymes and insulin are created through a process of fermentation, the residue from which is rich in nutrients. After lime and heat treatment, it makes an excellent fertilizer. Some 1.5 million cubic metres a year are delivered to local farmers, free of charge.

b. The power station produces other valuable by-products including 170,000 tonnes a year of fly ash, which is used in cement manufacturing and road building.

c. The power station also provides gypsum from its sulphur di oxide scrubber plant to Gyproc, a wall board manufacturer. Gyproc purchases about 80,000 metric tons of this material each year, meeting almost two-thirds of its requirement.
d. The refinery's desulfurization operation produces pure liquid sulfur, which is trucked to Kemira, a sulfuric acid producer.
e. Surplus yeast from insulin production at Novo Nordisk goes to pig farms as pig food.
f. A biotechnical firm that joined the symbiosis in 1999, uses municipal sewage sludge as a nutrient to decompose pollutants in contaminated soils. This facilitates beneficial reuse of another material stream drawn from the city's wastewater.

Table 35. 4 Significant Environmental Beneficial Impact of Industrial Ecology at Kalundborg

Reduction in Consumption of Resources	
Oil	45000 tonnes per year
Coal	15,000 tons per year
Water	600,000m^{3}per year
Reduction in waste emission	
Carbon di oxide	175,000 tons per year
Sulphur di oxide	10,200 tons per year
Value form Wastes	
Sulphur	4500 tons per year
Calcium sulphate(gypsum)	90,000 tons per year
Fly ash (for cement)	130,000 tons per year

Source: UNEP Environmental Management for Industrial Estates – Information and Training Resources

Learning from the experience of Kalundborg even developing countries are exploring the possibilities for developing industrial ecosystems. In India the initiative at Naroda Industrial Estate in Gujarat is an industrial ecology networking project, seeking a cooperative approach to achieve pollution prevention. Naroda Industrial Estate is one of the largest sites for eco-industrial development in the world. 700 companies with 35,000 employees operate on 30 km² of land. The industries functioning in the estate are: Chemical pharmaceutical, dyes and dye intermediaries, engineering, textile and food production. Local leadership from the Naroda Industrial Association, and the Local Bureau of the Confederation of Indian Industry (CII) have taken the initiave with technical assistance from University of Kaiserslautern, Germany. The initiative at Naroda Industrial Estate show that companies which were isolated once can work effectively in a collaborative approach and improve their environmental and financial performance.

Industrial Symbiosis is possible only if there is basic awareness of the value of an effective environmental management programme. Industrial ecosystems result in elimination of waste and maximizing efficiency which paves the way for sustainable industrialization.

Conclusion

The concept of eco efficiency has proved to bc a win-win situation for companies enabling them to minimize their environmental impact at least cost using the various strategies, discussed in this chapter. An environmentally responsible attitude and environmentally friendly production methods will confer substantial benefits in the long run to the company as well as to all the stake holders.

Questions

1. Explain the various theories of corporate environmental strategies.
2. What are the various tools in use by business enterprises towards environmental management.
3. Make a note on industrial ecology using an example.

Exercise

1. Search the internet and find at least 15 products that have had an LCA done for them.
2. From the internet find out various ecolabels and write a brief note on them.
3. Prepare an essay on scope of industrial ecosystems in India through any case study.
4. Make a detailed updated study of the Kalundborg industrial ecosystem.
   Reference website: www.symbiosis.dk/en
5. Prepare a detailed report on the Naroda industrial estate in Gujarat and application of the concept of industrial ecology there.
   Website for reference:
   https://study lib.net/doc/5914623/eco-industrial-estates-handbook.

SECTION 9

ENVIRONMENTAL POLICY IN PRACTICE

36

ENVIRONMENTAL CHALLENGES AND POLICY IN INDIA

The earth lies polluted under its inhabitants; For, they have transgressed laws, violated the statutes, broken the everlasting covenant.

—Prophet Isaiah

The environmental problems of a country is attributable to a number of factors – the stage of economic growth of the country, whether the country is a developing nation or a developed nation, the population of the country, production technologies of the country and the environmental policy of the country. In developed countries, environmental problems are largely the by-products of affluence accompanied by resource wasteful life-styles. Poverty, rising population, efforts to achieve development are contributing factors to environmental challenges of underdeveloped and developing economies. Some environmental issues arise predominantly in underdeveloped and developing countries – such as inadequate sanitation and water shortage. In developed nations on the other hand environmental issues such as pollution, waste generation and resource depletion are exacerbated by the growth of economic activity.

36.1 A Profile of India's Major Environmental Issues

India is the second most populous country in the world accounting for about 17% of the world's population with over 1.2 billion people; In the last two decades India experienced phenomenal economic growth to become world's seventh largest by nominal GDP and third largest in terms of purchasing power parity. India's GDP averaged 7% in the last 15 years. The commendable performance of the Indian economy in the recent decades is the result of unsustainable use of natural resources which has resulted in widespread environmental degradation at alarming rates,making people vulnerable to serious health issues caused by air and water pollution.

With nearly 17 per cent of the world's population on just 2.4 per cent of world's land area, India is causing a heavy pressure on the environment. This coupled with rapidly increasing rural industrialization and urbanisation is posing a challenge to sustainability of India's development efforts. According to a World Bank report (2013) the total cost of environmental degradation in India is about Rs. 3.75 trillion (US $ 80 billion) annually, equivalent to **5.7** percent of **GDP** in **2009.**

Some of the major environmental issues faced by India include:

- Resource depletion problems - land degradation
- Deforestation and biodiversity
- Air pollution from industries and households

- Water pollution and water scarcity
- Waste management issues
- Soil erosion
- Coastal environmental Issues
- Climate change due to green-house gas emissions

36.1.1 Resource depletion – Land degradation and deforestation:

The main causes of the land degradation include climate change, land clearance and deforestation, depletion of soil nutrients through poor farming practices, and overgrazing, inappropriate irrigation, urban sprawl and commercial development and soil pollution. Of India's total geographical area of 328.73 million hectare (mha), 304.89 mha comprise the reporting area and only 264.5 mha is under use for agriculture, forestry, pasture and other biomass production. DOEF (2001) Degraded land includes eroded lands, saline / alkaline lands, water logged lands and mined lands. Of the total land area of 304.89 million hectares, about 187.8 million hectares (57%) is degraded in one way or the other. This also includes about 40 million hectares of degraded forest. According to National Bureau of Soil Survey and land use Planning (2005), in India, water erosion is the most prominent reason of land degradation contributing to 93.8 million hectares (mh) of land degraded. Other factors include: wind erosion (9.48mh) water logging (5.95mh) and soil acidity (16.03mh). The total cultivable land of the country is about 144 million hectares of which 56% (80.6 million hectares) is degraded due to faulty agricultural practices. Around 7.4mh of land is degraded due to other causes.

36.1.2 Deforestation: Mismanagement and overuse of India's once abundant forests has resulted in desertification, contamination and depletion of soil throughout the sub-continent. Increasing industrialisation, urbanisation and infrastructural development, extraction of wood from forests for fuel and the occurrence of frequent forest fires are the major causes of degradation of forest land in many parts of India. Percapita forest land in India is only 0.08 ha against the requirement of 0.47 ha to meet basic needs, creating excessive pressure on forest lands.

India's forest cover is about 21% of total land area (about **69** million hectares). Due to deforestation, the forest cover of India has fallen below the minimum recommended level. According to experts, forests should cover about one-third of the total area of country. Dense forest constitutes only 12% of total forest cover area. Based on a figure of 28 million hectares of degraded forest (2009) and about 0.6 million hectares of deforested lands (2006-2009), the total annual losses from degraded forest land and annual deforestation losses are reported to be in the range of **0.1- 0.3%** of **GDP.**

According to FSI (Forest Survey of India) estimates, 78% of India's forests are affected by the impact of grazing. Overgrazing and over extraction of green fodder and increasing demand for commercial timber from industries is another contributing factor for decrease in forest cover. It is reported that an estimated 0.7 mha of forest lands are encroached upon for agriculture by the people living in the areas closer to forests.

Over-exploitation and loss of forest cover has led to the extinction of various plants, animals and microbial species. It is reported that over 1500 plant species are endangered and about 79 mammals, 44 birds, 15 reptiles, 3 amphibians and several insects are listed as endangered.

36.1.3 Air Pollution

According to World Health Organisation (WHO), more than 20 cities in India with population over a million are among the world's most polluted cities. A study released recently in 2014 by the WHO observed that, of, 1600 cities across the world, New Delhi has the world's dirtiest air. It further observes that 13 of the 20 cities with most polluted air are in India. According to the Environmental

Performance Index, India ranks 141 out of 180 countries in terms of air pollutionin 2016. WHO (2007) reported that air pollution contributes to the death of 0.52 million people annually in India. The International Energy Agency (IEA) reports that, by 2040, around 9 lakh premature deaths are likely to happen due to drastic air pollution in India and average life expectancies are likely to decrease by 15 months due to air pollution. Air pollution caused by vehicle exhaust increased eight-fold in the last twenty years; Many studies observe that air pollution in Indian cities are higher than in Chinese cities.

The WHO's "Global Burden of Disease Assessment" reports that outdoor air pollution in India causes 620,000 premature deaths per year in India, which is a six fold increase since 2000. This is mainly due to the emissions of particulates from transport and power plants.India is the third largest emitter of carbon di oxide and accounts for about five percent of global carbon dioxide emissions, roughly a quarter of the emissions of China and the United States. India has had the fastest growth in emissions, which have tripled since 1981. More than 60 percent of emissions in India come from energy sector.

36.1.4 Water Pollution and Water Scarcity

Almost 70 per cent of India's surface water resources and a growing percentage of its groundwater reserves are contaminated by biological, toxic, organic, and inorganic pollutants. Due to uncontrolled dumping of chemical and industrial waste, fertilizers and pesticides, 70% of the surface water in India is polluted. All of India's fourteen major river systems are heavily polluted. In 2011, the Central Pollution Control Board (CPCB) identified 150 polluted river stretches in the country. Nearly 23% of these were found to have BOD levels higher than 30 milligrams per litre (mg/l).

Wastewater generation from industrial sector has been estimated to be 55,000 million m3 per day, of which 68.5 million m3 are dumped directly into local rivers and streams without prior treatment. Nearly 40-45 per cent of the total pollution from industrial sector is caused by the processing of industrial chemicals and 65 – 70 percent of the total industrial waste water interms of organic load is from food products and agro-based industries.

Groundwater pollution is also a major concern. Groundwater in 122 districts are affected by salinity, by chloride in 66 districts, by fluoride in 224 districts, by arsenic in 35 districts and by nitrate in 368 districts. Arsenic contamination in groundwater has been found in the states of West Bengal, Bihar, Chhattisgarh, Uttar Pradesh and Assam. Due to high concentrations of fluoride in groundwater beyond the permissible limits, an estimated 44 million people in 19 states are affected with fluorosis, and another 66 million are at risk.

The domestic sector is responsible for the majority of waste water generation in India. Each year nearly 50 million cubic meters of untreated sewage is discharged into the rivers. The municipal wastewater treatment in India can treat only about 29 per cent of wastewater generated in the urban centres, calling for urgent attention.

Only 19.2 per cent of the rural and 70 per cent of the urban inhabitants have access to adequate sanitation facilities. The result of unclean water and poor hygiene are diarrheal diseases and typhoid. A World Bank (2013) report observes that the estimated annual cost associated with inadequate water supply, sanitation and hygiene averages to around Rs 540 billion. Nearly 0.4 million lives are lost annually in India due to lack of water, sanitation, and hygiene (WHO 2007).

Water scarcity: The per capita water availability in India in 1951 was 5177 m3 per year when the total population was only 361 million. In 2001, when India's population increased to 1027 million, the per capita water availability decreased to 1820 m3 per year. It is reported that by 2025, the per capita water availability will decrease to 1341 m3 and to 1140 m3 in 2050. Water stress condition refers to a situation when the per capita water availability ranges from 1000 to 1700 m3 per year and water scarcity exists when the availability reduces to 1000 m3 per year.Within the country, water availability varies widely as a result of rainfall, ground water reserve and proximity to river basins. It is reported that most of the Indian States will have reached the water stress condition by 2020 and water scarcity condition by 2025 (N G Hedge, 2012). Increase in population, urbanization, rising per capita income that promotes affluent consumption style and increased industrialization and agricultural development have contributed to increase in demand for water in the country. Over exploitation of ground water,inefficient use of water by industries and households, water pollution from agricultural run-off, pollution by industries and households, deforestation and resulting monsoon failure are responsible for decreasing water availability.

36.1.5 Waste Disposal

India's rapid urbanization and increasing economic growth has resulted in phenomenal increase in solid waste generation in urban areas. More than 377 million people live in 7935 towns and cities. These urban towns and cities generate 62 million tonnes of municipal solid wastes per annum. Only 43 million tonnes of the waste is collected, 11.9 million tonnes is treated and 31 million tonnes is dumped in land fill sites (Planning Commission Report , 2014). Planning Commission projects that that by 2031 these urban centers will generate 165 million tonnes of waste annually and by 2050 it could reach 436 million tonnes. Nearly 50% of the wastes are compostable, around 16 -21% are recyclable. About one third of total wastes are inert wastes. The composition of waste is also changing – the share of paper and plastics are increasing. Central Pollution Control Board reports that during the last decade, solid waste generation has increased 2.44 times. The e-waste inventory based on the obsolescence rate in India for the year 2005 was estimated to be 1,46,180 tonnes, and was expected to exceed 8,00,000 tonnes by 2012.

36.1.6 Soil Erosion: It is reported that India is losing 5,334 million tonnes of soil every year due to soil erosion. The factors responsible for this massive erosion of soil in India are indiscreet and excessive use of fertilisers, insecticides, and pesticides. A study conducted by the Central Soil Water Conservation Research and Training Institute observes that the loss due to soil erosion is 16.4 tonnes per hectare every year.

36.1.7 Coastal Environment

India's marine environment, supports productive and protective habitats such as mangroves, coral reefs and sand dunes. Its long coast line of more than 7500 km include a wide range of mangroves, coral reefs, sea grasses, salt marshes, estuaries, lagoons, and unique marine and coastal flora and fauna. India's coastal and offshore environment supports rich biodiversity. Bacteria, fungi, and zooplankton species are abundant. However, in spite of their contribution to the national economy, India's coastal and marine areas are under threat from economic activities such as offshore drilling, aquaculture, port activities. Studies reveal that about 34% of India's mangroves were destroyed during 1950-2000. More than 65 % of the mangroves and associated plant species are endangered and 97% of the plant species are threatened. Indiscriminate cutting, reclamation for agriculture and urbanization, fuel and overgrazing by domestic cattle and aquaculture have severely degraded mangroves in India.

A World Bank report observes that almost all coral areas are threatened and marine fish stocks are declining. Such rapid depletion and degradation, unless controlled, will adversely affect the livelihood, health and well-being of the coastal population.

36.1.8 Climate change and India: India relies a lot on traditional sources of energy such as fuelwood, crop residue and dung cake. In rural India, traditional energy sources dominate domestic energy use and accounts for about 90 per cent of the total. In urban areas, nearly 24 per cent of the total energy use is from traditional sources of energy. These traditional sources of energy contribute heavily to air pollution, particularly to emissions of greenhouse gasses. India was the third largest emitter of total carbon dioxide in 2009 at 1.65 Gt per year, after China (6.9 Gt per year) and the United States (5.2 Gt per year). With 17 percent of world population, India contributed some 5 percent of human-sourced carbon dioxide emission.

36.2 India's Environmental Policy

Population pressure and development needs are having adverse impact on India's environment. Indian government has responded with policy statements, legislation and provisions under five year plans to tackle the pressure on environment. Though measures were taken to preserve and protect environment even as early as 1900, it is only after the Stockholm conference that specific policy measures and legislations were introduced.

36.2.1 Evolution of India's Environmental Policy – Prior to Stockholm Conference (1972)

In India environmental protection has received specific attention though for different reasons. In ancient India, respecting and worshipping the environment was the essence of culture. This was reflected in the daily lives of the people. The Vedas and Upanishads upheld a worshipful attitude towards earth, sky, air, water, all flora and fauna and preached environmental harmony and conservation. For example a hymn in Vedas in praise of nature goes as follows: "I worship the Lord of Air and Water...I worship these again and again". The Arthasastra prescribed various punishments for cutting trees, damaging forests, and for killing animals.

With the establishment of British Colonial rule, many changes were brought in the religiously oriented indigenous system. Forestry, wildlife and water pollution specifically attracted the attention of the British Government. The Forest Act of 1927 specifically denied people any rights over the forest produce simply because they were domiciled there. There were specific laws such as:

- The Shore Nuisance (Bombay and Kolaba) Act of 1853 and the Oriental Gas Company Act of 1857 for controlling water pollution.
- the Merchant Shipping Act of 1858 which dealt with prevention of pollution of sea by oil.
- the Indian Penal Code, 1860 that attempted to control water and atmospheric pollution through criminal sanctions.
- the Easement Act of 1882 allowed a prescription right to pollute the water going against the prohibitive provisions under the IPC, 1860.
- the Bengal Smoke Nuisance Act of 1905 and Bombay Smoke Nuisance Act of 1912 to control air pollution.

Inspite of these regulations, conservation of nature was not the focus under the British regime, the intention of which was only exploitation of India's natural resource for its own benefit. The Indian Constitution, adopted in 1950, did not deal with the subject of protection of environment. There were select provisions such as the Factories Act of 1948 and the River Boards Act of 1956 for checking pollution of air, water, etc., but there was no serious effort to design and implement an environmental policy.

36.2.2 India's Environmental Policy 1972 – 1990

The UN Conference on Human Environment held at Stockholm in 1972 paved the path for environmental policy and environmental legislation in India. A number of steps were initiated by the Government of India to implement the decisions taken at the conference, such as, amendments to the constitution, new legislations for environmental protection and creation of institutions for implementing the new legislations.

India is the first country to make amendments in its Constitution for the protection and improvement of its natural environment. The 42nd amendment to the Constitution in 1976, inserted specific provisions for environmental protection in the form of Directive Principles of State Policy and Fundamental Duties. The 'Constitution's Forty-second Amendment stated: "*The State shall endeavour to protect and improve the environment and to safeguard the forest and wild life of the country.*" The forty second amendment was implemented from January 3rd, 1977. While Article 48A (Directive Principles) provided for the protection and improvement of the environment by the State, Article 51.A (g) (Fundamental Duties) enunciates that it shall be the duty of every citizen of India to protect and improve the natural environment including forests, lakes, rivers, and wild life and to have compassion for living creatures. Besides these Constitutional Provisions which provide for environmental protection, the three lists of the Seventh Schedule of the Constitution of India- namely, the Union List, the State List and the Concurrent List - contain specific entries which permit the Union or the State or both, to make laws having a bearing, directly or indirectly, on environment.

Recognizing the need for comprehensive and integrated view of environmental protection and improvement with emphasis on the sustainable use of natural resources for development, the Government set up a National Committee on Environmental Planning & Co-ordination (NCEPC) in 1972; the Committee was to advice the Government on environmental problems and suggest solutions after consultation with experts and the concerned Ministries/Departments.

During the seventies the country got two important environmental Acts - **the 'Wild Life Protection Act, 1972; and the Water (Preservation & Control of Pollution) Act, 1974.** The Water Act paved the way for the establishment of Central and State Pollution Control Boards (CPCB and SPCBs) which were responsible for implementing legislations relating to prevention and control of pollution. However the increase in the complexity of environmental issues and the rising number of environmental conflicts necessitated the need for an exclusive department to deal with environmental protection. Hence the Government constituted a High Level Committee under the Chairmanship of Shri N.D. Tiwari, Deputy Chairman, Planning Commission, to recommend legislative measures and an administrative machinery for ensuring environmental protection. The Committee submitted its report to the Prime Minister on September 15, 1980. On the recommendations of the Committee, the **Department of Environment** (DoEn) was set up in November 1980, to provide explicit recognition to environmental protection. In January 1985 the Department of Environment became part of the Ministry of Environmentand Forests. The Ministry of Environment and Forests (MoEF) is the nodal agency in the administrative structure of the Central government for the planning, promotion, coordination and ensuring the implementation of India's environmental and forestry policies and programmes.

The chief functions of the Department of Environment are:

- To serve as a nodal agency for environmental protection and eco development in the country;
- To play a 'watch dog' role to study and bring to the attention of government and Parliament, instances, causes and consequences of environmental degradation in all sectors;
- To carry out environmental appraisal of development projects;
- To carry out administrative responsibility for:
  a. Conservation and survey of flora, fauna, forests and wildlife
  b. Prevention and control of pollution
  c. Afforestation and regeneration of degraded areas
  d. Protection of the environment and
  e. Ensuring the welfare of animals

The Department of Environment conducts environmental impact assessments of major development projects and strengthens the capabilities of State Governments in carrying out environmental planning, protection and review. The Department of Environment has set up a computerised Environmental Information System (ENVIS) with a network of distributed information centres all over the country. This helps in the collection, processing and dissemination of information related to environment in order to promote research.

In September 1985 the Department of Forests and Wildlife, which was also under Ministry of Environment and Forests, was merged with the Department of Environment to constitute a single department – Department of Environment, Forests & Wildlife.

The Ministry of Environment and Forests consisting of the Department of Environment, Forests & Wildlife areas perform vital functions. The main objectives of the Ministry of Environment and Forest are conservation and survey of flora, fauna, forest and wildlife, prevention and control of pollution, afforestation and regeneration of degraded areas, protection of environment and ensuring the welfare of animals. The objectives are well supported by a set of legislative and regulatory measures aimed at the preservation, conservation and protection of environment. Beside these legislative measures, National Forest Policy-1988, a National Conservation Strategy and Policy Statement on Environment and Development, 1992, a Policy Statement on Abatement of Pollution-1992, and National Environment Policy-2006 have also been evolved.

During 1980s important central legislations were implemented such as **the Forest Act (1980), the Air Act (1981), the Wild Life Protection Act (1986) and the Environment act (1986). The National Forest Policy, 1988** is a major policy initiative during the eighties. India has had a forest policy as early as 1894. The policy was revised in 1952 and again in 1988. The main aim of the revised forest policy of 1988 is protection, conservation and development of forests. The major objectives of the policy are:

- Maintenance of environmental stability" through preservation and restoration of ecological balance;
- Conservation of natural heritage by preserving the remaining natural forests and protecting the vast genetic resources;
- Control of soil erosion and denudation in catchment areas of rivers, lakes and reservoirs;
- Maintaining intrinsic relationship of forests and tribal & other people living in and around forests
- Involvement of people in forest management under joint forest management (JFM) scheme.

This policy gave priority to the ecological value of forests over economic benefits of forests. The policy upheld the rights of local communities to fuel wood, fodder and other produce of forests. Most importantly, the Policy introduced community approach to forestry rights.

36.2.3 India's Environmental Policy from 1992

In the period following the Rio Summit in 1992, the concern for environment strengthened among policy makers in all countries. India is no exception. The Ministry of Environment and Forests in India came out with the Policy Statement for Abatement of Pollution and the National Conservation Strategy and Policy Statement on Environment and Development. The National Environmental Policy, 2006 was the first initiative in strategy-formulation for environmental protection in a comprehensive manner.

36.2.3.1National Conservation Strategy and Policy Statement on Environment and Development, 1992

The primary purpose of the strategy and the policy statement is to "include & reinforce our traditional ethos and to build up a society living in harmony with Nature and making frugal and efficient use of resources guided by the best available scientific knowledge". The policy thoroughly studied the prevailing environmental situation in India and reviewed the prevailing policies and in view of the context of enormous challenges and prepared an agenda for action. The agenda aimed to:

- ensure sustainable and equitable use of resources for meeting the basic needs of the present and future generations without causing damage to the environment.
- prevent and control future deterioration in land, water and air which constitute our life-support systems.
- take steps for restoration of ecologically degraded areas and for environmental improvement in our rural and urban settlements.
- ensure that development projects are correctly sited so as to minimize their adverse environmental consequences.
- conserve and nurture the biological diversity, gene pool and other resources through environmentally sustainable development.
- protect the scenic landscapes, unique and representative biomes and ecosystems and wildlife habitats, heritage sites/structures and areas of cultural heritage importance.

To implement the agenda the strategy and policy statement recommended:

- Environmental impact assessment of all development projects right from the planning stage and integrate it with their cost-benefit considerations.
- All projects above a certain size and were subject to compulsory prior environmental clearance in certain ecologically sensitive areas.
- Incorporating environmental safeguards and protection measures in policies, planning, site selection, choice of technology and implementation of development projects.
- Research, development and adoption of environmentally compatible technologies to be encouraged.
- Create environmental awareness among people and improve people's participation in environmental improvement programmes.
- Effectively implement the various environmental laws and regulations for environmental protection through creation or strengthening of the requisite enforcement machinery.

36.2.3.2 Policy Statement on Abatement of Pollution-1992

The objective of the Policy Statement on Abatement of Pollution is to integrate environmental considerations into decision- making at all levels. The policy statement emphasized on actual implementation. The policy statement stressed on preventive aspects of pollution abatement and promotion of technological inputs to reduce pollution. To achieve this it recommended the following:

- prevention of pollution at source instead of end of the pipe treatment;
- application of the best available practical technical solutions
- adoption of the polluter pays principle in policy for pollution control
- protection of heavily polluted areas and river stretches
- Involve public in decision making on issues related to environmental improvement.

The 1990s saw many major actions and policies and legislative measures for environmental protection. The following Acts were enacted during 1990s.

- The Public Liability Insurance Act, 1991
- The National Environment Tribunals Act, 1995,

- The National Environment Appellate Authority Act, 1997
- Biological Diversity Act (2002)
- National Green Tribunal Act (NGTA) (2010)

Most of these were response to the United Nations Conference on Sustainable Development, more popularly known as the Earth Summit or Rio Conference. The Rio conference laid the foundation for serious environmental thinking and action by policy makers in all nations. Liability for compensation, establishment of Green tribunal, exclusive legislation for protecting biodiversity of the nation, inclusion of polluter pays principle and precautionary principle etc are some of the major policy actions that evolved after the Rio Summit.

36.2.3.3 National Environmental Policy 2006 (NEP, 2006)

The National Environmental Policy (2006) builds on the earlier policies extending their coverage, and filling in the existing gaps, using the accumulated experience and additional new knowledge. As mentioned by the MoEF, the NEP 2006 "does not displace, (displace other national policies), but builds on the earlier policies". It is a response to national commitment to a clean environment, mandated in the Indian Constitution in Articles 48A and 51A(g), strengthened by judicial interpretation of Article 21. According to the policy, development is sustainable if and only if it respects ecological constraints, and the imperatives of justice. The policy highlighted the need to ensure that people dependent on particular resources obtain better livelihoods through conservation of rather than from degradation of the resource. The policy recommended measures to enhance and conserve environmental resources.

Objectives of the Policy include:

- Conservation of Critical Environmental Resources
- Intra-generational Equity:
- Livelihood security for the poor.
- Integration of Environmental Concerns in Economic and Social Development
- Efficiency in Environmental Resource Use
- Environmental Governance
- Enhancement of Resources for Environmental Conservation

To realize the objectives stated above, the policy enumerated 14 principles. Of these seven major principles are adopted from Agenda 21 principles. The Principles are given below: (Ministry of Environment and Forests, 2006)

1. Human Beings are at the Centre of Sustainable Development Concerns.
2. The Right to Development.
3. Environmental Protection is an Integral part of the Development Process.
4. **The Precautionary Approach**.
5. **Economic efficiency** which includes **Polluter Pay's** and **cost minimization** principles.
6. Entities with "Incomparable": Incomparable entities refer to those entities which the society will not accept for any amount of real or pecuniary benefits; such entities pose risks to human health and environmental support systems. They should be given priority in the allocation of society's scarce resources while considering economic benefits.
7. **Equity** in the context of this policy refers to both equity in entitlements to and participation of, the relevant public, in the processes of decision-making over use of environmental resources.
8. **Civil liability** to supplement the principle of legal liability on which regulation is based since civil liability would deter environmentally harmful actions, and compensate the victims

of environmental damage. There are two approaches to civil liability concept, namely fault based liability and strict liability. In fault based liability, a party is held liable if it breaches a pre existing legal duty, for example, an environmental standard. Strict liability, on the other hand, imposes obligation to compensate the victim for harm resulting from actions or failure to take action, which may not necessarily constitute a breach of any law or duty of care.

9. **Public Trust Doctrine** which implies that State is only a trustee of all natural resources, which are by nature meant for public use and enjoyment, subject to reasonable conditions.
10. **Decentralisation** which implies transfer of power from a Central Authority to State and Local Authorities for more effective and timely decisions in matters if environmental issues.
11. **Integration** referring to the inclusion of environmental considerations in sectoral policy making, as well as all possible linkages among various decision making units with reference to environmental policy making.
12. **Environmental Standard Setting** must take into consideration socio economic differences in the areas they are applied.
13. **Preventive Action:** Prevention of environmental damages must get priority over restoring damages after allowing damages to occur.
14. **Environmental Offsetting:** If for some reason environmental protection of any specific natural system is overlooked, cost effective offsetting measures must be undertaken by the proponents of the activity to restore as nearly as possible and feasible, the lost environmental services to the same public.

The National Environment Policy is intended to be a guide to action in regulatory reform, programmes and projects for environmental conservation; and review and enactment of legislation, by agencies of the Central, State, and Local Governments. NEP 2006 states: "Action plans would need to be prepared on identified themes by the concerned agencies at all levels of Government - Central, State/UT, and Local. In particular, the State and Local Governments should be encouraged to formulate their own strategies or action plans consistent with the National Environment policy". The policy highlighted the need to empower Panchayats and Urban Local Bodies particularly, in terms of functions and funds. Reforms of existing laws were underlined by the policy. The policy encouraged partnerships of different stakeholders - national and international - to use their respective resources and strengths for the environmental management of the nation. NEP 2006 stated policy related strategic themes and outlines of actions.

The strong points of the 2006 Environmental Policy if implemented with perseverance will pave the way for sustainable development in India. As recommended by the policy, reforming of existing laws and new laws to fill gaps in the environmental context are necessary. Public involvement and public partnership are positive measures towards this end.

The National Green Tribunal Act (2010) added dynamism to the policy. Judicial activism is visibly seen now in the context of environmental protection and conservation of resources. The various policies and policy statements related to environmental protection are strengthened by the implementation of the various Acts which are discussed below in Section 36.2.1.

36.3 Environmental Legislation in India

The Stockholm Declaration of 1972 was a motivating force in the enactment of environmental legislation and designing environmental policy in India. The Stockholm Conference on Human Environment highlighted the need for having uniform laws throughout the country for dealing with environmental issues that had serious impacts on the health of the people and of flora and fauna. The major environmental legislations enacted by the Government of India since 1972 are:

- The Wildlife (Protection) Act, 1972
- The Water (Prevention and Control of Pollution) Act, 1974
- The The Forest (Conservation) Act, 1980
- The Air (Prevention and Control of Pollution) Act,1981
- The Environment (Protection) Act, 1986
- The Public Liability Insurance Act, 1991
- The National Environment Tribunals Act, 1995,
- The National Environment Appellate Authority Act, 1997
- Biological Diversity Act (2002)
- National Green Tribunal Act (NGTA) (2010)

36.3.1 The Wild Life (Protection) Act, 1972

This Act was enacted under the provisions of Article 252 with the objective of effectively protecting India's wild life and to control poaching, smuggling and illegal trade in wildlife and its derivatives. The major motives for the passing of the Act are:

- The rapid decline of India's wild animals and birds, one of the richest and most varied wildlife resources of the country.
- Increase in the number of extinct species of flora and fauna and the threat of more becoming extinct.
- Outdated existing laws in terms of coverage as well as punishments for non-compliance.

The Act prohibits hunting of animals, except with permission from the concerned authority, when an animal becomes dangerous to human life or property or becomes disabled or diseased beyond recovery. The Act empowers central and State governments to declare any area as a wild life sanctuary, national park, or closed areas if the area has adequate ecological significance in terms of flora and fauna for protecting them. Industrial activity is banned in these areas.

36.3.2 The Water (Prevention and Control of Pollution) Act, 1974

The Water (Prevention and Control of Pollution) Act was enacted in 1974 to provide for the prevention and control of water pollution and for maintaining or restoring of wholesomeness of water. All human activities having a bearing on water quality are covered under this Act. It also provides for the establishment of Boards both at the Central and State level for carrying out the provisions of the Act. The water act of 1974 along with amendments in 1978 is an extensive legislation for prevention and control of water pollution. The Act is the first specific and comprehensive legislation. The salient features of the Act are:

- The Act prohibits any discharge of poisonous, noxious, or polluting water in excess of predetermined standards from entering into any water body.
- The Act prescribed effluent standards.
- The Act is responsible for the creation of the Central and State Pollution Control Boards (CPCB and SPCB).

The pollution control boards at the central and state levels (CPCB and SPCB) are empowered to prevent, control, and abate water pollution, and to advise governments on matters pertaining to such pollution. CPCB is to coordinate the activities of the state boards. The main function of the CPCB 'is to promote cleanliness of 'streams' and wells in different areas of the states. The term 'stream' includes river, watercourse, inland water, subterranean waters, and sea or tidal waters.

Water Act requires that any industry likely to discharge waste water in to a water body can do so only with the previous consent of the State Pollution Control Boards. In granting consent orders, the Board may lay down conditions for the quality of waste water discharged. The consent granted by the State boards is conditional, and may be withdrawn in the event of non-compliance with the prescribed standards.

Penalties for non-compliance with the standards prescribed for polluting any water body are imprisonment and / or fine. In addition any expense incurred by the Board for sampling, analysis, inspection etc. must be paid by the polluter.

The penalties for non-compliance are imprisonment from 18 months to 6 years with a fine for the first violation of the rules and additional fine upto Rs.5000 per day till the failure continues. For making new outlets and thus discharging effluent without consent of the SPCBs, the penalties are imprisonment from 2 to 6 years and fine for the first contravention and imprisonment from 2 to 7 years and fine after the first conviction.

The Act is not without limitations. The major limitation is the omission of groundwater pollution in the Act. Further the penalties for non-compliance with the standards or directions are independent of the extent of violations.

36.3.3 Water Cess (Prevention and Control of Pollution) Act, 1977, amended in 1991

The Act was enacted to levy and collect cess on water consumed by certain categories of industry specified in the schedule appended to the Act. The money thus collected is used by CPCB and SPCBs to prevent and control water pollution. The Act was passed to enable the state Boards to overcome financial burden which were overburdened and underfunded. The revised rates of water cess varied between 1.50 paise to 5.00 paise for kilo litre for various uses. These rates are too low compared with the opportunity costs of water. Out of cess collected and credited to consolidated fund of India (CI), 80 percent of cess is reimbursed to SPCBs to augment the resources of Boards.

The Water Cess Act grants exemption to all industries consuming water less than ten kilo litres per day from the levy of cess. However the Act clearly states that no such exemption shall be applicable in case of industries generating 'hazardous waste' as defined in Hazardous Wastes (Management and Handling) Rules, 1989. An industry which installs and operates its effluent treatment plant is entitled to a rebate of 25% on the cess payable.

36.3.4 The Air (Prevention and Control of Pollution) Act, 1981 (Amended in 1987)

The objective of the Air Act 1981 is to prevent, control and reduce air pollution. The Act defines air pollutant as 'any solid, liquid or gaseous substance (including noise) present in the atmosphere in such concentration as may be or tend to be injurious to human beings or other living creatures or plants or property or environment'. The CPCB and SPCBs are entrusted with the responsibility of implementation of the Act.

The **penalties** for violation of the rules specified in the Act are:

- Imprisonment for a term between 18 months and 6 years and a fine;
- If non- compliance continues, an additional fine will be imposed which may extend to Rs.5000 for every day during which such failure continues after conviction.
- If the failure continues beyond one year after the date of conviction, the offender shall be punishable with imprisonment for a term between 2 years and 7 years and with fine.
- For further failure to intimate the occurrence of the emissions in excess of the standards, giving false information for obtaining consent to operate, are imprisonment for a term which may extend to 3 months with fine which may extend to Rs.10000 or both.

36.3.5 The Environment (Protection Act) 1986

The Environment (Protection) Act, 1986 was introduced as an umbrella legislation that provides a holistic framework for the protection and improvement to the environment. The Act was framed after the Bhopal Gas Tragedy in 1984. The Act empowers the central government to take all measures that are necessary for the purpose of protecting and improving the quality of the environment and preventing, controlling and abating environmental pollution.

The main objective of the Act is protecting and improving the environment. The Government enacted this Act under Article 253 of the constitution. The act provides a framework for preventing and controlling air, water and land pollution and empowers the government for setting national ambient and emission standards, establishing procedures and regulations for inspection and checking pollution sources. The Act empowers the government to appoint officers for performing various functions and for issuing various directions for the control and abatement of pollution. The Act empowers the central government to plan and execute a nation-wide programme for the prevention, control and abatement of environmental pollution; It also empowered central government to prepare manuals, codes or guides regarding the prevention, control and abatement of environment pollution.

The Environment (Protection) Act, 1986 provided for specific rules which complement the provisions under the Act: -

- The Environment (Protection) Rules, 1986
- The Manufacture, Storage and import of Hazardous Chemical Rules, 1989 amended 2000
- The Hazardous Wastes (Management & Handling) Rules, 1989 amended 2000, 2003
- The Manufacture, Use, Import, Export and Storage of Hazardous micro-organisms, Genetically engineered organisms or cells Rules, 1989
- The Chemical Accidents (Emergency Planning, Preparedness and Response) Rules, 1996
- The Bio – Medical Waste (Management and Handling) Rules, 1998 as amended 2000 and 2003.
- The Ozone Depleting Substances (Regulation) Control Rules, 2000

The 1986 Environment Act thus provides a holistic approach for controlling pollution and improving India's environment.

36.3.6 Public Liability Insurance Act (PLIA), 1991

The Public Liability Insurance Act 1991 is in line with the spirit of Principle 13 of the Rio Declaration, which states that 'States shall develop national laws regarding liability and compensation for the victims of pollution and other environmental damage'. The Act was passed in the aftermath of the Bhopal Gas Tragedy at Bhopal in Madhya Pradesh in India in 1984 involving the leakage of toxic gas Methyl isocyanide (MIC) from the Union Carbide's Indian Subsidiary and the Oleum gas leak in the public Ltd Company Shriram Ltd situated in Delhi in 1985. The objective of the Act is to 'provide for public liability insurance for the purpose of providing relief to the persons affected by accidents while handling any hazardous substance connected therewith or incidental thereto'..

This Act makes it mandatory for the business owners who operate in hazardous substances to:

1. take out insurance policies for covering potential liabilities from an accident or incidents involving these hazardous substances; and
2. establish environment relief funds for dealing with accidents arising from the mishandling of hazardous substances.

The PLIA is based on 'no fault' liability and is not applicable to workmen since their interests are covered by the labour laws. The rule currently stipulates that the owners are liable to pay not more than Rs 50 million for any one accident and not more than Rs 150 million for any one-year.

The reimbursement of relief to the extent of Rs.25,000/- per person is admissible in case of fatal accidents in addition to the reimbursement of medical expenses up to Rs.12,500/-. Any claim in excess to this liability will be paid from the ERF. In case the amount exceeds, the remaining amount shall have to be met by the owner.

For permanent total or permanent partial disability or other injury or sickness, the relief will be:

(a) reimbursement of medical expenses incurred up to a maximum of Rs.12,500 in each case and

(b) cash relief on the basis of percentage of disablement as certified by an authorised physician. The relief for total permanent disability will be Rs.25,000;

For loss of wages due to temporary disability, compensation will be Rs.1000 per month for a maximum of 3 months; and for damage to property up to Rs.6000 depending on the damage.

The PLIA was amended in 1992, and the Central Government was authorized to establish the Environmental Relief Fund, for making relief payment.

Environment Relief Fund

An amount equal to the annual premium is to be paid by the owner to the insurance company and the insurance company deposits this amount into a special pool called the Environment Relief Fund. This fund will be utilised for paying the relief to be given as mentioned in the Act. If the amount of relief awarded by the Collector exceeds the amount payable under the insurance policy purchased by the owner or exceeds the liability of the insurance company, ERF is to be utilized for paying claims.

The Act prescribes a criminal sentence of up to six years with a minimum mandatory sentence of one and a half years for persons who do not takeout insurance policies and fail to adhere to directions with a fine of a minimum of a lakh of Rupees.

36.3.7 The National Environment Tribunal Act, 1995

This Act is structured on the same line as PLIA. The Act "provides strict liability for damages arising out of any accident occurring while handling any hazardous substance." The Act also provided for the establishment of a National Tribunal "for effective and expeditious disposal of cases arising from such accident, with a view to giving relief and compensation of damages to persons, property, and the environment and for matters connected therewith or incidental thereto".

36.3.8 The National Environment Appellate Authority Act, 1997: The Act established the National Environment Appellate Authority to hear appeals with respect to restriction of areas in which any industry operations or processes or class of industries, operations or processes, shall or shall not be carried out, subject to certain safeguards under the Environment (Protection) Act.

36.3.9 Biological Diversity Act, 2002

The Act was enacted under the United Nations Convention on Biological Diversity signed at Rio de Janeiro on the 5th day of June, 1992 of which India is also a party. Objective of this act is to regulate the access to genetic resources and protection of biodiversity. As per the provision of Act, certain areas, which are rich in biodiversity and encompasses unique and representative ecosystems are identified and designated as biosphere reserve to facilitate its conservation. This act provides for establishment of statutory bodies such as National Biodiversity Authority, State Biodiversity Boards, National and State Biodiversity Funds, Biodiversity Management Committee etc. This Act provides for:

- conservation of biological diversity
- sustainable use of its components
- fair and equitable sharing of the benefits arising out of the use of biological resources.

The NBA deals with the requests for access to the biological resources as well as transfer of information of traditional knowledge to foreign nationals, institutions and companies. This confers two important benefits:

- Prevention of piracy of Intellectual Property Rights in and around India
- Protects the indigenous people from exploitation.

The recent developments relating to NBA implementation include the establishment of Designated National Repository (DNR) as an important aspect of infrastructure for biodiversity conservation. This DNR facilitates service providers for preserved specimen consisting all fauna, herbarium (dried plant material for research), living cells, genomes of organisms and information relating to hereditary and function of biological system.

36.3.10 National Green Tribunal Act (NGTA) (2010)

The act was enacted under constitutional provision of Article 21, which assures the citizens of India the right to a healthy environment. When this Act came into force, the National Environmental Tribunal Act and the National Environment Appellate Authority Act were repealed.

The National Green Tribunal Act 2010 established the National Green Tribunal for:

- effective and expeditious disposal of cases relating to environmental protection
- conservation of forests and other natural resources
- enforcement of any legal right relating to environment
- giving relief and compensation for damages to persons and property and for matters connected therewith or incidental thereto.

The Green Tribunal is a specialized body equipped with the necessary expertise to handle environmental disputes involving multi-disciplinary issues. According to the Act, the Tribunal is not bound by the procedure laid down under the Code of Civil Procedure, 1908, but will be guided by principles of natural justice. National Green Tribunal is India's first dedicated environmental court with a wide jurisdiction to deal with not only violations of environmental laws, but also to provide for compensation, relief and restoration of the ecology in accordance with the 'Polluter Pays' principle and powers to enforce the 'precautionary principle'. The NGT has the power to hear all civil cases relating to environmental issues and questions that are linked to the implementation of laws listed in Act.

Section 26 in the Act, specifies penalty for failure to comply with orders of Tribunal. According to the Act, "whoever, fails to comply with any order or award or decision of the Tribunal under this Act, he shall be punishable with:

- imprisonment up to three years, or a fine of rupees ten crore or both.

In case the failure or non-compliance with the order or decision of the Tribunal continues, then he is punishable with additional fine which may extend to twenty-five thousand rupees for every day during which such failure or non-compliance continues."

The Act further provided that "In case a company fails to comply with any order or award or a decision of the Tribunal under this Act, such company shall be punishable with fine which may extend to twenty-five crore rupees, and in case the failure or contravention continues, with additional fine which may extend to one lakh rupees for every day during which such failure or contravention continues".

NGT's action – select case studies

In April 2014, the NGT said that the health of Yamuna will be affected by the proposed recreational facilities on the river, and recommended the Government to declare a 52 km stretch of the Yamuna in Delhi and Uttar Pradesh as a conservation zone.

In March 2015, NGT imposed a fine of Rs 5 crore on Art of Living Foundation because it organized World Cultural Festival on Yamuna flood plain and affected the environment.

The National Green Tribunal cancelled the clearance given to the Parsa East and Kante-Basan captive coal blocks in the Hasdeo-Arand forests of Chhattisgarh. The coal block required clearance of 1989 hectares of forest land in an area considered to be a patch of valuable forest and demarcated as a 'no-go' area. The Government had initially barred the coal block in this area and demarcated it as a 'no-go' area.

The NGT and the NGTA are important landmarks in the development of environmental legislation in India.

36.4 Environmental Protection under Twelfth Five Year Plan – a brief note

India's efforts to protect environment has relied on legislation. The various Acts and the policy statements have created the necessary environmental institutions for managing environmental issues. These have been strengthened adequately by support from Five Year Plans. It was the Fourth plan that explicitly mentioned about the need to protect the environment. It mentioned about the "obligation of each generation to maintain the productive capacity of land, air, water and wildlife in a manner which leaves its successors some choice in the creation of a healthy environment." Thereafter, environmental protection has been included under five year plans. For example the Sixth Five Year Plan (1980-85), devoted an entire chapter on "Environment and Development". It stated that "… a concern for environment is essentially a desire to see that national development proceeds along rational sustainable lines." The eleventh plan envisaged a commitment to promote environmentally sustainable development. The Eleventh Plan (2007-2012) mentioned specific targets towards environmental protection:

The eveventh plan emphasised on four environment related targets, in the environment and forest sector:

- Increase forest and tree cover by 5 percentage points
- Treat all urban waste water by 2011–12 to clean river waters
- Attain World Health Organisation (WHO) Standards of air quality in all major cities by 2011–12.
- Increase energy efficiency by 20 percentage points by 2016–17.

36.4.1 The Twelfth Plan (2012 -2017)

The Twelfth Plan (2012 -2017) aims to change the environmental governance system towards a holistic approach. The basic theme of the Twelfth Plan Document, approved by the National Development Council (NDC) on 27th December 2012, is "Faster, Sustainable, and more inclusive growth". It lays out major targets, key challenges to meet them, and the broad strategy to achieve the objectives stated.The twelfth plan outlay for Ministry of Environment and Forests is Rs`17,874 crores which is 0.41% of the Plan allocation across various Ministries. At current prices, the enhancement in this Ministry's Twelfth Plan outlay over the Eleventh Plan outlay, however, works out to 109%.(MoEF Annual Report 2014-15).

The vision statement of the twelfth plan is:

"Managing Environment, Forests, Wildlife and challenges due to Climate Change for faster and equitable growth, where ecological security for sustainability and inclusiveness is restored, equity in access to all environmental goods and ecosystem services is assured through institutionalisation of people's participation;

AND

A future in which the nation takes pride in the quality of its environment, forests, richness of its biodiversity, and efforts by the State and its people to protect, expand and enrich it, for intra and inter-generational equity and welfare of the local and global community".

In the 12th Five Year Plan managing the Environment is one of the "**Twelve Strategy Challenges** " that is, one of the core areas that require new approaches to produce the desired results. After an in-depth analysis of the prevailing policies and programmes towards environmental protection, the twelfth plan set twelve monitorable targets. Of the twelve, three relate to environment and climate change, four to forestry, and three relate to wild life and ecotourism and animal welfare and two under ecosystem and bio diversity. The targets are:

Environment and Climate Change

- Assess and remediate 12 identified contaminated sites (hazardous chemicals and wastes) with potential for ground water contamination by 2017.
- Clean 80 per cent of critically polluted stretches in rivers by 2017 and 100 per cent by 2020.
- States to meet National Ambient Air Quality Standards (NAAQS) in urban areas by 2017.
- To reduce emission intensity of Gross Domestic Product (GDP) in line with the target of 20 to 25 per cent reduction over 2005 levels by 2020.

Forests and Livelihood

- Greening 5 million ha under GIM including 1.5 m.ha. of degraded lands, afforestation and eco-restoration of 0.9 m.ha. of ecologically sensitive areas.
- Technology-based monitoring of forest cover, biodiversity and growing stock through dedicated satellite by 2017 and establishment of open web-based National Forestry & Environmental Information system for research and public accessibility by 2015.
- Engagement of village Green Guards/ Community Foresters for every Joint Forest Management (JFM) village by 2016.
- Establish forestry seed bank in forest circles and Model Nursery in every district with information on public portal by 2014.

Wildlife, Ecotourism and Animal Welfare

- Twenty per cent of veterinary professionals in the country will be trained in treating wildlife.
- Integrated Ecotourism District Plans covering 10 per cent of all potential Protected Areas (PAs) by 2017.
- Promoting participation of private sector, civil societies, NGOs and philanthropists in animal welfare.

Ecosystem and Biodiversity

- Restore 0.1 mha. of wetlands/ inland lakes/ water bodies by 2017.
- Mapping and preparation of biodiversity management plans for deserts (both cold and arid), coastal areas, important coral zones, wetlands, mangroves and so on to be completed by 2017.

Besides completing the unfinished tasks of the eleventh plan, the twelfth plan committed to new initiatives too. These are:

- Recasting the scheme of Common Effluent Treatment Plants (CETPS)
- National Plan for Conservation of Aquatic Eco-Systems (NPCA)
- National Environmental Monitoring Programme
- National Forestry Information System
- Invasive Species Management
- Coastal and Marine Conservation

- Valuation of Ecosystem Services and Biodiversity
- Environmental Performance Index (EPI)
- Rangeland and Silvi-Pasture Development Scheme
- Satellite Based Forest Resource Assessment
- Green India Mission

A comprehensive review and reform of laws concerning Environment, Forests, Wildlife and Biodiversity is an important strategy of the12th Plan, in order to make them more effective. It suggested the amendment of the Environment Act of 2006 to include an upward revision of the penalties and also to include fast-track levy of penalty. The plan suggested many initiatives for improving the existing system of monitoring and control of pollution, strengthening existing institutions, rules and policy statements and achieving infrastructure/technology upgradation and directing investment in the environment, forest and wildlife sectors.

36.5 Fiscal Incentives for Environmental Protection in India

Though India relies more on command and control regulations introduced through the various legislations and Rules, there are few fiscal incentives too. For example the Water Cess Act (1977) provides for a 25% rebate on the cess payable if the person or local authority concerned installs a plant for treatment of sewage or trade effluent.

The customs duty on some specified pollution control equipment has been reduced to a concessional rate of 35%. Since March 1992, a rebate of over 5% has been allowed on excise duty of over 5%. In addition to the rebate on customs and excise duties levied by the Central Government, certain states too have offered concessions on Sales Tax for specified pollution control equipment.

The 1993-94 budget provided for 100% rate of depreciation for pollution control equipment.A provision is available in the Income Tax Act under which a companv can deduct up to 35% of the actual cost of some specified new assets for computation of taxable profit.

The income Tax Act allows deduction of contribution made by tax payers to any institution engaged in the conservation of natural resources while computing taxable income. It also provides for exemption of capital gains arising from transfer of building, land, machinery etc., for establishing business in a new place to reduce industrial congestion.

Conclusion

It is clear that so far India's environmental policy has relied more on regulation to protect environment. Considering the complexity of the issues involved, the performance of environmental governance in India has been incredible in spite of several drawbacks. A market oriented approach that enables application of polluter pay's principle will strengthen the policy and make it more effective and complete.

Questions

1. Discuss the salient features of India's Environmental Policy.
2. Enumerate and give a brief note on the various legal provisions in India for protecting the environment.
3. What are the outstanding features of the National Environmental Policy 2006.
4. Highlight the environmental initiatives under the Twelfth Plan.

Exercise

1. Identify some major environmental issues in your state and discuss the measures being taken to respond to them.
2. Explain judicial activism in India using case studies.

37

GLOBAL ENVIRONMENT: PROBLEMS AND POLICIES

"For the first time we have clearly realised that in the absence of any global control, man's so called peaceful constructive activity is turning into global aggression against the very foundations of life on earth."

—*Eduard Shevardnadze*

One of the prominent issues of the 1990's has been the concern for the state of global environment. On account of the growing awareness of the environmental crisis that is happening, these issues are today assigned top priority in national and international agendas. Global environmental issues include both pollution related issues such as global warming, acid rain and stratospheric ozone depletion and resource depletion problems such as deforestation and extinction of species besides other biodiversity issues. The adverse effects of these environmental problems on the global ecosystem, necessitate global cooperation to prevent the degradation of the global ecosystem from pollution, and to promote efficient use of our natural resource base so that the needs of the present generation may be met 'without compromising the ability of the future generation to meet their own'.

Global environmental problem poses two types of issues:

1. Environmental issues for which the source and impact are not confined to the same country or region. The source could be in one country and effects in another country. Such issues are generally termed as transfrontier issues. Example is Acid Rain and Hazardous wastes. Solution to this is multilateral treaties among countries emitting the pollutant and countries suffering the impact.
2. Environmental issues arising in several countries but the impact are global. Issues such as global warming, ozone depletion etc belong to this type. Global agreements among nations are required to solve these issues. Examples include Montreal Protocol and Kyoto Protocol.
3. There are certain environmental issues for which the effects are confined to the source country or region. But the impact of the issue is so complex that global solution is required. Example: Bio diversity loss.

This chapter focuses on four important global environmental issues: They are:

- Global warming/ climate change
- Ozone depletion
- Biodiversity loss
- Hazardous wastes

37.1 Global Warming

One of the major global problems is the threat of a long-run increase in the surface temperature of the earth. Global warming must be considered on an entirely different scale from that of most other environmental issues. The effects of global warming, or 'greenhouse effect' as it is popularly called, are long-term and largely irreversible. Carbon dioxide, methane, CFCs and nitrous oxides act like a greenhouse, warming the earth's surface. Hence global warming is also referred to as greenhouse effect. In a greenhouse the enclosing glass panels (which are replaced in the modern times by plastic) allows the passage of incoming sun light, but traps a portion of the reflected infrared radiation, which warms the interior of the greenhouse. The greenhouse gases like carbon dioxide, methane, CFCs and nitrous oxides play a similar role, keeping the earth warm and making it habitable. In the absence of such greenhouse gases, the earth's surface would be 30°C cooler than it is today, making human life impossible. The principle of 'greenhouse effect' explains the cold climate of Mars (where water vapour, a highly efficient greenhouse gas, is virtually absent), the hot climate of Venus (where the atmosphere is thick with carbon dioxide).

37.1.1 Greenhouse Gases

The most important greenhouse gases are CO_2, Methane, Nitrous Oxides, ChloroFluoro Carbons (CFCs) and Fluorinated gases. Nearly 76% of global greenhouse gas emissions are carbon-di-oxide (CO_2). Of the remaining 24%, methane accounts for 16% and nitrous oxide for 6 % and fluorinated gases account for 2% (IPCC, 2014). There are two main sources of greenhouse gas emissions. One is through human or anthropogenic activities and the other is natural processes. The major human sources of greenhouse gas emissions are: fossil fuel use, deforestation, livestock farming, use of synthetic fertilizers and industrial processes. Natural processes include animal and plant respiration. The table 37.1 shows the major greenhouse gases and their primary sources.

Table 37.1 Sources of Greenhouse Gases

Greenhouse gas	Source	Specific source
Carbon dioxide	Natural sources	Decomposition, ocean release, respiration and volcanoes.
	Human sources	Cement production, deforestation and the burning of fossil fuels.
Methane	Natural sources	Wetlands, termites and the oceans
	Human sources	landfills, livestock farming, production, transportation and use of fossil fuels.
Nitrous Oxides	Natural sources	Soils under natural vegetation and the oceans.
	Human sources	Agriculture, fossil fuel combustion and industrial processes.
Fluorinated gases such as hydro fluorocarbons (HFCs), perfluorocarbons (PFCs) and sulphur hexafluoride (SF6)	Human sources	HFCs are used inside of products like refrigerators, air-conditioners, foams and aerosol cans and are emitted throughout the product's life. PFCs are released during the production processes of aluminum and semiconductors. SF_6 used by electric power industry as an insulator.

Based on information from the site:
Source: http://whatsyourimpact.org/greenhouse-gas-emissions

Data on sources of greenhouse rom the IPCC (2014) 5th Assessment Reprot, reveal that electricity and heat production, agriculture and forestry and other land use sources and industry are responsible for 25%, 24% and 21% respectively of 2010 global greenhouse gas emissions. Of the remaining 30%, transportation accounts for 14%, buildings for 6% and other energy sources for 10% of 2010 global greenhouse gas emissions.

Carbon dioxide (CO_2) is the most important of the greenhouse gases. The rise in earth's temperature due to increase in carbon dioxide emission has been speculated since 1800s, and its effect have been analysed for almost a century. As early as 1896, a Swedish chemist, Svante Arrhenius, estimated that a doubling of CO_2 emissions in the earth's atmosphere would warm the earth's surface by 7° to 10°F. However, it was only in 1957, after the publication of a classic paper by Roger Revelle and Hans Suess of Scripps Institute of Oceanography, that the issue was taken for any serious discussion by the scientific community. In an article published in a European meteorology and oceanography journal in 1957, Revelle and Hans Suess demonstrated that the use of fossil fuels has resulted in an increase in the atmospheric concentration of CO_2. Since 1958, the atmospheric concentration of CO_2 has been continuously recorded at an observatory, 11000ft high on the slope of Mauna Loa in Hawaii, thanks to the foresight of C.D. Keeling of the Scripps Institute. Keeling's observations when plotted illustrated a graph showing rising CO_2 concentrations.

CO_2 is released through human activities as well as from natural processes. Nearly 42.8 percent of all naturally produced CO_2 emissions come from ocean-atmosphere exchange. Other important natural CO_2 sources include plant and animal respiration (28.56%) as well as soil respiration and decomposition (28.56%).

Nearly 87% of CO_2 emissions from human sources come from the burning of fossil fuels like coal, natural gas and oil. Other sources include deforestation (9%), and industrial processes such as cement manufacturing (4%).

The amount of CO_2 in the atmosphere is by convention expressed in terms of the carbon component. An estimate reveals that about 6 billion tonnes of carbon from burning fossil fuels is emitted into the atmosphere annually. The worst offender in terms of CO_2 emission is coal which is responsible for one-third of fossil fuels' share of world total primary energy supply and for 43% of carbon dioxide emissions from fossil fuel use.

37.1.2 Global Warming Potential of Greenhouse Gases

GWP is a reporting mechanism developed by the IPCC to standardize the impact of GHGs on climate. GWP is a measure of how much energy the emissions of one tonne of a gas will absorb over a given period of time, relative to the emissions of one tonne of CO_2. The global warming potential (GWP) of any gas depends on the timespan over which the potential is calculated and is generallyexpressed over a 100-year time horizon. GWP is expressed is interms of units of carbon dioxide equivalency and is referred to as CO_2 equivalent or as CO_2e. The GWP of other greenhouse

Table 37.2 Global Warming Potential GWP for select Greenhouse Gases

Greenhouse gas	Chemical formula	GWP for 100 year time horizon
Carbon dioxide	CO_2	1
Methane	CH_4	25
Nitrous Oxide	N_2O	298
CFC -11	CCl_3F	4750
CFC-12	CCl_2F2	10900
Hydrofluorocarbons HFC-23	CHF_3	14800
Sulphur hexafluoride	SF_6	22800

Source: Adapted from IPCC Fourth Assessment Report

gases is determined by the GWP of CO_2 which is assigned a 100-year GWP of 1. For example, a gas with a GWP of 50 has an impact on warming 50 times greater than that of CO_2 across a 100-year time span. Table 37.2 includes the direct 100 year time horizon global warming potential (GWP) relative to CO_2.

Though carbon dioxide is the most plentiful and effective greenhouse gas, the trace gases like CFCs, methane and nitrous oxides absorb radiation much more effectively than carbon dioxide. A molecule of methane is nearly 21 times as effective as carbon dioxide at trapping heat, while a molecule of nitrous oxide has 250 times the capacity of carbon dioxide to trap heat. CFCs are the most effective of all trace gases. The two most prevalent CFCs are CFC11 and CFC12. CFC-11 is a common chlorofluorocarbon that depletes the ozone, has a 100-year GWP of approximately 4,750 CO2e.

Apart from Methane and Nitrous oxides, there are three key types of high GWP gases. These are: sulfur hexafluoride (SF6), perfluorocarbons (PFCs), and hydrofluorocarbons (HFCs). All of these gases contain fluorine. Fluorinated compounds are very potent GHGs because of their long lifetime in the atmosphere and high heat absorption potential. The use of PFC and HFC usage has increased in the last decade since they are the replacement (substitutes) for ozone depleting substances (ODSs) being phased out of production under the Montreal Protocol.

PFCs, HFCs are emitted during evaporation of the solvents designed for electronics and metals cleaning. HFC is released from refrigeration, heat pumps and air conditioning equipments during operation, repair, or disposal at the end of a unit's useful life. HFCs have now replaced halons in fire extinguishers as well. These HFCs are emitted when a fire extinguisher is discharged.

SF_6 is usedas an insulator in electric transmission and distribution equipment and in the manufacture of magnesium production. HFCs, PFCs, and SF6 are used in the manufacture of semiconductors.

37.1.3 Effects of Global Warming

One important impact of accumulation of greenhouses gases in the atmosphere is the resulting climate change. Climate change is not a new phenomenon. The Earth's climate has changed throughout history. But, as pointed out by IPCC, Fourth Assessment Report's summary for policy makers, the current warming trend is of particular significance because most of it is very likely human-induced and proceeding at a rate that is unprecedented in the past 1,300 years. Climate scientists warn that the world we live in will be warmer by atleast eight degrees by 2100, if global emissions of greenhouse gases continue unabated. This small rise in temperature will have far reaching consequences, some of which are already felt. There is evidence that the period 2000 to 2009 was hotter than any other period in the past 1300 years.This warming is altering the earth's climate system, in far-reaching ways.

It is predicted that global warming will have far-reaching, long-lasting devastating consequences on planet Earth. The potential effects of climate change are dramatic. The temperature of the earth is rising at nearly twice the rate it was 50 years ago. According to the Fifth Assessment Report of the Inter-governmental Panel on Climate Change (IPCC), during the 21st century the global surface temperature is likely to rise a further 0.3 to 1.7 °C (0.5 to 3.1 °F) for their lowest emissions scenario and 2.6 to 4.8 °C (4.7 to 8.6 °F) for the highest emissions scenario.. The rate of heating is put at 0.3^{0}C per decade, which is expected to be very much faster than in the past when the rate of climatic change was just 0.05°C per decade. An increase in temperature has been registered all over the world. Researchers observe two phases of global warming. The first phase from 1919 to 1940, registered an average temperature gain of 0.35°C, and the second phase from 1970 to the present, exhibiting temperature gains of 0.55°C. Records show that the last 25 years have been the warmest period of the past 5 centuries. The result of this increase in temperature is warming of the oceans, rising of the sea levels, melting of glaciers, and diminished snow cover in the Northern Hemisphere.

Rise in sea level worldwide: Global warming is expected to bring about a rise in the sea level because of the expansion of sea water, caused by the melting of glaciers and the melting of even polar ice, with a rise in temperature. There is considerable uncertainty about how fast and how much the sea level will rise. A recent estimate puts it at "a one foot rise by 2050", the effects of which are far from negligible. The first effect would be increased flooding of many of the coastal wetlands. This coastal erosion is expected to create shoreline losses of between 10 and 100 ft depending on local conditions. Shoreline losses will aggravate storm damages. Low lying island nations like Maldives and Bahamas may disappear. Studies suggest that up to 18 per cent of Bangladesh could be under water by 2050. It is further estimated that the sea level rise will make many homeless.

The worst impact is on agriculture, horticulture and ecosystem. Global warming results in substantial decline in soil moisture due to higher temperature and reduced rainfall; besides it will also cause increased pest and weed growth due to higher CO_2 concentration in areas that are world's bread baskets. Altered rainfall is the most unpredictable and deleterious effect of greenhouse related climate change on agriculture. Since with higher global temperature more water will be evaporated from the oceans, average rainfall worldwide is bound to increase. But the rainfall pattern will be disrupted, varying widely among regions and between times. It is reported that in the northern hemisphere for example, polar regions will warm faster than equatorial zones and in the continents the centers will become drier than peripheries. This varying climate change will drastically affect agriculture because of the inability of crops to withstand changes in temperature. It is observed that global warming results in desertification as a result of which severe drought and famines are bound to happen. As a result of these climatic changes, the developing countries will be worst hit. Areas that are already arid like Tunisia, Algeria, Ethiopia and Somalia will dry out further. In agriculture too much water or water delivered at the wrong time is more difficult to cope up with than too little water. However agriculture could be adapted to these climate changes through crop development and technology, which of course needs more time. Global warming has strong impact on ecosystem, leading to a decline in biodiversity and provision of ecosystem service. More rapid the climatic change is, more severe will be the pressure towards extinction and more serious will be the assault on ecosystem. According to research published in *Nature*, by 2050 rising temperatures could result in the extinction of at least a million species. WWF report of coral reefs observes that coral populations are likely to collapse by 2100 due to increased temperatures and ocean acidification. In addition species in the oceans which rely on coral reefs for their survival are also at risk.

Threats to health may also accompany global warming in the form of an increase in disease carrying vectors, such as mosquitos that carry diseases like malaria, dengue fever, encephalitis and yellow fever, particularly in the temperate regions. Already in the United States, a tropical mosquito specie associated with dengue fever has been found.

37.1.4 Contribution to Global Warming

According to the World Resource Institute CAIT Climate Data Explorer, the top 10 emitters contribute 72.78 percent of global greenhouse gas emissions (excluding land use change and forestry). On the other hand, the lowest 100 emitters contribute less than 3 percent.

Six of the top 10 emitters are developing countries.The share of the energy sector is more than 75 percent of global greenhouse gas emissions. Industrial emissions in China contribute to more than

TABLE 37 .3 Top Ten Countries with the Highest Greenhouse Gas Emissions, 2012

Country	Contribution to Global Greenhouse gas emission (in percentage%)
China	25.36
United States	14.4
European Union	10.16
India	6.96
Russia	5.36
Japan	3.11
Brazil	2.34
Indonesia	1.76
Mexico	1.67
Iran	1.65
Others	27.22

Source: http://www.ecowatch.com/top-10-greenhouse-gas-emitters-find-out-which-countries-are-most-respo-1882054580.html

3 percent of global emissions and new data from the UN Food and Agriculture Organisation indicate that agriculture contributes a notable share of Brazil's and Australia's emissions.

Per capita emissions are distributed unequally. Emissions per person vary among the top 10 emitters - the per capita emissions of the U.S. is eight times those of India. Canada, the United States, and Russia emit more than double the global average per person. India's per capita emissions are only one-third of the global average.

Responses to Greenhouse Effect

The consequences of global warming and data on country/region wise contribution to global warming clearly indicate two things (1) that both developed and developing nations have good reason to worry about global warming. (2) that global cooperation is an important consideration when addressing global warming issues. In line with this the responses to the global warming issue can be analysed as **technical** response and policy response.

Technical response attempts at reducing at emission of greenhouse gases and at increasing the carbon dioxide absorbing **capacity** of the earth.

Reduction in the Emission of Greenhouse Gases Calls for

1. Increased energy efficiency in consumption and production.
2. Switch over to low or no carbon fuels.
3. Using substitutes of CFCs in refrigerants, airconditioners, etc.
4. Promote complete combustion in vehicles used for transport through proper maintenance and increase fuel efficiency in vehicles.
5. Reduce methane production from livestock and rice fields.
6. Switch over to non-fossil fuel sources of energy such as solar, nuclear, hydro, etc.
7. Increase afforestation & decrease deforestation since, forests absorb CO_2.

Economists have suggested two policy tools for reducing CO_2 emissions that may be globally effective. They are:

a. A transferable discharge permit (TDP) and
b. Carbon tax

TDP requires that countries would be allocated CO_2 emission permits equal to their permitted base level emissions, that is determined by any of the following four criteria:

- Equi proportionate reduction in emission.
- Ability to pay criteria.
- Polluter pay principle.
- Equal per capita consumption.

Initially developing countries should be allocated more permits and therefore developed nations would transfer income to developing countries in buying the extra permits from them. Thus TDP are considered to be efficient and equitable.

The other policy option is carbon tax, a tool expected to provide an incentive to reduce fuel consumption and to shift to lower carbon forms of energy. Such a tax would be levied on the carbon content of the fuels consumed. A single tax to all sources in all countries to reduce CO_2 emission globally has been suggested to achieve cost effectiveness among countries and within each country among the different sources. Prof. Nordhaus has calculated that to reduce CO_2 emission by 20 per cent worldwide would require a tax of about \$45 per tonne of carbon, while a reduction of 50 per cent of CO_2 will require a tax of \$ 140 per tonne of carbon. Thus progressively large taxes would be required for deeper CO_2 reduction, which may be burdensome for developing countries. Besides equity consideration, monitoring of emission and enforcement of such a carbon tax are complicated.

Besides these technological and policy options, a worldwide cooperation is required to reduce emissions of the greenhouse gases and to prevent further warming of the globe. The formation of the Intergovernmental Panel on Climate Change (IPCC) in 1988 is an attempt at achieving this global cooperation. The second climate conference of 1990 concluded that nations should take steps to reduce greenhouse gases at source. The Kyoko protocol is yet another milestone to reduce global warming.

37.1.5 The Kyoto Protocol

The Kyoto Protocol which emerged from the UN Framework Convention on Climate Change (UNFCCC), is one of the three conventions adopted at the Rio Earth Summit in 1992. The other two are the UN Convention on Biological Diversity and the Convention to Combat Desertification.

The United Nations Framework Convention on Climate Change (UNFCCC) is an international environmental Treaty negotiated at the Earth Summit in Rio de Janerio in 1992. It entered into force on 21 March 1994. The framework pledges to stabilize greenhouse-gas concentrations "at a level that would prevent dangerous anthropogenic interference with the climate system". The ultimate objective of UNFCCC is to prevent "dangerous" human interference with the climate system and stabilize greenhouse gas concentrations "at a level that would prevent the interference of human beings with the climate system." It states that "such a level should be achieved within a time-frame sufficient to allow ecosystems to adapt naturally to climate change, to ensure that food production is not threatened, and to enable economic development to proceed in a sustainable manner." The countries that have ratified the Convention are called as Parties to the Convention. There are now 197 parties to the convention. Parties to UNFCCC are classified as:

- Annex I countries – industrialized countries and economies in transition
- Annex II countries – developed countries which pay for costs of developing countries
- Non Annex I countries - Developing countries.

The parties to the convention meet annually in Conference of the Partiers (COP) to assess progress in dealing with climate change and to discuss how to achieve the treaty's aims. The first COP was held in Berlin, Germany in 1995. The twenty-second session of the Conference of the Parties (COP 22) was held in Marrakech, Morocco in North Africa. COP 23 was held on 6–17 November 2017 in Bonn, Germany.

The third COP was held in Kyoto, Japan in 1997 where the member countries prepared the Kyoto Protocol. **The Kyoto Protocol** was adopted in Kyoto, Japan, on 11 December 1997 and entered into force on 16 February 2005. The Kyoto Protocol set emissions targets for developed countries which are binding under international law. The detailed rules for the implementation of the Protocol were adopted at COP 7 in Marrakesh, Morocco, in 2001, and are referred to as the "Marrakesh Accord." There are two commitment periods to the Kyoto Protocol, the first of which lasted from 2008-2012. The second one runs from 2013-2020.

The Kyoto Protocol committed the industrialized nations to specify, legally binding reductions in emissions of six greenhouse gases. The 6 major greenhouse gases covered by the protocol are carbon dioxide (CO_2), methane (CH_4), nitrous oxide (N_2O), hydrofluorocarbons (HFCs), perfluorocarbons (PFCs), and sulfur hexafluoride (SF6).The Kyoto Protocol states that developed countries (Annex I countries) are committed, individually or jointly, to reducing their overall emissions of greenhouse gases by at least 5% below 1990 levels by 2012. Towards fulfilling this requirement, the Kyoto Protocol provided three flexible mechanisms. These are:

a. Clean development mechanism
b. Joint implementation
c. Emissions trading

Clean Development Mechanism (CDM):

CDM provides for Annex I countries to invest in emission reduction projects in non-Annex I countries which do not have an emission reduction target, in return for Certified Emission Reductions (CERs). These projects should reduce the emission of greenhouse gases and contribute to the sustainable development of the host country involved. The achieved emission reductions can be purchased by the Annex I country in order to meet its reduction target. An example would be an investment in clean energy production plant to replace a proposed coal-fired plant.

In order to be accepted as CDM-projects, the projects have to be accepted by both the parties in advance. It also has to be proven that the projects will lead to emissions reductions that are higher than what otherwise would have been obtained. In otherwords an investor from a developed country, can invest in, or provide finance for a project in a developing country that results in emission reductions which is greater than levels that can be achieved without the CDM project. The investor then gets credits - carbon credits - for the reductions and can use those credits to meet their Kyoto target. Projects included for emission reduction under CDM include:

- End-use energy efficiency improvement
- Supply side energy efficiency improvement
- Renewable energy
- Fuel switching
- Agriculture - facilitating reductions of NO_x and CH_4
- Industrial processes
- sink projects like afforestation

Joint Implementation (JI): JI provides for any Annex I country to invest in an emission reduction project in any other Annex I country in order to reduce emissions domestically. By investing in projects that reduce greenhouse gas emissions in an Annex I country where reducing emissions may be cheaper is hence an efficient method of complying with the Kyoto Protocol. These countries which are bound by the Protocol are eligible to transfer and/or acquire emission reduction units (ERUs) and use them to meet part of their emission reduction target. JI is an innovative approach that encourages transfer of technologies.

JIs are similar to CDM with the main difference that the projects will take place in Annexure I countries (developed nations). The sponsoring governments will receive credits that may be applied to their emissions targets; the recipient nations will gain foreign investment and advanced technology.

Emission credits ("Emission Reduction Units", ERUs) can only accrue from 2008.

International Emission Trading

The Kyoto Protocol sets limits on total emissions by the world's major economies which is expressed in terms of a prescribed number of "emission units". It allows countries that have surplus emission units -emissions permitted to them but not "used" - to sell this surplus emission units to countries that need more. This creates a market where, a new commodity, created in the form of emission reductions or removals, is traded. Since carbon dioxide is the principal greenhouse gas, Carbon is popularly traded like any other commodity. This is known as the "carbon market. Countries which are not able to meet their commitments will be able to "buy" emission units from those willing to sell. With increase in demand for emission units, its price increases and the buyers of the emission units will use energy more efficiently and engage in research and promote the development of alternative sources of energy that have low or no emissions.

UNFCCC clearly stated that the units which may be transferred under the scheme, each equal to one tonne of CO_2, may be in the form of:

- A removal unit **(RMU)** on the basis of landuse, landuse change and forestry (LULUCF) activities such as reforestation
- An emission reduction unit **(ERU)** generated by joint implementation project
- A certified emission reduction **(CER)** generated from a clean development mechanism project activity.

The operation of the emission market is complex since emissions have to be constantly monitored and checked with reported emission levels. Hence the 2001 Marrakesh Accords specified rules of operation for the emission market.

The European Union's Emission Trading System (ETS) is the world's biggest scheme for trading greenhouse gas emissions allowances. It was launched in 2005 and covers some 11,000 power stations and industrial plants in 31 countries. Carbon emissions of these 30 countries make up almost 50% of Europe's total. ETS set a cap on half of Europe's carbon emissions, which were previously unregulated. It operates through a mandatory carbon dioxide (CO_2) cap-and-trade system, in which sources are allocated a certain number of emission allowances based on historic performance and other parameters. The European ETS is now in its third phase, running from 2013 to 2020. The program covers about 45% of the EU's GHG emissions. ICAPC (International Carbon Action Patnership) (2016) Status Report provides data on emission trading.

Evidence across the world indicates that carbon trade is growing – nationally and internationally. By December 2013, 17 countries had either running or planned carbon pricing mechanisms. These cover greenhouse gas emissions of 10 GtCO2e/y, equal to 21% of the 50 GtCO2e emitted globally. China is expected to become the world's epicenter of carbon trading. China developed atleast seven pilot emission trading schemes in order to cut its carbon intensity by 40-45% by 2020 from 2005 levels. In 2015, all seven of China's pilot schemes completed their annual compliance cycles and as of 31st December 2015, the accumulated secondary market trading value of the pilot schemes had reached CNY 1.41 billion (EUR 198 million). It is reported that by 2020 China's carbon trading could be worth US$ 3.5 trillion. China intents to launch a unified national carbon market by 2017.

India too has initiated positive response in abating climate change. India has committed to reduce emissions intensity by 20-25% of 2005 by 2020. India has decided to develop pilot projects of emission trading schemes in three states - Tamil Nadu, Maharashtra and Gujarat covering 1000 industries.

The Paris Agreement which came into force in November 2016 provided new impetus for a dynamic global carbon market and for the proliferation of domestic carbon pricing systems post 2020. The International Carbon Action Partnership (ICAP) Status Report 2016 makes the following observations on Global Emission Trading:

- With 17 systems now in operation around the world, ETSs are currently pricing more than four billion tons of GHG emissions. In 2017, two new systems are to be launched in China and Ontario.
- More than a decade after its launch, the EU ETS is preparing for its fourth phase. A link with the Swiss ETS has been negotiated.
- Countries like Ukraine are also taking steps towards cap-and trade
- Turkey made its first year of mandatory emission reporting.
- Asia is rapidly establishing itself as a new ETS hub, with the newest system launched in the Republic of Korea in 2015.

Currently, there are six exchanges trading in UNFCCC related carbon credits like the Chicago Climate Exchange, European Climate Exchange, and the NASDAQ.

In October 2016, 197 countries agreed under the Montreal Protocol in Kigali, Rwanda to phase down HFCs which are thousands of times more dangerous than carbon dioxide in causing global warming (discussed in Section 37.2.3)

37.2 Ozone Depletion

Yet another global 'green issue' is the steady depletion of the ozone layer. Ozone, chemically is 'an irritating pale blue gas with a chlorine like odour'. At sea level ozone is a pollutant which is produced when emissions of hydrocarbon and nitrogen oxide interact in the presence of sunlight forming smog and causes respiratory problems. Ozone depletion is about the thinning of the ozone layer in the stratosphere.

37.2.1 Depletion of Ozone – Causes

Most of the ozone in the earth's atmosphere is in the stratosphere, a zone extending from about 15 km to about 30 km above earth. The ozone layer is a belt of the naturally occurring gas "ozone." This stratospheric ozone is critical in maintaining the earth's radiation balance. Stratospheric ozone acts as a filter blocking a large percentage of incoming harmful ultraviolet radiation emitted from the sun. It protects all terrestrial life.

Increasing concentrations of the synthetic chemicals known as Chloroflurocarbons (CFCs) and halons are breaking down the ozone layer, allowing more of the solar U-V rays to penetrate to the earth's surface. CFCs are compounds that consist of chlorine, fluorine and Carbon. CFCs are used as coolants for refrigeration and air-conditioners, propellants for aerosol sprays, agents for producing plastic foam and cleaners for electrical parts.

CFCs are stable in the troposphere. In the stratosphere they are broken down by U-V radiation from the sun, into substances that include chlorine. The chlorine reacts with the oxygen atoms in ozone and rips apart the ozone molecule. Chlorine and hallons catalytically destroy ozone.

It is estimated that each 1 per cent drop in stratospheric ozone will produce a 2 to 3 per cent increasing in U-V radiation on the earth and U-V radiation is expected to increase by 3 to 4 per cent at the tropics and 10-12 per cent at the higher altitudes.

Figure 37.1 Depletion of Ozone

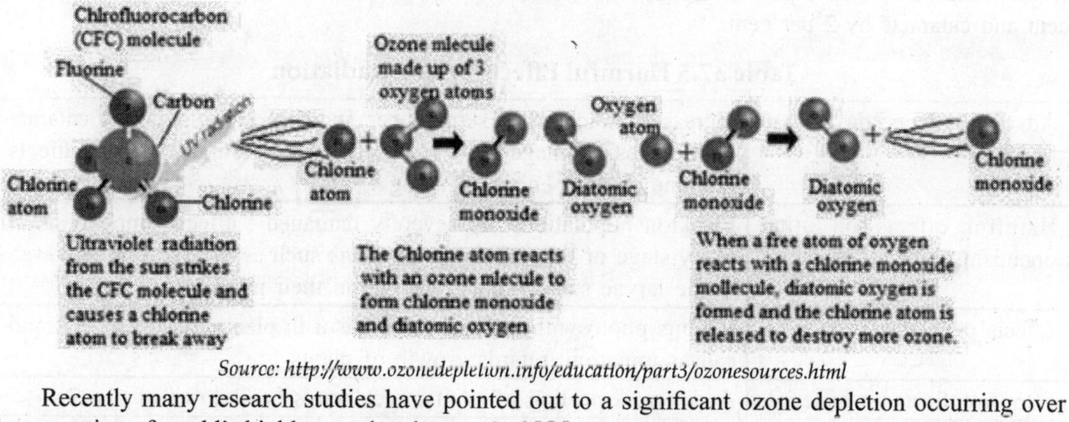

Chlrofluorocarbon (CFC) molecule
Fluorine
Carbon
UV radiation
Chlorine atom
Chlorine
Ultraviolet radiation from the sun strikes the CFC molecule and causes a chlorine atom to break away
Ozone mlecule made up of 3 oxygen atoms
Chlorine atom
Chlorine monoxide
Diatomic oxygen
The Chlorine atom reacts with an ozone mlecule to form chlorine monoxide and diatomic oxygen
Oxygen atom
Chlorine monoxide
Diatomic oxygen
Chlorine monoxide
When a free atom of oxygen reacts with a chlorine monoxide mollecule, diatomic oxygen is formed and the chlorine atom is released to destroy more ozone.

Source: http://www.ozonedepletion.info/education/part3/ozonesources.html

Recently many research studies have pointed out to a significant ozone depletion occurring over large portion of world's highly populated areas. In 1985 an ozone hole was observed over Halley Bay in Antartica, caused by chlorine from CFCs. It is now said that some 10.0(H) to 100,000 ozone molecules are destroyed for each chlorine atom that is released into the stratosphere by the gradually ascending CFC molecules.Table 37.4 gives vital information on the most common ozone depleting chemicals.

TABLE 37.4 The Most Common Ozone Depleting Chemicals

Name of the ODS	Chemical formula	Life time	Source gas	Used in
Chlorofluro carbon - CFC11	CCl_3F	45 years	Long-lived ODS, chlorine source gas	Refrigeration,Aerosol, foam, food freezing, warming devises, cosmetics, fire fighting.
Chlorofluro carbon - CFC 12	CCl_2F_2	100 years	Long-lived ODS, chlorine source gas	
Chlorofluro carbon – CFC 113	CCl_2FCClF_2	85 years	Long-lived ODS, chlorine source gas	
Halon 1301	$CBrF_3$	65 years	Long-lived ODS; bromine source gas	Fire fighting
HCFC -22	$CHClF_2$	11.9 years	CFC replacement – Chlorine source gas	Refrigeration, aerosol, foam, fire fighting
Methyl Chloroform	CH_3CCl_3	5 years	Long-lived ODS, chlorine source gas	Solvent
Carbon Tetrachloride	CCl_4	35 years	Long-lived ODS, chlorine source gas	Solvent

Source: SPARC Report on the Lifetimes of Stratospheric Ozone-Depleting Substances, their Replacements, and Related Species, M. Ko, P. Newman, S. Reimann, S. Strahan (Eds.),
SPARC Report No. 6, WCRP-15/2013. Available at http://www.sparc-climate.org/publications/sparc-reports/sparc-report-no6/
Global Environmental Issues Module 4 available at http://download.nos.org/333courseE/14.pdf

37.2.2 Effects of Ozone Depletion

Depletion of stratospheric ozone exposes the population, flora and fauna to UV radiation. In humans, exposure to UV causes skin cancer, eye damage and damage to human immune system. U-V rays can disintegrate important biological molecules, including DNA. Increased exposure to U-V rays will result in greater incidence of cancer, cataracts and immune deficiencies, to acceleration of the aging process of the skin. It is said that, for every 1 per cent increase in U-V radiation, base cell cancer would increase by 1 to 2 per cent, while melanoma (skin cancer) would increase by less than 1 per cent and cataracts by 2 per cent.

Table 37.5 Harmful Effects of U V Radiation

Adverse effects on human health	Increased incidence of skin cancer; increase in incidence of cataract of the eyes; Damage to DNA; Cornea and Retinal damage: affects immune system; enhances aging
Harmful effects on other organisms	Plankton populations are severely damaged ; affects amphibians at every stage of life; affects amphibians such as fish, shrimp and crab in the larvae stage –causes decline in their numbers.
Effects on plants	Inhibits photosynthesis and metabolism in plants; destroys cells and causes mutation; retards growth of plants
Harmful effects on materials	Accelerates peeling of paints; accelerates breakdown of plastics.

UV rays results in decreased crop yields and reduced population of certain fish larve, phytoplankton and zooplankton that are vital to the food chain. The impact of phytoplankton and zoo planktons, in turn, affects the food chain and oceanic carbon cycle. UV radiations can alter the time of flowering in plant species besides affecting the plant growth.

UV rays affect the whole ocean ecosystem. It affects the amphibians in every stage of their life cycle. By hampering the growth and development in the larvae stage, UV rays results in decreasing the number of the amphibian specie. It is also held responsible for the deformities and decreases immunities in some species and to even retinal damage and blindness in some species.

37.2.3 Policy Response to Ozone Depletion

In response to the intensified public concern about stratospheric ozone depletion caused by CFCs, the use of CFCs as aerosol propellants was banned in 1978, by the US, Canada and a few European nations. However the other uses of CFCs continued to grow. In the 1980s, the continued scientific evidence of ozone depletion led to international action. In 1987, 24 nations, representing the majority of the CFC producing countries signed the *Montreal Protocol,* on substances that deplete the ozone layer. The high CFC using signatories of the protocol agreed to phase down use of CFCS and Halons to 50 per cent of 1986 levels by 1998, while low CFC using countries were given a grace period of 10 years. Starting in 1999, these countries had to reduce CFC use to 1995-1997 levels.

The Montreal protocol provided for periodic assessments and rapid revision if scientific research indicated the need for revision; but this was partly because, some high CFC producing countries had not signed the original agreement. Hence in 1990, the agreement was revised to regulate 10 additional substances including carbon tetrachloride. Besides, the Montreal protocol countries agreed to phase out the production of CFCs completely by the year 2000. The 1990 Agreement provided for the following:

1. Regulation of 10 additional substances, including carbon tetrachloride.
2. High-using countries with consumption of CFC greater than 3 kg per person, to bring about,
   a. 20 per cent reduction in production and consumption from 1986 levels by 1993.
   b. 50 per cent reduction in production and consumption from 1986 levels by 1997.
   c. 100 per cent reduction in production and consumption from 1986 levels by 2000.
3. Halons to be phased out by 2000, except for certain “essential uses”.
4. Methane to be phased out by 2005.
5. 20 Years grace period to Low CFC using countries on phase out schedules.
6. Multi-lateral fund to aid developing countries with phase out problem and to foster technology transfer.
7. No imports or exports of controlled substances with non-parties after 1990.

In subsequent years, more countries signed the agreement. By 1992, 110 countries including India and China had become party to the protocol. The basic problem in phasing out CFCs is looking for substitutes, with shorter life time and lower ozone depleting potentials than CFC 11, 12 and 13. Some of these substitutes developed are variety of hydro chloro fluorocarbons (HCFCs) and hydro fluorocarbons (HFCs). Some of these substitutes replace the original chemical with ease while others require the installation of new capital equipment. Hence the cost of developing substitutes and costs of change over to the new chemicals is a serious obstacle to the objective of protecting stratospheric ozone.

To meet the phase out schedules spelt in the Montreal Protocol, each country will have to adopt some explicit control policy on production, imports and exports of ozone depleting substances. The US for example, introduced transferable production quotas among the five domestic CFC producers. Each of these firms is required to reduce its CFC production in stages to meet the objective of the protocol.

The Montreal Protocol suggests the use of trading of emission reduction among countries for switching out of substances covered by the agreement. Thus, the country, which is unable to fulfill the requirement of the agreement, is to offset the excess emissions by getting comparable reduction in other countries.

Since its initial adoption, the Montreal Protocol has been amended several times to enable, the control of new chemicals and the creation of a financial mechanism to enable developing countries to comply. Specifically, four Amendments to the Protocol were adopted in the Second, Fourth, Ninth and Eleventh Meetings of the Parties to the Montreal Protocol adopted. These are the London Amendment (1990), the Copenhagen Amendment (1992), the Montreal Amendment (1997) and the Beijing Amendment (1999). The London, Copenhagen, Montreal and Beijing Amendments entered into force in 1992, 1994, 1999 and 2002 respectively, only for those Parties which ratified the particular amendments. In October 2016, 197 countries adopted an amendment to phase down HFCs under the Montreal Protocol in Kigali, Rwanda. The amendment is for phasing out HFCs which are thousands of times more dangerous than carbon dioxide in causing global warming.

The Kigali Amendment (2016) to phase down HFCs was the result of years of negotiation by Parties to the Montreal Protocol. Under the Amendment, countries committed to cut the production and consumption of HFCs by more than 80 percent over the next 30 years.The amendment provided for developed countries to reduce HFC consumption beginning in 2019 and most developing countries to freeze consumption in 2024. Few developing countries with unique circumstances were to freeze consumption in 2028.

The amendment to the legally-binding Montreal Protocol ensures that:

- the rich and industrialised countries bring down their HFC production and consumption by at least 85 per cent compared to their annual average values in the period 2011-2013.
- Select developing countries which include China, Brazil and South Africa will reduce their HFC use by 85 per cent of their average value in 2020-22 by the year 2045.
- India and some other developing countries — Iran, Iraq, Pakistan, and some oil economies like Saudi Arabia and Kuwait — will cut down their HFCs by 85 per cent of their values in 2024-26 by the year 2047.

It is estimated that the complete elimination of HFCs by the year 2050 will prevent about 0.5 degree Celsius rise in global temperatures by the end of this century. For this reason, the Kigali Amendment, is considered absolutely vital.

According to a report in Indian Express by Amitabh Sinha (October 15, 2016), "the phase-out scheduled under the amendment is estimated to avert 70 billion tonnes of carbon dioxide equivalent emissions between 2020 and 2050. This is considered equivalent to shutting down more than 750 coal power plants, each of 500 MW capacities, or taking off about 500 million cars off the road from now to 2050".

The Montreal Protocol is a successful international environmental policy. The NASA scientist Pawan Batra observes "The Antartic hole is stabilizing and may be slowly recovering. Our focus now is to make sure that it is healing as expected." Many research studies observe that the quantity of Ozone Depleting Substances (ODS) in the atmosphere has not been increasing in the recent years and remark that they may indeed be decreasing. A 2009 research study observed that without the Montreal Protocol global ozone depletion would be at least 10 times worse than current levels by 2050.

37.3 Biodiversity Loss

Biodiversity is a natural wealth essential for survival. It is the term given to the variety of life on Earth. It is the sum of all life on Earth. The term bio diversity encompasses different ecosystems, species, genes, and their relative abundance. Peter H. Rogan defines biodiversity as "the sum total of all the plants, animals, fungi and microorganisms in the world, or in a particular area; all of their individual variation; and all of the interactions between them. It is the set of living organisms that make up the fabric of the planet …"

37.3.1 Classification and Important Concepts related to Biodiversity

Biodiversity may be classified as:

Genetic diversity defined as the variations within and among species in the form of the genetic makeup. It is the variation of the set of genes carried by different organisms. According to an estimate there are some 109 different genes present in the world's biota.

Species diversity is the variation and variability of species in a particular area or volume at a particular time. It refers to total number of different biological species. It is a composition of species richness and species evenness. Species richness is the total number of species while species evenness is an indication of their abundance. World-wide, just 1,75 million of the estimated 13 to 14 million species have so far been described.

Ecosystem diversity includes the many differences among ecosystem types, including diversity of habitats and ecological processes.

Extinction is a process that happens when an entire species permanently disappears from the biosphere due to the death of the species' last member. Humans have increased the extinction rate by a factor of 1,000. More than 1100 species are known to have gone extinct in the past 400 years.

Endangered: Species whose habitats have been so drastically reduced that they are deemed to be in immediate danger of extinction. Examples: Bengal Tiger, Asian Elephant

Vulnerable: Species likely to move into the endangered category in the near future if the casual factors continue operating. Examples: African elephant, polar bear

Biodiversity hotspots: A biodiversity hotspot is an area of rich biodiversity that faces serious threats to its existence due to habitat loss, climate change, or extensive species loss. Around 25 sites worldwide are recognized as such hotspots. In order for a region to be included in this category, it must be biologically diverse, with a high proportion of species that are not found anywhere else on Earth, and the security of the region must be threatened. Losing more than 70% of native vegetation, for example, is a clear example of a threat. Examples include the Atlantic Forest in South America, and the countries of New Zealand and Japan, Caribbean Islands, Guinean forests of West Africa, Indo Burma, Madagascar and Indian Ocean Islands

Concepts related to Conservation of Biodiversity

There are two types of biodiversity conservation approaches – **In-situ conservation and Ex-situ conservation.** In the in-situ conservation approach, plants and animals are conserved in their native ecosystems or even man made ecosystems where they naturally occur. Examples include National Parks, Sanctuaries, Biosphere reserves, etc. Ex-situ conservation is conservation outside habitats by perpetuating sample populations. It is conservation in an artificially created environment. Example include Zoos, botanical gardens, seed banks, Aquarium etc

37.3.2 Benefits of biodiversity

Biodiversity provides several direct and indirect benefits to the homosapiens. The direct benefits include the supply of a variety of products like food, medicinal plants, firewood, timber and raw materials by plants and trees. Some plant extracts are used in the manufacture of glue, soaps, cosmetics, dyes, lubricants and polishes. The plants also provide an important source of renewable energy. Some plant extracts are used in the manufacture of glue, soaps, cosmetics, dyes, lubricants and polishes. The plants also provide an important source of renewable energy

Indirect benefits include ecosystem functions related to flood control, soil fertility, pollution control, pollination, reducing pollution etc. Biodiversity is involved in water purification, recycling nutrients and providing fertile soils. Most indirect use values are non-consumptive use values referring to ecological services provided by biodiversity that are not consumed in the typical sense; ecological services such as nitrogen fixation by bacteria is an example of non-consumptive use value. Environmental functions support economic activity by recycling important elements like carbon, oxygen and nitrogen and by acting as buffer against excessive variations in weather, climate and other natural events outside the control of human beings. As natural habitat declines, the ecological processes slow down.

a. Ecosystem services

The stability of ecosystems is also related to biodiversity, with higher biodiversity producing greater stability over time. Rich and vast biodiversity reduces the chance that ecosystem services will be disrupted as a result of disturbances such as extreme weather events or human exploitation.

Ecosystem Services are the processes by which the environment performs the source function and the sink function. The source function of the environment refers to the production of resources such as clean water, timber, and habitat for fisheries, and the sink function of the environment refers to assimilation of wastes. The United Nations 2005 Millennium Eco System Assessment (MEA), grouped the ecosystem services into four broad categories:

- *provisioning*, such as the production of food and water;
- *regulating*, such as the control of climate and disease;
- *supporting*, such as nutrient cycles and crop pollination;
- *cultural*, such as spiritual and recreational benefits.

Provisioning Services: These are the products obtained from ecosystems, and include food and fiber, fuel, genetic resources, bio chemicals, natural medicines, and pharmaceuticals, energy, ornamental resources and fresh water..

Regulating Services: These include the regulation of ecosystem processes and include the following: carbon sequestration and climate regulation, waste decomposition and detoxification, purification of air and water, pest and disease control, erosion control, biological control, pollination and storm protection.

Cultural Services are the non-material benefits people obtain from ecosystems through spiritual enrichment, cognitive development, recreation, aesthetic experiences and scientific discovery.

Supporting Services / Habitat services Supporting services such as nutrient cycles and pollination are necessary for the production of all other ecosystem services.

b. Supply of food

Biodiversity is essential for supply of food to both humanbeings and non human creatures. At global level, there are around 250,000 species of flowering plants. Of these around 3000 are food sources. It is reported that 75% of the world's food comes from just a dozen crops & five animal species. Nearly 70% chocolate's vital ingredient is grown from a single species in Ghana and ivory coast.

c. Supply of Medicines: Genetic resources, taken from the wild, sustain modern societies, providing medicines, food and raw materials for industries. A significant proportion of drugs are derived, directly or indirectly, from biological sources. Nearly 80% of the world population depends on medicines from nature (used in either modern or traditional medical practice) for primary healthcare. Worldwide, medicines from wild products are worth atleast $40 billion a year. Foxglove can save the lives of millions of sufferers from heart disease, by providing digitoxin and digitalis. The snake root plant from Indian forests relieves high blood pressure and hypertension. Bee venom is used to treat arthritis. Codeine and morphine are yielded by poppies. Quinine to fight malaria comes from an Amazonian tree. In all, 1400 tropical forest plants and 500 marine organism yield chemicals that control and cure cancer—but at the present rate of harvest, many may be driven to extinction before their potential can be assessed or tapped.

Indian medicine system relies on medicinal plants. An estimate observes that of the top 150 drugs prescribed in the US, 74% are from plants, 18% from fungi, 5% from bacteria & 3% from 5 snakes species (ESO 2000)

d. Supply of Industrial Materials: Biodiversity's vast ecosystems provide material for construction and fuel industry. Supply of wood and non-wood forest products is the primary commercial function of nearly one third of the world's forests. Oflate forests are useful for the production of bio fuels.

e. Leisure, Cultural and aesthetic values: Leisure activities such as hiking, bird watching or natural history study, are possible only due to the presence of forests and parts. These are known as non-consumptive use values. Biodiversity has inspired musicians, painters, sculptors, writers and other artists. Many cultural groups view themselves as an integral part of the natural world and show respect for other living organisms. Popular activities such as gardening, caring for aquariums and collecting butterflies are all strongly dependent on biodiversity. A visit to a botanical garden or zoo is as much an aesthetic or cultural experience as it is an educational one.

37.3.3 State of Biodiversity

The United Nations' 1995 Global Biodiversity Assessment estimated the total number of species at 14 million of which nearly 1.7 million species have so far been identified and scientifically described, but this represents only a fraction of life on Earth.

The identification of an exact estimation of species is not possible. So far only 1 per cent of the world's specie has been studied for their potential value to humanity in medicines, food or industry.

Table 37.6 Number of described Species on Earth

Specie	Number
Bacteria	4000
Proctoctists (algae, protozoa)	80,000
Animals - vertebrates	52000
Animals - invertibrates	1,272,000
Fungi	72000
Palnts	270,000
Total	1,750,000
Possible total of all species (including unknown species)	14,000,000

Source: UNEP/ WCMC, (2000)
Global Biodiversity: Earlt's Living Resources in the 21st century, World Conservation Press

The loss of valuable specie of flora and fauna is often referred to as 'bio diversity loss ' or 'genetic loss'. By the turn of the century, a million kinds of animals, plants and insects are expected to be driven to extinction; by the year 2050, half of all the species alive today could be lost for ever. Pollution, overhunting, over fishing, and the trade in wild life are partly responsible for this phenomenon, but, by far, the greatest cause of extinction is the destruction of the wild habitats for farming, fuel, industry and a host of other uses.

The Millennium Ecosystem Assessment Report (2005) concludes that the irreversible changes caused by the society are degrading the ecological processes that support life on Earth. According to the report, the changes in important components of biological diversity were more rapid in the past 50 years than at any time in human history.

The *Living Planet Report 2008*, published by the WWF report, tracks population trends for more than 1,600 freshwater, marine and terrestrial species. According to the report:

- An estimated 58 per cent of the world's coral reefs are at risk from human activities.
- Just one-fifth of the world's original forest cover remains in large tracts of relatively undisturbed forest.
- Between 1970 and 2005, populations of terrestrial species dropped by 33 per cent. Populations of marine species dropped by 14 per cent, and freshwater species by 35 per cent.

37.3.4 Causes for Bio diversity Loss

There are six specific types of human actions that threaten species and ecosystems

- Over hunting
- Habitat loss/degradation/fragmentation
- Invasion of non-native species
- Pollution
- Climate Change

Over hunting has resulted in the extinction of hundreds of species and the endangerment of many more. Over-harvesting for food, fashion, and profit have caused extinction of species. Species are now becoming extinct at 25,000 times the natural rate. Poaching and hunting for food is a major factor. The different species are so interlinked and interdependent in maintaining the ecological balance that the loss of one plant can cause the loss of as many as 30 kinds of animals and insects which **depend upon** it. Even the loss of a single species is a tragedy because each form of life is a store house of irreplaceable substances. Principal threat is from commercial hunting, both legal and illegal (poaching). Snowy egret, passenger pigeon, heath hen are few examples. Rhino species are on the verge of becoming extinct since they are hunted for their horns which fetch a price of $ 40,000 to $100,000 per horn. Trade of pet animals and decorative exotic plants is an important reason for illegal commercial hunting. Trade for these activities is estimated to be worth at least $5 billion.

Habitat loss/degradation/fragmentation: Human interference is the predominant cause of habitat loss/ degradation and mass extinctions of species. Over-harvesting by (illegal) hunting and the systematic cutting of wood for heating purposes, or charcoal production are other reasons for biodiversity loss. Habitat damage, especially the conversion of forested land to agriculture is an important factor causing biodiversity loss. Development policies are responsible for most of the deforestation occurring worldwide. Loss of tropical forest is causing most concern because they contain atleast 50%, of world's biodiversity. Nearly 50% of tropical forest is already lost due to population pressure, commercial activities and development policies. It is estimated that tropical forests will be reduced to 10-25% of their original extent by late 21st Century.

Table 37.7 shows the significant impact of human activity on world ecosystems. The table classifies existing habitats as undisturbed, partially disturbed and human dominated.

Fragmentation: Biodiversity loss is further accentuated by fragmentation. Fragmentation refers to breaking down of habitat into pieces or fragments for either a dam or road construction. Fragmentation decreases habitat simply through loss of land area. This reduces the probability of maintaining effective reproductive units of plant and animal populations.The maintenance of adequate pollinator population levels is essential for forest health. Due to fragmentation of forest area, many species of trees become isolated since their pollinators cannot cross the unforested areas. Therefore, the trees in the fragments lose genetic variability and vigor.

Large animals require extensive areas of intact forest to obtain sufficient food, or to find suitable nesting sites and their migrations are likely to be interrupted by fragmentation. These animals are also much more susceptible to hunting in forest fragments, as result of which species extinctions occur more rapidly in fragments. Fragmented bits of land are easily vulnerable to extinction due to environmental fluctuations, disease, and other factors.

Invasion of non-native species is an important and often-overlooked cause of extinctions. Non-native species introduced either by humans or through habitat modification, cause extinction of native plants and animals. Essentially four impacts can be seen:

Table 37.7 Human Disturbance of Habitat

Region / Country	Undisturbed	Partially disturbed	Human dominated
Europe	15.6	19.6	64.9
Asia	43.5	27.0	29.5
North America	48.9	35.8	15,4
South America	56.3	18.8	24.9
Australia	62.3	25.8	12
Antarctica	100	00	00

Source : OECD, Saving biological diversity. Economic incentives, 1996

- **Predation**:Non-native species often reproduce in large numbers because of a lack of predators. Further, the introduction of a non-native species which is a predator profoundly affects food chains.
- **Competition**: Non-native exotic species can often out-compete native species for food and habitat acquisition.
- **Hybridization**: Introduction of non-native species has resulted in the decline of native species due to the interbreeding of native and non-native species. It is observed that 37% of American fish species became extinct due to hybridization. In Lake Victoria, the purposeful introduction of the exotic specie, the Nile Perch, for subsistence and sports fishing has caused the extinction of most of the native species, by simply eating them all. Similarly, it is reported that, Eucalyptus an indigenous specie in Australia, behaves merely as a pest upon being introduced in many tropical and subtropical regions in the world.
- **Homogenization of ecosystems**: Introduction of non-native species decreases the number of native species in a habitat which are replaced with widespread species. This causes regional homogenization of ecosystems. Diversity of species is thus lost.

In **agriculture** and animal husbandry, the introduction of mono cropping and the use of relatively few plants for food and other uses is held responsible for the loss of biodiversity and genetic variability. Green revolution promoted hybridization which has resulted in several of the indigenous breeds becoming extinct or threatened. This has resulted in widespread genetic erosion and genetic pollution due to uncontrolled intentional and unintentional cross-pollination and crossbreeding.Genetic erosion coupled with genetic pollution is reported to be the cause of destruction of unique genotypes, thereby posing a severe threat to our food security.

Pollution by chemical contaminants pose a serious threat to species and ecosystems, particularly for species whose range is extremely small. Pollution of water in lakes and rivers has degraded waters so that many freshwater ecosystems are dying. Since almost 12% of animals species live in the aquatic ecosystems, and most others depend on them to some degree, this is a very serious matter. Air pollutants adversely affect biodiversity through acid rain.

Climate change: The impact of **global warming** on biodiversity has been reported from many parts of the world. Plants and animals are sensitive to fluctuations in temperature and climate. Species and ecosystems are threatened by the changing global climate. The distribution of species is largely determined by climate. Climate change causes shift in these distributions to which plants and animals are not able to adjust.

Costa Rica's golden toad has become extinct, at least partly because of the decrease in mist frequency in its cloud forest habitat; Climate change is causing shift in the migratory patterns of birds as a result of which the birds arrive at their breeding grounds at an inappropriate time. Many migratory species are in decline; birds such as the great tit in Scotland and the Mexican jay in Arizona are beginning to breed earlier in the year; butterflies are shifting their ranges northwards throughout Europe; alpine plants are moving to higher altitudes in Austria; and mammals including polar bears, walrus and caribou - in many parts of the Arctic - are beginning to feel the impacts of reduced sea ice and warming tundra habitat.

It is reported that Russia, Canada, Kyrgyzstan, Norway, Sweden, Finland, Latvia, Uruguay, Bhutan and Mongolia are likely to lose 45 per cent or more of current habitat. The rare Gelada baboon of Ethiopia, the Andean spectacled bear, Central America's resplendent quetzal, the mountain pygmy possum of Australia and the monarch butterfly at its Mexican wintering grounds are threatened by global warming.

Many coastal and island species are reported to be at risk from the combined threat of warming of oceans, sea-level rise and range shifts, all of which can add significantly to existing human pressures. Scientists fear that by end of next century, perhaps 25% of existing species will be lost. The rate of global warming may be a critical determinant in the future of the global biodiversity.

The underlying common factor in all these causes is that they are all human induced. Therefore human activity is the most important source for biodiversity loss.

37.3.5 Policy Response to Protect Biodiversity

Ecosystems and species are threatened with destruction to an extent rarely seen in the history of civilization. The loss of species and ecosystems is attributed to the accelerating transformation of the earth by a growing human population. Dealing with this problem will require greater efforts to preserve habitats. According to the Millennium Assessment Report (2005) "The drivers of loss of biodiversity and the drivers of changes in ecosystem services are either steady, show no evidence of declining over time, or are increasing in intensity." At the same time it is also true that less biodiversity would exist today but for the actions taken by the communities, NGOs, governments, and business and industry, to conserve biodiversity and promote its sustainable use. Many traditional cultural practices, a number of community-based resource management programs and substantial investments by NGOs, governments, and the private sector have slowed the loss of biodiversity.

Protecting global biodiversity is one of the major global challenges to day. More than ten global biodiversity-related treaties have been negotiated besides hundreds of regional and bilateral agreements. Governments have also initiated action plans based on the Agenda 21, which set forth a blueprint for implementing sustainable development.

According to Mireille Jardin (2010), a former UNESCO civil servant, bio diversity related global conventions evolved in three distinct phases.

The first phase focused on specific species or habitats in view of their perceived importance. The important conventions during this period include:

- Convention on Wetlands of International Importance (Ramsar Convention),
- Convention on International Trade in Endangered Species of Wild Fauna and Flora (CITES)
- Convention on the Conservation of Migratory Species of Wild Animals (CMS).

These conventions complemented each other and emphasized on conservation of biodiversity. The First phase also includes the **World Network of Biosphere Reserves (WNBR),** of the MAB (Man And Biosphere) Programme of UNESCO.

The second phase saw the shift in its focus to a global or holistic concept including all ecosystem services. During this phase the Convention on Biological Diversity (CBD) in 1992 was adopted. The CBD dealt with the biodiversity issue in a holistic way, setting new principles and new global ambitions for its protection. This phase addressed the issue of "Access and Benefit Sharing (ABS)". **The Third Phase** which is the current phase, "aims to improve the scientific basis for decision-making on biodiversity issues and to give these issues a higher profile on the international agenda" (Jardin, 2010). The land mark of this phase is the Intergovernmental Science-Policy Platform on Biodiversity and Ecosystem Services (IPBES) which was established in 2012. The IPBES provides policymakers with objective scientific assessments about the state of knowledge regarding the planet's biodiversity, ecosystems and the benefits they provide to people; it also provides the tools and methods to protect and sustainably use these vital natural assets.

The First Phase of Bio Diversity Protection

During this phase the focus was on conservation of biodiversity. The first phase is important for three major Conventions, namely

- Convention on International Trade in Endangered Species (CITES) -1975
- Convention on Wetlands of International Importance (Ramsar Convention), 1975
- Convention on the Conservation of Migratory Species of Wild Animals (Bonn Convention) -1983

This phase also witnessed the creation of the World Network of Biosphere Reserves which consists of a dynamic and interactive network of sites of excellence. The WNBR combines conservation with the sustainable use of natural resources. It fosters the harmonious integration of people and nature for sustainable development through participatory dialogue and knowledge sharing.

Convention on International Trade in Endangered Species (CITES) -1975

CITES is an international agreement that regulates and monitors trade in animal and plant species to ensure that such trade in animal and plant species does not threaten their long-term survival in the wild. CITES entered in to force on 1st July 1975. It has now 183 members.

CITES imposes controls on international trade in specimens of selected species. All import, export, re-export and "introduction from the sea" of species covered by the Convention has to be authorized through a licensing system. Over 34,000 species are covered by CITES which monitors and regulates trade in endangered species through a system of permits and certificates. These documents are needed to cross borders with any CITES species or any product containing CITES species. Species are listed in three different 'Appendices', depending on their conservation status and how much they are traded. Permit requirements are different for each Appendix.

- Appendix I species are the most endangered, and trade is more restricted for those species.
- Appendix II species can withstand more trade.
- Appendix III species are those where individual countries have asked for help to protect those species.

CITES maintains a close cooperative relationship with the World Customs Organization (WCO) and INTERPOL. CITES has been successful in the safeguard of the vicuna, the South American caiman or the Nile crocodile. However it failed to regulate or stop the killing of tigers and rhinoceros for trade purposes.

Convention on the Conservation of Migratory Species of Wild Animals (Bonn Convention) -1979 aims to conserve terrestrial, aquatic and avian migratory species throughout their range. It is an inter governmental treaty, concluded under the aegis of the United Nations Environment Programme, It is concerned with the conservation of wildlife and habitats on a global scale. Since the Convention's entry into force, its membership has grown steadily to include 120 Parties (as of November 2014) from Africa, Central and South America, Asia, Europe and Oceania.

The Convention held that migratory species should be considered as shared resources. The CMS covers those species of migratory animals whose populations regularly migrate across or outside of national boundaries. The animal species are listed in two different appendices according to their threat status.

- Appendix I covers species which are threatened with extinction and require the protection of all states within whose boundaries, habitats of the species in question are located. Conservation measures include the maintenance or restoration of habitats along migratory routes.
- Appendix II covers migratory species which have an unfavourable conservation status and which require international cooperation for their conservation.

The Conference of the Parties (CoP), the principal decision-making body of the convention, meets every three years.

Convention on Wetlands of International Importance (Ramsar Convention)

The Ramsar Convention, adopted in the Iranian city of Ramsar in 1971, came into force in 1975. The Convention arose out of the concern about the increasing loss and degradation of wetland habitats for migratory water birds. UNESCO is the depositary of the Convention. As of 2017, 169 states are Parties to the Convention and 2279 sites are included in a "Ramsar List of Wetlands of International Importance". The Convention's mission is "conservation and wise use of all wetlands through local, regional and national actions and international cooperation, as a contribution towards achieving sustainable development throughout the world" (COP, 2002).

Under the Convention, the Contracting Parties commit to:

- work towards the wise use of all their wetlands through national plans, policies and legislation, management actions and public education;
- designate suitable wetlands for the list of Wetlands of International Importance (the "Ramsar List") and ensure their effective management;
- Co-operate internationally on trans-boundary wetlands, shared wetland systems, shared species, and development projects that may affect wetlands.

The Second Phase of Biodiversity Conservation

The second phase is broader in scope. It delth with wider varieties of species & aimed at conservation of biological diversity in general. The focus shifted from protection of "exceptional nature" to "ordinary nature".

The second phase is very significant and it includes:

- TheConvention on Biological Diversity(CBD) – 1992
- Cartagena Protocol on Biosafety (CPB) -2000
- The Strategic Plan for Biological Diversity 2011-2020, a 10 years action program which provided for:
  a. The Aichi Targets
  b. The Nagoya Protocol, 2010.

The Convention on Biological Diversity(CBD) – 1992

Convention on Biological Diversity (CBD) was born at the 1992 UN Conference on Environment and Development (the Earth Summit). The Convention provides the framework for 196 parties to guide efforts to conserve, and sustainably use biological diversity and equitably share the benefits from the use of genetic resources. In April 2002, the Parties to the Convention committed to significantly reduce the loss of biodiversity by 2010. The Convention was opened for signature at the Earth Summit in Rio de Janeiro on 5 June 1992 and entered into force on 29 December 1993. The CBD is now one of the most widely ratified international treaties on environmental issues, with 196 member countries.

The objectives of the Convention on Biological Diversity are expressed in its article 1:

- the conservation of biological diversity;
- the sustainable use of its components; and
- the fair and equitable sharing of the benefits arising out of the utilization of genetic resources, by appropriate
  - * access to genetic resources,
  - * transfer of relevant technologies,
  - * funding.

The Convention is the first agreement to address all aspects of biological diversity: species, ecosystems and genetic resources. It is indeed the first time that genetic diversity is specifically covered in a binding global treaty. The Convention is legally binding; countries that are Parties to it are obliged to implement its provisions.

So far there have been twelve meetings of the Conferences of the Parties. Some of the output of these meetings are:

- Programmes to conserve marine and coastal biodiversity, inland water ecosystems, forest biodiversity, dry and sub-humid lands and mountain biodiversity.
- Sharing, in a fair and equitable way, the results of research and development and the benefits arising from the commercial and other utilization of genetic resources with the Contracting Party providing such resources
- Decision to specify guiding principles on invasive alien species;
- Access to and transfer of technology, including bio technology, to the governments and/or local communities that provided traditional knowledge and/or biodiversity resources.
- a decision to initiate negotiations on an international regime on access and benefit-sharing (ABS).
- Technical and scientific cooperation
- Integrate the knowledge of tribal communities
- Education and public awareness.
- Provision of financial resources.
- National reporting on efforts to implement treaty commitments.

In the COP-10 meeting, the parties agreed to come up with new plans and targets since the previous biodiversity protection targets are not achieved. The countries adopted the Strategic Plan for Biological Diversity 2011-2020.

The Strategic Plan for Biological Diversity 2011-2020 is a 10 years action program aimed at saving biodiversity. This short term plan provided a set of 20 ambitious, yet achievable targets known as the Aichi targets. The mission of the Strategic Plan is to "halt the loss of biodiversity in order to ensure that by 2020 ecosystems are resilient and continue to provide essential services, thereby securing the planet's variety of life, and contributing to human well-being ..,"

Aichi Targets, one of the two important features of COP10, is a short term plan that provides a set of **20** ambitious yet achievable **targets in five sections**. They are a set of 20 Targets grouped into five Strategic Goals that shall be achieved by 2020. They are part of the Strategic Plan for Biodiversity 2011-2020, which was adopted in 2010 by the 10th Meeting of the Conference of Parties of the Convention on Biological Diversity at Nagoya, Aichi Prefecture, Japan from 18th to 29th October 2010. The five strategic goals (A to E) of Aichi Targets are:

a. Address the causes of biodiversity loss
b. Reduce the direct pressure on biodiversity and promote sustainable use

c. Safeguard ecosystems, species and genetic diversity
d. Biodiversity benefits to all from biodiversity and ecosystem services
e. Enhance implementation through participatory planning, knowledge management and capacity building

A second important outcome of the COP 10 is the Nagoya Protocol

The Nagoya Protocol on Access to Genetic Resources and the Fair and Equitable Sharing of Benefits from their Utilization was adopted at the tenth meeting of the Conference of the Parties on 29 October 2010, in Nagoya, Japan. It is a supplementary agreement to the Convention on Biological Diversity. The Protocol provided a strong basis for greater legal certainty and transparency for both providers and users of genetic resources.

The Nagoya Protocol provided for access to traditional knowledge of genetic resources held by indigenous and local communities. It strengthend opportunities for fair and equitable sharing of benefits from the use of biological diversity.

The protocol aimed at generating incentives to conserve biological diversity and enhance the contribution of biological diversity to sustainable development and human well-being.

COP 11 held at Hyderabad, India in 2012 and COP-12, held at Pyeongchang (Republic of Korea), in October 2014 and COP14 held at Cancun, Mexico in December 2016, reviewed the progress towards the achievement of the Aichi Biodiversity Targets. These meetings assessed the progress in the implementation of the Convention and the Strategic Plan for Biodiversity 2011-2020.

Cartegena Protocol

The Cartagena Protocol on Biosafety to the Convention on Biological Diversity was adopted on 29th January 2000 and entered into force on 11th September 2003. The Biosafety Protocol, facilitates the environmentally sound application of biotechnology. It created avenue for maximizing the benefit from the application of biotechnology while minimizing the possible risks to the environment and to human health. The Protocol applies to the trans-boundary movement, transit, handling and use of all living modified organisms that may have adverse effects on the conservation and sustainable use of biological diversity. The Protocol seeks to protect biological diversity from the potential risks posed by living modified organisms resulting from modern biotechnology. The Protocol contains reference to a precautionary approach. The Protocol also establishes a Biosafety Clearing-House to facilitate the exchange of information on living modified organisms and to assist countries in the implementation of the Protocol. As on Mar 12th 2015, 170 countries were parties to the Protocol.

The Third Phase of Biodiversity Conservation

The third phase begins with the establishment of the Intergovernmental Science-Policy Platform on Biodiversity and Ecosystem Services (IPBES). This is an independent intergovernmental body to strengthen the science-policy interface for biodiversity and ecosystem services for the conservation and sustainable use of bio diversity, long term human wellbeing and sustainable development. The IPBES was established in Panama City, on 21st April 2012. IPBES is placed under the auspices of four United Nations entities: UNEP, UNESCO, FAO and UNDP and administered by UNEP. The IPBES performs four interdependent vital functions: They are:

- Assessments
- Policy Support
- Capacity Building
- Knowledge Generation

IPBES prepares global and regional reports on the state of knowledge on biodiversity and ecosystem services and on specific topics related to biodiversity, based on requests from all stakeholders.

Policy Support: IPBES supports policy decisions and their implementation by identifying appropriate policy instruments that can help in the application of the results of assessments into policy.

Capacity Building: IPBES identifies the capacities and competencies that are required to work with IPBES and provides support for the most urgent measures and / or call on other organisations to support these efforts.

Knowledge Generation: IPBES will identify knowledge gap with regard to biodiversity, and support research facilities and other knowledge generators to fill in these gaps.

37. 4 Hazardous Wastes

A hazardous waste is any solid or liquid waste that is considered toxic, chemically reactive, flammable or corrosive. Hazardous wastes are harmful to human health and to the health of ecosystems on exposure. They are by-products of industrial and manufacturing processes and discarded products from commercial and industrial sectors. Examples include waste acids, contaminated sludges, spent chemicals, pesticides, unused cleaning products, paints, certain parts of end of life vehicles, industrial equipment, and electronic goods.

Hazardous wastes possess specific properties. They are toxic, corrosive, reactive and ignitable.

- Toxic wastes: Toxic wastes are harmful or fatal when ingested or absorbed (e.g., containing mercury, lead, etc.)
- Corrosive wastes include strong acidic or alkaline substances. They destroy solid material and living tissue upon contact, by chemical reaction. They are capable of corroding metal containers, such as storage tanks, drums, and barrels. Battery acid is an example.
- Reactive wastes are unstable under "normal" conditions. They can cause explosions, undergo violent reactions, generate toxic fumes, gases, or vapors or explosive mixtures when heated, compressed, or mixed with water. Examples include lithium sulphur batteries and explosives
- Ignitable wastes which can create fires under certain conditions, are spontaneously combustible, or have a flash point less than 60 °C (140 °F).

Though industries are mostly responsible for generation of hazardous wastes, households also contribute to the generation of such wastes. Examples of hazardous wastes generated from households include:

- Paints and solvents
- Used motor oil in Automotive wastes
- Pesticides
- Mercury containing wastes such as thermometers, fluorescent lighting
- Electronics or e-wastes from computers, television, mobile phones)
- Aerosols / Propane cylinders
- Cleaning agents
- Refrigerant containing appliances
- Specific batteries (e.g. lithium, nickel cadmium, or button cell batteries)

The main challenge posed by hazardous waste is the safe disposal of such wastes and international trade of hazardous wastes. The export of hazardous waste, particularly from richer Northern countries to poorer Southern countries is a serious problem for more than one reason:

First, the recipient developing or underdeveloped country is not given the complete and correct information about the true content and characteristics of the waste.

Second, the recipient developing country does not have the required technology for the safe handling and disposal of the wastes.

The tightening of environmental regulations in the advanced countries in the 1970s and 1980s increased public resistance to disposal of hazardous wastes. Hence the industrialized nations searched for cheap options for waste disposal; the developing nations with weak environmental regulations and weaker implementation provided them a solution for easy and cheap disposal of hazardous wastes. There are several instances where the wastes from industrialized rich nations have tried to dump hazardous wastes in a developing or underdeveloped nation. Examples include:

1. Barrels of hazardous waste from Singapore labeled for a false destination remained unclaimed on a Bangkok, Thailand dock for years releasing their toxic contents to the environment.
2. Between 1987 and 1988, around 4000 tonnes of hazardous wastes containing polychlorinated biphenyl (PCB) from Italy was deposited at a site near the town Koko in Nigeria. The improperly marked barrels of hazardous waste leaked into the environment. Italy ultimately agreed to repackage the wastes and return them to Italy after other countries refused to accept the waste.
3. The *Khian Sea, a* freighter ship from Philadelphia, carrying 14000 tonnes of toxic incinerator ash, dumped 4000 tonnes on a beach in Haiti which is yet to be cleaned. The Ferry travelled around the world for several years and as nation after nation refused to let it dispose of the waste, it changed its name to *Pelicano* and finally illegally dumped the toxic wastes into the open sea near Singapore.
4. The tragedy at Abidjan, the economic Capital of Ivory Coast August 19-20, 2006 when toxic wastes were illegally disposed of by an European multinational Company, Trafigura,.through a local private contractor in Ivor Coast. Alteast 15 people were reported to be killed in the incident. (See Box 37.1)

Trafigura, a Netherlands/Switzerland/UK based multinational corporation specialized in trading raw materials and in particular oil, instead of refining the oil normally, used a chemical process called caustic washing, onboard the ship Probo Koala, to cut down on cost and make profits. But the Company realized the difficulty in dealing with the wastes. Having failed in its attempts to get it treated it managed to get rid of it at Ivory Coast by paying a contractor just around 20 euro/m3, while treating it at The Netherlands would have cost around 1000 euro/m3. Tragedy struck the Abidjan, the economic capital of Ivory Coast. Approximately 400 metric tons of hazardous waste was secrctly discharged at open air sites around the city of Abidjan, the economic capital of Ivory Coast. The waste was spread around the city, and exposing ten thousands of people to toxic fumes. Atleast 15 deaths were reported and around 100,000 people were hosptalised.

Source: http://www.greenpeace.org/international/en/campaigns/detox/trafigura/

Box 37.1 Illegal Disposal of Toxic Wastes

The Secretariat of the Basel Convention estimated that countries exported 7.5 million tons of industrial and chemical waste in 2003 of which only one million tons was disposed of properly which implies that 6.5 million tons of hazardous waste are being illegally disposed of. It is reported that nearly 30 industrialised nations produce 90% of the world's hazardous wastes. The export of hazardous waste, particularly from industrialised developed nations to poorer Southern countries is an issue of environmental justice.

Thus the Basel Convention on the Control of Trans-boundary Movements of Hazardous Wastes and their Disposal was born. The Basel Convention was born in response to a public uproar following the illegal disposal of hazardous wastes in the Southern poor countries from the Northern rich indusrialised nations.

The Basel Convention as it is popularly known was adopted in 1989, and entered into force in 1992. It addressed the increasing concerns over the management, disposal and trans-boundary movements of hazardous waste. The main objective of the Basel Convention is to protect human health and the environment against the adverse effects of hazardous wastes. The Basel Convention regulates, rather than bans, the export of hazardous waste. As of May 2011, 176 countries, including the European Union were parties to the Convention.

The principal aims of the Basel Convention are:

- Minimize the generation of hazardous waste and hazardous recyclable materials;
- Ensure they are disposed in an environmentally sound manner and as close to the source of generation as possible;
- Minimize the international movement of hazardous waste and hazardous recyclable materials.

Under the Convention's provisions, trade in hazardous wastes generally cannot take place:

- without the importing country's written consent to a particular export; or
- where the exporting country has reason to believe that the particular wastes will not be handled in an environmentally sound manner.

Under the provisions of the Basel Convention, Parties to the Convention may not carry out or authorize trans-boundary movements (imports, exports or transits) of hazardous waste or hazardous recyclable material:

- to States that are not Parties to the Convention unless they have a bilateral agreement under Article 11.
- to Antarctica;
- if the prospective State of destination has prohibited such imports;
- if appropriate disposal or recycling facilities are available in the State of origin unless the waste is needed as a raw material for recycling or recovery industries in the state of import;
- if there is reason to believe that environmentally-sound management/disposal options are not available in the prospective State of destination. (importing country).

In the first decade after it entered into force, the Basel convention focused on setting up a framework for controlling the movement of hazardous wastes across international frontiers, developing the criteria for "environmentally sound management" and establishing a Control System based on prior written notification. This was stressed in the various Conference of Parties meeting held periodically.

The twelfth meeting of the CoP of the Basel Convention was held at Geneva in Switzerland from 4th to 15th May 2015, along with the seventh CoP Meeting of the Rotterdam Convention and seventh meeting of the Stockholm Convention.

Rotterdam Convention on the Prior Informed Consent Procedure for Certain Hazardous Chemicals and Pesticides in International Trade was adopted in 1998 in response to dramatic growth in chemicals trade, and vulnerability of developing countries to uncontrolled imports. It entered into force on 24 February 2004 and in 2011 there were 143 Parties.

Stockholm Convention on Persistent Organic Pollutants was adopted in 2001 in response to an urgent need for global action on "POPs". POPs are persistent chemicals and they "bio accumulate in fatty tissues and biomagnify through the food chain". The Stockholm Convention entered into force on 17 May 2004 and in 2011 there were 173 Parties.

The Basel Convention's 12th CoP meeting adopted 25 decisions including six identical ones for the three Conventions. Most importantly the Basel Convention's 12th CoP meeting included the adoption of the e-waste technical guidelines and updated the technical guidelines on mercury wastes, and adopted technical guide lines for seven POPs.

The thirteenth meeting of the Conference of Parties (COP13) to the Basel Convention was held from 24th April to 5th May, 2017, at Geneva, Switzerland along with the eighth CoP Meeting of the Rotterdam Convention and Eighth meeting of the Stockholm Convention to discuss joint issues shared among the Conventions and for discussing respective Convention specific issues. It decided on the establishment of an expert working group (lead country: China) to look further into the Technical Guidelines on Transboundary Movements of Electrical and Electronic Waste and Used Electrical and Electronic Equipment.

The three Conventions together – The Basel Convention, the Rotterdam Convention and the Stockholm convention - work for the sound management of hazardous chemicals and wastes. While, the Basel covers hazardous wastes that are explosive, flammable, reactive, poisonous, infectious, corrosive, toxic or ecotoxic, the Rotterdam Convention covers pesticides and industrial chemicals that have been banned or severely restricted for health or environmental reasons, the Stockholm covers 14 pesticides, and 7 industrial chemicals and by-products. Most POPs are covered by all the three Conventions.

37.5 Major International Conferences on Environmental Protection

Since 1972 the world has witnessed the active participation of many national and international environmental non-governmental organizations. Two important conferences played an important role:

- The United Nations Conference on the Human Environment held in 1972 in Stockholm.
- The United Nations Conference on Environment and Development (UNCED), Popularly known as the Earth Summit, held in Rio de Janeirio in June 1992.

The UN Conference on Human Environment – the Stockholm Conference (1972)

The Stockholm Conference is a landmark in the emergence of global environmentahsm. It was after the Stockholm Conference that for the first time, environmental issues gained legitamacy in international relations. The theme of the Conference - "Only One Earth" - was chosen to emphasize that man would have no other place to live if he ruined his surroundings through his selfish abuse of the environment. The Stockholm Conference was attended by not less than 113 countries and atleast 19 intergovernmental agencies and 400 non-governmental organisations. One of the post Stockholm achievement has been the setting up of the United Nations Environmental Programme (UNEP), which in 1977, commissioned the IUCN (International Union for the Conservation of Nature) to prepare the World Conservation Strategy.

The Stockholm Conference had several important outcomes. It promoted the development of national environment policies, notably the creation in many countries of environment agencies and ministries. Several initiatives on the international environment and development issues followed in the 1970s and 1980s.

The agreed documents were the Stockholm Declaration on Human Environment and the Action Plan for the Human Environment. The Stockholm Declaration consisting of a preamble and 26 principles, addressed the major areas related to environmental issues, ranging from education and science to social and economic development and from resources to pollution. The Action Plan was a functional framework of 109 recommendations and consisted of three parts; (i) a global assessment programme (ii) environmental management activities and (iii) supporting measures, such as education and training. The 26 principles relate to safeguarding and conserving the natural resource, international co-operation for improving the environment, recognize environment – development interaction and interdependence, maintain pollution within the assimilating capacity of the environment, and use of science, technology and research to promote environmental protection.

The interaction of environment and development was formally recognised in the final documents, notably in several principles of the Stockholm Declaration. However, in terms of real commitments in the Action Plan, development issues were not covered in much detail, and only the human settlement policies were addressed in depth.

Rio Summit(1992)

The United Nations Conference on Environment and Development (UNCED) that was organised in Rio de Janeiro, in June 1992, marking the 20th anniversary of the Stockholm Conference, was a unique event in the annals of international affairs. The 'Earth Summit', as it is popularly called was the largest conference ever staged by the United Nations. Over 178 governments attended the Summit and official delegates numbered almost 10,000 and number of non-governmental organisation were also present.

Several major agreements were reached at the RIO conference; some of the highlights of the summit are:

- A convention on Biological diversity.
- A framework Convention on climate/Change.
- Forest Principles.
- The RIO declaration of 27 principles.
- Agenda 21.

The framework convention on climate change provides a legal framework and process intended to address the problem of human interference with the Earth's climate system. The text accepts that climate change is a serious problem, requiring a 'precautionary approach', 'that is cost effective'. It accepted that developed countries shall take the lead and they agreed to fund the 'full agreed upon incremental cost' of the measures taken by developing countries, initially through the Global Environmental Facility (GEF). The convention established the 'decade-stabilisation' of carbon dioxide and other greenhouse gas emissions from industrialised countries' as an initial 'aim'. At Rio, the climate change convention was signed by 153 governments plus the EC, and others have joined later.

The convention on Biological diversity was negotiated to conserve the biological diversity of the planet, through the protection of species and ecosystems and to establish terms for the associated uses of biological resources. Parties are to develop 'national strategies, plans or programmes' for protecting biodiversity and communicate information on them to the Conference of Parties.

The RIO declaration on Environment and Development presented 27 principles of "Environment and Development" intended to build upon the Stockholm Declaration of 1972. It differs from the Stockholm Declaration in giving greater emphasis to developmental issues and less to ecological issue. The RIO declaration recognised the sovereign rights of the countries to exploit their resources provided such exploitation does not cause damage to the environment of other states.

The Agenda 21 is an action plan to achieve sustainable development. It consists of 40 chapters covering 500 pages, which address (i) general issues of social and economic development; (ii) issues of specific national and other resources; (iii) the role of different major groups; and (iv) means of implementation.

Agenda 21 emphasised on:

a. A 'bottom-up' approach of putting emphasis upon people,communities and NGOs;
b. The need for 'open governance';
c. The importance of adequate information;
d. The need for adequate cross-cutting institutions;
e. The complementarity between regulatory approaches and market mechanisms for addressing development and environmental needs.

Agenda 21 called for a 'Commission on Sustainable Development' as the major follow-up institution within the UN system. More specific results of the Agenda 21 include recommendations to start negotiation on a desertification convention and to hold conferences on the sustainable development of small island states and on the management of migratory fish stocks.

The final agreement at UNCED was a statement on Principles of Forest Management. This emphasised that governments have the sovereign right to exploit the forests within their national boundaries, and also the responsibility to ensure that their activities do not negatively affect other countries.

The other resolutions followed through the specific recommendations in Agenda 21. The longest and the most important, is the 'Institutional Arrangements to Follow up the UNCED' that endorsed the recommendations of Agenda 21 and directed the Economic and Social Council to set up a high-level Commission on sustainable development in order to ensure the effective follow-up of the conference.

Rio+20 Summit (2012)

The United Nations Conference on Sustainable Development - or Rio+20 - took place in Rio de Janeiro, Brazil on 20-22 June 2012. In this Conference, the Member States decided develop a set of sustainable Development Goals which will be built upon the Millennium development Goals. The focus of the Conference was making sustainable development a reality. With this focus the Conference urged the Member Countries to adopt the 10-year framework of programmes on sustainable consumption and production patterns. The Conference resulted in over 700 voluntary commitments and witnessed new partnerships to achieve sustainable development.

Conclusion

Since 1970s one of the major challenges in international relations has been environmental protection. Since the Stockholm Conference, several bilateral and multilateral treaties have been signed, several Conventions have been held and important resolutions adopted to protect the environment, several action plans have been designed, including the Agenda 21, which proposed a blueprint for achieving sustainable development. The result of all these is mixed; unfortunately we are not able to say that we have curtailed resource depletion and controlled pollution and saved genetic and biodiversity. The threat to environment continues still. What is required is a whole hearted understanding and conviction from all nations irrespective of their stage of development to implement sustainable development.

Questions

1. How serious is the issue of climate change. What are the predicted impacts of climate change? Present a time line of the major initiatives to arrest climate change.
2. Summarise the salient features of the Montreal Protocol
3. Highlight the current trends in biodiversity loss. Bringout the impact of bio diversity loss on humanity.
4. Summarise the measures taken globally to conserve biodiversity.
5. Why is trans-boundary movement of hazardous wastes a critical issue at international level. Give examples.
6. What are the international rules and regulations to adopted on the issue of trans-boundary movement of hazardous wastes.

Exercise

1. Prepare a case study that will highlight the impact of bio diversity loss.
2. Make out a case study of dumping of hazardous wastes in to underdeveloped nations by developed nations.
3. Read the latest report by the UN on climate change and summarise the findings.

GLOSSARY

1. **Abatement:** The reduction in degree or intensity of pollution.
2. **Acid** Rain: A decrease in the p^H of rain water, which may be caused by the emission of sulphur or nitrogen oxides into the atmosphere.
3. **Aichi Target:** Aichi target is a short term plan for biodiversity conservation. It is officially known as "Strategic Plan for Biodiversity 2011-2020". It includes a set of 20 targets grouped into five strategic goals that shall be achieved by all countries. The five strategic goals are:
   a. address the cause of biodiversity loss;
   b. reduce the direct pressure on biodiversity and promote sustainable development;
   c. safeguard ecosystems, species and genetic diversity.
   d. biodiversity benefits to all from biodiversity and ecosystem services
   e. enhance implementation through participatory planning, knowledge management and capacity building
4. **Albedo Effect:** A phenomenon that refers to the proportion of sunlight that the earth's surface reflects back into the space. It is believed that deforested land would reflect more solar heat than land with vegetation or crops.
5. **Anthropocentrism:** Anthropocentrism is a philosophical view point arguing that human beings are the central or most significant entities in the world. Anthropocentrism regards human beings as superior to nature and hence the exploitation of other entities such as animals, plants mineral resources etc are justified.
6. **Basel Convention:** An international agreement on the control of transboundary movements of hazardous wastes and their disposal, drawn up in March 1989 in Basel, Switzerland, with over 100 countries as signatories.
7. **Benefit/CostAnalysis:** The systematic comparison of the benefits and costs of undertaking a project to determine the efficient level of activity for that project.
8. **Benefit transfer:** Estimating the economic contribution of ecosystem services by applying the value identified in one primary research study to another location.
9. **Bio-chemical Oxygen Demand (BOD):** The dissolved oxygen required to decompose organic matter in water. It is a measure of pollution because the demand for oxygen increases when there is an increase in effluents discharged into water.
10. **Bio-degradable Material:**Organic waste materials that can be broken down into their basic elements by the action of micro-organisms.
11. **Biodiversity:** Biodiversity, a contraction of the phrase "biological diversity," is often used to describe all the species living in a particular area. Biodiversity can be summarized as "life on earth." At a much broader level biodiversity refers to the variety of life on Earth at all its levels, from genes to ecosystems, and the ecological and evolutionary processes that sustain it.
12. **Biodiversity Hotspot**: A biodiversity hotspot is an area of rich biodiversity that faces serious threats to its existence due to habitat loss, climate change, or extensive species loss. Around 25 sites worldwide are recognized as such hotspots. In order for a region to be included in this category, it must be biologically diverse, with a high proportion of species that are not found anywhere else on Earth, and the security of the region must be threatened.
13. **Bubble Concept:** A form of regulation that allows all sources within a plant to be treated as one source, as if they were in a bubble with one point of escape.
14. **Carrying capacity:** The number of people that can be supported within an ecosystem, based on the average level of consumption and the environmental impacts of the prevailing technology.It is the maximum number of individuals of a defined species that a given environment can support over the long term

15. **Cartegena Protocol:** The Cartagena Protocol on Biosafety to the Convention on Biological Diversity is an international agreement which aims to ensure the safe handling, transport and use of living modified organisms (LMOs) resulting from modern biotechnology that may have adverse effects on biological diversity, taking also into account risks to human health. It was adopted on 29 January 2000 and entered into force on 11 September 2003.
16. **Chipko Movement:** The Chipko Movement, started in the 1970's, was a non-violent movement aimed at protecting, and conserving of trees and forests from destruction.
17. **Chemical Oxygen Demand (COD):** A measure of the oxygen required to oxidise all organic and inorganic compounds in water.
18. **Chlorofluorocarbons:** A family of inert, nontoxic, and easily liquefied chemicals used in refrigeration, air conditioning, packaging, and insulation or as solvents and aerosol propellants. Because CFCs are not destroyed in the lower atmosphere, they drift into the upper atmosphere, where their chlorine components destroy ozone.
19. **Clean Development Mechanism:** The CDM of the Kyoto Protocol allows projects in developing countries to generate emission credits if they result in emission levels lower than would otherwise be the case; these credits can be marketed and eventually counted against a developed country's emission obligation.
20. **Command and Control**: Command and Control is "the direct regulation of an industry or activity by legislation that states what is permitted and what is illegal.With reference to pollution control it involves the government or the assigned institution to "command" the reduction of pollution by setting emissions standards and to "control" the manner in which emission reduciton is achieved - specification of pollution abatement technology.
21. **Compensatory damages:** Payment for damages to ecosystems, to compensate stakeholders for loss, injury, or harm suffered as a result of oversight or inaction by another.
22. **Compensation Variation:**Compensation Variation is the sum of money required to compensate an individual or a group or an economy for the welfare effects of a change in the economy. It is the monetary measure of a change in welfare.
23. **Common Property Resources:** Common property resources are natural resources owned and managed collectively by a community or society rather than by individuals. They are different from public goods since they posess the feature of rivalry in consumption.
24. **Consumer's Surplus:** Consumer's surplus is the economic measure of consumer benefit measured as the difference between what the consumer is willing to pay for a good relative to its market price.
25. **Contingent Valuation Method:** The Contingent Valuation Method (CVM) is an economic, non-market based valuation method especially used to infer individual's preferences for public goods, notably environmental quality.
26. **Convention on International Trade in Endangered Species of Wild Fauna and Flora** (CITES) is an international agreement between governments. Its aim is to ensure that international trade in specimens of wild animals and plants does not threaten their survival.
27. **Cradel to Grave Approach:** Cradle to Grave Appraoch to sustainable business is the full Life Cycle Assessment from manufacture ('cradle') to 'use phase' and disposal phase ('grave').
28. **Damage Function:**A function revealing the relationship between emissions and the resulting ambient quality.
29. **Deep Ecology :** Deep ecology is a holistic approach to the environment that argues for the equal rights of all species including human beings. It stresses the inherent worth of non-human living beings regardless of their instrumental utility to human needs.
30. **Deforestation:**Deforestaiton is the permanent removal or clearance of forests and make the land available for non-forest uses.
31. **Dissolved Oxygen:** Dissolved oxygen (DO) is the amount of oxygen that is present in water. It is measure of the amount of oxygen available for bio-chemical activity in a given amount of water. When wastes discharged into water increases, DO will decrease.
32. **Deposit Refund System**: Deposit refund System is a monetary deposit (charge / fee) at the time of sale of a product. The deposit is returned when the item is returned at the end of its useful life. The fees are partly used to subsidize the administrative costs associated with the return, recycling and reuse of the products.
33. **Discount rate:** The rate of time preference that equates present value and future value.

34. **Ecocentrism:**Ecocentrism is a philosophy that places intrinsic value on all living organisms and their natural environment, regardless of their perceived usefulness or importance to human beings.

35. **Ecology** Study of relationship or interdependencies between living organisms and their environment.

36. **Ecological footprint**: The ecological footprint measures human demand on nature, i.e., the quantity of nature it takes to support people or an economy. The ecological footprint is defined as the biologically productive area needed to provide for everything people use: fruits and vegetables, fish, wood, fibers, absorption of carbon dioxide from fossil fuel use, and space for buildings and roads. Biocapacity is the productive area that can regenerate what people demand from nature.

37. **Eco-sphere:** The layer of earth and troposphere. Suitable for the existence of living organisms.

38. **Ecosystem:** An ecosystem is a community of living organisms (biotic) in union with the non-living components (abiotic) of their environment (things like air, water and mineral soil), interacting as a system. These biotic and abiotic components are linked together through nutrient cycles and energy flows. Examples of ecosystem include: a pond, a lake, a forest, an estuary etc.

39. **Efficient Environmental Quality**: The level of quality of the environment, measured according to some set of physical indicators, that maximises total net benefits.

40. **Effluent Fee (Charge):** A charge or fee imposed on the polluter for every unit of pollutant discharged.

41. **Emission Standard:** The maximum amount of a pollutant that is permitted to be discharged from a single polluting source over a specified period of time.

42. **Emission Trading:** Emission trading is a market-based approach to controlling pollution by providing economic incentives for achieving reductions in the emissions of pollutants. It is also known as "cap and trade" system. Inthis a cap on emissions is set and permits are created up to the limit set by the cap. These permits are distributed to the firms emitting the specified pollutant.Allowing trading of these permits puts a price on pollution.

43. **Endangered Species:**Endangered species are those considered to be at risk of extinction, meaning that there are so few left of their kind that they could disappear from the planet altogether. Examples include: Bengal Tiger, Asian Elephant

44. **Entropy :**A measure of the qualitative state of energy in a system. It is a measure of the unavailable energy in a closed thermodynamic system. It is is also usually considered to be a measure of the system's disorder

45. **Environmental Damage:**The reduction in the value of the environment to society as a result of pollution.

46. **Environmental Auditing:** Environmental audits are reviews of a company's operations and processes to verify compliance with environmental regulations.

47. **Environmental Kuznet's Curve:**The environmental Kuznets curve explains the relationship between various indicators of environmental degradation and income per capita.

48. **Environmental Labelling**: Environmental labelling also referred to as Ecolabels are seals of approval given to products that are deemed to have fewer impacts on the environment than functionally or competitively similar products.It indicates to the customer that a product has certain environmentally friendly benefits.

49. **Environmental Impact:** Any alteration of environmental conditions or creation of a new set of environmental conditions, adverse or beneficial, caused or induced by the action or set of actions under consideration.

50. **Environmental Impact Assessment (EIA):** Environmental Impact Assessment [EIA] refers to the evaluation of the effects of a major project on a man-made natural environment. It is a decision making tool that predicts both the beneficial and adverse environmental consequences of policies, programmes, plans and projects..

51. **Environmental Management Accounting (EMA):** EMA is the identification, collection, analysis, dissemination, and use of information related to:

    a. physical flow information on materials, energy and water and waste flows.

    b. monetary information related to costs and revenue necessary for environmental decision-making within an organisation.

52. **Environmental Marketing: Environmental or Green marketing** is the marketing of products that are environmentally safe. It is a new marketing approach that promotes "reconsumption", the ability to use and reuse goods in whole or in parts.

53. **Environmental Quality Standards:** Rules prescribing a particular level of physical quality for the environment. Also called as environmental standards or ambient standards, it refers to the permissible level of pollution in the environment.

54. **Eutrophication:** Excessive flow of nitrate and phosphates into a water way which leads to growth of algae. Decomposition by the micro-organisms depletes the oxygen content of the water and leads to death of the water way.

55. **External Cost:** Cost imposed by consumption and production activities on third parties towards which no compensation is paid.

56. **Externality:** Costs/benefits imposed by consumption and production decisions on third parties not directly participating in the decision.

57. **Extinct Species:** Extinct species refer to those species that no longer exist in the planet earth.

58. **Free Riders:** Individuals with a positive demand for a public good who do not express that demand in order to avoid paying for the supply of the public good.

59. **Gaia Hypothesis:** The Gaia Hypothesis proposes that our planet functions as a single organism that maintains conditions necessary for its survival. It was formulated by James Lovelock in the mid-1960s.

60. **Global Warming:** Global warming is the gradual heating of Earth's surface. Also referred to as climate change, it is the observed century-scale rise in the average temperature of the Earth's climate system and its related effects.

61. **Global Warming Potential: Global warming potential** (GWP) is a relative measure of the heat trapping potential of greenhouse gases. It compares the amount of heat trapped by a certain mass of the greenhouse gas such as Methane to the amount of heat trapped by a similar mass of carbon di oxide. It is expressed as a factor of carbon di oxide.

62. **Green Belt Movement:** is a non-governmental organization founded in 1977 by Prof Wangari Maathai. The movement takes a holistic approach to development by focusing on environmental conservation, community development and capacity building. The Green Belt Movement organises women in rural Kenya to plant trees, combat deforestation, restore their main source of fuel for cooking, generate income, and stop soil erosion.

63. **Greenhouse Effect:** The warming effect of the atmosphere by carbon dioxide and other gases such as Methane and CFCs, is referred to as greenhouse effect. Shortwave solar radiation penetrates to the planet's surface and is reradiated into the atmosphere as infrared waves that are then absorbed by carbon dioxide, Methane, CFCs water vapor, etc. It is similar to the effect occurring inside a green house in which the radiant heat from the sun passes through the glass, warming the contents and is trapped by the glass.

64. **Hazardous Waste:** Pollutants that can cause very serious damages even at relatively low concentrations.

65. **Hedonic valuation:** Estimating the value of a service based on the observed willingness-to-pay for that service through purchases of correlated goods (e.g., the effect of open space on nearby housing prices).

66. **Index of Sustainable Economic Welfare (ISEW):** An alternative to the GNP, calculated by adjusting personal consumption for various factors known to impact human welfare or sustainability (e.g., environmental degradation, income inequality).

67. **Industrial Ecology:** Industrial ecology conceptualises industry as a man-made ecosystem that operates in a similar way to natural ecosystems, where the waste or by product of one process is used as an input into another process. *The concept of industrial ecology owes its origin to the concept of industrial ecosystem developed* by Robert Frosch and Nicholas Gallopoulos.

68. **Inter-generational Equity:** Intergenetrational equity is about equity between present and future generations.

69. **Intra-generational Equity:** Intragenerational equity is concerned with equity between people of the same generation.

70. **ISO14000:** ISO 14000 is the world's most recognized EMS framework that helps organizations manage the environmental impact of their activities and to demonstrate sound environmental management. It was adopted by the International Organization for Standardization (ISO), as an approach to improved environmental performance.

71. **Joint Implementation:** JI provides for any Annex I country to invest in an emission reduction project in any other Annex I country in order to reduce emissions domestically.

72. **Kyoto Protocol:** The Kyoto Protocol is an international agreement linked to the United Nations Framework Convention on Climate Change, which **commits** its Parties to internationally binding emission reduction targets, to prevent climate change. The Kyoto Protocol was adopted in Kyoto, Japan, on 11 December 1997 and entered into force on 16 February 2005.

73. **Liability Rules:** Liability Rules are based on the faith that if polluters are made liable for the damages they cause, they will have an incentive to limit pollution. The liability rules provide incentives for socially responsible behavior by polluters through **legal liability** for environmental damages or the consequences arising from any environmental damage.

74. **Lifecycle Assessment:** Life cycle Assessment, also known as the "cradle to Grave Approach" examines every significant environmental impact of a product from the extraction and use of raw materials through to the final disposal of the product and its decomposition. It helps in tracing the environmental impact of the products and services throughout their life (from cradle to grave).

75. **Limits to Growth:** Limits to Growth is a study about the future of our planet and on the predicament of mankind. The basic thesis in the Limits to Growth model is that infinite growth is impossible on a finite planet.

76. **Marginal Benefits of Pollution Control:** The reduction in all environmental damages by the removal of an additional unit of pollution.

77. **Marginal Costs of Pollution Control:** An increase in total cost of pollution control as an additional unit of pollution is removed.

78. **Market Based Instruments (MBIs): MBIs** are policy instruments that use markets price, and other economic variables to provide incentives to polluters to reduce pollution. MBIs seek to address the market failure of negative production externality such as pollution, by internalising the externalities. MBIs are classified as market using instruments and market creating instruments. .

79. **Market Creating Instruments:** Market creating instruments refer to those policy instruments which internalise the externalise or achieve the target of pollution control by creating a market for pollution rights. Example: dischargeable pollution permits.

80. **Market Using Instruments:** Market using instruments are those policy instruments which control pollution by bringing about changes in the market forces of demand and supply. The market based instruments internalise the externality by placing a cost on the release of pollutants. Examples include, emission and effluent charge and subsidies.

81. **Market failure:** A market failure is a situation where free markets fail to allocate resources efficiently. Price mechanism fails to account for all the costs and benefits involved. As a result market will not provide the socially optimum supply of the good. The good will be either over produced or under produced.

82. **Minamata Tragedy:** Minamata tragedy refers to mercury poisoning of the Minamata bay by the Chisso Chemical Corporation located on the Japanese island of Kyushu. The Chisso Corporation is believed to have discharged between 70 and 150 tons of methyl mercury (an organic form of mercury) into Minamata Bay between 1932 and 1968 exposing thousands of Minamata Bay residents to methyl mercury poisoning.

83. **Monetary Damage Function:** Refers to the amount necessary to compensate those who suffer from such a change in environmental quality.

84. **Montreal Protocol:** The Montreal Protocol, finalized in 1987, is a global agreement to protect the stratospheric ozone layer by phasing out the production and consumption of ozone-depleting substances (ODS).

85. **Nagoya Protocol:** The *Nagoya Protocol* is a supplementary agreement to the Convention on Biological Diversity. Its objective is the fair and equitable sharing of benefits arising from the utilization of genetic resources, thereby contributing to the conservation and sustainable use of biodiversity. The Nagoya Protocol on ABS was adopted on 29 October 2010 in Nagoya, Japan and entered into force on 12 October 2014,

86. **Narmada Bacaho Andolan:** Narmada Bachao Andolan is a peoples movement formed from local peoples movements in Madhya Pradesh, Maharashtra, and Gujarat in protesting against the building of a World Bank-funded dam along the Narmada River. The project - which has displaced hundreds of thousands and has imposed stunning environmental costs without reaping the promised benefits of modernization - has been the source of constant controversy.

87. **Non-renewable Resource:** Resources that exist as finite deposits in the Earth's crust which do not get replenished. Resources that get depleted by use. For example fossil fuels.

88. **Opportunity Cost:** The sacrifice of some good or service made because of a decision to acquire some other good or service.
89. **Optimum Pollution:** Optimum pollution, in economics, refers to the level of pollution where total costs of pollution is the least. It refers to the level of pollution where marginal pollution damage cost is equal to the marginal pollution abatement cost.
90. **Pareto Optimum:** Pareto optimum is a situation in which it is not possible to make any individual better off, through changes in production or consumption activities of firms and households respectively, without making at least another individual worse off.
91. **Physical Damage Function:** It refers to the relationship between changes in the ambient environmental quality and physical effects on health, materials and productivity.
92. **Pollution:** Pollution is the introduction of contaminants into the environment resulting in adverse impacts on the health of human beings, flora and fauna and on properties.
93. **Polluter Pays Principle:** The Polluter Pays Principle (PPP) was first clearly formulated by the OECD Secretariat in 1972. It states that whoever is responsible for damage to the environment should bear the costs associated with it.
94. **Precautionary Principle:** The Precautionary Principle states that whenever there is risk of severe damage to humans and/or the environment, absence of scientific conclusive proof is not a reason for inaction. It is a better- safe – than – sorry approach, in contrast to the traditional wait and watch approach to environmental protection.
95. **Private Costs:** A firm's cost of production—a cost that excludes external costs.
96. **Private Goods:** Goods for which the consumption of a unit by one person precludes the consumption of that same unit by another person.
97. **PROPER:** PROPER is Indonesia's Programme for Pollution Control Evaluation and Rating, used public disclosure, environmental awards and reputational incentives for motivating the manufacturing firms to be more environmentally conscious. PROPER rates factories on the basis their compliance with national standards for waste water discharge
98. **Public Goods**: Goods for which two or more individuals can consume the same unit at the same time and not reduce its availability to others.
99. **pH**: A scale use to designate the acidity or alkalinity of solutions or soil. pH=7 is neutral. Value of pH<7, reflects acidic nature of the solution. Value of pH>7 indicate increasing basicity.
100. **Ramsar Convention:** The Ramsar Convention, the **Convention on Wetlands of International Importance,** adopted in the Iranian city of Ramsar in 1971, came into force in 1975. The Convention arose out of the concern about the increasing loss and degradation of wetland habitats for migratory water birds. The Convention's mission is "conservation and wise use of all wetlands through local, regional and national actions and international cooperation, as a contribution towards achieving sustainable development throughout the world.. As of 2017, 169 states are Parties to the Convention and 2279 sites are included in a "Ramsar List of Wetlands of International Importance".
101. **RECLAIM:** RECLAIM (Regional Clean Air Incentives Market) is the world's first comprehensive emissions market programme for reducing air pollution. It is a "cap and trade" permits program implemented in the Los Angeles River Basin in the US to reduce emissions of SO_X and NO_X annually by the amounts necessary to achieve the AQMP (Air Quality Management Plan) targets: to reduce SO_2 emissions by 75% and NO_2 emissions by 60% by 2003.
102. **Reclamation**: The restoration of land, water or waste materials to usefulness through methods like land filling, waste water treatment and materials recovery.
103. **Recycling**: Converting solid wastes into new products by using the resources contained in discarded materials.
104. **Refuse:** A term generally used for all solid wastes.
105. **Renewable Resource :** Resources which may be replenished by natural cycles. Resources that may be used without depletion. For example solar energy.
106. **The Rio Summit:** the Rio Summit, also known as the U N Conference of Environment and Development (UNCED), popularly known as the Earth Summit was held in Brazil's Rio de Janeirio in 1992 . The two major outcomes of the Earth Summit were: the Rio Declaration and the Agenda 21. The Rio declaration called for global partnership to conserve, protect and restore the health and integrity of the Earth's ecosystem. The Agenda 21 is an action plan to achieve sustainable development.

107. Stockholm Conference: The Stockholm Conference, known as the United Nations Conference on the Human Environment was held in Stockholm, Sweden, from June 5–16 in 1972.It was the UN's first major conference on international environmental issues, and marked a turning point in the development of international environmental politics. The Stockholm Conference was a landmark in the history of environmental movement by giving the peoples group greater involvement in discussion

108. Shallow Ecology: Shallow Ecology is an environmental Philosophy which assumes that human beings are the central species in the Earth's ecosystem, and that other beings and parts of systems are resources for human use, and of less importance or value. Shallow ecology is anthropocentric and accepts that nature may be harnessed to meet human needs and ends.

109. Sludge: Any solid, semi-solid or liquid waste generated from a municipal, commercial or industrial waste water treatment plant.

110. Smog: A mixture of fog and smoke.

111. Social Cost: Sum of private cost and external cost.

112. Sustainable Development: Sustainable development is defined as the development that meets the needs of the present generation without compromising the ability of the future generation to meet their needs.

113. Sustainable Industrialisation: Sustainable industrialisation requires integrating environmental considerations at every stage of decision-making in the supply chain of the product, from resource extraction to disposal of the product

114. Total Benefits of Pollution Control (TBC) : The reduction in all environmental damages as pollution is controlled.

115. Total Costs of Pollution Control (TCC): The value to society of all resources used to control pollution.

116. Total Net Benefit: Difference between TCC and TBC.

117. Tradable Discharge Permit: Tradable Discharge Permit is a market based pollution control policy instrument. Tradable permits work by addressing the *property rights* problem. Permits give a firm a property right to emit a certain level of a pollutant. Thus the approach is based on the allocation of property rights and the creation of a market that did not exist earlier.

118. **Tragedy of Commons:** "The Tragedy of the Commons" is a term used to describe what happens to common resources as a result of human greed. It was first coined in an article in *Science* in 1968 by Garrett Hardin. It refers to a situation in which the self- dominated rational acts of human beings can destroy a common resource.

119. Urbanisation: Re-distribution of population from rural to urban areas.

120. Urban Sprawl: Developing suburban communities or new urban communities away from city, outward or horizontal expansion of urban areas.

121. Urban Renewal : Renewal of life in urban areas suffering from neglect and decay due to industrialisation, technological factors and other such factors, through measures like slum clearance, construction of new houses etc.

REFERENCES – WEBSITES

SECTION 1

http://www.tutorvista.com/content/biology/biology-iv/ecosystem/ecosystem-components.php

http://web.ead.anl.gov/ecorisk/fundamentals/pdf/ecofund.pdf

http://www.globalchange.umich.edu/globalchange1/current/lectures/kling/ecosystem/ecosystem.

http://www.globalchange.umich.edu/globalchange1/current/lectures/kling/ecosystem/ecosystem.

http://ecosystem.pollutionsitesite.com/permalink.php?article=Rainforest+Ecosystem.txt

http://darwin.bio.uci.edu/~sustain/issueguides/TimberCert/forestfunc.html

http://darwin.bio.uci.edu/sustain/global/sensem/S98/Ohara/EnvEthics.html

http://www.indiaonline.in/About/Profile/Geography/Wet-Lands/index.html

http://www.wwfenvis.nic.in/pdf/land.pdf

http://www.millenniumassessment.org/documents/document.300.aspx.pdf. http://www.millenniumassessment.org/documents/document.353.aspx.pdf. http://en.wikipedia.org/wiki/Ecosystem_services.

http://www.millenniumassessment.org/documents/document.299.aspx.pdf. http://www.tropical-rainforest-animals.com/Environmental-Pollution.html

http://www.ejfoundation.org/pdf/tsunami_report.pdf

https://www.nap.edu/read/11139/chapter/4#35

http://earthobservatory.nasa.gov/Features/WorldOfChange/aral_sea.php

http://visearth.ucsd.edu/VisE_Int/aralsea/index.html

http://unimaps.com/aral-sea/index.html

http://www.columbia.edu/~tmt2120/introduction.htm

http://www.dailymail.co.uk/news/article-1263516/How-Aral-Sea--half-size-England--dried-up.html

http://www.nato.int/science/publication/pdf/water-e.pdf

http://www.jcu.edu.au/jrtph/vol/v01whish.pdf

http://www.mpsaz.org/stapley/staff/dsbloom/study_guides/files/ecology_picture_vocab_study_guide.pdf

http://welkerswikinomics.com/blog/2012/01/11/the-tragedy-of-the-commons-as-a-market-failure/

http://www.eoearth.org/article/The_Economics_of_the_Coming_Spaceship_Earth_(historical)

https://www.goodreads.com/book/show/1675564.Respect_for_Nature

http://www.panarchy.org/boulding/spaceship.1966.htmlhttp://en.wikipedia.org/wiki/Deep_ecology

http://www.gutenberg.org/etext/11238

http://www.iep.utm.edu/envi-eth/

http://www.schumachercollege.org.uk/learning-resources/from-gaia-theory-to-deep-ecology

http://plato.stanford.edu/archives/fall2011/entries/ethics-environment

https://plato.stanford.edu/entries/ethics-environmental/

http://www.sustainablescotland.com/general/the-simple-life-environmental-ethics

http://gadfly.igc.org/e-ethics/ee-topic.htm

http://cw.routledge.com/textbooks/9780415366311/resources/chapter15.pdf

http://www.gaiatheory.org/synopsis.htm

http://www.gaiatheory.org/overview/

http://www.bibliotecapleyades.net/gaia/esp_gaia01.htm

http://www.mrgscience.com/uploads/2/0/7/9/20796234/intrinsic_value_article.pdf

http://www.school-portal.co.uk/GroupDownloadFile.asp?ResourceId=3989568

http://environment-ecology.com/deep-ecology/63-deep-ecology.html

https://learn.saylor.org/mod/page/view.php?id=8353

http://conferinta.management.ase.ro/archives/2014/pdf/81.pdf

http://www.animalethics.org.uk/deep-ecology.html

http://www.env-ethics.com/en/html/92/e-book/
http://www.aeseonline.org/aeseonline.org/Ecology_and_Ethics.html
http://www.austlii.edu.au/au/journals/MqJlICEnvLaw/2005/4.html
http://en.wikipedia.org/wiki/Paul_R._Ehrlich
http://en.wikipedia.org/wiki/Barry_Commoner
http://www.britannica.com/EBchecked/topic/189205/environmentalism>.
Ecology, Global network, http://ecology.com/featuresarchive/henrydavidthoreau/, site accessed on 28.08.09
http://www.ecology.com/
http://en.wikipedia.org/wiki/John_Muir
http://en.wikipedia.org/wiki/Aldo_Leopold accessed
http://www.uh.edu/engines/epi595.htm accessed
http://en.wikipedia.org/wiki/Gifford_Pinchot accessed
http://www.edwardgoldsmith.com/
http://www.iph.ufrgs.br/posgrad/disciplinas/hidp04/Boulding,
%20The%20Economics%20of%20Spaceship%20Earth.PDF
http://nilesema.com/nuclearradio.htm
http://chernobyl486.tripod.com/
http://www.earthmind.net/earthmind/docs/boulding-1965.pdf
http://www.earthmind.net/earthmind/docs/boulding-1966.pdf
http://www.earthmind.net/sustainability.htm
http://www.myhero.com/myhero/hero.asp?hero=c_mendes
http://www.shvoong.com/social-sciences/sociology/1677251-tragedy-commons/
http://www.theecologist.info/page34.html
http://en.wikipedia.org/wiki/Small_Is_Beautiful
http://june2008.unric.org/index2.php?option=com_content&do_pdf=1&id=227
28 http://www.pacificislandtravel.com/south_america/brazil/about_destin/nature.html
http://www.cook.rutgers.edu/~humeco/COURSES/GMCLASSES/GLOBAL/TRANSPARE/WEEK9AND10_FOREST/CHICOMENDEZ_CASESTUDY.DOC
http://ecovista.wordpress.com/2007/09/28/emergence-of-environmental-movements-in-indiaan-analysis/.
http://en.wikipedia.org/wiki/Kyoto_Protocol
http://www.berr.gov.uk/whatwedo/sectors/ccpo/kyotoprotocol/page20655.html
http://www1.american.edu/TED/ice/ogonioil.htm
http://fading-hope.blog-city.com/shellbp.htm
http://iimk.ac.in/gsdl/cgi-bin/library?e=d-000-00---0econom--00-0-0--0prompt-10---4------0-0l--1-en-50---20-about---00031-001-1-0utfZz-8-00&cl=CL2&d=HASH01cd404093e5e58a37ea7f10.3&x=1
http://www.humansandnature.org/aldo-leopold-reconciling-ecology-and-economics
https://www.linkedin.com/pulse/ethics-environment-focus-aldo-leopolds-land-ethic-lisa-andrews
https://www.world-religion-watch.org/index.php/book-reviews-on-relevant-religious-and-cultural-issues/178-nature-by-ralph-waldo-emerson-transcendentalism-at-the-core-of-american-identity
Thoreau's Environmental Ethics in Walden (PDF Download Available). Available from: https://www.researchgate.net/publication/241078795_Thoreau%27s_Environmental_Ethics_in_Walden
http://www.nytimes.com/2012/09/23/magazine/how-silent-spring-ignited-the-environmental-movement.html
https://www.nrdc.org/stories/story-silent-spring
https://www.thenation.com/article/remembering-barry-commoner/
http://www.elearnportal.com/courses/science/environmental-science/environmental-science-history-of-the-modern-environmental-movement#sthash.COsN10rS.dpuf
http://www.edwardgoldsmith.org/1128/
https://www.theguardian.com/environment/2016/dec/23/john-vidal-environment-editor-greatest-job-on-earth?CMP=Share_AndroidApp_Tweet
http://www.lenntech.com/environmental-disasters.htm#1._Bhopal:_the_Union_Carbide_gas_leak
http://www.lenntech.com/environmental-disasters.htm#2._Chernobyl:_Russias_nuclear_power_plant_explosion
http://www.lenntech.com/environmental-disasters.htm#3._Seveso:_Italys_dioxin_crisis
http://www.yesmagazine.org/issues/media-that-set-us-free/the-green-belt-movement-the-story-of-wangari-maathai

http://www.garretthardinsociety.org/articles/art_tragedy_of_the_commons.html
http://www.investopedia.com/terms/t/tragedy-of-the-commons.asp
http://www.ecofriends.org/main/eganga/images/Critical%20analysis%20of%20GAP.pdf
http://reli350.vassar.edu/gosselin/gangatoday.html
http://www.apnauttarakhand.com/chipko-movement/
http://edugreen.teri.res.in/explore/forestry/chipko.htm
http://www.iisd.org/50comm/commdb/desc/d07.htm
http://www.ecoindia.com/education/chipko-movement.html
http://www.greenbeltmovement.org/who-we-are/our-history
http://en.wikipedia.org/wiki/Green_Belt_Movement
http://www.care2.com/causes/how-the-green-belt-movement-in-kenya-fights-climate-change.html#ixzz22IvsbQ6J
http://www.womenaid.org/press/info/development/greenbeltproject.html
http://www.greenbeltmovement.org/who-we-are/our-history
http://www.yesmagazine.org/issues/media-that-set-us-free/the-green-belt-movement-the-story-of-wangari-maathai
http://unesdoc.unesco.org/images/0023/002301/230122e.pdf
http://chingaree.blogspot.in/2011/10/narmada-bachao-andolan-analysis.html
http://chingaree.blogspot.in/2011/10/narmada-bachao-aandolan-case-study.html*http://www.geocities.com/CapitolHill/6027/Narmada.html*
http://www.ecoindia.com/education/narmada-bachao-andolan.htmlwww.egyankosh.ac.in/bitstream/123456789/33151/1/Unit16.pdf
http://www.myhero.com/go/hero.asp?hero=c_mendes
http://www.chicomendes.com/
http://library.thinkquest.org/26026/People/chico_mendes.html
http://greenliving.about.com/od/greenprograms/a/Rainforest-Activist-Chico-Mendes.htm
https://ratical.org/corporations/OgoniFactS.html
https://www.theguardian.com/commentisfree/2015/nov/10/ken-saro-wiwa-father-nigeria-ogoniland-oil-pollution
http://stream.aljazeera.com/story/ogoni-vs-oil-giant-shell-0022089
https://www.controllingpollution.com/forest-ecosystem/
http://sherinrafi.blogspot.com/2011/05/forest-ecosystem.html?m=0
https://www.huffingtonpost.com/peter-dreier/barry-commoner-dead_b_1928377.html (The Blog – Peter Dreier, updated Dec 2012.)

SECTION 2

http://csep10.phys.utk.edu/astr161/lect/earth/atmosphere.html
http://library.thinkquest.org/CR0215471/acid_rain.htm
http://www.edu.pe.ca/gulfshore/Archives/ACIDSBAS/scipage.htm
http://geography.about.com/od/globalproblemsandissues/a/acidrain.htm
http://www.epa.gov/apti/course422/ap7a.html
http://www.tropical-rainforest-animals.com/Air-Pollutants.html
http://coe.mse.ac.in/taj.htm
http://www1.american.edu/TED/taj.htm
http://www.4to40.com/Qa/index.asp?id=3002
http://en.citizendium.org/wiki/Taj_Mahal#The_Taj_today_and_its_future
www.unesco.org/courier/2000_07/uk/signe.htm
http://www.nlsenlaw.org/air-noise/case-laws/supreme-court/m-c-mehta-v-union-of-india-air-1997-sc-734/
http://www.rrcap.unep.org/male/baseline/Baseline/India/INCH4.htm
http://www1.american.edu/ted/bhopal.htm
http://www.hu.mtu.edu/hu_dept/tc@mtu/papers/bhopal.htm
http://www.icmrindia.org/casestudies/catalogue/Business%20Ethics/BECG009.htm
Moral Inquiry by White Ronald F., Ph.D. Professor of Philosophy College of Mount St. Joseph downloaded from the site: http://faculty.msj.edu/whiter/ETHICSBOOK.pdf
http://en.wikipedia.org/wiki/Bhopal_disaster
http://cpcbenvis.nic.in/ar2000/annual_report1999-2000-try2.htm
http://corbettfoundation.org/Water_contents.pdf

http://www.fao.org/docrep/W2598E/w2598e04.htm
http://www.safewater.org/PDFS/resourcesknowthefacts/Oil_Spills.pdf
http://www.tutorvista.com/content/biology/biology-iv/environmental-pollution/water-pollution-effects.php
http://cbcs.km.nccu.edu.tw/xms/read_attach.php?id=232 http://www.env.go.jp/en/chemi/hs/minamata2002/
http://rarediseases.about.com/od/rarediseases1/a/102304.htm
http://www.soshisha.org/english/10tishiki_e/10chisiki_3_e.pdf
http://www.lenntech.com/electrodialysis.htm#ixzz1uSTo12qB
http://www.fibre2fashion.com/industry-article/9/840/effluent-treatments-coagulation1.asp
http://www.lenntech.com/water_reuse_food_industry.htm#ixzz1uSyWL4c7
http://www.indiatogether.org/environment/articles/wastefact.htm
http://www.devalt.org/newsletter/jun04/lead.htm
http://edugreen.teri.res.in/explore/solwaste/types.htm
http://www.actionbioscience.org/environment/hinrichsen_robey.html
http://sovereignty.net/p/gov/rise/g_part12.html
http://www.mumbaisuburbs.com/articles/ngo-environmental-conservation.html
http://www.seas.columbia.edu/earth/wtert/sofos/Sustainable%20Solid%20Waste%20Management%20in%20India_Final.pdf
http://www.wgea.org/media/2905/eng04pu_guidewaste.pdf
http://edugreen.teri.res.in/explore/ngos.htm
www.chennaicoproration.com
http://envis.maharashtra.gov.in/envis_data/newsletter/msw/mswgeneration.html
http://www.nswai.com/waste-municipal-solid-waste.php
http://www.unep.or.jp/ietc/publications/spc/solid_waste_management/Vol_I/5_6- Part1_Section-chapter1.pdf
http://www.cpcb.nic.in.
www.tn.gov.in/cma/swm_in_**india**.pdf
www.sandracointreau.com/CointreauComplexitiesandChallenges.ppt
http://sovereignty.net/p/gov/rise/g_part06.html
http://www.prb.org/Publications/Lesson-Plans/HumanPopulation/PopulationGrowth.aspx
http://news.nationalgeographic.com/news/2014/09/140920-population-11billion-demographics-anthropocene/
http://www.footprintnetwork.org
http://www.21stcentech.com/human-population-update-carrying-capacity-planet-earth/
http://science.jrank.org/pages/1244/Carrying-Capacity.html
http://www.in-iwla.org/waltonian/fall2001-5.htm
http://www.sustainablescale.org/ConceptualFramework/UnderstandingScale/MeasuringScale/CarryingCapacity.aspx
http://www.sustainabilityed.org/pages/example2-2.htm)
http://www.sierraclub.org/population
http://www.globalissues.org/article/214/stress-on-the-environment-society-and-resources
https://na.unep.net/geas/archive/pdfs/geas_jun_12_carrying_capacity.pdf
http://www.ncbi.nlm.nih.gov/pmc/aAnnAticles/PMC2792934/
http://www.ncbi.nlm.nih.gov/pmc/articles/PMC1891640/
http://journalistsresource.org/studies/environment/cities/economic-growth-developing-world-cities-benefits-urban-clustering#sthash.axkMDTgn.dpuf
http://www.igbp.net/news/features/features/urbanairpollutionanewlookatanoldproblem.5.19895cff13e9f675e253f0.html
http://asiancenturyinstitute.com/development/224-urbanization-and-slums-in-asia
http://www.business-standard.com/article/opinion/shankar-acharya-india-s-urbanisation-challenge-114050701457_1.html
http://www.nature.com/news/environment-waste-production-must-peak-this-century-1.14032
http://www.epj-conferences.org
http://www.epj-conferences.org/articles/epjconf/abs/2015/17/epjconf_eps-sif_01001/epjconf_eps-sif_01001.html
http://www.ei.lehigh.edu/learners/energy/impacts1.html
http://www.economicsdiscussion.net/notes/conventional-and-non-conventional-sources-of-energy/2177
http://www.ces.iisc.ernet.in/energy/paper/alternative/classification.html
https://energy4me.org/all-about-energy/sustainability/environmental-impact-by-source/
http://www.bp.com/content/dam/bp/pdf/energy-economics/statistical-review-2015/bp-statistical-review-of-world-energy-2015-full-report.pdf

http://www.epj-conferences.org/articles/epjconf/pdf/2015/17/epjconf_eps-sif_01001.pdf
http://www.leonardo-energy.org/blog/sustainable-energy-definitions-focus-and-social-dimension
http://environ.andrew.cmu.edu/m3/s3/09fossil.shtml
http://ifs.nic.in/Dynamic/misc/apfisn/apfisn2005.pdf
http://www.nucleartourist.com/basics/reasons1.htm
https://saferenvironment.wordpress.com/2008/08/18/effects-of-envedugreenironmental-degradation/
http://www.ipcc.ch/pdf/assessment-report/ar4/wg3/ar4-wg3-chapter10.pdf
www.sandracointreau.com/CointreauComplexitiesandChallenges.ppt
http://www.unep.or.jp/ietc/publications/spc/solid_waste_management/Vol_I/5_6-Part1_Section-chapter1.pdf
http://urbanindia.nic.in/publicinfo/swm/chap2.pdf
http://www.sustainabilityed.org/pages/example2-2.htm
http://viso.ei.jrc.it/iwmlca/
http://davidsisler.com/07-01-2001.htm www.hu.mtu.edu/hu_dept/tc
https://climatism.wordpress.com/2014/01/13/shock-news-heat-island-effect-warms-temperature-data/
http://ilmastotyokalut.fi/kaupungin-lampotilaerot/mika-on-lamposaareke/urban-climate-research-in-the-city-of-turku/
https://sustainabledevelopment.un.org/content/documents/2539journal.pone.0023777.pdf
http://urban.yale.edu/research/theme-4
https://ourworldindata.org/world-population-growth/
https://www.wilsoncenter.org/sites/default/files/Report6-1.pdf
http://www.rand.org/pubs/research_briefs/RB5045.html
http://www.actionbioscience.org/environment/hinrichsen_robey.html
http://www.prb.org/Publications/Lesson-Plans/HumanPopulation/PopulationGrowth.aspx
http://news.nationalgeographic.com/news/2014/09/140920-population-11billion-demographics-anthropocene/
from http://ourworldindata.org/data/population-growth-vital-statistics/world-population-growth/[onlineresource]
http://www.footprintnetwork.org
http://www.21stcentech.com/human-population-update-carrying-capacity-planet-earth/
http://science.jrank.org/pages/1244/Carrying-Capacity.html
http://www.in-iwla.org/waltonian/fall2001-5.htm
http://www.sustainablescale.org/ConceptualFramework/UnderstandingScale/MeasuringScale/CarryingCapacity.aspx
http://www.sierraclub.org/population
http://www.globalissues.org/article/214/stress-on-the-environment-society-and-resources
https://na.unep.net/geas/archive/pdfs/geas_jun_12_carrying_capacity.pdf
http://www.ncbi.nlm.nih.gov/pmc/articles/PMC2792934/
http://www.peopleandtheplanet.com/index.html@lid=26385§ion=38&topic=44.html
https://www.newscientist.com/article/mg22430005-200-mangrove-forest-planted-as-tsunami-shield/
https://na.unep.net/geas/archive/pdfs/geas_jun_12_carrying_capacity.pdf
http://urban.yale.edu/research/theme-4.
http://www.nature.com/news/environment-waste-production-must-peak-this-century-1.14032
http://www.ncbi.nlm.nih.gov/pmc/articles/PMC1891640/
http://journalistsresource.org/studies/environment/cities/economic-growth-developing-world-cities-benefits-urban-clustering#sthash.axkMDTgn.dpuf
http://www.hindustantimes.com/india/urbanisation-in-india-faster-than-rest-of-the-world/story-IdmQ4BSqxEZe874AprzfnL.html
http://dish.andrewsullivan.com/2013/11/01/hitting-peak-garbage/
http://www.livemint.com/Politics/XsXf3cmvKjaoHPnlo31Y0H/South-Asia-to-become-fastest-waste-producer-by-2025.html
http://urban.yale.edu/research/theme-4
http://www.business-standard.com/article/opinion/shankar-acharya-india-s-urbanisation-challenge-114050701457_1.html
https://www.iea.org/publications/freepublications/publication/WEO2015 Special Reporton Energy and ClimateChange.pdf http://www.epj-conferences.org
http://www.epj-conferences.org/articles/epjconf/abs/2015/17/epjconf_eps-sif_01001/epjconf_eps-sif_01001.html
http://www.demographia.com/db-worldua.pdf
http://www.ei.lehigh.edu/learners/energy/impacts1.html
http://www.economicsdiscussion.net/notes/conventional-and-non-conventional-sources-of-energy/2177

http://www.ces.iisc.ernet.in/energy/paper/alternative/classification.html

https://energy4me.org/all-about-energy/sustainability/environmental-impact-by-source/

http://www.bp.com/content/dam/bp/pdf/energy-economics/statistical-review-2015/bp-statistical-review-of-world-energy-2015-full-report.pdf

http://www.epj-conferences.org/articles/epjconf/pdf/2015/17/epjconf_eps-sif_01001.pdf

http://www.leonardo-energy.org/blog/sustainable-energy-definitions-focus-and-social-dimension

http://environ.andrew.cmu.edu/m3/s3/09fossil.shtml

http://www.mnn.com/earth-matters/wilderness-resources/blogs/21-reasons-why-forests-are-important

http://ifs.nic.in/Dynamic/misc/apfisn/apfisn2005.pdf

http://www.amosweb.com/cgi-bin/awb_nav.pl?s=wpd&c=dsp&k=market+failures

https://saferenvironment.wordpress.com/2008/08/18/effects-of-environmental-degradation/

http://ihttp://indiasendangered.com/facts-you-did-not-know-about-biodiversity-of-india/ndiasendangered.com/facts-you-did-not-know-about-biodiversity-of-india/

http://www.bagheera.com/inthewild/ext_dodobird.htm

Hinrichsen Don and Bryant Robey,2000. Population and the Environment:The Global Challenge. Accessed via: http://www.actionbioscience.org/environment/hinrichsen_robey.html . (October , 2017

https://www.ipcc.ch/publications_and_data/ar4/syr/en/spms5.html

Dennis Dimic on, " As World's Population Booms, Will Its Resources be Enough for Us? (2014) Downloaded from: https://news.nationalgeographic.com/news/2014/09/140920-population-11billion-demographics-anthropocene/ (Accessed in December 2017) .

www.worldenergy.org

http://www.worldenergy.org/publications/2013/world-energy-resources-2013-survey

http://www.worldenergy.org/publications/2013/world-energy-resources-2013-survey

http://www.worldenergy.org/publications/2013/world-energy-resources-2013-survey

SECTION 3 Economic Development and Environmental Quality

http://www.unece.org/fileadmin/DAM/ead/pub/032/032_c2.pdf

http://www.edwardgoldsmith.org/1125/introduction-the-need-for-change/

http://geog.utm.utoronto.ca/ecofootprint/efbackground.html

http://coe.mse.ac.in/dp/Paper%2017.pdf

http://data.footprintnetwork.org/

http://www.precaution.org/lib/06/econ_growth_and_carrying_capacity.pdf

http://www.ktu.lt/lt/mokslas/zurnalai/inzeko/57/1392-2758-2008-2-57-15.pdf

http://www.ceepa.co.za/docs/PolicyApplicationsofEnvAcct-WB2003.pdf

http://ndctws.org/newsletters/2004-2-may.pdf.

http://www.footprintnetwork.org/en/index.php/GFN/page/footprint_for_cities/

http://www.mnforsustain.org/meadows_limits_to_growth_30_year_update_2004.htm

http://www.eoearth.org/article/Macroeconomics_and_the_environment

http://www.eoearth.org/article/Environmental_dimensions_of_macroeconomic_measurement

faculty.washington.edu/…dy/SciencePolicy/**Growth**.rtf

http://donellameadows.org/archives/a-synopsis-limits-to-growth-the-30-year-update/

http://isecoeco.org/pdf/stern.pdf

http://media.hoover.org/sites/default/files/documents/0817944826_83.pdf

http://steadystate.org/wp-content/uploads/Stern_KuznetsCurve.pdf

http://www.unece.org/fileadmin/DAM/cad/sem/sem2003/papers/panayotou.pdt

http://www.cid.harvard.edu/archive/esd/pdfs/iep/643.pdf http://www.macalester.edu/~wests/econ231/yandleetal.pdf

ftp://131.252.97.79/Transfer/ES_Pubs/ESVal/EnviroKuznetCurve/unruh_kuznetandabruptchange_1998_ecolecon_v25_p221.pdf

http://documents.worldbank.org/curated/en/1992/06/699664/economic-growth-environmental-quality-time-series-cross-country-evidence

http://citeseerx.ist.psu.edu/viewdoc/download;jsessionid=A69006A651F8C1E69DB12766B2A931A2?doi=10.1.1.595.2879&rep=rep1&type=pdf

http://citeseerx.ist.psu.edu/viewdoc/download?doi=10.1.1.495.6098&rep=rep1&type=pdf
http://www.wseas.us/e-library/conferences/2011/Angers/ELA/ELA-01.pdf
http://gredi.recherche.usherbrooke.ca/wpapers/GREDI-0703.pdf
http://web.econ.ku.dk/nguyen/teaching/Grossman%20and%20Krueger%201995.pdf
www.AtKisson.com.
http://www.eeeee.net/sd_manifesto.htm
http://www.uvm.edu/~jashman/CDAE195_ESCI375/What_is_Sustainable_Development.html
http://bioscience.oxfordjournals.org/content/62/3/251.full
https://tonystoneblog.wordpress.com/2012/11/10/models-of-development-tony-stone/

SECTION 4 Welfare Foundations of Environmental Economics

http://www.amosweb.com/cgi-bin/awb_nav.pl?s=wpd&c=dsp&k=market+failures
http://www.tutorsonnet.com/kaldor-hicks-compensation-criteria-homework-help.php
http://www.economicsdiscussion.net/welfare-economics/criterion-of-welfare-with-diagram/18937
http://www.yourarticlelibrary.com/economics/new-welfare-economics-compensation-principle-with-diagram/37588/
http://christpgmicro1.blogspot.in/2007/11/module-6-welfare-economics.html

SECTION 5 ENVIRONMENTAL ECONOMICS

http://www.all-recycling-facts.com/recycling-statistics.html#ixzz4KFOsMffw
https://perfectrubbermulch.com/blog/u-s-recycling-compare-rest-world-infographic-2/
http://samples.sainsburysebooks.co.uk/9781135036621_sample_529192.pdf
http://coe.mse.ac.in/dp/DISSEMINATION%20PAPER%20-%2022.pdf.
http://www.supersystems.in/bank/accounting3.htm
http://articles.economictimes.indiatimes.com/2009-06-11/news/27645573_1_natural-resources-national-income-green-gdp
http://dx.doi.org/10.1787/9789264060265-en
http://www.globalization101.org/the-tuna-dolphin-case/
http://www.globalization101.org/are-international-trade-and-protection-of-the-environment-enemies/
http://www.iisd.ca/process/chemical_management-baselintro.html
http://www.basel.int/theconvention/overview/tabid/1271/default.aspx
http://www.mfa.gov.tr/basel-convention-on-the-control-of-transboundary-movements-of-hazardous-wastes-and-their-disposal.en.mfa
https://www.cbd.int/intro/default.shtml
https://www.cbd.int/history/
https://www.cbd.int/abs/about/default.shtml
https://www.cbd.int/abs/
http://www.iisd.ca/process/climate_atm-fccintro.html
http://www.unido.org/resources.html
http://www.unido.org/what-we-do/environment/capacity-building-for-the-implementation-of-multilateral-environmental-agreements/the-stockholm-convention.html
https://www.epa.gov/international-cooperation/minamata-convention-mercury
https://www.britannica.com/topic/General-Agreement-on-Tariffs-and-Trade
https://www.wto.org/english/tratop_e/envir_e/issu3_e.htm
http://repiica.iica.int/docs/B0733i/B0733i.pdf
http://www.wto.org/english/tratop_e/envir_e/envir_e.htm
http://www.iisd.ca/process/chemical_management-picintro.html
http://ase.tufts.edu/gdae.
http://www.apec.org.au/docs/oxley2001.pdf
http://unep.ch/etb/areas/pdf/MEA%20Papers/TradeRelated_MeasuresPaper.pdf
http://www.oecd- org/docserver/download/0109121e.pdf?expires=1474724318&id=id&accname=guest&checksum=DB993C1B5EF4CCA08493DFEF9C76CD46

SECTION 6

http://www.envfor.nic.in/divisions/cltech/ac.htm
http://www.un.org/documents/ga/conf151/aconf15126-1annex1.htm
http://nptel.ac.in/courses/Webcourse-contents/IIT- delhi/environment%20and%20ecology/mod4/mod4_4.htm

http://www.pattfoundation.org/10-interesting-pollution-facts/#sthash.9pIhOZk4.dpuf
http://coin.wne.uw.edu.pl/tzylicz/irere-www.pdf
http://www.thestatesman.com/mobi/news/marquee/making-the-polluter-pay/103254.html#Eju3SHAdmsh6SjtX.99
http://www.legalservicesindia.com/article/article/fundamental-principles-of-environmental-protection-755-1.html
http://www.ejolt.org/2013/05/polluter-pays-principle/
http://ec.europa.eu/environment/legal/law/pdf/principles/2%20Polluter%20Pays%20Principle_revised.pdf
http://paralyzingprecautionprinciple.com/problems-with-the-precautionary-principle.html
www.unescap.org/drpad/publication/dp21_1990/dp21_vi.PDF -
http://www.unep.org/documents.multilingual/default.asp?documentid=78&articleid=1163
http://chemicalspolicy.org/downloads/Issue%20Report%20No%2022.pdf
http://www.psrast.org/precaut2.htm
http://classes.maxwell.syr.edu/ppa777/lectures/envlct6.html
http://classes.maxwell.syr.edu/pai777/lectures/envlct5.html
http://www.treasury.govt.nz/publications/research-policy/wp/2003/03-02/09.htm
http://www.heritage.org/Research/Lecture/The-Perils-of-the-Precautionary-Principle-Lessons-from-the-American-and-European-Experience
http://documents.worldbank.org/curated/en/421701468772781985/pdf/multi-page.pdf
http://www.un-documents.net/a21-08.htm
http://acts.oecd.org/Instruments/ShowInstrumentView.aspx?InstrumentID=41&InstrumentPID=38&Lang=en
http://www.iisd.ca/consume/skou.html
https://books.google.co.in/books?id=G3fsAgAAQBAJ&pg=PA7&lpg=PA7&dq=Applying+economic+instruments&source=bl&ots=jauYbodI6v&sig=Kl2i_JrFUkmDAUw4Ex3Fi0F-Gyo&hl=en&sa=X&ved=0ahUKEwj4rrKwl8bPAhXBP48KHcBIBug4ChDoAQgsMAQ#v=onepage&q=Applying%20economic%20instruments&f=false
www.carbontradewatch.org
http://www.statensnet.dk/pligtarkiv/fremvis.pl?vaerkid=4973&reprid=0&filid=32&iarkiv=1
http://documents.worldbank.org/curated/en/770561468038722316/Indonesias-program-for-pollution-control-evaluation-and-rating-PROPER
http://www.env.go.jp/earth/coop/oemjc/ind/e/indonee2.pdf
http://erb.umich.edu/News-and-Events/news-events-docs/11-12/eco-labels2011/JorgeGarciaLopez.pdf
aep.alberta.ca/.../documents/Emissions_Effluent_Trading.pdf
http://www.aqmd.gov/search?q=RECLAIm
http://www.sustainabilitydictionary.com/pollution-offset/
http://www.forest-trends.org/documents/files/doc_541.pdf
https://www.epa.gov/cwa-404/mitigation-banking-factsheet
http://carboncreditnetwork.org/carbon-trading
http://www.ecospecifier.com.au/knowledge-green/technical-guides/technical-guide-9-introduction-to-ecolabels-and-environmental-product-declarations.aspx
http://www.iso.org/iso/iso14000
http://www.horizons.gc.ca/eng/content/feature-article-voluntary-approaches-environmental-policy
http://www.neuralenergy.info/2011/06/carbon-offsets.html
http://erblegacy.snre.umich.edu/News-and-Events/news-events-docs/11-12/eco-labels2011/JorgeGarciaLopez.pdf
https://www.commdev.org/userfiles/files/1428_file_RFF_2DDP_2D04_2D34.pdf

SECTION 7

http://www.sjsu.edu/faculty/watkins/cba.htm
http://www.ejolt.org/2012/12/cost-benefit-analysis-cba/
http://cals.arizona.edu/classes/rnr485/ch1.htm
www.sljol.info/index.php/JEPSL/article/view/5144
http://www.rri.wvu.edu/WebBook/garrett/chapterfive.htm
www.oecd.org/environment/tools-evaluation/36190261.pdf
http://www.oecd-ilibrary.org/content/book/9789264010055-en
https://cals.arizona.edu/classes/rnr485/title.htm
https://www.nap.edu/read/11139/chapter/6
http://www.fao.org/docrep/003/X8955E/x8955e03.htm

https://www.environment.gov.au/resource/techniques-value-environmental-resources-introductory-handbook
https://wiwi.uni-kl.de/fileadmin/wiwi.uni-kl.de/downloads_pdf_doc/blank/umwelt/envecon_01.pdf
https://www.nap.edu/read/11139/chapter/6
http://www.fao.org/docrep/V8350E/v8350e08.htm#final report environmental impact statement
http://www.ece.ubc.ca/~leos/pdf/a230/notes/t2/EIA.pdf
http://www.cseindia.org/node/383
http://eia.unu.edu/course/index.html%3Fpage_id=102.html
http://arthapedia.in/index.php?title=Environment_Impact_Assessment_(EIA)_in_India
http://www.cseindia.org/programme/industry/eia/introduction_eia.htm#hist
http://awsassets.wwfindia.org/downloads/session_13_1.pdf
http://www.os.is/gogn/unu-gtp-sc/UNU-GTP-SC-05-28.pdf
http://www.entek.chalmers.se/~anly/miljo/EIA.pdf
http://www.doe.ir/portal/theme/talab/0DB/2-BS/WMRA/SO/bs-wmra-so-1997.pdf
http://www.rlarrdc.org.in/images/Introduction%20EIA.pdf retrieved on 1st March 2017.
https://www.iaia.org/uploads/pdf/principlesEA_1.pdf retrieved on 1st March 2017.
http://www.cati.org.pl/download/MCA/multicriteria_analysis.pdf
http://simple.werf.org/simple/media/documents/BCT/stepThreeALinks/12A.html

SECTION 8

http://pernerscontacts.upce.cz/24_2011/Micietova.pdf
https://www.kent.ac.uk/scarr/events/ahteensuu.pdf
https://ratical.org/co-globalize/MaeWanHo/PrecautionP.html
http://study.com/academy/lesson/full-cost-accounting-definition-example.html
https://www.epa.gov/ems/learn-about-environmental-management-systems
http://www.conserve-energy-future.com/environmental-management-systems.php
http://www.gdrc.org/uem/iso14001/info-7.html
http://www.environmentalmanagementsystem.com.au/what-is-an-environmental-management-system.html
https://www.scribd.com/document/62579326/Environmental-Audit
http://smallbusiness.chron.com/basics-environmental-accounting-4932.html
http://www.un.org/esa/sustdev/publications/proceduresandprinciples.pdf
https://www.scribd.com/document/320392536/Environmental-Management-Accounting
http://www.unido.org/fileadmin/import/26164_EMApartIcropped.5.pdf
https://www.scribd.com/document/320392536/Environmental-Management-Accounting
http://www.lifecycleinitiative.org/starting-life-cycle-thinking/life-cycle-approaches/
http://www.umich.edu/~nppcpub/resources/compendia/CORPpdfs/CORPlca.pdf
http://www.levistrauss.com/wp-content/uploads/2015/03/Full-LCA-Results-Deck-FINAL.pdf
http://www.lifecycleinitiative.org/starting-life-cycle-thinking/what-is-life-cycle-thinking/
http://www.referenceforbusiness.com/encyclopedia/Gov-Inc/Green-Marketing.html#ixzz4cEFKBoAi
http://www.uow.edu.au/~sharonb/STS300/market/green/article2.html
http://www.fao.org/docrep/005/y2789e/y2789e06.htm
https://center.sustainability.duke.edu/sites/default/files/documents/ecolabelsreport.pdf
http://www.iso14000-iso14001-environmental-management.com/index.htm
http://dnr.wi.gov/topic/SmallBusiness/documents/caseStudies/IndustrialEcologyInPractice.pdf
https://www.iisd.org/business/viewcasestudy.aspx?id=77 (International Institute for Sustainable Development, 2013)
http://www.environmental-mainstreaming.org/documents/EM%20Profile%20No%205%20-%20EMS%20(6%20Oct%2009).pdf
www.environmental-mainstreaming.org
https://cdn.iccwbo.org/content/uploads/sites/3/2015/01/ICC-Business-Charter-for-Sustainable-Development.pdf

SECTION 9

http://www.envfor.nic.in/soer/2001/ind_land.pdf
http://www.nationsencyclopedia.com/Asia-and-Oceania/India-ENVIRONMENT.html
http://www.gktoday.in/blog/causes-and-consequences-of-land-degradation-in-india/

http://www.millenniumpost.in/indias-challenges-in-waste-management-178385
http://www.importantindia.com/16100/deforestation-in-india/ http://planningcommission.gov.in/hackathon/Environment.pdf
http://www.worldbank.org/en/news/feature/2012/10/11/protecting-indias-coastline
http://documents.worldbank.org/curated/en/354091468269139836/pdf/793170NEWS0WB000PUBLIC00Box0377368B.pdf
http://nptel.ac.in/courses/Webcourse-contents/IIT- Delhi/Environment%20and%20Ecology/mod1/1.htm
http://wmc.nic.in/chapter1-legal-aspects.asp
http://mjcetenvsci.blogspot.in/2014/11/salient-features-of-environmental-acts.html
http://envfor.nic.in/legis/others/tribunal.html
http://envfor.nic.in/rules-regulations/national-environment-appellate-authority
http://www.nbaindia.in/uploaded/pdf/know.pdf
http://www.drishtiias.com/upsc-exam-gs-resources-NATIONAL-GREEN-TRIBUNAL-NGT#sthash.J3uAgDro.dpuf
http://www.thehindu.com/news/national/green-tribunal-cancels-forest-clearance-for-chhattisgarh-coal-blocks/article5826314.ece
http://shodhganga.inflibnet.ac.in
http://www.gktoday.in/blog/biological-diversity-act-2002/
https://www.lawctopus.com/academike/biodiversity-act-2002-analysis/
http://www.envfor.nic.in/divisions/iwsu/induction.pdf
http://www.planningcommission.nic.in/plans/planrel/fiveyr/welcome.html, accessed on 16.04.2010.
http://www.envfor.nic.in/sites/default/files/introduction-csps.pdf
http://iced.cag.gov.in/?page_id=1034
http://www.gktoday.in/national-environment-policy-2006/#Objectives_of_the_Policy
http://planningcommission.nic.in/plans/planrel/fiveyr/7th/vol2/7v2ch18.html
http://envfor.nic.in/division/introduction-2
https://www.iucn.org/content/facts-and-figures-biodiversity
http://12thplan.gov.in/forum_description.php?f=10
http://planningcommission.gov.in/hackathon/Environment.pdf
www.envfor.nic.in/report/0607/chap04.pdf
http://envfor.ni c.in/rules - regulations /national -environment-appellate-authority
http://planningcommission.gov.in/aboutus/committee/wrkgrp12/enf/wg_envr.pdf
http://blogs.worldbank.org/endpovertyinsouthasia/indias-air-pollution-woes
http://www.moef.nic.in/downloads/public-information/Strategic_Plan_MoEF.pdf
https://earthobservatory.nasa.gov/Features/Revelle/revelle_2.php
http://www.nmsea.org/Curriculum/Primer/Global_Warming/fossil_fuels_and_global_warming.htm
https://www.nrdc.org/stories/are-effects-global-warming-really-bad
https://www.epa.gov/ghgemissions/global-greenhouse-gas-emissions-data
http://www.wri.org/blog/2015/06/infographic-what-do-your-countrys-emissions-look
https://ssrn.com/abstract=2168859
http://carbonmarketwatch.org/category/additionality-and-baselines/joint-implementation/
http://unfccc.int/kyoto_protocol/mechanisms/emissions_trading/items/2731.php
http://www.ecowatch.com/top-10-greenhouse-gas-emitters-find-out-which-countries-are-most-respo-1882054580.html
https://www.theguardian.com/environment/2011/jun/07/ets-emissions-trading
https://www.c2es.org/technology/factsheet/high-global-warming-potential-gas-abatement%20
http://www.business-standard.com/article/markets/price-of-carbon-credits-may-rebound-this-year-112052500017_1.html
http://whatsyourimpact.org/greenhouse-gas-emissions
http://www.climatechangenews.com/2013/12/02/worlds-carbon-markets-now-cover-20-of-emissions/
https://icapcarbonaction.com/images/StatusReport2016/ICAP_Status_Report_2016_Online.pdf
https://www.lawctopus.com/academike/emission-trading-scheme-overview-indian-perspective/
http://download.nos.org/333courseE/14.pdf
http://www.ozonedepletion.info/education/part3/ozonesources.html
http://www.ozone.unep.org/en/treaties-and-decisions/montreal-protocol-substances-deplete-ozone-layer
http://sedac.ciesin.columbia.edu/ozone/docs/UNEPsummary96.html
http://www.ozone.unep.org/en/handbook-montreal-protocol-substances-deplete-ozone-layer/41453

http://www.ozone.unep.org/en/handbook-montreal-protocol-substances-deplete-ozone-layer/27608
http://www.sparc-climate.org/fileadmin/customer/6_Publications/SPARC_reports_PDF/6_SPARC_LifetimeReport_Web.pdf
http://indianexpress.com/article/india/india-news-india/kigali-delivers-second-big-climate-deal-montreal-protocol-amended-to-eliminate-hfcs-3083930/
http://www.differencebetween.com/difference-between-genetic-diversity-and-vs-species-diversity/
http://www.scidev.net/global/biodiversity/feature/biodiversity-facts-and-figures-1.html
http://www.rainforestconservation.org/rainforest-primer/2-biodiversity/g-recent-losses-in-biodiversity/5-causes-of-recent-declines-in-biodiversity/
http://redpath-museum.mcgill.ca/Qbp/3.Conservation/impacts.htm
http://www.rainforestconservation.org/rainforest-primer/2-biodiversity/g-recent-losses-in-biodiversity/5-causes-of-recent-declines-in-biodiversity/
https://www.cbd.int/abs/doc/protocol/nagoya-protocol-en.pdf
http://biodiversity.de/sites/default/files/products/reports/nefo_giz_values_eng_2_ansicht.pdf
https://www.cbd.int/abs/
http://www.pmindia.gov.in/en/government_tr_rec/namami-gange/
https://www.cbd.int/doc/legal/cartagena-protocol-en.pdf
https://www.informea.org/en/treaties/cartagena
http://www.doc.govt.nz/cites-
http://www.nmfs.noaa.gov/ia/agreements/LMR%20report/convention_on_ the_ conservation_of_migratory_species_of_wild_animals_pd
http://www.greenpeace.org/international/en/campaigns/detox/trafigura/
http://www.ec.gc.ca/gdd-mw/default.asp?lang=En&n+1C6F3B4C-1
http//www.academia.edu/688422/International_Hazardous_Waste_Trade
http://www.enb.iisd.org'process/chemical_management-baselintro.html
http://news.national geographic.com/news.2004/01/0107_040107_extinction.html
http://en.wikipedia.org/wiki/Environemntal_governance
http.www.cop19.gov.pl/unfcc
http://planningcommission.gov.in/plans/mta/11th_mta/chapterwise/chap22_envir.pdf
https://www.wri.org/blog/2014/11/6-graphs-explain-world-s-top-10-emitters
http://www.fao.org/docrep/019/i3671e/i3671e.pdf
http://www.fathom.com/course/21701785/session2.html
http://conservationbiology404.blogspot.com/
https://www.ipbes.net/about
https://www.ifri.org/sites/default/files/atoms/files/hereport6biodiversitygouvernance.pdf
http://www.unesco.org/new/en/natural-sciences/environment/ecological-sciences/biosphere-reserves/world-network-wnbr/

Articles, Reports and Books

Abrahammson, K. V. 1997. Paradigms of Sustainability. In S. Sorlin, ed. The Road Towards Sustainability, A Historical Perspective, A Sustainable Baltic Region, The Baltic University programme,Uppsalla University, pp. 30-35. 2. Hanna, S. & Munasinghe, M. 1995. eds.

Agarwal V.K., 2005. "Environmental Laws in India: Challenges for Enforcement" in *Bulletin of the National Institute of Ecology* 15: 227-238

Ahmad Furgan,2008. "Legal Parameters of the National Environmental Policy, 2006" in "Problems and Prospects of Environment Policy: Indian Perspective" edited by Dr. M. S. Bhatt, Shahid Ashraf, Asheref Illiyan, Aakar Books.

Alam Md Khorshed, 2003, PhD thesis submitted to Murdoch University, *Cleanup of the Buriganga River- Integrating Environment into Decision Making.*

Ameen Muhammad Riyazul and Abhinav Dahariya, 2014,"Critical Appraisal of National Tribunal Act, 2010" International Journal of Academic Research, ISSN: 2348-7666 Vol.1 Issue 2(3), pp 69 -84.

Anbumozhi, V., Q. Chotichanathawong, and T. Murugesh. 2011. Information Disclosure Strategies for Green Industries. ADBI Working Paper 305. Tokyo: Asian Development Bank Institute. Available: http://www.adbi.org/working-paper/2011/08/22/4678.info.disclosure.strategies.green.industries/

Anderson C Robert,2002, Incentive-Based Policies for Environmental Management in Developing Countries, Resources for the Future: Issue Brief, 0 2 – 0 7.

Anderson Karen (2000) Environmental Impact Assessment retrieved from http://www.entek.chalmers.se/~anly/miljo/EIA.pdf on 1st March, 2017.

Andersen M S 2007 "An Introductory Note on the Environmental economics of the Circular Economy" in Sustainability Science 2:133–140

Andy, G., and Keolelan, G.A., "Industrial Ecology an Introduction", National Pollution Prevention Centre for Higher Education, University of Michigan, (1995).

Annepu, R. (2012) Sustainable Solid Waste Management in India. Master of Science in Earth Resources Engineering. Columbia University in the City of New York.

Archie B. Carroll and Ann B. Buchholtz, Business and Society: Ethics and Stakeholder Management, fourth edition, Springer Netherlands Volume 5, Number 1/February, 2001

Arora, S., Cason, T.N., "Why do firms volunteer to exceed environmental regulations? Understanding participation in EPA's 33/50 program", *Land Economics* 72, (1995); 413-432.

Arrow Kenneth, Bert Bolin, Robert Costanza, Partha Dasgupta et al, (1995), "Economic Growth, Carrying Capacity, and the Environment" in Science, Vol. 268

Asian Development Bank 2013, Cost Benefit Analysis for Development – A Practical Guide.

Austin Duncan, (1999) Economic Instruments for Pollution Control and Prevention – A Brief Overview, World Resource Institute.

Atkinson G and S Dietz 2009. "Progress in the Measurement of Sustainable Development" in Welfare Economics and Sustainable Development, Vol I, E book, (Eds) Yew-Kwang Ng and Ian Willsayloan, Encyclopedia of Life Support Systems (EOLSS).

Atkinson Giles and Susana Mourato,2008, Environmental Cost Benefit Analysis, Annu. Rev. Environ. Resour. 33:317–44

AtKisson Alan, R. Lee Hatcher, and Sydney Green, 2004. Introducing *Pyramid*: A Versatile Process and Planning Tool for Accelerating Sustainable Development, © AtKisson, Inc.available @ http://citeseerx.ist.psu.edu/viewdoc/download?doi=10.1.1.521.595&rep=rep1&type=pdf

Banerjee Somdutta and Prasenjit Sarkhel,(2012) "Biases and reliability of WTP estimates from Contingent Valuation responses: A Study Based on Solid Waste Management Services in Bally Municipality, India", in *Arthaniti* 11 (1-2)/78.

Baqui Abullah, 2009, Global Urbanisation: Trends, Patterns, Determinanta and Impacts, The Johns Hopkins University and Abdullah Baqui..

Bartling Jonathan, 2016, Valuing Nature -Ethical Considerations of Biodiversity in Sustainability Science, Masters Programme Thesis, Lund University.

Bhattacharya Rabindra N, 2012, Economics of Natural Resources, Dissemination Papers -22, Centre for Excellence in Environmental Economics, Madras School of Economics downloaded from http://coe.mse.ac.in/dp/DISSEMINATION%20PAPER%20-%2022.pdf

Beckerman.W, 1992. "Economic Growth and the Environment: Whose growth? Whose environment?", *World Development, Vol. 20, No. 1, April 1992, pp. 481-496.*

Bedajna Sutirtha ,2012. "Between Ecology and Economy Environmental Governance in India" in New Subjects and New Governance in India, (Eds) Ranabir Samaddar and Suhit K. Sen, Taylor and Francis.

Benedic R E, 2000. Human Population and Environmental Stresses in the Twenty first Century, in Environmental Change & Security Project Report, Issue 6 (Summer 2000) Available @ https://www.wilsoncenter.org/sites/default/files/Report6-1.pdf.

Bennet Jeff, 2005. "Choice Modelling – Step by Step Guide. Economics Techniques Series: Fact sheet No.1 The Economics Branch, Policy Division, EPA,Queensland Government. available @ https://www.gbcma.vic.gov.au/downloads/sircs_review_2005_env_2/Choice_modelling_A_stepbystep_guide_by_Jeff_Bennett.pdf

Bergh, J.C.J.M. van den, (2000) Themes, Approaches and Differences with Environmental Economics, Tinbergen Institute Discussion Paper, TI2000 -080/3 available @ at http://ftp.tinbergen.nl/discussionpapers/00080.pdf

Blackman Allen, 2007, "Colombia's Discharge Fee Programme, Discussion Paper, Resources for the Future. DP 05-31 REV

Blackman A. (2007), Can Voluntary Environmental Regulation Work in Developing Countries? Lessons From Case Studies, Discussion Paper, Resources For Future, DP 07-10 REV

Blackman A. (2009),Alternative Pollution Control Policies in Developing Countries: Informal, Informational and Voluntary. Resource for the Future DP 09-14

Boardman, Greenberg, Vining and Weimer. 1996. *Cost-Benefit Analysis: Concepts and Practice*. Prentice-Hall. Upper Saddle River, NJ.

Boos Adrian, 2015. Genuine Savings as an Indicator for "Weak" Sustainability: Critical Survey and Possible Ways forward in Practical Measuring in Sustainability, 7; 4146-4182 downloaded from: http://www.mdpi.com/2071-1050/7/4/4146/htm

Boulding K.E(1973): *The Economics of the Coming Spaceship Earth,* in The. *Environmental Quality in a Growing Economy.* Ed. Henry Jarrett. Baltimore: Johns Hopkins Press, 1966

Boutwell James L. and John V. Westra (2013) "*Benefit Transfer: A Review of Methodologies and Challenges*", *Resources, 2*, 517-527; doi:10.3390/resources2040517.

Brack Duncan & Thomas Branczik,2004. "Trade and Environment in the WTO: After Cancun", Briefing Paper No. 9, Sustainable Development Programme, Royal Institute of International Affairs.

Brack Duncan and Kevin Gray,2003, Multilateral Environmental Agreements and the WTO - Report, Royal Institute of International Affairs and International Institute for Sustainable Development.

Brennan, Andrew and Lo, Yeuk-Sze, "Environmental Ethics", *The Stanford Encyclopedia of Philosophy* (Fall 2015 Edition), Edward N. Zalta (ed.).

Brennan, Andrew and Lo, Yeuk-Sze, «Environmental Ethics», *The Stanford Encyclopedia of Philosophy* (Winter 2016 Edition), Edward N. Zalta (ed.), URL = <https://plato.stanford.edu/archives/win2016/entries/ethics-environmental/>.

Brown C Thomas and Robin Gregory, 1995.Why the WTA–WTP disparity matters, in Ecological Economics 28: 323–335

Brown R C P, J. Asafu-Adjaye, M. Draca and A. Straton

Brown R C P, J. Asafu-Adjaye, M. Draca and A. Straton, How Useful Is The Genuine Savings Rate As A Macroeconomic Sustainability Indicator For Countries And Regions?: Australia And Queensland Compared, 2003. Discussion Paper No 331, School of Economics The University of Queensland Australia

Budholai Bharat, "Environment Protection Laws in the British Era" available @ http://www.legalserviceindia.com/articles/brenv.htm

Caldwell Lynton K , Principles of Sustainable Development, Vol I, 2009, (Ed) Giancarlo Barbiroliayte, EOLSS.sample available @ http://www.eolss.net/sample-chapters/c13/e1-46a.pdf

Carson Richard T and Robert Cameron Mitchell, (1993) *The Value of Clean Water : The Public Willingness to Pay for Boatable, Fishable and Swimmable Quality Water.* Water Resources Research Water resources Research Vol 29,No7, 2445 -2454

Carson Richard T and W. Michael Hanemann (2005) "Contingent Valuation" chapter in Handbook of Environmental Economics, Volume 2.Edited by K.-G Mäler and J.R. Vincent (Ed) Elsevier B.V.

Chakravarty Sumit, S. K. Ghosh, C. P. Suresh, A. N. Dey and Gopal Shukla, 2012. Deforestation: Causes, Effects and Control Strategies Chapter 1(Open Access) in Global Perspectives on Sustainable Forest Management, (ed) Okia Clement Akais © Authors. Available @ http://cdn.intechopen.com/pdfs-wm/36125.pdf

Centre for Science & Environment, 2006 Introduction to EIA , Compiled by Industry & Environment Unit, Retrieved from http://www.rlarrdc.org.in/images/Introduction%20EIA.pdf on March 1st, 2017.

CEL, WWF-India & National Law University Delhi 2011. "Law and Policies Pertaining to Environment."

Centre for Science & Environment, 2014,Strengthen Institutions Reform Laws and Streamline Processes, Agenda for Improving Environmental Governance in India.

Centre for Development, Environment and Policy (CeDEP) P563: "Ethics for Environment and Development" prepared by: Bindi Clements, with Unit 10 contributed by Nigel Poole SOAS 3736. Downloaded from: https://www.soas.ac.uk/cedep/programmes/modules/file38130.pdf

Chakravarty Sumit, S. K. Ghosh, C. P. Suresh, A. N. Dey and Gopal Shukla, 2012. Deforestation: Causes, Effects and Control Strategies Chapter 1(Open Access) in Global Perspectives on Sustainable Forest Management, (ed) Okia Clement Akais © Authors. Available @ http://cdn.intechopen.com/pdfs-wm/36125.pdf

Chieng, S. *(———), Environmental Impact Assessment EIA retrieved on* March 2nd 2017 from http://www.ece.ubc.ca/~leos/pdf/a230/notes/t2/EIA.pdf

Chowdhury Nupur, 2014, Environmental Impact Assessment in India: Reviewing Two Decades of Jurisprudence in IUCN Academy of Environmental Law eJournal Vol.5, pp 28-32

Chuhan Kirti Singh and Surender Singh Chauhan, 2009. "Ecological Destruction vis-à-vis Environmental Jurisprudence in India: A Survey" in Journal of Human Ecology, 27(3): 207-216

Čiegis Remigijus, and Raimondas Čiegis (2008), Laws of Thermodynamics and Sustainability of the Economy in Engineering Economics, No 2 (57), ISSN 1392-2785 No 2 (57).

Clerici and G. Alimonti , 2015, "World Energy Resources" EPJ Web of Conferences Volume 98, 001001 published by EDP Sciences, available at http://www.epj-conferences.org

Cochrane Alasdair "Environmental Ethics" , Internet Encylcopedia of Philosophy downloadable at:

http://www.iep.utm.edu/envi-eth 21/07/2017

Cohen, J. E. (1995a). Population Growth and Earth's Human Carrying Capacity. Science, 269(5222), 341-346. doi: 10.1126/science.7618100

Cole, M., A. Rayner, and J. Bates. 1997. "The Environmental Kuznets Curve: an Empirical Analysis" from *Environment and Development Economics 2*. pgs 401-416

Connolly, S. & Munro, A. (1999). 'Public Choice', Chapter 8 in *Economics of the Public Sector*, Pearson, Harlow, Essex

Cordero Paula, *Sergio Sepulveda and Adrian Rodriguez,2004. "Trade and Environmental Issues"* Rural Development Technical Handbook No. 25, Inter-American Institute for Cooperation on Agriculture (IICA). 2008

Cox J Linda and John Cusick, 2006. "What is Sustainable Development?" in Resource Management, RM-14. College of Tropical Agriculture and Human Resources, University of Hawai, (UH–CTAHR), downloaded from http://members.hawaiiecotourism.org/resources/Documents/WhatisSustDevelopment.pdf

Cristian Duran Dan, Luminita Maria Gogan, Alin Artenea,Vasile Duran,2015, The Components of Sustianable Development- A Possible Approach, in Procedia Economics and Finance 26 (2015) 806 – 811© Authors 2015.

Daniel Bodansky, and Rajamani Lavanya, The Evolution and Governance Architecture of the United Nations Climate Change Regime (November 14, 2016).

Darnall, N., "Why Firms Mandate ISO 14001 Certification", *Business and Society* 45 (3), (2006); 354–381

Datta Pranati, 2006. Urbanisation in India, Paper presented in the Regional and Sub-Regional Population Dynamic Population Process in Urban Areas European Population Conference 21-24 June, 2006

Dayo B Felix Babajide I. Alo and Adeolu Ojo, Hazardous Waste Management – *International Issues in* Hazardous Waste Management, Encyclopedia of Life Support Systems (EOLSS)available at http://www.eolss.net/Sample-Chapters/C09/E1-08-02-00.pdf

De Sherbinin A, Carr D, Cassels S, Jiang L. Population and Environment. *Annual review of environment and resources*. 2007;32:345-373. doi:10.1146/annurev.energy.32.041306.100243.

De Sherbinin A, Carr D, Cassels S, Jiang L. Population and Environment. *Annual review of environment and resources*. 2007;32:345-373. doi:10.1146/annurev.energy.32.041306.100243.do

De Steiguer, J. E. "A Student's Guide to Cost-Benefit Analysis for Natural Resources." The University of Arizona. downloaded from: https://cals.arizona.edu/classes/rnr485/ch1.htm

Desvousges, W. H., Johnson, F. R., Dunford, R. W.,Boyle, K. J., Hudson, S. P., Wilson, K. N. (2010). *Measuring Nonuse Damages Using Contingent Valuation: An Experimental Evaluation of Accuracy*, 2nd ed. RTI Press publication No. BK-0001-1009.Research Triangle Park, NC: RTI International. Retrieved [date] from http://www.rti.org/rtipress.

Devall Bill, The Deep, Long-Range Ecology Movement 1960 -2000 - A Review, Ethics & The Environment, 6(1), Indiana University Press.

DeWitt, C. B. 1995. Ecology and Ethics: Relation of Religious Belief to Ecological Practice in the

Biblical Tradition. *Biodiversity and Conservation* 4:838-848.

Diamond, P.A. and J.A. Hausman (1994) "*Contingent Valuation: Is Some Better than No Number*" Journal of Economic Perspectives 8, 45-64.

Dietz Simon and Eric Neumayer, 2006. A Critical Appraisal od Genuine Savings as an Indicator of Sustainable Development" in Sustainable Development Indicators in Ecological Economics (Ed) Philip Lawn© Philip Lawn.

Di Falco Salvatore , **2012.**"Economic Incentives for Pollution Control in Developing Countries: What Can We Learn from the Empirical Literature?"Politica Agricola Internazionale, International Agricultural Policy, Edizioni LaC™ Informatore Agrario,Issue2.

Dinda S.2004. Environmental Kuznets Curve Hypothesis: A Survey, *Ecological Economics*49, pp 431– 455

Dupre, Kenneth, (1994) The Environmental Movement: A Status Report and Implications for Pricing, Sam Advanced Management Journal available at the site: http://www.allbusiness.com/sales/453046-1.html

Eduard Pestel Abstract established by. A Report to The Club of Rome (1972), by Donella H. Meadows, Dennis l. Meadows, Jorgen Randers, William W. Behrens III

Ehrenfeld John and Nicholas Gertler, 1997, Industrial Ecology in Practice The Evolution of Interdependence at Kalundborg, Journal of Industrial Ecology, Vol 1, No 1.Massachusetts Institute of Technolcgy and Yale University. Available @ http://www.johnehrenfeld.com/Kalundborg.pdf

Dosi Cesare,2000, Environmental Values, Valuation Methods, and Natural Disaster Damage Assessment, for UN Economic Commission for Latin America and the Caribbean.(UN ECLAC).

E. E. (Stathis) Michaelides, 2012.Alternative Energy Sources, Green Energy and Technology, Springer-Verlag Berlin Heidelberg .

Elkington, J., "Toward the Sustainable Corporation: Win-Win-Win Business Strategies for Sustainable Development", *California Management Review* Vol. 36, (1994).

Elliott Lorraine 2009 "Environmentalism" in Encyclopaedia Britannica. 2009 "Environmentalism" downloaded from: https://www.britannica.com/topic/environmentalism

Ellerman Denny A, Paul L. Joskow and David Harrison, Jr,2003."Emission Trading in the US -Experience, Lessons, and Considerations for Greenhouse Gases" Prepared for the Pew Center on Global Climate Change.

Larderel J. Aloisi De, 2009. Sustainable Development: The Role of Business in Public Administration and Public Policy – Vol. II. Book (Ed) Krishna K. Tummalaaytex, Encyclopedia of Life Support Systems (EOLSS),

Ebook. Environmental Management , 2002. ISO and the Environment.

Eskeland, Gunnar S., and Emmanuel Jimenez. 1991. "Choosing Policy Instruments for Pollution Control." Policy Research Working Paper 624. World Bank, Policy Research Department, Washington, D.C

Farrow, Scott and Michael Toman. 1999. "Using Environmental Benefit-Cost Analysis to Improve Government Performance," *Environment* 41, 12–37.

Gadgil Madhav and Raamachandra Guha, 1994, Ecological Conflicts and the Environmental Movement in India", in Development and Change 1994, Special Environment Issue, Vol 25 pp 101-136 , © I*nstitute of Social Studies; Published by* Balckwell Publishers.

Gadgil, Madhav and Ramchandra Guha, 1998 'Towards a Perspective onEnvironmental Movements in India',The Indian Journal of Social Work, Vol.No. 59, Issue I, Part 2, pp. 450-472.

Garcia Grossman, Gene Lopez Jorge, Thomas Sterner, and Shakeb Afsah,2004, "Public Disclosure of Industrial Pollution: The PROPER Approach for Indonesia" , Discussion Paper 04-34, Resources for the Future

Georgescu-Roegen, N.1971. *The Entropy Law and the Economic Process* (Cambridge, Harvard University Press.

Geert van Calster, 2009, "International Trade and the Environment", in International Law and Institutions, Edited by : Aaron Schwabach,and Arthur John Cockfield, Encyclopedia of Life Support Systems (EOLSS) .

Georgieva Kristalina and Muthukumara Mani,2006. "Trade and the Environment Debate: WTO, Kyoto and Beyond", in Trade Policy and WTO Accession for Economic Development in Russia and the CIS: A Handbook (Ed) David Tarr, World Bank Institute. Available @ siteresources.worldbank.org/…./TradeEnvironment.doc

Gleick, P. H., 1996: Water resources. In Encyclopedia of Climate and Weather, ed. by S. H. Schneider, Oxford University Press, New York, vol. 2, pp.817-823

Government of United Kingdom (2007), 'An Introductory Guide to valuing eco system ' , Department of Environment , Food and Rural Affairs, available @ http://webarchive.nationalarchives.gov.uk/20140608205842/https://www.gov.uk/government/publications/an-introductory-guide-to-valuing-ecosystem-services

Gundimeda Haripriya, Contingent Valuation Method, Dissemination Paper – 6, Madras School of Economics.

Gundimeda Haripriya, Environmental Accounting – Concept Note, Madras School of Economics.

Güneralp, Burak, and Karen C. Seto. "Can gains in efficiency offset the resource demands and CO_2 emissions from constructing and operating the built environment?" *Applied Geography* **32, no. 1 (2012): 40-50.**

Gunningham Neil and Darren Sinclair, 2002. "Voluntary Approaches to Environmental Protection: Lessons from the Mining and Forestry Sectors" Paper presented in the Conference on Foreign Direct Investment and the Environment, OECD Global Forum On International Investment.

Golden S Jay (Ed) 2010, "An Overview of Ecolabels and Sustainability Certifications in the Global Marketplace Corporate Sustainability Initiative", Nicholas Institute for Environmental Policy Solutions, Duke University and the Sustainability Consortium.

Goodward, Jenna; Kelly, Alexia (August 2010). *"Bottom Line on Offsets"*. World Resources Institute. *Retrieved 2010-09-08.*

Golden S Jay (Ed) 2010. An Overview of Ecolabels and Sustainability Certifications in the Global Market place, Corporate Sustainability Initiative, Nicholas Institute for Environmental Policy Solutions, Duke University, and the Sustainability Consortium.

Grossman, Gene M. and Alan B. Krueger (1995), 'Economic growth and the Environment', Quarterly Journal of Economics, 112, 353–77.

Guillermo, E., and Richards, B., (2002), Fundamentals of Environmental Impact Assessments– Basic Text prepared for Trainers' Course on Environmental Management and Assessment for Investment Projects, Inter American Development Bank – IDB, Inter-American Association of Sanitary and Environmental Engineering – AIDIS

Gunawardena, U.P. 2013. An Inquiry into Ethical Foundations of Cost Benefit Analysis. Journal of Environmental Professionals Sri Lanka. 1(2), pp.1–15.

DOI: http://doi.org/10.4038/jepsl.v1i2.5144

Håkan Nordström and Scott Vaughan 1999, WTO, Special Studies - Trade and Environment.

Hanemann, W.M. (1991). "*Willingness to Pay and Willingness to Accept: How Much Can They Differ?*" American Economic Review 81, 635-47.

Hanley, N., Mourato, S., & Wright, R. E. (2001). "Choice Modelling Approaches: A Superior Alternative for Environmental Valuatioin" Journal of economic surveys, 15(3), 435-462

Harris Jonathan M and Anne-Marie Codur 2004, Macro Economics and the Environment, A GDAE Teaching Module on Social and Environmental Issues in Economics, Global Development and Environment Institute, Tufts University.

Harris Jonathan M 2004, Trade and the Environment, A GDAE Teaching Module on Social and Environmental Issues in Economics, Global Development and Environment Institute, Tufts University.

Harris Jonathan M,2000. Basic Principles of Sustainable Development, Working Paper, Global Development and Environment Institute, Tufts University, USA.

Hardoy J, Satterthwaite D. Squatter Citizen—Life in the Urban Third World. London: Earthscan; 1995:301. Cited by http://www.ncbi.nlm.nih.gov/pmc/articles/PMC1891640/

Hecht E Joy, 1999. "Environmental Accounting: Where We Are Now Where We Are Heading", Resources for The Future, Issue 135, Resources 14.

Hegde N G (1999) Challenges oof Community Forestry in India, Asia Pacific Forestry Research – Vision 2010. Proc. of the Regional Seminar. Kuala Lumpur, Malaysia, 2000. Mar.26-27, 1999.: 11-20.

Heinzerling Lisa and Frank Ackerman. 2002 "Pricing the Priceless – Cost benefit Analysis of Environmental Protection", Georgetown University.

He Jie. 2007. Is the Environmental Kuznets Curve Hypothesis Valid for Developing Countries? A Survey, Working paper 07003 GREDI

Hens Luc and Emmanuel K. Boon, 2003, "Causes of Biodiversity Loss: a Human Ecological Analysis; :O Futuro dos Recursos # 1, outubro de,MultiCiencia

Hilson Gavin, 2000, Thesis for Master of Arts (Graduate Department of Geography and The Institute for Environmental Studies, University of Torrento) on An Examination of Environmental Performance and Eco-Effaciency in the North American Gold Mining Industry

Hood Laura , 2010. Biodiversity Facts and Figures, Greenfleet Australia available @ http://www.scidev.net/global/biodiversity/feature/biodiversity-facts-and-figures-1.html

Hoornweg, Daniel; Bhada-Tata, Perinaz. 2012. "What a Waste : A Global Review of Solid Waste Management". Urban development series; knowledge papers no. 15. World Bank, Washington, DC. © World Bank. https://openknowledge.worldbank.org/handle/10986/17388 License: CC BY 3.0 IGO.

Hoornweg Daniel, Bhada-Tata Perinaz, & Chris Kennedy 2013, Environment: Waste Production Must Peak This Century downloaded from http://www.nature.com/news/environment-waste-production-must-peak-this-century-1.14032

Hoornweg D and Laura Thomas, 1999, What A Waste: Solid Waste Management in Asia, Urban Development Sector Unit, World Bank, East Asia and Pacific Regional Office.

Jantzen Jochem, 2006, "Economic Value of Natural and Environmental Resources" TME, Institute for Appli54ed Environmental Economics available @http://i-tme.nl/pdf/assessment%20of%20econ%20value%20of%20environment%20final.pdf

Jardin Mireille, 2010,Global Biodiversity Governance: The Contribution of the Main Biodiversity Related Conventions in IFRI's Health and Environment Reports, "Global Governance of Biodiversity New Perspectives on a Shared Challenge."

Jérôme Ballet, JérômePelenc. Strong sustainability, critical natural capital and the capability approach. Ecological Economics, Elsevier, 2015, 112, pp.36-44.

IGBP's (International GEosphere Biosphere Programme) Global Change magazine. Downloaded from the site: http://www.igbp.net/news/features/features/urbanairpollutionanewlookatanoldproblem.5.19895cff13e9f675e253f0.html

International Association for Impact Assessment, 1999, Principles of Environmental Impact Assessment – Best Practices retrieved on 1st March, 2017 from https://www.iaia.org/uploads/pdf/principlesEA_1.pdf

International Institute for Sustainable Development & United Nations Environment Programme. (2014). *Trade and Green Economy: A Handbook.*Published by the International Institute for Sustainable Development, Geneva.

Jeffery, Michael 2005, "Environmental Ethics and Sustainable Development: Ethical and Human Rights Issues in Implementing Indigenous Rights" Macquarie Journal of International and Comparative Environmental Law (MqJIIC Env Law) 4; (2005) 2(1)

Johnston Robert J , John Rolfe, Randall S. Rosenberger and Roy Brouwer,2015, "Introduction to Benefit transfer Methods" Chapter 2 in 'Benefit Transfer of Environmental and Resource Values –A Guide for Researchers and Practitioners', (EDs) **Johnston, R.J., Rolfe, J., Rosenberger, R., Brouwer,** R, Springer.

Joseph J. Domask, 1998, Evolution of the Environmental Movement in Brazil's Amazonia, Global Forest Programme, WWF

Joshi Rajkumar and Sirajuddin Ahmed, 2016. "Status and challenges of municipal solid waste management in India: A Review", *Cogent Environmental Science* , 2: 1139434

Kahneman, D., & Knetsch, J. (1992). *Valuing public goods: The purchase of moral satisfaction*. Journal of Environmental Economics and Management, 22, 57±70.

Kaika D and Efthimios Zervas. 2013. Searching for an Environmental Kuznets Curve (EKC)-pattern for CO_2 Emissions, Recent Researches in Energy, Environment and Landscape Architecture, ISBN: 978-1-61804-052-7.

Kaivo- Jari, Jyrki Luukkanen and Penetti Malaska,2009. Advanced Sustainability Analysis" in Dimensions of Sustainable Development, Vol II, (Eds) Kamaljit S. Bawa and Reinmar Seidler. EOLSS E book.

Kamal Kumar, 2014," Environmental Movements in India: Re-Assessing Democracy", International Journal of Scientific Engineering And Research (IJSER), ISSN(Online) 2347- 3878, Volume 2: Issue 2. Paper ID: J2013136

Kathuria Vineesh, 2006, Public Disclosures – Using Information to Reduce Pollution, Madras School of Economics.

Kathuria V and N A Khan, 2002. "Environmental Compliance vs. Growth: Lessons from Malaysia"s Regulation of Palm Oil Mills (with Nisar Khan)", Economic and Political Weekly, 37(39), September 28, 3393-99 (2002).

Kathuria, Vinish (2001): "Pollution: Prevention v/s Control," EPW Vol 36, No. 29 (July 21 - July 27).

Kathuria, Vinish and Haripriya G.S. (2000): "Industrial Pollution Control - Choosing the Right Option," EPW Vol XXXV, No. 43 and 44 (October 21- 27 / October, 28).

Kaseke Nyasha, 2003, The Use of Deposit Refunds as Pollution Control Policy in Urban Areas: The Case of Zimbabwe (Harare), Environmental Paper, final Report, University of Zimbabwe.

Kavi Kumar, K.S (-------) Precautionary Principle, retrieved from http://coe.mse.ac.in/dp/Precaution-Kavi.pdf

Keiner Marco,2005. "History, Definition(s) and Models of Sustainable Development" ETH Zurich Research Collection. available @ https://www.research-collection.ethz.ch/bitstream/handle/20.500.11850/53025/eth-27943-01.pdf

Kellett, B. M., Bristow K L, & Charlesworth P B,2004. Indicator Frameworks for Assessing Irrigation Sustainability. CSIRO Land and Water Technical Report No. 01/05, CSIRO.Available @ http://www.clw.csiro.au/publications/technical2005/tr1-05.pdf

Kohrshed Alam Md, 2003, Cleanup of Buriganga River: Integrating the Environment into Decision Making. PhD Disssertation, Murdocuh University, Perth.available @ http://researchrepository.murdoch.edu.au/id/eprint/22/1/01Front.pdf

Kotchen Matthew J. 2011. "Cost – Benefit Analysis" in *Encyclopedia of Climate and Weather 2nd Edition*, Stephen Schneider (ed.), New York: Oxford University Press.

Kundu Amitabh, 2011. Trends and Processes of Urbanisation in India, © IIED and UNFPA 2011

Kuznets, S. 1955. Economic Growth and Income Equality, *American Economic Review* **45** (1), 1-28.

Leib Christoph M. 2003.The Environmental Kuznets Curve – A Survey of the Empirical Evidence and of Possible Causes, Discussion Paper Series No 391, Department of Economics, University of Heidelberg.

Lohani, B., J.W. Evans, H. Ludwig, R.R. Everitt, Richard A. Carpenter, and S.L. Tu. 1997. Environmental Impact Assessment for Developing Countries in Asia. Volume 1 - Overview. 356 pp.

Love, P. and R. Lattimore (2009), *International Trade: Free, Fair and Open?*, OECD Publishing, Paris. http://dx.doi.org/10.1787/9789264060265-en

Lundin Margareta,1999. Assessment of the Environmental Sustainability of the Urban Water Systems, Chalmers University Of Technology, Sweden.

Lvovsky, Kseniya. 1996. *Effective pollution charges : lessons of worldwide experience*. Washington, DC: World Bank .Downloaded from: http://documents.worldbank.org/curated/en/157721468761126924/Effective-pollution-charges-lessons-of-worldwide-experience

Markandya, A., and A. Shibli. 1995. *Industrial Pollution Control Policies in Asia.* Environmental Discussion Paper no. 3. *Harvard Institute for International Development, Cambridge, Mass.*

Markandya A and A Shibli, 1995. Industrial Pollution Control Policies in Asia: How Successful are the Strategies" Asian Journal of Environmental Management ,Vol 3 No 2, 87-117

Mathews Freya, 2001. "Deep Ecology" in Jamieson Dale (Ed) 2001. A Companion to Environmental Philosophy Copyright © 2001 by Blackwell Publishers Ltd.

Mathur Aditi and Siddharth Dang2009. Multilateral Environmental Agreements versus World Trade Organization System: A Comprehensive Study, American Journal of Economics and Business Administration 1 (3): 219-224.

Montague Peter,1999, Rachel's Environment & Health Weekly #657, downloaded from http://www.psrast.org/precaut2.htm

Max Roser(2015) – 'World Population Growth' published online at: OurWorldInData.org. Retrieved from http://ourworldindata.org/data/population-growth-vital-statistics/world-population-growth/[onlineresource]

McShane Katie 2009, "Environmental Ethics – An Overview" in *Philosophy Compass* 4/3 (2009): 407–420.

Meadows, D H, Meadows,D L, Randers J and Behrens.W 1972. The Limits to Growth:A Report for the Club Rome's Project on Predicament of Mankind, Earth Island Limited, London.

Meadows, Donella H.1998. "Indicators and Information Systems for Sustainable Development." A Report to the Balaton Group, The Sustainability Institute. Available for download from: http://www.iisd.org/pdf/s_ind_2.pdf

Meyer, John M. 1997 "Gifford Pinchot, John Muir, and the Boundaries of Politics in American Thought" in Polity (Palgrave MacMillan) **30** (2): 267–284.

Mishra Mrutyunjaya and Nirmal Chandra Sahu, Environmental Governance and State Pollution Control Boards, Conference Paper.

Morrisette, P. M. 1989. The Evolution of Policy Responses to Stratospheric Ozone Depletion. *Natural Resources Journal* 29: 793-820.

Munasinghe M, Economics of the Environment, Chapter 3available @ http://www.mohanmunasinghe.com/pdf/Sust-SecEd-Ch03-EnvEcon-v5F-S.pdf

Murti M N and SurenderKumar "Water Pollution In India- An Economic Appraosal" available @http://www.idfc.com/pdf/report/2011/Chp-19-Water-Pollution-in-India-An-Economic-Appraisal.pdf

Naess, A. 1973. 'The Shallow and the Deep, Long-Range Ecology Movement' *Inquiry* 16: 95-100

Narula Smita, 2008, "The Story of Narmada Bachao Andolan: Human Rights in the Global Economy and the Struggle Against the World Bank", *New York University Public Law and Legal Theory Working Papers.* Paper 106. Down loaded from;http://lsr.nellco.org/nyu_plltwp/106

National Focal Point for Asia Pacific Forest Invasive Species Network (APFISN), India Ministry of Environment & Forests, GOVERNMENT of India, "Stocktaking of National Forest Invasive Species Activities" downloadable @ http://ifs.nic.in/Dynamic/misc/apfisn/apfisn2005.pdf

Naevdal Eric, 2012. Safe Minimum Standards, in The Berkshire Encyclopedia of Sustainability; The Future of Sustainability, Vol 5© Berkshire Publishing Group.

Nayga, Jr., Rodolfo M., Richard Woodward, and Wipon Aiew, (2005) "*Experiments on the Divergence between Willingness to Pay and Willingness to Accept: The Issue Revisited.*" Economics Bulletin, Vol. 17, No. 4 pp. 1–5 URL: http://www.economicsbulletin.com/2005/volume17/EB–04Q00002A.pdf

Neumayer Eric, 2000, "Scarce or Abundant? The Economics of Natural Resource Availability" Journal of Economic Surveys, Vol 14. No 3

Nordström Håkan and Scott Vaughan, 1999, Trade and Environment , Special Studies, WTO.

O'Connor D. (1999), "Applying Economic Instruments in Developing Countries: from Theory to Implementation". Environment and Development Economics 4.

Ohara Mari, 1998, Environmental Ethics, Students Papers, Spring, 1998 downloaded @ http://darwin.bio.uci.edu/sustain/global/sensem/S98/Ohara/EnvEthics.html on 21/7/2017

Oliphant Jill, 2011. AQA Religious Ethics for AS and A2, Eds Jon Mayled and Anne Tunley, Chapter 15, Environmental and Business Ethics. Routledge

Ooi GL, Phua KH. Urbanization and Slum Formation. *Journal of Urban Health : Bulletin of the New York Academy of Medicine*. 2007;84(Suppl 1):27-34. doi:10.1007/s11524-007-9167-5.

Ogola Achieng PF, 2007, *Environmental Impact Assessment general Procedures,* Presented at Short Course II on Surface Exploration for Geothermal Resources, organized by UNU-GTP and KenGen, at Lake Naivasha, Kenya.Retrieved on March 1st, 2017 from http://www.os.is/gogn/unu-gtp-sc/UNU-GTP-SC-05-28.pdf

Orbach, Barak (2013). "What Is Government Failure," *Yale Journal on Regulation Online*, 30, pp. 44-56.

Ott, E Hermann,1998. "Emissions Trading in the Kyoto Protocol - Finished and Unfinished Business" Linkagages Journal, Volume 3 No 4 available @ http://enb.iisd.org/journal/ott.html

Oxley Alan, 2001, WTO and the Environment. International Trade Strategies available @ http://www.apec.org.au/docs/oxley2001.pdf

Panayotou Theodore 1994, Economic Instruments for Environmental Management and Sustainable Development, Environmental Economics Series Paper 16, background paper for discussion for the UNEP sponsored Consultative Expert Group Meeting on "the Use and Application of Economic Instruments for Environmental Management and Sustainable Development.

Panayotou T.1997. "Environmental Kuznets Curve" Environment and Development Economics 2 (1997): 465-484

Panayotou, T.1997. Demystifying the Environmental Kuznets Curve: Turning a Black Box into a

Policy Tool, Environment and Development Economics

Panayotou, T.2003. Economic Growth and the Environment, Economic Survey of Europe, no 2, pp 45-72

Panigrahi Jitendra K.and Susruta Amirapu,2012, An assessment of EIA system in India in Environmental Impact Assessment Review Vol 35.

Pascual, U., Muradian, R., Brander, L., Gómez-Baggethun, E., Martín-López, B., Verma, M (2010). "The Economics of Valuing Ecosystem Services And Biodiversity" in *The Economics of Ecosystems and Biodiversity: Ecological and Economic Foundations (*Chapter 5) Available @ http://teebweb.org/wp-content/uploads/2013/04/D0-Chapter-5-The-economics-of-valuing-ecosystem-services-and-biodiversity.pdf

Pathak Hemant, 2015. "Effect of Water Borne Diseases on Indian Economy: A Cost- Benefit Analysis", in Analele Universităţii din Oradea, Seria Geografie, XXV, no. 1/2015 (June) Article no. 251108-678 pp. 74-78.available @ http://geografie-uoradea.ro/Reviste/Anale/Art/2015-1/8.AUOG_678_Hemant.pdf.

Paula Cordero-Salas, Sergio Sepulveda, Adrian Rodriguez. 2004. "Trade and Environment Issues" Rural Development Technical Handbook No. 25 Inter-American Institute for Cooperation on Agriculture (IICA). 2008

Pearce Davis and Giles Atkinson " The Concept of Sustainable Development: An Evaluation of Its Usefulness Ten Years After Brundtland"CSERGE Working Paper PA 98-02

Pelenc Jérôme, Jérôme Ballet, and Tom Dedeurwaerdere, 2015. "Weak Sustainability versus Strong Sustainability" Brief for GSDR. Downloaded from: https://sustainabledevelopment.un.org/content/documents/6569122-Pelenc-Weak%20Sustainability%20versus%20Strong%20Sustainability.pdf

Pellus, Chiara, 2014 "Regulations, Watchdogs, Eco-labels, oh my!:The Highly Fragmented and Uncoordinated State of Anti-Greenwashing Efforts" (*Law School Student Scholarship* Paper 619).

Pichl, H. (1997) Basic philosophy for environmentalists. *Verge (Amsterdam)*, **October**, 25–27.

Raffensperger Carolyn, Ted Schettler, , Nancy Myers, 2000. International Journal of Occupational Environmental Health, VOL 6/NO 3, OCT/DEC pp 266-269.

Rahmatian Morteza, 2005, " Contingent Valuation Method" Caspian Environmental Programme, UNDP and World Bank Institute available @ iwlearn.net/resolveuid/68f0313f42a531088300e467dca9d00c

Ramachandra T. V and Shruthi Bachamanda, 2006, EnvironmentalAudit of Municipal Solid Waste Management, Technical Report 118

Ramasamy Ramesh, 2004. Industrial Ecology for Planning Sustainable Societies In: Klaus Jacob, Manfred Binder and Anna Wieczorek (eds.). Governance for Industrial Transformation. Proceedings of the 2003 Berlin Conference on the Human Dimensions of Global Environmental Change, Environmental Policy Research Centre: Berlin. pp. 448 - 458.

Reagan Tom, 1985, "The Case for Animal Rights" from "In Defmce ofAnimals", ed. Peter Singer, pp. 1>-26.Blackwell Publishers. downloaded from http://rintintin.colorado.edu/~vancecd/phil3140/Regan.pdf

Reddy C S , Kalloli Dutta and C. S. Jha 2013, Analysing the gross and net deforestation rates in India, Current Science, Vol. 105, No. 11, 10.December 2013.

Reddy, V. Ratna (1997) Environmental Movements in India: Some Reflections Discussion Paper 64, Heidelberg (URL: http://www.rzuscr.uni-hcidelberg.de/-t08).

Revesz, Richard L. and Nash, Jonathan Remy, Markets and Geography: Designing Marketable Permit Schemes to Control Local and Regional Pollutants. Ecology Law Quarterly, Issue 28, July 3, 2001. Available at SSRN https://ssrn.com/abstract=261756 or http://dx.doi.org/10.2139/ssrn.261756

Rietbergen-McCracken Jennifer, Hussein Abaza, 2000, P, Economic Instruments for Environmental Management: A Worldwide Compendium of Case Studies, UNEP Earthscan.

Rolston Holmes,III, 2003, "Environmental Ethics, in Blackwell Companion to Philosophy 2nd ed. Nicholas Bunnin and E. P. Tsui-James, eds.Blackwell Publishing.

Roome, N (1992), 'Developing Environmental Management Strategies', Business Strategy and the Environment, Vol 1 (1), 11-24

Roth Kellyn, 2001. "Policy Options for Environmental Pollution Control Including A Case Study: Road Transport Alternatives" Sustainable Energy ESD166J. available @ http://web.mit.edu/10.391J/www/proceedings/Pollution_Roth2001.pdf

Rourke O'Dara, Lloyd Connelly, Catherine Koshland 1996 "Industrial Ecology: A Critical Review" in International Journal of Environment and Pollution, Vol. 6, Nos. 2/3, pp. 89-112.

Sahzabi H Yousefi , 2004, Application of GIS in The Environmental Impact Assessment of Sabalan Geothermal Field, NW-Iran, report presented in the Geothermal Training Programme, in United Nations University

Sandhu Vikram Er. and A.S.Sidhu, 2015. "Environmental Governance in India: A Systematic Review of the Initiatives" in Pacific Business Review International, Volume 8, Issue 4,pp49-57.

Sangeetha Bhargava and Richard Welford, 1996 "Corporate Strategy and the Environment – the Theory" Chapter 2 in Corporate Environmental Management – Systems and Strategies", Earthscan Publications Ltd.

Sankar, U. (1998), "Laws and Institutions Relating Environmental Protection in India", available at http://www.crrid.res.in/keyurban.pdf http://www.mse.ac.in/pub/op_sankar.pdf

Sankar U, ----------, Environmental Externalities. Madras School of Economics.

Sankar U, 2007, Trade and Environment : A Study of India's Leather Exports, OUP.

Saunders Peters T, 2000, Use and Abuse of the Precautionary Principle, ISIS submission to US Advisory Committee on International Economic Policy (ACIEP) Biotech. Working Group. Retrieved from http://www.i-sis.org.uk/prec.php, 1st March2017.

Sawhney Aparna (Indian Council for Research on International Economic Relations) 2004, WTO-Related Matters in Trade and Environment: Relationship Between WTO Rules And MEAs, Working Paper 133.

Sayman S and Onculer A, 2001, INSEAD Working Papers,2001/71/MKT/TM.available @ https://flora.insead.edu/fichiersti_wp/inseadwp2001/2001-71.pdf

Selden, T.M., and D. Song.1995. "Neoclassical Growth, the J Curve for Abatement and the Inverted U Curve for Pollution" *Journal of Environmental Economics and Environmental Management,* Vol.29, pp.162-168.

Sengupta Meghna, 2017," EIA Process in India", in Business Environment available @ http://www.pocketlawyer.com/blog/environmental-impact-assessment-india-eia-process/

Seto, Karen C., and Peter Christensen, 2013. "Remote Sensing Science to Inform Urban Climate Change Mitigation Strategies." *Urban Climate* 3: 1-6.

Seto, Karen C., Burak Güneralp, and Lucy R. Hutyra, 2012. "Global Forecasts of Urban Expansion to 2030 and Direct Impacts on Biodiversity and Carbon Pools."Proceedings of the National Academy of Sciences of the United States of America .

Shafik, N., and Bandyopadhyay, S., 1977. Economic Growth and Environmental Resources, Journal of Environmental Economics and Management 4, 1-24.

Shafik, N., Bandyopadhyay, S., 1992. Economic growth and environmental quality: Time Series And Cross-Section Evidence. World Bank, Policy Research Working Paper (WPS904)

Shandilya Raghwendra Narayan and Rakesh Lala, "Evolution of Environmental Policy in India and Salient Feature of the Policy" available @ https://fenix.tecnico.ulisboa.pt/downloadFile/563568428721347/Environmental%20Policy%20India.pdf

ShankarAcharya 2014. India's Urbanisation Challenge, Business Standard , May 7, 2014,

Sharma, Aviram , 2007 'Emergence of Environmental Movements in India: An Analysis', Downloaded from, ecovista.wordpress.com/2007 /09 /28 /emergence-of environmental-movements-in-indian-analysis

Sharma, R C (1975) "Population Resources and Environment" paper presented to the Group Traning Course on Population Education at the UNESCO Regional Office, Bangkok

Sherbinin de Alex, David Carr, Susan Cassels, and Leiwen Jiangm, 2007, "Population and Environment",Annual Review of Environment and Resources, Vol. 32: 345-373 (First published online as a Review in Advance on July 16, 007DOI: 10.1146/annurev.energy.32.041306.100243 http://www.ncbi.nlm.nih.gov/pmc/articles/PMC2792934/

Shiva Vandana, 1991,Ecology and the Politics of Survival: Conflict over Natural Resources in India, New Delhi: Sage Publications.

Shreekant GUPTA (2014) Environmental Policy and Governance in a Federal Framework: Perspectives from India. Environmental Policies in Asia: pp. 15-42.

https://doi.org/10.1142/9789814590488_0002

Simona Margareta Busoi, 2014, "Ethical Dimensions of Sustainable Development", Proceedings of the 8th International Management Conference "Management Challenges for Sustainable Development", November 6th-7th, 2014, Bucharest, Romania

Smith Carl, 2000, The Precautionary Principle and Environmental Policy Science, Uncertainty, and Sustainability in International Journal of Occupational Environmental Health, VOL 6/NO 3, OCT/DEC pp 263-264

Singer, Peter,1974, "All Animals Are Equal", *Philosophical Exchange,* Vol. 1. No. 5 (Summer,1974): 243-257.downlaodable @ https://greencurriculumsc.files.wordpress.com/2012/04/singer_all_animals_are_equal.pdf

Singh P Suresh, 2009, "India 2006, National Environmental Policy Not a Paradigm Shift" CUTS Hanoi Resource Centre available at http://www.ieepa.org/news/Other/20100917175453892.pdf

Singh Govind, 2007, "To Study the Inception and Evolution of Environmental Impact Assessment in the World and in India and to Analyze and Comment upon the Environmental Clearance Process in the Country" – Masters Thesis , School of Environmental Studies, New Delhi.

Sinha Amitabh (2016) "Kigali Delivers Second Big Climate Deal; Montreal Protocol Amended to Eliminate HFCs", IE Online Media Services Pvt Ltd, downloadable at:

http://indianexpress.com/article/india/india-news-india/kigali-delivers-second-big-climate-deal-montreal-protocol-amended-to-eliminate-hfcs-3083930/

Sivasakthivel.T and K.K.Siva Kumar Reddy, 2011, "Ozone Layer Depletion and Its Effects: A Review" in International Journal of Environmental Science and Development, Vol.2, No.1ISSN: 2010-0264

Srivastava, D K, Rita Pandey and C. Bhujanga Rao ,2012, "Environmental Subsidies in India: Role and Reforms', Technical Paper 4 of the project "Integrating Pollution-abating Economic Instruments in Goods and Services Tax (GST) Regime" Madras School of Economics, Monograph 12

Stavins N Robert, 2001. Experience with Market-Based Environmental Policy Instruments", Discussion Paper:01-58, Resources for the Future.

Stern, D.I., 1998. "Progress on the Environmental Kuznet Curve?" *Environment and Development Economics*, Vol 3, pp.173-196.

Stern, D.I., 2003. The Environmental Kuznets Curve, International Society for Ecological Economics Internet Encyclopaedia of Ecological Economics.

Stern D.I., 2004. The Rise and Fall of the Environmental Kuznets Curve. *World Development*, vol 32, No. 8, pp 1419– 1439.

Stern, D. I., and Michael S. Common. 2001. Is there an environmental Kuznets curve for sulfur? Journal of Environmental Economics and Management 41: 162–78.

Sterner T, 2003, "Instruments of Environmental Policy" Environment Policy Division, Department for Natural Resources and the Environment, Art No:SIDA2384en, SIDA.

Strange, T. and Bayley, A. (2008) OECD Insights Sustainable Development Linking Economy, Society, Environment. OECD Report, Geneva

Svedsater, Henrik, (2000) "*Contingent Valuation of Global Environmental Resources: Test of Perfect and Regular Embedding.*" *Journal of Economic Psychology* 21, no.6 (2000): 605–623.

Szoke Alpar , 2013. " Environment, Sustainability and Economic Performance – The Case of the Northern Aral Sea Region" in East European Studies No. 4 – *Zsuzsa Ludvig (ed.),* Eurasian Challenges – Partnerships with Russia and other issues of the post-Soviet area, Institute of World Economics, Research Centre for Economic and Regional Studies of the Hungarian Academy of Sciences.

Tilt Ann Carol, (____), Organisational Change in Response to the Environmental Agenda: Some Developments Research Paper Series: 99-3 School of Commerce Flinders University.

Taylor Bron and Michael Zimmerman, 2005 "Deep Ecology" in Encyclopedia of Religion and Nature ,Vol I, Ed Bron R Taylor and Jeffrey Kaplan, Downloaded from http://users.clas.ufl.edu/bron/pdf--christianity/Taylor+Zimmerman--Deep%20Ecology.pdf

Ten Brink, P., Lutchman, I., Bassi, S., Speck, S., Sheavly, S., Register, K., and Woolaway, C., 2009. *Guidelines on the Useof Market-based Instruments to Address the Problem of Marine Litter*. Institute for European Environmental Policy (IEEP), Brussels, Belgium, and Sheavly Consultants, Virginia Beach, Virginia, USA. 60 pp.

The Indian Institute of Ecology and Environment (IIEE), Environmental Governance in India" available at: www.ecology.edu

The Royal Institute of International Affairs,& International Institute for Sustainable Development, 2003, Multi National Environmental Agreements and the WTO – Report by Duncan Brack and Kevin Gray.

Torres, Magui Moreno; Kanungo, Parameeta. 2003. *Indonesia's program for pollution control, evaluation, and rating (PROPER)*. Empowerment case studies. Washington, DC: World Bank.

Umashankar, Saumya, Evolution of Environmental Policy and Law in India (October 2, 2014). Available at SSRN: https://ssrn.com/abstract=2508852 or http://dx.doi.org/10.2139/ssrn.2508852

Unruh, G.C., Moomaw, W.R., 1998, "An alternative analysis of apparent EKC-type transitions", Ecological Economics, Vol.25, pp.221-229.

Unsworth E Robert and Timothy B. (----) A Manual for Conducting Natural Resource Damage assessment: The Role of Economics prepared for Division of Economics, Fish and Wild Life Service ,U S Department of the Interior.

Venkatachalam L, 2004. "The Contingent Valuation Method: A Review", in Environmental Impact Assessment Review Volume 24, Issue 1, January 2004, Pages 89-124

Venkatachalam L , 2005. "Damage Assessment and Compensation to Farmers Lessons from Verdict of Loss of Ecology Authority in Tamil Nadu" Economic and Political Weekly April9,2005., pp 156-1560.

Vuletic Mark, 2010/2016, Philosophy notes on Peter Singer's "All animals are equal"(1974) downloaded from http://www.vuletic.com/hume/ph/singer.html

Walls Margaret, 2011, Deposit - Refund Systems in Practice and Theory, Discussion Paper, November 2011, Resources for the Future.

Warford, J.,M.Munasinghe, and W. Cruz,1997, The Greening of Economic Policy Reform, (Vol I) (P,2005,) World Bank, Wahington D.C.

Watson David, "The Distinction Between Deep and Shallow Ecology" Essex Graduate Journal of Sociology volume 10.downloaded at : http://www.school-portal.co.uk/GroupDownloadFile.asp?ResourceId=3989568

Wattage Premachandra, (2011), A Targeted Literature Review – Contingent Valuation Method, Research Gate. downloaded from https://www.researchgate.net/publication/267855582_A_targeted_literature_review_-_contingent_valuation_method.

West John, 2014 "Urbanization and Slums in Asia downloaded from the site: http://asiancenturyinstitute.com/development/224-urbanization-and-slums-in-asia

Whittington, D., (1998), "Administering Contingent Valuation Surveys in Developing Countries." *World Development* 26 (1), 21-30.

Williams Tim, 2014, Climate Change Negitiations, United Nations Framework Convention of Climate Change in Context, Publication Number 2014-03-E, Library of Parliamnet, Ottawa, Canada.

Woods Mark 2010, "Intrinsic Value" in 'Green Politics: An A to Z Guide' edited by Dustin Mulvaney, Sage Publications.

Yakhou Mehanna and Vernon P. Dorweiler, 2004. "Environmental Accounting: An Essential

Component of Business Strategy" in Business Strategy and the Environment, 13, 65–77.

Yandle Bruce, Maya Vijayaraghavan, and Madhusudan Bhattarai .2002. The Environmental Kuznets Curve- A Primer , PERC Research Study.

World Bank, 2006, State and trends of the Carbon Market 2006.Authors: Karan Capoor and Philippe Ambrosi.

Yang T (2006). "Towards an Egalitarian Global Environmental Ethics." in Environmental Ethics and International Policy. Paris: UNESCO.

Yavapolkul Navin. 2005. Environmental Kuznet Curve: Empirical Investigation Using Non-parametric Approach , ol.32, n.8, pp.1419-1439.

Yeung Y-M. 1991 "The Urban Poor and Urban Basic Infrastructure Services in Asia: Past Approaches and Emerging Challenges" Occasional Paper No. 7, Hong Kong Institute of Asia-Pacific Studies. Hong Kong: The Chinese University of Hong Kong; 1991:7

Zutshi P.K.: "Making It Unfit to Breathe", *Science Today* (October 1970).

Zylicz Tomasz, 2010, "Goals and Principles of Environmental Policy", International Review of and Resource Economics, Vol. 3, No 4. pp. 299-334; [http://dx.doi.org/10.1561/101.00000028]

Reports

1. Centre for Environment Education, 2007. Sustainable Development – An Introduction, Internship Series, Volume I.
2. Central Pollution Control Board (CPCB) 2005. Status of Sewage Treatment in India.
3. Central Pollution Control Board CPCB, 2009-10. Status Of Water Supply, Wastewater Generation And Treatment In Class-I Cities & Class-Ii Towns Of India.
4. Demographia World Urban Areas,. Thirteenth Annual Edition. Available @ http://www.demographia.com/db-worldua.pdf
5. Environment Canada, University of Jounsuu and UNEP, 2007. Multilateral Environmental Agreements – Negotiator's Handbook.
6. European Environment Agency, 2001. "Late Lessons From Early Warnings: the Precautionary Principle 1896–2000, Edited by Paul Harremoës, David Gee Malcolm MacGarvin Andy Stirling, Jane Keys , Brian Wynne and Sofia Guedes Vaz ; downloaded from: http://chemicalspolicy.org/downloads/Issue%20Report%20No%2022.pdf
7. FAO 2010 *The Global Forest Resources Assessment 2010,*© FAO
8. FAO 2015 *The Global Forest Resources Assessment , "How are the World's Forests Changing?" © FAO.*
9. FAO 2001, Fisheries Technical Paper 422 on "Product Certification and Ecolabelling for Fisheries Sustainability".
10. Government of India, Ministry of Environment and Forests. "India's Green House Gas Emissions Profile –Results of Five Climate Modelling Studies"
11. Government of India, 2013. Ministry of Statistics and Programme Implementation, "Green National Income in India – A Framework".
12. Government of India, Ministry of Environment and Forests, Chapter 11 on Marine Environment, available @ http://envfor.nic.in/sites/default/files/ch11.pdf
13. Government of India 2006, Ministry of Environment and Forests, National Environmental Policy, Available @ http://envfor.nic.in/sites/default/files/introduction-nep2006e.pdf
14. Government of India, Ministry of Environment and Forests, Strategic Plan. available @ http://www.moef.nic.in/downloads/public-information/Strategic_Plan_MoEF.pdf
15. Government of India 2014, Ministry of Environment, Forests and Climate Change, "India's Progress in Combating Climate Change, Briefing Paper for UNFCCC COP20 Lima, PERU. Available at http://envfor.nic.in/sites/default/files/press-releases/Indian_Country_Paper_Low_Res.pdf
16. Government of India, 2010, Ministry of Forest and Environment "Forest Sector Report-India 2010", Indian Council of Forestry Research and Education.
17. Government of India 2013, Ministry of Housing and Urban Poverty Alleviation National Buildings Organisation 2013, "Status of Slums in India – A Statistical Compendium".
18. Government of India 2013, Ministry of Statistics & Programme Implementation, 20th Conference of Central and State Statistical Organistions.
19. Government of India 2012, Ministry of Housing and Urban Poverty Alleviation, Report of the Technical Urban Group (TG-12) on Urban Housing Shortage 2012-17.
20. Government of India, Tenth Five Year Plan, Section IX, Forests and Environment.
21. Håkan Nordström And ScottVaughan, 1999. "Trade and Environment, Special Studies", World Trade Organisation (WTO).
22. IPCC, 2014: Climate Change 2014: Synthesis Report. Contribution of Working Groups I, II and III to the

Fifth Assessment Report of the Intergovernmental Panel on Climate Change [Core Writing Team, R.K. Pachauri and L.A. Meyer (eds.)]. IPCC, Geneva, Switzerland, 151 pp.

23. ICAP (2016). Emissions Trading Worldwide: Status Report 2016. Berlin: ICAP
24. IFRI, 2010, Health and Environment Reports, "Global Governance of Biodiversity: New Perspectives on a Shared Challenge" by Billé Raphaël, Lucien Chabason, Claudio Chiarolla, Mireille Jardin, Gilles Kleitz, Jean-Patrick Le Duc and Laurent Mermet,available @ http://re.indiaenvironmentportal.org.in/files/globalgovernanceofbiodiversity.pdf
25. International Institute of Sustainable Development, 2013. Business and Sustainable development – A Global Guide, available @ http://www.iisd.org/business/
26. IPCC, 2014: Climate Change 2014: Mitigation of Climate Change. Contribution of Working Group III to the Fifth Assessment Report of the Intergovernmental Panel on Climate Change [Edenhofer, O., R. Pichs-Madruga, Y. Sokona, E. Farahani, S. Kadner, K. Seyboth, A. Adler, I. Baum, S. Brunner, P. Eickemeier, B. Kriemann, J. Savolainen, S. Schlömer, C. von Stechow, T. Zwickel and J.C. Minx (eds.)]. Cambridge University Press, Cambridge, United Kingdom and New York, NY, USA.
27. International Energy Agency 2015, Energy and Climate Change, World Energy Outlook Special Report downladable at https://www.iea.org/publications/freepublications/publication/WEO2015SpecialReportonEnergyandClimateChange.pdf
28. Inter-American Development Bank – IDB Inter-American Association of Sanitary and Environmental Engineering – AIDIS, 2002 "Trainers' Course on Environmental Management and Assessment for Investment Projects" Basic Text by *Guillermo Espinoza and Barbara Richards*
29. International Organisation of Supreme audit institutions (INTOSAI) (2002) 'Towards auditing waste management', Report of INTOSAI Working Group on Environmental Auditing, INTOSAI, Norway.
30. IUCN — The World Conservation Union , Red List of Threatened Species
31. IUCN — The World Conservation Union , 1994, Economic Value of Bio Diversity by Davis Pearce and Dominic Moran, Earthscan Publications Ltd, London.
32. IUCN, The World Conservation Union , Environmental Accounting: What's It All About?
33. Millennium Ecosystem Assessment, 2005. Ecosystems and Human Well-being: Biodiversity Synthesis. World Resources Institute, Washington, DC.
34. Maharashtra Pollution Control Board, 2005.Institutional Capacity Building, Final Report.
35. Organisation for Economic Co-operation and Development (OECD) 2006. Cost-Benefit Analysis and the Environment: Recent Developments. (Report prepared by Pearce D, Giles Atkinson and Susana Mourato)
36. OECD Environment Directorate, 1992, Environment Monograph, The Polluter-Pays Principle OECD Analyses and Recommendations
37. OECD (2006) report on "Environmental Compliance and Enforcement in India: A Rapid Assessment" pp 1-31.
38. OECD. 1991. *Environmental Labelling in OECD Countries,* OECD Report 12, written by James Salzman.
39. OECD,2002. Climate Change: India's Perceptions, Positions, Policies And Possibilities by Parikh KK Jyoti and Kirit Parikh.
40. OECD/IEA, 2014 Energy Climate Change and Environment
41. OECD/IEA, 2015, World Energy Outlook, Special Report.
42. OECD/IEA, 2015, India Energy Outlook.
43. Planning Commission, Govt of India, "Climate Change & 12th Five Year Plan" Report of Sub-Group on Climate Change
44. Report on the Lifetimes of Stratospheric Ozone-Depleting Substances, their Replacements, and Related Species, M. Ko, P. Newman, S. Reimann, S. Strahan (Eds.), SPARC Report No. 6, WCRP-15/2013. Available at http://www.sparc-climate.org/publications/sparc-reports/sparc-report-no6/
45. Torres, Magui Moreno; Kanungo, Parameeta; Torres, Magui Moreno; Kanungo, Parameeta;. Indonesia's program for pollution control, evaluation, and rating (PROPER) (English). Empowerment case studies. Washington, DC: World Bank. 2003.
46. United Nations, Department of Economic and Social Affairs Population Division(2001) Population, Environment and Development – The Concise Report , ST/ESA/SER.A/202
47. United Nations, Department of Economic and Social Affairs Population Division, 2001, Population, Environment and Development – World Population Monitoring, ST/ESA/SER.A/203

48. United Nations, 2001, UN Division of Sustainable Development, Environmental Management Accounting : Procedures and Principles: Prepared for the Expert Working Group on "Improving the Role of Government in the Promotion of Environmental Management Accounting"

49. United Nations, 2001, Population, Environment and Development, The Concise Report, ST/ESA/SER.A/202.

50. United Nations,2014, Department of Economic and Social Affairs, Population Division (2015). World Urbanization Prospects: The 2014 Revision, ST/ESA/SER.A/366.

51. United Nations, 2015, Department of Economic and Social Affairs, Population Division (2015). *World Population Prospects: The 2015 Revision, Key Findings and Advance Tables*. Working Paper No. ESA/P/WP.241

52. UNEP, 1972, **Declaration of the United Nations Conference on the Human Environment**, Chapter11 downloadable from the site:
http://www.unep.org/documents.multilingual/default.asp?documentid=97&articleid=1503

53. UNEP, Environmental Management for Industrial Estates: Information and Training Resources: Case Study /Kalundborg - 1.

54. UNEP 2002, EIA Training Resource Manual, Second Edition, available @ http://unep.ch/etu/publications/EIA_2ed/EIA_E_top1_tit.PDF

55. UNEP, 2004, The Use of Economic Instruments in Environmental Policy, Opportunities and Challenges.

56. UNEP, 2007, Global Environmental Outlook ©UNEP

57. UNEP, 2010, Auditing the Implementation of Multilateral Environmental Agreements (MEAs): A Primer for Auditors

58. UNEP ,2011. Valuing Ecosystem Services: Benefits, Values, Space and Time by Brendan, Fisher Ian Bateman and R. Kerry Turner

59. UNEP Global Environmental Alert Service, 2012. "One Planet, How Many People?" A Review of Earth's Carrying Capacity,A discussion paper for the year of RIO+20, available @ https://na.unep.net/geas/archive/pdfs/GEAS_Jun_12_Carrying_Capacity.pdf

60. UNEP – WCMC (2000) Global Biodiversity: Earth's living Resources in the 21st Century. Cambridge, World Conservation Press

61. UNOPS, 2009, A Guide to Environmental Labels - for Procurement Practitioners of the United Nations System.

62. USEPA, 2005, International Experiences with Economic Incentives for Protecting the Environment.

63. World Commission on the Ethics of Scientific Knowledge and Technology (COMEST) 200. "Precautionary Principle". UNESCO

64. World Bank, 1992. "World Development Report 1992", Oxford University Press, New York, USA.

65. World Bank,2002, "Contingent Valuation" Environmental Economics and Development Policy CourseWorld Bank Institute. UNEP – WCMC (2000) Global Biodiversity: Earth's living Resources in the 21st Century. Cambridge, World Conservation Press.

66. World Commission on Environment and Development (WCED), *Our Common Future*. Oxford: Oxford University Press, (1987). UNEP – WCMC (2000) Global Biodiversity: Earth's living Resources in the 21st Century. Cambridge, World Conservation Press.

67. World Bank (1997), *Five Years after Rio: Innovations in Environmental Policy,* Environmentally Sustainable Development Studies and Monograph Series No. 18.

68. World Bank 2000 "Greening industry – New Roles for Communities, Markets and Governments" Oxford University Press: New York downloaded from @
http://documents.worldbank.org/curated/en/421701468772781985/pdf/multi-page.pdf

69. World Bank (2000) "The Policy Matrix" downloaded from: siteresources.worldbank.org/.../PolicyMatrix2000.pdf

70. World Bank,2012,"Protecting India's Coast Line" in The World Bank in India,Vol 11 Number3.

71. World Commission on the Ethics of Scientific Knowledge and Technology (COMEST), 2005. "Precautionary Principle" UNESCO

72. World Energy Resources, 2013, World Energy Council.

73. World Energy Issues Monitor, 2015, World Energy Council

74. World Resource Institute 2002-2004, "International Environmental Governance" in Decisions for the Earth: Balance, Voice, and Power, World Resource Institute. Available @ http://pdf.wri.org/wr2002_fullreport.pdf.
75. WWF, Zoological Society of London, Global Footprint Network 2008, Living Planet Report
76. USIAD, 2005.Biodiversity Conservation A Guide for USIAD Staff and Partners.
77. PROPER-PROKASIH Team, BAPEDAL, Jakarta and PRDEI, World Bank, "What is Proper?
78. PBL Netherlands Environmental Assessment Agency, The Hague, 2016, "Trends in Global CO_2 Emissions -2016 Report".

Books

79. Anderson A David, Environmental Economics and Natural Resources Management, Routledge, 2010.
80. Asafu-Adjaye John, Environmental Economics for Non Economists, World Scientific Publishing Company,2000.
81. Atkinson, G. Doubourg, W.R. Hamilton, K. Munasinge, M Pearce,D.W. and Young C.E.F. (1997), "Measuring Sustainable Development". Macroeconomics and the environment; Cheltenham
82. Barrow,C J, Environmental Management for Sustainable Development, Routledge,2006.
83. Baumol, W.J., and Oates, W.E., *The Theory of Environmental Policy*. Cambridge: Cambridge University Press, 1975/1988.
84. Blank E Jürgen, Environmental Economics, downloaded on 28/5/2016 from the website https://wiwi.uni-kl.de/fileadmin/wiwi.uni-l.de/downloads_pdf_doc/blank/umwelt/envecon_01.pdf
85. Beder, S., *Environmental Principles and Policies: An Interdisciplinary Introduction*. London: Earthscan, 2006.
86. Benson, J. Environmental Ethics, London, Routledge, 2000.
87. Bhattacharya, N. R., *Environmental Economics - An Indian Perspective*. New Delhi: Oxford University Press, 2001.
88. Bhatt M S, Shahid Ashraf, Asheref Illiyan, 2008. Problems and Prospects of Environment Policy: Indian Perspective, Aakar Books.
89. Boardman A, David Greenberg, Aidan Vining and David Weimer. 2011. Cost-Benefit Analysis: Concepts and Practice, (Prentice Hall1996), Imprint by Pearson.
90. Brennan, Andrew and Yeuk-Sze Lo, "*Environmental Ethics*", in The Stanford Encyclopedia of Philosophy, Edited by Edward N. Zalta Stanford CA :Stanford University ,(2011).
91. Callan Scott J and Jannet M Thomas, Environmental Economics and Management South Western Cengage Learning. 2010
92. Cassels, Jamie, The Uncertain Promise of Law: Lessons From Bhopal. University Of Toronto Press Incorporated, 1993.
93. Clifford, R.S., and William J. Vaughan, "The Choice of Pollution Control Policy Instruments in Developing Countries: Arguments, Evidence and Suggestions" in "International Yearbook of Environmental and Resource Economics", Vol. VII, Ed. Henk Folmer and Tom Tietemberg Cheltenham , U.K: Edward Elgar, (2003).
94. Daly (Ed.), *Toward a Steady-State Economy*. San Francisco: Freeman, (1973).
95. Daly, H. E., and Cobb, J. B., *For the Common Good: Redirecting the Economy toward Community, the Environment and a Sustainable Future*. Boston: Beacon Press, (1989).
96. Devall, B, Sessions, G . *Deep Ecology*. Gibbs M. Smith.(1985).
97. Eckholm P. Erik: *Down to Earth*; Affiliated East West Press Ltd. (1991).
98. Ehrlich, Paul and Anne Ehrlich: *Population, Resources and Environment—Issues in Human Ecology;* W.S. Freeman (1970).
99. Elliot A Jennifer, An Introduction to Sustainable Development, Routledge, 2006.
100. Field, Barry, Environmental Economics – An Introduction, McGraw - Hill Inc. 1994.
101. Foreman, D., *Confessions of an Eco-Warrior*. New York: Crown Publishers, (1991)
102. Fox. W., "*From Anthropocentrism to Deep Ecology*", *Re-vision* Vol. 16, (1993).
103. Fox. W, *Toward a Transpersonal Ecology: Developing New Foundations for Environmentalism*. Boston and London: Shambhala Publications, (1990).
104. Georgescu-Roegen, N. *The Entropy Law and the Economic Process* (Cambridge, Harvard University Press 1971.

105. Getzner Michael, Clive L. Spash and Sigrid Stagl (Ed), Alternatives for Environmental Valuation, Roultledge, ISBN 0-203-34079-5 (Adobe eReader Format)2005.

106. Guha, R *Environmentalism : A Global History*, OUP, New Delhi,(2000)

107. Guillermo, E., and Richards, B., *Fundamentals of Environmental Impact Assessments*– Basic Text prepared for Trainers' Course on Environmental Management and Assessment for Investment Projects, Inter American Development Bank – IDB, Inter-American Association of Sanitary and Environmental Engineering – AIDIS(2002).

108. Hackett C Steven, *Environmental and Natural Resource Economics –Theory, Policy and the Sustainable Society*, M E Sharp, (2006).

109. Hanley, N., Jason, F., Shogren and Ben White, *Environmental Economics in Theory and Practice*. Macmillan, (1997).

110. Hardin, G., *Living Within Limits*. USA: Oxford University Press, (1995).

111. Hardoy J, Satterthwaite D. Squatter Citizen—Life in the Urban Third World. London: Earthscan; 1995:301. Cited by http://www.ncbi.nlm.nih.gov/pmc/articles/PMC1891640/

112. Harris Jonathan, Environmental and Natural Resource Economics, A Contemporary Approach, Global Development and Environment Institute, Tufts University, 2011.

113. Harvey, Brian and John D. Hallet: *Environment and Society: An Introductory Analysis*; Macmillan (1977).

114. Helmer Richard and Ivanildo Hespanhol, (Eds), "Water Pollution Control - A Guide to the Use of Water Quality Management Principles" , UNEP AND WHO, E. & F. Spon, 1997.

115. Herbert Bormann and Stephen R Kellert (eds), *Ecology, Economics, Ethics*: The Broken Circle (1991).

116. Hill M K Understanding Environmental Pollution, Cambridge University Press, 2004.

117. Hunter Lori M, The Environmental Implications of Population Dynamics, RAND, 2000.

118. Hussen, M.A., *Principles of Environmental Economics: Economics, Ecology and Public Policy*. London: Roultledge, (2000).

119. Isacat Ben, How to do Animal Rights Legally with Confidence PDF edition downloaded from http://www.animalethics.org.uk/ 2015.

120. Jamieson Dale (Ed), A Companion to Environmental Philosophy Copyright © 2001 by Blackwell Publishers Ltd,2001.

121. Jeroen, C.J.M., van den Bergh, *Handbook of Environmental and Resource Economics*. Springer Netherlands, (1999)

122. Kaivo-oja, Jari, Luukkanen, Jyrki and Malaska, Pentti ; Advanced sustainability analysis. In M.K. Tolba (Ed.) Our Fragile World, Challenges and Opportunities for Sustainable Development. Encyclopedia of Life Support Systems and Sustainable Development. Vol 2. Oxford: EOLSS Publishers Co. Ltd. UNESCO, 2001.

123. Karpagam M and Geetha Jaikumar, *Green Management Theory and Applications*, Ane Books Pvt. Ltd, New Delhi (2010)

124. Kerry, T.R., Pearce, D., and Bateman, I., *Environmental Economics - An Elementary Introduction*. Johns Hopkins University Press, (1993).

125. Kibert C J, Leslie Thiele, Anna Peterson and Martha Monroe, Ethics of Sustainability, ____

126. Kuik, O.J., Nadkarni, M.V., Oosterhuis, F.H., Sastry, G.S., Akkerman, A.E., *Pollution Control in the South and North, A Comparative Assessment of Environmental Policy Approaches in India and the Netherlands*. Sage Publications, (1997).

127. Kula E, Economics of Natural Resuorces and the Environment, Springer Netherlands, 1994.

128. Kumar, A., *Industrial Pollution: Problems and Solutions*. New Delhi: Daya Books, 2006.

129. Lakshmi Narasaiah M, 2006, Population and Bio Diversity, Discovery Publishing House.

130. Lawn A Philip, Towards Sustainable Development= An Ecological Economics Approach, Ecological Economics Series (International Society for Ecological Economics), CRC Press, LLC, 2001.

131. Leopold, Aldo, *A Sand County Almanac*. Oxford University Press (1949).

132. Martinez-Alier, J., *The Environmentalism of the Poor: A Study of Ecological Conflicts and Valuation*. New Delhi:Oxford University Press, (2004).

133. McCormic, J., *Reclaiming Paradise –The Global Environmental Paradise*. Blackwell Publishing, (1991) Perman, R., Yue Ma, McGilvray, J., *Natural resource and Environmental Economics*. Longman Ltd., (1996)

134. N.de Sadeleer, *Environmental Principles: From Political Slogans to Legal Rules*. Oxford: Oxford University Press, 2002.
135. Mac Neill Jim, Pieter Winsemium and Taizo Yakushiji: *Beyond Interdependence*; OUP (1991).
136. Mani, Muthukumara S. Greening India's Growth: Costs, Valuations and Trade-offs. New York: Routledge. © World Bank. 2014.
137. Markandya A and Shibli (1995) "Using Environmental Regulations – Malaysia Experience in Effluent Control in the Palm Oil Industry: Specific Approach: Standards and Charges" in Five years After Rio – Innovations in Environmental Policy , Environmentally Sustainable Development :Studies and Monograph Series 18 World Bank.
138. Mukherjee Roma, Environmental Management and Awareness Issues, Sterling Publishers Pvt. Ltd, 2002 .
139. Oliphant Jill , OCR Religious Ethics for AS and A2 Edted by Jon Mayled, Routledge, 2014.
140. Palmer, Clare Contemporary Ethical Issues, .BC-CLIO (1997).
141. Planisamy P N, Manikandan P, Geetha A , and Manjula Rani I, Environmental Science, Pearson, 2012.
142. Pearce, D W., Barbier, E., and Markandya, A., *Sustainable Development: Economics and Environment in the Third World*, Edward Elgar, (1990).
143. Pearce, D., *Blueprint 3: Measuring Sustainable Development*. London: Earthscan, (1994).
144. Pearson Charles S, *Economics and the Global Environment*, Cambridge University Press, (2010).
145. Perman Roger, Yue Ma James McGilvray Michael Common, Natural Resource and Environmental Economics, Pearson Education Limited,(2003).
146. Roodman, M.D., *The Natural Wealth of Nations*. New York, London; W.W. Norton & Company, (1998).
147. Rootes, C., *Environmental Movement – Local, National and Global*. London: Frank Cass Publishers, (1999).
148. Roszak, Theodore, *The Voice of the Earth: An Exploration of Ecopsychology*. USA: Phanes Press, Inc., (1992)
149. Sharma, A., *Emergence of Environmental Movements in India: An Analysis*. Eco Vista, ecovistawordpress.com, 2007.
150. Taylor, Paul W., *Respect for Nature: A Theory of Environmental Ethics,* (Princeton NJ: Princeton University Press, 1986)
151. Thomas A Garrett and John c Leatherman, An Introduction to State and Local Public Finance, Regional Research Institute, West Virginia University, (2000).
152. Tickner Joeln, Carolyn Raffensperger and Nancy Mayers, The Precautionary Principle in Action – A Hand Book, First Edition, Windsor, North, Dakota: Science and Environmental Health Network – SEHN , (1999)
153. Tietenberg, T.H., *Environmental and Natural Resource Economics*. (4th Ed), New York: HarperCollins College Publishers, (1996).
154. Tolba M K (Ed.) Our Fragile World, Challenges and Opportunities for Sustainable Development. Encyclopedia of Life Support Systems and Sustainable Development. Vol 2. Oxford: EOLSS Publishers Co. Ltd. UNESCO, 2001.
155. Tongjing Yang, "Towards an Egalitarian Global Environmental Ethics" in Environmental Ethics and International Policy, Edited by Henk A. M. J. ten Have. UNESCO ,2006
156. Turner, R.K. (Eds), *Sustainable Environmental Economics and Management. Principles and Practice*, Belhaven Press, London, (1993).
157. Paul M Rikhardsson, Martin Bennet, Jan Jaap Bouma and Stefan Schaltegger (Eds), Implementing Environmental Management Accounting: Status and Challenges, Springer, 2005.
158. Shakeb Afsah, Allen Blackman, Jorge H. Garcia, Thomas Sterner, Environmental Regulation and Public Disclosure, RFF Press, 2013.
159. United Nations, 2000. Department of Economic and Social Affairs, Statistics Division and UNEP Division of Technology, Industry and Economics, Hand Book of National Accounting Integrated Environmental and Economic Accounting An Operational Manual , United Nations.
160. UNDP and ASCI (Administrative Staff College of India), "Analysis of Existing Environmental Instruments in India" Series F, No. 78, 2009.
161. United Nations Environment Programme, International Institute for Sustainable Development, Environment and Trade - Handbook, 2000.

162. UNEP and International Institute for Sustainable Development (IISD). Trade and Green Economy, A Handbook. IISD, 2014.

163. Weimer, David L. and Aidan R. Vining, Policy Analysis: Concepts and Practice. Fourth edition. Upper Saddle River, NJ : Pearson Prentice Hall, 2004.

164. Weir, David. The Bhopal Syndrome: Pesticides, Environment, And Health. Sierra Club Books, San Francisco. 1987

165. Welford, R., *Corporate Environmental Management: Systems and Strategies*. Universities Press (India) Ltd., 1993.

166. Welford, R J Environmental Strategy and Sustainable Development: The Corporate Challenge of the 21st Century, London Routledge, 1995.

167. Welford, R J, and Gouldson, A P Environmental Management and Business Strategy, Pitman Publishing, 1993.

168. Yew-Kwang-Ng, Welfare Economics, Macmillan, 1983.